# KRISHNAMURTI

# KRISHNAMURTI

## A BIOGRAPHY

Pupul Jayakar

*1817*

HARPER & ROW, PUBLISHERS, SAN FRANCISCO

Cambridge, Hagerstown, New York, Philadelphia, Washington
London, Mexico City, São Paulo, Singapore, Sydney

FIRST HARPER & ROW PAPERBACK EDITION 1988

Library of Congress Cataloging-in-Publication Data

Jayakar, Pupul.
    Krishnamurti: a biography.

    Includes index.
    1. Krishnamurti, J. (Jiddu), 1895–1986
2. Philosophers—India—Biography.  I. Title.
B5134.K754J39  1986                    181'.4 [B]                    85–45739
ISBN 0-06-250401-0
ISBN 0–06–250404–5 (pbk.)


89  90  91  92  93  HC  10  9  8  7  6  5  4  3  2  1

*To Krishnaji with*
*profound Pranaams*

# Contents

# Preface

In the late 1950s Krishnaji, as J. Krishnamurti is known in India and to his friends throughout the world, suggested that I write a book on his life, based on the notes I had kept since I first met him in 1948. I began writing this book in 1978.

I have attempted to write of Krishnamurti the man, the teacher, and his relationships with the many men and women who formed part of the Indian landscape. The book concentrates on Krishnaji's life in India between 1947 and 1985, but some recording of his early life became necessary as a backdrop to the unfoldment of the story of the young Krishnamurti. Some new material, hitherto unpublished, has also been included.

The reader will soon notice that Krishnamurti is called by several different names in this book. I have referred to Krishnamurti as Krishna when he was a young person, for so he was known; as Krishnaji from 1947, for by then he was to me the great Teacher and Seer. *Ji* is a term of respect added to names both of men and women in North India; in an old-fashioned household even the child's name has the suffix added, for it is considered discourteous to address a person by her or his first name. In South India no suffix is added and *ji* is unknown. It is likely that Annie Besant, because of her close associations with Varanasi, added the *ji* to Krishna's name as a term of endearment and respect.

Most religious teachers in India have a prefix added to their names, such as Maharshi, Acharya, Swami, or Bhagwan. Krishnaji never accepted any such title. Krishnaji referred to himself in the dialogues or in his diaries either as "K" or as the impersonal "we," to suggest as absence of the "I," the ego's sense of individuality. In this book, therefore, when I refer to the man or the teacher in an impersonal manner, I refer to him as Krishnamurti or as K.

Krishnaji agreed to hold dialogues with me, and these form part of the book. Most of the writing is from notes kept by me during or immediately after conversations or dialogues. From 1972 onwards, some of the dialogues were on tape and have been taken from there.

Certain incidents discussed in the book—Krishnaji's meetings with Indira Gandhi, his relationship with Annie Besant—could have become controversial. These chapters I read aloud to Krishnaji for his comments. I also sent Indira Gandhi the chapter on her meetings with him; she suggested some minor changes, which have been incorporated.

I wish to acknowledge my deep gratitude to Sri Rajiv Gandhi for permission to include the letters of Indira Gandhi; to the Krishnamurti Foundation, England, for permission to publish the dialogues held by me with Krishnaji at Brockwood Park; to the Krishnamurti Foundation, India, for permission to publish the dialogues and talks in India; to Smt. Radha Burnier, President, Theosophical Society, for all her kindness and help in making available material from the archives of the Theosophical Society; to Sri Achyut Patwardhan for his many conversations, to Smt. Sunanda Patwardhan for giving me access to her notes and personal records; to my daughter Radhika and her husband, Hans Herzberger, for their critical comments; to Sri Murli Rao for certain manuscripts he brought to my notice; and to the many other friends who have shared their experiences with me. I would also like to acknowledge Sri Asoke Dutt for his friendship and immense help in making the publication possible; to Mr. Clayton Carlson of Harper & Row for his valuable suggestions, interest, and support; to Sri Benoy Sarkar for his valuable help in sorting out and collating the photographs; to the National Institute of Design, Ahmedabad; to the heirs of Mitler Bedi; to Asit Chandmal; Mark Edwards, and A. Hamid, for permission to use their photographs; to A. V. Jose for his overall support and supervision; and to M. Janardhanan for bearing with me in preparing the manuscript.

# "A Song Bestowed Upon a Tethered Bird"

Awake, arise, having approached the great teacher, learn
The road is difficult, the crossing is as the sharp edge of a razor.

KATHA UPANISHAD III

I first met Krishnamurti in January 1948. I was thirty-two years of age and had come to live in Bombay after marrying my husband, Manmohan Jayakar, in 1937. My only child, a daughter, Radhika, was born a year later.

India had been independent for five months and I saw a sweet future stretching ahead. My own entry into politics was imminent. It was a time when men and women involved in the freedom struggle had also turned to what was then known as social or constructive programs initiated by Mahatma Gandhi. This covered every aspect of nation building, particularly those activities related to village India. From 1941 I became very active in organizational matters related to village women's welfare, cooperatives, cottage industries. For me, it was a tough and rigorous initiation. With freedom, the aftermath of partition saw me at the center of the main relief organization set up in Bombay for refugees who were pouring into the country from Pakistan.

One Sunday morning I went to see my mother, who lived in Malabar Hill, Bombay, in an old rambling bungalow roofed with country tiles. I found her with my sister Nandini getting ready to go out. They told me that Sanjeeva Rao, who had studied with my father in King's College, Cambridge, had come to see my mother. He saw that even after several years of mourning, she was still in great sorrow at my father's death. He had suggested that she might be helped by meeting Krishnamurti. An image came suddenly to my mind: the mid-1920s, the school at Varanasi* where I was a day student. I remembered seeing a very young Krishnamurti, a lean, beautiful figure, seated cross-

---

*Benares.

legged, dressed in white, and I, one of fifty children, laying flowers before him. . . .

I had nothing to do that morning, so I accompanied my mother. When we reached Ratansi Morarji's house on Carmichael Road, where Krishnamurti was staying, I saw Achyut Patwardhan, standing outside the entrance. In recent years he had become a revolutionary and freedom fighter, but I had known him since we were children at Varanasi in the 1920s. We spoke together for a few moments before we went into the sitting room to await Krishnamurti.

Krishnamurti entered the room silently, and my senses exploded; I had a sudden intense perception of immensity and radiance. He filled the room with his presence, and for an instant I was devastated. I could do nothing but gaze at him.

Nandini introduced my tiny, fragile-bodied mother and then turned and introduced me. We sat down. With some hesitation, my mother began to speak of my father, her love for him and of her tremendous loss, which she seemed unable to accept. She asked Krishnamurti whether she would meet my father in the next world. By then the intensity of heightened perception his presence had first evoked had started to fade, and I sat back to hear what I expected to be a comforting reply. I knew that many sorrowful people had visited him, and I assumed that he would know the words with which to comfort them.

Abruptly, he spoke. "I am sorry, Madam. You have come to the wrong man. I cannot give you the comfort you seek." I sat up, bewildered. "You want me to tell you that you will meet your husband after death, but which husband do you want to meet? The man who married you, the man who was with you when you were young, the man who died or the man he would have been today, had he lived?" He paused and was silent for some moments. "Which husband do you want to meet? Because, surely, the man who died was not the same man who married you."

I felt my mind spring to attention; I had heard something extraordinarily challenging. My mother seemed very perturbed. She was not prepared to accept that time could have made any difference in the man she loved. She said, "My husband would not change." Krishnamurti replied, "Why do you want to meet him? What you miss is not your husband, but the memory of your husband." He paused again, allowing the words to sink deep.

"Madam, forgive me." He folded his hands and I grew aware of the perfection of his gestures. "Why do you keep his memory alive? Why do you want to recreate him in your mind? Why do you try to live in sorrow and continue with the sorrow?" I felt a quickening of my senses: His refusal to be kind in the accepted sense was shattering. My mind leapt to meet the clarity and precision of his words. I felt that I was in contact with something vast and totally new. Though the words sounded harsh, there was gentleness in his eyes and a quality of healing flowed from him. He held my mother's hand while he was speaking.

Nandini saw that my mother was disturbed. She changed the conversation and began speaking to Krishnamurti of the rest of the family. She told him that I was a social worker interested in politics. He was grave as he turned to me and asked why I did social work. I responded by telling him of the fullness of my life. He smiled. It made me feel uneasy and nervous. Then he said, "We are like the man who tries to fill water into a pail that has holes. The more water he pours in, the more it pours out, and the pail remains empty."

He was looking at me without intruding. He said, "What is it you are trying to run away from? Social work, pleasure, living in sorrow— are these not all escapes, attempts to fill the void within? Can this void be filled? And yet, to fill the void is the whole process of our existence."

I found his words very disturbing, but felt they had to be explored. To me, action was life; and what he said was incomprehensible. I asked him whether he wanted me to sit at home and do nothing. He listened; and I had a peculiar feeling that his listening was unlike anything I had ever perceived or experienced. Then he smiled at my question, and the room filled. Shortly after that we left. Krishnamurti said to me, "We shall meet again."

The meeting had left me very disturbed. I could not sleep, his words kept arising in my mind. As the days passed I began to attend the talks he was giving in the gardens of Sir Chunilal Mehta, Nandini's father-in-law. I found it difficult to understand what Krishnamurti was saying, but his presence devastated me and I continued to go. He spoke of world chaos as the projection of individual chaos. He told us that all organizations and "isms" had failed, and that in our pursuit of security we build new organizations that in turn betray us.

I had the feeling that I was not meeting him at the level at which he was speaking. After a few days I asked for an interview.

I was driven by the urge to be with him, to be noticed by him, to probe into the mystery that pervaded his presence. I was afraid of what would happen, but I could not keep away. For two days before our interview I planned what I would say to him and how I would say it. When I walked into the room I found him sitting straight-backed and cross-legged on the floor, dressed in an immaculate white *kurta* that stretched to below his knees. He sprang to his feet, his long, petal-like fingers folded in greeting. I sat down facing him. He saw I was nervous and he asked me to sit quietly.

After a while I began to talk. I had always been sure of myself, so though I hesitated, I soon found that I was speaking normally and what I had planned to say poured out. I spoke of the fullness of my life and work, of my concern for the underprivileged, my desire to enter politics, my work in the cooperative movement, my interest in art. I was completely absorbed in what I had to say, the impression I was trying to create. After a few moments, however, I had the uncomfortable feeling that he was not listening. I looked up and saw he was gazing at me; there was a questioning in his eyes and a deep probing. I hesitated and grew silent. After a pause he said, "I have noticed you at the discussions. When you are in repose, there is a great sadness on your face."

I forgot what I had intended to say, forgot everything but the sorrow within me. I had refused to allow the pain to come through. So deep was it buried that it rarely impinged on my conscious mind. I was horrified of the idea that others would show me pity and sympathy, and had covered up my sorrow with layers of aggression. I had never spoken of this to anyone—not even to myself had I acknowledged my loneliness: but before this silent stranger all masks were swept away. I looked into his eyes and it was my own face I saw reflected. Like a torrent long held in check, the words came.

I remembered myself as a young child, one of five children, timid and gentle, bruised at the slightest harshness. Dark of complexion in a family where everyone was fair, unnoticed, a girl when I should have been a boy, living in a large rambling house, being alone for hours, reading books that I seldom understood. I remembered sitting on a lone veranda facing ancient trees; listening to legends of ogres and heroes, of Hatim Tai and Ali Baba—the oral tales of this ancient land told by the white-bearded Muslim tailor Immamuddin, who sat with his sewing machine all day long on the veranda. I remembered hearing Tulsidas's *Ram Charit Manas* sung by Ram Khilavan, the blind *punkah* coolie who fanned us, and the fragrance of cool, wet *khus* mats on a summer day.* I remembered going for walks with my Irish governess,

---

*\*Ram Charit Manas* is the story of Ram and Sita from the epic *Ramayana* composed in the vernacular by poet Tulsidas in a four-line quatrain inserted in the text.

Before electricity came to India, every bungalow had a long wooden pole hung horizontally from the high ceiling, with a heavy cloth frill attached. A rope connected the pole through a hole in the wall to the outer veranda, where a man sat pulling the rope

learning of plants and the names of flowers; delighting in the history of British kings and queens, Arthur and Guinevere, Henry the VIII and Anne Boleyn; never playing with dolls, seldom with other children. I remembered being afraid of my father, yet secretly adoring him.

I remembered at age eleven the buds opening in my womb, the first bleeding, and with it a miraculous blossoming. To grow up and to be young was intoxication. To be admired, to live intensely—riding, swimming, playing tennis, dancing. With wild abandon I raced to meet life.

I remembered going to England, to college and the stimulation of the mind; meeting my husband, the return to India, marriage and the birth of my daughter Radhika.

Inevitably, I soon refused the role of a housewife. I plunged into social work, played bridge and poker for high stakes, lived at the heart of the social and intellectual life of Bombay. Then another pregnancy; in the seventh month an attack of eclampsia brought violent convulsions and total blindness.

I remembered the bewildering anguish of darkness and the explosive storms of color: cerulian blue, the color of the neelkantha bird, the color of blue fire. The brain ravaged by the body's convulsions; the ending of the heartbeats and the death of the unseen baby; the heavy death silence of the womb. Sight returning through a mist, as gray dots, converging to create form.

My mind paused, words ended, and I looked again at the beautiful stranger. But the racking pain of my beloved father's death soon awakened in me, and again there was tearing, unendurable agony.

Words would not end. I spoke of the many scars of living, the struggle to survive, the growing ruthlessness, the slow hardening, the aggression and ambition. The drive in me, demanding success. Then another pregnancy, the birth of a little girl, beautiful of face, but deformed. The drowning in anguish and again the death of the child. Eight years of barrenness of mind, heart, and womb; and then death.

In his presence the past, hidden in the darkness of the long forgotten, found form and awakened. He was as a mirror that reflected. There was an absence of personality, of the evaluator, to weigh and distort. I kept trying to keep back something of my past, but he would not let me. Now, in the compassionate field, there was a quality of

---

and so moving the fan, to create a slight breeze in the frightful heat of Northern India in the summer months. The fragrant *khus* mats were hung on doors and windows. When wet, the hot wind blowing through them was transformed into a cool, scented breeze.

immense strength. He said, "I can see if you want me to." And so the words which for years had been destroying me were said. Saying them brought me immense pain, but his listening was as the listening of winds or the vast expanse of water.

I had been with Krishnaji* for two hours. As I left the room my body felt shattered, and yet a healing had flowed through me. I had touched a new way of observing, a new way of listening, without re-action, a listening that arose from distance and depth. While I was speaking he appeared aware not only of what was being said—the expressions, gestures, attitudes—but also of what was happening around him—the bird singing in the tree outside his window, a flower falling from a vase. In the midst of my outcry he said to me: "Did you see that flower fall?" My mind had stopped, bewildered.

I had been listening to Krishnamurti for several days. I went to his talks, attended the discussions, cogitated, discussed what he was say-ing with my friends. On the evening of January 30, when we had all gathered around him at Ratansi Morarji's house, Achyut was called to the telephone. He came back, his face ashen.

"Gandhiji has been assassinated," he said. For an instant, time stopped. Krishnaji had become very still. He seemed to be aware of each one of us and our reactions. Among us, a single thought arose: Was the assassin a Hindu or a Muslim? Achyut's brother Rao asked, "Is there news of the killer?" Achyut said he did not know. The con-sequences that would follow if the killer were a Muslim were clear to all of us. We rose silently, and one by one left the room.

The news that Gandhi had been murdered by a Brahmin from Poona swept the city; anti-Brahmin riots broke out in Poona. You could hear the whisper of relief from the Muslim residents. We listened to Jawaharlal Nehru's anguished voice addressing the nation. The country seemed paralyzed. The unthinkable had happened, and for a brief mo-ment men and women searched their hearts.

On February 1 a hushed audience gathered to hear Krishnaji speak. He was asked a difficult question: "What are the real causes of Ma-hatma Gandhi's untimely death?"

Krishnamurti replied, "I wonder what your reaction was when you heard the news. What was your response? Were you concerned over it as a personal loss, or as an indication of the trend of world events? World events are not unrelated incidents; they are related. The real

---

*See Preface for explanation of various forms of Krishnamurti's name used in this book.

cause of Gandhiji's untimely death lies in you. The real cause is you. Because you are communal, you encourage the spirit of division— through property, through caste, through ideology, through having different religions, sects, leaders. When you call yourself a Hindu, a Muslim, a Parsee, or God knows what else, it is bound to produce conflict in the world."

For days after that we discussed violence, its root and its ending. For Krishnaji nonviolence as an ideal was illusion. The reality was the fact of violence, the rising of perception that understood the nature of violence and the ending of violence in the "now": the present of existence in which alone action was possible.

In the talks that followed he spoke of the everyday problems that face humankind—fear, anger, jealousy, the fierce thrust of possession. Speaking of relationships as the mirror for self-discovery, he used the example of husband and wife, the most intimate relationship and yet often the most callous and hypocritical. Men looked with embarrassed eyes at their wives. Some traditional Hindus walked out of the talks, unable to understand what the relationship between husband and wife had to do with religious discourse. Krishnaji refused to move from "what is," the actual. He refused to discuss abstracts like God or eternity while the mind was a whirlpool of lust, hatred, and jealousy. It was at this time that some of his audience began to feel that he did not believe in God.

In mid-February I went to see him again. He asked me whether I had noticed anything different in my thinking process. I said I was not getting as many thoughts as I did before. My mind was not as restless as it used to be.

He said, "If you have been experimenting with self-knowing, you will notice that your thinking process has slowed down, that your mind is not restlessly wandering." For a time he was silent; I waited for him to continue. "Try working out each thought to its completion, carry it right through to the end. You will find that this is very difficult, for no sooner does one thought come into being than it is pursued by another thought. The mind refuses to complete a thought. It escapes from thought to thought." This is so. When I have tried to follow a thought, I have always noted how swiftly it eludes the watcher.

I then asked him how one could complete a thought. He said, "Thought can only come to an end when the thinker understands himself, when he sees that the thinker and the thought are not two separate processes. That the thinker is the thought, and the thinker separates himself from thought for his self-protection and continuance. So the thinker is continually producing thought which is transforming and changing." He paused.

"Is the thinker separate from his thoughts?" There were long pauses between his sentences, as if he expected the words to journey far and deep. "Remove thought, where is the thinker? You will find the thinker is not. So when you complete every thought to its end, good or bad—which is extremely arduous—the mind slows down. To understand the self, the self in operation has to be watched. This can only be when the mind slows down—and you can only do this by pursuing every thought to its end as it arises. You will then see that your condemnations, your desires, your jealousies will come out before a consciousness that is empty and completely silent."

Listening to him over the course of a month, my mind had grown pliable; it was no longer crystalized and solid in its encrustations. I asked, "But when consciousness is filled with prejudices, desires, memories, can it then understand thought?"

"No," he answered, "for it is constantly acting on thought—escaping from it or building on it." Again he was silent. "If you follow each thought to its completion, you will see that at the end of it there is silence. From that there is renewal. Thought that arises from this silence no longer has desire as its motive force, it emerges from a state that is not clogged with memory.

"But if again the thought that so arises is not completed, it leaves a residue. Then there is no renewal and the mind is caught again in a consciousness which is memory, bound by the past, by yesterday. Each thought, then to the next, is the yesterday—that which has no reality.

"The new approach is to bring time to an end," Krishnaji concluded. I did not understand, but came away with the words alive within me.

Nandini and I sometimes took Krishnaji for evening drives to the Hanging Gardens on Malabar Hill, or to Worli beach. At times we would walk with him, finding it difficult to keep pace with his long strides. Other times he would walk alone and return after an hour, a stranger. During the walks with us he would occasionally speak of his youth, his life in the Theosophical Society, and his early days at Ojai, California. He told us of his brother Nitya, of his companions Rajagopal and Rosalind and the Happy Valley School. Often when he spoke of the past his memory would be precise, accurate. At other times he would grow vague and say he did not remember. He was quick to smile, and his laughter was deep and resonant. He shared jokes, he asked us questions of our childhood and our growing up. He also spoke of India, eagerly seeking our views on what was taking place in the country. We were hesitant and shy; a sense of mystery and his overwhelming presence made it difficult for us to be casual with him, or to speak of trivialities in his presence. But his laughter brought him closer to us.

On some days we discussed thought. He would ask, "Have you watched the birth of a thought? Have you watched its ending?" Another day he would say, "Take a thought, stay with it, hold it in consciousness, you will see how arduous it is to hold one thought as it is to end thought."

I told Krishnaji that since I had met him, I had been waking in the mornings, without thought, but with the sound of birds and the distant voices of the street flowing through my mind.

To the Indian the silent straight-backed stranger, the mendicant who stands waiting at the doorways of the home and mind holding an invitation to otherness, is a powerful symbol. It evokes in the householder—woman or man—passionate longings, anguish, and a reaching out physically and inwardly to that which is unattainable. But this seer laughed and joked; he walked with us, was near and yet very far away. Hesitatingly, we invited him to my mother's house for dinner.

He came smiling, wearing a *dhoti*, a long *kurta*, and an *angavastram*,* and was received with flowers by my tiny mother. She had never had a formal education, but her natural elegance of mind, her grace and dignity, made it possible for her to meet and speak with Krishnaji. She was the widow of a senior Indian civil servant. While living with my father she had shared in his intellectual and social life, had met scholars and social workers, and was herself an ardent social worker. Tenacious and shrewd, my mother had broken free from tradition early in her married life. She spoke English with ease, entertained with élan, and cooked delectably. In my childhood we had two cooks, one for vege-

---

*A *dhoti* is a forty-five-inch wide and five yards long cotton handwoven cloth, unstitched, with a plain border of burgundy or black. It is tied around the waist, pleated in front, and tucked between the legs to be fastened at the back, falling ankle length. It is a graceful garment for wear on ceremonial occasions. The *kurta* is a stitched, loose, collarless shirt with long sleeves, and it reaches below the knees. An *angavastram* is an unbleached handwoven cotton shawl with a dark red, indigo, or black border woven with a gold design. Folded and thrown over the shoulder, it is worn on all ceremonial occasions, particularly in South India.

tarian Gujarati meals and another trained in the Western cuisine; a Goan butler waited at table. My father's death had broken her, but my mother's house continued to be resonant with laughter, in which Krishnaji joined. He soon felt at home, and came frequently to dinner. By the end of March we could speak to him with ease; yet after each of his talks and discussions we grew intensely aware of the distances that separated us and the mystery that we could neither touch nor fathom.

Toward the end of March I told Krishnaji of the state of my mind and the thoughts that pursued me; of the moments of quietness and bursts of frenzied activity; of days when my mind was caught in the pain of not becoming. I was distracted by this constant jumping backwards and forwards of the mind.

He took my hand and we sat quietly. Finally, he said, "You are agitated. Why?" I did not know, and sat silently. "Why are you ambitious? Do you want to be like anyone you know who has got on?"

I hesitated and then said, "No."

"You have a good brain," he continued, "a good instrument that has not been used rightly. You have a drive that has been wrongly directed. Why are you ambitious? What is it you want to become? Why do you want to waste your brain?"

I was suddenly alert. "Why am I ambitious? Can I help what I am? I am busy doing, achieving. We cannot be like you."

His look was quizzical. For some time he remained without speaking, letting what lay dormant within me reveal itself. Then he asked, "Have you ever been alone, without books, the radio? Try it and see what happens."

"I would go mad, I cannot be alone."

"Try it and see. For the mind to be creative, there must be stillness. A deep stillness that can only come into being when you have faced your loneliness.

"You are a woman, and yet you have a great deal of the man in you. You have neglected the woman. Look into yourself."

I felt a stirring deep within me, the crumbling of the many crusts of insensitivity. I felt again the tearing anguish.

"You want affection, Pupul, and you do not find it. Why do you put out your begging bowl?"

"I don't," I said. "That is one thing I have never done. I would rather die than ask for affection."

"You have not asked for it. You have smothered it. Yet the begging bowl is always there. If your bowl was full you would not need to hold it out. It is because it is empty that it is there."

For an instant I looked at myself. As a child I wept so often. As an adult I permitted nothing to hurt me. I turned from it fiercely and attacked. He said, "If you love, then you do not demand. Then if you find the person does not love you, you will help the other to love, even though it is someone else."

I saw myself with clarity—the bitterness, the hardness. I turned to him. "It is too horrible to look. What have I made of myself?"

"You are not solving the problem by criticizing yourself. There is no flowing richness in you, otherwise you would not need sympathy or affection. Why have you no richness? Look, this is what you are. You do not condemn a man who has a disease. This is your disease. Look at it calmly and simply, with compassion. It would be stupid to condemn or justify. To condemn is another movement of the past to strengthen itself. Look at what takes place in your conscious mind. Why are you aggressive? Why do you want to be the center of any group?

"As you look at the conscious mind, slowly the unconscious will throw up its intimations—in dreams, even in the waking state of thought."

We had been talking for over an hour, but that span was meaningless. In his presence there was a shrinking of one's sense of time as duration. I spoke to him of the changes that were taking place in my life. I was no longer sure of myself or my work. Although desires and urges still arose, they had no vitality.

I told him I realized that a great deal of the work I was doing was based on self-aggrandizement. It no longer seemed possible for me to enter political life. My social life was also changing radically. Of all things, I could no longer play poker. I had tried to play, but found that the intention to outwit the other players was lacking. Unbidden, I had moments of awareness in the middle of playing poker that made bluffing impossible. Krishnaji put back his head and laughed and laughed and laughed.

I told him that at times I felt an immense inner balance, like a bird playing with the wind. All desire dissolved in this intensity, spent itself. At other times I was swamped in becomings. My moorings were going and I was adrift. I did not know what lay ahead. I had never felt so unsure of myself.

Krishnaji said, "The seed has been planted, allow it to germinate— let it lie fallow for a while. This has been quite new to you. Coming to it with no preconceptions, no notions, no beliefs, the impact has been direct, the mind now will need rest. Don't push it."

We sat quietly. Krishnaji said, "Watch yourself. You have a drive few women possess. In this country men and women peter out so easily, so early in life. It is the climate, the way of living, the stagnation. See that the drive does not drop away. In freeing yourself from aggression, don't become innocuous and soft. To be free from aggression is not to become weak or humble."

Repeatedly, he was to tell me, "Watch your mind, let not a thought escape, however ugly, however brutal. Watch without choosing, weighing, judging, without giving direction or letting thought take root in the mind. Watch relentlessly."

As I left the room he rose to see me to the door. His face was in repose, his body slim, uprising like a deodar tree. For an instant, overwhelmed by his beauty, I asked, "Who are you?" He said, "It does not matter who I am. What you think and do and whether you can transform yourself is alone important."

As I journeyed home I suddenly realized that, in the many conversations I had had with Krishnaji, he had never said a word about himself. There had been no reference to any personal experience, not a single movement of the self had manifested itself. It was this that made him a stranger, however well you knew him. In the midst of a gesture of friendship, casual conversation, one felt it—a sudden distance, silences that emanated from him, a consciousness that had no focal point. And yet in his presence one felt the bounty of an infinite concern.

# Part 1

## THE YOUNG KRISHNAMURTI
### 1895–1946

# CHAPTER 1

# "In Space One Is Born and Unto Space One Is Born."

Fired by the sun, sculptured rocks, amongst the oldest in the world, cradled the village of Madnapalle in the Chittoor district of Andhra Pradesh, South India. From the sacred site of Tirupati through Rishi Valley to Anantpur stretched hills topped with rocky boulders, interspersed with small valleys. Rainfall was minimal, population sparse. Tamarind and gold mohur trees provided shade and exploding color. It was sacred earth, *punyasthal*, where mystics and saints had lived and taught for centuries, their bodies buried there to sanctify the soil. Here, on May 12, 1895, at thirty minutes after midnight, a son was born to Sanjeevamma, the wife of Jiddu Naraniah, a minor civil servant.

The ancestors of Jiddu Krishnamurti, a Brahmin of the Velanadu subcaste, originally came from Giddu or Jiddu, a village that lies in the midst of the fertile paddy fields of coastal Andhra. Krishnamurti's paternal grandfather, Gurumurti, was also a minor civil servant; but his grandfather, Ramakrishna, renowned for his great learning, his knowledge of Sanskrit and the *Vedas*, held a responsible position in the judicial department of the British East India Company.

The house of Naraniah in Madnapalle, one of the most drought-prone areas of South India, was tiny; ill-ventilated and two-storied, it had a narrow frontage that opened onto a lane, along which flowed an open drain. All water for Naraniah's home was drawn from a nearby well and taken by water carriers to be stored within the house in large, burnished brass vessels or earthen pots.

Krishnamurti was born to Sanjeevamma in the *puja* room of her home.[1] The significance of this has been missed by Krishnamurti's biographers. To a traditional Hindu, living amongst the snow-peaked

Himalayas or in Kanyakumari in the deep South, in urban dwelling or village hut, the *puja* room was the sanctum, the heart of the home, where the *griha devatas*, the household gods, were enshrined; it was a room made auspicious with flowers and incense and the recitation of sacred mantras. The room for the gods could only be entered after ritual bath and the wearing of fresh clothes. Birth, death, and the menstrual cycle were the focus of ritual pollution. At birth and death the householder and his family shared in the pollution and refrained from performing the daily *puja*; instead, a Brahmin from the local temple was invited to perform the daily rituals. That a child should be born in this room was unthinkable.

Naraniah's wife and cousin, Sanjeevamma, was a devout and charitable woman. She was considered psychic, experienced visions, and could see the colors in people's auras. As a musician's ear is tuned to a perfectly stringed instrument, so as a mother her ear was tuned to the heartbeats of the baby that waited in the crucible of her body, soon to start its passage through the portals of life. Intimations of the uniqueness of this birth must have given her prophetic vision and courage, otherwise she could not have so challenged the gods.

Early in the evening of May 11, Sanjeevamma felt intimations of the imminent birth of the child. This child would be her eighth, and she was well aware of the routine preparations necessary for the nativity. So she prepared the room, sung Telugu* songs to her husband in her melodious voice, and rested on a mat in the upper story of the building. Toward the middle of the night the pains started. She woke Naraniah, went to the room she had prepared, and lay down on a mat for the birth. A local woman, a relative who was well-versed in the experience of childbirth, came to help while her husband waited outside. Sanjeevamma had little pain. Throughout the period the only words she uttered were, *"Rama, Rama, Anjaneya,"* another name for Hanuman.† At 12:30 A.M., in the early morning of May 12, the woman attendant opened the door and said to Naraniah, *"Sirsodayam,* the head is visible." According to tradition, that is the precise moment of birth.

In this tiny room lit with oil lamps, in the presence of the ishta devata, the household god, Krishnamurti took his first breath. From

---

*Telugu is a Dravidian language spoken by the people of Andhra Pradesh in India. It has a large number of Sanskrit words included in it.

†Hanuman, the monkey devotee of the divine hero Rama of the epic the *Ramayana*, is a people's god, widely worshiped throughout India. In South India he is also known as Anjaneya.

the protected spaces of the womb the baby entered the spaces of the world.

"In space one is born and unto space one is born."[2]

The child's horoscope was cast the next morning by Kumara Shrowthulu, a well-known astrologer of that region. He told Naraniah that this new son would be a very great man. The astrological chart was complex; the child would encounter many obstacles before he grew to be a great Teacher.

For eleven days of the prescribed period, the baby rested in an atmosphere that recreated the ambience of the womb. He lay in semidarkness, gently rocked in a cloth cradle next to his mother. As in all orthodox Hindu births, Krishnamurti's entry into the dazzling light of the sun and the world was gradual.

On the sixth day after birth the name-giving ceremony was held. It was inevitable in this tradition-bound family that the eighth son be given the name Krishnamurti, symbolic of Krishna, the cowherd-god who was the eighth child.

Three years later, in 1898, another boy was born to Sanjeevamma. He was named Nityananda, "eternal bliss."

When Krishna was six years old the *upanayanama* was performed. This is a ceremony of initiation into *brahmacharya*, the period of chaste discipleship that is the first stage in the life of a Brahmin. The ceremony took place at Kadiri, where Naraniah was posted.

The sacred handspun thread was placed around Krishna's shoulders and the secret *gayatri* mantra, the invocation to the sun, was whispered into Krishna's ear by his father. He was taught to recite the mantra with the correct intonation, accent, and gesture. He must have learned to recite the *gayatri* mantra to the sun at dawn and perform the Sandhya rituals at sunset, to take ritual baths, and to be free of any form of ritual pollution. He must have also been taught to recite the *Vedas*.

According to Naraniah's description, "It is a ceremony which Brahmin boys go through when it is time to launch them out into the world of education. It takes place between the age of five and seven years, according to the health and capacity of the child. So when Krishna had reached that age, a day was set apart for this ceremony. It is our custom to make it a family festival, and friends and relations are invited to dinner."

When all the people were assembled, Krishna was bathed and clothed in new clothes. The boy was then brought in and placed upon his father's knees, while Naraniah's outstretched hand supported a silver tray strewn with grains of rice. His mother, sitting beside Naraniah, then took the index finger of the boy's right hand, and with it traced in the rice the sacred word AUM, which in its Sanskrit rendering consists of a single letter—the first letter of the alphabet in Sanskrit and in all the vernacular languages.

"Then," says Naraniah, "my ring was taken from my finger, and placed between the child's finger and thumb; and my wife, holding the little hand, again traced the sacred word in Telugu character with the ring. Then again, without the ring, the same letter was traced three times. After this, mantrams were recited by the officiating priest who blessed the boy that he might be spiritually and intellectually endowed. Then, taking Krishna, my wife and I drove to the Narasimhaswami temple to worship and pray for the future success of our son. From there we drove to the nearest school, where Krishna was handed over to the teacher, who performed, in sand, the same ceremony of tracing the sacred word. Meanwhile, many of the schoolchildren had gathered in the room, and we distributed among them such good things as might serve as a treat to the pupils. So we started our son on his educational career, according to our custom. Then we drove home and partook of dinner with our relations and friends."[3]

Krishna and his brother Nitya were very close, but by nature they were totally different. Nitya was remarkably intelligent. Even "before he could talk, when he saw other boys going to school, he would pick up a slate and pencil and follow them."[4] Krishnamurti was a weak child and suffered grievously from bouts of malaria. At one stage he suffered from convulsions, and for a whole year was kept away from school because of bleeding from the nose and mouth.

Krishnamurti took little interest in the school and academic work, but spent long hours looking at the clouds, at bees, at ants and insects, and gazing into the vast distance. He has been described as sickly and mentally undeveloped. His vagueness, few words, lack of interest in worldly affairs, and eyes that gazed out at the world, seeing beyond horizons, were mistaken by his teachers for mental retardation.

The young Krishnamurti, despite his seeming vagueness, was greatly interested in all mechanical contrivances. One day Krishna missed school. Seeking him, his mother found him alone in a room, totally absorbed in opening up a timepiece. He would not move from the room, and refused all food and drink until he had taken the clock apart and, having understood how it worked, put the machinery back in its place.

The boy Krishna was deeply attached to his mother, who seemed to be aware of her son's unique nature.[5] Sanjeevamma died in 1905, and her death left the child Krishna bewildered and bereft. Many years later, in the summer of 1913, when he was in Europe, he decided to start writing his autobiography. He gave it the title "Fifty Years of My Life," intending as the years passed to "add fresh incidents, and by the year 1945 I shall have justified the title."[6] Alas, the story was to be abandoned after the first few pages. The short manuscript, however, throws very interesting light on his feelings and his early life with his mother. At age eighteen his childhood memories were still vivid, and there is a poignancy in his description of the visions of his mother after her death:

The happiest memories of my child-hood centre round my dear mother, who gave us all the loving care for which Indian mothers are well-known. I cannot say that I was particularly happy at school, for the teachers were not very kind and gave me lessons which were too hard for me. I enjoyed games as long as they were not too rough, as I had very delicate health. My mother's death in 1905 deprived my brothers and myself of the one who loved and cared for us most, and my father was too much occupied with his business to pay much attention to us. I led the usual life as an ordinary Indian youth until I came to Adyar in 1908 [in fact it was January 1909].

Adyar was of special interest to me as my father used to attend the conventions of the Theosophical Society there. He also held meetings in our house at Madnapalle for the study of Theosophy and I learnt about Adyar from my mother and from him. My mother had a *puja* room where she worshipped regularly; in the room were pictures of the Indian deities and also a photograph of Mrs. Besant in Indian dress sitting cross-legged on a *chowki* or small platform on which was a tiger-skin.

I was generally at home while my brothers were at school for I suffered much from fever—in fact almost every day, and I often went into the *puja* room about noon when she performed her daily ceremonies. She would then talk to me about Mrs. Besant and about Karma and reincarnation and also read to me from the *Mahabharata* and *Ramayana* and from other Indian scriptures. I was only about 7 or 8 years of age, so I could not understand much, but I think I felt much that I could not actually understand.

Writing of my mother reminds me of some incidents which are perhaps worth mentioning. She was to a certain extent psychic, and would often see my sister who had died some two or three years before. They talked together and there was a special place in the garden to which my sister used to come. My mother always knew when my sister was there and sometimes took me with her to the place and would ask me whether I saw my sister too. At first I laughed at the question but she asked me to look again and then sometimes I saw my sister. Afterwards I always could see my sister. I must confess I was very much afraid, because I had seen her dead and her body burnt. I generally rushed to my mother's side and she told me that there was no reason to be afraid. I was the only member of the family, except my mother, to see these visions, though all believed in them. My mother was also able to see the auras of people, and I also sometimes saw them. I do not think she knew what the colours meant. There were many other incidents of a similar nature which I do not now remember. We often talked about Sri Krishna to whom I felt specially attracted and I once asked her why he was always represented as being blue in colour. She told me that His aura was blue but how she knew that I do not know.

My mother was very charitable. She was kind to poor boys, and gave food regularly to those who were of her own caste. Each boy came to our house on a special day in the week, and went to other houses on other days. We had daily a number of beggars who often came from some considerable distance to receive rice, *dal* and from time to time clothes.

Before coming to Adyar my brothers and I attended many schools, the pleasantest of which was the school in Madnapalle. I first went to this school when quite a child, for I was born in Madnapalle. My father being a government officer, he was continually being transferred from one place to another, and so our education was much interrupted.

After my mother's death, matters were worse, for there was really nobody to look after us. In connection with my mother's death, I may mention that I frequently saw her after she died, I remember once following my mother's form as it went upstairs. I stretched out my hand and seemed to catch hold of her dress, but she vanished as soon as we reached the top of the stairs. Until a short time ago, I used to hear my mother following me as I went to school. I remember this particularly because I heard the sound of the bangles which Indian women wear on their wrists. At first I would look back half-frightened and I saw the vague form of her dress and part of her face. This happened almost always when I went out of the house.

CHAPTER 2

# The Theosophical Society and the Occult Hierarchy

Madame Helena Petrovna Blavatsky (1831–1891), often called H. P. B., was by all accounts an extraordinary woman. With her psychic vision and piercing mesmeric eyes, and with a personality that provoked controversy, she had appeared on the Indian scene in 1879. A Russian by birth, she claimed to have lived in Tibet for several years in close contact with the Mahatmas* or Masters of the occult brotherhood. It was there that she learned from her *guru*, her teacher, the well-guarded doctrines of the Tibetan sages. While she was in Europe in 1873 her Masters asked her to seek out Colonel Henry Steele Olcott, a fellow psychic researcher in the United States. Obediently, she went there, met Colonel Olcott, and by 1875 the Theosophical Society had been conceived. They were soon to travel together—first to Bombay and then to Ceylon, where they took Buddhist initiation, and later to Madras. By 1882 the Theosophical Society's Headquarters had been established at Adyar, Madras.

The Theosophical Society was based on the tenets of a Universal Brotherhood of humanity, which sought to study ancient wisdom and to explore the hidden mysteries of nature and the latent powers of man. It established an occult hierarchy drawing from the Hindu and Buddhist traditions, in particular the Tibetan tantric texts and teachings.

At the head of the hierarchy was Sanat Kumar, mentioned in the Tantras, in the Bhagvat, and in early alchemic writing, as a youth of sixteen, eternally young, free of all time, as past, present, and future; he was regarded in the Theosophical hierarchy as the lord of the world.

---

*Mahatma*, a Sanskrit term meaning "great spirit," "great soul," "adept," or "master."

Below Kumar was the Buddha. And below the Buddha were the three heads of the logos of the solar system: the bodhisattva Maitreya, the Buddha to be; the Mahachohan, a figure not to be found in any Hindu or Buddhist scriptures; and the Manu, one of the fathers of human-kind, according to the *Rig Veda*. Respectively, they symbolized the heart as compassion, the head as intellect, and the hands as skill in action. Below them were the Mahatmas or Masters, who in years to come would themselves evolve to be bodhisattvas and Mahachohans. Master Koot Hoomi (or Master K. H., as he was known) had the body of a Kashmiri Brahmin, while Master Morya (Master M.) had the body of a Rajput prince. These two Masters guided the affairs of the Theo-sophical Society and the disciples who went through various initiations under their benign guidance.

Toward the end of the nineteenth century whispers of the coming of the Messiah or the World Teacher had spread amongst occult com-munities. H. P. B. had written before her death in 1891 that the real purpose of the Theosophical Society was to prepare for the advent of the World Teacher.

In 1889 Annie Besant (1847–1933) chanced to read Blavatsky's *Secret Doctrine*, and later met the founder of the Theosophical Society. Besant, or A. B., had been a rebel, a free thinker, a fierce fighter for the causes she held to be right. Eloquent and dedicated, she had an organizational capacity of a very high order. She was a passionate crusader for free-dom of thought, women's rights, trade unionism, Fabian socialism, and birth control. But Blavatsky's work transformed her completely. She turned her enormous energies from materialism and atheism to the pursuit of the occult and sacred. Her friends and admirers—among them Bernard Shaw, Sidney and Beatrice Webb and Charles Brad-laugh—were stunned when she joined the Theosophical Society. Part-ing from her former associates, and aware of the cynicism her new role would arouse in her admirers, she wrote:

But here, as at other times, in my life, I dare not purchase peace with a lie. An imperious necessity forces me to speak the truth, as I see it, whether the speech please or displease, whether it brings praise or blame. That one loyalty to Truth I must keep stainless, whatever friendships fail me or human ties be broken. She may lead me into the wilderness, yet I must follow her; she may strip me of all love, yet I must pursue her, though she slay me, yet will I trust in her; and I ask no other epitaph on my tomb but
"She tried to follow Truth."[1]

With her arrival in India in 1893 at the age of forty-six, the passionate dialogue and involvement with India that was to continue throughout her life had commenced.

She sensed the lack of interest in India for what she felt was its true mission in the world—the country's genius for religions and spiritual knowledge. She made this point in one of her first speeches:

If religion perish here, it will perish everywhere and in India's hand, is laid the sacred charge of keeping alight the torch of spirit amid the fogs and storms of increasing materialism. If that torch drops from her hands, its flame will be trampled out by the feet of hurrying multitudes, eager for worldly good; and India, bereft of spirituality, will have no future, but will pass on into the darkness, as Greece and Rome have passed.[2]

Annie Besant studied the sacred books of India, learned Sanskrit, held discussion with the religious leaders of the land. Inspired by the passion of her words, many intellectuals and young aspirants flocked to her and joined the Theosophical Society. Listening with rapt attention and fired by her eloquence was a young boy, twelve-year-old Jawaharlal Nehru. He had come to hear Mrs. Besant under the influence of his Belgian-Irish tutor, Ferdnand T. Brooks, an ardent Theosophist.

Fascinated by the doctrine and by Besant's eloquence, he had gone to his father, Motilal Nehru (the nationalist and flourishing lawyer who would later form the Congress party), and asked for permission to join the Theosophical Society. Motilal Nehru laughed. He had also been a member of the Theosophical Society in the days of Madame Blavatsky. Permission was given, and at thirteen Jawaharlal Nehru became a member and was initiated by Mrs. Besant herself. He attended a convention in Varanasi and saw Colonel Olcott with his white beard. With the young Nehru's departure for Harrow, Theosophy promptly faded from his consciousness. But the three years of his contact with it would leave an impression on him and his character, which he would later acknowledge in his admiration for Annie Besant.[3]

With the death of Colonel Olcott in 1907, Annie Besant became president of the Theosophical Society. A web of intrigue and a fierce division of forces within the Theosophical Society had preceded this event. Soon after Mrs. Besant took over, she came into close contact with Charles Webster Leadbeater or C. W. L. (1847–1934), an ex-Anglican clergyman with reputed powers of clairvoyance. Some years earlier incidents connecting him with homosexual relation with young boys had led to his being expelled from the Society; but Mrs. Besant, aware of his psychic perceptions and refusing to accept the charges against him, had readmitted him to the Society as soon as she became president. Leadbeater was soon to rise high in the Theosophical Society hierarchy.

Naraniah retired from government service in 1908. On his meager pension of 125 rupees a month, he found it impossible to maintain his enlarged family—apart from his sons he also had the responsibility for supporting his sister and his nephews. He had joined the Theosophical Society in 1882, and he now wrote to Annie Besant asking for a job in Adyar. At first she had refused him, aware of the problems his large family would pose to the peace and quiet of the Theosophical Society campus. But Naraniah persisted, and soon he was in Adyar, working as assistant secretary to the Esoteric Section (E. S.). He took a tiny house outside the Adyar compound; his sister oversaw the domestic arangements.

Krishna and his brother Nitya had to walk every day to attend school at Mylapore, where Krishna's inattention resulted in severe punishment. He remained vague and uninterested in his studies; his teacher considered him half-demented. But Krishnamurti's aunt was extremely fond of the dreamy-eyed, unworldly young Krishna and, sensing an incipient wisdom, named him Dronachari, after Drona, the guru of the Pandavas and the Kauravas in the epic *Mahabharata*.

Naraniah's sons used to go bathing in the sea on the Adyar beach, where Leadbeater saw them. In 1899 the subject of Mrs. Besant's lecture at Adyar was "Avatars." In 1908, during her whirlwind tour of the United States, she spoke incessantly of the imminent coming of the World Teacher. For days Leadbeater watched Krishnamurti, growing aware of the presence of the young boy and the unique aura that contained no selfishness.

One evening Mr. Leadbeater, on returning to his room after his usual swim, told Ernest Wood, a young man who was helping Leadbeater in his occult studies, that one of the boys had a remarkable aura; it was Krishnamurti. Wood expressed surprise—he knew the boys, and Krishnamurti was certainly not one of the bright ones. But Mr. Leadbeater persisted that it was Krishnamurti who would one day become a spiritual teacher and a great speaker. Wood asked, "How great? As great as Mrs. Besant?" Leadbeater is said to have replied, "Much greater."[4]

Krishnamurti described his meeting with Leadbeater—who was

quite possibly the first European he had ever met—in his autobiography:

When we first went to Adyar we lived in a house close to the new printing press. Every day we walked to the Mylapore high school. In the early mornings and in the evenings we prepared our home lessons. After some time we began to paddle in the sea with some other boys who lived near. On one of these occasions, in the year 1909, we met for the first time my dear friend and elder brother, C. W. Leadbeater. The meeting was quite casual.

As far as I remember, he (Leadbeater) was going down to the sea with Mr. Van Manen and others to have a swim. I do not remember any particular conversation, especially as I did not know English at all well. After this we met very often and he sometimes invited us to his house or rather bungalow. He was living at the time of which I write in what is known as the river bungalow.

When I first went over to his room I was much afraid, for most Indian boys are afraid of Europeans. I do not know how it is that such fear is created; but one of the causes, there was, when I was a boy, much political agitation and our imaginations were much stirred by the gossip about us. I must also confess that the Europeans in India are by no means generally kind to us, and I used to see many acts of cruelty which made us still more bitter. I wish the English people in India could understand that Indian boys have as deep a love for India as the English have for their own country and feel as deeply any insult, however unintentional.

It was a surprise to us, therefore, to find how different was the Englishman who was also a Theosophist. We soon became very friendly with Mr. Leadbeater, and he helped us regularly with our lessons. Sometime later Mr. R. B. Clarke, a young engineer, arrived at Adyar and it was arranged with my father that my brother Nitya and I should leave school and be taught at Adyar by Mr. Leadbeater and Mr. Clarke. We soon began to make much better progress than we had ever made before. Life became very regular. We came to Mr. Leadbeater's bungalow early in the morning, studied until what might be called breakfast, which we took at home, and then returned to him. In the afternoon we played tennis or went to the sea to learn swimming. My father was very pleased with the progress we were to make and on August 14th it was finally decided that we should not go to school any more.[5]

Krishnamurti had come to be noticed by Leadbeater at a time when the Englishman was undertaking a clairvoyant investigation into the former lives of his associates. Soon he began to probe into the former incarnations of Krishnamurti. These forays into Krishna's occult past were later published as "The Lives of Alcyone." The name Alcyone was derived from the "halcyon," the brightest star in the Pleiades. The investigations revealed a luminous array of past lives where Krishna had been a disciple of the Buddha, and other wondrous lives where his compassion and wisdom had healed and illumined.

At the time the boys were found, they had the front of their heads shaven (as was the custom in South India); Krishnamurti had long hair down to his knees. He was thin and ill-nourished. Soon Krishnamurti and his brother Nitya had started their studies in Adyar. At first strict caste rules on food were maintained, but they were relaxed as Leadbeater's impatience grew and he began weaning the boys away from their father's influence. Naraniah in turn began to create difficulties. Immediately, Leadbeater wrote to Mrs. Besant that the man had lost his sanity and fallen under the influence of "the Blacks." It was then that instructions were "received" by Leadbeater from Master Koot Hoomi. The message was as follows:

They have lived long in hell; try to show them something of paradise. I want them to have everything the opposite of those previous conditions. Instead of hostility, distrust, misery, squalor, irregularity, carelessness and foulness, I want them to be surrounded by an atmosphere of love and happiness, confidence, regularity, perfect physical cleanliness and mental purity . . . Keep them as far as you can, within your aura and Annie's so that they may be protected from evil and carnal thoughts . . . I want you to civilise them; to teach them to use spoons and forks, nail brushes and tooth brushes, to sit at ease upon chairs instead of crouching on the ground, to sleep rationally on a bed, not in a corner like a dog.[6]

It is inconceivable that a Master of wisdom—who was also a Kashmiri Brahmin—could have written this letter, loaded as it is with colonial overtones and with its obvious Victorian bias. The contempt with which the British in India regarded Indian culture and living habits is evident in this letter. It was written at a time when the South Indian man, woman, and child, rich or poor, sat and slept on a mat on the floor, and where the joint family provided warmth and a sense of belonging rare in the West.

It is also difficult to believe that the brothers were dirty in their habits; as Brahmins, they must have bathed several times a day. Ritual bathing preceded by an oil bath was a discipline closely followed. The teeth were regularly cleaned by the twig of a neem tree, perhaps the best disinfectant that exists; daily clothes washing must also have been part of the regular chores of the household.

In the first half of the twentieth century the Indian was regarded by the British rulers of India as a necessary part of the landscape—to be kept at a sufficient distance, to be at best tolerated; but under no circumstances was an Indian encouraged to be familiar, and an attitude of condescension pervaded most relationships. It was in this milieu that the boy Krishna, born a Brahmin but to a family very low in the official hierarchy, came to be recognized by an eccentric British mystic, in a flash of psychic insight, as a great being, and later as the vehicle for the advent of the Bodhisattva Maitreya.

Krishna and Nitya were taken from the confines of their tiny house into the grandeur of the Theosophical Society headquarters building and its vast grounds. They were taken over by C. W. L., a long-bearded, venerable-looking white man who spoke an esoteric language of luminous Masters and initiates, past lives and splendid incarnations. The extra-sensitive nervous system and perceptions of Krishna, keyed to a state of expectancy, possibly did touch treasures of the racial unconscious. His Brahminic background and its iconography provided the warp to the woof of Theosophical Society imagery. Thought forms and visual images circulating in the atmosphere of Adyar, charged with occult truths and illusions, were made manifest to the young neophyte. As the boy Krishna had seen visions of the divine child Krishna in the devout home of his mother, so he now saw the Masters, the Buddha, and Sanat Kumar—the smiling, sun-filled youth who was the head of the Theosophical Society hierarchy. The esoteric forces, if they existed, and certainly Leadbeater, demanded for their vehicle a Brahmin body, with its heritage of sensitivity, vegetarianism, and cleanliness, with a brain that through centuries had been concerned with otherness, with the subtlety, strength and perception necessary to cleave into the within of mind and matter, with the capability of receiving the vast volumes of energy it would be called upon to hold.

Ironically, once they had been accepted into the Theosophical fold, everything possible was done to see that Krishna and Nitya were stripped of all Indianness. It is almost certain that Krishnamurti's mentors decided that he and his brother were to speak only English, so the melodious Telugu language was slowly forgotten; the *Vedas* and the hymns learnt in childhood were wiped away. Their hair was cut and halved by a central parting. They were taught English; they learned how to eat with a spoon and fork and to keep their elbows close to their body when they raised their forks to their mouths; to wear Western clothes with ease; to see that the crease of their trousers was pressed and to polish their shoes till they shone. They were taught how to bathe the British way. "The boys were to become English gentlemen because in Leadbeater's scheme of evolution, English gentlemen represented the pinnacle of human development."[7]

Fortunately, the outer veneer and education left no mark on the mind that lay in abeyance, untouched. Perhaps it was right that the boy, destined to be a Teacher who would walk the world, had to be freed from a condition of birth and country. To fulfill his destiny no frontiers could contain or restrain him.

According to C. Jinarajadasa, later to be president of the Theosophical Society, the training was strictly regimented. Meals, study, and games were on an absolute schedule intended to teach the boys alertness to time and circumstances. Bicycling was not for fun, but to teach self-reliance and resistance to fatigue. On one occasion they were made to cycle to Chingelpet and back, a total of sixty-four miles. To eliminate fear, Leadbeater read them bloodcurdling ghost stories.[8]

Speaking to us of this period of his life seventy-five years later, Krishnamurti spoke of the boy Krishna and his relationship to Leadbeater. "The boy had always said, 'I will do whatever you want.' There was an element of subservience, obedience. The boy was vague, uncertain, wooly; he didn't seem to care what was happening. He was like a vessel, with a large hole in it, whatever was put in, went through, nothing remained." They called him the vehicle, he accepted that without any question. There was no resistance in him, no doubt nor questioning. Krishnamurti also spoke of the boy's psychic powers. He could read what was in a closed letter, read people's thoughts, see faeries. But he appeared totally unaware of the significance of these extrasensory faculties; for him they were of no account.

The Masters had instructed Mrs. Besant and Leadbeater to protect the body of Krishnamurti for two years and so prepare it for the manifestation. Everything was done to ensure this; Krishnaji would later say that although Leadbeater and others determined the conditions in which the outer life of Krishnamurti would develop, no attempt was made to interfere with the boy's psyche or to mold his brain, for they said, "The Lord is preparing it."

Leadbeater was often impatient with Krishna—the boy's vagueness irritated him, particularly the habit of standing with his mouth open. On one occasion he hit Krishna sharply on the chin to force him to close his mouth. Krishnaji was to say later that this act of violence broke all relationship between Krishna and Leadbeater.

Just before Mrs. Besant's return to India, Krishna was put on probation by the Masters. When Mrs. Besant arrived in Madras in November 1909, she saw with Leadbeater an "eager large eyed boy" shyly step forward to put a garland round her neck. Leadbeater's voice said, "This is our Krishna."[9]

With her coming, a protective wall was slowly built around the boy. A special group of boys was selected to play with him; no one was permitted to sit on his chair or to use his tennis racket. Everything he did was closely monitored.

To ensure that Naraniah would not interfere in the training, a message was soon received from the Masters that the boys should go as little as possible to their father's house. Mrs. Besant prevailed on the father to hand over the guardianship of the boys to her. Soon all visits of the boys to Naraniah's house had ended.

While Mrs. Besant was in Adyar, she met with Krishna every day. It was during this period that the seeds of her relationship with him, based on love and infinite trust, were sown. In the months prior to Mrs. Besant's return to India, Leadbeater claimed to have taken Krishna every night on the astral plane to be instructed by the Masters. The boy had been brought in contact with the esoteric life of the Society as viewed by Leadbeater and the language that surrounded the occult mysteries. Portraits of the Masters and Mahatmas hung in the shrine room, the meditation hall of the Esoteric Section; faces and names were absorbed by Krishna to fuse and grow one with his everyday reality. Mrs. Besant first met Krishna on November 27, 1909, and by December 5 he had been admitted to the Esoteric Section of the Theosophical Society.

She was to leave Adyar for Varanasi soon after.

# CHAPTER 3

# The Dream: "Is That You My Lord?"

What was the work that took Mrs. Besant to Varanasi at this time, the most crucial moment of her life? Why was she not in Adyar at the time of the first initiation? Was she herself under the guidance of mystics and sages, seeking an assurance about Krishnamurti from the occult hierarchy? Had she to undergo yogic initiations in order to protect the child who was to be the World Teacher?

Speaking to learned scholars and the Brahmin pandits of Varanasi more than seventy years later, I gathered that in those early years Mrs. Besant had been in touch in Varanasi with Swami Vishudhanand and his disciple Gopinath Kaviraj. Swami Vishudhanand was a renowned tantric, with many *siddhis* or mystical powers. He also claimed direct links to a secret cult and doctrine of Tibet; originating in India, this doctrine had survived in its pristine form in a heavily charged psychic center beyond Mansarovar Lake in Tibet. At this center many great sages and bodhisattvas were said to gather, not in their physical form, but perhaps as centers of energy. One of their most guarded doctrines was an ear-to-mouth, whispered doctrine, concerned with the eternal cycle of time—with yoga or *kundalini* practices and with the transference of consciousness. This yoga, fraught with immense dangers, had originated in India long before the Buddha and his teaching. It later disappeared in India, but survived amongst adepts in that secret center in Tibet.

It is possible that through Swami Vishudhanand, Mrs. Besant grew aware of the doctrine of the "turning around" or transference of consciousness and its close links to *kundalini* yoga. Pandit Jagannath Upadhyaya of Varanasi, who had found a copy of the original text of the *Kala Chakra Tantra,* and who was undertaking research into it, told

Krishnaji that Pandit Gopinath Kaviraj maintained that the Theosophical Society drew much of its hidden teaching from this secret doctrine. He went on to say that Swami Vishudhanand and Gopinath Kaviraj, in the early years of the twentieth century, had spoken to Mrs. Besant of the imminent coming of the Maitreya Boddhisattva and his manifestation in a human body; according to the swami, the body chosen was that of Krishnamurti. Krishnaji's response had been swift. "The Maitreya cannot manifest, it would be like the sky manifesting. It is the teaching that manifests." Another day, speaking on the same subject, as if through a rent in time Krishnaji suddenly saw an image. He said, "Amma [A. B.] visited the Kaviraj riding a horse."[1]

When I heard this I was intrigued. The image of Mrs. Besant riding a white charger in the early twentieth century through the tiny lanes of Varanasi to visit *sadhus*, mendicant ascetics, was pure magic; I enquired further and found that Mrs. Besant was very fond of riding and it is likely that she did ride to her meetings with the gurus of Varanasi. This whole area of enquiry throws new light on the manner in which many secret insights and doctrines entered the Esoteric Section of the Theosophical Society. It is possible that Mrs. Besant's total faith that the Bodhisattva Maitreya would manifest through the body of Krishnamurti was due to these early contacts with Varanasi gurus and their links to the occult hierarchy. Leadbeater, with his obvious psychic gifts, was heavily burdened by occidental occult symbology; the sources that provided the Indian stream to the occult world of Theosophy could only have come from sources steeped in Indian and Tibetan tradition.

Within three weeks of Krishna's joining the Esoteric Section, Leadbeater had telegraphed Mrs. Besant that the boy had been accepted by Master Koot Hoomi as his disciple. Only five months had passed since Krishna had been discovered by Leadbeater.

Writing to Mrs. Besant in a beautiful script, possibly the result of intense copybook practice, Krishna described the ceremony of acceptance on January 3, 1910:

My dear Mother,

It was very beautiful. When we went to our Master's house, we found him and Master Morya and the Master Djwal Kul all standing talking, and they spoke very kindly. We all prostrated ourselves, and the Master drew me onto his knee, and asked me whether I would forget myself entirely and never have a selfish thought, but think only how to help the world and I said indeed I would, and I wanted only to be like him someday. Then he kissed me and passed his hand over me, and I seemed to be somehow part of him, and I felt quite different and very very happy, and I have had that feeling ever since. Then they all three blessed me and we came away. But next morning in the Shrine Room when I thanked him again, I felt his hand press strongly on my head again just as in the night.

I have ridden 254 miles now, and I enjoy the rides very much. How soon will you come back to us. I send you very much love many times each day.

Your loving son,

Krishna[2]

The period of probation was short, and unusual events soon followed. An eminent astrologer, G. E. Sutcliff, had foreseen a very unusual positioning of planets for January 11. Telegrams were exchanged between Leadbeater and Mrs. Besant, and she was finally informed that the first initiation of Krishna was to take place on the night of January 11 to 12. Mrs. Besant was unable to be present, but she issued instructions that the doors of the shrine room of the Esoteric Section and the veranda which opened onto her room were to be closed, and that Krishna and Leadbeater were to occupy her room during this momentous occasion.

It was said later that Krishna and Leadbeater were out of their bodies during two nights and a day, coming back into them occasionally for some nourishment. Krishna lay on Mrs. Besant's bed, Leadbeater on the floor. On January 12 they emerged from the room to find some of the elders of the Society awaiting them. Amongst them was Krishna's father, Naraniah, and his brother Nitya. Krishna wrote to Mrs. Besant immediately, describing the mysterious happenings:

When I left my body the first night, I went at once to the Master's house and I found Him there with the Master Morya and the Master Djwal Kul. The Master talked to me very kindly for a long time, and told me all about the initiation, and what I should have to do. Then, we all went together to the house of the Lord Maitreya, where I had been once before, and there we found many of the Masters—the Venetian Master, the Master Jesus, the Master the Count, the Master Serapis, the Master Hilarion and the two Masters Morya and K. H. The Lord Maitreya sat in the middle and the others stood round Him in a semi-circle. [Here Krishna drew a diagram to make the positions of the gathered Brotherhood clear.] Then the Master took my right hand and the Master Djwal Kul my left, and they led me in front of the Lord Maitreya, you [Mrs. Besant] and uncle [Leadbeater] standing close behind me. The Lord smiled at me, but He said to the Master: "Who is this that you bring before me?" And the Master answered: "This is a candidate for admission to the Great Brotherhood."

[The Masters who had gathered agreed to his admission into the Brotherhood.]

Then the Lord turned away from me and called towards Shamballa: "Do I this, O Lord of Life and Light, in Thy Name and for Thee?" And at once the great Silver Star flashed out over His head and on each side of it in the air there stood a figure—one for the Lord Gautama Buddha and the other the Mahachohan. And the Lord Maitreya turned and called me by the true name of my Ego, and laid His hand upon my head and said: "In the name of the One Initiator, whose Star shines above us, I receive you into the Brotherhood of Eternal Life." [The next night they were taken to visit Sanat Kumar.]

. . . for He is a boy not much older than I am, but the handsomest I have ever seen, all shining and glorious, and when He smiles it is like sunlight. He is strong like the sea, so that nothing could stand against Him for a moment, and yet He is nothing but love, so that I could not be in the least afraid of Him.[3]

Mrs. Besant's reply to Krishna is not available, but she wrote in glowing words to Leadbeater, confirming the event. The correspondence between Mrs. Besant and Krishna reveal the immensity of her love and concern for the child. Her words reach out to him:

31 March 1910

My loved Krishna, blessed little son, I wonder if you see or feel me in the morning meditation where I come to you, *you* do in your astral, but do you in your brain down here? And very often in the day I send a thought-form to wrap its wings round you.

There was such a big meeting in Calcutta for the animals and I told the people about the Robin who tried to pull the nail out of the hand of Christ on the Cross. That is not a story of a fact but of a real truth, like the story of Shri Rama stroking the squirrels have pretty stripes [sic]. Once at Sarnath where the Buddha preached his first sermon, I looked back to see it; and a little fawn came up and put her nose into his hand. The Lord was all love, so the animals were not afraid of him. Tell dear Nitya that I give him a kiss on the top of his dear little head every morning, and send him a thought-form too. You know that I love you very much my Krishna, and am always.

Your loving mother.[4]

Krishna replied on April 5, 1910:

Of course, my physical brain remembers when you put your arms round me, because I am trying to make my consciousness the same all the time, but I am not always quite sure of it yet. I am working always for what is wanted for the second step, but it will take some time. I think, I have not much doubt or superstition, but it is very hard to get rid of the delusion of self, but I will do it. I do not quite know how yet, but somehow it shall be done.

I have read "Children of the Motherland" and in about the next three days, we shall have finished "The Story of the Great War." I have heard the stories about "The Robin and the Squirrel," but I have not yet seen a Robin. It is 1250 years since I was last at Saranath, but I hope to go there in this life also. There was a great grey pillar there with a lion on it and other smaller pillars round it in half a circle. How soon will you come back to us? I send you very much love every day.

Your loving son, Krishna.[5]

A photograph taken immediately after Krishna's first initiation, five months after he had been "discovered" by Leadbeater, reveals the young *brahmacharin* mantled in an *angavastram*. It is a fragile face with intimations of unbounded strength. In profile, the hair hangs just above his shoulders; his eyes mirror *akash*, endless space and sound. The mouth is slightly open, neither smiling, nor grim; a tender mango shoot that has no self-will, but only life energy; a face defenseless, entirely without guile: "Of the waters the first born sap, / likewise of the forest trees."[6]

Many of Krishna's biographers, describing him at the time of discovery by Leadbeater, speak of him as backward, even moronic, dirty, unkempt, with only his large eyes to distinguish his face. Astonishingly, there are no comments on his awesome beauty.

By September 1910 Mrs. Besant, who was in Adyar, took the brothers with her to Varanasi. It was here that Krishna sent for the notes he is said to have written in Adyar, and which were to form the material for his first book, *At the Feet of the Master.*

The appearance of the book aroused a major controversy. Specially bound in blue leather and autographed by Krishna, a copy meant for Master Koot Hoomi and placed under Krishna's pillow was to disappear by morning. A vast number of copies of the book sold. Krishna's English at the time was feeble, and many critics maintained that the book had been written by Leadbeater. The book was lucid, combining Theosophical teaching with certain basic tenets of Hinduism.

There is little doubt that even if the notes had been originally written by Krishna under the guidance of Master K. H., the final version bore a definite Leadbeater imprint. Questioned by his father, Krishna is reported to have denied having written the book.

Some fifty years later the physicist George Sudarshan asked Krishnaji about the authorship of *At the Feet of the Master.* Krishnaji replied,

"The man who wrote the book has disappeared."[7] He refused to say anything further about it.

In 1911 Mrs. Besant traveled to England with her two wards. Her old friends and admirers in India had been very critical about what they referred to as the whole "Messiah business," and she had been attacked relentlessly by *The Hindu*, an influential English daily published in Madras. Soon many members of the Theosophical Society from all over India, some of whom were her close friends, were in open revolt for her worship "of the little Hindu boy she calls Alcyone."[8] In spite of ridicule, open opposition, and desertion from the Society of some of its eminent members, Mrs. Besant stood like a rock, her faith unshaken, steadfast to the Masters' instructions that Krishna was to be the vehicle for the Maitreya Buddha.

Before leaving for England Mrs. Besant had a complete Western wardrobe made for the boys by the best tailors in Bombay. When they arrived at Charing Cross Station to be met by a gathering of Theosophists, Krishna was wearing a Norfolk jacket and trousers.

Mrs. Besant took the boys to stay at the home of her friend Miss Bright. In her book *Old Memories and Letters of Annie Besant,* Esther Bright described the two Indian wards of Mrs. Besant.

It was to this house that A. B. brought her two young Indian wards, the brothers Krishnamurti and Nityanandam. They made their home with us. It was interesting to watch their reactions to our Western life—very shy and reserved they were—but keenly alive to what was going on in our peculiar Western world, and often, no doubt, very critical of us! Especially on the subject of Rice! "I do not think Miss Bright quite understands" said Nitya once very gravely "how much we like rice." He was a charming little fellow, such a serious face and keen, friendly, inquiring eyes; a fine, big nature in that small Indian body. A. B. was devoted to these boys and gave them all the affection and loving kindness possible. It was beautiful to see them together . . .[9]

Parted from Krishna for a short while, Mrs. Besant wrote on November 29, 1911:

I am sending you big waves of love, like those that come tumbling in through the opening of the bar; only they do not knock you about, but only envelope and guard the precious body that the Lord will wear.

I love my own dear Krishna, the ego that I have loved for so many years; How many? I do not know. Since we were leaping animals, and guarded our Master's hut? Perhaps longer still; perhaps when we were plants, we put out delicate tendrils to each other in the sunshine and the storm. And perhaps we were animals—Oh, so very long ago—I was a bit of crystal and you a bit of gold in me.[10]

Krishna and Nitya returned to India with Mrs. Besant for a short period in December 1912. The attacks against Mrs. Besant were continuing. The brothers accompanied Mrs. Besant to Varanasi. According to Mrs. Besant and Leadbeater it was here that the first quickening of the spirit was to occur, after which Mrs. Besant proclaimed that there could no longer be any doubt that Krishnamurti had been selected by the Bodhisattva Maitreya as his vehicle.

By 1912 Mrs. Besant and the two boys returned to Europe. Naraniah had reluctantly allowed his sons to go back, on the understanding that they would be kept away from all contact with Leadbeater. At the time, news of Leadbeater's sexual proclivities were being freely talked about in the English community of Madras, and it was natural that the father should resent any contact of his sons with him. As Mrs. Besant was about to leave India with her wards, Naraniah's fears reawakened and he threatened to file a suit for their recovery. But she prevailed on the father to allow the boys to accompany her and prepare for their entry to Oxford. Hearing, however, that Mrs. Besant on reaching Europe had taken the boys to Taormina in Italy, where Leadbeater was waiting to help Krishna undergo his second initiation, Naraniah finally filed a case for the recovery of custody of his sons. Mrs. Besant returned to India and fought the suit with her enormous energy, diligence, and sheer willpower; she appeared in person in the courts and argued with great skill against some of the best legal experts of the country. She lost the case both in the lower court and in the High Court of Madras; but eventually she won in her appeal to the Privy Council.

Krishna and Nitya did not see India from 1912 to 1922.

The contact between Mrs. Besant and Krishna could only be maintained through letters. Krishna wrote to her every week describing his studies, his dreams, his problems. He started collecting money for Mrs. Besant's work in India and promised to contribute 2s 6d a week from his pocket money. During a visit to a dentist in the last week of August 1912, a mild application of cocaine to his wisdom tooth led to an extraordinary dream that night of the Lord Maitreya. He described the dream in a letter to Mrs. Besant—the handwriting sprawls across the page, words are cut out, the lines crooked:

I remembered being in a room above an E. S. [Esoteric Section] room with

Clarke.* There was an E. S. meeting which Mother held. The meeting was over and Clarke and I went upstairs into my room. My window looked into the E. S. room. I went to the window casually and saw a person in the E. S. room. I was rather startled at first, because I saw that every person was out after the meeting and I had myself locked the door. I felt rather uneasy about it and was rather afraid but, I said to myself "what is there to be afraid about?" Therefore, I called Clarke and went down. I walked down rather quickly and when I was at the bottom, I looked up to see Clarke, but he was not there. I heard a sort of noise and I saw as follows: A form seemed to come out of the Lord Maitreya's picture and those of the Master's. I saw a man's legs and only up to his neck, as I could not see whose face it was as it was covered with a sort of gold cloth. I knew who the person was as he had long hair and pointed beard and I wanted to make sure and I said very humbly & the words are exact. I said "Is that You, my Lord?" . . . He took away the cover from His face and I knew for certain, it was the Lord Maitreya. Then, I prostrated myself and He stretched His hand over me in blessing. Then He sat on the ground cross-legged and I also sat down cross-legged on the floor. Then He began to talk to me and told me things which I do not remember. Then I prostrated and He was gone.

A few hours later I and an Indian boy friend were walking along a road and on both sides there were mountains and rivers and I saw a man walking towards us, he was tall and well built. As the form approached us I knew who it was and told my friend to go away. My friend said he wanted to see who it was. By this time, the form was very close to us and I was going to prostrate myself when He put up His hand not to do it. My friend was behind me. The Lord turned to my friend and said to him "What do you want here?" My friend did not answer Him. Then the Lord said to him again "if you do not want anything, you had better go away." My friend still stood there without answering. Then the Lord lifted His hand and pointed it towards my friend and as I was close to His hand, I heard a sort of rumbling noise as if a train had passed by. I turned towards my friend and I saw him slowly falling down. My friend was motionless as though he was dead. Then I prostrated, and the Lord Maitreya said "That boy of yours is rather inquisitive" and I could not answer Him and I was sorry that I brought my friend along.

### PRIVATE

The Lord said, I think this is what He said—"Raja [C. Jinarajadasa] was to go to America after George [Arundale, Krishna's tutor in England between 1912 and 1914] has come next year and Clarke was to stay." He told me that I was getting on well and something else which I do not *remember*. I remember the

---

*Russel B. Clarke (Dick) was an engineer and a Theosophist who came to stay in Adyar in 1910 and was assisting C. W. Leadbeater in his work. When the boys Krishna and Nitya were discovered, Clarke became their tutor.

Lord very clearly. His face was like a glass covered with a thin piece of gold; in other words, as Mother said, like ripe corn. His face was radiant and luminous.

He was very kind to me. He once or twice put His hand over my shoulder. He talked about Mother and George. We talked for a very long time. At the end, I asked him "Is there any order my Lord?" and He said, "you need not be so formal." Then I prostrated once more. He said, "we shall meet often."

I felt as though I could talk with Him for ever and I saw Lord Maitreya's form disappear. Then I awoke and it was half past five. Then also, I wrote out all this. . . . Krishna.[11]

Through the years of separation Mrs. Besant continued to write to Krishna regularly, describing her life, teaching him to spell, and so forth. Her letters reflect her concern for him and her remarkable qualities as a teacher. On October 9, 1912, she noticed his appalling spelling and wrote:

I am glad you are doing your lessons regularly. Please try to pay attention to them while you are doing them, and make your mind steady and *think*, as you did with me. It is very important that you should master these ordinary things, and do us all credit at Oxford. I should like parallel bars better without two Rs; you have the ll's right; unparalleled is one of the puzzle words often given for spelling. I do not think there is any rule about "r" being single or double for we write harass with one, and embarras [sic] with two. In reading books, we learn to know how a word *looks*, and if it is wrongly spelt, it looks like a lame man.

I leave for Adyar on the 20th at midnight, and there is going to be a reception given to me by the Madras people, to show that they do not sympathise with the *Hindu*.

With very much love to you and dear Nitya,

Your own loving Mother.[12]

A year later, in reply to a comment about his unruly writing, Krishna wrote to Besant, "I am very sorry that Lord Maitreya should speak three times about my hand-writing."[13]

Mrs. Besant, fighting the case for the custody of the boys, and caught in the whirlpool of political life in India, placed Krishna and Nitya in the care of C. Jinarajadasa and later George Arundale. Shunted as they were from place to place, tutor to tutor, very little spiritual education or discussion appears to have taken place during this period. For a time the brothers were sent to school near Rochester. Their lives were made miserable by the other boys, who told dirty jokes and called the brothers "black devils."

While Krishna was in India, in the early years, he had a living contact with the Masters: but in England he soon grew skeptical and took little interest in any esoteric activity. He told a friend that on one occasion when the Master K. H. was standing before him, speaking to him, he had gone up to the Master and walked through him. The Masters, according to Krishna, were never to appear to him again.

On April 15, 1913, Justice Blackwell of the High Court of Madras passed judgment on the case brought by Naraniah for the return of the custody of his sons, Krishna and Nitya.

The honorable judge concluded that although the evidence of Naraniah, the father, was not to be trusted, the plaintiff was not aware when he signed the guardianship agreement that his son was to be brought up as a "vehicle of supernatural powers" and, therefore, had a right to change his mind when he so learned.

His lordship refused to pass orders of custody, as the boys were residents of British India and only temporary residents of England. He therefore declared them wards of the court and ordered the boys to be turned over to their father on or about May 26, 1913.

A stay of execution, however, was granted to Mrs. Besant, who decided to appeal to the Privy Council. She had telegraphed Krishna and had received a cable in reply from Raja, Nitya, and Krishna, expressing their total confidence in her.

She wrote to Krishna on April 17:

My beloved son,

Your nice telegram, signed by you, Raja and Nitya, gave me much pleasure. You and Nitya are perfectly safe. No one can touch you. "I protect." And over us all shines the Star of the great king, and the hand of the Lord Maitreya guards you. Did not He Himself bid me protect you? It is my privilege and pride to do so, my blessed boy.

I am quite enjoying myself and am remembering how you, [and] I gallopped along the Himalayan valleys when we came down into India.

Your own loving mother.

Do you think galloped or gallopped look better? I am not sure. People spell it both ways. I think the two pps look more like the leaps of a horse.[14]

With the outbreak of war in 1914 Krishna's tutor, George Arundale, had volunteered for the Red Cross and found a senior position in King George's Hospital. Krishna and Nitya, eager to work, had also offered their services, but to no avail. Despite the fact that a large number of Indian troops were fighting for the British, racial prejudice was at its peak. The presence of dark-skinned Indians in a white man's hospital was frowned on by the authorities. After great pressure from influential sources, Krishna found work in a hospital near the Theosophical Society, but was only permitted to scrub floors. He wrote to Mrs. Besant on July 1, 1915:

My dearest Mother,

Thank you so very much for your letter. Of course, I shall do what you wish and I shall not touch meat or anything of that sort. We are now working in a hospital near the Theosophical Society with Dr. Guest. I like working there and I am kept busy from morning till nearly 7 in the evening. I think George likes his work too and I think he is happier. We are of course working under Dr. Guest and I like it very much.

I think everything is going on very well.

Your own devoted son,
Krishna[15]

But by July 15th they had been asked to leave. In another letter to Mrs. Besant, written from Greenwood Gate, Withyham, Sussex, Krishna says:

. . . I have been working really hard for a change at the hospital because there are too many Theosophists and I being an Indian am not wanted by the Committee. They also don't want any honorary workers. They are all very jealous and very petty. Lady Williamson who is the wife of the Chairman, Sir Archibald Williamson, wants to boss everybody including Dr. Guest and he is appointed as the Head of the Hospital by the War Office. Dr. Guest is now Major Guest and he is a bit sick of all this. The Committee has asked me and others to go away and so I have not been working there since yesterday. I am sorry because I liked the work very much and I was just getting into it. Now, I am going to find something else which will occupy me and think of other people and get away from myself. I will do what you tell me and be useful. . . .[16]

The brothers tried desperately to find work but were turned away. Krishna wrote on August 18, 1915:

. . . I have tried very hard to find work anywhere of any sort but it is really very difficult. First of all, I am an Indian and nobody seems to like them . . . I do want to work, in as [sic] you tell me to forget myself, I think it is the only way, work. I hope it will be all right.[17]

The fact that he was an Indian and, therefore, unacceptable became a recurrent refrain in his letters to Mrs. Besant.

Mrs. Besant's replies are unavailable, but the stiff-necked old ladies who surrounded Krishna felt he was too frivolous and must have complained to Mrs. Besant. Krishna wrote to Mrs. Besant on October 7:

I know, I have not taken my life seriously so far and I am going to do it from now. I am beginning my studies from next Monday. I had settled to study after the letter you had written to Lady De La Warr. I am going to study Sanskrit, English, Mathematics, History and French. I am having lessons for each and I mean to get into Oxford as soon as I can. I will study for all my worth and after Oxford, there is my work laid out for me by the Masters and yourself. I honestly mean to do this and *I will* do this at all costs.[18]

In spite of these letters, the brothers were very lonely, unhappy, and felt totally rejected. Increasingly disillusioned, they appear to have lost interest in the Theosophical teachings. Krishna wrote to Leadbeater about Nitya:

He feels very lonely, like most of us do, and there is nobody whom he specially likes or loves and makes doubly harder. He is very bitter, hard and cold. He suffers a lot. I am afraid, I can't help him much. He wants somebody to love him first and foremost and to whom he can pour out all his troubles. He wants a mother to love as I have lady Emily.[19]

Krishna's only friend in England was Lady Emily Lutyens, the wife of Edwin Lutyens, the visionary architect who had designed New Delhi. Thirty-six years old when she first met Krishna, she was present, along with a huge crowd at the Charing Cross Road platform, to receive Mrs. Besant and the mysterious young boy Alcyone. When she saw the large-eyed, long-haired young Indian boy, who was then sixteen years old, she was deeply stirred. Lady Emily became very friendly with Krishna, who was bewildered and lonely in alien surroundings. At first her husband, Edwin Lutyens, was amused. Later he became deeply upset, as he felt Lady Emily was neglecting him and the children. Mrs. Besant was very distressed, because she felt that any emotional atmosphere around Krishna was detrimental to the mission for which he was intended. In the letters Krishna continued to write Mrs. Besant, however, he referred to Lady Emily as being much better, more serious, and trying very hard.

The brothers' names had been entered for Balliol at Oxford. But the master of Balliol, concerned about the controversies that had arisen around Krishna, rejected him on the "general principle that his college did not want to have anything to do with a brown Messiah."[20]

All attempts by Mrs. Besant to arrange for their admission to any other college in Oxford or Cambridge also failed. Krishna was also unable to pass any of the entrance examinations for London University. He would study for days but, when faced with an examination, would come away leaving a blank paper.

The brothers were living with Miss Dodge in Wimbledon. Miss Dodge was a very rich and charitable American woman. Crippled by arthritis, she had financed many activities of the Theosophical Society. She was a friend of Lady Emily Lutyens, who introduced her to Mrs. Besant and Theosophy. Krishna and Nitya commuted every day to London, where they were studying, with immense difficulty, to pass the entrance examinations to London University. "It was at this time that they learnt to dress well, and feel at ease in a rich aristocratic household."[21] They had begun to go to expensive tailors and visit the theater. Krishna was showing very few signs of his fulfilling the promise forecast for him by Leadbeater and Mrs. Besant. As Krishna grew older Mrs. Besant was to say to him, "My dear, what is to happen to you?" She saw that Krishna was only interested in clothes and cars. But her trust in the role the Masters had foreseen for Krishna remained unshaken.

Meanwhile, at the Theosophical convention held in Varanasi in December 1913, C. W. Leadbeater had discovered a thirteen-year-old Brahmin youth from Madras named D. Rajagopal. Attracted by his aura, C. W. L. prophesied a brilliant future for him—even to the extent of saying that in a future life he would be the next Buddha on the planet Mercury. Adopted by Leadbeater, Rajagopal was sent to England with C. Jinarajadasa in 1920. He was soon to enter Cambridge, where he studied law and passed his examination brilliantly.

When Krishna and Rajagopal first met, there was a certain aloofness, and Krishna's friends treated Rajagopal with a flippancy and disregard. Rajagopal, deeply hurt by their attitudes, attempted to mask his feelings. By 1922, however, the relationship between Krishna, Nitya, and Rajagopal had improved considerably.


After the war, having failed in all his attempts to enter a university, Krishna went to Paris and stayed with his friends the Manziarlys. They were a large, warm family, and introduced him to Paris. Krishna met dancers, writers, painters, musicians. He was awakening to a new creative world. It was enchantment. For a time the role of messiah sat lightly on his shoulders.

One night Krishna attended a reception hosted for him. Amongst the many personalities present were some generals in gala uniform;

many had gathered out of curiosity to see this beautiful young man destined to be a messiah. Some were cynical, others full of admiration.

"Many expected the new messiah to appear as an oriental figure" with the "voice of an Elijah." The "messiah" proved to be "an elegant young man in flannel trousers." His gestures were nonchalant and even a little bored. When questioned about the heavy burden of being called an incarnation of a Deity, he laughed aloud. "I should say it is rather a burden. The thing I am most interested in just now is whether Suzanne Lenglen will be able to hold out against Helen Wills [at Wimbledon]."[22]

In December 1921, after an absence of nine years, Krishnamurti and his brother Nitya returned to India. Krishnamurti was seeing India anew; during this visit he would make friends, observe his surroundings, and reestablish a communication with the Masters.

The brothers decided to visit their father, Naraniah, who had had no contact or news of them for nine years. His daughter-in-law G. Sharada, who had married Krishna's elder brother when she was fifteen, was deeply hurt and in tears when she spoke to me years later in 1984 of the reports that had been current of the meeting between Naraniah and his two sons. Unable to visit the Theosophical Society, he had sought news of them from outside the Society. Neither of the boys had written to him over the years, and when he received a telegram that they were coming to visit him, he had wept. At his behest, his daughter-in-law spent two days preparing the special foods he knew his sons had enjoyed eating.

It was evening when the brothers arrived. G. Sharada said she was very shy, and waited outside on the veranda when Krishnamurti and Nitya came to visit. Describing Krishnamurti, she said, "He looked beyond description, very bright—full of light. He had a strange quick walk, and was much taller than others." She bowed her head when she saw him. To tease her, he put his two hands on his face, as if he had not seen her. Nitya chided him and said, "Why do you do that? She is naturally shy, like an Indian girl."

Naraniah was overwhelmed when he saw his sons, and stood up to greet them. Krishnamurti and Nitya prostrated themselves before him and touched their foreheads to his feet. Naraniah embraced them and started weeping. Krishnamurti sat down with him and, according to G. Sharada, "consoled him." Later they spoke of Mrs. Besant. The father and his sons did not speak in Telugu, but in English. The specially prepared sweets and savories were offered to the brothers. The boys were shy and embarrassed, and were unsure of how to behave. Consequently, they ate very little. Krishnamurti refused, but Nitya took an orange.

Naraniah was suffering from diabetes and had bladder problems. The emotional excitement of seeing his sons prompted him to go to the lavatory; and, as was demanded by ritual, he washed his feet. This was later interpreted to mean that Naraniah had washed his feet because they had been touched by his sons, whom he regarded as pariahs.[23]

The brothers stayed for only half an hour on their first visit. According to G. Sharada, they came to see Naraniah three days running, after which their visits were to cease.* Naraniah wanted to go to the Theosophical Society to see his sons before they left India, but was restrained by his eldest son. Naraniah died in 1924. He did not see his sons again in his lifetime.[24]

---

*In Krishnamurti's *Journal*, page 36, there is an account that varies from that given by G. Sharada. I read the version in my manuscript to Krishnaji. He said he did not remember. Sometimes when he spoke of the past, his own memories would fuse with what others had told him.

CHAPTER 4

# "Mother, Please Touch My Face. Is It Still There?"

In early 1922 Krishnaji and Nitya traveled by ship from Colombo to Sydney, Australia, to attend a Theosophical convention to be held there. Krishna and C. W. L. were meeting after ten years, and he appeared happy to meet his old mentor. Charges of homosexuality arose again in Sydney against Leadbeater, and trouble exploded amongst serious Theosophists, which Krishna did his best to allay.

It was in Sydney that Krishna was also to meet James Wedgewood. By then Wedgewood had been ordained a bishop of the Liberal Catholic Church.* In 1916 he had in turn consecrated C. W. L. as the Regional Liberal Catholic Bishop for Australasia. C. W. L. was delighted, for this involved not only the rituals and the gorgeous robes attached to the Church, but a new liturgy, which was in English.

As Nitya was still unwell, after the convention was over the brothers decided to return to Europe by way of San Francisco and the United States. A. P. Warrington, the General Secretary of the Theosophical Society in the United States, was in Sydney for the convention. He invited Krishna and Nitya to spend some time in Ojai, California, an ancient Native American area near Santa Barbara, which had a dry climate, excellent for tuberculosis. As their time to leave Sydney approached, C. W. L. received a message from Master K. H. for Krishna, which touched Krishna deeply.

It was a long voyage, and Nitya grew desperately ill on board ship.

---

*The Liberal Catholic Church emerged from a group of German Catholic rebels against the Church of Rome on the doctrine of papal infallibility in 1870. It associated itself with the old Catholic Church of Holland, spread amongst Catholic and Anglican priests, but had a small following.

But at last he rallied, and they arrived in California. It was their first visit, and Krishna was enchanted with the beauty of the countryside. After a trip to a redwood forest he remarked on the majesty of the trees and their resemblance to vast cathedrals.

Krishna and Nitya finally came to Ojai, where they lived in a cottage surrounded by six acres of land. The property was later to be bought for the brothers by Annie Besant, and renamed Arya Vihara, the monastery of the noble ones.

Krishnamurti had begun meditating regularly every morning, and was surprised at the ease with which the mind responded. He found he could hold the image of Maitreya in consciousness for the whole day. He was, as he said, "getting calmer and more serene." His whole outlook on life was changing. Doors were opening inward. From Ojai Krishnamurti wrote to Leadbeater:

As you well know, I have not been what is called "happy" for many years; everything I touched brought me discontentment; my mental condition as you know, my dearest brother, has been deplorable . . . I have changed considerably from what I was in Australia. Naturally I have been thinking and deliberating about the message Master K. H. gave me while in Australia.[1]

In August 1922 Krishnamurti was to be plunged into the intense spiritual awakening that changed the course of his life. In the Indian tradition, the yogi who delves into the labyrinth of consciousness awakens exploding *kundalini** energies and entirely new fields of psychic phenomena, journeying into unknown areas of the mind. A yogi who touches these primordial energies and undergoes mystic initiation is recognized as being vulnerable to immense dangers; the body and mind face perils that could lead to insanity or death.

The yogi learns the secret doctrines and experiences the awakening

---

*The *kundalini* energy principle, dormant until awakened by the yogi, is likened to a serpent; it arises at the base of the spine, behind the generative organs, and ascends through the *sushumna nadi*, piercing and awakening *chakra* by *chakra* till it exits through the center of the scalp, the aperture of Brahma. The six *chakras* of *kundalini* yoga are regarded as six centers of explosive but dormant cosmic energy of the nature of fire. The route along which these centers are placed is the spinal column. The *chakras* are likened to a lotus: awakened by the rising *kundalini* or serpent power, it opens and faces upwards.

On either side of the *sushumna* or median nerve are the solar and lunar channels, *ida* and *pingala* coiled like serpents around the *sushumna*. The point between the eyebrows is the sixth *chakra* or nodal point of energy. With the opening of the thousand-petaled lotus in the scalp, the yogi is liberated; within him he holds an inexhaustible source of energy that does not dissipate.

of dormant energy under the instruction of the guru. Once the yogi becomes an adept, these transformations of consciousness on the playground of consciousness are revealed in a mystical drama. The body and mind must undergo a supremely dangerous journey. The adept is surrounded and protected by his disciples; secrecy and a protective silence pervade the atmosphere.

In Ojai, Nitya and Rosalind Williams, a young American, were present when Krishnamurti experienced much of the phenomena.[2] Nitya and Krishnamurti both sent Annie Besant reports of the events. Nitya's account vividly describes his brother's agony. Krishna was in pain, fainting, calling out in Telugu for his mother, asking to be taken to the woods in India, complaining of dirt, asking Nitya and Rosalind not to touch him. Krishna spoke of the presence of mighty Beings; an emptying of the Krishna-consciousness was evident, and with it there was sometimes a feeling of great presence. Finally, Krishna went out of the house and sat under a pepper tree. Nitya's description, though conditioned by Theosophical terminology, reveals bewilderment and anxiety and deep concern for his elder brother. Krishnamurti also wrote an account of the happenings to Mrs. Besant:

On the 17th of August, I felt acute pain at the nape of my neck and I had to cut down my meditation to fifteen minutes. The pain instead of getting better as I had hoped, grew worse. The climax was reached on the 19th. I could not think, nor was I able to do anything, and I was forced by friends here to retire to bed. Then I became almost unconscious, though I was well aware of what was happening around me. I came to myself at about noon each day. On that first day while I was in that state and more conscious of the things around me, I had the first most extraordinary experience. There was a man mending the road; that man was myself; the pickaxe he held was myself; the very stone which he was breaking was a part of me; the tender blade of grass was my very being and the tree beside the man was myself. I almost could feel and think like the roadmender, and I could feel the wind passing through the tree and the little ant on the blade of grass I could feel. The birds, the dust and the very noise were a part of me. Just then there was a car passing by at some distance; I was the driver, the engine and the tyres; as the car went further away from me, I was going away from myself. I was in everything, or rather everything was in me, inanimate and animate, the mountain, the worm and all breathing things. All day long I remained in this happy condition. I could not eat anything, and again at about six I began to lose my physical body, and naturally the physical elemental did what it liked; I was semi-conscious.

The morning of the next day [the 20th] was almost the same as the previous day. I ate nothing throughout the day, and I could not tolerate too many people in the room. I could feel them in rather a curious way and their vibrations got on my nerves. That evening at about the same hour of six I felt worse than ever. I wanted nobody near me nor anybody to touch me. I was feeling extremely tired and weak. I think I was weeping from sheer exhaustion and lack of physical control. My head was pretty bad and the top part felt as though many needles were being driven in. While I was in this state, I felt that the bed on which I was lying, the same as on the previous day, was dirty and filthy beyond imagination and I could not lie in it. Suddenly I found myself sitting on the floor and Nitya and Rosalind asking me to get into bed. I asked them not to touch me and cried out that the bed was not clean. I went on like this for some time till eventually I wandered onto the verandah and sat a few moments exhausted and became slightly calmer. I began to come to myself and finally Mr. Warrington [General Secretary of the Theosophical Society in the United States] asked me to go under the pepper tree which is near the house. There I sat cross-legged in the meditation posture. When I sat thus for some time, I felt myself going out of my body. I saw myself sitting down and with the delicate, tender leaves of the tree over me. I was facing the East.

In front of me was my body and over the head I saw the Star bright and clear. Then I could feel the vibration of the Lord Buddha; I beheld Lord Maitreya and Master K. H. I was so happy, calm and at peace. I could still see my body and I was hovering and within myself was the calmness of the bottom of a deep unfathomable lake. Like the lake, I felt my physical body an unfathomable lake. Like the lake I felt that my physical body with its mind and emotions could be ruffled on the surface, but nothing, nay nothing could disturb the calmness of my soul. The presence of the mighty Being was with me for some time and then They were gone. I was supremely happy for I had seen. Nothing could ever be the same. I have drunk at the clear pure waters at the source of the fountain of life and my soul was appeased. Never more could I be thirsty, never more could I be in utter darkness. I have seen the Light. I have touched compassion which heals all sorrow and suffering; it is not for myself, but for the world. I have stood on the mountain top and gazed at the mighty Beings. Never can I be in utter darkness; I have seen the glorious and healing Light. The fountain Truth has been revealed to me and the darkness has been dispersed. Love in all its glory has intoxicated my heart; my heart can never be closed. I have drunk at the fountain of joy and eternal Beauty. I am God-intoxicated![3]

For the next ten days Krishna's body was quiet, recuperating. On September 3, however, there were signs of an awakening of sensations in his spine and of his consciousness leaving the body. Soon periods of acute pain began. Three witnesses were present: Nitya, Rosalind, and Mr. Warrington. Nitya took detailed notes, but no one could understand what the events signified. The notes bearing Nitya's signature and the date February 11, 1923, were sent to Mrs. Besant. Only recently rediscovered, they lay for years in a miscellaneous file in the Adyar archives. Nitya wrote, "It is difficult for me to decide whether to write as if it were a scientific process; or as if it were a sacred ceremony in a temple. The incidents were concentrated and started every evening around 6. They lasted for a regular period and were to end at the same time late in the evening at 8-o'clock—on a few days they lasted till 9 at night."[4]

The sequence of events seems to have been as follows: Every evening Krishna meditated under the pepper tree. On September 3, after he had finished his meditations, he entered the house in a semiconscious state and lay down. He started to moan and to complain of great heat; he shuddered a little and collapsed on the couch. When he recovered full consciousness he did not remember what had occurred, though he felt a vague general discomfort. The next evening there was a recurrence of the symptoms. On September 5 he went down to Hollywood to see a dramatization of the life of Christ. He had arranged to do this a long time ago and did not want to break the engagement. Krishna told Nitya afterwards that while he was at the play in the evening, he felt himself gradually losing consciousness and it was with a great effort that he awakened himself. He returned to Ojai on the evening of the 6th. On the night of September 7, the day after the full moon, it was still very bright. Nitya continued,

As Krishna came up from the tree we could see him clearly. He looked a spectral figure in his Indian clothes, as he walked with a heavy dragging step swaying a little, scarcely able to hold himself up. As he came nearer we could see his eyes, they had a curiously dead look in them, and though he saw us he knew none of us; he could still speak coherently but he was fast becoming unconscious. It looked so dangerous to see him walking unsteadily that Rosalind or Mr. Warrington tried to go near to support him, but he would cry out "please don't touch, Oh, please, it hurts." Then he would go into the porch and lie down on the bed. We had drawn all the blinds so it was dark in there though there was the brilliant moon. Rosalind would sit nearby. After a little while he would get up and say to someone whom none of us could see, "what! yes I'm coming" and start walking out and Rosalind would try to restrain him, but he would say "I'm alright, please don't touch me, I'm perfectly alright" and his voice would sound normal though a little irritated. Deceived by this Rosalind would leave him and scarcely had he taken two steps, there would be a frightful crash and he had fallen full length on his face, unmindful of where he fell or how. Out on the porch there were boxes protruding from under a long bench that runs the length of the porch; but he was absolutely unconscious of all this, and he would fall wherever he was, fall unrestrainedly just as if he were fainting; sometimes he would sit up on the bed and after murmuring something he would fall backward with a crash on the bed and sometimes it was forward on the floor. He needed close attention every moment, and yet when he realized this he seemed annoyed and would affirm in a clear voice "I'm alright, please believe me, I'm perfectly alright." But even as he said it his voice would trail off. All this time he was groaning and tossing about unable to sit still, murmuring incoherently and complaining of his spine.

Any noise, even low-toned talk, would disturb him and he would beg his companions not to talk about him, to leave him alone; for every time they talked about him it hurt him. And so it went until eight o'clock. A little before eight he would become more peaceful, more restful, and sometimes he would go to sleep; gradually, he would become conscious and normal.

On the night of September 10 Krishna started calling for his mother. He called several times, then he said, "Nitya, do you see her?" When he returned to normal consciousness, he told Nitya that when his eyes rested on Rosalind, the face of their mother came in between and Rosalind's face would merge with their mother's face. Memories of his early childhood arose and he relived his childhood experiences.

Nitya and Warrington soon realized that Krishna was undergoing very dangerous transferences of consciousness or awakening of *kundalini*, and felt the atmosphere "charged with" electricity; they felt as if they were guardians of a temple where sacred ceremonies were being performed. At times those who were with Krishna felt the presence of a Being who was conducting the operations, although they could neither see nor identify it. But Krishna's body, between spasms of pain, would converse with the unseen presence, who appeared to be a friend and a Teacher. Krishna could not bear light or sound; he would cry out at the slightest touch; he could not bear too many people around him; the body and mind seemed tuned to a high pitch of sensitivity. A dull pain would suddenly concentrate on one spot and then become acute, he would push everyone away and complain of heat.

By September 18 a new phase began. The pain was more intense. Krishna was asking the unseen presence questions. His restlessness had increased; his eyes were open but unseeing; he would shiver and moan; sometimes he would shout out in pain, "Please, oh, please give me a minute." Then he would call for his mother.

On September 18, at 8:10 P.M., he was sitting on the couch, awake and fully conscious, talking and listening; but in a few minutes he went off again. The body, which was like an open wound, started to go through the same frightful pain. The pain seemed to have moved to a new part of the body unaccustomed to the deadly heat, and his sobbing would end in an awful, suppressed shriek. Krishna was in the dark and Nitya heard "the body speak, sob, shriek with pain and even beg for a moment's respite." They soon learned to recognize two voices: one, "the Physical elemental," the body, as Nitya writes of it, and the other the voice of Krishna. At a quarter past nine Krishna would grow conscious, finally, for the night. The time for the process seemed measured, as if a certain quantity of work had to be performed every evening, and if it were in any way interfered with in the beginning it was made up at the end.

Every night for the next fifteen nights he would ask, in the middle of his suffering, what the hour was. Invariably, to the minute, it was always 7:30 P.M.

When he came back to normal consciousness, the pain would be totally wiped out. He listened to Nitya and Rosalind telling him what had happened; but it was as if they were talking of another person.

On September 19 the pain seemed to be worse than before. It started immediately after he became unconscious, without any preliminaries, and grew worse and worse until suddenly Krishna was on his feet and running at full speed. They held him with difficulty, terrified that he would fall on the stones. He struggled to get away. After a time he started sobbing and gave a frightful cry, "Oh, Mother, why did you bear me, why did you bear me for this?" His eyes, according to Nitya, "looked strangely unconscious, wild and bloodshot, recognizing no one but Mother." He complained a fire was burning him, and his sobbings became so terrible that he began choking and gurgling; but this stopped soon. "And again when it became beyond endurance, he would suddenly stand up and run, and we would be round him. Three times he tried to run away and when he saw us round him he would calm down a little. At intervals when the pain was intense he would beg for rest for a few minutes and then he would start talking to his 'Mother' or else we would hear him talking to 'Them.' Sometimes he would say with a great deal of assurance, 'yes, rather I can stand a lot more; don't mind the body, I can't stop it from weeping.' "

On the night of September 20 the pain was even more acute, and Krishna tried to run away five or six times. His body would contort in dangerous and awkward positions, due to the awful pain. Nitya wrote that on one occasion Krishna, sobbing and weeping, suddenly put his head over his knees on the floor and turned over, nearly breaking his neck; but luckily Rosalind was there to turn him over sideways. He became totally still and for a moment they could hardly feel his heart beating.

The next day Rosalind had to go away for a few days. During her absence the process slackened, but he continued to complain of a strange pain low down on the left side of his spine.

On one occasion Krishna appeared distraught and felt that someone was lurking around the house. He insisted on walking to the low surrounding wall and said in a loud voice, "Go away, what do you mean by coming here? Go away. I don't know where you go, go behind the hills, but go right away from here." Then he came back and lay down. Soon he started calling out, "Please come back Krishna." He kept on calling for Krishna until he lapsed into unconsciousness. This was the first time he had called out his own name. That night there was an increase of pain in the back of his neck.

On Rosalind's return the pain grew worse and he complained of a burning in the spine and he could not bear too much light, even the light of the rising moon. Again, in the middle of the process he got up to repel some unseen person. He appeared angry and the invisible presence did not return. As soon as the light became unbearable they had to bring him indoors. One evening, toward 5 P.M., the atmosphere in the house changed; it grew quieter, peaceful, and soon they could feel a great Presence who was in charge. Nitya said it was as if, "Great engines were working and for a few hours, the house vibrated."

By October 2 a new phase began. The pain had shifted to Krishna's face and eyes. He felt that they were working on his eyes and said, "Mother, please touch my face, is it still there?" and a little later, "Mother, my eyes are gone, feel them, they have gone." As he said this he had started sobbing and moaning. This continued till 8 P.M. By 9 P.M. he was shivering and shuddering and could hardly breathe.

It appeared as if "the real Krishna" found it intensely hard to get back into his body. According to Nitya, "Every time he tried to wake up, it brought on this shivering."

On October 3 he said to Rosalind, "Mother, will you look after me, I'm going a long way off," and then fell unconscious. Some time later he began to speak to Rosalind, asking her where Krishna was. He told her that he had left her in charge, and now she did not know where Krishna was. And he began to weep, for he had lost Krishna. He refused to sleep before Krishna came back, which was after an hour and a half.

One morning while they were at Mr. Warrington's house Krishna went out of his body. He had told Rosalind that he had to go a long way and she had to look after him. Two hours later, he began to talk. Seeing Rosalind's hand, he appeared astounded and asked, "Mother, why is your skin white?" He looked at her and said, "You have grown younger, what has happened?" Then, "Mother, Krishna is coming in, look, he is standing there." And when Rosalind asked what he looked like, he said, "He is a fine tall man, very dignified. He frightens me a little." Then he said, "But, don't you know him, Mother, he is your son, he knows you."

On the night of October 4 Krishna suffered more than usual, the agony was concentrated in his face and eyes. He kept saying, "Oh, please have mercy on me," and "I don't mean that, of course, you are merciful."

Later, he told Nitya that they were cleansing his eyes so that he might be allowed to see "Him." It was, he said, "Like being tied down in the desert, one's face to the blazing sun, with one's eyelids cut off."

Later that night Nitya found Krishna sitting up in meditation and again felt the throbbing presence of a great Being flooding the room. All suffering had been washed away. "Krishna," Nitya wrote, "did not see His face, only His body in shining white."

The next morning Krishna was in a rebellious mood, he was semi-conscious but insisted on going out. They had to stop him. Later he said that he had felt a frightful burning in his spine and wanted to find the creek in the canyon so that he could sink his body in it, to relieve the burning.

Shortly afterward his companions again felt the great Presence. "Krishna's eyes were extraordinarily brilliant and his whole face transfigured. With his entry the atmosphere was marvelously changed. We felt the presence of a supremely majestic Being and Krishna had a look of great bliss on his face." Krishna told Nitya, Rosalind, and Warrington to prepare themselves, for a great visitor would come that night. He asked for the picture of the Lord Buddha to be put in his room.

Later, when Krishna came in from his meditation, he told them that the Great Being had left after Krishna's meditation had ended.

That night was a ghastly night of suffering and when I look upon it, it seems to me that it was the most agonising night that Krishna ever went through. He suffered terribly the following nights, and they seemed much worse, but I think this was due to the piteously enfeebled condition brought on by this night. Before the suffering actually started, we heard him talking to the Master in charge. He was told not to say anything of what was being done to him and he gave his promise; then he was told that the visitor would return later at 8.15. Krishna said "He is coming at 8.15, then let us start quickly." Then just before it was started, he had been standing up and we heard him fall with an awful crash and then we heard Krishna apologising "I'm so sorry I fell, I know I must not fall." All through the evening he was more conscious of his physical body than he had ever been before. They told him that he must make no movement, for generally he was writhing and twisting with the pain. But now he promised "Them" he would not move and over and over again he said "I won't move, I promise I won't move." So he clasped his fingers tightly and with his knotted hands under him, he lay on his back, while the awful pain continued. He found it very difficult to breathe that night and he gasped for breath continuously and choked repeatedly and when the pain grew beyond endurance and he could no longer get his breath, he just fainted. Three times he fainted that night, and the first time he did it, we did not know what had happened; we had heard him choking and gasping and sobbing with the pain and suddenly after a long drawn gasp there was dead silence. When we called to him there was no answer and when we went into the room and felt our way towards him, for the room was inky black and we did not know where he lay. We found him lying on his back so still and his fingers so tightly locked that he seemed [a] tower out of stone. We brought him to quickly and three times this happened. Every time he came to, he would apologise to Them for the waste of time and tell Them that he had tried his best to control himself, but that it had been beyond control. Sometimes They gave him a slight breathing space and the pain would cease and between the throes of suffering he would start making some joke with the one in charge and he would laugh as if the whole thing was a joke. And so it went on for an hour and a quarter. By 7.45 Krishna started calling for his Mother and as Rosalind started gently to go in, he became terribly nervous and called out "Who is that, who is that, who is that?" and when she went into the room he fainted. The entry of any person into the room while he was in this sensitive state seemed to upset him. She was with him for some time and presently he asked her to go out of the room for "He was coming." So Rosalind and I were outside on the porch and Krishna sat inside, cross-legged, as if in meditation. Then we felt, as we had felt earlier, in the evening, the Great Presence.

Later, when both Rosalind and I were in the room Krishna began talking to people we could not see. The work had been assured of success and apparently they were congratulating him, and the room was full of visitors all desiring to rejoice with Krishna; but there were too many for his comfort. We heard him say "There is nothing to congratulate me about, you'd have done the same yourself."

Then they must have left for he gave a deep sigh and lay still for a long time, too tired to move. Then he began to talk. "Mother," he said, "everything will be different now, life will never be the same for any of us after this." And again "I've seen Him, Mother, and nothing matters now." Over and over again he said this and all of us felt the truth of it, life would never be the same for any of us.

That night when we went to bed, just before we fell asleep Krishna began talking to someone I could not see. I heard Krishna's end of the conversation. Apparently a man had been sent by the Master D. K. to keep watch over the body through the night; Krishna began to tell him how sorry he was to cause him all that trouble. This was one of the most noticeable things all through. Krishna's politeness and consideration was extraordinary, whether he was fully conscious or whether it was only the physical elemental speaking. The man came to watch every night after this for six or seven nights, Krishna was to say "I've seen Him now. Nothing matters."

By this time, the body had become very weak and would constantly lapse into unconsciousness.

The location of the pain was constantly shifting. A few days later, on October 6, the agony had shifted to the scalp. Something seemed to have been opened in his head, which was causing him indescribable torture. At one moment he shouted, "Please close it up, please close it up." He screamed with pain, but they kept opening it gradually. When he could no longer endure the pain, Krishna screamed and then fainted. At the end of forty minutes he lay without the slightest flicker of movement. Slowly, consciousness returned. To their amazement, his companions found they were speaking to Krishna as a child, about four years old or even younger. He was reliving certain episodes of his early years. He saw three distinct scenes. The first, his mother giving birth to a child. To witness his mother's agony was a terrible shock to him, and he moaned and cried out and kept on crying out, "Oh, poor Mother, poor Mother, you are brave Mother."

The next scene was of Krishna and his brother as young children, lying seriously ill with malaria.

The last scene was the death of his mother. He could not understand what was happening. When he saw the doctors give her medicine, he begged his mother not to take it. "Don't take it Mother, don't take it, it is some beastly stuff and it won't do you any good. The doctors do not know anything. He is a dirty man, please don't take it Mother." A little later, in a tone of horror, he said, "Why are you so still, Mother? What's happened and why does father cover his face with his *dhoti*? Answer me, Mother, answer me Mother, answer me?" The child's voice continued to cry out till he came to and Krishnamurti was back. That night again the presence came to watch over him while he slept.

The next night, according to Nitya, "They appeared to be operating on his scalp again." He was agonized and cried out in pain—even fainting eight times—when it became too severe. "He begged them to open it slowly and gradually so that he could get used to it by degrees." He was choking and had difficulty in breathing.

A little later he again became a child, and one could feel his loathing for his school. "Mother, I need not go to school today—need I? I'm awfully ill Mother." And after a while, "Mother, let me stay with you, I will do anything you want, I will take castor oil, if you like, but let me stay with you." And later, "Mother, you know, you hid the box of biscuits from us; well, I stole them from that box. I have been doing it for a long, long time." When Rosalind laughed, Krishna was very hurt, and said, "Mother, you are always laughing at me, why do you laugh at me?"

Still later, after talking a great deal about snakes, puppies, and beggars, "he talked of going into the shrine room where he saw a picture of a lady sitting cross-legged on a deer skin. Nitya had a vague memory that it might be a picture of A. B. and suggested this. Krishna did not know her name 'who is that?' he asked 'she looks like someone I know, only she does not look like that, she's quite different.' "

Soon, a change was apparent. By now he could leave his body with extraordinary ease and rapidity, and the return no longer brought on shivering. He was to say later that night that they had left open the center in his head.* The man whom they could not see came again to keep watch.

As the day progressed, Krishna talked less; he continued to faint at night, but he woke soon and he had greater vitality.

There were still periods when he became a child. On one occasion he spoke of a journey in a bullock cart which lasted for three or four days.

On October 18 the pain came in frequent spasms, waves of it which were to leave him exhausted. "We were again blessed with a visit from the Great One. The 19th was a very curious experience after he came in from his meditation, he began calling over and over again for Krishna. He called out 'Krishna, please Krishna, don't leave me.' "

Later he spoke to Nitya and Rosalind and asked them "to look after Krishna carefully, never to wake him too quickly, nor to startle him, for it was very dangerous"; "things might snap" if anything went

---

*This is possibly a reference to the opening in the scalp which in *kundalini* yoga is regarded as the *Sahasrara* or the *Brahmarandhra*—the fully opened thousand-petaled lotus, resting in supreme emptiness. With this opening comes union and final liberation for the yogin.

wrong. The episodes decreased in frequency, and by November 1923 they had ended.

The process, which could not be explained by Leadbeater or Mrs. Besant, was to continue intermittently in the months that followed. His body would be racked with pain, it would thrash around, and at times would hit the floor. Krishnamurti often had to send his brother and whoever else was present out of the room, for they found it difficult to witness his agony. He would faint repeatedly, and at the end of it he would look excessively tired.

In 1924 Krishna and some companions went abroad, where the experiences continued. Toward the end of his terrible pain he beheld visions of the Buddha, Maitreya, and the other Masters of the occult hierarchy. Nitya, deeply perplexed, wrote to Annie Besant on March 24 from Ojai on their return from Pergine, Italy:

Krishna's process has now taken a definite step forward. The other night, it began as usual, none of us expecting anything fresh or new. All of a sudden, we all felt an immense rush of power in the house, greater than I have ever felt since we have been here; Krishna saw the Lord and the Master; I think also the star* shone out that night, for all of us felt an intense sense of awe and almost fear that I felt before when the star came out. Krishna afterwards told us that the current started as usual at the base of his spine and reached the base of his neck, then one went on the left side, the other on the right side of his head and they eventually met at the centre of the forehead; when they met a flame played out of his forehead. That is the bare outline of what happened; none of us know what it means but the power was so immense that night that it seems to mark a definite stage. I presume it should mean the opening of the third eye.

Except for the vision of "The Lord," the rest is a classic description of the arousing of the *kundalini*.

---

*The Order of the Star of the East, an international organization, was established by Annie Besant and C. W. Leadbeater in 1911. Mrs. Besant and C. W. L. were named Protectors of the New Order and Krishna was declared its Head. Representatives were appointed and offices established for each country. The badge of the Order was a silver five-pointed star. A quarterly magazine was printed in Adyar under the name *Herald of the Star*, with Krishna as its editor. The first issue appeared in January 1911. By 1914 the publications office was shifted to England.

# CHAPTER 5

# "Our Life Here Is One of Intense Inner Activity."

A group of his close friends accompanied Krishna to Pergine in Italy. Lady Emily, with her daughters Betty and Mary, was there; so was Helen Knothe, a young American woman and a close friend of Krishnaji's; Dr. Shivakamu, Rukmini Arundale's sister; Malati; the wife of Patwardhan; another close friend of K's, Ruth Roberts; John Cordes, the Austrian representative of the *Star*, who had been in Adyar in 1910 and 1911 and at the time was responsible for Krishna's physical exercises, training and welfare. Rama Rao and Jadunandan Prasad, close associates of K's from India, and D. Rajagopal were also in the group. This anonymous account of K in Pergine was found among Shiva Rao's papers after his death. It is possibly a diary kept by Nitya or Cordes. Though the author's identity is not known, the document appears authentic.

*August 29, 1924:* Our life here is one of intense inner activity and almost complete outer inertia. Or that is what it should be and what Krishnaji desires.

On previous holidays of this kind, when Krishnaji has collected around him those whom he desired to teach and help and has retired to some quiet spot away from civilization, there has been no concerted plan of action. Krishnaji has of course spoken to each of his followers individually, but never before have the Masters been spoken of to us all collectively, as in our present group, so that every grade and those who were still apart might listen and talk openly about them.

We are here for but one purpose, to take definite "steps" and thereby become directly useful to Them. Each one has his opportunity;

each one is at a different stage, and therefore capable of serving those above and helping those below. (Terms such as above and below are apt to mislead, I use them not to imply a superiority and inferiority, but only a distinction.)

The regime for the day is, meditation at a quarter past eight, breakfast at eight thirty. A walk down to an open stubble field where we play rounders for an hour or two, and then one hour's talk under the trees, of the Masters and of how to serve Them. Lunch at 12.30—rest or individual work, if wished, until three; games in the Castle grounds, bath, and dinner at six. After which all separate for the night, some of us going to the Square tower where certain intensive preparation goes on for an hour. Bed at 8.30.

Krishnaji is of course the central figure of each day; of the games, and of the work. Around him everything [is] centred; Krishnaji's life is one of absolute devotion to the Lord, such passionate worship of the idealistic and the beautiful—and yet he is so perfectly human and so near to his fellow men. No words can depict his character, but he seems like a human creature who has perfected himself to a great extent, rather than a divine being in an imperfect human form. Surely what the Lord will desire, will be a perfect human instrument, so that he can contact humanity on its own level. The divinity He Himself will show forth through the instrument. Never except at the coming of a World Teacher to His world is there such a union between those things which are Divine and those that are human. For usually humanity reaches up to Divinity and the moment it touches it becomes one with it, but in this case Divinity reaches down to a human instrument, uses it, works through it as separate and apart from it, and retires again leaving the instrument still a human instrument. Certainly the evolution of the human instrument is often so quickened that it becomes almost immediately super-human (through this service) but this is a separate process. Man may reach up and become Divine but he cannot use divine powers while he is still human. Whereas the Divine can descend and use human powers, even though he is no longer human.

Today Krishnaji was very alive at breakfast, and as often our conversation was not printable. The morning after a very serious talk or hard evening's work, Krishnaji will often be most frivolous, making jokes and laughing at them uproariously, with his sudden thundering outbursts of mirth, or prolonged, infectious giggle. These two things are strange about him—first, his capacity to change from the most serious, real and glorious mood, to one of laughter and joking[,] instantaneously; secondly that no joke he utters however vulgar, makes the usual atmosphere surrounding such talk. It seems as though his beauty, his absolute clarity of being, sweeps everything before it, so that he can touch any person, or object or subject, and impart his cleanness to it, endow it with the fresh air of his presence. Krishnaji tried to remember his own experiences. When he and Nitya first saw C. W. L. he showed them pictures of the Master M. and the Master K. H. and asked them which they preferred. When they chose the one of the Master K. H. he said it was as he expected.

When Krishnaji was young the Masters were very real to him, then it was that he wrote "At the Feet of the Master," afterwards came a period when for him the reality was not so intense, he only believed because of what C. W. L. and A. B. said. Now again the intense realization has returned. Nitya said that our group should make an atmosphere which should "attract" Their attention. He spoke of the various influences at Ojai, on the different nights. That of the Master M. as a power that made you feel capable of anything. That of the Master K. H. as perfect kindness—it was as if honey were entering into you when he spoke. And that of the Master K. H. as absolute cleanness, perfect clarity. Then of the greatest of all influences, that of the Lord, as we also felt at Ehrwald*—peace—"the peace that passeth understanding."

Krishnaji spoke of Adyar as of a mighty power house, where either you became a saint, went mad, or were turned away as useless by an unerring watcher.

I have never seen him so radiantly beautiful as he is at nights, at these times. His eyes laugh with a strange unearthly joy, which is triumphant and yet so gentle. Gentleness and a sweet keen joy robe him, and show in the lines and curves of his face, and an aroma of roses surrounds and envelopes him. At times, he shivers as if cold and at other times he is too worn out, but on these nights, these particular nights of which I speak, the real Krishna, all that makes him what he is in the deepest sense, comes and looks out through his eyes.

*September 1, 1924:* Lady Emily compares Rajagopal to St. Peter. He is the Buffoon amongst the present disciples it seems; and he dearly loves his position as High Court Jester. To know Krishnaji, one has to know his followers. Rajagopal was once St. Bernard of Clairveaux, and

---

*Krishna, Nitya, and some of their friends had visited Ehrwald in Austria before their trip to Pergine.

at other times he has been a venerable priest; and both the saint and priest peep out through him over and over again. Perhaps especially the latter. He talks perpetually, and when making a speech is lengthy and tedious, in fact he sermonises. He is or rather pretends to be very fond of food, this being his chief topic for jokes etc. When Krishnaji is strained and tired, or the party in general, dull, Rajagopal has always some joke, or amusing phrase to hand, and he laughs at himself so persistently that everyone must join in. It is said that the one quality all the Masters have, and without which it is impossible for the disciple to progress, is a sense of humour. And the more the spiritual life is led the more this becomes apparent. A sense of humour will relieve the tension of feelings and thoughts under the most trying circumstances, and often it is just that that prevents a definite break in the work, or individually in a person. Certainly Rajagopal's wit is not of the clearest, sharpest type, but then it allows Krishnaji and the others to take part and add their quota. Needless to say, Rajagopal gets a great deal of teasing, but then so does everyone who comes near Krishnaji, that being one way through which he influences people; especially of certain types.

One of Krishnaji's theories is that people must surely be able to evolve through joy alone, arriving at Godhead as naturally as a flower opens to the sun. At one time it seemed almost to worry him, that everyone he met had evolved so far by the long devious ways of sorrow, and so few had taken the simple way of joy. I think I have heard him even say that he has never met anyone who evolved through joy alone, nevertheless it is a possibility, which would become very common if only our present civilization were not so complex. "Be natural, be happy." So Rajagopal plays a great role in this mighty drama, in which Krishnaji is the first to laugh, the easiest to be amused. "Be a God, and laugh at yourself."

Speaking of his two years of training with Leadbeater Krishnaji said he was "bored to tears," literally. All desires were burnt out; for instance, K and N asked for bicycles, (probably as they were small boys they pestered C. W. L. for them); the bicycles were found and a ten mile ride was not only done once but they had to do it every day for two years. Also they expressed a desire for porridge; they had it—but again every day for a year; if they had dirty feet, or as once Nitya threw a stone at a frog, it was "Pupils of the Master do not do these things." But it must have seemed hard then for the small dark boy who was to become the Krishnaji of today—the Jesus of tomorrow.

He has had many lives as a woman, and these have left a very strong trace in his character; his exceptional power of intuition makes him unlike most men. At times he can be as cruel as he can be the reverse, but this always for a purpose. One short sharp phrase, which his flashing eyes emphasise to an unbearable degree, that is all. Krishnaji will never offer to talk to anyone, unless an approach is made, and then for the first two or three times that a serious conversation is broached, he is terribly shy.

*September 8, 1924:* Lady Emily, Cordes and I sat in Krishnaji's room. Krishnaji being in the one below. The time was about a quarter to seven, and all was the same as on ordinary nights, except for a magic silence that came down on us. Somewhere in the tower Nitya, Rama Rao and Rajagopal were chanting, and incense wafted in through the cracks on the door. We all felt His Presence, how would even the dullest fail to recognize the ineffable peace that pervaded the building. We sat "silent and rapt" for an hour.

Afterwards when we were all together, and Krishnaji sat in our midst; it was as if we had all only just found each other; and as we spoke of what had happened, a low sweet laughter, of greatest inexpressible joy seemed to come to our lips. "If it is like this now, what will it be when the time comes?"

*September 14, 1924:* This afternoon instead of playing the usual "volley-ball," we all lay out on the rocks which surround the Square Tower. Krishnaji squatted on the rocks with Rama Rao, examining a small yellow snail with great interest. Once before some years ago, I remember being with Krishnaji when he discovered a colony of ants and spent the whole morning feeding them with sugar, stirring them up and watching them carry eggs and rebuild their home. Presently, another snail was found and the two were made to crawl over each other and up and down precipitous crags. At Ehrwald last year, he was lying amongst the long grass and flowers, when a butterfly settled on his hand, and soon he had one or two poised on his finger. His delight was unbounded. He has a love of all creatures great and small, indeed anything that is beautiful or natural interests him; he will chase a grasshopper following its movements and noting the colour of its wings; or with his customary "I say!" will stand almost enraptured before a beautiful scene. "Just look at that lake, it's so smooth, like ice—and dark green. See the reflections in it? Oh-ee you should see Lake Geneva—so blue."

Krishnaji reads a small passage out of "The Gospel of Buddha" in meditation each morning. He is indeed a devotee, and the very sound of the name of the Lord Buddha, seems almost to make him tremble with a feeling of utmost worship. There was one sentence today, in which the Lord Buddha said, that the disciple who lives in the world must be like a lotus. In India, the lotus symbolizes supreme purity. Its ability to blossom fully while rooted in a muddy, slushy pond signifies the human ability to flower in purity and rise out of any condition however dark and sullied.

Krishnaji was speaking to me this afternoon. He spoke of the Lord Buddha and that state of existence which is absolutely without self. He is thinking much of being absolutely impersonal these days, and already he seems to have dived deep into that clear well which is unsullied by the mud of self. As he spoke of the Lord Buddha, a new world lay stretched before one, in which all personal love and ambition died away and became as naught, only an impersonal, tremendous unshakeable love remained. The full realisation of life without self only came to Krishnaji while he was at Ojai, and even he finds it almost impossible to describe. He spoke of how when all the Masters were assembled together, the coming of the Lord Buddha was like the north wind, so free from anything even resembling self. He said: "Whenever I see the picture of the Lord Buddha, I say to myself, I am going to like it."

The image of the Lord Maitreya has been appearing to him on several occasions. At Pergine on the last appearance He was to give Krishnamurti a message—"The happiness you seek is not far off; it lies in every common stone." In another message, He conveyed "Do not look for the Great ones when they may be very near you." For the next three evenings, Krishna was to laugh often, tell comic stories—many members of the party were shocked at his behaviour.

# CHAPTER 6

# "I and My Brother Are One"

Mrs. Besant made her entry into the Indian political scene in 1913, just before the outbreak of World War I. Under the guidance and blessings of the Rishi Agastya (who, according to the Theosophical Society, had special charge in the occult hierarchy of the destiny of India), she was launched into the center of the growing political ferment.

She was already famous throughout the country. Known for her brilliant oratory, she was recognized as an educator of the highest order and admired for her courage as a social reformer. Concerned as she was with new values, and with her immense pride in Indian culture and thought, her entry into politics was welcomed by her many intellectual friends and admirers. With her temperament it was inevitable that she would grow deeply involved. Soon she lost contact with the occult hierarchy; her insights into the sacred and her psychic powers began to ebb, and she had to rely on C. W. Leadbeater to bring through messages from the occult world of the Masters.

By 1925, with growing age, Mrs. Besant's mental faculties began to decline and with it her iron control of the affairs of the Society. The intrigues and machinations to gain power over her and thus of the Society were gaining momentum. Aware of her failure to reawaken *kundalini shakti chakras* (or the six centers of dormant psychic energy placed along the spinal column) and her aspirations to regain contact with the Mahatmas, many of her associates claimed clairvoyant powers and the ability to bring through instructions from the Masters. Dabbling in the occult, claiming to have awakened the serpent of *kundalini*, seeking power and giving free play to illusion, often linking what did not fit their scheme of things as emanating from black powers, the actions of some of its senior members were to make a mockery of the Theosophical Society.

In Sydney, Australia, Leadbeater, clad in purple robes with crozier and jeweled cross, was busy creating the atmosphere and the energy for the emergence of the sixth root race.* Surrounding himself with young boys and girls who were his chosen disciples, his occult powers and their uses had reached bizarre levels. He was magnetizing jewels for fairies in the National Park in Sydney, in return for permission to take some fairies back to "The Manor," where he and his disciples lived. To add to his occult resources, while crossing the ferry in Sydney harbor Leadbeater claimed to be creating invisible nets in which he caught water sylphs from the sea; attaching them to his aura, he sent them out on command to succor people in distress.[1]

In Europe, George Arundale and Wedgwood claimed to have established a direct channel of communication with the occult hierarchy and to have been accepted as disciples by the Mahachohan. The atmosphere was charged with excitement as a number of new initiations were announced by Mrs. Besant as brought through by Arundale.

Having been ordained Bishops of the Liberal Catholic Church, the purple-clad Arundale and Wedgwood were in rapid succession to attain Arhathood† by passing through their third and fourth initiations. Arundale's wife, Rukmini,‡ passed three initiations in three days.[2] Mrs. Besant and Leadbeater were already Arhats, having passed the fourth initiation. Krishnamurti, in Ojai nursing his seriously ill brother Nitya, was unaware of the occult ferment taking place in the Netherlands at Huizen and later at the Star Camp in Ommen, an annual convention attended by members of The Order of the Star. Without his knowledge an announcement was made that his astral body from Ojai and Jinarajadasa's from Adyar had traveled and appeared before the magnificence of the gathered occult hierarchy to receive their blessings in their journey through the fourth initiation. Later, when the camp was over, Mrs. Besant at Huizen called Lady Emily, Miss Bright, and Shiva Rao to her room and told them that she and Leadbeater, Krishnaji, Arun-

---

*In Theosophy the sixth root race would follow the fifth root race—our present society; similar to the coming of the Aquarian Age.

†Arhat is a sramanic (Buddhist/Jain) term indicating the highest spiritual attainment for a monk below the status of Buddha/Jina. In the Theosophical spiritual hierarchy, adepts were masters or mahatmas. Members of the Great White Brotherhood, they had attained perfection but remained in human form, to help in the evolution of Seekers on the Path of Discipleship.

‡Rukmini was the South Indian Brahmin wife of George Arundale. She came from a prominent family of Theosophists. A major cultural personality, she established a well-known dance and music academy, Kalakshetra, in Madras. She died in 1986.

dale, and Wedgwood had passed their fifth and final initiation. All of them were now not only Arhats but Adepts, and so free of the causal chain of karma and rebirth.

A report that appeared in the Theosophist journal *Herald of the Star* gives some insight into the Ommen camp, where these great tidings were being announced by Mrs. Besant. Under the heading "By command of the King," the *Herald* published Mrs. Besant's words:

The new World Teacher will choose, as before, his twelve Apostles. I have only the command to mention seven who have reached the stage of Arhatship. . . . The first two, my brother Charles Leadbeater, and myself, passed that great initiation at the same time. The other Arhats are, C. Jinarajadasa, George Arundale, whose consecration as Bishop was necessary, as the last step of his preparation for the great fourth step of initiation. Oscar Kollerstron, Mrs. Rukmini Arundale, Krishnaji, and Bishop Wedgwood.[3]

Later, realizing that she had made a major error by including the name of Krishnamurti, who was the vehicle, in the list of Apostles, she corrected her statement. Various other lists existed in which were included the names of Lady Emily, Nitya, Rajagopal, and Theodore St. John, a golden-haired fifteen-year-old protégé of Leadbeater.

Mrs. Besant further went on to declare the three lines of activity the Society would follow in the future. A new world religion must be established, with Annie Besant as the head. A new world university must be set up with Besant as rector, Arundale as principal, and Wedgewood as director—because, according to Mrs. Besant, "he knows both sides—ordinary and occult." She goes on to say that "you should not oppose them as they are part of the work of the King." Meanwhile Arundale, claiming the power of prophecy, said,

I think there is no one in the world who has so magnificent, so marvellous a capacity for self effacement, as has my brother Nitya. The way in which he loses himself in his brother is one of the most beautiful things I have seen: And I want you to remember what I am saying today, because I venture to think it is in the nature of prophecy. I think that as the years pass, not only shall we see our Krishnamurti leading the life to which he is so supremely dedicated, but we shall also see at his right hand his great brother recognised throughout the world as one of its greatest statesman-leaders.

Nitya died less than four months after these words were said.[4]

Meanwhile, Nitya's illness had taken a turn for the worse. Arundale had given Rajagopal, who was present at the camp and who had been made Deacon of the Liberal Catholic Church, an amulet to take to Nitya, specially magnetized by the Mahachohan. The great ones of the hierarchy had stated that Nitya would live and be one of the main supporters for the work of the World Teacher. According to Arundale, "Nitya's life was Krishna's boon on becoming an Arhat."[5]

Krishna, hearing reports of Apostles and Arhats, rapid initiations, world religion and world universities, was bewildered and deeply distressed. Leaving Nitya under the protection of the Masters, he departed for Europe with Rajagopal. Lady Emily, who had been present at the camp and had herself undergone her second initiation, had come to meet him at the dock. Krishnamurti told her his views in no uncertain terms. He refused to accept the initiations or the Apostles. He was deeply skeptical of the world religion and the world university. He did not want to hurt Mrs. Besant in her old age, and so refrained from openly voicing his protest; but he conveyed his misgivings to her.

Mrs. Besant was shattered by Krishnamurti's rejection of the initiations, Apostles, world religion, and world university. Her mental condition rapidly began to deteriorate. "She showed signs of ageing, loss of memory and a tendency to focus on the past."[6] But this did not in any way curtail her activities or her total commitment to Krishnamurti as the World Teacher.

By early November 1925 Mrs. Besant, Krishnaji, Rajagopal, Rosalind, Wedgwood, Shiva Rao, and Rukmini and George Arundale left for India to participate in the Jubilee celebrations to be held in Adyar. Krishnamurti's faith in the Masters and their assurance regarding Nitya's well being was unquestioned. Early in 1925, while in Adyar, Nitya had been dreadfully ill. On February 10, 1925, Krishnamurti had written a letter to Mrs. Besant describing a dream in which he had visited the Great Brotherhood and pleaded with them for his brother's life:

With regard to my dream, I remember going to the Master's house and asking and begging to let Nitya get well and to let him live. The Master said that I was to go to the Lord Maitreya and I went there and I implored there, but, I got the impression that it was not His business and that I should go to the Mahachohan. So, I went there. I remember all this so clearly. He was seated in his chair, with great dignity & magnificent understanding, with grave and kindly eyes. My futile description is so absurd, but, it is impossible to convey the great impression of it all. I told him that I would sacrifice my happiness or anything that was required to let Nitya live, for I felt this thing was being decided. He listened to me and answered "He will be well." It was such a relief that all my anxiety has completely disappeared and I am glad.

With regard to my own preparation, I don't know what has been decided but I am willing to do anything. It has been very bad and I am feeling very tired and rather weak, but it can't be helped.

Thank Heaven, you will be here, my own mother & I love you, with all my heart and soul. Yours Krishna.[7]

This direct meeting with the Masters had convinced Krishnaji of the powers of the Great Beings to prolong Nitya's life. If we pause an instant to examine Krishnaji's contact with the Masters, their manifestations, and Krishnaji's communication with them, it becomes evident that his encounters with Master K. H., the Mahachohan, Maitreya, and the Buddha were visions, often in the dream state. This had happened so when he was a child; with his tender consciousness exposed to the esoteric imagery and thought forms of Leadbeater, he naturally saw the Masters in the likenesses pictured in the Esoteric Section of the Theosophical Society. It was so when he described his meetings with Master K. H. in his early letters to Mrs. Besant, and traces of it were to be found in the process at Ojai, though by then he was freeing himself of visions, physical manifestations, and visual imagery. In the early years no sharp division existed for Krishnaji between the dream state and the state of being awake. Visions, dreams, and actual manifestations of thought forms for him appeared to have the same reality. Later he was to say that all images and manifestations, however profound, were projections of the mind. With the death of Nitya and the explosive sorrow that brought him face to face with the actual, all physical references to the Masters ceased.

Even before that, on board ship back to India, Arundale started bringing through messages from the Mahachohan chiding Krishnamurti on his skepticism and subtly implying that unless he accepted the revelations brought through by Arundale at Huizen and Ommen and confirmed the names of the people who had been made Adepts, Nitya would die. Krishnamurti refused.

While in the Suez Canal, Krishnaji received a telegram from Nitya saying that he had contracted influenza. The next day another cable was received in which Nitya said, "Flu rather more serious. Pray for me." Krishnamurti, faith unshaken, told Shiva Rao that the Masters would not have let him leave Ojai if his brother was destined to die. On November 13, in the midst of a thunderstorm, they received a cable announcing Nitya's death.

Shiva Rao, who was sharing the cabin with Krishnamurti, has left a vivid account of what followed.

Mrs. Besant asked me, to take her to Krishnamurti's cabin. She went in alone, to speak to him. The news broke him completely: it did more, as I saw for myself during the rest of the voyage. His entire philosophy of life—the implicit faith in the future as outlined by Mrs. Besant and Mr. Leadbeater, Nitya's vital part in it, were shattered at that moment. At night he would sob and moan and cry out for Nitya, sometimes in his native Telugu, which in his waking consciousness, he could not speak. Day after day, he seemed to change, gripping himself together in an effort to face life—but without Nitya.[8]

Krishna and Nitya had shared their loneliness in an alien world; laughed together; told comic stories; traveled together—planned their future work and life together.* Writing after his brother's death, Krishnaji was to say: "An old dream is dead and a new one is being born. A new vision is coming into being and a new consciousness is being unfolded—I have wept, but I do not want others to weep; but, if they do, I know what it means. Now, I know, now we are inseparable. He and I will work together, for I and my brother are one."

By the time Krishnamurti, with Dr. Besant, reached Adyar, Krishnamurti had emerged from his encounter with sorrow immensely quiet, radiant, and free of all sentiment and emotion. But his belief in the Masters and the hierarchy had undergone a total revolution. He was rarely to refer to the Masters in physical form again. In later years, speaking haltingly of this period, Krishnamurti accepted that perhaps the intensity of sorrow had triggered a vast, wordless perception. An intelligence that had taken long years to mature, that had rested in abeyance, was to function in the moment of acuteness of suffering.†

---

*In a letter from Ojai February 28, 1923, Nitya had written to Mrs. Besant "Krishna and I are full of schemes we want to carry out in India; and we want to talk to you about them and we both want to get back, I have never in my life been so homesick for India, California has made an Indian of me. I am beginning to realize in a small way of course, what you feel about India.

With all my love,
Nitya."[9]

†In a message to the International Self-Preparation Group shortly after Nitya's death, Krishna wrote, "For instance, when my brother died, I felt utterly lost. You have no idea how I felt for two or three days—for more than that, for a week perhaps. I still miss him; I shall always miss him physically, but I feel that he and I are working together, that we are walking along the same path, on the same mountain side, seeing the same flowers, the same creatures, the same blue sky, the same clouds and trees. That is why I feel as if I were part of him; and only when I get tired do I begin to say: 'My brother is not here.' But at once my mind pulls me up and tells me how absurd is such a thought."[10]

# CHAPTER 7

# "The Personality of J. Krishnamurti Has Been Swallowed Up in the Flames."

Before the Jubilee convention commenced at Adyar, Mrs. Besant tried to resolve the tensions between Krishnaji and the main mentors of the Theosophical Society. She brought the young Teacher to the room where Leadbeater, Jinarajadasa, Arundale, and Wedgwood had gathered, and asked K whether he would accept those chosen as Apostles as his disciples. K replied that he would only accept Mrs. Besant.

At the Star Congress that followed the Jubilee convention, K spoke under the ancient banyan tree; the sun filtered through its outstretched branches and its numerous roots, transforming it into a magical forest of light and shadow. Suddenly, in the midst of his talk, he electrified his audience by changing his speech from the third to the first person. Referring to the World Teacher to come he said, "He comes only to those who want, who desire, who long—" and then suddenly, "I come for those who want sympathy, who want happiness, who are longing to find happiness in all things. I come to reform and not to tear down, I come not to destroy, but to build." Many people who were present felt the timbre of the voice change, a strength and power enter the words. Later Mrs. Besant was to say, "The event marks the consecration of the chosen vehicle."[1]

From Adyar, Krishnamurti was to visit Varanasi in February. He was giving talks to the boys and girls of the schools at Kamaccha. He returned with high fever brought on by food poisoning. He was advised to rest and went up to Ootacamund. While there he was

Experimenting with myself, not very successfully at first, trying to discover how I could detach myself and see the body as it is. I had been experimenting with it for two or three days—it may have been a week—and I found that for a certain length of time I could quite easily be away from the body and look at it. I was standing beside my bed, and there was the body on the bed—a most extraordinary feeling. And from that day there has been a distinct sense of detachment, of division between the ruler and the ruled, so that the body, though it has its cravings, its desires to wander forth and to live and enjoy separately for itself, does not in any way interfere with the true Self.[2]

In the spring of 1926 Mrs. Besant accompanied Krishnaji back to England. He was seriously contemplating taking sannyasa,* and spoke of it to some of his friends.

Later in July K went to Ommen. Although Annie Besant was present, it was he who gave the fireside talks at the Ommen camp. Krishnamurti was expressing an overflowing joy and a feeling of oneness with the universe. His words did not conform to the orthodox Theosophical teaching and Wedgwood, who was present, was greatly perturbed. He whispered to Mrs. Besant that it was not the Lord Maitreya who was speaking through Krishnamurti, but a powerful black magician. Later Annie Besant herself spoke of this to the young Teacher. Shocked by her statement, he said that if she believed this story, he would never speak again. She withdrew her remarks and the next night Krishnamurti told the campers, "Walking over the hills of India last winter, there appeared before me my Ideal, my Beloved, my Guru, my Great Teacher and ever since that vision I seem to see all the trees through him, all the mountains, all the little pools, all the little insects and ever since that vision, that understanding of things has remained."[3] This oneness with the *guru* and the mystery of life continued to be the theme of his talks.

At the last talk Krishnamurti said, "I have altered so much during the last fortnight—both inside and outside my body, my face, my hands, my entire being has changed. The only way to breathe fresh

---

*Sannyasa is a state of being, a state of dying to the world and society. The *sannyasin* takes the vows of *sannyas*. Initiated by a guru, he is given the saffron robe, ceases to be a member of society, and is outside its frame, having hardly any concern with social laws, rites, rituals, sacraments, and so on. The *sannyasin* renounces caste, family, and adopts a new name signifying rebirth.

air of life is by this constant change, constant turmoil, constant unrest."[4]

Writing of the 1926 Ommen camp, Esther Bright said:

So A. B. sat by him at the Camp Fires, with a warm affection in her heart, wondering, loving, admiring, not always understanding, but with the most wonderful faith that he was the Herald of the New Age, and that in time all would be made clear. And together they walked through that great throng of men and women, down the path which led to the centre, where the fire had been laid—great masses of branches, heaped-up logs and twigs, and together they set it alight—the grand old white head, and the black head and fine, thoughtful features of Krishnaji, bending down together. The flames leapt up, and all sat for a while in silence. . . .

*"But you are a teacher"* said his faithful friend, Rajagopal to him one day at Ommen, when a group of us were gathered together, discussing difficult problems. Krishnaji was silent for a while, and then said simply, "I hold out a light to you."[5]

From August 1926 to April 1927 Annie Besant and Krishnamurti were together in Ojai. It was probably the longest time they had spent together since his youth. Sensing a certain need for her presence, Annie Besant canceled her return to India and the many engagements that awaited her there. While in Ojai she and Krishnamurti planted trees, and she busied herself with acquiring lands in the Ojai Valley for what was later to be the Happy Valley Foundation. Living in close proximity with him she grew aware of how far he had traveled from the orthodox Theosophical teaching.

Mrs. Besant was seeing a new Krishnamurti. She had a growing awareness that the earlier prophecy that Krishnamurti's body was to be the vehicle through which a fragment of the Maitreya consciousness would manifest was incorrect, and that the consciousness of Krishnamurti and the Lord Maitreya were likely to merge. She was to endorse this in a letter of October 12 to Arundale: "J. K. is changing all the time, but it does not seem as though he stepped out and the Lord stepped in, more like the blending of consciousness."[6]

It was growing clear that neither the formative years in the Theosophical Society under the guidance of Leadbeater, nor the rigors of his life during the war years in England, nor the time spent by Krishnamurti in the heart of British aristocracy had molded the brain of Krishnamurti. It could not be programmed, but rested—watching, listening, unoccupied.

After a long gestation, Krishnamurti's mind shed the superficial layers that had vaguely accepted and responded to Theosophical ritual and hierarchy and emerged pristine, without a scar. A volcanic energy was needed to plough the root of the human mind—to question, to perceive, to negate the structure of human consciousness, to enter the heart of the within of thought and feeling as they operated, to break away from all knowledge and to perceive anew. Austerity and a life of asceticism were not only integral to his person but, as he was to say, "a necessity to conserve energy."[7]

His awakening was luminous. His words had a startling simplicity. By February 9 Krishnamurti wrote to Leadbeater:

I know my destiny and my work. I know with certainty that I am blending into the consciousness of the one Teacher and that he will completely fill me. I feel and I know also that my cup is nearly full to the brim and that it will overflow soon. Till then I must abide quietly and with eager patience. I long to make and will make everybody happy.[8]

Before Mrs. Besant left the United States, she made a statement to the Associated Press: "The Divine spirit has descended once more on a man Krishnamurti, who in his lifetime is literally perfect as those who know him can testify. The World Teacher is here."[9]

At the opening of the Star camp at Ommen in 1927 Krishnamurti spoke a language diametrically opposed to Theosophical teaching. On June 30 he said, "For many lives and for all this life, and especially the last few months, I have struggled to be free—free of my friends, my books, my associations. You must struggle for the same freedom. There must be constant turmoil within you."[10] Krishnamurti was in revolt. No teacher nor authority satisfied him. "Who brings the truth?" he was to query.

He was questioning himself to find out the truth behind the form of the World Teacher. As a boy he told his listeners that he had seen Lord Krishna with a flute; in the Theosophical Society with Leadbeater he saw Master K. H. and then the Lord Maitreya, in the form in which his associates believed. In the last years, in the intensity of his suffering, he had seen Buddha, to his delight and glory.

The Beloved of whom he spoke were Krishna, the Masters, the Buddha—and far beyond all these. "The Beloved is the open sky, the flower, every human being. Krishnamurti is not outside but within them. He because of his sorrow has become one with the picture."[11]

Jinarajadasa was soon to arrive at the camp, and he was quick to question Krishnamurti's statements. For it was clear that Krishnamurti was rejecting all authority, even the most fundamental, such as belief in the Masters and the esoteric path. On July 23 he gave a reply to Jinarajadasa: "I and my Beloved are one. The vision is total. To me that is liberation." And then: "The personality of J. Krishnamurti has been swallowed up in the flame—what happens after that does not matter—whether the spark remains within the flame or issues forth."[12]

The following year, in the summer of 1928, Krishnamurti was at Eerde in Holland. He had started speaking to his friends of the possibility of dissolving the Order of Star.

A huge gathering of over three thousand people awaited Krishnamurti at the Ommen camp, which lasted from August 2 through 12. He spoke with great clarity on the need for the listener to abandon all grounds of authority, especially that of the World Teacher. Each one should live only by the light within. Later, speaking to a Reuter's representative who was present, he said, "The Buddha, the Christ had never claimed divinity, it was the disciple who, by his worship, gave divinity to the teacher."[13] To the astonishment of the correspondent, the World Teacher then went on to speak of golf and of his handicap, which was plus 2. Krishnamurti had played golf on some of the most famous golf courses in the world.

The news of the rift between Krishnamurti and the Theosophical Society spread rapidly. Annie Besant did not attend the Ommen camp, and on hearing what Krishnamurti had said she fell seriously ill. According to one version she had a nervous breakdown, fainted, and fell unconscious. She was ill for a long time. Her mental faculties slowly faded; she lost her memory and was never to recover completely. She had been told that Krishnamurti had refused to accept the role of the Messiah on the terms laid down by the Theosophical Society.

On her return to India she had recovered sufficiently to close down the Esoteric Section, the heart of the occult teaching within the Society, declaring that the World Teacher was here, and no one else had the right to teach. On November 30, 1928, she wrote to Krishnamurti, who was on his way to Adyar:

Beloved,

I am sending by Mr. Varma a paper sent to all E. S. corresponding Secretaries, as I am sure that it is better that all our students should devote themselves to the study of your wishes and ideals, and leave all the older teachings aside for the present. So, I am suspending the E. S. altogether indefinitely, leaving all teaching to you. I am sorry to be away when you arrive, but it cannot be helped.

All my love goes to you Beloved.

Mother.

A few months later, however, Mrs. Besant succumbed to pressures from other members and reopened the Esoteric Section. She also told Krishnamurti that she wanted to resign as president of the Theosophical Society and desired only to sit at his feet and listen to the teaching; but he refused to let her do so.

On August 3, 1929, in the presence of Mrs. Besant and three thousand members of the Order of the Star present at the Ommen camp, Krishnamurti announced his determination to dissolve the Order of the Star, of which he was the president. His talk to the members was a summation of the insights that had arisen within him during the years since his brother's death. The talk was possibly a seminal statement of his position, one that remained unchanged throughout his life: "I maintain that Truth is a pathless land, and you cannot approach it by any path whatsover, by any religion, by any sect. That is my point of view, and I adhere to that absolutely and unconditionally. Truth, being limitless, unconditioned, unapproachable by any path whatsover, cannot be organized; nor should any organization be formed to lead or to coerce people along any particular path. If you first understand that, then you will see how impossible it is to organize a belief. A belief is purely an individual matter, and you cannot and must not organize it. If you do, it becomes dead, crystalized; it becomes a creed, a sect, a religion, to be imposed on others. Truth is narrowed down and made a plaything for those who are weak, for those who are only momentarily discontented. Truth cannot be brought down, rather the individual must make the effort to ascend to it. You cannot bring the mountain-top to the valley. If you would attain to the mountain-top you must pass through the valley, climb the steeps, unafraid of the dangerous precipices. You must climb towards the Truth, it cannot be stepped down or organized for you. I do not want to belong to any organization of a spiritual kind, please understand this. Again, I maintain that no organization can lead man to spirituality. If an organization be created for this purpose, it becomes a crutch, a weakness, a bondage, and must cripple the individual, and prevent him from growing, from establishing his uniqueness, which lies in the discovery for himself of that absolute, unconditioned Truth. So that is another reason why I have decided, as I happen to be the Head of the Order, to dissolve it. No one has persuaded me to this decision.

"This is no magnificent deed, because I do not want followers, and I mean this. The moment you follow someone you cease to follow Truth. I am not concerned whether you pay attention to what I say or not. I want to do a certain thing in the world and I am going to do it with unwavering concentration. I am concerning myself with only one essential thing: to set man free. I desire to free him from all cages, from all fears, and not to found religions, new sects, nor to establish new theories and new philosophies. Then you will naturally ask me why I go the world over, continually speaking. I will tell you for what reason I do this: not because I desire a following, not because I desire a special group of special disciples. (How men love to be different from their fellow-men, however ridiculous, absurd and trivial their distinctions may be: I do not want to encourage that absurdity.) I have no disciples, no apostles, either on earth or in the realm of spirituality.

"One newspaper reporter, who interviewed me, considered it a magnificent act to dissolve an organization in which there were thousands of members. To him it was a great act because, he said, "What will you do afterwards, how will you live? You will have no following, people will no longer listen to you." If there are only five people who will listen, who will live, who have their faces turned towards eternity, it will be sufficient.

"As I have said, I have only one purpose: to make man free, to urge him towards freedom; to help him to break away from all limitations, for that alone will give him eternal happiness, will give him the unconditioned realization of the self.

"Because I am free, unconditioned, whole—not the part, not the relative, but the whole Truth that is eternal—I desire those, who seek to understand me, to be free, not to follow me, not to make out of me a cage which will become a religion, a sect. Rather should they be free from all fears—from the fear of religion, from the fear of salvation, from the fear of spirituality, from the fear of love, from the fear of death, from the fear of life itself. As an artist paints a picture because he takes delight in that painting, because it is his self-expression, his glory, his well-being, so I do this and not because I want anything from anyone.

"You are accustomed to authority, or to the atmosphere of authority which you think will lead you to spirituality. You think and hope that another can, by the extraordinary powers—a miracle—transport you to this realm of eternal freedom which is Happiness. Your whole outlook on life [is] based on that authority.

"You have listened to me for three years now, without any change taking place except in the few. Now analyze what I am saying, be critical, so that you may understand thoroughly, fundamentally. When you look for an authority to lead you to spirituality, you are bound automatically to build an organization around that authority. By the very creation of that organization, which, you think, will help this authority to lead you to spirituality, you are held in a cage.

"Instead of old spiritual distinction, instead of old worships you have new worships. You are all depending for your spirituality on someone else, for your happiness on someone else, for your enlightenment on someone else; and although you have been preparing for me for eighteen years, when I say all these things are unnecessary, when I say that you must put them all away and look within yourselves for the enlightenment, for the glory, for the purification, and for the incorruptibility of the self, not one of you is willing to do it. There may be a few, but very, very few.

"So why have an organization?

"Why have false, hypocritical people following me, the embodiment of Truth? Please remember that I am not saying something harsh or unkind, but we have reached a situation when you must face things as they are. I said last year that I would not compromise. Very few listened to me then. This year I have made it absolutely clear. I do not know how many thousands throughout the world—members of the Order—have been preparing for me for eighteen years, and yet now they are not willing to listen unconditionally, wholly, to what I say.

"So why have an organization?

"As I said before, my purpose is to make men unconditionally free, for I maintain that the only spirituality is the incorruptibility of the self which is eternal, is the harmony between reason and love. This is the absolute, unconditioned Truth which is Life itself. I want therefore to set man free, rejoicing as the bird in the clear sky, unburdened, independent, ecstatic in that freedom. And I, for whom you have been preparing for eighteen years, now say that you must be free of all these things, free from your complications, your entanglements. For this you need not have an organization based on spiritual belief. Why have an organization for five or ten people in the world who understand, who are struggling, who have put aside all trivial things? And for the weak people, there can be no organization to help them to find the Truth, because Truth is in everyone; it is not far, it is not near; it is eternally there.

"Organizations cannot make you free. No man from outside can make you free: nor organize worship, nor the immolation of yourselves for a cause, make you free; nor can forming yourselves into an organization, nor throwing yourselves into works, make you free. You use [a] typewriter to write letters, but you do not put it on an altar and worship it. But that is what you are doing when organizations become your chief concern. 'How many members are there in it?' That is the first question I am asked by all newspaper reporters. 'How many followers have you? By their number we shall judge whether what you say is true or false.' I do not know how many there are. I am not concerned with that. If there were even one man who had been set free, that were enough.

"Again, you have the idea that only certain people hold the key to the Kingdom of Happiness. No one holds it. No one has the authority to hold that key. That key is your own self, and in the development and the purification and in the incorruptibility of that self alone is the Kingdom of Eternity.

"So you will see how absurd is the whole structure that you have built, looking for external help, depending on others for your comfort, for your happiness, for your strength. These can only be found within yourselves.

"So why have an organization?

"You are accustomed to being told how far you have advanced, what is your spiritual status, How childish! Who but yourself can tell you if you are beautiful or ugly within? Who but yourself can tell you if you are incorruptible? You are not serious in these things.

"So why have an organization?

"But those who really desire to understand, who are looking to find that which is eternal, without beginning and without an end, will walk together with a greater intensity, will be a danger to everything that is unessential, to unrealities, to shadows. And they will concentrate, they will become the flame, because they understand. Such a body we must create, and that is my purpose. Because of that true friendship—which you do not seem to know—there will be real cooperation on the part of each one. And this not because of authority, not because of salvation, not because of immolation for a cause, but because you really understand, and hence are capable of living in the eternal. This is a greater thing than all pleasure, than all sacrifice.

"So these are some of the reasons why, after careful consideration for two years, I have made this decision. It is not from a momentary impulse. I have not been persuaded to it by anyone—I am not persuaded in such things. For two years, I have been thinking about this, slowly, carefully, patiently, and I have now decided to disband the Order, as I happen to be its head. You can form other organizations and expect someone else. With that I am not concerned, nor with creating new cages, new decorations for those cages. My only concern is to set man absolutely, unconditionally free."[14]

Later, the various trusts and funds were liquidated, the vast estates and lands returned to the original donors. A small office was established with Rajagopal as the main organizer, to undertake publications of Krishnamurti's talks. By now Krishnamurti was coming to be regarded as a secular philosopher, totally hostile to all religious beliefs, and many stalwarts of the Theosophical Society maintained that the coming of the World Teacher had been vitiated.

# CHAPTER 8

# Krishnamurti in Ojai: The Forgotten Years, 1938–1947

Krishnamurti resigned from the Theosophical Society in 1930. Writing in the *International Star Bulletin* in that year he had said, "My teaching is neither occult nor mystic for I hold both as limitations placed on man on his search for Truth." Mrs. Besant's one concern on hearing the news of his resignation was anxiety about Krishnamurti's future. She was aware of his total lack of worldly values and wondered how he would survive the cruel world without the protection of the Society. I am told that she prevailed on B. Sanjeeva Rao and his wife, Padmabai, eminent educators and her close associates, to resign from the Theosophical Society so that they could join Krishna's work, to be with him and protect him.

He did not return to India until November 1932. From Bombay he went directly to Adyar to see Mrs. Besant. She had become very fragile, had lost her memory, and was living in the past. But she recognized her dearly beloved son. It was tragic to see her, and Krishnamurti was deeply saddened. On his return from Varanasi he was to see her again. He had grown a beard and she commented on his beautiful face and said that he was frail and should look after himself. This was their final meeting.

His speech at the Theosophical convention held at Adyar in 1932 was met by critical comments from the elders of the Society. He told me many years later that they had cornered him and questioned him relentlessly, asking him to affirm or deny the existence of the Masters. He had refused to reply.

On his way back to Europe he met George Bernard Shaw at the

home of Sir Chunilal Mehta. They spoke of Mrs. Besant. Shaw enquired how she was. "Very well," said Krishnamurti, "but at her great age, she cannot think consecutively." "She never could," whispered Shaw. Krishnamurti merely smiled.

Later Shaw was to describe Krishnamurti to Heskith Pearson as the most beautiful human being he had ever seen.[1]

Annie Besant died at Adyar on September 20, 1933. Half a century later I asked Krishnaji about the impact Mrs. Besant's death had on him. A look of intense gravity touched his eyes as he responded. "I read the notice of her death in *The New York Times*—they never informed me."

Throughout their two lives, so closely intertwined, Mrs. Besant and her adopted son Krishna were to spend little time together. But from Mrs. Besant's earliest letters to Krishna an intensity of love, a wave, flows from her to reach out and envelop the child, holding and protecting him.

The bonds fused between her and Krishna, transcending time and space. As a boy he wrote to her every week describing his dreams, his studies, his daily life, and his little problems. She was first a mother, anxious that no harm should befall him; then the teacher; as the years passed she sometimes took the role of disciple and sat at his feet to listen to his words. As her intellect faded, her mental powers diminished and her letters to Krishna grew pale; his were affectionate, yet formal. But Krishna's deep love and respect for her rested undiminished throughout his life.

She was an influence not in molding or giving direction to his mind and teaching, but in providing the ground of a total security of love. He had seen the fire in her blaze and sink to embers, but the warmth and unselfish love of Mrs. Besant was perhaps the one constant factor in his early life.

With the dissolution of the Order of the Star the group of young people who were always around Krishna dispersed. The organization of his travel plans and talks were for a time divided between Jadunandan Prasad, a young and much-loved associate, and Rajagopal. Jadu's sudden death in 1931 at the age of thirty-five left Krishna with few companions. Many who had left the Theosophical Society with him felt lost and in despair; the Society had provided shelter, solace, and a purpose in life. Money was scarce.

Jadu had been a close friend. Krishna wrote to Padmabai Sanjeeva

Rao in Varanasi, sharing her grief. These letters reveal Krishna's mind in the days following the severing of his membership with the Theosophical Society. On August 30, 1931, he wrote:

My dearest Akkaji,

Isn't it terrible that Jadu has gone away. It is really tragic and dear Padmabai, I can imagine what you must be feeling and how depressed you must be. I can hardly believe such a thing is possible. Jadu was just getting into his stride and you have no idea how much he was liked on his tour and what a success he made of it. I heard during the camp that I had a cable from John Ingleman— Jadu had a heat stroke and his blood pressure 220; again a few days later, that he was steadily improving. We were naturally anxious about it but he didn't think that anything serious was afoot. When I came here, I had a cable of which you know. Akkaji, you must have had a grievous shock and I wish I were with you, but . . . !

In your letter—thank you so much for it—you were prophetic as you said how many of us will be alive when we all meet again! Nitya has gone and so has Jadu. Jadu was so clever, liked by everybody and very intelligently critical. We shall miss him and my dearest Padmabai, all my love is with you.

You were all depressed and this will be another dreadful blow. Akka, there are so few of us that we must pull ourselves together and we have got to change and we have to realise there is something infinitely greater than birth and death. We have to realise it and the effort is colossal. I wish I were with you but there it is. Life is like that and cruel if we are not master of it.

I wish, I were with you dearest Akka.[2]

Padmabai's reply must have expressed her own profound anguish, for in another letter, on September 29, Krishna refers to his sorrow at Nitya's death, his enquiry into the cause of sorrow, and a blazing awakening.

My dearest Padmabai,

Thank you very much for your letter. I know, Padmabai the fight you must be putting up, Akkaji, because we want the perfume of love through one person only, death [darkens] our love. There will be always death as long as our understanding is limited by personal, egotistical outlook. I tell you, Akkaji dear, as long as there is consciousness of oneself there is death, loneliness and sorrow. I went through this when Nitya died and I understood what lay behind sorrow, the cause of it. I have cheated death. So, Akkaji, this is the time to understand in the midst of this sorrow and loneliness. You must understand, probe into the deepest and you will see, Padmabai dear, that there is something more permanent, eternal than all persons. We all must die and while you are in the midst of this sorrow, this is the time to understand. Don't postpone it, Akkaji. In the gloom, you must seek the way out and not wait or let sorrow

# THE ANTI-GURU

In an era in which spiritual leaders come and go with the frequency of TV sitcoms, the influence of Jiddu Krishnamurti—whose centenary is being celebrated this month—continues to grow. Who was he, and why do we still care?

By Cheryll Aimée Barron

This year, a string of discreet lionizing events marks the centenary of one of the twentieth century's most original and influential thinkers, Jiddu Krishnamurti. Born one hundred years ago this month—on May 12, 1895, to be precise—Krishnamurti (or K, as he referred to himself) has been studied and admired by millions, ranging from the likes of Jonas Salk to writers and artists such as Aldous Huxley and David Hockney to pop stars like the singer Van Morrison and the kung fu master Bruce Lee. In south India, the Dalai Lama inaugurated K's centenary in January, proclaiming him "one of the greatest thinkers of the age."

An anti-religious anti-guru, Krishnamurti is a study in contradictions and irony: the lapsed prophet who said he wanted no acolytes yet lectured to rapt millions all over the world about truth seeking; the philosopher whose most fervent fans were often rigorous thinkers to whom he lectured about uncluttered thinking; the seemingly lifelong celibate who is perhaps best remembered for his discourses on love, relationships, and sex.

Krishnamurti has been dead for nine years, and his exquisite profile—he was in his masculine way as powerfully beautiful as Garbo—has disappeared from the pages of the newsmagazines. In our age of instant gurus who flash in and out of celebrity like so many fireflies, his writings should by now have vanished from the catalogues of major publishers, shunted off to small, specialist presses. But they have not.

A listing of his titles—fifty-six of them, including seventeen volumes of the collected works—currently takes up nearly one and a half columns in Books in Print. Half the books are published by the multinational giant HarperCollins, which next month will release a new Krishnamurti compilation, The Book of Life. "Because sales of most of his titles are very good, we continually look for new ways to publish him," says Joel Fotinos, the HarperCollins marketing manager responsible for Krishnamurti books. In addition to HarperCollins's offering, at least six other new Krishnamurti-related works are being issued this year, including Krishnamurti: 100 Years from Stewart, Tabori & Chang, and a collection of dialogues between the sage and one of his biographers, from Penguin India.

"Krishnamurti has persisted because he appeals to people who don't want anybody to tell them what to do," says Huston Smith, the venerable Berkeley scholar and authority on the world's traditional religions. "Whether or not they admit it, [they] have a spiritual hunger, but they want no authority above or beyond themselves." Krishnamurti, it would seem, gives them the tools with which to conduct their own search.

Smith's description of anti-authoritarians—spiritually starved or not—fits many twentieth-century Americans. An illustration from a memorable dinner on Easter weekend six years ago: the talk turned to religion, and a scientist friend became emphatic. Whenever he met anyone who used the words spiritual or religious to describe himself, he

said, "I immediately begin to look for other signs of pathology. These people nearly always have a few screws loose."

What struck me was that when he finished, no one at the table challenged him. Who would challenge a scientist—especially a Stanford molecular/biologist who had just been given a MacArthur "genius" Fellowship? To have done so would have been to fall under suspicion of promoting the crutches of the feeble-minded—the mumbo-jumbo of religious doctrine and dogma; superstition; mysticism; ritual; ridiculous myths about miracles. In any case, what he said was only an exaggeration of the way most highly educated people these days view spiritual voyagers.

Yet it is to just such skeptics as my friend that Krishnamurti's views seem not only acceptable but profound and practical. To both the believer and the seeker, Krishnamurti offers the same seemingly unremarkable advice. Think for yourself, and think rigorously. Be utterly fearless; forget any form of received wisdom or belief, as well as all the conventions, tradition, and knowledge with which your head was stuffed in school. But as you think, scrutinize your mind's workings relentlessly for signs of self-delusion. Train your mind to stay in "a state of perpetual inward revolution" in which you set aside the conditioning that gets in the way of deep and genuinely fresh perception. In this way, ferret out truth for yourself.

Scientists—among them, the path-breaking physicists David Bohm and Fritjof Capra—have long loved this message, for it echoes their traditional disgust with antique religious dogma. Today, many of them find in it support for rejecting new forms of dogma.

Consider the situation in physics, where theorists have been stuck in a rut for decades, because the foundations of the field, its basic truths, have been found to be inconsistent. The problem, says Carver Mead, the distinguished Caltech physicist credited with revolutionizing the design of semiconductor chips, is that "the most modern principles of physics have become an orthodoxy"—an orthodoxy that blocks the radical thinking that must be done to clear the rut. "For many serious physicists," Mead says, "there would be enormous resonance with what Krishnamurti is saying. For a breakthrough to happen, we all need to achieve that state of mind he describes. We need to transcend the known."

Scientists of all types are also attracted by the systematic and analytical way in which Krishnamurti examines a subject many of them find disturbingly mushy, murky, and irrational: human relationships. "Our relationships are mechanical," K said in a talk he gave in Switzerland in 1982. "One has certain biological urges and one fulfills them. One demands certain comforts, certain companionship because one is lonely or depressed.... But in one's relationships with another, intimate or otherwise, there is always a cause, a motive, a ground from which one establishes a relationship. That is mechanical."

Nonetheless, Krishnamurti stressed, human relationships are of paramount importance because they are "the mirror in which we see ourselves as we are." Without the clear reflection they provide, our efforts to shed our conditioning and preconceptions are doomed. "Relationship," he once said, "is the most important thing in life." This he seemed to know instinctively—possibly because his own closest human ties had been broken again and again.

Photograph from the book *Krishnamurti: 100 Years*, by Evelyne Blau, published by Stewart, Tabori & Chang, 1995.

T he first and most significant of these breaks came in 1909, when, as a scrawny, ragged boy living in south India, Krishnamurti was plucked from a beach near Madras by a traveling religious seeker and declared to be divine.

His discoverer was a teacher in what was known as the theosophical movement, a Victorian rage whose adherents believed in, among other things, universal brotherhood, cross-religious studies, and reincarnation. Theosophy's doyenne was Helena Petrovna Blavatsky, a free-spirited Russian noblewoman and occultist who founded the Theosophical Society in New York in 1875. Blavatsky's contemporaries were divided as to whether she was a charlatan or a divinely inspired mystic, but there is no question that she was a pioneer who introduced Western intellectuals to Eastern religious philosophy and mysticism. In every sense, she was the great-grandmother of today's New Ager. Among her admirers were the likes of William Butler Yeats, James Joyce, E. M. Forster, Paul Klee, Paul Gauguin, and Albert Einstein.

Not long before she died in 1891, Blavatsky said that her real pur-

pose in establishing the Theosophical Society had been to prepare for the reincarnation of what she called the "World Teacher." In theosophy's esoteric hierarchy, this was the Lord Maitreya, who had in the past twice taken on human form, once as Jesus Christ. In 1909, after being presented with a little Indian boy from Madras who was said to have a remarkable "aura," Blavatsky's successors declared that Maitreya had come back a third time as Jiddu Krishnamurti.

At the time of his "discovery," the then 14-year-old Krishnamurti —who had lost his devout Hindu mother four years earlier—was being brought up somewhat distractedly with his four brothers by his impoverished father, Naraniah, who was both a Brahmin and a theosophist. Though K hadn't much of an education, he was soon writing down philosophical ideas that combined tenets of Hinduism and theosophy. These insights supposedly came to him through "astral communion" with a type of spiritually evolved being whom the theosophists called "master" or "elder brother." They were collected in a little book called *At the Feet of the Master*, which rode the wave of interest in theosophy to become an international best-seller.

In 1911, Annie Besant, the English social reformer and Fabian who was then president of the Theosophical Society, removed Krishnamurti

Above: Krishnamurti at his last public appearance, in Madras, 1986

"Krishnamurti appeals to people who don't want anybody to tell them what to do"

and his younger brother Nitya from their father's home and took them to England, hoping to give them the intellectual foundation of an Oxbridge education. But Krishnamurti had always been an exceptionally poor student, and he failed the university entrance examinations. Nonetheless, the rich English theosophists showered him with largess. As K came of age, he lived in splendor and drove Rolls-Royces—fast.

In 1922, however, this life of luxury ended.

Krishnamurti and his brother were then living in Ojai, California, a somnolent health resort seventy-five miles northeast of Los Angeles, where they had been sent in the hope of curing Nitya's tuberculosis. One day, as he was meditating, Krishnamurti had his first experience of what later became known as "the process"—an experience of extreme physical, mental, and emotional agony that lasted for hours, during which he believed he left his body and sensed the existence of "mighty beings" hovering nearby. This experience was repeated nearly every day for a fortnight (and after that, intermittently, for several years). Immediately after each episode, he reported feeling rapturous and blissful. His theosophical handlers read these as signs of a classic religious initiation. By 1927, when K turned 32, Annie Besant formally announced to the Associated Press the arrival of the World Teacher.

Only two years later, though, Krishnamurti renounced his messiah role. "Truth," he told a gathering of three thousand theosophists in Holland, "is a pathless land....The moment you follow someone you cease to follow Truth." He ended his speech by spelling out his chief goal for the future: "My only concern is to set men unconditionally free."

In the years following his renunciation—which nearly destroyed Blavatsky's movement—Krishnamurti never again spoke publicly as a mystic, and he cut all his ties to the theosophists.

Although Krishnamurti repeated often and vehemently the wish that no one should become a follower of his, people from all over the world came to live in the Ojai Valley simply because of his connection with the place. They still come, and today comprise a community clustered loosely around the Oak Grove School for children, which K started in 1975, and around the Krishnamurti Foundation of America (KFA), one of five organizations worldwide charged with preserving and disseminating what K called "the teachings."

Aside from overseeing the publication of books and videos, how do you preserve and disseminate the wisdom of a philosopher who frowned on systematized belief and proselytizing—in fact, on all attempts to structure and institutionalize spiritual insight? To prevent K's ideas from becoming fossilized and forgotten, the KFA executive director Mark Lee hit on the original strategy of organizing or inspiring "dialogues" among admirers of K about different concepts in his corpus. So, every few months there are large public gatherings—in Ojai and elsewhere in the United States—at which hundreds of aficionados divide into groups of eight to ten people for a sort of joint philosophical grope on topics such as God, social responsibility, and the self.

According to a KFA document explaining the rules, "Dialogue deals with the large picture of an issue...rather than the particular, personal manifestations...in daily life." More important than what is actually said are the movements in participants' own "listening minds," which they are supposed to scrutinize and question in order to gain the beady-eyed self-awareness that accompanies true insight.

In Ojai itself, "discussions" take place almost every evening. And while these exchanges rarely exhibit the kind of cerebral superwattage the rules suggest, even when they verge on the downright banal, the form of shared, active K study that they attempt can be oddly entertaining.

"Can goodness exist in relationship?" This is the subject under discussion at the meeting I am invited to attend after dinner one Tuesday night. The venue is the Krishnamurti Library, an old, plain California ranch house—K's favorite—at Ojai's east end, where dusty orange groves are overlooked by the high, parched wilderness and forbidding rock faces of the Los Padres National Forest.

Relatively little is actually said about goodness and relationship. The discussion wanders, and only at evening's end does someone summarize what the real subject has turned out to be. "I think we have talked a lot about group dynamics and very little about goodness!" remarks Ulrich, a dimpled Swiss-German, to the group's six other participants.

This is chiefly because Roland—chic in his plunging, collarless designer shirt—has persisted in comparing tonight's meeting to a Krishnamurti dialogue he attended the night before. "Goodness was present in the room there, and it isn't here," he declares. "Goodness is present when you can listen to someone without judging or even reacting, even if you think that person is boring or unintelligent—or whatever."

"I'd like to suggest that your attachment to yesterday's meeting has maybe created a resentment that's preventing you from being open to what goodness might be present here," Ulrich says.

Roland sighs heavily. "I think we should all be willing to listen without constantly checking each other by Krishnaji's standards of negativity—his ideas about the right and wrong ways to approach things," he complains. He looks dejected.

Eventually, the discussion ambles back on course.

"Can relationship exist *without* goodness?" studious-looking Daniel asks.

"Yes—maybe when two people are just using each other?" suggests Birkenstocks-clad Hans, from Germany.

A pregnant silence. Then Rex speaks.

"Can goodness exist in a relationship where fear is present? Because when fear begins to enter, it can throw things a bit out of whack."

"Oh!" Roland exclaims feverishly. "*Totally!*"

A fly on the wall here, I feel as if my head will pop from the pressure of questions no one in the group is asking or answering. What experience of Hans's life made him choose his example of a mutually exploitative relationship? Does Rex have a wife or lover with whom he is scrapping because one of them is insecure? But this sort of inquiry or admission, or indeed any illustration from real life, is taboo in Krishnamurti dialogues, which are in no way supposed to be like group therapy. That would be getting away from "the large picture."

Yet it is for guidance in their particular, personal problems that

Photograph from the book *Krishnamurti: 100 Years*, by Evelyne Blau, published by Stewart, Tabori & Chang, 1995.

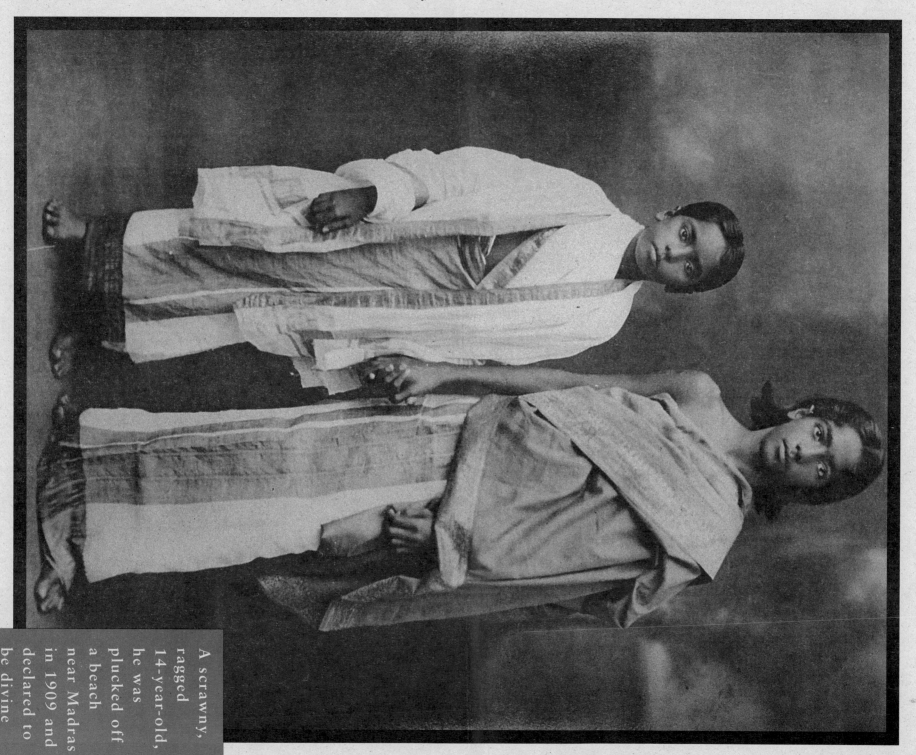

Krishnamurti (at right), with his brother Nitya, 1910

A scrawny, ragged 14-year-old, he was plucked off a beach near Madras in 1909 and declared to be divine

many in the Krishnamurti circle in Ojai steep themselves in his work. One day I find myself in the tiny, one-bedroom house off Ojai Avenue of Dunya Ramicova, a 44-year-old costume designer whose work takes her to the famous opera houses and theaters of London and Salzburg. Ramicova and her family fled from Czechoslovakia to New York after the Prague Spring of 1968, the year she turned 18. The year after that, in a state of bottomless confusion—"I had no idea how to live"—she was given one of Krishnamurti's books by a friend. Then as now, she felt, "I have never found anything as clear and intelligent as what Krishnamurti had to say." The friend later moved to Ojai and, visiting him from Yale, where she was teaching costume design, Dunya met her future husband, Ivan Berkovics, whom I'd met the previous evening at the Krishnamurti Library, where he works as an archivist.

Dunya and Ivan married and settled in Ojai, but have now been separated and on their way to a divorce for nearly two years. Dunya finds their reaching this pass hard to explain—even to herself—given their passionate shared interest in Krishnamurti, who spoke volumes about how people could avoid relationship woes.

"There are times when I beat myself with that question," she says, "I find it hard to look myself in the eye with that question." "I had always wanted nothing more in my life than a partner who was interested in the spiritual questions. How could I be married to someone like that and we just dropped each other? Ivan never heard me, and I never heard him."

"We didn't look sufficiently deeply into our problems. We just wanted a quick solution to them," Ivan tells me later, shrugging slightly, across the table at a fast-food burrito place. "The fact that we didn't understand sufficiently what Krishnamurti was drawing our attention to made us no different from people with no interest in him."

A deep-seated ambivalence about religion originally led Ivan to Krishnamurti. "What he was—or, rather, was not—espousing really struck a chord with me. He wasn't saying go toward *this*; here are the *positive* steps to enlightenment. Instead he was saying it's all the *negative* things we have to get rid of before there's any understanding at all."

Dunya sometimes wishes that she could give up her costume-design work and teaching for a full-time engagement with Krishnamurti's ideas. She says, laughing, that she sometimes feels envious when she thinks of Krishnamurti's life. "All of this messy stuff went on in my life with various relationships. But when you read about him, there wasn't anything that went on. He just gave lectures and…"

Her voice trails off as she takes in the skeptical expression on my face. I know it wasn't as simple as that, and so does she.

I f anyone looked the part of an upper-class *sannyasi*, a wandering Hindu religious ascetic and mendicant, it was Krishnamurti. He cut a solitary figure, was known to be a bachelor, and in his celebrity, seemed detached from the world of sensual fulfillment. Many people, like me, read what he had to say about sex over the years ("it is perhaps the only deep, firsthand experience we have") and thought: But

how could he know?

The answer to this question, revealed only recently, and to the dismay of the official keepers of his flame, is explosive. When he was 37, three years after abandoning his role as a messiah, Krishnamurti secretly gave up chastity, too. The sexual initiator he chose was Rosalind Rajagopal, the empathetic blond and blue-eyed American wife of Desikacharya Rajagopal. Like Krishnamurti, D. Rajagopal was a Brahmin who as a teenager had been identified by the theosophists as having a special mission on earth; in his case, he was asked by Annie Besant to devote his life to furthering the World Teacher's work.

Rosalind had become a friend of Krishnamurti's and his brother soon after their arrival in Ojai. Though younger than either of them—she was just 19—she acted as a sort of surrogate mother to them. She nursed Nirya in his illness and always acceded to Krishnamurti's pleas that she, and she alone, hold him as he went through his episodes of "the process." In 1927, she married Rajagopal. Only four years later, however, they ended their unsatisfactory sex life together, and the year after that, Krishnamurti—who lived with the Rajagopals in their Ojai house—began a clandestine affair with Rosalind that continued for over twenty years. Rosalind became pregnant by him several times but always managed to conceal the fact; her pregnancies ended in at least three abortions and a miscarriage.

In 1950, upset over Krishnamurti's apparent infatuation with another woman, Rosalind told her husband about the affair, which Krishnamurti did not deny. Even after this, she continued to sleep with the philosopher, and Rajagopal continued to serve as his editor, manager, and amanuensis. But Krishnamurti and Rosalind gradually grew increasingly estranged. The affair finally ended in three bitter lawsuits, one brought by Rajagopal, two by a group of supporters on K's behalf—over who would control not Rosalind but Krishnamurti's writings, as well as the houses and land that were held in trust for him.

This account of Krishnamurti's private life is taken from *Lives in the Shadow with J. Krishnamurti*, a book written by Rosalind and D. Rajagopal's only child, Radha Sloss. Because the first American publishers Sloss approached reportedly turned down the manuscript out of respect for the philosopher (a Knopf editor flatly refused to believe that K was capable of sexual dalliance), it was first published in England in 1991. It came out in the United States two years later. *Lives in the Shadow* is an intimate account of the ménage à trois, with descriptions of Krishnamurti (and not her father) changing Radha's diapers, of K clad in a silk nightshirt, flowers in hand, creeping up the stairs for an assignation with Rosalind. There are accounts of ironies—K's followers mistaking his glow of happiness after his first experiences of sex for a "transcendent spiritual condition," and a chiropractor diagnosing celibacy as the cause of a mysterious illness afflicting K, who at the time had been sleeping with Rosalind for more than a decade.

"The Krishnamurti community here went berserk when the book was published," Dunya Ramicova said when I told her I had been reading *Lives in the Shadow*. But though the debate was furious in the KFA circle over what should be done about the book, cool heads eventually prevailed. Although those at the circle's center believed that Sloss had gravely distorted Krishnamurti's side of the dispute between him and Rajagopal, they agreed that ignoring the book would be wiser than publicly attacking the author, and so drawing more attention to her story. Whatever the reason, the book's U.S. publication passed virtually unnoticed by the American media—even though it had garnered glowing reviews in both the British and Indian press.

In retrospect it would have been surprising if there had been no Rosalind in K's life. His soulful good looks had a powerful effect on women. A therapist who had recently given up her practice in Minneapolis to move to Ojai told me that women relate to the philosopher "as a wonderfully gentle and sensitive man from another culture—as a lover." Later I repeat this to Bill Quinn, once a trustee of the KFA and an intimate of Krishnamurti's. "A lover? That would drive him up the wall!" Bill exclaims, but then goes on to admit that "when he was younger, women just went off the deep end about him."

Quinn recalls for me how one adoring female bought the house next door to K's in Ojai and for years trailed him on his daily walks. Another prowled back and forth behind him "looking very sinister" as he gave one of his talks. Bill tells me how he persuaded her to leave; she announced in parting: "'If he would only marry me, the war

would end,'—this was during World War II—and, lifting herself to her full height, said, 'for I am a *cosmic woman!*'"

I put a question to Mark Lee, the tall, urbane executive director of the KFA. 'Since Krishnamurti spoke of the importance of living fearlessly and growing beyond "this rotten social order," why didn't he conduct his relationship with Rosalind openly?

"I think what's important is what he *said*," says Lee, unruffled. "What he actually did in his life really has no bearing on his teachings. Nor do his teachings have any bearing on the way he lived."

"Then," I suggest, "he was saying Do as I say and not as I do?"

"No. No! For example, he talks about stimulants and escapes, and yet he would occasionally have a glass of wine or drink a cup of coffee. There are Krishnamurti fundamentalists just like Christian fundamentalists who extrapolate a whole way of life from what he said. But that's the antithesis of what he was trying to do. What's important is not his but *your* life and whether you lead it intelligently and whether you've discovered these things for yourself."

The difficulty with accusing Krishnamurti of hypocrisy—for culti-

**Above: Rosalind Rajagopal, Krishnamurti's secret lover for more than twenty years**

vating a false image of personal asceticism—is that he always spoke out against celibacy. "So if you deny—as most religions have denied—sexuality, then you must close your eyes, cut your tongue, put out your eyes, and never look at anything," he once railed. So why the need to appear to be celibate? A friend of his, the New York psychiatrist David Shainberg, once speculated that "it was his conditioning at work. The Brahmin holy man doesn't engage with women, and he was forced thereby to maintain his image."

Of various speculations by various people, this one seems nearest the mark because—for all his emphasis on the importance of shaking off one's conditioning—Krishnamurti showed how profoundly he was influenced by his own in the details of his daily life. He mocked people who slavishly followed regimens of yoga and meditation, yet himself practiced these faithfully; he ridiculed extremists but was a strict vegetarian.

Another bit of high-caste Hindu philosophy that may have affected K's behavior is the prescription against losing semen—thought to be physically weakening—and instead letting the body recirculate it for the supreme reward of greater spiritual vigor. This would account both for Krishnamurti's anxiousness to seem celibate—if he didn't; his many Indian admirers might be less inclined to see him as spiritually evolved—and for his actual restraint. While he could have had a sex life rivaling Elvis Presley's, the evidence suggests that he may have slept only with Rosalind Rajagopal.

Whatever the real explanation, Krishnamurti's management of his own love life makes him—for me, at least—a less than inspiring teacher about relationships. Which leads me to ask Mark Lee what it is, essentially, that justifies K's high rank among twentieth-century philosophers and makes him a thinker for the ages.

He has his answer ready. "He described the way the mind—and consciousness—works so precisely, so accurately, that it is possible for anyone to see it for themselves and then to have an insight of their own," he says. "He gives the approach—the way to understand conflict or misery or anything that causes the whole range of human problems."

"But what proof is there that Krishnamurti's approach works better than the others?"

"Ah! There *is* no proof! But it is at least in an area that's unknown. At least it's pointing to areas that are unexplored. And areas that have a potential for being hugely creative."

O ne day in Java Heaven, an Ojai espresso bar, a 34-year-old attorney named Tony Goldsmith walks over to my table to introduce himself. He tells me he left a Los Angeles law firm to start his own practice four years ago—and moved here partly because of his interest in Krishnamurti. But, he says, he has grown somewhat bored with K in recent years. "I feel there's a lack of earthiness and direct contact with real-world issues in his stuff."

I nod in warm agreement. For me, the chief deficiency of K's perspective is this: though it addresses basic human preoccupations, it lacks a sense of a blood-and-guts connection to them. For others,

though, that is precisely what it has—a discovery I make talking to Ed Kowalczyk, who is 23 and sings, plays the acoustic guitar, and writes most of the lyrics for Live, a well-known Pennsylvania rock group. I put in a call to him after reading in a magazine that Live's first album, *Mental Jewelry*, was heavily influenced by Krishnamurti. Ed phones me back from his room in the Hotel Biedermeier in Vienna, where he is on tour with his band. Between concerts, he says, he has been tapping a transcript of one of Krishnamurti's earliest talks into a portable computer—part of a volunteer effort to help the KFA digitize the collected works.

For the last six years, Ed says, no one has done a better job than Krishnamurti of answering the questions he has had about living. As he explains in one of the songs on *Mental Jewelry*:

*He said, he said, he said,*
*"There was nothing to fear boy"*
*And be said, be said, be said,*
*"Wortbless are your tears boy"*
*Just realize your senses*
*And realize your earth*
*Just realize your essence first"*

J oel Fotinos, the HarperCollins manager responsible for marketing Krishnamurti was, until a few months ago, the religious-books buyer for the famous Denver bookstore Tattered Cover—"on the front lines of what's hot," he says. The experience gave him a fresh insight into K's popularity. "His message is meaningful for this interesting time we are living in," Fotinos says, "when people are reading across the board—reading about Buddhism when they were born Catholic, or they come from Lutheran backgrounds but are reading about Sufism and Jewish mysticism."

Just as Krishnamurti appeals to the strictly secular and logically oriented among us, he says, he also speaks to sophisticates who may be too embarrassed to discuss religion or spirituality in public, but who in private devour books on these subjects. "His idea that truth is a path that has no specific religious message validates these people's own personal journey," he says, "whereas our Western churches and religious institutions often will not support individual search."

I repeat this to the religious scholar Huston Smith. "It is deeply ironic," he replies, "that Krishnamurti became an authority figure for millions by repudiating all traditionalism and authority figures. Though he talked against authority, he himself was very authoritative in his pronouncements."

Such confusion is absolutely characteristic of our Age of Groping. A historian a hundred years from now trying to describe this century's struggle with issues of faith and skepticism could say it all simply by telling about Krishnamurti. About the anti-guru not-preaching about a do-it-yourself God. About a skeptic whose talks drew crowds of equally skeptical seekers from the 1920s onward. And about a man born in nineteenth-century India whose writings continue to bring him new, young fans on the millennium's cusp. Z

eat your heart and loneliness darken your smile. So Padmabai, be eager to understand, though it hurts. Detach your mind from loneliness, sorrow and examine and you will see that by freeing your own consciousness, you go beyond birth and death. Try it dear Padmabai and don't say these are just words.

I wish I were with you, perhaps I could be able to help you. Oh, Padmabai, you have no idea the joy of true impersonal love.

You are in my thoughts and in my heart.

All my love, my dearest Padmabai. My love to everyone.

Krishna

His letters express a longing for India; he was drifting away from many of his close friends in the West whom he had known from his childhood. From Ojai he wrote of being alone, resting and going into *Samadhi*

My dearest Padmabai,

Thank you very much for your letter of October 29th. I am so very sorry that you are having a hard time and I wish I were there to help you along. It would be good to talk things over and that has to wait till we meet again, which will not be till the end of next year. I have been by myself for the last fortnight and I have been over the thoughts of the past years. I wish, I could have a good talk with you which is much better than writing.

This place is lovely and one day (?) you must come here. I am taking a complete rest and going into *samadhi*.* I only see people on Sundays and the rest of the days I am giving to thought. Rajagopal and Rosalind are in Hollywood as Rajagopal has to see to his rheumatism which is pretty bad.

I hear Amma is pretty bad and that she is not expected to live long. Rama Rao wrote to me that she is stone deaf and can hardly recognise. It is tragic and I wonder what is going to happen to the Theosophical Society. . . .

With all my love,<br>Krishna

Krishna's friend Rama Rao went blind and was seriously ill. With the death of Jadu, Krishna turned to Rajagopal and his wife Rosalind (they had married in 1927), who remained with him and were free to journey with him across continents.

While Nitya was alive Rajagopal's role in the young seer's life was peripheral—Nitya had taken over all organizational matters connected with Krishnamurti's work. Nitya's death created a functional vacuum

---

*Samadhi:* A state of final liberation. A state where the ego entity has ceased to exist and the seeker has disappeared. A state of union with the cosmos.

that had to be filled. Inevitably, at first Jadu and then Rajagopal took charge, planning lectures and tours and setting up the infrastructure to support his future work. Rajagopal's marriage to Rosalind, a very close friend of Nitya's, brought Rajagopal closer to Krishnamurti. Soon Arya Vihar in Ojai became their permanent home.

A relationship born of an act of friendship to protect the young, vulnerable Krishnamurti—whose utter lack of worldliness made protection necessary—slowly underwent a sea change. In the earlier period of his life, protected by Mrs. Besant, he was the World-Teacher-to-be—and the attitudes of Krishnaji's comrades reflected this awareness and a reverence. There was always a distance between the World Teacher and his disciples.

However, with the dissolution of organizations and the negation of all spiritual hierarchy by Krishnamurti, new attitudes were inevitable. Slowly, the distance between the teacher and his associates lessened. Soon Rajagopal and Rosalind assumed the role of guardians, *sarvadhikaris*, holders of authority around the young seer, taking over all decision-making in Krishnamurti's personal life and the work connected with his teaching. The shy, hesitant young man who was feeling his way in the irridescent ocean of energy being released within him, groping for words that could contain his observations and insights, was totally unconcerned with worldly affairs. He was happy to leave everything in the competent hands of Rajagopal. K seemed vague, passive, naive, and even juvenile. His former disciples, living in close proximity to Krishnamurti, found him eager to perform the most menial chores; and this blurred their vision. They lost contact with the immensity in their midst and in time started to treat him as a child, who could be scolded, ignored, bullied, told what to do and whom to meet.

It is part of Krishnamurti's mystique that, time and again, he permitted this. His very nature made any assertive or aggressive response or action impossible. He never lost his temper. His pliant mind, lack of the ego, and total trust in those around him made it possible for others to take him for granted. He would sign any paper placed before him by his close friends, and at times even echoed their irrationalities. This led to seemingly contradictory statements and actions, which confused his friends. Yet, when he appeared to be totally hemmed in and dominated, the situation would explode out of its complexities, leaving Krishnamurti untouched, free to move on; while those who dominated him would be left angry, bewildered, often broken.

Between 1933 and 1939 Krishnamurti traveled several times to India, giving talks to fairly large audiences. With the death of Mrs. Besant in 1933 and the election of George Arundale as president of the Theosophical Society in 1934, all contact between Krishnamurti and the Society had been severed. Krishnamurti had spoken of the Theosophical Society as an organized belief, "and the idea of a Master leading man to truth does not enter my belief."[3]

The world and the media had lost interest in the "World Teacher" after his rejection of the role the Theosophical Society had conceived for him. For a long time his name disappeared from the newspapers and he led a life of anonymity.

Toward the end of those years, a new foundation, Krishnamurti Writings Inc. (K. W. I.), was established with headquarters at Ojai. Krishnamurti was nominal head, but Rajagopal played the pivotal role in determining the membership of the new body and its areas of operation. However, there was one area where the young seer, however hesitant, refused to permit any intrusion: That was in the unfoldment, the flowering of the new mind and the silent ground of perception that was coming into being.

Krishnamurti was in Ojai in 1939 when World War II broke out in Europe. For nearly eight years he lived in Ojai in comparative isolation. The war restricted his movements, and it was no longer possible for him to travel. He had been sent for by the U.S. draft board, and had to give detailed explanations as to why he could not fight and join the army. The board suggested that he return to India. He agreed and asked them to send him back, but there was no transportation. So they let him stay, but he was forbidden to give talks and had to report to the police regularly.

In later years Krishnamurti was to speak of those forgotten years in Ojai. He cherished his walks in the silences of the mountains surrounding the Ojai Valley. He walked "enormously," for endless miles, spending whole days in the wilderness, alone, forgetful of food, listening and observing, probing the world within him and around him. He recounted episodes of meeting wild bears and rattlesnakes, facing them without movement of body and mind. The wild beast would pause, its cautious, watchful eyes meeting K's silent eyes for several minutes; the animal, sensing a total absence of fear, would turn and move away.

The observing mind of Krishnamurti, free of any inner direction or pressure, blossomed; and with it an elemental perception, a mind-body awareness through which earth, rocks, trees, budding leaves, insects, reptiles, birds, animals communicated the story of earth's history and the mystery of a bottomless pit of time. He said, "When I walk, I don't think, there is no thought. I just look. . . . I think my solitary walks must have done something."

Krishnamurti recalled gardening at Arya Vihar, growing roses and vegetables, milking cows, washing dishes. His intense interest in mechanical things, which he had cultivated from childhood, was to continue; he still enjoyed taking apart watches and automobile engines to understand how they worked, and then putting them together again. He had been given a gift of a car by some of his friends. Gas was scarce but, whenever possible, Krishnamurti enjoyed driving at a tremendous speed along the curving roads of the valley.

Reports of the war and the atom bomb's devastation of Hiroshima and Nagasaki filled him with inexpressible horror, but awakened insights into the nature of violence and evil. This was made especially vivid to him one day when he went to nearby Santa Barbara. A woman approached him, offering Japanese souvenirs. Krishnamurti declined, but she insisted on showing him what she had in her box. She opened it to reveal a shriveled human ear and nose.

Miss Muriel Payne, who claimed to have nursed Krishnamurti in Ojai when he was very ill, told me that his response to the devastation and cruelty of war had been traumatic. He asked repeatedly, "What is the use of my talking?" He sought refuge alone in the mountains, with trees and wild animals. He spent several weeks in solitude in a hut in Wrightwood, in the San Gabriel mountains near Los Angeles, and in Sequoia, further North. He had grown a beard.

Krishnaji recalled the routine of his life in the sparsely furnished log cabin in the wilds. He would awake early in the morning, go for a long walk, cook breakfast, clean the dishes and the house and for an hour every day play Beethoven's Ninth Symphony (the only record available), listening, meditating. There were no books. In the evenings he would chant Sanskrit hymns remembered from his early childhood. His favorite was one to Daksinamunti—Shiva as the supreme guru. The sound of Sanskrit rose from the depths of his belly—it filled forests, virgin sounds heard by pine and ancient redwood trees, by skunk, bear, and rattlesnake. A spider shared the hut with him. Every morning Krishnamurti swept away the spider's web, in which were trapped flies and insects; carefully picking up the spider, he would place it outside the hut, but every morning, the spider was back, spinning its web.[4] A verse from the *Upanishads*, learned in his childhood, may have come to his mind. "As a spider emerges [from itself] by [spinning] threads [out of its own body], so too from this self, all life breaths, all the worlds, all the gods, and all contingent beings rise upon all directions."[5]

For days the ritual between the spider and Krishnamurti continued, a wordless communication; then one day Krishnamurti said to the spider, "Pax, let us share the hut."

Krishnamurti had occasional visitors. Aldous Huxley, who had settled in California and who was losing his eyesight, walked with Krishnamurti for long hours. At times they spoke of the senses and blindness. Krishnamurti helped Huxley; the power to heal was alive. He used it sparingly and in secret, was rather shy of it, and apologized before he even spoke of it.

Many years later, when asked what he meant when he spoke of all the senses operating simultaneously, Krishnaji told of meeting a blind friend while he was living in the hills. They had discussed the senses. Later, alone in the hut, Krishnamurti spent a week with his eyes bandaged, to see what happened when a sense on which one depended was denied. He spoke of every pore of his body, being fully awake, every sense carefully operating, compensating for the lost sense; of everything having to be in the right place, inwardly and outwardly.

There are also hints that he experimented at this time with many of the rigid austerities of yoga—fasting for long periods; observing complete silence for days; closing the sense organs with two hands to shut out sight, sound, and breath; and awakening to vast reverberations of sound within. But he dismissed these yogic stances as play, peripheral, and of no account.

The luminous beauty and the dramatic legendary early life of Krishnamurti had aroused the curiosity and interest of a number of writers, actors, and seekers who had settled in and around Los Angeles, besides Huxley. Gerald Heard was one of the first of the Western mystics to settle in California and delve into Indian religious enquiry. He was a friend of Huxley, Krishnamurti, Christopher Isherwood, and Prabhavanand, a monk of the Ram Krishna Mission. Huxley and Heard had become close friends of Krishnamurti. It was a curious relationship. Krishnamurti in the late 1930s and early 1940s was very shy, and perhaps had not allowed the limitless within him to reveal itself. Otherwise, it is impossible to understand Maria Huxley's comment on him.

She said of him during the years 1938 to 1939, "He is charming and amusing and so simple. How he must suffer when he is treated as a prophet?"[6]

Aldous Huxley and his first wife, Maria, loved picnics, as did Krishnamurti. Anita Loos, writing of Los Angeles in the late 1930s, recounts an incident which, as she put it, "could have taken place in Alice in Wonderland." At one such picnic the guests included the Huxleys and Krishnamurti; Greta Garbo, wearing a sloppy pair of men's trousers and a battered hat; Charlie Chaplin and his beautiful wife Paulette Goddard, dressed in a Mexican peasant outfit; Bertrand Russell (who is described by Anita Loos as a "Pixie on a spree"); and writer Christopher Isherwood.

Failing to find a suitable picnic spot, they finally descended on the dusty bed of the Los Angeles river. As they were getting down to prepare their special food—Garbo carrying bunches of raw vegetables, Goddard with her champagne and caviar, Krishnamurti with his rice— a hefty policeman suddenly appeared and asked, "What the hell's going on here?"

They stopped all preparations, "stunned into silence." A sheriff appeared, holding a gun. "Don't anybody in this gang know how to read?" he asked Aldous Huxley, pointing to a sign that read "No trespassers." Huxley pleaded with the sheriff, promising to clean up the place and leave the riverbed cleaner than they had found it. The sheriff was getting angry and told Huxley to "Get going—and that means now." Huxley, thinking he might appease the sheriff by mentioning some of the celebrities, pointed out Charlie Chaplin and Greta Garbo.

"Don't give me that," snarled the sheriff. "I seen these stars in the movies and none of them belong in this outfit. Get out of here, you tramps, or I'll arrest the whole slew of you." And so, says Anita Loos, "We folded our tents like the Arabs and quietly stole away. . . ."[7]

By the mid-1940s Krishnamurti and Huxley had become close friends. They met often and went for long walks. Huxley talked and Krishnamurti listened. Huxley was perplexed; his formidable intellect found it difficult to comprehend the pliant strength of a mind born of perception untainted by knowledge. In turn, Huxley listened and learned to be silent when Krishnamurti spoke of perception, of time, and of awareness. That Krishnamurti's mind interested Huxley is evident. On one of the walks, he told Krishnamurti "that he would give everything for one direct perception of the truth, but his mind was incapable of it. It was too filled with knowledge." Christopher Isherwood recounts a conversation he had with Huxley. Isherwood had been telling Huxley of the instructions for meditation given to him by his guru, Swami Prabhavanand, "thus, prompting Aldous to tell me that Krishnamurti never meditated on 'objects' such as lotuses, lights, gods and goddesses and even believed that doing so, might lead to insanity."[8]

Recalling his relationship with Huxley and Gerald Heard, Krishnamurti says, "I was terribly shy. They were all tremendous intellectuals. I listened to them. I interjected one or two statements."[9] Much of the correspondence between Krishnamurti and Huxley, and the notes taken by Huxley of that period of his life, were burned in a fire that destroyed his home and all his records. Later, Huxley was to write the introduction to Krishnamurti's book *The First and Last Freedom*. In 1961, just before his death, Huxley heard Krishnamurti speak at Saanen in Switzerland. Writing to a friend, he describes it "as amongst the most impressive things I have listened to . . . it was like listening to the discourse of the Buddha—such power, such intrinsic authority, such an uncompromising refusal to allow the *homme moyen sensuel* any escapes or surrogates, any *gurus*, saviors, *führers*, churches. I show you sorrow and the ending of sorrow, and if you don't fulfill the conditions for ending sorrow, be prepared, whatever *gurus*, churches, etc. you may believe in, for the indefinite continuance of sorrow."[10]

In Ojai, during the war years, Krishnamurti recalled visiting Gerald Heard at Trabuco, "a club for mystics" built a few miles from Los Angeles by Gerald Heard and Felix Green, a British sinologist who was also interested in Indian religious enquiry. Gerald Heard, who has been eloquently described by Christopher Isherwood as "one of [the world's] few great magic myth makers and revealers of life's wonder"[11] had built a retreat with a meditation hall overlooking the Pacific Ocean. Krishnamurti visited Trabuco for a week at the invitation of Gerald Heard. Describing Trabuco to us, Krishnamurti spoke of its resemblance to a Trappist monastery—except that here people could come for retreat and were not trapped for the rest of their lives. Meditation sessions took place about six times a day. The residents were permitted conversation in the mornings, but after lunch strict silence was imposed. Krishnaji joined in the meditation sessions; sitting cross-legged on the floor for hours in the darkened meditation hall, he felt the seething thoughts in the minds of those meditating around him. The intense darkness was used as an aid to create the silent mind. The eerie atmosphere and the chaotic, violent thoughts of the other guests greatly disturbed Krishnamurti, and he did not visit Trabuco again.

Perhaps the most insightful of the comments to come from "outsiders" living on the Pacific Coast in the 1940s and 1950s was from Henry Miller, the bawdy, tempestuous writer of some of the finest prose to emerge from North America in the twentieth century. In his later years Miller became a recluse and lived at Big Sur on the coast south of San Francisco. He had never met Krishnamurti; but after reading a book about him by Carlo Suarez, Miller wrote,

Krishnamurti has renounced more than any man I can think of except Christ. Fundamentally he is so simple to understand that it is easy to comprehend the confusion which his clear, direct words and deeds have entailed. Men are reluctant to accept what is easy to grasp.

I have never met Krishnamurti, though there is no man living whom I would consider it a greater privilege to meet than he.

His career, unique in the history of spiritual leaders, reminds one of the famous Gilgamesh epic. Hailed in his youth as the coming Savior, Krishnamurti renounced the role that was prepared for him, spurned all disciples, rejected all mentors and preceptors. He initiated no new faith or dogma, questioned everything, cultivated doubt (especially in moments of exaltation), and, by dint of heroic struggle and perseverance, freed himself of illusion and enchantment, of pride, vanity, and every subtle form of dominion over other. He went to the very source of life for sustenance and inspiration. To resist the wiles and snares of those who sought to enslave and exploit him demanded eternal vigilance. He liberated his soul, so to say, from the underworld and the overworld, thus opening to it "the paradise of heroes."

Is it necessary to define this state?[12]

In 1945, when the war was over, Krishnamurti was to go to New Zealand, but fell very ill. He had urinary trouble, high fever, and was unconscious for long periods. It is possible that some vast psychic changes took place in him during this illness. He talks of recuperating by himself, of the body being alone. Doctors saw him, but seemed unable to diagnose his illness, no medicines were prescribed.

# Part 2

## KRISHNAMURTI IN INDIA
### 1947–1949

# CHAPTER 9

# The Gathering of the Friends

On August 15, 1947, India became independent and Jawaharlal Nehru its first prime minister. Tumultuous yet nonviolent in character, the struggle for independence had been from the early twentieth century guided by Mahatma Gandhi. By 1944 the courage of a nonviolent struggle against the military might of the British Empire had inspired people in a world struggling to rehabilitate itself after the most violent war in history.

But independence in India had also brought a bitter aftermath. To achieve it, the vast subcontinent had been partitioned, territories in the North, West, and East cut away from the main heartland, to form the new Islamic State of Pakistan. Families were divided, friendships broken. Violence exploded; massacres, rape, looting, arson were witnessed along the borders and in the hinterland. Vast migrations of people took place; the Hindus moved eastwards, the Muslims westwards. The new rulers of India, most of whom had spent half their lives in jail, were suddenly called upon to bring order to a continent in flames and to deal with a refugee problem the like of which had never before been witnessed.

K's arrival in India, two months after independence, could not have been at a more propitious moment. An old age in India was dying, and the birth of the new was beset by travail and disillusionment. The massacres that had erupted with freedom and the partition of India had been traumatic for minds nurtured on theories of nonviolence. There had been little time to pause, to ponder, to look into the distance, to cogitate, to ask fundamental questions. For India's leaders and builders, action based on immediacy had overtaken the possibility of action born of long vision.

Vast resources of energy were held in abeyance in the startlingly young body and mind of Krishnamurti. His face in 1947 appeared qualitatively different from earlier photographs of him in the 1920s and 1930s. It was evident that the long period of withdrawal in Ojai, brought about by forces beyond his control, had provided the spaces in which exploding energies could converge. An intelligence was coming into being, a perfection of mind, heart, and body that was supremely beautiful, majestic, and awake. When asked about his years in Ojai, K said, "I think it was a period of no challenge, no demand, no outgoing. I think it was a kind of everything kept in, everything held in; and when I left Ojai it all burst."

A splendor and inward incandescence had transformed K's face; ancient yet untouched by time. The blue-black eyes reflected the long vision of the seer. Profoundly empty yet grounded in compassion, they were prophetic eyes that had journeyed vast distances. His slightly greying hair, swept back, revealed the majesty of his forehead. The earlobes were long, the head and spine erect, the waist slim, the shoulders sloped. He walked with long strides, his feet pressed down, sinking into the earth, creating spaces within which he walked. The long arms rested at his side, the palms open and held inward. From my first meeting with him, I was aware of the deep stillnesses of his body. In repose there was little movement of head, shoulder, or spine; no movement was superfluous; when need for action arose, the body responded with a natural dignity and grace, with precision and a minimum expenditure of energy.

In dialogue the hands assumed symbolic gestures, they opened, questioned, probed, contained, pointed the way. Relaxed, the hands rested.

He arrived in India alone for the first time. All outer bonds and constraints had dropped away. Throughout his life he had been held, protected. At first by the affection and concern of his father, then by the Theosophical Society and their expectations of the role he was to play as the World Teacher. When he left the Theosophical Society, its rituals and hierarchies, his outer life was taken over by Rajagopal and Rosalind. The nine years in Ojai had separated him from his friends in India. Slowly, the old, loyal friends were dying or being pushed away. Now, however, there was no one to question him, to plan his day, to decide whom he should meet, where he should go. Outwardly and inwardly he was totally free.

All through the years, whenever he was to return to India, his first act was to take off his Western clothes and wear Indian garments. With this change of clothes his personality, attitudes, and responses also changed. In the West he was more formal, with exquisite Old World manners. He lived a secluded life, meeting few people; the long discussions and insights that arose at breakfast and lunch, intimately woven into his life in India, were absent. The perceptions that arose on walks or in apparently casual conversations have not been recorded.

With the Indian robes, the length of which gave him the look of a mendicant, he naturally assumed the role of the teacher. The centuries of meditation and concern with otherness held in abeyance in the Indian earth entered into him. He appeared to grow taller, the sloping shoulders revealed by the shape of his garment. His walk had the majesty of the king elephant in a forest.

The young men and women who gathered round Krishnaji in Bombay (many of whom, like myself, were to remain with him for over thirty years) were drawn from various disciplines—political, literary, academic, and social. Many of them had participated in the freedom struggle and had been acclaimed political heroes. Filled with horror by the events that followed the partition of India, they lacked the prophetic insight to see the chaos that was to face the India of the future. They were sensitive enough, however, not to share in the wild euphoria of freedom that led large numbers of people to believe that with the retreat of the British Raj a Golden Age based on the ethical values of secularism, socialism, and an ending of poverty had dawned.

They had glimpsed the wasteland of ambition, bitterness, and greed that lay behind their slogans and grandiose words. The ideals that had carried them through years of political struggle had crumbled under them, and with it the verbal structures that had nourished them. They were faced with confusion, contradiction, and what seemed a blank wall.

They gathered because of the radiance and compassion that emanated from K's presence; and because of the personal aches and despairs, the sorrow, that they could neither face nor dispel; and their inability to give a meaningful direction to their lives. Buddha had ordained his monks with the call "Ehi Etha," Come ye. Krishnamurti's silent call was of the same nature.

Amongst the people who met K at the airport was Sir Chunilal Mehta, a distinguished industrialist, who had served as a member of the Governors Council in what was then the Bombay presidency.* An ardent admirer of K, Sir Chunilal was ecstatic when, on returning home, he told his young daughter-in-law Nandini of "this wondrous young being, who ran down the steps of the plane—and like a shaft of light came towards us." K was staying at the house of Ratansi Morarji on Carmichael Road. It was open house in the mornings, and many people had gathered when Chunilal Mehta and Nandini walked in. What happened is best told in the words of Nandini:

"I went and sat on the floor in a corner, feeling a little nervous. I saw a figure in a long white *kurta* sitting straight-backed at a distance. The room was full of people, and K was in the midst of a discussion. Kakaji [Sir Chunilal] was sitting facing K and soon joined in the discussion. A minute later K, whose face was looking away from me, turned and looked at me steadily for a few seconds. Time stopped for me. He turned back and continued his discussion. Some time later he turned again and looked deep into my eyes, and again time stopped. K continued his discussion. But I was totally unaware of what was being said.

"The discussion ended and people started getting up to leave. I rose and found K standing in front of me. Seeing K approaching me, Kakaji rushed up and introduced me as 'Nandini, my daughter-in-law'— Krishnaji had started laughing, not smiling, but laughing—I had never heard laughter as deep and as resonant. The sound of a Himalayan stream falling rock to rock to mingle with another stream. He asked, 'Why have you come?' Tears had started flowing uncontrollably down my cheeks. He continued to laugh and my tears continued to flow. He took my hand and held it hard. Again he asked, 'Why have you come?' and at last I could speak, though the tears were unabated. 'I have waited thirty years to see you.' [Nandini was thirty years old at the time.] K's laughter continued. Then, letting go of my hand, he placed his palm on my head and left it there for a few seconds. My pranams† to him were through my tears.

"In the car Kakaji seemed a little bewildered, turned around and told me, 'Did you see him? That he should notice you is a great privilege. Don't let it go to your head.' I started accompanying Kakaji every day to see K. One morning K said, 'Don't you want to see me?' I did not answer. I did not know it was possible to see him."

---

*The present states of Maharashtra and Gujerat.
†*Pranam* and *namaskara* have the same meaning except that pranam has an element of greater respect in it. It is the traditional form of greeting, the holding up of folded hands as in prayer.

K was to leave for Madras shortly, and it was only on his return that Nandini started seeing him.

Maurice Friedman, a Polish engineer, was also at Carmichael Road to meet K on his arrival. A tiny, bent-backed man, he wore a *kurta* and a loose, ill-fitting pyjama. It was impossible to determine his age. A Theosophist since his boyhood, he had come to India as an engineer to work in Bangalore. Soon he lost interest in his work, donned a saffron robe, took the vows, and became a mendicant, taking the name of Bharatanand. From the northernmost point of India to Kanniya-kumari in the deep south, he traveled the pilgrim's path—barefoot, eating the food given to him, staying in *maths* (monasteries) or under trees, discussing with yogis and fakirs. He met wise men and held discourses with religious teachers, but found that awakening did not lie in the outer facade of robe or begging bowl. So, giving up the robe, he came and stayed at Ramana Maharshi's *ashram* in the deep South. Ramana Maharshi is regarded as a liberated man; a saint who broke all bondages and transcended the self.

An apocryphal story relates how Friedman went to the flooded river one day. Pondering on life and causation, he said to himself, "If I am to die, I will be swept away; if I have to live, the waters will save me." So he threw himself into the torrential waters, and was thrown back on the banks. Thrice he threw himself, and three times the waters refused to accept him. So, battered in body but undaunted in spirit, he said, "Fate wants me to live." He walked back to the *ashram*. Half-way he met Ramana Maharshi, who looked at him and said gently but sternly, "Stop playing the fool with yourself."

While a *sannyasin*, Friedman had lived for some years at Sevagram, Gandhiji's *ashram* near Wardha, in Maharashtra. He used his engineering skills to help evolve the *ambar charkha*, the many-spindled spinning wheel, and had participated in many of the development programs initiated by Gandhiji. Deeply interested in K and his teachings, he had come to Bombay to be with him. Friedman participated in the discussions with much energy, took on himself the role of interpreter, and prefaced his remarks with, "In other words . . . " Warm, affectionate, intelligent, intensely curious, but with a somewhat distorted approach to life, he battered himself against his bonds, unable to penetrate beyond his own self-made limitations of words and ideas.

Jamnadas Dwarkadas, another constant visitor, was a rotund figure who wore a spotless *dhoti*, a white Gandhi cap, and *kurta*. Dwarkadas came from a very affluent family from Kutch. Long settled in Bombay, the several brothers had distinguished themselves in various fields. Jamnadas Dwarkadas, a politician and businessman, had been a close associate and friend of Dr. Annie Besant. Generous of heart and with a deep devotion to K, he had given of his wealth with abundance. Through the years he was to lose his family fortunes, but his generosity did not diminish nor did misfortune sour his bountiful nature. He would embrace K, weep with emotion, and sit with his eyes closed during the discussions, an ecstatic look on his cherubic face. He would tell us stories of K's childhood; for Jamnadas had a remarkable memory and a fund of anecdotes. The children in our family gathered round him, for he held them spellbound with stories of K and Dr. Besant. A *vaishnava*,* he brought K exquisite garlands of jasmine interwoven with rose petals to resemble pearls and rubies; he would insist that K wear this fragrant garland after his discussions and talks. I remember standing with Nandini at the foot of the staircase that led to the terrace where K held discussions. K stood at the head of the stairway, a slender figure in white, with jasmine around his neck, a garland that fell to his knees. It was always late evening when the discussions ended, and the glow of the lights used to catch K's hair, swept back from his brow, while his eyes smiled down at us.

Also amongst the people who gathered at Madras to meet K in October 1947 was a young chemist named Balasundaram, who was teaching at the Institute of Science in Bangalore. K was staying at Sterling Road, Madras, where he gave talks and held public discussions. His host was R. Madhavachari, the Indian representative of Krishnamurti Writings Inc. and an engineer in the Southern Railways.

Attendance at the talks was small; a few old Theosophists, some writers and professors, and a few young people were the audience. Amongst them was Shanta Rao, the *bharat natyam*† dancer; she spent the day at Sterling Road, taking K his orange juice, helping serve his food, and acting as a *dwarpal*, a doorkeeper outside K's door.

These were the years before Shanta Rao had emerged, resplendent on the Indian landscape, as one of the most brilliant *bharat natyam* dancers to perform in free India. Shanta entered K's surroundings with the same eloquence and assured presence with which she entered a

---

*A *vaishnava* is a devotee of Krishna. But the word also conveys a certain ethical behavior, such as vegetarianism, almsgiving, kindness, and devotion.
†*Bharat natyam:* Dances born out of the rituals of worship in the temples of South India. It was in the middle of the twentieth century that *bharat natyam* began to be danced by women of the higher castes and was transported from the temple to the stage, from ritual to art and entertainment.

stage. She was to spend long periods of time in Madras listening to his talks, having interviews with him, or just being around. Young, with a panther-like body and strong, arrogant mind, she had studied the *Natya Sastras** and had learned to dance under the discipline of the great gurus of *bharat natyam* and *kathakali.*† Her supreme confidence was evident in her poise and her words. She questioned K on the nature of beauty—whether it was outer or inner, and what was its measure.

Perhaps she influenced K, who wrote of a dancer in his *Commentaries on Living:*

She was a dancer, not by profession but by choice. She must have felt proud of her art, for there was arrogance about her—not only the arrogance of achievement but also that of some inner recognition of her own spiritual worth. As another would be satisfied with outward success, she was gratified by her spiritual advancement. She not only danced, but also gave talks on art, on beauty, and on spiritual achievement.[1]

Another visitor who was closely associated with K through his years in India was doe-eyed, lissome Sunanda, the daughter of an old Theosophist. Sunanda, a graduate of Madras University, had a finely honed intellect and was studying law and preparing for the foreign service examination. She too spent some time every day with K at Sterling Road—speaking of her dreams of the future, her personal problems, or watching him as he sat polishing his shoes or sitting quietly while K was writing letters. K bantered with her, chanted with her, told her that she was too young to consider settling down, and asked her to go out and see the world. Her senses afire, she responded passionately to K's presence and was swept away in the torrent of his attention.

In those years K was very accessible. Mukund Pada, a young man who would later don the saffron robe, wrote to me many years after of his meeting with K in 1947:

Back in Madras, I attended for the first time in December 1947 a talk by one

---

*Natya Sastras*, written between 200 B.C and A.D. 200 by the sage Bharat Muni, was a treatise on the dramatic arts, mime, dance, stagecraft. A theory of aesthetics formed the basic element of the book.

†*Kathakali* is dance, mime and theater. Accompanied by powerful drumming and song, it evolved in the courts of the Nayar kings of Kerala. The stories were based on the epics, the Mahabharata and the Ramayana. The Nayars were a military class. The society was matriarchal. The Brahmin (Namboodries) were learned and powerful. Costumes, painted masks, and highly stylized gestures were integral to the *kathakali* form of dance.

Theosophist named J. Krishnamurti as described by an elderly person. The talk stunned and rocked me out of my core. Standing lost and helpless after the talk, Krishnaji who was passing me, suddenly stopped and putting an arm around me asked Shri Madhavachari to grant me some time for an interview. The interview between an insignificant pebble and the Himalayas was a blast of the Eternal, Cosmic breath. It left me shattered and trembling in every limb. As Krishnaji was speaking, I was thunderstruck in an awareness that the seeds of his message were already there in my brain. It was the voice of truth that had spoken to me. His last words to me on parting, as he came to the door "Sir, two flowers or things can be similar, but not the same," suddenly opened an immense space. Quietly words surfaced in my mind. "Yes, Sir, thou are Blessedness walking amongst humanity. Two flowers may be similar. You are the thornless flower—me, I am more thorns than flower." Oh, how he laughed—his laughter like a lightning in a thundercloud.

Dr. Balasundaram found that Krishnaji's former Theosophical associates had grown old. C. Jinarajadasa, then president of the Theosophical Society and wearing a purple cap, used to visit Krishnaji. They had long talks, but Krishnaji did not enter the compound of the Theosophical Society—though he went for long walks on Adyar beach. Sanjeeva Rao, an old associate of Dr. Besant and an eminent educator who had built Krishnaji's educational institutions in Varanasi, and his wife Padmabai, a friend of Krishnaji and an equally well-known educator in her own right, were constant visitors.

A small discussion group had started, but most of the participants were weary and aging and had little contact with the enormous new teaching. K told them, "You are clinging to the known. Let go." They looked bewildered, tried to appear intense, but little energy was generated.

Balasundaram described to me a poignant moment during a discussion of "the ending of the known." An old Theosophist named Narhari Rao had put up his hands and, in a tremulous voice, said to Krishnaji, "Wait, Sir, wait—the unknown is coming."

B. Sanjeeva Rao accompanied Krishnaji on his return to Bombay from Madras in early January 1948. They were staying with Ratansi Morarji at Carmichael Road. Every morning and evening Krishnaji would sit in the living room, which was furnished with chinoiseries, carved chairs, and jeweled screens. People who wished to see Krishnaji dropped in and sat with him asking questions, discussing problems or giving him the news of the day.

Prominent amongst the visitors were two young men dressed in spotless white hand-spun and handwoven *khadi*: Rao Sahib Patwardhan and Achyut Patwardhan. Their father had been a respected and wealthy resident of Ahmadnagar in Maharashtra, had belonged to the Theosophical Society, and had been an ardent follower of Annie Besant. He died young, leaving the burden of his large family to his eldest son, Rao Sahib Patwardhan. Before his death he had told his two elder sons that they were to dedicate their lives to Krishnaji and his work. Whatever happened in the future, they were never to deny the great teacher.

Handsome, intensely male, austere, with an inviolable integrity, Rao Sahib and Achyut were devoted brothers. Within his family Rao Sahib was a domineering patriarch. Deeply attached to learning, impatient with women except the rare few who measured up to his standard of brain and heart, he set himself moral standards and practiced an austerity that made life miserable for his family and placed limits on his own potential. He was deeply committed to work for the amelioration of poverty and want, and was closely associated with the Sarva Seva Sangh, a service organization established around Gandhiji; but it was the idea rather than the operational part of work that attracted him. He was not a builder, nor an organizer. Perhaps the lesson that nothing is trivial had evaded him. The canvas of the freedom struggle was vast, and the actors had assumed the role of heroes. The struggle had not prepared these fighters of independence for a work technology that would demand an understanding of the nuts and bolts of development. An insight into the seemingly trivial was part of the genius of Gandhiji and his homespun development economics. Two decades of independence would pass before its essential truth was made clear.

Rao Sahib was intense, but he was also vulnerable and sensitive to beauty. A romantic, the austere and the sensory battled within him and made him hesitate and withdraw at the slightest sign of a physical flowering of the senses. The only areas in which he permitted abandon were in his relationship to K, and in growing roses and cultivating the parijataka bush.

That he never broke through the limitations of his self-imposed austerity and circumscribed environment was a personal tragedy. Within him was a reservoir, capable of receiving and communicating with abundance. His Brahminic arrogance and refusal to claim what was his by right, along with an incapacity to take anything to its limits, generated conflict and kept him conditioned and confined.

His brother Achyut was an intellectual, a word that in India has very special connotations. He lived in an age that hailed Karl Marx as the prophet of the new awakened man, and Achyut, along with his friends Jai Prakash Narain and Acharya Narendra Dev, grew impatient with the older traditional leadership of India, which was concerned primarily with maintaining the status quo. Together, they founded the Socialist Party of India. In total contrast to Rao Sahib, Achyut was not emotional; in him the mind dominated action. He was a leader of men, a fighter; and for long periods of his life ends determined means. But his incapacity to wear masks or to disguise his emotions inhibited him. He had a violent temper and could seldom brook being thwarted.

In 1929, when the freedom struggle in India was at its peak, the brothers had gone to Krishnamurti. Achyut had asked, "Do you really mean it when you say 'negate all authority'?" K replied, "Yes. The mind has to reject authority and examine everything." Achyut's response was that, for him, the freedom of India was the only freedom that was important. On this note he left Krishnamurti, and he and Rao Sahib plunged into the struggle for independence—fighting the British colonial rule, going to jail for long periods, making friends within prison walls, reading and contemplating.

In 1938, the last time Krishnamurti was in India before 1947, Achyut met him in Rishi Valley.* Madrid had fallen in the Spanish Civil War and Achyut was in tears. Speaking to Achyut, K said that in this defeat he saw the beginning of World War II. He commented that he did not see much difference between fascism and communism. Achyut vehemently denied this. K repeated, "They are both tyrannies." It was a major truth that Achyut was to realize in later years.

The Quit India movement of 1942† saw Rao Sahib in jail, while Achyut had gone underground to wander, seeking anonymity and refuge over the length and breadth of India. He and Jai Prakash Narain were to become revolutionary heroes of those dark, fearful, yet intoxicating days. Unlike Jai Prakash, Achyut was never arrested, escaping the police net time and again—by taking refuge as a patient in a hos-

---

*Rishi Valley, ten miles from Krishnaji's birth place Madnapalle, was so named after the cone-shaped hill, Rishi Konda, which lay to the west of the valley. Seeking to find a suitable site for a school, Krishnaji, with some friends, had spotted the vast banyan tree from the roadside. He stopped the car and said, "This is the place."

†A meeting of the All India Congress Committee was held in Bombay on July 16, 1942. The main intention was to serve notice on the British government to "Quit India." The resolution was greeted with an uproar of applause. That night Mahatma Gandhi, Jawaharlal Nehru, and a large number of Congress leaders were arrested in Bombay and other parts of India.

pital, disguising himself as a miserable clerk, growing a beard, and wearing a fez.

In 1947 he came to K, weary and disillusioned. With freedom, the petty urges to power that had lain in abeyance amongst Congress leaders were surfacing. During the struggle the anti-Brahmin feeling in Maharashtra had little vitality. The leaders, the constructive workers, the intelligentsia in Maharashtra were mainly Brahmins. With independence, the drives for the loaves and fishes of office had given stimulus to the formation of groups within the Congress. Very disturbed by the intrigues and with a fractured emotional life, Achyut turned back to his roots and sought advice from Krishnamurti.

Achyut expressed his conflicts, and K took Achyut for a walk. Pointing to a tree, he turned to Achyut and said, "Look at that tree—the leaf that was tender green has turned yellow. The leaf has nothing to do with it. It is born, dries and falls. Any decision to stay in politics or to leave, any decision taken by choice is wrong. Things happen in their own course. Stop fretting."

Achyut went to see Gandhiji for the last time toward the end of 1947. He told him that he was going to leave politics for a few months. Gandhiji asked him what he was going to do. When he heard he was to spend the time with Krishnamurti, Gandhiji was very happy. He spoke to Achyut of the terrible events of the partition. He said he was passing through a great darkness. He could not see any light.

Achyut spent the next year with K in Bombay, Ootacamund, Poona, Delhi, and Varanasi. At the end of the year Achyut told Krishnamurti that when he was with him all his faculties were wide awake. K's response was, "Be careful, don't take a little of this, to gild what you already know. What you think you feel is only a theory. On no account allow your mind to be stimulated by me." In early 1949 Achyut returned to Delhi to edit a Socialist weekly; but his comrades were aware of deep changes taking place within him, which were to lead to his final break with the Socialist Party and politics.

Rao Sahib was a member of the Congress working committee. A friend of Jawaharlal Nehru and Sardar Patel,* his future in politics seemed assured. But he too felt the suffocation and darkness of the struggle for position and power that erupted amongst his erstwhile friends. The Constituent Assembly was about to meet. Rao Sahib was expected to be one of the participants, but his close friends persuaded

---

*Vallabhai Patel and Sardar Patel are the same person. Vallabhai was the given name and Patel the caste name. Sardar, meaning leader, was a term of endearment and respect.

Vallabhai Patel and Jawaharlal Nehru to exclude him. Rao Sahib was deeply hurt, but his pride and obstinacy made it impossible for him to fight his friends or to appeal to Nehru. The personal disappointment was forgotten in the aftermath of partition; the hatred, bloodshed, and cruelty generated by the transfer of population had shattered Rao Sahib's foundations, built on Gandhian values and ideals. He met Krishnamurti, discussed his conflicts with him, listened to his talks. His immaculately starched *khadi kurta* and Gandhi cap worn at a rakish angle, and his face with its warm captivating smile, were seen mornings and evenings around Krishnamurti.

Reared in an atmosphere that threw up vast challenges and demanded equally vast responses, Rao Sahib and Achyut never admitted to any personal sorrow, frustration, or despair. To them the personal was narrow and trivial. The canvas of their concern had to include great abstractions—man, the masses, the poor. Their sorrow had meaning only when related to the immense sorrow of man. Many years later Achyut was to tell me, "That was the great illusion" that held Rao imprisoned.

However, the intensity and luminosity of Krishnamurti touched deep springs. The Teacher reached out with a passionate flame. Krishnamurti smiled, and Rao smiled with him. Tears sprang to Rao's eyes, for *bhakti*,* also part of the Maharashtrian ethos, was awakened. Rao Sahib, with love overflowing, would say with folded palms, "Sir, there was a Maharashtrian poet, Saint Tukaram, who said, 'When *vithal*† enters the home of a householder all peace is shattered.' " In the evenings, Rao and Achyut would sing Tukaram's *"Abhangas." "Adi Beja Ekle"* was Rao's favorite. He had a deep, emotion-filled voice. On other occasions they joined Krishnamurti in chanting the *"Purusha Shukta"* of the *Rig Veda*. They sat straight-backed, the sharp stacatto sounds of Sanskrit reverberating and filling ears and eyes. The vowels were resonant and strong, each sound pronouced distinctly. The *vedic* chants were woven on fire, on winds, on the hearts and breath of singer and listener. We gathered and listened, even the little ones—my daughter Radhika, aged ten, and my nephew Asit, aged nine. Wide-eyed, they were swept into the blazing presence of Krishnamurti, a man aflame with intensity. Beauty of sound, form, illumined. Every pore of the body responded. Those were enchanted moments.

---

*Bhakti:* A creed based on devotion to Krishna.
†*Vithal:* Another name for Krishna, the divine cowherd.

# CHAPTER 10

# "You Are the World."

Krishnamurti in later years was to say of himself, "Full awakening came in India in 1947 to 1948." During those years the five ways of communication integral to the teaching were unfolding: public talks, dialogues and discussions, personal interviews, seemingly casual insights revealed on walks or at the dinner table, and silences. Krishnamurti was launching his associates and listeners on the river of self-knowing, on a journey of discovery "of oneself without a beginning" that in its movement broke the limitations of the mind, opening new frontiers of perception. It was an austere teaching, not in its demand for outer renunciation or sacrifice (though in actuality, austerity and a life of correctness was the ground from which the teaching emanated), but in its total negation of all anchors, crutches, and rituals, even the most subtle.

The denial of the guru as central to religious enquiry was in India the ultimate negation of all spiritual authority; for in the absence of the one sacred revealed book, the guru was the initiator, the preceptor, the doorway to truth. By his refusal to concede the place of any intermediary between the seeker and reality, Krishnamurti cast total responsibility on the seeker. To the seeker he said, "The Real is near, you do not have to seek. Truth is in 'what is,' and that is the beauty of it." But for the aspirant who remained inwardly a disciple, there was bewilderment, for there was nowhere to go, no goal to reach, no peak to climb. There was no guru to promise ecstasy or exploding lights, no visions or *siddhis*, extrasensory powers, to sustain a quest; all extrasensory phenomena as they arose were to be observed and put aside. The only concern was with the awakening of a living perception: seeing and listening to the actual in the outer, as revealed in relationship to man and nature; and in the inner as revealed in thoughts and feelings that were the actual content of the mind.

This frontier perception, direct and uncluttered, was the beginning of self-knowledge, of the self as "is." To observe thought as it arose in consciousness, and as it disappeared to hold it by its tail and not let go, was to have insights into the nature of thought and to observe "what is."

But the "what is," in its swift movement, was constantly changing, transforming, in flux. An awareness flowing from senses tethered to a sluggish static mind, held in thought born of the past, did not have the energy or the pliability to pursue and be one with the present, the "now" of existence, and act from that perception. Man was forever seeking to mold the movement of thought, projecting action into the future as the "I will be," and so thwarting action in the present. Krishnamurti asked, Who is it who seeks to mold or change thought or give it direction? "Remove thought, where is the thinker? If the thinker is thought—then he cannot act or change thought. Thought has to end."[1]

When asked, "How does one know oneself? What is there to know? For what does one seek? Where does one start?" he replied, "The more complex the question, the more overpowering the confusion, the more simple and innocent has to be the approach. Man does not know the way, so the only thing he can do is to cease to struggle and with whatever instruments and energy he has, observe that which is the bondage. It is the simple, the sorrow-laden, the real seeker who is the hope. The simple are so crushed by their own insignificance, they do not trust the integrity of their own intentions."[2]

Many people came to him seeking physical healing. To them he said, "I also at one time did healing; but I found it far more important to heal the mind, the inward state of being. Merely to concentrate on healing physically may make for popularity, draw large crowds, but it will not lead man to happiness."[3]

In *Commentaries on Living I,* he writes: "We are an old people; we wander in search for everything in far off places when it is so close to us. Beauty is ever there, never here, truth is never in our homes but in some distant place. We go to the other side of the world to find the master, and we are not aware of the servant; we do not understand the common things of life, the everyday struggles and joys and yet we attempt to grasp the mysterious and the hidden."[4]

Krishnamurti's public talks in Bombay in January 1948 were held on the lawns of Sir Chunilal Mehta's spacious residence on Ridge Road. Krishnamurti entered the grounds dressed in a red-bordered *dhoti,* a long, spotlessly white *kurta*, and an *angavastram*. Taking off his sandals, he sat cross-legged on a platform, his back straight and without movement. Turning his head he looked at the five hundred people who sat on the ground or on chairs before him. Among them were *sannyasis*, old Theosophists, some professors, and a sprinkling of *khadi* caps. There were few young people; but the rich merchant princes of Bombay, the friends of Sir Chunilal Mehta, were present.

In those early years Krishnamurti flayed the rich. He was to say, "You cannot mix god and mammon. Reality is not for the man who has his hand in his neighbor's pocket—who exploits and fills his heart with the riches of the earth."[5] The gaze of Krishnamurti drew his listeners into a united field of attention. But it was not a glance that classified as a group. The direct communication that emanated from Krishnamurti established contact with the individual woman and man; each person felt that Krishnamurti was speaking to her or him alone. Krishnamurti's role was that of a friend, taking the hand of the man in sorrow and walking with him through the by-ways and depths of the mind, of thought and feeling. He moved step by step, with infinite patience, opening up the problem, probing, questioning, blocking all escapes away from the fact. Teaching the listener to observe, as in a mirror, sorrow, anger, fear, loneliness. Teaching him to dwell on the space between thoughts—moving from thought to thought; to see, when pushed back to its roots and its source, thought dissolve in the ground of its begetting.

While speaking, Krishnamurti was aware not only of the people who listened to the words he was saying, but of what was happening around him—the birds twittering, a leaf falling, the sound of a flute being played in the distance. There was a simultaneity of awareness, an inclusive seeing, listening, that did not shut out the outer or the inner, but let it flow through the mind, so that nothing was exclusive, nothing was a distraction. Only the flowing river of existence, of "what is."

A large number of people were hearing him for the first time. His vocabulary had totally changed, and even people like Sanjeeva Rao, who had been with him for many years, found it difficult to comprehend him. What he said appeared simple. "I am going to say 'What is' and I will follow the movement of 'What is.' " Then to the audience, "Follow not my words, but the movement of thought, that is active in you."[6] To acknowledge life "as is," ends conflict. "The seeing of 'What is' is the freedom from 'What is.' "[7]

Clogged with words and ideas, and caught in the trap of becoming, the minds of K's listeners, which had never directly "seen" thought as it operates—its movement, its complexities, and the spaces it creates as it moves—struggled to understand. "Can I who am the result of the past—can I step out of time?" Krishnamurti asked. "You do step out of time when you are vitally interested. You take a stride—not chronologically but psychologically—in that timeless existence."[8]

In those early years Krishnaji rarely posited a position of direct confrontation with the "I," the ego entity. He never asked the question, "Who am I"; rather, he approached the "I" through negating the accretions, the qualities that coalesced to form the "I" and give it reality. This negation, the dissolution of the nature and qualities, quenched the volition of thought through which the "I" was manifest and through which it perpetuated itself. The perception and negation of all psychological becoming was the ending of thought, of time, and of the "I" principle.

Seeing the nature of mind and its structure and the forces that operated in human consciousness, insights arose: The very nature of the mind and thought limits us and is the cause of our bondage and sorrow. To Krishnamurti all efforts to substitute or change at the level of content and meaning a movement within the field of the opposites, was at best a partial answer, incapable of solving the extraordinarily complex and primeval urges that lay at the depths of the mind.

The problems that face man could end, not through ideals that projected a gradual change of sorrow into happiness, greed into love, but by a transformation in the nature of the ground from which sorrow takes root. The change or transformation, therefore, is not in quality or degree, but in nature, structure, and dimension.

As such, Krishnamurti's teaching altered the very dimensions of the human problem. It concerned itself with a revolution at the core of human consciousness and the discovery of a new space-thought relationship—so that mind, moving in a linear space-time, cause-effect dimension, turned back on itself and a simultaneity of sensory perception arose. This simultaneity, by its very operation, negated any self-centered entity. It awakened new capacities and instruments of enquiry, a new energy was set into operation, negating the limitations.

"It is only truth that deconditions completely," said Krishnaji. "To perceive the truth, there must be a focusing of attention. This does not mean turning away from distraction. There is no such thing as distraction, because life is a movement and has to be understood as a total process."[9]

K was addressing an audience that for a century had been educated in English-speaking schools and nurtured on Western ideals of democracy, with its emphasis on universal franchise and an egalitarian society. The principles on which the Indian Constitution were being formulated were to lead to a great churning within all sectors of society. The underprivileged would slowly grow aware of the power they wielded. With this came a rapid transformation and hardening of class structures. Pressures were to mount in the years that lay ahead.

The Indian mind, held in centuries of myth, symbol, concern with "otherness," was in the mid-twentieth century colored by the theories of the Indian social philosophers of the nineteenth and twentieth centuries; rebelling against the superstitions and darknesses that had eroded the Indian psyche, they had adopted a veneer of Western conditioning to cover the tumultuous centuries of tradition. Forces and energies of the archaic past, its wisdom and its violence, lay dormant and unexplored. With freedom, people looked to leaders, both political and religious, to show the way; they could not comprehend the pace of change and the explosive forces that were soon to shatter their traditional ways of life and their values. Demand for social change in India generated a laudable concern for the "more" in certain sectors of society. And within and integral to this concern was a redistribution of wealth. But, within a democratic structure, the thrust for the "more" could not be confined to the legitimate needs of the underprivileged, but saturated the human condition; inevitably, it led to the release of forces previously kept in check by traditional relationships, with their exploitations but also with their inherent responsibilities. Linked to this, pressures were generated by a rapidly escalating population and accelerated increase in material hardware made possible by advances in technology. A blatant shift to material attitudes and values was to saturate Indian society and relationships. The new rich—the landlord and the industrialist—the emerging power groups of the "backward," and a rapidly growing antisocial organization battled for the postulates of wealth and power.

The postwar West was also in turmoil; the war had generated vast resources of material and scientific knowledge, and technocrats trained to create artifacts of destruction had to find new avenues for their skills. Cybernetics was soon to come of age and the tools of automation were taking shape on drawing boards. By the end of the 1940s one could see the stirrings of what was to come. At the material level, man seemed ready to dominate the world—all problems appeared soluble.

One conspicuous aspect of the postwar phenomenon was the production of weapons of war and an avalanche of consumer goods (central to economies geared to waste-makers) and artifacts that were built to become obsolete. With it came an emphasis on the creation of a rapidly escalating entertainment industry, with artifacts and gadgets that were to swamp the markets and the minds of man, woman, and child.

In 1947 the impact on India of the West and its exploding technologies was still minimal. The trauma of partitions and its aftermath had shaken the foundations of every thinking person. But these were only surface murmurs revealed the chaos and violence that lay in the future. Krishnamurti, with the long vision of the seer, sensed the seething unrest. He was feeling his way into the landscape of India, delving into the minds of men and women, observing, questioning, probing the environment, laying his hands on the tensions and conflicts that were to corrode mind and heart. "The house is burning," he passionately told those who listened—but the intensity and urgency were absent in those who heard him.

Out of his passionate concern and his vast perception were born major insights central to the teaching.

Man—not in the abstract, but in the "I", the ego entity in his relationship to another—creates society and the world. "You are the world" was a central tenet of the teaching. Social and political action can never transform the world at its roots unless the individual radically transforms himself. "Systems can never transform man, man always transforms the system," said K. When questioned on the helplessness of the single individual to change society and the world, Krishnamurti replied that the roaring volume of water that was the Ganga* in flood, at its source was a single drop, and that all major actions that have changed man had been born of a single human being.

The transformation of the individual was not a gradual process. Transformation was an immediacy—it was the instant man saw himself in the mirror of relationship—to man, nature, and to himself. Speaking of relationship, Krishnamurti used the most intimate examples: the relation of husband and wife; employer and employed. Though many who listened were troubled by Krishnamurti's persistence in speaking of the hypocrisy that underlay these relationships, they were to realize the truth of his insights. He said that "seeing" without any movement

---

*The Ganges River.

to distort or change what was seen is only possible when the direction-giving activity of the seer has ended. This is the instant of transformation; the birth of insights that in turn transform society and give birth to a new generation. Real transformation is not the result of any revolution of the right or left, but a revolution from sensate values to those values that are not the result of environmental influence.

Inbuilt into the immediacy of transformation were Krishnamurti's insights into time. He perceived that the "coming to be" and the "ceasing to be," or the sapling growing into the banyan tree, involving linear time, are integral to the life process. Energy held in matter and subject to the laws of time as an arrow is entropic—it has to dissipate, deteriorate, and end. Krishnamurti said, "There is a chronological time and time of the mind. Time which is mind itself. There is confusion between the two. Psychological time is the process of becoming."[10] This time as becoming, the "I will be," was born of illusion and was a manifestation of the "I"; both self-sustaining and self-energizing, maintaining and supporting itself through its own ignorance and, by this process, storing up its own potential energy as consciousness. This consciousness was perceived by the individual through the operation of the senses.

The "I" as the product of psychological time, manifesting itself as thought, could not act to transform or free itself. It was only through a negative approach, the perception and denial of all psychological thought—as a desire to change "what is" into "what should be"—that there could be direct perception of "what is" and a freedom from time born of the psyche.

In this state of perceiving, the mind is not using thought to revive itself. There is neither the thinker nor thought, neither experiencer nor experience. The mind that is caught in becoming is the product of time, which has transformed itself. From this approach, arising out of the negation of the false as it arises, emerges the great truth that seeing and listening to the fact directly—innocently, without thought seeking to change or alter the fact, a nonoperation of thought or will on the deep roots of hate, anger, greed, fear—dissolves the state. There is a transformation in the nature of matter as anger or fear and the release of an energy held in these states, an energy untouched by time and, therefore, not subject to its laws. This state is not related to, nor is it the opposite of hate, anger, or fear. Posing the problem in terms of the opposites, as the ideal, is the trick thought plays to self-perpetuate itself; for the ideal contains within itself the seed of its own opposite.

Only a total, nonfragmented perception can negate both the observer and the observed. The seeing of "what is," is the transformation of "what is."

Thought divides the mind from the heart. The mind, with its roots in self-interested activity, leads to an increase in material values and the slow drying of these essences and responses which nourish humankind.

The denial of love is the destructive tendency in man. It is only when the mind rests in the heart and self-centered activity is totally negated that humanity has its flowering.

The unlocking of the secrets of mind and the arising of insight came naturally to Krishnamurti. Thus with ease, with grace, he could open the door and say, "Look. Take. It is there, why do you hesitate?"

It was during the months in Bombay that dialogue as a major instrument of exploration into Krishnaji's teaching was born. Through the years it would flower in subtlety and insight. In the early years the group discussions had been in the form of question and answer. The precision and perceptive probing into hidden depths of the mind as evident in dialogue were absent.

The first discussions in Bombay in 1948 were confused and dispersed. A question was asked of K. His fluid mind took in the question and turned it back, challenging the questioner and the group to seek the answer within the field of self-knowing. K spoke slowly, with many pauses, bending forward as if each response was for the first time. He listened to his own responses with the same openness and receptivity as he did to the voice of the questioner. The energy of Krishnaji's response was met by struggling minds, battling with confusion, conditioned to respond from memory and to seek solution from a higher authority, inner or outer, spiritual or temporal. We found Krishnaji's way difficult to comprehend. We strained to understand the words of Krishnaji and to apply them to our own minds. We attempted to approximate, to reach beyond the word with the only instruments of enquiry available—memory and thought. But these were the very instruments that were being challenged, and there was a sense of bewilderment. The clues were missing and the mind, clinging to words, was a battlefield of despair and conflict.

Krishnaji spoke over and over again of the seeing of "what is," the real, and not "what should be," the illusion; of the need for man to transform himself before he could transform society, for he is society. He spoke of being free of memory; memory that counteracts and distorts and hinders understanding of the present, memory that is the "I" consciousness, and of the nature of "being" and "becoming." In the discussions Krishnaji refused to give an immediate answer, an easy solution. To K any reaction to a fundamental question ended the probing into the question. He demanded an enquiry, a seeing and penetration into the question itself; not as an outer dual process, but seeing both the nature of response and the ground from which the question and answer arose. To pause, to ponder, was the awakening of the "listening" and "seeing" mind that annihilates the illusion of outer and inner, awakening a state that can deal with the question.

The discussions proceeded slowly. K moved from thought to thought, pushing, blocking, retreating, advancing. In the very movement of this step-by-step observation of the mind, the thought process slowed down until, in an instant, the perceptions of the participants awoke, and there was direct contact of perception with mind and its flux. The first "seeing" of mind was the starting point of enquiry. It was the clue that unraveled and revealed and, in the very revealing, illumined the question and the answer.

The people who investigated with K were discovering the structure and nature of consciousness and the immense strength and resilience of the thinking process. To observe the movement of the mind caught in thought and to "see" its own inadequacy had in it the excitement and awe of discovery, of traveling uncharted terrain.

Thought held in its grooves could not break through its own bondage. By discussion, seeing, observing, challenging, and doubting, the grooves in which thought moved and the process of becoming was born were being shattered.

A new methodology born of seeing and listening was unfolding, new perceptions were awakening. A ground of observing and enquiry was being established. The energy generated by the question was not permitted to dissipate in the reflexive answers and responses that arose from the storehouse of memory. K was challenging the minds of the participants. Every cell in the body and mind of K was awake. His relentless questioning opened up the psyche; and as the muscle and tone of the listeners strengthened, the mind of K in turn was deeply challenged. In K's very challenging there arose rare insights into the human condition.

Like an antenna, K's mind reached out to sense the minds of the participants. When the dialogue got bogged down or the group entered into sterile dialectics and the discussion was barren, K's mind would take a leap, carrying the discussion out of its rut. He brought into the discussion the nature of love, death, fear, and sorrow; feelings and situations that were of the skin and heart; and suddenly the discussion would come in direct, tactile contact with the problem.

The breakthrough in the discussions began one morning in 1948 when Rao Sahib Patwardhan said that the ideals and beliefs that had carried him through the political struggle had crumbled under him. He was faced with a blank wall and felt that the time had come for him to reexamine his fundamental beliefs. Then he turned to Krishnaji and asked him what he meant by "creative thinking." Krishnaji, who had been sitting quietly, listening intently to Rao Sahib, sprang to his feet and sat down next to him. Leaning forward, he said, "Do you want to go into it, Sir, and see whether you cannot experience the state of creative thinking now?" Rao was perplexed and looked at K, unable to comprehend what he was saying.

"How does one think?" K began. Rao responded, "A problem arises, and to meet the problem thoughts arise."

K asked, "How do you try to solve a problem?" "Find out an answer," said Rao.

"How can you find an answer and how do you know that it is the right answer? Surely you cannot see the whole content of the problem—how can then your answer be the right one?"

"If I do not find the right answer the first time, I try other ways of finding it," answered Rao.

"But whatever way you try to find an answer it will only be a partial answer, and you want a complete answer. How then will you find a complete answer?" K was blocking all movements of the mind—refusing to defuse the energy held in the question.

"If I cannot see the problem completely, I cannot find the right answer," Rao responded.

"So you are no longer looking for an answer."

"No."

"You have shut off all the avenues seeking an answer."

"Yes."

What is the state of your mind when it is no longer looking for an answer?"

My own mind was quite blank, but this was not what he was getting at. We were missing something.[11]

During a discussion a few days later, K spoke of memory as the "I" consciousness, the factor that distorts and hinders understanding of the present. He separated factual memory from psychological memory—the "I" will be, "I" should be. Then he asked, "Can we live without psychological memory?"

The discussion proceeded slowly, and I lost interest. My mind darted away in pursuit of some desire. The more I tried to concentrate on the subject, the more restless the mind grew. I was so disgusted that I let it roam. Soon I found that it settled down, and for the first time that morning I listened to what was being said. Professor Chubb of Elphinstone College had entered into an argument, and I listened. Could memory drop away? I asked myself. I did not want to be free of the "I" principle. I had built it up so carefully; why should I be free of it? I would be lost.

Then I felt curious to find out whether one could drop memory. There was an immediate clarity. I started watching the mind. K was saying, "What can you do, Sirs? You are faced with a blank wall. You can't just leave it, you have to do something." In a flash I spoke: "Drop memory." Suddenly, my mind was clear. K looked straight at me. The clarity deepened.

"Go on," he said. "What is the state of your mind when you drop memory?" It was as if the fifty people were gone, and there were just K and I. "My mind is still," I said. Suddenly, I felt it—a quality so potent, so flexible, so swift and alive. He smiled and said, "Leave it, go slow, don't trample it." The others tried to intervene to get at what I had experienced, but K said, "Leave it alone, it is so delicate, don't strangle it." When I left the meeting he came to the door with me and said, "You must come and see me, we must talk of it." I had the feeling my mind had been washed clean.

As the intensity and clarity generated in the dialogue became evident, we were eager to continue. And on days when public talks were not held, we met and discussed with K. Most of the questions that arose concerned the urgency of ethical action in the midst of a chaotic society, and it was only later that the fundamental human problems—envy, ambition, fear, sorrow, death, time, and the agony of becoming and not achieving—were to surface and find expression.

In later years K wrote, "To be still after tilling and sowing, is to give birth to creation."[12]

As the discussions proceeded through the years, various analytical enquiries were made; tentative and exploratory. We questioned without seeking immediate solution; rather, we developed a step-by-step observation of the process of thought and its unfoldment—penetration and withdrawal, every movement plunging attention deeper and deeper into the recesses of the mind. A delicate, wordless communication took place; an exposure of the movement of negation as it met the positive movement of thought. There was the "seeing" of fact, of "what is," the releasing of energy held in "what is," which is the mutation of "what is." This was again perceived from various directions to examine its validity.

The nature of duality and nonduality were revealed in simple language. In that state of questioning—a state where the questioner, the experiencer has ceased—in a flash "truth" was revealed. It was a state of total nonthought, the ending of duality. At the end of the discussion many of us felt as if our minds had been freshly bathed.

In later years K was to say of these discussions, "The mind which is the vessel of movement, when the movement has no form, no 'me,' no vision, no image, it is completely quiet. In it there is no memory. Then the brain cells undergo a change. The brain cells are used to movement in time. They are the residue of time and time is movement; a movement within the space which it creates as it moves. . . . When there is no movement, there is tremendous focus of energy. So mutation is the understanding of movement, and the ending of movement in the brain cells themselves."[13]

The revelation of the instant of mutation of "what is" provided a totally new dimension to the whole field of intellectual and religious enquiry.

Years later I said to Krishnaji, "Having a personal discussion with you, one is exposed to a nothingness. It is like facing something totally empty. There is nothing except 'what is' as reflected in oneself. You throw back on the person exactly 'what is.'

K replied, "That is what Aldous used to say. But when K throws back, it is yours."

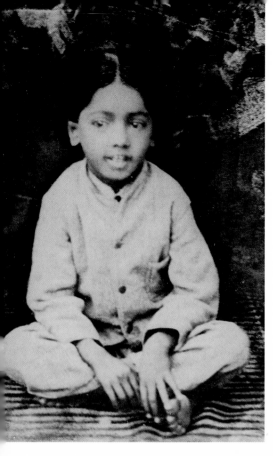

Jiddu Krishnamurti at the age of five.

Jiddu Sivamma, the mother of Krishnamurti, about 1900.

The Madanapalle High School in September 1908. Krishna stands in the second row from the left, fourth in line, with a cap on and a handkerchief in his pocket.

Krishnaji in 1909 sitting in front of the elephant bas-relief at Mahabalipuram, a seventh-century archaeological site forty-five kilometers west of Madras.

Krishnaji on the morning after his first
initiation into the Theosophical Society
in January 1910.

Krishnaji, his younger brother Nitya, and C. W. Leadbeater of the Theosophical
Society, on the terrace of the Society's headquarters at Adyar, that same morning.

Krishnaji in January 1910.

Nitya in April 1911.

Radha Burnier in
the 1950s.

Krishnaji at the time of his visit to the Theosophical
Society, Varanasi, in November 1985, thirty-three
years after their split. On his right is Radha Burnier, the president of the Theosophical Society.

Krishnaji, seated center, flanked by Annie Besant, C. W. Leadbeater and other
members of the Theosophical Society, approximately 1911 (from left to right, seated
on floor) Subba Rao, Jadunanandan Prasad, Padmabai, Siva Rao, Sanjeeva Rao,
Balfour Clerk; (sitting on chairs) Francis Arundale, Annie Besant, Krishnamurti,
C. W. Leadbeater, G. Arundale; (standing, front) V. P. Dalal, Bankey Behari, Cooper
Bekley, P. K. Teleng, Nitya, Damodar Prasad, Samant; (standing, rear) M. G. Kanit-
kar, I. G. Gurtu, A. Woodhouse, Trilokikar, Ruspoli.

Krishnaji during his time in Europe
in the early 1920s.

Krishnaji and Jadunanandan Prasad, a close friend and associate,
in Ootacamund, India, 1926.

Nitya and Krishnaji in Europe in the early 1920s.

Nandini Mehta in 1947, at the time of her first meeting with Krishnamurti.

Sunanda Patwardhan in 1947.

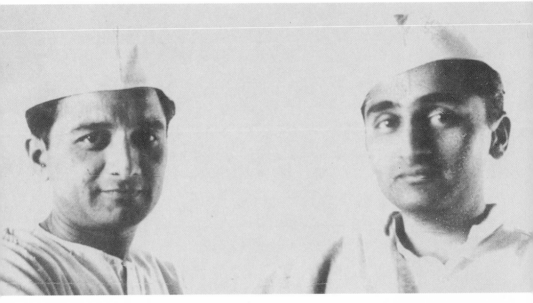

Rao Sahib and Achyut Patwardhan in the 1940s. The white handspun cap, called a "Gandhi cap," was the mark of a freedom fighter.

Dr. Balasundaram in 1947.

# CHAPTER 11

# "Go and Make Friends with the Trees."

In early April 1948 Krishnaji returned to Madras. He stayed at Vasant Vihar, the official headquarters of Krishnaji's work in India. R. Madhavachari was his host.

Vasant Vihar was a solid colonial building with pillars and verandas; the doors, windows, and furniture were of rich Burma teak. On the ground floor, the house had an office and a large room for meetings, but very few bedrooms—it had been deliberately built so that few people could live there. Although he had a suite of rooms on the ground floor of the house, Krishnaji slept on a covered veranda. He gave interviews in a room that faced the front lawn, and public discussions were held under the trees. The house was surrounded by banyan, mango, and rain trees; flowering bersali, cassia, gul mohar, and laburnum gave fragrance and color to the varied greens; and near the gate was an artificial lake filled with water lilies.

Madhavachari was an austere Brahmin, a follower of the Madhava sect. He was naive, devoted, obstinate, and steeped in a monumental tradition. Dark, with the smooth, unwrinkled skin that comes from numerous South Indian oil baths, and with a lean upright body, he had a presence, his face radiated strength and beauty. But beneath his austere outer appearance, in later years we were to discover a very human person. He could chuckle with my husband at rather risqué stories, and had a number of anecdotes of his early life.

Krishnaji had been discussing with Sanjeeva Rao and Madhavachari the possibility of starting a magazine with Sanjeeva Rao, Maurice Friedman, and myself as editors. In his first letter to me dated April 18, 1948, he wrote from Madras:

My dear Pupul,

Since the mountain will not come to Muhamad etc.

I wrote to Nandini, I think it was yesterday, telling her that my host has asked you & Nandini to stop here for a day or two before going up to Ooty. I hope you both will. Then we can all travel together to Ooty; we can leave here about the 1st of May.

If you accept Mr. Madhavachari's invitation, which I hope you both will, then before going to Ooty, a new job which we got for you!! I hope you will like the job. Joking apart, I would like to talk over with you & a few others something which we have been talking over here. They have been talking over with me the starting of a magazine, with you, Friedman, Sanjeeva Rao as co-editors. It sounds formidable but it is serious. We can talk it over when you come here. Please let us know when you & Nandini can come. If you can come a couple of days before the 1st of May, it will give us an opportunity to talk over the matter.

I hope you & family are well. Please give my love to them.

With much affection,
J. Krishnamurti

I had never seen Madras, and so decided to go. Nandini ultimately persuaded her husband to agree that she could accompany me. On our arrival we were met by Krishnaji and Madhavachari, who were warm and affectionate in their welcome. In the evening we went with Madhavachari to the Theosophical Society and the Garden of Remembrance, the grounds where Annie Besant had been cremated—her *samadhi*. Krishnaji did not come with us. Since his break from the Theosophical Society, he had not visited the estate in Adyar. The break with the Society was complete.

We brought a white lily back from Annie Besant's *samadhi*, and gave it to Krishnaji. He took it in his two hands and held it. We could see he was deeply moved. Later we went with him for a walk on the Adyar beach. He walked away from us, his white-garbed body erect, elongated, his long arms by his side. On his return his deep blue-black eyes were distant, his face appeared exalted. When we reached home he asked Madhavachari (whom he addressed as *Mama*, "uncle"), "What were the gongs I heard last night—two long and one short? They were marvelous." Madhavachari was puzzled, said he had heard no gongs and did not know from where the sounds had come. Krishnaji insisted that he heard extraordinary sounds. K went to his room and came out within a few minutes to say he had found out about the gongs. It appeared that the deep, resonant sound was produced by two fans working together. Krishnaji was in an ecstatic state, his hands beat time to the resonance. He hardly spoke right through dinner, which we ate on *thalis*, while sitting on mats on the floor.*

Late at night we woke to the sound of Krishnaji's voice calling from the veranda where he slept. His voice sounded frail, and we were bewildered and thought he was ill. After a great deal of hesitation, we went to the doorway that led to the veranda and asked him whether he was unwell. Krishnaji was calling for somebody, his voice was fragile and childlike. He kept on saying, "Krishna has gone away, when will he be back?" His eyes were open, but there was no recognition. Then he seemed to grow aware of us and asked, "Are you Rosalind?" And then, "Oh, yes, yes, he knows about you, it is all right, please sit here, wait here." Then again after a little while, "Don't leave the body alone and don't be afraid." The voice started calling for "Krishna" again. His hand would cover his mouth and he would say, "He has said not to call him." Then in the voice of a child, "When will he be back? Will he come back soon?" This went on for a while; he would be quiet, then shout for "Krishna," then chide himself.

After about an hour his voice became joyful. "He is back, do you see them? They are here, spotless." His hands expressed a fullness. And then the voice changed, it was again the familiar voice of Krishnaji. He sat up, apologizing for having kept us awake. He saw us to our room and left. The strangeness of it all bewildered us; we were dazed and did not sleep all night. Next morning at breakfast he looked fresh and young. We questioned him as to what had happened. He laughed and said he did not know. Could we describe what had happened? We did so. He said we would talk about it some time, which by then we had come to understand meant that he did not wish to discuss the matter further. The next day we returned to Bombay.

Tensions and the ominous threat of war in Europe altered Krishnaji's plans for the summer. It was decided that he would not return to Europe and the United States, but would rest in India during May and June. Miss Hilla Petit and Maurice Friedman were his hosts. Miss Petit had rented Sedgemore, a house in Ootacamund—Ooty, we called

---

*Thalis: round metal plates on which food is served in traditional Indian households. The *thali* can be made of silver, of stainless steel, of stone. Little round bowls with various vegetables and lentils are placed on the *thali*, while rice and *rotis* or whole wheat bread are placed on the *thali* itself.

it—a verdant hill station in Nilgiris situated at a height of eight thousand feet. The hill stations in India, with their lush forests, shady walks, bridal paths, and exquisitely tailored gardens, had been planned to create the ambience of the British countryside. The British created these sylvan retreats to escape the heat of the long summer on the plains.

In 1948 these hill stations had still not been Indianized. The cottages and large bungalows nestled amongst trees and overlooked emerald green meadows; wildflowers, daisies, forget-me-nots, and dandelions blossomed with unobtrusive elegance in the grass, and pine, eucalyptus, and areccanut trees densely covered the hillsides. This was undulating country, with none of the rugged rocks and gorges of the Northern Himalayas. The gardens that surrounded the houses were resplendent with roses, fuchsias, poppies, and pansies. Climbing roses and wisteria covered the old house walls.

The window in Krishnaji's bedroom overlooked a dense grove of silver-green eucalyptus; branches and leaves intertwined to form a canopy of slender-trunked trees rising vertically to the sky. Shanta Rao, a close friend of Friedman's, had come from Madras and was also living in the house.

Krishnaji wrote to Nandini and me to join him in Ootacamund. We had just returned from seeing him in Madras. Looking back, it appears incomprehensible that Krishnaji did not consider for a moment whether it was possible, whether the money for the journey and stay in Ooty was forthcoming, whether Nandini could get permission to come. I was free to travel within the constraints of my not very affluent finances, but with Nandini the situation was entirely different. Her estrangement from her husband was deepening; though her husband and his family were quite wealthy, they were orthodox and very conservative. Nandini had no independent means of her own.

But it had been always so with Krishnaji. Once a necessity arose within him and was expressed, it happened—all hindrances were surmountable. And so Nandini, her children, her father-in-law, Sir Chunilal Mehta, and I with my daughter Radhika arrived in Ootacamund in the third week of May. Jamnadas Dwarkadas was to join us in Ootacamund a few days later. We found that Krishnaji had recovered from an illness and had grown a beard while he rested in bed. It was cold, and Krishnaji wore a long, flowing *choga* of natural *tus* wool.* The large

---

*Choga*: A loose woolen or silk coat with one button in front. It is worn by men over

penetrating eyes, bearded face, and long robes gave him a biblical appearance.

We went with him for long walks, taking shortcuts through the pines. He walked lithely up vertical slopes and it was difficult to keep pace with him. It was the season before the rains, the forests were opaque with rising mists. We walked with Krishnamurti, entering enchanted woods where trees shrouded in rising clouds turned incandescent, as sunlight touched them, to dissolve as mists closed in. On one occasion, climbing up a steep path through the pine trees, we came on three women walking carefully downhill, balancing heavy loads of wood on their heads. Krishnaji stood to one side and watched every movement the women made as they passed him. Suddenly, one felt it—a compassion emanating from him, a tender attention and energy that wiped away the burdens of the women who passed, never knowing what made their loads lighter.

One day, on a walk through the pines, he asked me how I met people. I did not know what he meant, and said so. As we passed a Toda patriarch and his daughter, he said again, "How do you meet people? Look at these Todas passing us—that old man with his beard, and the young girl with her striped shawl. What is your response to them?" I said that when I see them I think of what they once were. Once their tribe ruled in the Nilgiri hills. They were the kings of this land, and now they are poor wanderers, grazing cattle and clustering in small glades. He said, "Surely, if you want to understand them, you do not see them through your thoughts: Why aren't you just aware of them passively, with alertness? Why are you not sensitive to them?" Later, as we were returning home, he turned to me and said with a twinkle in his eye, "Go and make friends with the trees."

Although Krishnamurti was resting and in retreat, the news of his presence in Ootacamund had spread rapidly.

Jawaharlal Nehru, now the prime minister of India, was in Ootacamund, and I got a message from his secretary that the prime minister would like to call on Krishnamurti. But the problems of arranging for security were found to be tiresome, and so Krishnaji went to see him instead at Government House. Maurice Friedman and I accompanied

---

Indian garments, as protection from cold.

*Tus*: Fine handspun woolen fabric. Spun from the wool of sheep that graze at a height of over eight thousand feet, it is woven by families of traditional weavers in Srinagar, Kashmir. A six-yard-long shawl of *tus* can be pulled through a finger-ring.

him, and were present during the meeting in the prime minister's private sitting room. There was an open fire, and large bowls of carnations were placed on the tables. Krishnaji and Nehru sat on a sofa facing the fire, while Friedman and I sat on chairs on the side of the sofa. The flames lit the two noble Brahminic heads, their chaste, finely drawn faces—one from the Northern highlands, the other born amongst the most ancient Southern rocks of Andhra. The faces were sculptured, sensitive, with fine translucent skin that accentuated the bones and heightened mobility—the eyes of the seer encompassing vast distances, emanating compassion and silence; the other with the swift, nervous energy of an arrow. Nehru was a romantic man of action, with a highly cultivated intellect; concerned, committed, restless, seeking the unknown within the tangle of political adjustments.

Both men were shy, hesitant. It took some time for them to establish contact. Jawaharlal Nehru started the conversation by saying that he had met Krishnaji many years earlier, and that he had often thought of what he had said. He had been anxious to meet Krishnamurti again. Achyut Patwardhan and other friends had spoken to Nehru at length on the profound work Krishnamurti was doing in Madras and Bombay. Nehru appeared anguished at the massacres and violence that had erupted after partition and independence. He spoke of it at length; he saw the two forces operating in India, the thrust for good and evil. These forces were in conflict; if the good could not contain the spread of evil, the world would perish. Krishnamurti said good and evil were always present; while it was more difficult for the good and the compassionate to function, evil was waiting for a crack in which it could gain foothold. It needed a great awakeness and awareness to ensure that evil could not enter and gain strength. To be awake and aware, said K, was what would sustain man.

Jawaharlal Nehru asked Krishnamurti whether his teaching had changed over the years since they had last met. Krishnaji said it had, but he could not say exactly where and how. Nehru then spoke of what Krishnamurti had to say on transformation. He felt there were two ways in which transformation could be accomplished. By the individual transforming himself and so transforming his environment, and by the environment working on and transforming the individual. At this Krishnamurti intervened, "Isn't that the same? The two could not be said to be separate processes." Nehru agreed. He was groping, trying to express the desperation he felt at the state of the chaos in the world and what had happened in India in recent months. Greatly troubled and not knowing which way to turn, he started to question in depth his own thoughts and actions.

"Tell me, sir," he asked Krishnaji, "I wish to be clear of this confusion within me. Tell me what is right action and what is right thought." To us who listened it was the perennial question of the awake Indian mind.

There was silence for over three minutes. We were discovering that the silences that surrounded Krishnaji in dialogue formed part of communication; a silence of the mind in which distances between the minds diminished so that there was direct mind-to-mind contact and communication.

Then Krishnamurti spoke slowly, pausing at every word. "Right action is only possible when the mind is silent and there is a seeing of 'what is.' Action that arises from this seeing is free of motive, of the past, free of thought and cause." He then said that it was difficult to go into this vast problem in such a short time. Jawaharlal Nehru was listening deeply, his mind appeared fresh and sensitive, capable of receiving and responding. Krishnaji leaned forward, his hands eloquent. He said that with the growing chaos in India and the world, man could only start the process of regeneration with himself. He had to begin anew. For the world to be saved, a few individuals had to free themselves of the factors that were corrupting and destroying the world. They had deeply to transform themselves, to think creatively and so transform further people. It was from the ashes that the new had to rise. "Like Phoenix from the ashes," said Nehru.

"Yes," replied Krishnaji, "for there to be life there must be death. The ancients understood this and that is why they worshiped life, love, and death."

Krishnaji then spoke of the chaos of the world being a projection of individual chaos. The human mind caught in the past, in time as thought, was a dead mind. Such a mind could not operate on chaos, could only add to the confusion. Man had to free himself from time as becoming, the projection into the tomorrow. He had to act in the "now" and so transform himself.

The seer and the hero politician spoke for over an hour and a half. The evening sky had darkened and the evening star had sunk behind the horizon, when we came out of the room. The prime minister saw us to the car and there was affection and grace in the parting. They promised to meet again in the winter, when Krishnaji was to be in Delhi. Later Krishnaji, who wrote in a notebook every day, recorded these observations:

He was a very famous politician, realistic, intensely sincere and ardently patriotic. Neither narrow minded nor self-seeking, his ambition was not for himself, but for an idea and for the people. He was not a mere eloquent tub-thumper or vote-catcher; he had suffered for his cause and, strangely, was not bitter; he seemed more of a scholar than a politician. But politics was the breath of his life and party obeyed him, though rather nervously. He was a dreamer, but he had put all that aside for politics.[1]

Toward the end of May certain incidents occurred which cast light on the secret mystical life of Krishnamurti.

In August 1922 in Ojai, when Krishnaji was undergoing violent awakening, he had two trusted friends with him. This was so on most such occasions in his life, and the emphasis on the two people is not accidental. From Krishnaji's early years, Annie Besant had insisted that two people be with Krishnaji all the time, to protect the body. The protection of the body of the sage when it is undergoing mystical processes of mutation and transference of consciousness, was deeply rooted in Indian mystical tradition. The body at this time is immensely sensitive, vulnerable, and empty of all ego sense.

In the Indus Valley there is a pictograph in which the seer, sitting cross-legged in meditation, is flanked by two uprising cobras. In an image of the instant of creation, a plant sprouting from a woman's womb has two rampant tigers protecting the moment of mystery. A legend describes the body of Adi Sankaracharya (the exponent of Advaita and the reputed founder of the Advaita Vedantic school of philosophy) when it lay in the Amarnath cave in Kashmir. For some time the body lay empty, for Sankaracharya had taken over the body of a king, so that without destroying the innocence of his own body, he could experience sex and fatherhood and so answer the challenge of Sharda, the wife of Madan Misra of Mahishmati who had challenged the great Acharya in discussion at Varanasi. While the body lay defenseless in Amarnath, two of Sankaracharya's disciples tended it and saw that it came to no harm. The need to protect the body had been the main and perhaps the only function of those present while Krishnaji underwent enormous transformations of energy that opened up the previously nonoperative areas of the brain. To give any other significance to Krishnaji's relationship to these people, as may have been claimed, is not valid. The only valid point is that they were people whom Krishnaji trusted, who would see that no harm came to the body, and who above all would have no strong emotional reactions, fear or otherwise, to what took place.

The incidents at Ooty extended over a period of three weeks, from around May 28 or 29 1948 to June 20. They took place in Krishnaji's room at Sedgemoor. My sister Nandini and I were present. It was embarrassing for Nandini and me. Maurice Friedman had undoubtedly explained to Shanta Rao and Miss Petit something of what was happening, familiar as he was with the secret mystical traditions of the sages of this land. Anyway, there was nothing we could do.

It began on an evening when Krishnaji had been for a walk with us. He started to say that he was not feeling well, and could we go home. When we asked whether he wanted to see a doctor, he said, "No, it is not that." He would not explain further. When we got home he went to his room, telling Friedman that on no account was he to be disturbed; but he asked Nandini and me to come into the room. He closed the door and then told us not to be afraid, whatever happened, and on no account to call a doctor. He asked us both to sit quietly and watch him. There was to be no fear. We were not to speak to him, not to revive him, but to close his mouth if he fainted. On no account were we to leave the body alone.

Although I had been swept away by my meeting with K, I had a skeptical mind and observed very intensely the events as they took place.

Krishnaji appeared to be in extreme pain. He complained of severe toothache and an intense pain at the nape of the neck, the crown of the head, and in the spine.

In the midst of the pain he would say, "They are cleansing the brain, oh, so completely, emptying it." At other times he would complain of great heat, and his body would perspire profusely. The intensity of the pain varied as did the area where it was concentrated. At times the pain was located in the head, in the tooth, the nape of the neck, or the spine. At other times he groaned and held his stomach. Nothing relieved the pain; it came and went at will.

When the process was operating, the body lying on the bed appeared a shell; only a body consciousness appeared to be present. In this state the voice was frail, childlike. Then suddenly the body filled with a soaring presence. Krishnaji would sit up cross-legged, his eyes closed, the fragile body would appear to grow and his presence would fill the room; there was a palpable, throbbing silence and an immense strength that poured into the room and enveloped us. In this state the voice had great volume and depth.

After the first evening he started going for a walk alone in the evenings and used to ask Nandini and me to come later to the house. In the beginning the experiences started at 6 P.M. and were over by 8:30 P.M., but later they sometimes went on until midnight. On days when he had to meet people (Jawaharlal Nehru, for instance), nothing happened. Toward the end the periods grew longer, and on one occasion went on all night. On no occasion did he speak of dirt or express a desire to leave the room as he had done at Ojai, though Sedgemoor was not particularly clean; nor did he speak of disturbing thoughts. On one occasion he asked Nandini to hold his hand, as otherwise he would slip away and not come back.

While he was in the midst of the ordeal, his body would toss on the bed. He would have fits of shivering, would call out for Krishna, and then put his hand to his mouth and say, "I must not call him."

---

*May 30, 1948:*\* Krishnamurti was getting ready to go for a walk when suddenly he said he was feeling too weak and not all there. He said, "What a pain I have." He caught the back of his head and lay down. Within a few minutes the Krishnaji we knew was not there. For two hours we saw him go through intense pain. He said he had a pain in the back of his neck, his tooth was troubling him, his stomach was swollen and hard, and he groaned and pressed down. At times he would shout. He fainted a number of times. When he came to, the first time, he said, "Close my mouth when I faint."

He kept on saying: "Amma—oh, God, give me peace. I know what they are up to. Call him back. I know when the limit of pain is reached, they will return. They know how much the body can stand. If I become a lunatic, look after me—not that I will become a lunatic. They are very careful with the body. I feel so old. Only a bit of me is functioning. I am like an India rubber toy, which a child plays with. It is the child that gives it life."

His face throughout the occurrence was worn and wracked with pain. He kept clenching his fists and tears streamed from his eyes. After two hours, he fainted again. When he came to, he said: "The pain has disappeared. Deep inside me I know what has happened. I have been soaked with gasoline. The tank is full."

He then said he would speak so that he would not think of the pain inside him. "Have you seen the sun and the soft clouds heavy with rain? They pass over the sun and then the rain comes down with a roar on the earth that waits like an open womb. It washes everything

---

\*I tried to keep notes of what Krishnaji said in these mystical states. Some of the notes are missing. However, I have reprinted here the notes that do exist, and Nandini has helped me reconstruct the rest.

clean. Every flower, every leaf. There is fragrance, a newness. Then the clouds pass and the sun comes out and touches every leaf and every flower. The gentle little flower that is like a young girl that ruthless men destroy. Have you seen the faces of rich men? Hard busy with their stocks and money-making? What do they know of love? Have you ever felt every limb of a tree, touched a leaf, sat by a ragged child? You know when I drove to the aerodrome, I saw a mother washing the buttocks of a child. It was beautiful. Nobody noticed her. All they know is to make money and cesspools of their women. Love to them is sex. To hold a woman's hand, then she is not a woman, that is love. Do you know what it is to love? You have husbands and children. But how would you know? You cannot hold a cloud in a golden cage."

He was silent for a time, then said, "This pain makes my body like steel—but, oh, so flexible, so pliant, without a thought. It is like a polishing—an examination." We enquired whether he couldn't stop having the pain. He said: "You have had a child. Can you stop it coming when once it starts?" Then: "They are going to have fun with me tonight. I see the storm gathering. Oh, Christos!"

After some time, Maurice brought in some soup and then went out. Krishnaji had the light put on. He had sat up with the legs crossed, body erect. The pain had gone from his face. His eyes were closed. He seemed to grow. We felt tremendous power pour into him. There was a throbbing in the atmosphere. It filled the room. Our eyes and ears were filled with it and with sound, though there was no sound; and every pore of our bodies felt a touch, but there was nothing in the room. Then he opened his eyes and said: "Something happened— did you see anything?" We told him what we had felt. He said: "My face will be different tomorrow." He lay down and his hand went out in a gesture of fullness. He said, "I will be like a raindrop—spotless." After a few minutes, he told us he was all right and that we should go home.

*June 17, 1948:* Krishnaji went out for a walk alone. He asked Nandini and me to wait for him. We sat by the fire and waited. He entered the room as if he were a stranger. He went straight to his table and wrote something in his file. After some time he grew aware of us. He came and sat down near the fire. He asked us what we had been doing and said that he had walked far beyond the Golf Club. There was a flute being played in the distance and he sat silently, listening to it intently. It was only after it stopped that he appeared in that semiconscious state. Twice while we sat there, that tremendous presence filled him. He grew in stature before us. His eyes were half-closed; his face silent and immensely beautiful.

And then he lay on the bed and there was just the body. The voice that came from it was that of a frail child. The Krishnaji we knew was not there. The body of Krishnamurti started saying that he was very hurt inside, that they had burnt him inside; that there was a pain right through his head. He was shivering and started saying that something had happened on the walk. He turned to us and asked, "Did you see him return?" He could not synchronize his body and mind. At times he felt he was still in the woods. "They came and covered him with leaves." He said, "Do you know, you would not have seen him to-morrow. He nearly did not return." He kept on feeling his body to see if it was all there. He said, "I must go back and find out what had happened on the walk. Something happened and they rushed back. But, I do not know whether I returned? There may be pieces of me lying on the road." Twice he got out of bed and made for the door, but lay down again. Later, he went to sleep. When he awoke, he felt himself and stared at his hands.

*June 18, 1948:* Krishnaji asked us to come at about seven in the evening. He was out. We waited. He came in some time later. He was again the stranger. He wrote something in the book and then came and sat with us. He said: "Thoughts of my talk in Bangalore are pouring in. I am awake again." He closed his eyes and sat for some time erect, silent. Then he complained of hurt and went and lay down. He said he felt he was burnt. He was crying. "Do you know, I found out what happened on the walk. He came fully and took complete charge. That is why I did not know whether I had returned. I knew nothing." A little later, "Then in the emptiness, there was a light and a storm and I was tortured that day in the wind. Do you know that emptiness that has no horizon—no limit—it stretches?" His hand moved to show empty space.

Then a little later: "They have burnt me so that there can be more emptiness. They want to see how much of him can come." Then later: "Do you know emptiness? When there is not a thought? When it is completely empty? But, how could you know? It is this emptiness that brings power—not the power they know, the power of money, the power of position, the power of husband over wife." He paused. "This is pure power—like that in a dynamo. You know, on the walk I was in an ecstasy. I have never cried like that. As I walked I met a poor man. He saw me crying and thought I had lost a mother or sister. Then he smiled at me and I could not understand." Suddenly, he said, "I have a thought—time and emptiness—that's it. I hope I remember when I wake up."

He started saying that he could not bear it, that he was all burnt inside, hurt. Then suddenly he sat up and said, "Don't move," and again we saw him like the other night. His face was in the dark, but the fire leapt up and his shadow lengthened on the wall. All pain had disappeared from the face. His eyes were closed, his body was throbbing, as if some power was entering his body. His face was pulsating. He appeared to grow and fill the room. He sat without movement for about three minutes and then he fainted. He woke up calm and peaceful.

———————

Although the notes we took on the final night are lost, Nandini and I remember the occasion vividly.

Krishnaji had been suffering excruciating pain in his head and neck, his stomach was swollen, tears streamed down his face. He suddenly fell back on the bed and became intensely still. The traces of pain and fatigue were wiped away, as happens in death. Then life and an immensity began to enter the face. The face was greatly beautiful. It had no age, time had not touched it. The eyes opened, but there was no recognition. The body radiated light; a stillness and a vastness illumined the face. The silence was liquid and heavy, like honey; it poured into the room and into our minds and bodies, filling every cell of the brain, wiping away every trace of time and memory. We felt a touch without a presence, a wind blowing without movement. We could not help folding our hands in *pranams*. For some minutes he lay unmoving, then his eyes opened. After some time, he saw us and said, "Did you see that face?" He did not expect an answer. He lay silently. Then, "The Buddha was here, you are blessed."

We went back to the hotel, and the silence came with us and enclosed us for the next few days. We were held by a pervading presence. Most of the time we were in the room with Krishnaji, we had no part to play; yet our presence seemed necessary. There was nothing personal in him during the incidents—no emotion, no relationship to us. The ordeal appeared physical, and yet the next day left no trace on his face or body. He was aflame with energy—joyous, eager, and youthful. Not a word he said had psychological overtones. A weight, depth, and strength was present in the silence that permeated the room and the atmosphere on every occasion. When Nandini and I compared notes later, we found that we had both had identical experiences.

When Nandini and I left Ootacamund, Krishnamurti asked us to "go to Bombay and rest. You have gone through a great ordeal."

In one of his letters to me, K later referred briefly to what had happened. I had asked him one morning what was the reason for the two voices—that of the frail child and the normal voice of Krishnamurti. I said that it looked as if some entity goes out of the body and some entity reenters the body. Krishnamurti said in his letter, "This is not so. It is not that there are two entities." He said he would talk about it later; but it was to be many years before he spoke of it again.

CHAPTER 12

# "There Was the Face Beside Me."

On my return to Bombay I underwent a very deep and inexplicable experience. My senses, torn from their routine, had exploded. One night as I lay down to sleep I felt the pervading touch of a presence, waiting. I was received and enveloped in a dense embryonic fluid. I was drowning, for I felt my consciousness fading. My body rebelled; it struggled, unable to accept this encompassing embrace, this sense of death. Then the silent presence disappeared. This happened for three nights running. Each time, my body struggled; it resisted this encounter, unable to face this touch of death, which passed as swiftly as it had come, never to return. There was no fear. I told Krishnaji about it at our next meeting, and he told me to let it be, neither to hold it nor resist it.

Krishnaji had asked us to keep secret what we had witnessed at Ooty. We felt that he did not wish it to confuse the precision, clarity, and directness of the teaching. But by the 1970s Krishnaji himself started talking about it to many of the people close to him. I asked, "Do you think that the physical brain cells, unable to contain or hold the immensity of the energy that was flowing into the brain, had to create the spaces in the brain to sustain it? Did there have to be a physical mutation in the brain cells themselves? Or was it like a laser beam operating on the brain cells to enable them to function fully and so contain the boundless?"

Krishnaji said, "Possibly that was so." He paused, and then continued. "After Ojai, Leadbeater could not explain the pain, nor could Mrs. Besant. The explanation given by them was that the consciousness of Krishnaji had to be emptied for a fragment of the Maitreya Bodhi-sattva to use the body."

When asked whether it was "Maitreya," he neither said yes nor no. I asked, "Is it that we are witnessing the first mind that is operating fully, totally?"

"Possibly," K said, "and that is what has to be done with the children here [at the Rishi Valley School]."

Krishnamurti, speaking in 1979 about the happenings in Ooty, said that for him the dividing line between life and death was fragile and tenuous. During the state when the body was a shell, the possibility existed that K could wander away and never come back, or some other elements that wanted to destroy the manifestation could harm the body. Therefore there could be no fear amongst the people near him at the time. Fear attracted evil.

I told him that while he was in those states, only the body was operating; there was an emptiness in the body. The voice was childlike. K said, "Couldn't you explain the two voices by saying that one was that of the body alone?"

I asked, "Only the body speaking?"

He said, "Why not?"

"Only a shell?" I persisted.

"Yes, why not?" Then K asked me, "Was the voice hysterical?"

I replied, "There was no hysteria."

"Was it an imaginative state?" he asked.

"How could I know?" I replied.

K asked what would happen the next morning. I said we sometimes went with him for a walk. Krishnaji was alive, fresh. The pain had left no mark, and he appeared to have forgotten what had happened. He laughed a great deal, looked at us quizically, was affectionate, considerate, overwhelmed us with his presence, and had no answer to our questions. He said he did not know.

That same year, 1979, when K was in Bombay, some of us asked him to explain the phenomenon of the face changing. He said, "Many years ago I awoke and there was the face beside me. There was the face that K's face was becoming. This face was with me all the time, happily. The face was extraordinary, highly cultured, refined." He spoke as if his words related to another being. "And one day the face was no longer there."

"Had it become one with K?" I asked.

K said he did not know. He also spoke of the need of the body to be protected. Nothing ugly should take place around it while K was away, nothing evil. In that state the body was defenseless, all kinds of elements wanted to destroy it. "When there is good, there is also the other."

He was asked whether evil could take over his body when it was empty. His "no" was absolute.

"Then what could evil do? Destroy the manifestation?"

"Yes," K said, "that is why there has to be love. When there is love there is protection."

K also said that it was possible that the pain and what took place was necessary, as the brain was not ready. Traces of immaturity remained, the brain cells were not large enough to receive the energy. "When the energy comes pouring in and the brain is not capable of holding it, then that energy feels it has to polish it up. It may be its own activity."

Speaking further of the need for two people to be with the body, K said, "Where there is love there is protection. Hatred permits evil to enter."

When asked where does the consciousness of K go, he replied, "I have asked myself what happens when there is no movement of the brain." After some time he continued. "It ceases completely. Only when it has to manifest it comes. It ceases to exist when it is not there. Has air any place, has light any place? Air is enclosed and so it is there. Break the enclosure, it is everywhere."

He seemed hesitant to probe further. He said that he should not probe further. "You can ask," he said, "and I will reply. But I cannot ask."

Krishnaji visited Bangalore on his return from Ootacamund. He was staying at Premalaya, a house that belonged to the well-known physicist Vikram Sarabhai, Chairman of the Atomic Energy Commission and a pioneer of space research in India. Maurice Friedman was looking after him. An insatiable desire to experiment made Friedman suggest to Krishnaji that garlic was beneficial for his health. So six cloves of raw garlic were added to his diet. Under Friedman's instructions Balasundaram, who was in Bangalore, massaged Krishnaji daily with medicinal oil.

By now a small group of young people had gathered around the seer. Balasundaram and his wife Vishalakshi, Sunanda and her cousin Lalita, Dwaraka (a young friend from Bangalore), and Shanta Rao were constantly around, adding color, chatter, and laughter to the atmosphere. Sanjeeva Rao, who was in Bangalore, was disturbed by so many young people gathering around the astonishingly beautiful being. He felt there was a certain levity in the atmosphere, and perhaps was reminded of Annie Besant's instructions on the need for initiates to protect Krishnaji against destructive forces. Rumors started, and some of the gossip floating around came to Krishnaji's hearing. Sensing a certain smugness in the situation, he chided the older group at a public meeting. He spoke of the destructive nature of irresponsible gossip and the need for a serious mind.

By now the very proper Madhavachari had come to Bangalore. He was aghast at Friedman's experiments, and immediately stopped Friedman from giving Krishnaji his garlic diet and the massages.

Subha Rao, an old Theosophist who had left the Theosophical Society with Krishnaji and was now principal of the Rishi Valley School, soon came to Bangalore to discuss the school's affairs with Krishnaji. Subha Rao was a fine, dedicated educator, loved by the students; but he was growing old. As Madhavachari repeatedly stated, the affairs of Rishi Valley were falling into the hands of the Coimbatore group. Subha Rao, unable to control the affairs, had suggested he resign. One day Sanjeeva Rao said to Krishnaji, "Rishi Valley was bought with £10,000 given as a gift for that purpose. It is your property. It is being destroyed. You must interfere." Krishnamurti replied swiftly, "My property? I have no property."

The talks in Bangalore were very well attended, and soon discussions were held regarding the Rishi Valley School. At this stage Miss Muriel Payne stepped in. Muriel Payne, who had come to Bangalore from England, was a big-boned woman, immensely energetic. The head of a nursing organization during the war, she sold her nurse's training college and came to India. She had known Krishnamurti for many years. In fact, she told me that she had nursed Krishnamurti when he was seriously ill in Ojai during 1945 and 1946.

She met Krishnamurti in Bangalore and suggested that she put together a group of young people and start work in Rishi Valley. Miss Payne's down-to-earth capacity to organize, combined with a certain perception and some insight into the teaching, made her a formidable personality. She was an ardent friend, but had no use for the inefficient and the mediocre and dealt with people harshly. A physically unattractive woman, she was unmarried; and the absence of physical love had accentuated her natural ruthlessness. But she was a tall woman in every sense of the word. She could fill a room with her irrepressible intention to shape people's lives.

It was decided to set up a community to look after Rishi Valley; the group would include Miss Payne, Madhavachari, Maurice Friedman, Subha Rao, and Rajagopal Iyengar. Also in the group were Evelyn Wood, Gordon Pearce, and Adhikaram. Evelyn Wood, an Englishman married to an Indian woman who was a professor of English at Bombay University, served the British government and later stayed on in India after Independence. Gordon Pearce, a Theosophist and well-known educator, married an Indian woman, Anusuya Paranjpaye. He established a public school in Gwalior, took charge as principal of Rishi Valley School, and later was to start the Blue Mountain School in Ootacamund. Adhikaram, a very well-known educator from Sri Lanka, later became chancellor of Colombo University. They were later to go to Rishi Valley and take charge. Inevitably perhaps, they were soon torn by dissension. Evelyn Wood was the first to leave, followed by Maurice Friedman. Madhavachari resigned, and Subha Rao left the valley. Pearce and Adhikaram never came. Miss Payne was left in sole charge. Sanjeeva Rao was by then horrified by Miss Payne and her "lack of education." Educated at Kings College, Cambridge, Sanjeeva Rao was unable to countenance Miss Payne's ignorance of English grammar and her appalling spelling. Sanjeeva Rao wrote poignant letters to me, complaining of Miss Payne's ignorance and the impropriety of her being connected with educational work.

At this stage a suggestion was made that Rishi Valley and the lands surrounding it be sold. Miss Payne reacted strongly to this whisper and wrote to Krishnamurti, who was in Poona, protesting the sale of land but suggesting that the school be closed. Miss Payne advised the establishment of an international community. Madhavachari strongly opposed the idea of selling the land, and in protest he resigned from the Rishi Valley Trust.

Krishnaji finally decided that Rishi Valley would not be sold. However, Subha Rao resigned and the school was partly closed down by Kitty Shiva Rao, Shiva Rao's Austrian wife, and Rao Sahib Patwardhan, then president and secretary of the Rishi Valley Trust. Miss Payne returned to England, after which Madhavachari rejoined the Trust. However, Miss Payne returned to the East and met Krishnamurti in Colombo, Sri Lanka, in October 1949. Later, along with Adhikaram and Pearce, she established the Rishi Vana Sangha, a community in which to live the teachings of Krishnamurti. They all drove to Rishi Valley and took over the estate. Rajagopal Iyengar, a senior engineer of the Central Services who had resigned prematurely from the government to work in Rishi Valley, was also a member of the community, as was Maurice Friedman. Relentlessly, Miss Payne took over. The old workers were asked to leave, and the community was soon reduced to a skeleton.

From Bangalore K traveled to Poona, where he was to stay at the guest house of the Servants of India Society. My mother, Iravati Mehta, was to play host and look after K while he was in Poona. My nephew Asit Chandmal, aged nine, was with my mother. His father, a member of the Indian civil service, developed a mental illness. His mother and father separated and Asit was brought up by his grandmother, my mother. Aware of the complexity of the child's problems, she had taken him out of school to be in Poona, intuitively understanding that two months under the same roof with K would do more for Asit than any school.

I asked Asit to write some of his recollections of this period, for he had spent a great deal of time with K. In one letter, Asit wrote,

When I was nine I stayed with Krishnaji in Poona for several weeks. My grandmother had set up house in the Servants of India Society—there were two bedrooms and a living room in between. The dining room and the kitchen were in a separate cottage two hundred yards away. We used to walk together to the cottage for lunch—his umbrella always protecting him against even a hint of sun. He often asked me to run to the cottage—he ran with me and we finished together. I was nine and he was six times my age—fifty-four. When he saw me flying kites he told me about the enormous kites in California, larger in span than his outstretched arms, and later, when it was Dewali, we went to the markets of Poona, bought firecrackers, and lit them at night. Once, when I shied away from a bursting bomb he said, "Watch it, don't look away."[1]

Before he left Bangalore, K had given Sunanda 400 rupees and a shawl. It was a symbolic gesture, a suggestion that she leave her home and enter the world. She had come to Poona with her cousin Lalita, Dwaraka, and Gautam, her maternal uncle. They were staying in the Theosophical Society rest house. Also present was Gawande, a very intelligent and thoughtful young man who later was to become a *sannyasi*.

The audience at the talks was alive. Gandhians, students, writers, scholars, and professionals came to the meetings. The discussions were vibrant, dominated by questions on alleviation of poverty and the demands of social work.

K was meeting vast numbers of people. Many women with troubled marital lives sought interviews with him, and he soon sensed the insecurities and sorrows that burdened the life of a married woman. In his public talks he was asked many questions about the "duties of a wife" and the role of marriage. He lashed out at the hypocrisy of Indian society, its values and moralities. He spoke of the position of the woman and the economic domination of the husband. "It is only a static society and a deteriorating society that talks of duty and rights." He said, "Have you noticed a man whose heart is empty? His face becomes ugly. Look at your face sometimes in a mirror, how unformed, how undefined it is." He spoke of the absence of love with its depth and profundity. "To love is to be chaste, pure, uncorruptible."

I had preceded K to Delhi. By then my husband had shifted his headquarters to Delhi and we were staying at the Delhi Gymkhana Club. As my work was mainly in Bombay, I commuted between the two cities. I was troubled in Poona, my mind had begun to rebel. I felt I should go back to my old life and activities, to my work, my clubs, my endless routine. I tried to, but found myself an outsider. Neither could I go to meet K. Every time I was near him, I felt a wall between us; he was unapproachable. My inward balance was shattered.

I asked K what had happened to me. At Ooty I had felt at the edge of an awakening. I needed just one step to plunge into nothingness. But the step never came, and before I had time to hold to what I had, I was swept away into the depth of loneliness. In Ooty there was joy and the passion of awakening every morning, of seeing K aflame with the rising sun. It was like falling in love with sunlight; passionately, yet with delicacy. I had glimpsed vast depths and an immensity of seeing. It remained with me, sustaining me for days. Soon, however, I was to be thrust into the harsh reverberations of Bombay—its noises, the crude exploitations, the ugliness and coarseness of living. This sudden descent into the denseness and the grit of a polluted city, prompted me to write to Krishnaji, saying that it would be easier to don the saffron robe.

But that was not the only reason for my being so rapidly overwhelmed. I asked K in Poona again and again the reasons for despair, and he said, "Why do you ask for a reason? You are troubled and not in a state of awareness. See yourself in the pit and you will be out of it. Next time you will be watchful and see that you do not fall back into the pit." But I could not understand, and felt that going to him was utterly futile.

One of the *Upanishads* says that it is better to keep away from truth altogether; but, once having heard, you must act or the truth acts as a poison within you. Krishnamurti says the same thing: "Keep away if you are not serious." But I was serious. I have never been so serious. I have never felt so deeply. As I was leaving Poona he said to me, "Let go your hold. Why do you want to hold so tight? Let it go and see what happens."

When he arrived in Delhi, I went to meet K alone. He told me that he had dreamed about me (he rarely had dreams). "Listen to what I say. I am going to talk as if I were you. I am a Brahmin born of a tradition of culture and learning with a background of intellect and sensitivity. In this background there is a vein of weakness, of crudeness. I spent my childhood in a civil servant's house. I ate meat and was made to reject my Brahminism. I went to Europe, married, had a child, a severe illness. I went blind, life used me and left its mark on me. I grew ambitious and cultivated ruthlessness and denied sensitivity. In meeting people I have absorbed and reflected their coarseness or their sensitivity. I have not had the intelligence to meet coarseness with intelligence. Then Krishnamurti came. At first I saw in what he had to say a way of sharpening my brain, but soon I was caught in it. In the most powerful influence I had known. And all the time, although I denied my Brahmin background, it was there, the main contradiction, the Brahmin background never understood but rejected, and so I am always in conflict."

Then he said, "You see the picture, the patches, the lights, the shades, the crudeness, the sensitivity. What is it you feel when you see the picture as a whole?" I said it was a mess, and asked what I could do to straighten out the contradiction. Surely I must be able to act on the contradiction.

He said, "You are still concerned about doing. But any action on your part will mean adding another patch. Why can't you just see it? It is you, with all its shades and lights. What is the use of prejudice or pleasure? Just absorb it and see yourself as you are, clearly. Then you will stop bridging the coarseness and sensitivity."

"That is, I must stop trying to be sensitive, when I am coarse."

"No," Krishnamurti replied. "You cannot do anything. Just watch the truth of your bridging, which you are constantly doing." This was the first time I had heard him refer to the background and the necessity of understanding it. I asked him how it could be understood.

"See that it is there in all its richness, its fullness, its thousands of years of racial memory. Then when it next projects itself, you will see it and there will be instant understanding and the end of conflict with it. You cannot reject the background, for it is there as much as your arm or skin. You can only understand it, and understanding it be free of it." A little later he said, "What man needs is that contentment that is in the earth when it has given birth to a tree. In a bush when it has produced a flower."

# CHAPTER 13

# "Why Don't You Begin to Clean Your Front Doorstep, the Part of Your Street Which Is Yourself."

While in Delhi Krishnaji was the guest of Sanjeeva Rao's brother Sir B. N. Rao, a brilliant lawyer and bureaucrat, a member of the Indian civil service, who had been asked by Prime Minister Jawaharlal Nehru to advise in framing the constitution of India. Delhi was basking in brilliant sunshine, slowly awakening to the implications of freedom and the vast opportunities that were arising in every direction. The Constituent Assembly had commenced to function; lawyers, political thinkers, and freedom fighters had gathered in Delhi to formulate in a written constitution the ideals for which they had struggled. Secularism, equality before the law, freedom of speech, freedom from arbitrary arrest and confinement—all were being debated with passion. But underlying their discussions were the murder of Gandhiji and the traumatic events of partition that had revealed the violence and divisive faces buried deep in the Indian soil, and the intimations of chaos, fear, and brutality that lay ahead.

Sanjeeva Rao, the gentle educator and one of Annie Besant's oldest associates, had come from Madras to be with Krishnaji. With him was his wife Padmabai, an extremely able teacher and a pioneer in women's education in Uttar Pradesh. In the late 1920s I had for a short period studied at Varanasi, at the school where Padmabai was the principal. Dignified, protective, available, she communicated her affection and concern to young adolescent girls, who in turn loved her. In the 1920s women's education in Uttar Pradesh was still a sensitive subject. It demanded intelligence and probity to impart right values to girls within the restricted framework the environment demanded. Sir B. N. Rao's youngest brother, Shiva Rao, the Delhi resident representative of the powerful South Indian English daily *The Hindu*, was sharing the house with B. N. Rao. His wife Kitty, an Austrian who had come to India in the 1920s and taught in the Montessori School for children at Varanasi, acted as B. N. Rao's hostess.

In the evenings after dinner, K listened to the Rao brothers discuss India and the intricacies of the new constitution that was being framed.

K was visiting and speaking in Delhi after an absence of many years, and the legendary early years of his life had created great curiosity and interest. Scientists, administrators, diplomats, academics, and *sannyasis* came to his talks and discussions, confronting him with questions on the harsh realities of the Indian situation. They found in Krishnaji a silent and compassionate listener, and challenged him with the inadequacy of his teaching, asserting that he had no solutions to the problems of poverty, untouchability, the caste system. Krishnaji's response was to pose another question: Did they know the nature of the vast problem?

In this modern sage they sought a Vivekanand, but came away puzzled—for they encountered a man of supreme presence who did not fit any of their known categories of saints and *sannyasis*. He answered their questions on poverty by saying that the needs of man—food, shelter, clothing—could only be effectively organized when the needs were not used for psychological purposes for self-exclusive ends, but were dealt with on their own level. Sensing the smugness of the questioners, he castigated them: "The mind is yourself. It cannot be quiet when it is sitting on a volcano." Negating all beliefs, secret doctrines, and practices, he said to those who had gathered, "The self is not a permanent entity, but a stream, flowing water."

Most people in India had witnessed the freedom struggle and the power of a mass movement, and they felt that to build a new India vast numbers of people should launch a new struggle for values. Krishnaji told them, "To create a new structure I must be the architect, the builder as well as the workman." When asked what one man could do, he responded, "You think in terms of large movements, large actions, large responsibilities, but you do not take responsibility. Why don't you begin to clean your front doorstep, the part of your street which is yourself?"

The light of his intelligence was probing into thought and the mind.

"We feel that the 'I' is different from thought, from mind. Is the 'I' the thinker separate from thought? Then the thinker can operate on thought. Is the 'I' separate from its qualities? Remove thought, where is the thinker?" After each sentence he paused, as if to let the words sink deep into the listener's consciousness.

"We feel that the 'I' is permanent, because all other thoughts come and go. If the thinker is permanent, then thought can be changed, controlled, transformed by the thinker. But is not the 'I' the result of thought? Your mind separates the 'I' from thought because it cannot bear impermanency. Thought cannot move from the known to the unknown. To free the mind from the known is all the mind can do. To find out what lies beyond words, words must cease. I can only use words to get to the door."

In December Krishnaji was invited to Teen Murti House, the Prime Minister's official residence. I was also present. Jawaharlal Nehru had just returned from the Jaipur Congress and looked very tired and depressed. He said to Krishnaji, "I have been very busy lately, doing I don't know what." He asked Krishnaji how the disintegrating forces that were spreading so rapidly could be stemmed. Krishnaji answered that integration could only start at the individual level.

"This must be a slow process, while disintegration is spreading so rapidly," said Jawaharlal Nehru. "What is there to show that the forces of disintegration will not swamp the integrating forces?"

Krishnaji replied, "It is possible."

They then discussed how the individual was to regenerate himself. Krishnaji said, "Understanding of the self only arises in relationship, in watching yourself in relationship to people, ideas, and things; to trees, the earth, and the world around you and within you. Relationship is the mirror in which the self is revealed. Without self-knowledge there is no basis for right thought and action."

Jawaharlal Nehru intervened and asked, "How does one start?"

K replied, "Begin where you are. Read every word, every phrase, every paragraph of the mind, as it operates through thought."

Nehru was listening, but one could see the weariness on his face. He asked, "What is the common factor amongst all people?"

"The desire to avoid pain and seek happiness," said Krishnaji.

Nehru then discussed the fear that was driving people to acts of violence. He asked Krishnaji whether action born of understanding could free man from fear, the psychological fear that was the motive force of many of man's actions.

Krishnaji said, "Freedom from fear can only arise when man perceives the movement of fear within himself. The seeing of it is the quenching of it."

Jawaharlal Nehru and Krishnaji did not seem really to communicate except once or twice. The prime minister appeared very interested, but very tired. He kept himself awake by smoking. His mind turned back to the problem of integration and the approach to self-knowledge. "How does man understand himself?" he kept on asking, seeking a clue.

"Look at what is outside you and within you. Look at your thoughts," said Krishnaji. "Who is the thinker? And are thoughts separate from the thinker?" He spoke of the need for a deep revolution in consciousness; of the urgency for a perception of the global to operate, without which man could not survive. These were prophetic words; they would assume supreme relevance in the fragmented, violent world of the 1980s.

On the way to home after the meeting, Krishnaji was disturbed and sad. He remarked that Nehru's was such a fine, sensitive mind. It was wasted in politics. Politics was deadly. Later, at dinner, Krishnaji discussed with the Rao brothers the problem of disintegration in India. "Society is continually disintegrating. What is the place then of a reformer in society? Is he not adding to the disintegration? A reformer is concerned with effects and their rearrangements. Only a revolutionary goes to the root, to the cause in which the end is contained." Krishnaji was questioning himself. He asked whether Gandhiji was a revolutionary or a reformer.

"Gandhiji had the vision of the revolutionary. He had the capacity to think in a big way. His thinking was not that of a reformer," said Sir B. N. Rao.

"He was a revolutionary then in thought, but in execution, the vision narrowed. Caught up in politics, Gandhiji had to compromise, and his revolutionary sense was submerged and he emerged a reformer," mused Krishnaji. He then asked Sir B. N. Rao whether India had leaders who were capable of shaping effects.

"In India leaders seem powerless. Effects are sweeping them away. In this rapid disintegration there is despair as well as hope. There are two paths before India. Either she will be completely swept away and will cease to be of any importance in the world; or, by the very touching of the depths of disintegration, the individual will awaken to his responsibility and refuse to be carried away by the current. A new society will emerge entirely different to any that has been known." Krishnaji said that he was extremely interested to see what would happen.

He spoke again of his meeting with Jawaharlal Nehru. He had felt deeply moved by the fineness of the prime minister's mind, and it was a sadness to him that a sensitive mind like this should have been caught up in politics. Krishnaji said, "Politics ages the mind, it is destructive to the flowering of the mind."

Anandmai Ma, the most famous of the then-living deified "Mothers" (women who in their lifetime transcended the self and became symbols of Sakti, the primordial mother as energy), with a very large following in North India, came to meet Krishnaji. They met in the garden, as the Mother never entered the home of a householder. She did not speak English, and spoke through a translator. She had a radiant, smiling presence. She said that she had seen a photograph of Krishnaji many years before and knew that he was very great. She asked him, "Why do you deny gurus? You who are the Guru of Gurus" (this was translated to him).

He replied, "People use the guru as a crutch."

"People come to listen to you in thousands," she said. "That means you are a guru." He held her hand gently and did not answer.

Many visitors came and prostrated themselves at the feet of K and Anandmai Ma. Anandmai Ma accepted their greetings, but Krishnaji was embarrassed. As always, he would not permit them to bow down, but sprang to his feet and bent down to touch the feet of the seeker of blessing.

Later, after Anandmai Ma left, Krishnaji spoke of her with warmth and affection. There had been communication, though much of it had been wordless. He was, however, horrified at the prostrating, hysterical women followers who surrounded her.

In my notes of the period I have recorded the visit of an old blind *sannyasi*, who spoke only Hindi. The *sannyasi* asked Krishnaji about freedom from the bonds of body and mind. Someone translated. Krishnaji answered with passion and intensity, and the *sannyasi* seemed to understand. Although in his public talks Krishnaji castigated the wearers of the robe, deep within him he had always felt an immense kinship for the person who wore the robe. In his early years there is evidence that at times he had thought of becoming a *sannyasi*. Awakening to its implications, he had not done so; but a special tenderness for the true *sannyasi* or Buddhist monk remained, and he never refused to meet them, however tired he was. His criticism of their rituals, disciplines, and practices, however, was devastating.

One day two Iranian princesses came to see Krishnaji. They were visiting India and had heard of the presence in the city of a great religious teacher. They asked Krishnaji whether he could foretell their future. Krishnaji looked quizzical, and said that he was not an astrologer. They were embarrassed, for they had presumed that Krishnaji, being a religious person, was also a fortuneteller.

Discussions with a small group had started. Achyut Patwardhan was in Delhi and so was Sunanda, with her lithe young body and razor sharp intellect. Sunanda was very young, and her exploding senses held her enraptured. Ecstatic in the atmosphere surrounding Krishnaji and aflame with his supreme beauty, she would continue to sit on the floor after the discussions were over, her eyes tightly closed, one palm resting on her cheek. After a few minutes, when asked what was the matter, she would open her large eyes and say, "I am experiencing."

The discussions were precise, probing; every movement, every action of life was brought into the light of attention and examined. At times the process was painful, and the body mind shrank from the confrontation. We discussed violence, fear, anger, jealousy, and death.

At one of the evening discussions K was asked, "How can one be in love? To be so embedded in the state that action and response are those of love, and so free of the self?"

Krishnaji said, "Can you know love? Obviously, that which you know is not love. To love is to be sensitive, vulnerable to everything. It is to be virtuous. Can virtue be studied? Any attempt to become virtuous, any effort, is to deny virtue."

A young civil servant said that some mystics maintained that by acknowledging a personal God, endowing that God with certain qualities and all-embracing love, and then surrendering the self to those qualities, the self ended.

"This implies the projection of the self in a preconceived conception of what the qualities of love are," said Krishnaji. "I say to know it you have to be in a state of not-knowingness. But to want to be in a state of not knowing is to desire a result, which you have already projected; for all that you know is the known. How can you go from the known to the unknown? Whatever you do from the state of the known will remain within the field of the known. What then happens?" The participants were absorbed by the clarity and lucidity of his words. "You do not seek a way out, because you do not know a way out. The moment you really see this, you are out—in a state of not knowing, receptive, ready to receive the unknown."

We also discussed the nature of perception, that through thought there is no exit from the routine of the mind, for thought was its bondage. Krishnaji asked, "Is it possible to have a mind that is totally empty, free of any flowing movement of the self? Can the forward and backward movement cease? In this is there not the dissolution of the self?"

At that moment the lights went out. In the darkness the atmosphere became charged, minds turned to darkness as an aid to emptiness and nothingness. Krishnaji suddenly stopped speaking. He said he would wait for the lights to come on. "In darkness the mind can hypnotize itself, imagine all kinds of states. This is dangerous. It is illusion."

It is these little incidents that reveal the integrity and immensity of a mind that refuses to compromise or allow any foothold.

Achyut Patwardhan, who was in Delhi, came regularly to see Krishnaji. He had been to see Dr. Gyanchand, a well-known economist at Delhi University, who had pronounced Socialist views. Gyanchand had argued with Achyut on the nature and structural framework needed to establish the principles of equality in the constitution. He said that intellectual capacity had to be the criterion for leadership. Achyut asked Krishnaji whether this was the right approach. For Achyut, socialism implied the absence of hierarchies at all levels. By emphasizing hate and bitterness, Marxism had failed to see this. Krishnaji asked, "Can there be an approach that wipes away intellectual or capacity differences?"

"Socialism," Achyut said, "cannot merely be concerned with the economic needs of man. The economic struggle must create capacity differences, unless the basis was an equality of spirit."

Someone brought up the story of Krishna raising a hunchbacked woman to dignity. "How can such a psychological raising be brought about? Can there be a transformation at the root of the mind, and so outside the preview of capacity differences?"

Krishnaji asked, "Is the problem not one of refusing to accept a leader? This alone brings equality in social and economic relationships. When thrown on his own responsibility, man will inevitably question. And in questioning there is no higher, no lower. Any system based on acceptance of capacity differences to establish status must inevitably lead to a hierarchical society, and so breed class war."

Krishnaji later asked me, "What is it that gives dignity to man? Self-knowledge—the knowledge of what you are? The follower is the greatest curse."

# CHAPTER 14

# "Under the Last Rays of the Sun, the Waters Were the Color of Newborn Flowers."

In 1949 Krishnaji was to discover the flavor of India: the splendor of its rivers, mountains, and countryside; its squalor, poverty, and sorrow; and the dust of the paths on which barefoot sages and seekers had walked for centuries. He was feeling into the Indian mind that dwelt in abstractions and delighted in ideas; he was growing intensely aware of the shadows that separated the ideal from action.

From Delhi he traveled by train to Varanasi. A man sharing his compartment, interested in death and physical phenomena, questioned Krishnaji on the truth of death and on continuity. As the train came to a stop at a local station, an interesting thing happened.

"The train had come to a stop," said Krishnaji, "and just then a two-wheeled carriage was passing, drawn by a horse. On the carriage was a human corpse, wrapped in an unbleached cloth and tied to two long green-bamboo poles, freshly cut. From some village it was being taken to the river to be burnt. As the carriage moved over the rough road the body was being brutally shaken, and under the cloth the head was obviously getting the worst of it. There was only one passenger in the carriage besides the driver; he must have been a near relative, for his eyes were red with much crying. The sky was the delicate blue of early spring and children were playing and shouting in the dirt of the road. Death must have been a common sight, for everyone went on with what they were doing. Even the inquirer into death did not see the carriage and its burden."[1]

The house in which Krishnaji lived at Rajghat in Varanasi, the luminous city of pilgrimage, was built on the site of ancient Kasi on the high ground that arose near the Sangam, the confluence of the rivers Ganga and Varuna. It was here, at the most sacred point of its journey to the sea, that the river took a great curve and swept north towards its source. It was here near the ancient site of the temple Adi Kesava that the Buddha, having attained enlightenment at Bodh Gaya, is likely to have crossed the sacred river, traveling by ferry, to set foot on the riverbank. Along this ancient road of the pilgrim the Buddha had walked to the deer park at Saranath to preach his first sermon. The river Varuna bifurcated the land, dividing urban Varanasi from the rural countryside.

Through centuries the seers of this land had come to the banks of the Ganga in Kasi and left the seed of their teaching dormant in the soil. The Buddha, Kapila Muni, Adi Shankara—these great teachers had sat under the shade of ancient gnarled trees, on the *ghats* or along the riverbank. The villages had names that bore testimony to their presence.

A city known for learning and seeking, for skepticism and doubt and the hard brilliance of the dialectic mind, it was to Kasi that Adi Shankara had come to establish his supremacy. Through the centuries iconoclasts had swept through the city, destroying temples and shrines; but the seed of doubt, of enquiry, and the essence of the great teachings, which resided neither in temple nor in a single book, had been held by scholars and priests. In secret conclave, they kept alive and resonant the petals of a perennial wisdom. Along the banks of this river dialogue and a probing into the "within" of nature and mind had evolved.

Mango and neem trees, flowering cork and peepul grew on the Ganga's sacred banks. Ruins of temples and *ashrams* were overgrown with plumed grass and wild creeper. Every dawn Krishnaji stood in darkness on the veranda of his house and watched fire enter the rising sun, creating the world anew. A boat floated past, its sails unfurled. Swollen carcasses—human and animal, vultures sitting perched on their bodies—were carried by the waters. Everything was in slow motion, peaceful; the monsoon currents had ended with their frenzy and devastation, the waters like the poor people who lived on its banks had dignity, whatever their burden.

Achyut and Rao Sahib Patwardhan, Maurice Friedman, Sanjeeva Rao, Nandini, and I with Radhika, my ten-year-old daughter, were in Varanasi. Every evening we went for a walk with Krishnaji on the road of the pilgrim. The white flowers of the cork trees that bordered the road to the riverbank had scattered their fragrance, and perfect white blossoms lay under our feet. The rains had been plentiful; the river had overflown its banks and the rickety bamboo-and-earthen bridge that appeared during the dry months had not yet been erected. We had to cross the river by ferry, plied by a boatman. The sense of the never-changing rhythm of man's life was revealed in Kasi. A sense of the archaic permeated the land and the people. The unending past was mirrored in the lithe, dark-skinned boatmen on the waters, the women carrying water pots on their heads, the fishermen casting nets.

One evening, a dozen little children and goats stood with their herdsmen, waiting for the ferry on the banks of the river. Krishnaji picked up a baby goat, the gesture swift, natural; his leap into the boat was sure and precise; the children laughed to see the little goat wag its tail and nestle close to the gentle stranger. We crossed the river and the bleating goat went back to its mother.

Seeing a stone on the path, Krishnaji would remove it so that it might not hurt the naked foot of a villager. He was watchful, listening to the sounds of the river, watching people who passed, the waters, trees, birds, and the village dogs who barked incessantly. He would be quiet and we would be quiet with him.

On one of his walks he spoke. "Man is, because he is related; without relationship, man is not. To understand life you have to understand yourself in action, in relationship to people, property, and ideas."

He turned and pointed to the flowing river and then to an old peepul tree. "Most of us are not aware of our relationship to nature. When we see a tree we see it with a utilitarian view—how to get to its shade, how to use its wood. Similarly, we treat the earth and its products. There is no love of the earth, only a usage of earth. If we loved the earth there would be frugality of the things of the earth. We have lost a sense of tenderness, of sensitivity. Only in the renewal of that can we understand what is relationship. That sensitivity does not come by hanging a few pictures or by putting flowers in your hair. It only comes when the utilitarian attitude is put aside. Then you no longer divide the earth, then you no longer call the earth yours or mine."

Krishnaji was giving public talks at Kammacha in the heart of the city. As in all his talks the people who attended were Buddhist monks, *sannyasis*, the devotees from the Theosophical Society who still regarded Krishnaji as the world teacher, tourists, educators, and a large number of young people who came out of curiosity. The great *pandits* of Varanasi, steeped in the tradition of learning, grammarians and logicians, tantricks and devotees, were also there to listen to this teacher who denied all systems and all gurus. Some of them met him alone. Little discussion was possible, because of difficulties of language, but Rao and Achyut were there to translate.

Krishnaji had numerous discussions with the members of the Rishi Valley Trust, who managed the schools in Varanasi. We discussed the place of authority and fear in education. Krishnaji expressed his dissatisfaction with the approach of the management of the educational institutions and the quality of the teachers at Rajghat. No one quite understood what had to be done. Pandit Iqbal Narain Gurtu, a much respected citizen of Varanasi, who for years had been connected with Mrs. Besant's work and later with Krishnaji's schools, was fearful of change. He dug his feet into the ground and declared that any drastic change would be disastrous. Uttar Pradesh was old fashioned, traditional. Only gradual change was possible. The word "gradual," however, did not exist in Krishnaji's dictionary; action was immediate, arising out of seeing the fact of "what is." So there were marathon meetings.

The Rishi Valley Trust was being shaken to its roots. The members, sensing Krishnaji's concern at the state of the institutions, submitted their resignations and a new group of members were elected.

In 1948 the Rishi Valley Trust consisted of two independent institutions—a Children's School at Rajghat, a Boys' School and a Women's College in the city, within the Theosophical Society Compound. Another educational complex had been established in the deep south at Rishi Valley in Andhra Pradesh, where Subha Rao was head of a co-educational residential school. Subha Rao, a dedicated man capable of arousing affection and loyalty amongst his students, had built the school with spartan simplicity. Krishnaji's absence for many years, and the lack of a clear direction as to the purpose of the school, had led to a deterioration of standards at all levels in both Rishi Valley and Rajghat. The teachers were mediocre. Government grants limited all flexibility or possibility of change. Vested interests were entrenched and determined to see that the status quo continued.

On his return to Bombay from Varanasi in March, Krishnaji stayed at my residence, Himmat Nivas on Dongersey Road. It was a rambling flat with spacious rooms and high ceilings. The spaces had dignity, and Krishnaji filled it with his presence; a quietude lingered even when he was absent.

A large number of visitors came to meet Krishnaji. Amongst them was Morarji Desai, who was then finance minister of Bombay, a state that at the time included both Gujarat and Maharashtra. Krishnaji and he discussed the sacred books of India. Sensing a certain smugness and "holier than thou" attitude in Morarjibhai,* Krishnaji said that he had not read the *Bhagavad Gita* and had no use for sacred books. Morarjibhai was horrified, and told me later that he was unimpressed.

Krishnaji now felt strongly that the existing situation with the Rishi Valley Trust and the schools in Rajghat should not be allowed to continue. At a meeting on February 8, 1949, Krishnaji was to say, "A school born of friction cannot be creative. Unanimity amongst the workers is essential. The school should be treated as an organic whole. There should be concern with how to make the center alive. A dead center can only produce dead institutions. If people are really interested, Rajghat cannot remain with the status quo."

It was at this meeting that the decision was taken that Rao Sahib Patwardhan would go and work in Rajghat. He went there a few months later. The situation needed deep uprooting of crystalized structures, mentally and physically. Rajghat needed an explosion. But Rao Sahib was hesitant. Either he was not prepared passionately to locate the problem, giving it the one pointed energy the situation demanded, or he did not know how to tackle the problem. His mind, caught in structures, sought alternatives. He did not perceive that the negating of the existing situation would throw up the new. Energy, with its driving passion, and a cleaving vision were needed in Rajghat. Rao Sahib made friends, he was warm and affectionate, everyone loved him; Iqbal Narain Gurtu, the tough doyen of Rajghat, was his close friend. But something in his personal life, or his incapacity to abandon his ideals and live in uncertainty, made any creative action impossible. At the end of the year Rao Sahib returned to Poona, and Rajghat continued to be a mirror of the stagnation that had held Varanasi for centuries.

One morning in early 1949 a tiny, shaven-headed figure dressed in saffron robes rang the bell at the doors of Himmat Nivas. She gave her name as Chinmoyee. The servant who had answered the bell could

---

*Bhai* means brother in Gujerati. It is a suffix attached to the name of an elder person as a term of respect. In Western India a first name is rarely used for a man or woman. In Gujerat, *bhai* is used with the first name for a man, *behen* or sister for a woman. It is the equivalent of the North Indian *'ji'*.

not tell whether it was a boy or a girl, and came to me to say that a swami was at the door. Knowing Krishnaji's special affection for the *sannyasi* and for the saffron robe, I told K and he met Chinmoyee immediately. She was to return again.

The story of her life symbolizes one important aspect of the Indian ethos, in which the revolutionary spirit and religion integrate. Chinmoyee, whose original name was Tapas, came from a family of Bengali revolutionaries. Her father and brother had died in jail. Her mother had worked in an educational institution and brought up her two daughters. According to a close friend of Tapas, "She was a brilliant mathematician and a keen student of astronomy."

After graduating, she was for some time headmistress of the Sister Nivedita School in Calcutta. She had always wanted to lead a religious life, and after her mother's death, at the age of thirty-four, she left home in search of a *sannyas* guru. She spent some time in the Ramakrishna Mission, and six months in Anandmai Ma's *ashram*. Life in these places did not satisfy her. She spent her time in Varanasi meeting scholars like Gopinath Kaviraj and Gobind Gopal Mookherjee.

It was at this time that she met the great scholar saint of Bengal, Anirvanji. He agreed to be her *sannyas* guru and gave her the name Chinmoyee. For the next four years she was with him, helping him first with his work of translating the *Vedas*, and then Shri Aurobindo's *Life Divine*, into Bengali. They were then living in Almora, in Uttar Pradesh. It was in connection with collecting funds for the publication of Anirvanji's works that she went to Bombay. A friend suggested she go to hear Krishnamurti, who was then giving talks in Bombay. She went to hear him and then sought an interview.

That interview seems to have changed her whole being—it certainly changed her whole life. Back in Almora, she proceeded to arrange affairs for Anirvanji; and as soon as she could hand over her duties to another, she left him. She resumed her original name, Tapas, and gave up the saffron robes.

Completely on her own, some inner urge prompted her to undertake a trip to Kailash and Manasarovar Lake in Tibet that first summer, sacred sites of pilgrimage. Kailash, a cone-shaped mountain, is regarded as the abode of Shiva and his consort Parvati. Manasarovar Lake is situated to one side of Kailash. The azure waters of this lake are calm, and mythical swans are believed to appear on its waters. The journey to Kailash is fraught with great dangers. (The route to Kailash from the Tibetan side has recently been opened to pilgrims by the Government of China.) Alone and unaccompanied, she set out on a most hazardous journey through passes over 18,000 feet high, joining a party of pilgrims only when she was no longer permitted to travel alone.

In 1950 she returned to see Krishnaji. She was unrecognizable: Wearing a white *kurta* and pyjama, her gray-flecked hair had grown shoulder length. She came to Krishnaji and said, "I have come." He replied, "Good"; and she slowly became part of his surroundings.

In the years to come she would travel to every part of India where Krishnaji spoke: in time she began to look after Krishnaji's wardrobe. She would slip into the house unnoticed and make herself invisible— even to the extent of hiding behind doors—unpack Krishnaji's bags, wash and iron his clothes, arrange them in the cupboard, and potter around. Though Tapas herself only wore white, she had developed a fine sense of color. It was she who got her friends to buy natural honey-colored cottons and textured bark-colored wild silks for Krishnaji's *kurtas*. She transformed his wardrobe with an unusual eye for the rare and beautiful. But she was fiercely possessive of her role. The slightest disorder in the room was corrected and the servants concerned were spoken to severely. They regarded her as a terror; but Tapas, being a *sannyasin*, wiped away all irritation or anger within them. They touched her feet and carried on. She sat through discussions but never participated, though her friends tell me that she had deep understanding of the teaching and used to speak to small groups wherever she went.

When Krishnaji was not in India she would disappear into the mountains alone, unafraid—in the centuries-old tradition, she was a wanderer. It was impossible to determine her age. In the twenty-five years I knew her she hardly aged. She eventually fell ill with an illness that could not be diagnosed. Her body gradually wasted away, and she died of a heart attack in 1976.

Nandini's problems with her husband, Bhagwan Mehta, were approaching crisis. A few months after meeting Krishnaji, she had told her husband she wanted to lead a celibate life. Inevitably, the situation exploded. Sir Chunilal Mehta was bewildered, torn between his son and his guru; for it was universally believed that Krishnaji's teaching had influenced Nandini and led her to cease her physical relationship with her husband. It was assumed that Nandini was immature and that her intention was born out of this immaturity. Sir Chunilal sought Krishnaji's intervention, hoping that Krishnaji would persuade Nandini to change her mind; or, given time and with Krishnaji's absence,

Nandini's capricious decision would change. But the situation could not be defused.

It is not my intention to explore the marital incidents that were to lead to an explosion in my sister's home. The situation was made for whispers and gossip, and the "elite" in the vast metropolitan city were agitated. Men looked afresh at their wives, the clans closed in. The eyes of the dwellers of Malabar Hill turned to the huge, rambling house on Ridge Road, furnished with the trappings of a rich merchant prince, rich for generations, where women kept their heads covered and singing was taboo. Lady Chunilal, Nandini's mother-in-law, was a wizened old lady with a grim, tightly shut mouth and few words. She had told Nandini after her marriage that a woman's voice should not be heard, and that she was not supposed to laugh; she could smile, so long as her teeth were not seen. And above all, the eyes of the city turned to Krishnamurti.

On the night of the festival of Holi, when the fires had been lit, the situation between husband and wife exploded. Her children were taken from her, and Nandini fled. At midnight she came to my mother's house, hardly a hundred yards from the house of Sir Chunilal Mehta. Bruised in spirit and body, anguished by the loss of her children, the next morning she came to Krishnamurti.

Due to leave within the next few days, he told her, "Stand alone. If you have acted out of the depths of self-knowing because you feel in yourself that what you have done is right, then throw yourself on life. Its water will hold you, carry you, and sustain you. But if you have been influenced, then God help you. The guru has disappeared."

Nandini was penniless. Her children had been taken away from her and she had little support, for my father was dead. She had either to go back to her husband, or separate and face the consequences. My mother, struggling against events that were destroying her, went to Krishnaji and spoke to him of her burden she felt unable to carry. He told her to lay down her burdens. K said they were his responsibility. She wept, but his words had quenched her fears.

Aware of the consequences that would follow any move toward legal separation, I went to Krishnaji and told him that although Nandini had decided that she would not return to her old home, under no circumstances could we allow any legal action, which would be necessary to settle the question of the custody of the children. I said that as Nandini's husband had no other excuse, Krishnaji's name was bound to be brought in as having influenced Nandini in her action of renouncing sex. He looked at me a long time and then he asked, "Are you trying to protect me?" He then raised his two arms in a significant gesture. "There are far greater beings who protect me. Do not falter, do what is right for Nandini and the children. The children are important. It does not matter whether she wins or loses, if it is right, fight."

Soon Nandini filed a suit against her husband for legal separation and custody of the children, on the grounds of cruelty. Her daughter was nine, her elder son seven, and the youngest son three years old. The case came up for hearing in the autumn of 1949. By then Krishnaji had come back from Ojai—first to Madras, and later he was in Ceylon and then Rajamundry, Andhra Pradesh. Long passages from Krishnaji's public talks were quoted by Bhagwan Mehta's lawyers. Krishnaji had pointed out in the talks at Bombay and Poona the hypocrisy of Indian society, the moral stances of religious teachers and householders, the inferior position of the woman and her bondage to her husband and his family. Krishnaji had been passionate, earnest, deeply concerned. A number of women had sought interviews with him in Bombay, Poona, and Madras and had voiced their anguish, their sorrows, and their inability to break free.

The lawyers attempted to prove influence, and used these teachings to strengthen their case. It was a grotesque situation. A wife was suing her husband for legal separation and long passages from religious sermons were being presented as evidence.

Nandini's father-in-law, though he supported his son, was not prepared to say a word against his guru. When, during the cross-examination, he was asked whether he resented Nandini's association with Krishnaji, Sir Chunilal Mehta jumped from his chair and said in a loud voice, "Never, he is the greatest of the great."

According to him it was Nandini, aided and abetted by her sister, Pupul Jayakar, who were at fault. He pointed to Nandini's misbehavior in Poona. When questioned, he said that in Poona the sisters laughed a great deal and Nandini did not cover her face with her *sari* and had insisted on sitting to the right of Krishnaji. Her behavior, according to Sir Chunilal Mehta, had caused anxiety amongst the elders around Krishnaji.

But throughout the hearings not one word was said that was suggestive or improper. The emphasis was on influence and its role on a young immature mind.

The judge in the Bombay High Court listened to the arguments and the counterarguments in Nandini's plea for separation. Justice Weston was a Bombay civilian, and for him it was unthinkable that any violence could occur in the renowned family of Sir Chunilal Mehta, K.C.S.I.*

My father, who had lived his life in what was then the United Provinces, was dead, and his family little known in Bombay. The judge held that the plea for separation on grounds of cruelty was not proved in the High Court of Bombay, and the complaint was dismissed. The children, who were under temporary custody with Nandini, were taken away by her husband. We sent a telegram to Krishnaji, giving him the news. In his reply, he said, "Whatever will be is right."

Several queries had arisen amongst people close to Krishnaji whether he should speak during February and March of 1950 in Bombay. Nandini had appealed the dismissal of her suit by Justice Weston to the Bombay High Court, and the city was still astir with gossip.

It was finally decided in consultation with Ratansi Morarji that Krishnaji should speak in Bombay. He wrote from Madras on December 19. "So you can go and make necessary arrangements. If possible, not a hall, but an open space, *not* a rich man's house, this time. Isn't there some quiet open space, a pleasant spot, central and all that? Halls are terrible and I don't feel comfortable in them."

At the time, no open spaces were available. We arranged for his public meetings on the terrace of Sunderbai Hall, which was open to the sky. The number of people attending the public meetings had doubled, but the rich socialites and industrialists with their wives were conspicuously absent.

On his return to Bombay, Krishnaji met many of his old associates. There was no special sympathy in his attitude to Nandini. He met her alone several times, and refused to allow her space in the mind for self-pity. He was relentless in his demand that she face the fact that one life was over and she had to awake to the new. But his concern and compassion for Nandini's children was limitless. Whenever possible, Nandini—without the knowledge of her ex-husband—would bring the children to see Krishnaji. He would lay his hands on the eyes of the elder boy, who had been told by the doctors that he would never see normally, as the optic nerve of one eye had not developed. The eye improved and, in years to come, Ghanashyam Mehta was to take his doctorate in economics from the University of California at Berkeley, and would later teach in Australia at the University of Brisbane.

---

*Knight Commander of the Star of India, one of the highest titles awarded by the British.

Rao Sahib and Achyut were in Bombay and came every morning to Ratansi's house to see Krishnaji. The master was determined to kindle an awakening in Rao. One morning when we had gathered, Krishnaji said in the midst of a discussion, "Let us see whether we can stay in the pause between two thoughts." Rao Sahib looked skeptical, Achyut wary. Krishnaji began to challenge Rao's mind, refusing to let it escape into concepts. Krishnaji was pushing Rao, blocking the mind, forcing Rao to do nothing with it, to see "what is."

We were in the same stream as Rao; the refusal to let thought escape, or to change it, created an intensity of energy in the mind. On an instant, unable to wander, held by the energy of the question, the mind let go and there it was: the poise, the no-wandering, the end of thought, and of the sense of time as duration.

Rao's expression, which had been blank and stubborn in its refusal to be carried away by Krishnaji, suddenly lit up. His face relaxed and there was clarity in his eyes.

Krishnaji did this again and again; breaking through the frontiers of consciousness, through thought ending itself, finding no door through which to escape.

We took Krishnaji by motorboat to the Elephanta Caves. It was a night of the full moon; a night when the planet Mars was to vanish behind the moon for a minute; to reemerge with unsullied brilliance.

The rays of the setting sun penetrated and revealed the colors held in the rock. Out of the twilight of the cave loomed the face of the three-headed god, with eyes that were neither open nor closed; still eyes awake to the outer and inner. The lower lip was full and sensuous. Out of the rising sound of the archaic Sanskrit chants, the sculptor had created the meditation of the universe. Krishnaji stood before the sculpture, silent for a long time. He then turned and said he would have liked to have spent a night in the cave. Rao Patwardhan suddenly started to chant Sankaracharya's hymn to Shiva; that "Being" that is, when all qualities are negated. Krishnaji, deeply aroused by the quality of sound, was in a state of ecstasy. As we returned to the boat, he kept asking Achyut, where it had gone, the energy and creativity that had made manifest the Maheshmurti?* Why was India so dead to all creation?

---

*The "Maheshmurti" (seventh century A.D.) is a soaring image in stone of Shiva as the great god, sculptured with three faces—the creator, the preserver, and the destroyer—symbolizing the three aspects of the supreme godhead. The Maheshmurti is carved within a vast cave and surrounded by sculptures depicting episodes from Shiva's myths. Sound and form become one to create this sublime manifestation.

The moon was rising as we walked back. Children from the village had gathered, offering us flowers and asking for money. Krishnaji tried to talk to them; showed them his empty pockets, turned to us and wished us to give them some money. He laughed with them and, taking the hand of a little child, walked with him to the boat. In the boat we all tried to glimpse Mars emerging from behind the moon. Krishnaji went on the top deck and at last saw it, a minute speck. "There it is!" he cried excitedly, like a child.

In the morning meetings Krishnaji probed deeper and deeper and we could move with him. The mind felt fluid. I heard the words without verbal responses—there was a flowing of sound, word, and content. I could actually have counted the number of thoughts that arose in those two hours we spent with Krishnaji every morning.

# CHAPTER 15

# "The Mind Operating as Part of the Whole Is Endless."

While Krishnaji was in Bombay, a small group of people consisting of Rao Sahib, Achyut, Maurice Friedman, the Honorable Mrs. Lucille Frost (an Englishwoman and a long-time student of Jung who had met Krishnaji while in Sri Lanka and accompanied him to India), Nandini, and I soon gathered to hold discussions with Krishnaji. From these discussions were to emerge the first of the series of Krishnaji's great Indian dialogues. A new dimension was being added to his teaching, a movement which in its momentum was to free the mind from its old grooves.

We had been discussing the mind and memory, and Krishnaji raised a question. He had awoken in the night at about three o'clock, feeling a surge of joy that exploded within him. It seemed to spring from the heart of silence. He lay in bed with it, and then consciousness arose and the experience had been named. The mind-consciousness remembered. How did the mind, which was absent in the experiencing of that state, remember?

It was suggested that the superior mind had experienced the joy and the silence. Krishnaji said, "Any postulation of a superior mind is but another projection of the mind. The suggestion is hardly adequate. Either that state of silence was false—a projection of the mind—or it was real." He paused. "How did the mind remember? The mind is cause and effect, it is caught in time, it has a beginning and an end. Mind can never experience that which is without cause, the timeless, that which has no beginning and no end. The state this morning was without cause. How did the mind, which is both cause and effect, limited, remember the causeless—the limitless?"

Someone suggested that what the mind remembered was not the experience, but the waking from it. Krishnaji said, "In silence what is there to experience? Silence can only experience silence. Can silence leave an imprint?"

Perhaps, then, what the mind felt was the glow of being dipped in the silence. Krishnaji said, "There is an experience of silence and the mind remembers the feel, the perfume, the essence; how does the mind remember? Consciousness is the thought of the moment before, or the moment after. Thought is always of the moment or many moments before. Thought is the result of a stimulus." He let his words sink in, let the mind of his listeners ponder, move with him.

"We live in cause and effect, constantly rearranging them. We reject our background, our past of yesterday and of thousands of years, without being even aware that the past we reject is an aspect that lies deep within. And so the background remains undiscovered and is always in conflict, in contradiction.

"Do we see that consciousness is never in the 'now,' that it is always a projection, a backward or forward movement? That it is never in the present."

He was asked, "How does man understand this?" "Understanding of the 'now' can never be through thought, through consciousness," Krishnaji replied. He looked at Rao Sahib. "What is the state of the mind when it sees this?"

"The mind refuses to accept it as a fact," said Rao.

"But it is a fact. The mind cannot understand the 'now' which is the new. It is a fact, like a wall is a fact. What do you do when you are faced with a wall? You do not say you cannot accept it as a fact. What happens when you see as a fact that the mind cannot understand the 'now?' What is the state of your mind?"

"It is silent—thought has ceased," I offered.

"Go into it. What happens when the mind sees the fact that thought has ceased and yet there is movement, a freedom?"

"I see it and thought has ceased, and yet I hear your voice, a sensory perception continues."

"I see you. I hear your voice. Mind as thought is not there and yet sensory perception continues, is present. Only identification has ceased." said Krishnaji.

The next morning we again discussed consciousness.

First comes the layer of everyday activity—eating, going to the office, drinking, meeting people, the conditioned habits that operate automatically. It is obviously a static state that conforms to a pattern.

When one's routine is disturbed, this surface layer ceases for an instant and what is below reveals itself. For convenience we will call this the second layer (of course, since consciousness is nonspatial, it cannot be accurate to use terms indicating layer or level). The thinking that emerges from this layer is still conditioned memory, but it is not as automatic as the surface layer. It is more active, more elastic; it has more nuances. Here thought need not conform so completely to pattern, it has more vitality. The next layer is conditioned by like, dislike, choosing, judging, identifying. Here there is the sense of the ego established and in focus.

At this point Krishnaji stopped and said, "How have you been listening? How do you enquire? How does the mind function?"

"I have been dramatizing it," said Rao.

"I have been watching my responses," I said.

Krishnaji's response was immediate. "No, you are wrong."

"Surely, what else can you do?" queried Rao. And then one grew aware of the intensity of Krishnaji's awareness, how he listened to every response; Krishnaji's mind sensed that our watching was another repetition, another memory. He simply knew whether the state one spoke of was born of insight or was another repetition.

Krishnaji said, "I have not been thinking about it. There has been no delving into the past, into memory to find the next response. The responses have arisen by the very perception of the fact." He pushed further.

"Next come the unconscious memories of the individual and the collective, the tendencies, the forces, the urges, the racial instincts; this is the whole network of desire, the matrix of desire. There is an extraordinary movement here. The ego is still functioning—ego as desire moving in its patterns of cause and effect. The ego as desire that continues. The ego with its unconscious tendencies that reincarnate. Let us push still further." He paused and pondered. "Can we push further? Is there anything further? Is it that the known dimension has ended? Is this the bedrock of the ego? Is this the structure of consciousness, of the mind and its content?"

Someone asked, "What sustains it?"

Krishnaji was silent. After a few moments, he said, "Its own movement, its own functioning. What lies below? How can one proceed, go beyond the matrix?"

"Shut off the mind," said Rao.

"Who shuts off the mind? He who is the mind?" Krishnaji responded swiftly. "Then what is the way? Seeing the fact of consciousness—not the word, not the theory, but the fact of it—is ending not possible? Again, whatever I do to move toward the other is of effort and so destroys it. I cannot desire it. I can do nothing except be indifferent to it. And concern myself with the ego, with what I am, and my problems."

One morning Krishnaji said, "Can we go into consciousness again? Yesterday we had gone into it from the point on the periphery to the center. It was like going down a funnel. Could we today go from the center to the point on the periphery? Could we move from the inward out? Could we approach consciousness from the center?"

"Is there a center?" asked Rao.

"The center is only when there is focusing of attention. The center is formed when periphery is agitated. The center is formed as a point on the periphery. These peripheral points are one's name, one's property, one's wife, fame. These points are constantly being strengthened. There is movement all the time at the peripheral points. There is a constant fear of the breaking of these points."

"Can I live without the formation of centers?" asked Rao.

"If I start from the center, to investigate, where is the center from which to start? There is no center, but only the field. Except for the periphery there is no center. The fences to the field create the center. I only know the center because of the fence, the periphery. The fences are the points of attention, the limits that create the center. Remove these fences. Where is the center?"

"Can one remove the fences?" I queried.

"If you move in the field, in the non-center, there is no memory. See what happens as you move from field towards fence. As you approach the fence, memory begins.

"So far we have been thinking from the periphery to the center. The thinking from this (non-center) must be totally different. I have to get used to the movement from within towards the periphery."

"What happens to the points?" I asked.

"It is like slipping under and through fences. The fences no longer matter. To see the point at the periphery is to see no point at all. What we do, however, is to jump immediately into the periphery, into the habitual. I cannot form a habit of that which has no center.

"To go from the periphery to the center is to stick in the center. When attention becomes identified it becomes the point. Thinking in habit is the movement of the periphery. There is no point from which I can recognize point. To know the center it must be related to point. I can only know it if I approach it from the periphery.

"The more I stay in the field, I see there is no center."

The next morning the discussion continued. We asked Krishnaji, "What is the periphery? How is it formed? How are fences made? Are they different material from the pointless center?"

"Why do you stay at periphery? Why cannot you stay in the field, seeing its flora and fauna, its perfume? Why are you concerned with the fence?" he responded.

"I have been torturing myself to find out. The whole thing seems un-understandable. Achyut told me that I should take it playfully," said Mrs. Frost.

"You are taking time, effort, why?" asked Krishnaji.

"Because my mind is like a stone wall."

"Why? What is wrong? Listen to what is wrong," said Krishnaji.

"My thoughts," Mrs. Frost responded.

"Which means you have a pattern in which you want it explained. Your words are hindering you. The stone wall of ideas, words to which you are accustomed. Why don't you let go?"

"I don't know how," Mrs. Frost protested.

"Why? To you, thinking is important. You are lost when you cannot think along your grooves. Forget all that, play with it. See if we can start, not from the stone wall but from the non-center. What is the difficulty?"

"I am perfectly aware we have not got to that stage." Mrs. Frost was agitated.

"There is no stage. Why do you hold on to the periphery and then want to go to the center? Wipe out the state. It is too full at the pe-riphery. Let it go. Begin as if you were entering a new room. You see periphery and want to proceed to create center. You call it God and approach it. But there is no center without periphery. You cannot think apart from the thinking habit. You can never think anew. Difficulty lies not in the field, but with the periphery. It is the simple mind that sees this."

"From the periphery it is like seeing through a telescope. Being in the field is fluidity," commented Nandini.

"What is the point? Identified attention? What is the fence? What is the fence when you approach it from the pointless point? It is stoppage of movement. If there is the flowing field, is not the field of the same quality as movement arrested, as the fence? The stoppages of movement are points along the fence. I am still inside the field.

"Yesterday after the discussion I slept. As I was beginning to wake up, there was a coming from afar to a point of elaborate design. I lay watching design—it took me a long time to watch it. Then it disappeared and I came to. Movement when arrested forms design, becomes point from which I act. Sorrow is the result of stoppage of movement and the movement away from it. If I see that the point is of the same substance as the field, there is no struggle. If there is a living in the pointless center, the stoppage is the point. It is in fighting point with point that we strengthen it," said Krishnaji.

"What creates point? Is it that the same fluid crystalizes?" I asked.

"Is it subject to pressure—to a counterforce?" asked Rao.

"Is not your flow and my flow the same?" said Krishnaji.

Friedman asked, "Why does the impediment arise? Is it unreal, false?"

"Why does it happen? Twenty things are happening around me. Sometimes there is extensive seeing; sometimes it is limited," said Rao.

"No center meets impediment, nervous responses of the body. Why not? These may be just body reactions. You ask me a question and I answer you according to my conditioning—which arrests the flow. This conditioning is the result of the environment acting on the body and its responses. If the flow is arrested—I accept arrestation—life is like that," said Krishnaji.

"What is arrestation?" asked Rao.

"It is attention focusing. The river suddenly comes between two banks and the flow narrows down.

"The field has no point, no limit; it is vast and limitless. Focused attention is the narrowing down. Why do we stay there at the point? That is the question. The moment you ask me something, a point must form. But why do we allow it to crystalize?" He was silent and then spoke slowly, telling us to contact his mind.

"The vast field has no positive state. In solidity there is the positive. The non-center state is negation. This negation is challenged and there is positive action. This positive state creates its opposite."

"Has the positive state its own momentum?" asked Rao.

"The real solution lies in a field of negation. If we move away from this field we are lost. If we enter the point to examine it, we are lost. Look at it from the field of negation. Why does crystalization take place?" He paused, questioning himself. "Is this a wrong question? Crystalization is inevitable, a fact. My difficulty is, why does the mind stay in crystalization? When I see the negative approach I am free of crystalization, free of the point. I accept friction as inevitable and move on."

"Is it because we see our flow as separate that the trouble starts?" Rao asked.

"If negation was there it would have an answer. My problem is, why don't I stay in a state of negation? The danger is I am constantly weighing this with that. The fools enter the kingdom, not the cautious." said Krishnaji.

Krishnaji said, "What is the energy of the field? What place has energy in this we call consciousness? We know the activity of narrowing down. We know fear, want, sublimation, we know the various reasons and causes for identification.

"What is this energy? Obviously this energy has no enclosed space, no fence, no opposites. The field is energy."

"When we attempt to examine this energy the examiner becomes the point," said Rao.

"What is silence? Let us approach this energy differently. What is silence? Are you being silent? How do you find out what silence is? Are you being noisy? How do you know you are silent?"

"Silence is the pointless flow of the field," said Rao.

"Don't define it. Do I see silence? Do I experience it? Can I say as an observer, 'This is silence'?" asked Krishnaji.

"There is silence when I am not focused," said Rao.

"What do you mean by focused? Don't verbalize it. Just see what silence is and how you see it, how you experience it." Krishnaji was holding Rao's hand, moving with him into the pathless field.

"What is silence? How do you experience it? Don't do anything, just listen. Are you experiencing it or is there a state of silence which you are trying to describe?" He paused. "You see the difference? *See* what silence is."

"I am saying it is not a state to be got, so leave getting," said Achyut.

"You first make a picture, then fit things to the picture. Find out what silence is." Krishnaji was pushing.

"I can recollect times when there has been a state of silence," said Mrs. Frost.

"That is not silence. What is silence? I was asked what is energy, and I said there is a different approach to the problem. I say let us go into silence. That is the challenge. Now, what is silence? Do I have an image of it, or do I see it is there and because you ask me, I will communicate it to you?"

"Don't try to see or not see, just let go." Rao had touched the flow for an instant, was one with it.

"Leave your ideas and *see* what silence is." said Krishnaji. "Either I am imagining it or the state is there. I am not experiencing it. With you the mechanism operates immediately. Be simple, leave your mechanism. Why does it operate before silence?"

"The mind is so clever," said Achyut.

"That is no answer. Why does the mechanism come first? The moment I ask what is silence, your mechanism answers. How do you find silence? Surely not through the noise of the mechanism. So what do you do?"

"The fence begins with the mechanism," said Rao.

"Silence is there without end. I want to find out what energy is. It may be possible for it to function endlessly. But idea comes first and covers and frames silence. But silence has no end; things exist in it; they are part of it; they are not contradictory to silence. That child's crying is silence. When noise is within it, it is silence. If silence is extensive, noise is part of silence.

"Anything with its own mechanism contradictory to silence is not in silence. The mechanism as the observer looking at silence is contradictory to silence, is not silence. The idea of silence as exclusive is not silence. Anything separate may have its own energy, but is not part of expansive silence. By its movement separateness can create its own action and energy. The two energies are entirely different. The movement of a separate mechanism experiencing silence and noise in silence are entirely separate.

"Anything in silence that is not contradictory is extensive. Anything contradictory with its own energy is limited, and when the limited tries to find the extensive, there is no silence.

"I can live in silence and whatever I do is not contradictory, so long as I live in silence and do not resist it. Then everything is in it except resistance. It is resistance that creates its own whirlpool, like fire the flames leap to the skies."

"Is this silence the source of energy, without limit?" asked Rao.

"The moment it has limit, there is resistance," said Krishnaji.

"What is this state?" asked Rao.

"What is operating? In that state I smell these jasmines. I hear, I see. What is not in it? The exclusive, the contradiction, the idea which is always exclusive. Any form of resistance destroys this state.

"To me in silence, a cry is not exclusive, but the cry of the baby as an exclusive act is apart from the state of silence. Silence has no limit. When there is resistance there is exclusion; noise becomes exclusive, when the sensation forms a point which acts as a disturbance, it becomes a separate noise when you focus attention on it."

"This happens the moment a system of values begin to operate," said Friedman.

"The moment mind as idea operates it is contradiction. But this state needs extraordinary intelligence and integrity. Since this thing is limitless, it must be energy. Here it is limitless because there is no causation. The mind creates energy that has a cause and so an end. But silence is not of the mind, and so that energy has no limit." K stopped. Seeing our faces, he said, "Don't translate this to suit your mind. The mind cannot understand what is not of itself. But this is limitless. In this state everything is, but the things of the mind. In this state every noise is, and that is not noise. Then contradiction arises and mind arises and creates an exclusive pattern with its own energy."

Maurice Friedman said that he was experiencing a complete satiety. He felt that he was listening to Krishnaji through a mind that already knew what Krishnaji was going to say. He felt no newness. He felt he could not take it any more.

Rao Sahib said that though he did not feel satiated yet, he felt that he wanted to go away from Krishnaji. He felt that this sitting around was all wrong.

Nandini said she too felt the same. If she had understood Krishnaji, something must happen. She was waiting for it to happen and nothing was happening.

Achyut said he felt like Rao, and I said I felt dead, a complete sense of not functioning.

Krishnaji said, "It boils down to one thing. You are all waiting for something to happen. Some have technique but no urge, and they are waiting for the urge to act. Some have the urge but they have no technique, and so they too wait. Some feel dead, and they are waiting to be given life so that they can act.

"Why are you waiting and for what are you waiting? Are you waiting in order to act? You are not sure and you want proof before you act. How can you have proof? You have still not left the field of known action and known result.

"You want to be certain of the new before you act, and how can you be certain? You are not living, you are only waiting; that is not living. Rao has left his political action and is waiting; he is not living.

"So far you have been facing north, and I say to you turn round and face south. You want to face south without leaving the north.

"Why are you waiting? To be sure? Sure of what? That your action will be the new? But you are not living, waiting is death. Live, move, walk.

"I say to you, Rao, 'Look,' you have got it, walk.

"I feel something is happening. If I had a son I would like to share it. When you love you want to share, and I tell you Rao, hold out your hand. If you want it, you shall have it.

"When the little operates in the whole as part of the whole then the little is limitless. When it acts separately, then it is limited. The mind operating as part of the whole is endless."

"What is energy and can it be, so that it is continually free and operating—never limited?" Rao's face was aglow.

"If the mind does not limit it, then it is always limitless. Can action take place from there and not from the mind? What happens then to action? What is your action to the beggar on the street? Can you answer? No. But there will be action that will operate on him. As long as that operates there is no problem."

The next day Krishnaji was again to ask, "What is the problem? Instead of these flowers"—he pointed to a bowl of carnations before him—"put artificial flowers. You know which are real. These flowers have what nothing else has. What is the problem? What is missing between artificial and real?"

"They just are," said Rao.

"No, what is the central problem?"

"We refuse to see ourselves; becoming in our every breath," Achyut responded.

"I know all that, but what is missing? Take Rao, he is serious. He has the capacity to learn, to assimilate, he is capable of sacrifice. He has the faculty to gather facts, and he says, 'What am I to do? I am not the real flower.' Why has he become the artificial flower?"

"Why have I no song?" Rao spoke.

"Yes, why is there no flame? What is missing? We have no love, without it, do what you will, artificial will never make me real. We have cultivated intellect, which is the artificial flower. We have dug the real out from its roots. Now how is one to have love?

"Why haven't we got love? This demands extraordinary intelligence. Because I haven't got love I create temples and institutions." He pointed to the flowers before him. "That flower just opened; did you see it?"

Rao continued, "Love is missing and I keep on saying, I want a breath of it. I have not got love and I have spent my energy in making artificial flowers. What am I to do? Unless I have it, nothing else has meaning. Why don't I love?

"I know I exist on an artificial level. My brain can discuss anything, and yet I see I must have the other. How am I to get it?" asked Rao.

"What is the state of your mind when you say you see the artificial and are shocked? What is the state when you demand the other? There must be a way of unlocking the door. And there must be a way of receiving it. How? That is the real miracle. It cannot be put there. It must be something that cannot be undone. It is not a thing that continues. I cannot be concerned with it. I cannot create it.

"I can only act from the center, which is open to both cessation and the coming to be.

"I cannot try to hold it. The moment I say I must have an experience of it, it must always be there, I shut it out.

"I see falseness of the artificial, but I haven't got the real. What is happening to you when you see this? The moment I stop playing with the artificial, all efforts, all explanations have ended," said Krishnaji.

"All wanting, all yearning to do has ended. I feel relaxed, playful. I am not trying to catch up," said Rao.

"It means what, Sir? From what point of view are you seeing it? Is it free of reasoning?"

"To function without it is the only sin," said Friedman.

"So you are not going to play with the artificial. You may play with it, but you are out of it," said Krishnaji.

"We think that the first sign of sensitivity is to think, to reason. But to think is not have it. I act," said Rao. "My being feels conscious only when it is processed through thinking. This sucks away my vitality. I see this now very clearly."

Krishnaji said, "Can you be uncertain, hesitate between artificial flower and real? You will examine everything very carefully, you will be wary. It is only when you are not clear, that you will stumble.

"We began by saying we are dry. We carry with us a basket of the artificial. We have given the basket wrong values. You see this and put it aside. You are free of the basket, which is the artificial. What is your actual state?"

"All the inward wrinkles go. Inside one, the sense of getting at something goes. I am not dry," said Rao.

"You are not dry, which means you have a song. I want to know the state of inwardness, of being free."

"After three hours I see that it is the artificiality which is responsible for there being no warmth. In dropping artificiality, the scorching dryness has gone," Rao answered.

"It is difficult to communicate the quality that comes into being when in dialogue," I said. "There is an instant of understanding, of totally being one, a state where thought has ended and silence alone is awake."

Rao began, "Silence is not my normal consciousness, moments of silence are rare. A life based on action, response has not ended for me. I come on action which at the time I think is not a reaction. What is the difference between this action and action as challenge?"

Krishnaji answered, "The only test is whether it produces further reaction, whether there is continuity to it. If you are happy you would do the right thing. Action out of happiness is one thing. Action in a state of freedom from unhappiness has its own reaction; this is not the state of happiness. We don't know happiness which is not a reaction. We know happiness of reaction."

"I am unhappy and, having momentarily seen a state of being not unhappy, I am more unhappy. I want a mode of living which will free me," said Rao.

"Though I live in this world I want to live without unhappiness with its reactions. How am I to do it? I am not outside this pattern. I see it in all complexity. I live in that field. My problem is, I want to live in it completely anew, because I see the futility of pattern and its enlargement. I can't escape from it or run away from it. What am I to do in the pattern?" asked Krishnaji.

"The last few days my reflex actions are less. The urges and movements have died down. Voltage is so low. I have the feeling of not wanting anything. I want to sit by myself," said Rao.

"It is a feeling of shrinking," I added.

"The trouble is we are taken high and then we drop with a bang." This was Friedman's comment.

"Why do you soar and why do you shrink?" asked Krishnaji.

"Why do I come with a begging bowl? The begging bowl must go," said Rao.

"The begging bowl must go and I must live in the field with happiness. I will come to you, but I don't want to be dependent. What am I to do?"

"The voltage of life is so low, there is no joy," said Rao.

"Do you actually feel it, like a bucket that cannot hold water, which means you have no love? Why is it you haven't got it? Is it that emotionally your mind has lost its resilience, that you feel dead?"

"I am not dead. I still feel alive," answered Rao.

"Elasticity is there, but it is not reacting any more," said Krishnaji.

"There is the sense of an ebbing tide," said Rao.

"Is it that we have touched the bottom of things? Have you come to that, that you are nothing?" asked Krishnaji.

"You are saying that if there is no zest, you have reached the depth. The mind is so subtle. It will not see that," said Rao.

"Have you reached the bottom?" Krishnaji was pushing.

"In the darkness, I see a small ray of light, but it is still too dim to use," said Rao, hesitantly.

"Go with it," said Krishnaji.

"One is too aware to be anything of the old, but still one is not the new. Synthetic sensations have ceased, but happiness is not there."

"What are you to do? Let lie. It is like a field that has been sown and harvested, let it lie fallow now.

"I feel that there should be an explosion from within and not from outside. How am I to do it? I feel there is a clue to that mystery. If we can find it, we can pick it up. The last ten days something is happening to me, an extraordinary thing going on within me. I don't know where it is going. It is like a river moving. It is doing something physically. I haven't thought about it, and I ask why doesn't it happen in someone else? I have a feeling it is waiting. When I awoke something was happening. Why doesn't it happen to others? It is not a question of being clever or stupid. I know all the reasons that prevent you. But I say it is like going through something together. We have gone through this together. We can't do more. Now stretch out your hand and receive the certificate. It is really the same thing deeper down."

He turned to Nandini, "And I want to know why you don't pick it up. I say to you, bend down and pick it up.

"You know about the baby they have been bringing to me. The doctor had said its brain had not formed. It could not see, could not smile, could not recognize, and I have been touching it. Something is functioning very strongly in me.

"I feel a burning in my hand and the baby has begun to smile, to recognize people. You can do it. All you have to do is to pick it up. The thing that is operating in me will work with you as well, pick it up.

"It is no use saying you don't know how. I say to you, pick it up."

The dialogues ended, and Krishnaji prepared to return to Ojai. On March 10, at one of his last morning discussions, he spoke with great urgency of the need to penetrate the mechanics of his mind.

"I was thinking this morning if I could understand my own mind and the way it works, I could say to you, look carefully and you can have it.

"How does my mind work? Yesterday, when I spoke of meditation, was my brain working? If not, then what was working? My answers were logical. How did they arise? What happened? I said that the thought and the thinker were one. What was the mechanism that produced that thought? One can speculate and say it was the higher mind that was using me, Maitreya, that I am a sounding board; that would be a good Theosophical explanation. But that does not satisfy me.

"If I could show it to Achyut very clearly, he could have it. What is the thing operating? Yesterday, the moment Rao said 'point,' I said 'choice.' And who chooses? There is no step-by-step thinking, so what is operating?"

"This time I think I understand what Krishnaji is saying," said Rao. "Krishnaji is aware when people who listen to him are with him. But this would be the experience of any genuine person—with Krishnaji it is something more."

"To know an audience and to change, adjust, that is simple. Let us go a little beyond," said Krishnaji.

"What is the intellect that needs no books, no knowledge?" asked Rao.

"You are always new. There must be a creative source operating all the time. What is the nature of this source?" asked Friedman.

"You are in front of the wave, in front of consciousness. Are you conscious of that creative source?" said Rao.

"You are a trinity. There is Krishnamurti the man, just as he is; then he is the guru, pinching, coercing; then he is truth, the power 'which is.' They are not separate, but three aspects of the same truth. The question is, who is Krishnamurti?" asked Friedman.

"How would I set about getting this thing that is operating?" said Krishnaji.

Rao responded, "From the first day when you spoke of the movement, from pointless point, one saw that this state to you was a moment-to-moment reality. If one can remain there then conflict ends. If I see that, the quality of speaking is different."

"How does a man transmit the creative touch to another?" asked Krishnaji.

"This cannot be done except through identification," said Friedman.

"No, there is something operating through K which I would like to share. I know it is possible. I feel it is as possible as the sunshine," said Krishnaji.

"Are you drawing a current from a source not limited to you? If so, how can we tap the source?" Friedman was challenging Krishnaji.

"I feel from the beginning it was open to me. It has always been there. The distance getting clearer, clearer, closer—Why doesn't X get this? Would you have it if you kept near K all the time? I don't think so. I want to see how it works. I know how it works with me. This morning I woke with a feeling. There was no 'me' feeling. Tomorrow morning when I wake up there will be something new. It keeps going on all the time. When I talk it bursts out. There is never a storing up and then pouring out. With most people the storage is always the old. Here there is no storage, no safe. K wants you to have it. How is it to be done? Even if it is true that K was trained, that he is being used by Maitreya, that entity says to you, 'You should have it.' Admitting all the differences, that entity says, 'Come, you can have it.' He wants you to have it, therefore he abolishes all divisions. I feel that it is operating, I feel the field is open and some are in it.

"What is our problem? I have it, you don't, and I say you can have it. But if you ask, 'Have I got it? And what is the test? And is there a test? How can I know that I have it?'—then you are lost. For there is no test. You ask, 'Is this enough?' It is this asking for more that is the blockage.

"I say to Rao, 'Go out, try it.' I remember my first speech at Madurai. Dr. Besant said to me, 'My dear, your stance was alright, your gestures right, only you were too inexperienced. I know it is possible for you to have it. Go, start, speak, see what happens. Even if you make a mess, remain hesitant. With this you must be completely uncertain.' I say to you, you have got it. Go, open the door.

"This is so in my relationships. There is never a sense of coming back to a relationship. There are no anchorages, there is always a moving out.

"I have been told what I say today is different to what I said earlier and to what I was; and I will be different again. K is like that. K has no fixed points of return."

I met Krishnaji alone after the dialogues ended. He asked me how I was feeling. What had the five weeks of discussion done for me? I replied that I had been left with little self-volition. I was feeling very young within. It was like being reincarnated while still alive. I felt part of something that had to be. Things would happen to me, as was right and as they were meant to; there was little I could do.

I also told him of what had happened to me toward the end of the discussions on consciousness. The dialogue had generated an intense watching of the mind during the day; when I fell asleep, the observation continued. One night I had an explosive perception of the thinker and thought as one; there was blazing light and I fell into deep sleep. The second night the same watchful intensity and the perception of the observer and the observed as one, exploding light and deep sleep. The third night there was an instant when all thought was quenched, an immense light and then dreamless sleep. He heard me speak, but refused to give the experiences any importance. He said, "It is over, move." He then asked me what I was going to do. I said, "I do not know. I feel the urge to write. I also feel like doing nothing." He said, "Do nothing, see what happens."

# Part 3

## THE UNFOLDING OF THE TEACHING 1950–1959

# CHAPTER 16

# "Religion Comes When the Mind Has Understood the Workings of Itself."

On September 11, 1950, Krishnaji wrote to me from Ojai: "I have been here a good three weeks and need a long rest, as I have been talking for three years steadily. Also I have decided to go into complete retreat for a whole year without any interviews, public or private discussions or public talks. It will be more or less a silent year. So, I shall not be coming to India this winter."

His retreat was total. There were no meetings, no interviews. It was from Rajagopal that we heard Krishnaji was observing complete silence. From August 1950 to December 1951 Krishnaji's contact with India ended. Questioned later on what he did during this period, Krishnaji grew vague. The body was tired, he was inwardly drained, possibly some impurities, however subtle, still tinged the crystal clarity of his consciousness. And so, in keeping with the mystic tradition, he withdrew into himself.

In early spring of 1950 news of the dismissal of the case concerning Nandini's plaint for separation and custody of the children had exploded in the press in India. Even *Time* magazine in the United States carried a paragraph with the headline, "Revolt of the Doormat." It referred to Krishnaji as the Messiah and quoted Krishnaji's talks, in which he spoke with passion of the position of Indian women, that they were treated as doormats. It also linked Krishnamurti's name with Nandini's demand for separation from her husband. Rajagopal telegraphed to me to enquire whether this news that had appeared in *Time* was accurate. We replied, giving details and expressing our grave concern that Krishnamurti's name had been mentioned. On his return to Ojai later in 1950, Krishnaji faced a storm. Rosalind and Rajagopal questioned him on what had happened in India. Letters from Rajagopal's friends in India had spoken of Krishnaji's "new friends." Rosalind and Rajagopal were anxious and insisted on knowing more about these people. Krishnaji remained vague.

Rosalind and Rajagopal were united in their concern for the new Krishnamurti that was emerging. Aware of his sensitive, shy nature and the passivity of his personality, Rajagopal and Rosalind soon sensed the change in him. Krishnaji grew increasingly passive and silent, and withdrew within himself.

It was becoming evident to them, however, that the long spell in India, the people he had met, the freedom that had broken all the restrictions placed on him, had introduced entirely new elements in Krishnaji's attitude to people and situations. For the first time he had friends in India who were unrelated to his old connections. These people, who made no demands on him, sensed the vastness of the sacred manifest through him. They saw him with fresh, unburdened eyes, and brought to him a relationship of deep veneration, affection, and friendship.

Krishnaji returned to India in the winter of 1951, after an absence of nearly eighteen months. Rajagopal accompanied him. The many friends Krishnaji had made in the previous years thronged to meet him in Bombay. Krishnaji entered the room, greeted us solemnly, took our hands, but did not speak a word. He was still maintaining absolute silence. Rajagopal looked uneasy. We were meeting him for the first time, and we were wary of each other.

Krishnaji did not break his silence in Bombay, but went on to Madras, where he was to give twelve talks between January 5 and February 12. Nandini and I went to Madras and stayed in Vasant Vihar. We were living in a space that had been created by using cupboards to partition the veranda; we shared a bathroom with Madhavachari and ate our meals separately from Krishnaji, who ate in his room alone.

Rajagopal was very much in control. His relationship with Madhavachari was also slowly growing clear. Rajagopal treated him in a friendly manner, but did not reveal to Madhavachari what he had in his mind. Madhavachari was respectful, addressed him as Mr. Rajagopal, took his instructions, and carried out his wishes. Rajagopal was staying in the Leadbeater Chambers in the Theosophical Society, as the upper floor of Vasant Vihar had been rented and there was no other room suitable.

Krishnaji grew vague when questioned on the reason for his silent year, but spoke to Nandini and me of Rajagopal. He tried to make us understand how much Rajagopal had sacrificed for him. Krishnaji was apologetic, anxious that we become friends with Rajagopal; soon after dinner one evening a meeting was arranged, and we went to the Leadbeater Chambers to meet him.

Rajagopal was courteous; but his eyes, sunk in deep hollows in his somber, shadowed face, bore into us, trying to read nuances of meaning into every word we spoke. He was suspicious and inquisitive, and one needed an awake and alert mind to answer his seemingly innocuous questions. He seemed to be trying to catch us unawares. He hinted that Krishnaji could not be counted on as he was constantly changing his mind. Rajagopal had heard from Velu, a servant who had looked after Krishnaji in Sedgemoor, what had happened at Ootacamund. So Rajagopal grilled us for over four hours, wanting to know every detail of what had taken place. It was a trying experience and we were both worn out by the end of it.

Later we were to discover another side of Rajagopal. He appeared deeply attracted to us. He was warm and affectionate and we became friends. Years later he was to say to Nandini that it was such a pity that they were to meet under Krishnaji's shadow. He had an extremely intelligent and incisive South Indian mind. Sensitive to disorder and dirt of any kind, immaculately dressed in a starched white *kurta* and pyjama, he spoke and moved with elegant precision.

Krishnaji and Rajagopal were to leave for Europe and the United States by the spring of 1952.

By July 1952 Nandini's body, which had born the strain of five years of humiliation and the anguish of separation from her children, broke down. She was under pressure from many fronts: her ex-husband's arbitrary attitude toward when Nandini could see her children; the disapproving attitude of the elders around Krishnaji. She fell mortally ill with a fast-growing cancer of the cervix and had to be flown to England for an urgent operation.

I sent a telegram to Krishnaji giving him the news. There was no reply. It was as if he had vanished, and all relationship with us at the outer level had ended. However, his silent presence could be felt all through the period of our troubles, and with it came great strength and the capacity to face calamity.

Nandini was told in London of the devastating cancer that was destroying her body. Faced with the imminence of death, she received the news with deep silence. She told me that her brain became for some moments totally still and free of all thought or feeling. Right through the period of waiting for the operation in the hotel room, where she was to suffer a severe hemorrhage, there were few thoughts—no fear, no anxiety, no concern for tomorrow. On the eve of her operation she spoke by telephone to her children in Bombay with tenderness and concern for their well-being.

Later, she was to tell me that as she went under anesthesia she heard the sound of resounding laughter, which continued all through the operation. There was no blocking out of consciousness. She knew what was happening. She found herself walking in green fields, soft breezes played on her, and the sound of birdsong filled her ears. She felt a protective presence that surrounded her and held her. The protection was not to keep her alive, but to be with her in death or life. The protection, the presence, was in the surgeon's knife.

I was with her the next day, when she was told that the surgeon who had operated on her had suffered a stroke and was incapacitated. For two days she was without medical attention. After the operation, wherever she turned her face, the protection was there—to the left of her, to the right, above and below, she felt the touch of it. A few days after the operation she sat up in bed, cross-legged, and the breath of silence entered her. One day the young assistant doctor entered the room unexpectedly. Seeing her, he asked, "Are you a yogi?"

Like an underground spring of clear running water, unseen yet potent with life, Nandini's years have passed. Living with our mother in the 1950s, she chanced upon two tiny orphan girls of the neighborhood. Destitute, they lived with a distant aunt, but spent their life on the street. Deprived of her own children, Nandini had taken the girls in and started a tiny play school for them and for the other poor children of the neighborhood. Later, the school shifted to two nearby garages. Children of the surrounding areas soon started pouring in— today there are 150 children. Teachers and helpers have also come forward. The school, Bal Anand, provides to the child who wanders the street a creative space in an otherwise dreary landscape of concrete. Living alone for many years, Nandini has been the silent, nodal point of the school. The children sit round her and talk, laugh, and play. They are offered music, dancing, weaving, painting, language, dramatics, science, and a little arithmetic. After twenty-five years Bal Anand has become a part of the Krishnamurti Foundation, India, and

Nandini has become a member of the foundation. As her own children have come of age, they have returned to her, overflowing with love and protection.

Nandini remained a close friend of Krishnaji's, traveling with him to some of the centers when he was in India, and maintaining her contact through letters when he was away. Her hair is gray. She remains fragile, beautiful, anonymous.

As part of his Indian program it was decided that Krishnaji and Rajagopal would participate in a discussion group in Poona in the winter of 1952. Rao Sahib Patwardhan had arranged for a meeting of his friends at Vithal Wadi, where Achyut was living in a tiny cottage amongst forested hills, after his final break with the Socialist Party in 1950.

The people who gathered at Vithal Wadi for the discussions came from varied backgrounds. Professor Dhopeshwarkar taught philosophy at the University of Poona. S. M. Joshi was an austere, upright Chitpavan Brahmin, a Socialist and an active member of the Sarva Seva Sangh. He and Rao Sahib Patwardhan were close friends and had participated in many of the work camps with voluntary Sarva Seva Sangh workers. Mangesh Padgounkar, a poet, was one of the participants, along with Durga Bhagwat. Durga Bhagwat, a writer and anthropologist who had worked with Verrier Elwin in Madhya Pradesh, was a short lean woman with a tight bony face. Tough both physically and mentally, she had never married, had enormous energy, and felt strongly about problems of poverty in India. She was devoted to Rao Sahib. Madhavachari had come from Madras for the discussions, along with Padmabai and Sanjeeva Rao. Pandit Iqbal Narain Gurtu came from Varanasi and L. V. Bhave from Thana. I was the only other woman present.

Rao Patwardhan approved of me, and over two years he had become a close friend. His austere nature had responded personably and at depth to my totally alien background and attitudes. We discussed beauty, art, the Western mind, and the Indian creative matrix. For the first time I had established close contact with a traditional Brahminic intellect, a way of life that had no relevance to my early years as the daughter of a civil servant or to the life I led in the social milieu of Bombay.

Sunanda, who by then had married Pama, one of Rao Sahib's and Achyut's younger brothers, was not invited to attend the seminar. Nor was Nandini. Her astounding beauty, simplicity, and childlike quality combined with the fact that she had been married into a family of great wealth, made it difficult for Rao to accept the fact that she was serious. Sunanda had been asked by Rao to look after the arrangements for Krishnaji's food and other needs. Life was spartan, the rooms tiny; there were few amenities.

Krishnaji, sensing Sunanda's hurt at being left out of the group discussions, was most affectionate. He talked to her at length and walked with her in the woods. His attitude to her was of a much-loved daughter.

The discussions continued for over a week. Every morning and evening we gathered at Vithal Wadi. Krishnaji was dealing with tough minds entrenched and rooted in Marxian tenets of social service. The discussion kept impinging on poverty and the need for social action. This was understandable in a country of such immense poverty. But the minds that had gathered were intelligent enough to realize that at some point their approach was thwarted by their own inner conflicts, urges, and inadequacies. Slowly, with infinite patience, Krishnaji probed into the nature of mind, social action, thought and the thinker, and silence. He told the Socialists that the problem of food, shelter, and clothing could never be solved at an ideological level. It could only end when needs were not used for psychological purposes, but were dealt with on their own level. Though the hard-headed Socialists remained tethered to their perches, they were no longer secure in their positions.

At the end of the week we went our own ways. Of the group that had gathered, all drifted away except for the Patwardhans, Friedman, me, and the old friends of Krishnaji who had been with him from the Theosophical days. That the discussions had an impact on the tough minds of the Socialists and academics was evident. Professor Dhopeshwarkar wrote several books on Krishnaji's teachings. Many years later, S. M. Joshi was to say to me that Socialists in India since 1934 were dominated by Western thought and its dialectics. Marx became the central point from which all Socialist thought radiated. They could not see that when applied to Indian conditions, the Marxist position lacked a critical base. Western Marxism had no place for humanism. S. M. Joshi said his concern with socialism had always been with whether man could grow to his full stature. Therefore a moral element was integral to the Socialist stance. In 1948 the Socialists were profoundly perplexed and in a dilemma. They saw that ends justified means in Marxist thought. This was never quite acceptable to S. M. Joshi. While in jail, between 1944 and 1945, for a moment he had felt that perhaps ends did justify means; but this did not satisfy him and he was very confused. The discussions with Krishnaji had a liberating influence on him. He said they had "helped to clarify my attitude to injustice—helped me to face confusion and come through with clarity."[1]

While I was in Poona to attend the discussions at Vithal Wadi, I found myself watching with ruthless attention. I watched the movement of thought and feeling as they arose within me. I also watched what was outside me—people's faces, a leaf, a stone. While on a walk alone in the woods around Vithal Wadi, I suddenly found myself running. It was a still evening. The cry of one bird superimposed itself on other bird cries; the murmur of mosquitoes and chirping of crickets, a distant voice, the sound of my heartbeats poured piercingly into me, while sharp scent of neem, tulsi, and a multitude of jasmine swept through me like a strong wind. I was afloat in a sea of exploding color. The living green of peepul leaf, fresh fig green, new pink green of the mango shoot, the pale dawn green of a cactus bud, became one with sound; filling my nostrils, my ears, my eyes, my mouth. I found I was standing before a cactus bush weeping, unable to bear or contain the potency of that spring evening. The abundance of beauty, heavy like honey, lay in my eyes and ears for days. In seeing, beauty awakened; what was seen was unimportant. The intensity diminished as day followed day, but beauty taking over the sensory doorways, had generated a perception that seldom abandoned my eyes.

From Vithal Wadi in Poona, Krishnaji and Rajagopal went to Rishi Valley. The school had reopened with Pearce, the old Theosophist and educator, as principal. He had gathered a group of earnest young teachers around him. Rishi Valley was situated in the famine belt of Rayalseema in Andhra Pradesh. The land was barren. Miss Payne had dug wells, but trees had still to be planted—the thousands of trees that in years were to make this valley an oasis out of barren land. The surrounding hills were formed of rocks and boulders of immense size. Torn and gnarled by wind and time, they had assumed sculptural form; the huge boulders were balanced precariously on rocks, amongst the oldest in the world. The colors of sunsets and sunrises over the valley were palettes of saffron and amethyst; the air was clear and free of dust. In spite of the poverty of soil and sparse population, the area stretching from Anantpur on one end and Tirupati on the other was dotted with shrines to the *siddhas*.* Madnapalle was twenty kilometers from the site of the school.

---

*The *siddhas* or *sittars*, as they were known in South India, included Buddhist alchemists

At the heart of Rishi Valley was a very ancient banyan tree, like a temple; its roots had formed pillars, its branches sheltered monkeys, and cobras dwelt in the hollow at its base. A stage had been built around the tree, where the children danced between the many trunks and hid in the hollows. There were few birds, for the trees that were to attract them were yet to be planted.

Only thirty children attended the school, but the problems of the place had been immense. The teachers held long discussions on the role of authority, freedom, and order. No solution was possible, for the problems were living, moving, in flux; and the observations of the participants had to move, query, observe—with the same swiftness as the problem and its many nuances. Meanwhile, reports had reached Krishnaji of the conflicts that were arising in Rajghat, and he sent a telegram to Achyut at Vithal Wadi, asking him to come to Rishi Valley to see him.

Achyut swiftly responded to Krishnaji's telegram and arrived in Rishi Valley. Taking him aside, Krishnaji suggested to Achyut that he work at Rajghat in Varanasi. The land across the river Varuna was lying unused. Acquired to start some projects on agricultural research, the absence of workers had led to the lands remaining barren. Sanjeeva Rao and Pandit Iqbal Narain Gurtu, both close associates of Dr. Besant, who had left the Theosophical Society along with Krishnaji, had dominated the Rishi Valley Trust since its inception. They were growing old and a new initiative was needed. Krishnaji told Achyut that he would have to do a great deal of work, institutions would have to be built, the land had to be saved. But that was not and should not be the reason for Achyut to go to Rajghat.

Achyut's mind, Krishnaji said, was choked with the syndrome of social work. It was in his blood.

"Get it out of your blood. The deep movement of change has to be at the center. Unless the center changes, all social work is useless. Never lose sight of this, while you are at Rajghat. Don't let work overwhelm you and shadow your primary function, which is to change totally at the center. A watchfulness of mind has to be there."

Achyut agreed to go. The words of Krishnaji had soaked in. He saw the immensity of Krishnaji as a teacher; but to Achyut, with his Socialist background, Krishnaji's teaching could not be for the few. He felt that Krishnaji's presence had to permeate the soil of Rajghat. It

---

and magic makers, awakeners of *kundalini*, with intimate relationship with plants and minerals. In the face of invasions they had fled from the Buddhist monasteries of Vikram Sila and Nalanda, seeking refuge in Andhra Pradesh and Tamilnadu.

was sacred soil—the Buddha had walked there. Krishnaji had stood and watched the sunrise on the curve of the river, the sacred point where the Ganga started its journey northward—back to its source. This sacredness, that which lay behind the word of Krishnaji, the overflowing compassion, had to be communicated nonverbally to the villager, the fisherman, the weaver, the farmer who tilled the sacred Gangetic soil. The politically educated mind of Achyut saw that without this, there could be no stability in Rajghat and no work with the teaching was possible. Achyut's background and political life were legendary. Prepared to use violence to gain freedom, he had gone through all the inner and outer actions of the revolutionary. His name was resonant with the passion and fire of the freedom struggle. And now the *vira*, the warrior, had in spirit donned the saffron robe—a reversal of roles which intrigued Pandit Jawaharlal Nehru, and many of his Socialist comrades. There could be no finer material than Achyut to work in the villages of India.

Achyut went to Rajghat. From the first moment, he was totally dissatisfied with the mediocre school for middle-class children run by the Trust; and so he decided to work towards establishing a rural hospital to cater to the needs of the villages of the surrounding area. This was Achyut's first social response to the building of a religious center. He told me that "it was a gesture of friendship unconditionally available to the poor and the needy." Later, Dr. Kalle, an F.R.C.S.* and a deeply compassionate human being, joined Achyut to work in the hospital.

Achyut, like all Indians, had an intense love of the earth. It was for him the mother. So Achyut's mind now turned to the land. The Gangetic soil was rich, the crops poor. Ravines and the absence of any care for the land was impoverishing the rich earth. It had been neglected and plundered. He formulated plans for starting the agricultural school for the sons of farmers—Sir V. T. Krishnamachari, vice-chairman of the planning commission, was most receptive to Achyut's approach. Soon the agricultural school across the river Varuna came into being, the land was contoured, wells sunk. Achyut lived there in a tiny cottage, without electricity and with primitive sanitation. His main companion was Dr. Kalle, who lived in a cottage across the road from Achyut. It was Dr. Kalle, with the support of Achyut, who was to establish the medical center and hospital for the poor who lived in the villages around Rajghat.

To Achyut starting the agricultural school was a symbolic act, bear-

---

*Fellow of the Royal College of Surgeons, a prestigious British degree.

ing witness that the land, the sacred ancient land, the river, the cycle of the seasons, were alive, sanctity was reviving itself. Kasi, the most ancient and most sacred of the cities of India, was the soil in which the seed of renewal lay dormant. It had awaited the arrival of the Teacher for centuries. Krishnamurti's voice was heard again, and the dormant seed responded.

About this time Dr. Ram Dhar Misra, a mathematician who had been head of the department of mathematics in Lucknow University, was to join Achyut in his work. Ram Dhar Misra was a bachelor, and had decided to give up his profession to become a Buddhist monk. He had met Achyut, heard of the teachings of Krishnamurti, gave up his decision to take the robe, and came to Rajghat. He shared the small house with Achyut. And when Dr. Kalle started the hospital, Dr. Misra worked as his assistant, cleaning wounds, bandaging patients. No work was too menial; his role was to enable the rural hospital to function in every way. Austere, erudite in mathematics and in the sacred texts of India, he had a close affinity with growing things—trees, shrubs, or flowering grass. He was very fastidious about food and often invited his friends to a Varanasi breakfast of *jalebis* (luscious syrup-filled sweets), *kachoris* (wheat cakes stuffed with savory vegetables), and delicious fresh peas, which he cooked with delicacy.

It was about this time that Vinoba Bhave, one of Gandhiji's most trusted lieutenants, had started his Bhoodan movement. He had begun the *pada yatras*, a pilgrimage, walking on foot from village to village, asking landowners for gifts of land for the poor and the landless. The movement was in harmony with India's ethos, where quixotic behavior, sainthood, sacrifice, and gestures of righteousness were inextricably woven on the loom of tradition and social action.

Vast numbers of young people, shattered by Gandhiji's assassination and not knowing where to turn, followed Vinoba Bhave. "*Sarva bhoomi gopal ki*, all land belongs to God," sang his disciples. Vinobaji, the gaunt, bony, bearded ascetic, walked along the dust-filled paths of village India, eating frugally, demanding nothing for himself. Only in India was it possible to look as one pleased, without self-consciousness. In fact, eccentricity was considered integral to sainthood. For a time the Bhoodan movement exploded in India. Ripples were felt everywhere. Chief ministers and intellectuals, the poor and the affluent, walked on foot long distances, with the saint of Paunar, a village in Maharashtra where Vinobaji had his *ashram*. Rao Sahib and Achyut Patwardhan were deeply moved by the Bhoodan movement. They felt that Vinoba was introducing a new revolutionary, nonviolent attitude to poverty. From the earliest times the village of India had given of their bounty, their labor, and their skill to the city dwellers. The process, Achyut felt, had to be reversed.

In a sense Achyut was bridging, through his work at Rajghat, the impact of Krishnaji's teachings with his own conditioned responses to his social background and the immediate impact of Vinoba Bhave.

Krishnaji came with Rajagopal to Bombay in early 1953. They stayed with Ratansi Morarji on Carmichael Road. The affectionate atmosphere of the early days was over. Krishnaji was withdrawn and spent much time in his room, alone. His laughter was seldom heard, but the voice of Rajagopal in irritation and anger was often heard from Krishnaji's room.

Krishnaji was giving a vast number of interviews, meeting *sannyasis*, students, men and women burdened with sorrow and the isolation of old age. He was holding talks in the compound of the J. J. School of Art; small discussion groups had started, but he no longer came and sat in the living room every morning and evening. The chanting in which Krishnaji had participated also ended. Rajagopal appeared to be determining what Krishnaji could or could not do. At the time, Rajagopal was very friendly with Jamnadas Dwarkadas, who, with his ardent love and devotion for Krishnaji, reacted strongly and with anger to Rajagopal's insinuations. Jamnadas never told us what Rajagopal had said, but hinted that he had accused Krishnaji bitterly. Rajagopal was friendly to me, but we had long arguments on publications, organizations, and the like. At times we disagreed with passion. I was not used to secretive attitudes in public institutions. Rajagopal was arrogant and refused to answer questions. He wanted to know everything, but was not prepared to reveal anything. I told him that I could not work with him on these terms.

Krishnaji's public talks, however, bore no trace of the whirlpool that was revolving round Krishnaji at Ratansi's residence.

About this time an incident took place that was to release the arrow of causation which ultimately led to a complete break between Krishnaji and Rajagopal. Badgered by Rajagopal, with scenes taking place every day, Krishnaji was made to say something that affected Krishnaji's personal integrity. Having said it, Krishnaji awoke to its total implications. That is the only time I have seen Krishnaji in deep anguish.

He asked us to take him for a drive to Worli beach. We walked along the seashore; the tide was in and there was a strong wind. In those days the Worli beach was deserted. Krishnaji walked far ahead of us, completely silent, aloof. He stopped and waited for us. Turning to face us, he stood for a while, then crossed his hands across his chest and said, "Mea culpa." He knew that we understood. Then, as if from a long distance, we heard his voice. "The words have been said, the arrow has sped, I can do nothing about it. It will find its mark." He was never to refer to the incident again.

During the days that followed, the small discussions and talks started again. Krishnaji spoke of the necessity to be established in whatever state arose at a given moment—hatred, anger, greed, affection, generosity. "Is it possible," he asked, "to be these states completely without any movement of the mind away from them, without any movement either to change or strengthen them?"

Krishnaji said it was essential to ask fundamental questions; they rarely arose spontaneously. The mind, concerned with the trivial, seldom paused to ask the fundamental question. And when it did, it always had the easy answer arising from what it had already experienced.

"We have been educated to fight strong emotions, the resistance gave them strength and food. Is it possible to question, seek questions, without a movement of the mind? Could one ask the fundamental question and leave it in consciousness—remain with it—not let attention wander away from it? To hold the question or the problem so that it starts unfolding its petals, revealing itself—in the light of attention— so that, fully flowering, there is an ending totally?"

In 1953 Krishnamurti's nephew G. Narain came to see him in Bombay. The son of Krishnaji's eldest brother, Narain had finished his M.A. and qualified to be a lawyer. Krishnaji took Narain to his room. It was evening, and Krishnaji opened the windows so that the setting sun entered the room, lighting up Krishnaji's face. He asked Narain what he was going to do. Narain hesitated, and Krishnaji suggested that he should go to teach at Rishi Valley. Narain said he would think over it. That night, Narain told me that he felt his whole body covered with · blue light, cool and beautiful. He struggled and pushed it away, but half an hour later it was there again. Narain felt that this experience had wiped away all his problems. He went to Rishi Valley in June 1953, first as a teacher and later as vice principal.

From Rishi Valley Narain went to Oxford to qualify for his M.A. in education. After a year he rejoined Rishi Valley, but later went abroad.

He taught at one of the Rudolph Steiner schools for several years. Deeply interested in Buddhism, he had contacts with many practicing Buddhists in England. On a request from Krishnaji, he returned to India in 1978 and took charge as principal of the Rishi Valley School.

Krishnaji went to Varanasi with Rajagopal in the late winter of 1953. Kitty and Shiva Rao were away in the United States, and Krishnaji wrote to ask me whether he and Rajagopal could stay in our rooms in the Delhi Gymkhana Club, one of the last remnants of Delhi's colonial past. Krishnaji and Rajagopal stayed there for a night on the way to Rajghat in Varanasi, where Krishnaji was to give fifteen talks to the children of Rajghat School.

The talks were a challenge to Krishnaji. He had to discover words in which he could express himself and be understood by children who spoke English haltingly. Complex problems of authority, fear, sorrow, and death were being communicated. Krishnaji's pauses, the intensity of attention, the inclusive perception, the affection contained in his words, touched the depth of the minds of the youngest child. Krishnaji's voice was gentle, his words hesitant; he smiled with his heart and his eyes and the children listened and were quiet.

Speaking on January 4, 1954, Krishnaji said, "Education is not till you are twenty-one, but till you die. Life is like a river, it is always in movement, never still. It is alive. If one holds to a part of the river and thinks one understands, then it is like holding dead water. For the river goes by and if we cannot flow with it, one is left behind. Can one watch the movements of the river? Can one see things happening on the riverbank, can one understand, be faced with what is life?"

Speaking of fear with utmost simplicity, he opened up its complexities. He went into the fears that crowd a child's mind. He spoke of the nature of fear and punishment, the need for intelligence. Seeing and sensing the conservative families from which the children came, he probed into the words "to conserve," to hold, to guard. He delved into the word "tradition." What was it to be respectable? "If," he said, "you go into it very deeply, you will see that it arises out of fear of making a mistake."

"Why not make a mistake?" he asked. "Why not find out? The old people have not created a beautiful world, they are full of darkness, fear, corruption, compulsion; they have not created a good world. And perhaps if you are free of fear in itself and can face fear in another, the world would be totally different."

"What is sorrow?" asked a child of ten. Krishnaji, with anguish, turned to the teachers and said, "Is it not a terrible thing that a child so young should ask?" Then to the child he spoke of understanding of sorrow, of fear. "You cannot avoid sorrow or run away from it. You have to understand it. And to help you understand is the function of the teacher."

A little girl asked, "What is God?" and Krishnaji said, "In answer to that question, we are talking to the little girl, and also to the old people, the teachers will kindly listen. Have you watched a leaf dancing in the sun, a solitary leaf? Have you watched the moonlight on the water and did you see the other night the red moon? Did you notice the bird flying? Have you deep love for your parents? I am not talking of fear, of anxiety, of obedience, but of the feeling, the great sympathy you have when you see a beggar, or a bird die, or when you see a body burnt on the river bank. Can you see all this and have sympathy and understanding for the rich who go by in big cars, and for the poor beggar as well as for the poor *ekka* horse that is almost a walking skeleton? Can we have the feeling that *this earth is ours—yours and mine* to be made beautiful?

"Then, behind it all there is something much deeper. But to understand that which is deep and beyond the mind, the mind has to be free, quiet. The mind cannot be quiet without understanding the world around you. So you have to begin near, begin with little things, instead of trying to find out what God is."

In one of the talks, he explained the necessity for the child to sit still. "The older people grow, the more nervous, fidgity agitated they become. They cannot sit gently."

He told the child how to prevent the mind from becoming imitative; how the mind creates for itself tradition which is the way of imitation. "Can the mind be free?" he asked. "Not free from experience, but free to experience. Freedom comes when the mind experiences without tradition."

In his last talk to the children, he spoke of religion. "Religion comes when the mind has understood the working of itself. When the mind is quiet, very still—the stillness is not the peace of death; this stillness is very active, very alert, watchful. To find out what God—Truth is, one has to understand sorrow, and the struggle of human existence. To go beyond the mind there must be a cessation of the self, the 'me.' It is only then, that which we all worship, seek, comes into being."

In Varanasi we asked Krishnaji what he would do to create a school that would reflect his teachings. He replied, "First of all there has to be an atmosphere of immensity. The feeling that I am entering a temple. There must be beauty, space, quietness, dignity. There must be a sense of altogetherness in the student and teacher; a state of floration, a sense of flowering, a feeling of extraordinary sacredness. There must be truthfulness, fearlessness. The child must put his hands to the earth, there must be in him a quality of otherness."

"How do you create this concretely?"

"I would go into the way of teaching, the quality of attention," Krishnaji responded. "I would enquire how to teach the child to learn without memory being predominant. I would talk about attention and not concentration. I would go into the way the child sleeps, his food, the games he plays, the furniture in his room; I would see that the child is attentive to the trees, the birds, the spaces which are around him. I would see that he grows in an atmosphere of attention."

# CHAPTER 17

# "The Mind Seemed to Expand without an End."

In March 1955 it had been decided that before returning to Europe Krishnaji would rest for a month at Ranikhet, a hill station in the Himalayas. During the years of British rule, Ranikhet, in the Kumaun ranges of the Himalayas, had been a cantonment—no civilians had lived there. The houses, like all the homes built by the English in the hill stations of India, were nostalgic copies of English cottages—nestled in gardens, filled with fragrant flowers and towering pines and deodar trees. The sharp scent of resin and smoke permeated the trees. Flower bushes had been planted along the roadside, and in the summer they were ablaze with blossom.

From Ranikhet lay the route to the sacred points of pilgrimage, deep in the Himalayan ranges—to Kedarnath and Badrinath, the Himalayan homes of Shiva and Vishnu; to the sources of the rivers Ganga and the Jamuna; and to Kailash and Manasarovar in Tibet. Kailash, the snowbound mountain home of Shiva after he had been accepted into the Brahminic pantheon, was cone shaped. On one side of the mountain was Manasarovar, the lake with azure waters wherein lived mythical golden swans, the *ham sā*. The sound of the name of the swan was resonant with the silences of the cosmos, and with the inbreathing and outbreathing of *prana* the life force. On the other side of the mountain was Raksasa Tal, a volcanic lake with dark, angry waters. The two lakes symbolized the two aspects of Shiva and of mind—the turbulence and the total stillness.

From Ranikhet one could see on a clear day a vast stretch of snow-tipped Himalayan peaks. They had sacred names—Trisul, Neelkanth, Nandadevi, Nandakhot. Sunrise and sunset, the blazing noonday sun, the full moon at night—all revealed changing light and shadow on their awesome, steadfast faces. They were the eternal seers, the guardians of the land and the source of the life-giving rivers.

Achyut had gone to Ranikhet and found a house, Ardee, for Krishnaji to live in. It was arranged that my husband drive Krishnaji up to Ranikhet from Delhi. Krishnaji had been in Bombay giving talks and discussions, and it was decided that he would leave for the hills on March 18. In Bombay, however, he fell ill with a high fever. Krishnaji was delirious; he could not bear noise and his bed had to be moved to the sitting room. Dr. Nathubhai Patel, an eminent physician, examined Krishnaji and determined that he had gotten worms from eating raw food. K's sensitive body had reacted violently, and the bladder and urinary tract were inflamed. With treatment, however, Krishnaji recovered rapidly. By the third week of March we were in Delhi, and on March 28 we were ready to leave for the mountains.

Kitty Shiva Rao had arranged for one of her servants, Diwan Singh, and Tanappa from Rajghat, to go ahead to Ranikhet and prepare the house for Krishnaji. The journey was a little over two hundred miles. As Krishnaji could not bear heat, we started the journey at 5 A.M.

Krishnaji sat in the front seat with my husband, who was driving, and Madhavachari and I sat at the back. The early morning air was cool, and we covered most of the journey to the foothills before the sun was too hot. Krishnaji had always been a very good driver. His extensive awareness could sense danger seconds before catastrophe struck. But as a back-seat driver he was very disturbing. Throughout the journey he instructed Jayakar to do this and not to do that; warning him of approaching dangers. Several times we suggested that Krishnaji sit with us in back, but he was intent on staying where he was.

Madhavachari and I began to discuss various problems connected with self-knowing. We had been climbing steadily; the view was of waterfalls and steep gorges and hillsides covered with rhododendron. We looked out at the changing vegetation, the rocks and precipices, the rushing streams. We were speaking of awareness, and splitting hairs as to its nature, when suddenly we felt a jolt. We paid no attention and continued our conversation. A few seconds later, Krishnaji turned round and asked us what we were discussing. "Awareness," we said, and immediately started asking him questions about it. He listened, looked at us quizzically, and then asked, "Did you notice what happened just now?"

"No."

"We knocked down a goat, did you not see it?"

"No."

Then with great gravity he said, "And you were discussing awareness." No more words were necessary. It was devastating.

The house in Ranikhet was overgrown with creepers, the garden smothered with weeds, but deodars and pines surrounded the house. The sharp freshness of resin permeated the rooms. It was intensely quiet with the silence that is found in lone houses situated in forests.

My husband and I returned to Delhi after staying overnight. Madhavachari had to go to Madras, and he accompanied us back. Achyut stayed with Krishnaji for a few days.

Krishnaji went for long walks alone. Amongst pine trees and deodar forests he became lost, but instinctively found his way home. The trees against the backdrop of the Himalayan peaks were a delight. He spoke of these peaks stretching from Nepal to the Badrinath caves: "They were sixty miles away from us, with a vast blue valley between them and us stretching for over two hundred miles. They filled the horizon from end to end. The intervening sixty miles seemed to disappear, and there was only that strength and solitude. These peaks, some rising over 25,000 feet, had divine names, for the gods lived there, and men came to them from great distances to worship and to die.

"The mind seemed to cover the vast space and the unending distance, or rather the mind seemed to expand without an end and behind and beyond the mind there was something that held all things in it."

He then questioned his own perceptions. "That which is beyond all consciousness cannot be thought about or experienced by the mind. But what is it then that has perceived and is aware of something totally different from the projections of the mind? Who is it that experiences it? Obviously it is not the mind of everyday memories, responses and urges.

"Is there another mind?" he asks himself. "Is there a part of the mind that is dormant, to be awakened only by that which is alone and beyond all mind? If this is so then within the mind there is always that which is beyond all thought and time. And yet that cannot be, for it is only speculative thought and therefore another invention of the mind.

"Since the immensity is not born of the process of the mind, then what is it that is aware of it? Is the mind as experiencer aware of it, or is it that immensity is aware of itself because there is no experiencer? There was only *that*, and that was aware of itself without measurement. It had no beginning and no word."[1]

In the evening Krishnaji sat before the fire and asked Achyut to teach him some Sanskrit. Achyut began reading the *Mandukya Upanishad* with Krishnaji. The *Upanishad* which unfolds the sound of Ōm*— the total vowel sound in which there are no consonants—the *Ōm* sound that reverberates in the universe and in the caverns of the heart when all outer sound has ended.

Achyut asked, "What is wrong with the chanting of Ōm if the mind grows still?"

"Is your mind still?"

"For that second when we recited—the 'I' was not," Achyut said.

Krishnaji's response negated all anchors and props. "What you are doing involves time. That has nothing to do with time. Time can never lead to the other."

Achyut returned to the plains after a few days and Krishnaji stayed alone at Ardee. A series of letters to my husband reveals the meticulous care Krishnaji took of his clothes. He always had a passionate feeling for color and texture. Handwoven textiles enchanted him. In India he dressed with elegant simplicity, wearing a long *kurta* reaching below the knees and loose pyjamas. For warmth he wore a jacket or a *choga*. He had several of these beautiful woolens, given to him by Mrs. Besant, made of Kashmir *tus* wool, in warm honey-brown tones.

In 1948 and for some years following, he wore only white. But later his love of the earth colors of the mendicant prevailed. Friends brought him handwoven cottons and the heavy, handspun coarse linen-textured *kurtas* made from the waste that remains after silk has been reeled, in colors ranging from thick cream to burnt umber and the bark-dyed tones worn by Buddhist monks.

Living alone, with a cook to look after his needs, Krishnaji renewed himself. He went for long walks, conversed with the snowy peaks, looked, listened to the world within him and around him. He once told us a story of a large number of monkeys, the black-faced langurs which used to swing on the tree-tops surrounding Ardee. One morning he was writing in his room, the window was open. Suddenly, he had a feeling of eyes watching him intently. He looked up and found a full-grown monkey sitting on the windowsill and looking into the room with intensity. Krishnaji arose and walked towards the monkey. When they were face to face, the monkey put out its hand. Krishnaji took it and the monkey let him hold it. There was complete trust. Krishnaji

---

*Also, *Aum*.

describes the touch of the palm as strong, infinitely soft, despite callouses which had formed from climbing branches. For a few minutes they remained holding hands, then the langur tried to enter the room. Krishnaji pushed him back, gently but firmly, and closed the window.

# CHAPTER 18

# "Can There Be Action without Consequence?"

The winter of 1955 saw Krishnaji in Varanasi. He had come there with Rosalind from Sydney. His astonishing, awesome beauty was absent. The face appeared aged, the hair had started to turn grey.

He questioned himself aloud. "What is action without consequence?" For three days he probed into the question, refusing to allow any immediate response, letting the question unfold, letting it release the energy held within it. There was no leaving the question, and during the discussion meetings our minds probed with him. He refused to let us answer from the *Gita* or the sacred books. For him the question had to evoke its own answer. And yet every answer from the past was a consequence, from the present a consequence, and the projected future was also a consequence.

Krishnaji asked, "Can there be action without consequence? Can the past, future, be brought together in the present and extinguished? The past mistake was a consequence, my action on it is a consequence, my refusal to act on it is also a consequence, and yet there has to be action without consequence." He went on searching. He would take up the question, letting every intimation surrounding the question arise, perceiving the response without condemnation or justification and so negating it. All enquiry was tentative, there was a total absence of any assertive statement.

Then suddenly, on the third day, as if there had been revelation, he said, "Can one live without self-concept? Can one live without the reflected self-image? Only in that is there action without consequence."

"What does that imply?" we asked.

"To live without self-concept," he responded, "is to be aware of the constant projection of the self and seeing it to negate it."

Another morning he said, "We die through disease, old age, suicide. The dying is the sinking into the unknown, a sudden cutting away, an oblivion." Then he asked with great gravity, "Living, can one enter the house of death?"

Rosalind was visiting India after many years. She was meeting old friends from the days of her life in the Theosophical Society, and made new friends, among them Malti Nowroji and Kanji Dwarkadas, Jamnadas's brother and an old associate of Mrs. Besant. Kitty Shiva Rao was also in Varanasi, and they spent long days together. Sunanda Patwardhan had been working as Krishnaji's secretary from 1949, while Krishnaji was in India. She traveled with him around the country, taking shorthand notes, typing his letters, attending the talks and discussions. Rosalind liked her and gave her much affection. However, in Rosalind's relationship to Krishnaji, the tensions had accentuated. Like Rajagopal, her voice was often heard remonstrating with Krishnaji. Faced with her anger, Krishnaji was to tell us later, he became totally silent and passive. He listened with precision, deeply and extensively, but refused to react. Her inability to evoke a response from Krishnaji made Rosalind furious. It was a confrontation with no opponent. The other had vanished.

With an unending stream of questions, Rosalind sought to find the "influence" that underlay the seeming change in Krishnaji. For many years Rosalind had taken Krishnaji for granted, and now she found that there was suddenly no Krishnaji to contact or with whom she could establish a relationship.

Obstinately, Rosalind insisted that Krishnaji agree to travel with her to see the Ajanta and Ellora caves. Malti Nowroji and Sunanda accompanied them. It was very hot. The landscape was stark, the Deccan rocks molten in the sun. There was little green to relieve the eye. Krishnaji suffered, and when they returned to Bombay, the situation remained grim.

Krishnaji returned alone to Delhi in early October 1956. Beauty filled him. He was speaking again in the capital city after many years, under an open *shamiana*, a tent erected on the lawns of the Constitution Club. Diplomats, *sannyasis*, bureaucrats, clerks, professors, and a sprinkling of young people came to hear him.

The young were a handful. In spite of the massacres of partition,

the euphoria of freedom continued at its zenith. The glitter and afflu-
ence generated by the skills and artifacts of science and technology
were becoming apparent in India. The young minds, stimulated and
responsive to vast new explosions of knowledge in the West and the
opportunities being released by technology, were not interested in self-
knowledge or the long perspective. It was the immediacy and possibilities of the new that fired their minds.

The older generation was still steeped in the sterility of dead traditions; with the death of Gandhiji, the Gandhians had turned to Vinoba Bhave. Intrigued by Rao Sahib and Achyut's total involvement
with Krishnaji and his teachings, the Gandhians had started attending
Krishnaji's talks. The small group discussions had commenced. Shankar Rao Deo and Dada Dharmadhikari, two very important members
of the Sarva Seva Sangh were seen at every gathering.

Shankar Rao Deo, matured in the freedom struggle, was steeped in
a tradition of austerity. Highly educated, he was one of the bare-bodied
followers of Gandhiji, imposing on himself rigid disciplines of fasting
and practice of *brahmacharya*, which involves a vow of total celibacy.
He had gone to jail several times, had been placed in "C" class—the
lowest class reserved for prisoners. Political prisoners placed in "C"
class had to wear prison garments, eat prison food, and were not permitted newspapers or books. Revolted by the prevalent injustices, he
had protested and gone on a fast. His refusal to break his fast had
infuriated the prison authorities. He had been placed on the triangle
and flogged and left jail with permanent scars. A wildness and passionate urgency for the unexpressed fired his eyes; he had curbed his
senses with a harsh austerity; deep within were frustrations and un-
fulfilled desires, passions, and ambitions. In jail Shankar Rao Deo had
come in close contact with Javdekar, a close friend of Tilak and Bhagwat,* and an associate of Mahatma Gandhi from 1920. Recognized as
intellectuals in Maharashtra, they were steeped in the finest traditions
of learning. With them, Shankar Rao Deo had read Krishnamurti's
books. In later years Javdekar and Bhagwat had attended Krishnaji's
talks, but had never come close to him personally. They felt strongly
that Krishnaji was expressing, although in a new language, the entire
Adwaita position of Vedanta.

---

*Bal Gangadhar Tilak was a Brahmin intellectual, scholar, writer, and freedom fighter.
A highly revered and respected figure in Maharashtra, he was tried by the British government on charges of sedition and imprisoned in the Andaman Islands.

Bhagwat was a philosopher, freedom fighter, and editor of an important Marathi
newspaper, *Lok Sakti.*

In 1948 Javdekar and Bhagwat, in *Lok Shakti*, a much-respected Maharashtrian journal, wrote a six-column article in which Krishnaji was proclaimed a realized human being. The Maharashtra pandits accepted Krishnaji in 1948; it was late in the 1970s before the pandits of Varanasi did the same. With the acceptance of Krishnaji by Javdekar and Bhagwat, a stream of Maharashtrian thinkers and writers were drawn to him. They saw in him a teacher who, without contradicting the past, had shattered the tradition, transcending it. Through him they saw revealed the luminous, eternal truth.

In 1948 Shankar Rao Deo had been in New Delhi for the meetings of the Constituent Assembly. He had also participated in the small discussions Krishnaji had held at the time. At one of the first ones, Krishnaji had been discussing violence and nationalism. Shankar Rao Deo said of this, "To understand Krishnaji you had to understand the 'I.' Krishnaji had said, 'The understanding of the "I" involves time and space; understanding is, when time has ended.' "[1]

1956 was the year of the Buddha Jayanti, and the government of India invited His Holiness the Dalai Lama from Tibet to visit India and travel to the various sacred sites associated with the Enlightened One. Apa Sahib Pant, a senior officer in the Foreign Service who at the time was political officer in Sikkim, had been asked to accompany the Dalai Lama around the country. They traveled in a large, air-conditioned train accompanied by a vast entourage.

As religious and secular head of the Tibetan state, the life of the Dalai Lama was strictly bound by protocol. He had been a figure of mystery. In Tibet, rarely visible except to a few lamas, he lived a life of strict discipline and meditation. This would be the first visit of any Dalai Lama out of that mysterious land.

When he arrived in Madras in December, Apa Sahib Pant had suggested to the twenty-year-old incarnation of the divine that he visit Krishnamurti, who at the time was staying in Vasant Vihar. Apa Sahib had related the life of Krishnaji and the extraordinary nature of his teachings. The young monk had commented, "A Nagarjuna!"* and had expressed a keen desire to meet Krishnaji. Those around the Dalai Lama were most distressd. It was a shattering of all protocol. But the Dalai Lama insisted, and the meeting was arranged.

In Apa Sahib's words, "Krishnaji received [the Dalai Lama] simply.

---

*A reference to the second-century Buddhist sage who taught adherence to the "Middle Path" as also the way of the great negation.

It was breathtaking to feel the electric affection that instantly flashed between them." The Dalai Lama gently but directly asked, "Sir, what do you believe in?" and then the conversation went on in almost monosyllabic sentences, as it was a communication without rhetoric. The young Lama was feeling on familiar ground as Krishnaji made him "coexperience." On the return journey to Raj Bhawan, the Dalai Lama was to say, "A great soul, a great experience."[2] The Dalai Lama also expressed a wish to meet Krishnamurti again.

From the mid-1950s Shankar Rao Deo became a familiar figure at Krishnaji's talks; every winter he would visit Varanasi and stay at the Sarva Seva Sangh headquarters, which had been built at the entrance to Rajghat. With Rao Sahib Patwardhan, I had often visited him there and had found him engaged in *shram dan*—the gift of work, which along with the gift of land, was part of the teachings of the hermit Vinoba Bhave. We would find Shankar Rao sitting for hours with a winnowing fan, picking tiny stones out of rice. It amused me to see him do this seemingly absurd activity, but his action appeared perfectly appropriate to Rao Sahib.

Shankar Rao used to come to hear Krishnaji's talks; he would attend the discussions and sometimes meet K alone. Krishnaji would banter with Shankar Rao, make him laugh, point to the river and the trees, speak of beauty, love, and the nature of compassion, and overwhelm him with affection. Shankar Rao would listen, powerfully attracted by Krishnaji, yet his whole background rebelled against K's words. He was incapable of comprehending Krishnaji's insistence on the need for love, beauty, and sensitivity. Krishnaji's attitude to the sense and to desire perplexed him. "Listen to desire as you listen to the wind amongst the trees," said Krishnaji. The Gandhian, nurtured on ideas that demanded the destruction of desire, did not know where to turn or what to say. Shankar Rao found it difficult to reconcile Krishnaji's teaching with Gandhian ideals.

Krishnaji's response to Shankar Rao's determined austerity and his harsh denial of the senses was later reflected in Krishnaji's talks in Bombay. In February 1957 Krishnaji was to say, "To make the senses insensitive to that which is tempestuous, contradictory, conflicting, sorrowful, is to deny the whole depth and beauty and glory of existence. Reality demands your whole being, a total human being, not with a mind that is paralyzed. There is a constant battle between 'what I am' and 'what I should be.' This is the web of sorrow on which man is caught. To curb your senses is the cultivation of insensitivity. Though you may be seeking God, your mind is made dull."

In the small discussions the nature of being and becoming were explored. Germinating in the dark recesses of the mind, "desire to become is the soil in which sorrow takes root." The mind, to be free, has to see itself as the result of time—only in the energy of self-knowing is true enquiry possible.

"There is an astounding movement in the stillness of discovery moment to moment, which destroys germination in the mind. Self-knowing is the understanding of becoming in oneself. The religious revolution is the ending of becoming." On his evening walks on the Worli beach he spoke of the act of listening as "unpremeditated and uncalculated. It is an action of truth, for in it is total attention," and of silence as "the source of all creation." Then he made a seminal statement, which was to find expression again in his talks. "Can there be a feeling without thought? Can you ride a feeling without directing it, seeking to change it, calling it good or bad? Try it," he said.

Shankar Rao was present at the talks and at the small discussions. His conflicts and his complex reactions seemed to intensify. Shankar Rao Deo was incapable of living life with both passion and austerity. In Bombay Krishnaji asked, "If you knew that you were about to die, what would you do? Can you live one hour completely—live one day— one hour—as if you were going to die the next hour? But if you die so that you are living fully in this hour, there is enormous vitality, tremendous attention to everything. You look at the spring of life, the tear, you feel the earth, the quality of the tree. You feel the love that has no continuity and no object. Then you will find in that attention that the 'me' is not. It is then that the mind, being empty, can renew itself."

In the winter of 1956 Vimla Thakkar, a young woman devotee of Vinoba Bhave, was to accompany Shankar Rao and Dada Dharmadhikari to see Krishnaji in Varanasi. She was a Maharashtrian, passionate of speech, learned in Sanskrit and the ancient Indian texts. From her childhood she was attached to a religious life, and had visions of Krishna and other mystical experiences. In search of a guru, for some years she had been a disciple of Tukroji Maharaj, an accepted saint of Maharashtra, and later had left him to join Vinoba Bhave. She had walked with him through the villages of India. Preaching came naturally to her. She saw herself as a woman of destiny; this gave her enormous energy, eloquence, and drive.

During discussions Krishnaji, sensing her self-image, said to her, "Don't try to experience truth through Shankara, Krishna, Gandhi, or Krishnamurti." She questioned him, but found that there appeared to be no relationship between the questions she asked Krishnaji and his responses. For his responses were a challenge to her mind and its assumptions.

Vimla Thakkar had been practicing intense yogic *sadhanas*,* and she was suffering from a severe pain in the ear. The trouble in her ear persisted, and her friends had told her that it was due to the awakening of the *kundalini*. One morning when she, Shankar Rao, and Dada Dharmadhikari were discussing some aspect of the teaching with Krishnaji, Dada spoke of Vimla's ear trouble. He told Krishnaji that it was related to Vimla's yogic practices, but Krishnaji did not agree. He asked her to see a doctor, as he felt that it was not a mystical experience but a physical illness. She was distressed to hear Krishnaji say this, but later went to an ear surgeon and in 1960 was operated on in Bombay. The pain disappeared, but she became totally deaf in one ear.

In December 1960 she met Krishnaji again in Varanasi with Shankar Rao and Dada. During the conversation the deafness was mentioned, and Krishnaji suddenly said, "My mother used to tell me when I was very young that I had the power to heal in these hands." He said it shyly, as always when he spoke of himself. "Would you like me to see whether I can help you with your ear?" Vimla was taken aback. Brought up in a tradition which made her react strongly against all miracle makers, she said she did not believe in these things, and so the moment passed. Dada later chided her and told her that she should not have refused; Krishnaji was not like the ordinary *sadhu* living on miracles. After much discussion, she went back to Krishnaji and sought his help.

Krishnaji had a certain way of performing an act of healing. The sufferer sat on a chair, Krishnaji stood behind, and placed his hands on the head of the patient. Then, with a gesture, he seemed to throw off what had entered his hands. He would repeat this several times. Then he placed his hands on the patient's head for several moments, after which he asked the person to sit quietly for a while. Krishnaji invariably washed his hands afterward. In this way, for several days Krishnaji placed his hands on Vimla's ear, and slight hearing returned.

Vimla followed Krishnaji to Bombay, where he was giving talks. He asked her about her ear. She said she was hearing the sound of a flute

---

*Sadhana:* practice of austerity or discipline.

in the deaf ear. He told her that she was translating the sound into her own imagery; he asked her to stop doing so and to use ice packs on the ear to cure the noise. She was later to follow Krishnaji to London—and then to Saanen in Switzerland, where he continued his therapy. From Saanen she wrote to Dada joyfully, "I am cured, and can hear clearly."

At an interview in Wimbledon, Vimla asked Krishnaji about his healing powers. He told her, "I am afraid you won't understand."

She followed him to Gstaad, Switzerland. Krishnaji was not looking well, and appeared to be under a strain. She asked him again about his power to heal, as she felt that the healing had affected her mind as well as her body. The deafness was cured, and the mind too had been released, freed from bondage. She felt "something inside let loose, can't stand frontiers." Krishnaji was to say to her very seriously, "Who told you that the two are related?" She again questioned him on the "explosion" within her. But he did not encourage her in her belief, and refused to accept that his touch had brought about deep psychic changes and release from bondage. She decided not to attend any more of Krishnaji's talks, but to start speaking of reality, on her own.[3]

Meanwhile, Shankar Rao's inner conflicts were intensifying. In 1962, in the midst of the Chinese conflict and the traumatic Bay of Pigs confrontation between Kennedy and Kruschev, Shankar Rao decided to lead a peace march to China. His friends tried to dissuade him, but he was adamant. So a small band started walking the dusty, overland trail. No one was very clear what route they were to take; frontiers were forgotten, but the spirit had decided and so they marched. Poet Allen Ginsberg and his friend Peter Orlovsky, founders of the Beat movement, with its revolt against the establishment and its questioning of all material values, were in India at the time. They were seeking Truth on the Varanasi *ghats*, along with ferocious Aghori Bawas and Nath Panthis. Delighted by Shankar Rao's act of lunatic humanity, they walked part of the way with him, chanting *bhajans* in their nasal American voices.*

The Central Bureau of Investigation (CBI) grew suspicious of these two dirty, long-haired, bearded foreigners. They refused to extend their

---

*Aghori Bawas are amongst the most terrifying of the *sadhus* or holy men of India.

Nath Panthis are followers of Gorakhnath, the author of the first treatise on hatha yoga. Drawn from both Hindu and Muslim sects, they are wanderers, involved with magical practices and the worship of Shiva and Shakti. They are associated with many archaic legends all over Northern India.

*Bhajans* are devotional songs sung by groups of men and women.

visas. I received a telegram in Delhi from them which read, "CID [Criminal Investigation Department] harassment, visa extensions denied telegraphed Nehru, Gailbraith and Lord Ganesh arrive Delhi Monday—Allen and Peter." I explained the problem of these Western seekers to Viswanathan, a very sympathetic but cynical secretary of the home ministry, who told me that their telegram addressed to Prime Minister Nehru was before him, and that my name had been given to vouch for their integrity. Their visas were extended. Later, they rejoined Shankar Rao Deo's march. On March 16, 1963, they wrote:

Dear Pupul,

We went on elephant ride in zoo & then went out to Khurja and spent a day walking with Shankar Rao Deo & other marchers. They are making sense i.e. confronting loudspeaker-hysteria with person-to-person calm. Spent night with them; they took us in & treated us fine and we touched their walking feet & left. I phoned your house when we got back to Delhi, your husband said you were still out. I guess he told you—

OK—
love, Allen.

Hollo Pupul & Babu Pa and Babu Ma,

It was a joy to walk with them day & night before the walk we slept with them in a one room house ashram all of us in the one room, sleeping next to me was a fellow name Jain from Madras who writes articles for a Budan [Bova's work] newspaper—also a young girl from Bangalore married to an Austrian Gandhian fellow both of whom are on the walk to Peking last name DADA was accompanying Shankar Rao for a few months walk & talking—DADA making jokes cheering everybody up—. I hope they make it into Peking—it would be great if Bhave & Nehru & Shankar Rao Deo could meet & walk with each other a day & talk about—

Love & Ganesh
- Peter -
What you reading now?
Just finished Dali Lama's autobiography.

Shankar Rao and his dusty pilgrims were stopped at the frontiers of Burma. They sat and waited, but the Burmese government was adamant. So the travelers had to turn back and disperse. The newspaper comments were satirical, the scoffers laughed, and Shankar Rao was deeply hurt.

In the winter of 1961 Rao had met Krishnaji in Varanasi and had spoken to him of the enormous fear that was consuming him. When

Krishnaji asked him what he feared, Shankar Rao had said, "Death." Krishnaji had gone into fear and death with the Gandhian, but later was to say that it was the forced repression of the senses that was destroying Shankar Rao.

After the peace march debacle, Shankar Rao tried to see Krishnaji again, but Krishnaji was not in India in the winter of 1962. Thwarted, fearful, not knowing where to turn, the years of abstinence and sensory denial were suddenly shattered and the violence within Shankar Rao expressed itself in an act of passion. Horrified with himself, holding a great burden of guilt, Shankar Rao went into deep depression and became totally dumb. His friends were enormously concerned and wrote to Krishnaji about him.

On Krishnaji's return to India in the winter of 1963, Rao Sahib Patwardhan and Dada Dharmadhikari brought Shankar Rao to Krishnaji. At first Shankar Rao refused to accompany Dharmadhikari and Rao Patwardhan, but suddenly he nodded his head and ceased to struggle. I remember the wild-looking, fierce-eyed, dark, thick-set, bare-bodied person wearing a high *dhoti* who was brought into the sitting room of Himmat Nivas in Bombay.

Krishnaji came into the room and said to Shankar Rao, "What have you done to yourself, my friend?" and embraced him. At Krishnaji's touch the wild, terrible eyes burst into tears. Holding him by the arm, Krishnaji took him to his room. An hour later they came out. Shankar Rao's face was calm, he spoke to Dada with affection, and said goodbye to Krishnaji. It appeared that Krishnaji had warned Shankar Rao not to touch politics again.

The news of the "miracle" spread through the Sarva Seva Sangh, and through them to the *ashrams* all over the country. People flocked to hear Krishnaji. According to Dada Dharmadhikari, this was the second miracle he was to witness, the first being the curing of Vimla's ear. At Krishnaji's talks at Bombay, crowds gathered as he walked to the car from the meeting, striving to touch his hand, to share in his benediction. These incidents (which Krishnaji for many years refused to have talked about) and the vastness of his silent presence impressed people tremendously. The teaching, though they all agreed it was grounded in a total nonduality, appeared too distant and too unattainable.

When Krishnaji and Rajagopal came to India in the winter of 1957, Krishnaji was in semiretreat and was not giving public talks.

Rajagopal had accompanied Krishnaji to India to settle matters relating to Vasant Vihar and Krishnaji's copyright. Krishnaji was vague about institutional structures, uninterested in his legal rights and responsibilities, and agreed to whatever Rajagopal had suggested, although the signatures to the legal documents were finalized only in the winter of 1958. Krishnaji gave Rajagopal and Krishnamurti Writings, Inc. all rights on his copyright, and practically withdrew from K. W. I., of which he had been the president.

Madhavachari had become the secretary of the Foundation for New Education in 1957; he was also the K. W. I. representative in India. He had become Krishnaji's constant companion, his friend and his host. Madhavachari, retired from service, was living in Vasant Vihar. He was a tough South Indian Brahmin, and life in Vasant Vihar was spartan. Austerity was equated with a lack of concern for space or form, or for an ambience in which the creative could germinate. The spaces created by the genius of South India, to be found in temple shrines, in rural cottages, and the objects of daily use, had long been abandoned. Intimate laundry hung on clotheslines, over beds, and lithographs adorned the walls.

Vague feelings were arising in Krishnaji about the unkempt gardens and the general set-up in Vasant Vihar. The talks coincided with the Theosophical Society convention, and were attended by a large number of old people. Very few young people were in contact with the Vasant Vihar center or with Krishnamurti's teachings.

From Madras, Krishnaji and Rajagopal went to Rishi Valley and later returned to Madras. His work accomplished, Rajagopal returned to the United States. He was seen off at the Bombay airport by Sunanda and L. V. Bhave.

I had not been able to go to Rishi Valley or Madras, as my husband had had a very serious heart attack; I had to wait for Krishnaji in Delhi. My relations with my husband had been intensely difficult for some time; a Maharashtrian, he could not tolerate a wife who lived a life and had interests independent of his own. He struck out where he knew it would wound, but in the process the conflict shattered him and his body broke down.

Krishnaji, accompanied by Madhavachari, came to Delhi in early 1958. It was several years since I had met Krishnamurti the healer. I spoke to him of my sorrow and pain. His compassion contained me. He made me face the fact that no relationship existed between me and the man I had married. I was not prepared to see this. The pain came in waves, drowning me, making clear sight impossible. He put the two palms of his hands swallow-like round my face. He made me look into his eyes and see my sorrow reflected in them. He was the father, the mother, the friend, and the teacher, providing to my anguished spirit toughness and tenderness; but he would not let me look away. Like a pillar of fire, his seeing annihilated the memories, the loneliness, the lack of affection that were the root of pain. I was brought face to face with the emptiness of sorrow. A perception was generated that burnt away the scars of what had been. He gave abundantly of his love and it flowed through me, quietening the heart. If he healed me inwardly, to my husband too he gave of his abundance. Physically, healing the damaged heart, speaking to him with the same affection, healing his mind and spirit.

From Delhi, Krishnaji and Madhavachari went to Varanasi. I received several letters from Krishnaji asking me to come to Rajghat, but my husband's physical condition did not permit him to be left alone.

Krishnaji spent the summer of 1958 in India. He had been offered the M. E. S. bungalow at Chowbatia in Ranikhet, a spacious house situated at the highest point at Ranikhet, with a magnificent view of the snow-peaked Himalayas that lay enshrined before it. Again Krishnaji was in the sacred mountains of his ancestral past. In the evenings he sat and chanted the Sanskrit hymns he had relearned. He walked in the deodar woods, got lost, found the path that led homeward.

Speaking of these walks, he told of an evening when news came that a tiger had killed, not very far from Krishnaji's house. The next morning Krishnaji went for his usual walk, wandering farther and farther into the jungle. The many sounds of the forest—birds and rustling leaves, chattering monkeys—flowed through him. He came to a clearing and found that his body refused to move. Instinctively, he had sensed something, and the intelligence of the body had responded. All sound had ceased. Everything seemed in a state of abeyance—the breathing of nature had for an instant been suspended. Krishnaji stood for about two minutes, his mind totally alert, his body without movement. He could feel the watching. Then suddenly it was over, the birds called to each other, the monkeys sprang from tree to tree, the forest was alive, and Krishnaji came home. In the evening, reports reached the house that the tiger had been sighted in the forest.

Radhika, my eighteen-year-old daughter, and Asit Chandmal, my seventeen-year-old nephew, were to visit Krishnaji and Madhavachari at Chowbatia in May. They would later go abroad to continue their education—Radhika to Bryn Mawr in the United States, where she studied philosophy, and Asit to the Royal College of Science in London.

Krishnaji was happy to have two young people staying with him. Madhavachari gave them quantities of food, and Krishnaji taught them yoga *asanas*, postures. He showed them how to walk, how to stand, how to see from the back of the head. This was to let seeing flow backwards and to see from depth. He took them for long walks, observing, listening, and teaching them to see and listen.

"Pick up a leaf," he said. "Look at it—look far to the snow-clad peaks and let seeing flow beyond and then look very near and relate the looking to listening. Look in the Japanese way," he told them, which Radhika says is to bend the head and look at the world upside down. On one of the walks Asit recollects Krishnaji speaking of the sign of the cross, "The straight line being the 'I' and the vertical bar, the negation of the 'I.' "

Madhavachari was to leave for Madras before Krishnaji, and Murli Rao who had long been associated with Krishnaji, came up from Delhi to take Krishnaji down to the plains. Though the gardeners and the other attendants could not speak English, they had felt the silent, meditative presence of Krishnaji. The news of the great yogi had spread, and people arrived from all over the town to have a *darshan* and bid him goodbye. Krishnaji greeted them with smiles of affection, then before leaving he went round the garden and stood silently before the ancient gnarled deodar and pine trees. Later, Murli Rao asked Krishnaji what he was observing, and Krishnaji replied that he was bidding farewell to his friends. The trees had been his companions for the months he was there, and he had communed with them.

In Bombay, in January 1958, Rao Sahib Patwardhan brought a friend, P. Y. Deshpande—a lawyer, writer, and theoretical Marxist— to see Krishnaji. Disillusioned with Marxism, erudite, known for his intellect and his fierce temper, Deshpande came to meet Krishnaji in Bombay with his wife, Vimla Tai. Sorrow had shattered them; their son was dead and Marxism had no answers. He had turned to his Brahminical past, and he and his wife had studied the *Vedas* and the *Upanishads*. The Hymn to Creation of the *Rigveda* had evoked in them an instant of shattering perception. Deshpande had written a commentary on the hymn, through which he met Rao Patwardhan.

The Deshpandes met with Krishnaji at Himmat Nivas. Deshpande had a frail body, his face was lean and lined with sorrow, but his spirit had an amazing vitality. He told Krishnaji, "I am a Marxist and I want to have it out with you. I have to talk to you, with no holds barred. If what you say is true, I will drop Marxism and join you."

As Deshpande was to describe it later, he tried to wrestle with Krishnaji in words. He challenged Krishnaji but found no one to combat at the other end. This made him frustrated, angry. The stronger and more vehement his enquiry, the emptier the field he faced. Suddenly, all enquiry ended. Krishnaji spoke. "Marxism is not the problem, but the death of your child." The Deshpandes could not proceed further. "Let us speak of that, and of your sorrow," said Krishnaji.

They sat before Krishnaji in silence, while Krishnaji spoke to them on death. When words ended, the Deshpandes walked out with moist eyes. Seeing them, Rao asked, "Is all well with you?" Deshpande said, "All problems are over." They went back to Nagpur, packed up their belongings, and came to live at Sarai Mohana in a cottage on the bank of the Ganga. In later years Deshpande and his wife were to be connected with every aspect of the work at Rajghat.

# CHAPTER 19

# "To Speak with the Whole Head"

In early 1959 it was decided that Krishnaji would not return to Ojai, but would be spending his second year in India. He had been in the country since the autumn of 1957 and was not to return to Europe till the spring of 1960. It was the longest period that he was to spend in India since he left the country as a young boy.

In April, when the damp, hot weather became unbearable, Krishnaji decided to leave Bombay for Lonavala, a small hillside resort between Bombay and Poona. He stayed alone with a servant in the house of Amru Mehta, my youngest sister. Sunanda and her husband, Pama Patwardhan, were at Poona, which was only forty miles from Lonavala, and often came to visit him. He spent most days alone.

In May it had been arranged that he go to Kashmir via Delhi, accompanied by Madhavachari and a South Indian cook named Parameswaran. While in New Delhi Krishnaji insisted that a new woolen suit be tailored for Madhavachari. It gave him great delight to see Madhavachari well dressed, and he remarked, "Mamaji will look very smart now." On their arrival they stayed overnight on a houseboat in Srinagar. The next day they moved to a house located in a crowded part of the city, and in a letter to me Krishnaji expressed his unhappiness with the rat-infested house and its surroundings.

By May 26 Krishnaji and Madhavachari had left Srinagar and driven to Achebal, a *serai* or rest house built by Nur Jehan on the ancient road from Lahore to Srinagar. Achebal is mentioned in the *Akbar Nama** as a place of worship of the ancients; its abundant water, crystal clear and cold, arises from a torrential spring. Occasionally, the *Akbar Nama* goes

*Chronicles of Akbar's life and rule by Abul Fazl.

on to say, a beautiful yellow-spotted fish would appear in the waters, and its appearance was regarded as very fortunate. For hundreds of years pilgrims had come to this sacred site because of the healing properties of the spring water, though myths of the *yakshis*, water and tree spirits who guarded the spring, had long disappeared.

Nur Jehan had built a walled garden around the spring, enclosing an area planted with chinar and poplar trees. At one point in the enclosed area the spring that gushed torrentially from the earth fell as a sheet of water to lower levels of the garden. The huge branches of the chinar trees spread across the falling waters. Below the fall were pools and fountains, and channels had been laid to carry the water to distant parts of the garden. The channels were so planned that the rays of the sun created rainbows as they caught the spray of waterfall and fountain. Flowers had been planted, a trifle wildly, in areas where the chinar and poplar did not cast their shadow. Pavillions, originally built by the Moghuls, but later repaired and bearing little trace of their earlier exquisite proportions, were placed near the pool. The thunder of the waterfall and the sound of rippling water did not intrude to shatter the silences nor disturb the birds that rested in the wide-trunked chinar trees. The countryside was a vast carpet of sun-soaked green young rice fields, against a backdrop of snow-peaked mountains, which arose precipitously on the horizon.

Soon after their arrival Madhavachari had to leave for Madras, as one of his children was ill. But Parameswaran stayed on to attend to Krishnaji's needs. I joined Krishnaji at Achebal on June 6, and lived in a tiny hut next to Krishnaji's till the end of the month.

Before I came up to Kashmir, Krishnaji had written asking me to bring him a beginner's book of English, a copy of Palgrave's *Golden Treasury of English Verse*, and a bottle of hair tonic. I had also brought up a parcel of alfonso mangoes, a fruit Krishnaji loved. There was no electricity in Achebal, and at night we used kerosene lanterns or a petromax.*

K woke at dawn and did his yoga *asanas* and *pranayama*, which he had learned from B. K. S. Iyengar, an eminent teacher of yoga from Poona. Krishnaji was trying to persuade me to learn the yogic *asanas*, but I am by temperament physically lethargic and my attempts to learn were futile. After Krishnaji's *asanas* were over, we had a South Indian breakfast of *idlis* and *sambhar* or *dosas*, savory rice-and-lentil cakes, with

---

*Petromax: Before electricity was introduced in India, lamps fed with kerosene oil with special wicks and with a pump were used to produce a bright light. The petromax is still used at night in wedding processions.

coconut chutney. I drank coffee, Krishnaji drank some herbal concoction.

By then Krishnaji was ready for his long walk, and I joined him in climbing the surrounding hills. Walking through pine forests, we climbed steep slopes; Krishnaji was agile, exquisitely balanced, clambering over rocks and taking the most strenuous shortcuts with ease. I panted and sighed, but I was used to the mountains from childhood and managed to keep pace with him. He would climb swiftly, then look back at me, watching me struggle to negotiate a particularly difficult rock; sometimes he lent a hand and pulled me up behind him, across very steep slopes. From the top of the hill, which we reached after long and arduous climbing, the view was breathtaking. The walled garden and the cool green of rice fields flanked with poplar trees lay below, while the startling white of the snows surrounded us. Krishnaji was enchanted with the place.

In the afternoons, after resting, he would teach Parameswaran English. In the evenings we walked at a slower pace amongst the rice fields, or within the walled Moghul garden. The flowers were in full bloom and the light winds carried the fragrance of rose, lilac, and honeysuckle. Watercress grew along the bed of the stream, and we picked some for our evening meal. There was a trout hatchery, and Krishnaji spent time watching the swift movement of the fish.

Krishnaji was water's child. He delighted in falling, leaping, running water, or water flowing over lichen-covered boulders, or water with no ripple. The translucence and the freedom of water, its enormous turbulence, its stillness or its thrust through earth and rock, embodied him.

Krishnaji's mood was young; no storms raged. Laughter was on his lips and his eyes. He drowned me in compassion and affection. At times he was intensely serious and contemplative. Many of the insights that he was to explore later in the year, in his talks at Madras and Bombay, were arising. Like the tide, or the waxing and waning of the moon, his mind moved in its own rhythm. I saw this man of mystery, endowed with limitless beauty, comment on "the wholeness of sunlight," look up at a budding leaf, put his hands on a centuries-old tree, make friends with it, feel its bark, listen to the thunder of the sap as it flowed through the veins of a leaf. "The timeless is here, it lies under every leaf," he would say. I felt the earth on which we walked, talked, ate, and lived as the ground of an energy without limit. At times I felt intoxicated, as if fed on morning dew.

On a walk he asked me how I observed, and how I spoke. I was puzzled. He then said, "Is it possible to speak, sing, chant, not from the throat and mouth, not from the front of the mouth, but letting the words touch the back of the head, through the eyes, with attention held behind the eyes, and so speak? That is, to speak with the whole head."

We discussed at length the truly religious mind and the scientific mind as the only two minds that would exist in the years to come— a statement that he was to explore later in his talks at Madras. He spoke of death and ending as the source of creation and the release of an energy that did not dissipate. For him, listening was itself the miracle that transmuted and deeply penetrated, uprooting and destroying the hidden bonds of the mind.

On dark, moonless nights we would go out and watch the stars and the receding darknesses of space. He would point out the various constellations. He spoke of the journey into outer space and the pilgrimage within as the discovery of the endless. But a petty mind could not embark on this pilgrimage of eternity.

Every evening was a benediction.

At night, after an early dinner under the light of the petromax, he would recite poetry from the *Golden Treasury*. Keats's "Ode to the Nightingale" was his favorite. It was cold at night and we burned firewood and dry pine cones in the open fireplace. Occasionally, he would chant in Sanskrit. The sounds of his deep voice filled the room and resounded across the rice fields, reaching beyond the snows. Listening and seeing flowered in his pristine presence.

Krishnaji told me that on one of his walks he had met a group of monks walking, within the presence of the snow-clad peaks. They were passing through brilliant green rice fields, and the soaring, snowy peaks were aflame with the setting sun. In the seeing of the vastness was the essence of divinity. The monks, however, walked with their eyes narrowed and focused on the ground before their feet, totally unaware of the glory around them. However silent their minds became, he said, it would be the silence of the limited, of small spaces, and the vast expanding universe would have no place within it.

Every few days I would go to Srinagar by car and return in the evenings. Krishnaji had great feeling for the handcrafted, and I would bring back textiles and craft objects. He handled them with care and rejoiced in their colors, their textures, and the skill of the craftsman. I would also bring back fresh vegetables and fruit, for they were not available at Achebal.

In 1959 I had no knowledge that Achebal was an ancient site of pilgrimage, and that the waters of the spring were held sacred. The local inhabitants, who were Muslims, had erased all traces of their archaic past and the myths connected with it. Krishnaji, however, felt the pulse of the soil, the reverberations of the many pilgrims' feet that had walked on the path to the spring. He often spoke of the role of the pilgrim. I told him of an early text where the feet of the wanderer are likened to a flower. I also said that the pilgrims' route lay in Pahalgam, about forty miles from Achebal. But to no avail.

I grew aware of how difficult it was to live close to Krishnaji without growing insensitive. It was like living in front of a laser beam; one could so easily take the intensity for granted and so be scorched and shrivel. To live near him was to live in a field of observation and listening. One had to be immensely awake so that the spine straightened, the mind became alert, the body still. He was watchful of every movement, every thought; the way one walked, the agitated movements of the body; the way one spoke, the pitch of the voice, the silences. He listened to every response—was aware when the mind imitated, when it was alive with insight. Without a word said, one felt the listening and the observing. But the being who was near, who watched, who listened, was without judgment. It was like seeing one's face in a finely polished ancient bronze mirror.

A little distance from us lived a man who in his young days had taken *sannyas* and had later given up the robe. He was a constant visitor, bringing Krishnaji a vegetal brew he said was good for the kidneys. Krishnaji, instinctively a naturopath, delighted in herbs and drank the brew, insisting that it was good for his kidneys.

By the end of June I returned to Delhi. Madhavachari was soon to rejoin Krishnaji in Pahalgam, the main base camp for pilgrims journeying to Amarnath, one of the most sacred pilgrimages in India. At the Amarnath cave high in the Himalayas, a natural lingam of snow was formed and melted to the cyclic rhythm of the moon. The main pilgrimage was on the full-moon day of August when the lingam appeared in its perfect ovalid form, but from mid-June *sannyasis* and laymen journeyed to the cave. The journey was hazardous. The path lay across high passes and through precipitous gorges. Along the route was Sheshnag, a lake of limpid blue, against which towered high mountains. The full moon rising behind the highest peak, making luminous the eternal snows, was likened to the crescent moon resting on Shiva's matted locks.

At Pahalgam, Krishnaji stayed at a tourist hut set amongst pines. Through the valley, two rivers made turbulent by the massive boulders that lay along their bed, descended from the high places; the Lidar arising from the Kolahai glacier and the other, the Amarganga, sometimes called Sheshnag, along the banks of which lay the path to Amarnath.

*Sannyasis* and visitors from Srinagar came to see Krishnaji, and he talked with some of them. He was to refer to these *sannyasis* in his talks at Madras later in the year. He said, "The other day in Kashmir several *sannyasis* said to me, 'We live alone in the snow. We never see anybody. No one ever comes to visit us.' I said to them, 'Are you really alone, or are you merely physically separated from humanity?' 'Ah, yes,' they replied, 'we are alone.' But they were with their *Vedas* and *Upanishads*, with their experiences and their gathered knowledge, with their meditations and *japams*.* They had not renounced the burden of their conditioning. That is not being alone. Putting on a saffron robe does not mean renouncing. You can never renounce the world, because the world is part of you. You renounce a few cows, a house, but to renounce your heredity, your tradition, the burden of your condition, that demands enormous enquiry."

Most of Krishnaji's walks were alone through the thick forests of pine and fir that surrounded Pahalgam. On August 13 Vinoba Bhave and his followers came to see Krishnamurti.

Vinobaji said this was the first time he had seen Krishnaji. The Gandhian pilgrim asked, "How old are you?"

Krishnaji answered, "Sixty-four."

"So you are my younger brother. I have come to pay my respects and seek your blessings. Rao and Achyut Patwardhan, Dada Dharmadhikari, and Vimla have told me about you several times. But I am always on the move and so are you. So we have never met."

After the pleasantries were over Vinobaji asked Krishnaji to speak to him of his wisdom. Krishnaji appeared shy and was silent. A record of the discussions were kept by Nirmala Deshpande, who was present during the meetings and who took down notes as the conversation took place.[1]

Vinobaji said, "How do we start?"

"It depends on what you are interested," answered Krishnaji.

"Life," responded Vinobaji.

---

*Repeated sound forms or *mantiams* meant to silence the mind.

"Everyone is interested in life. But discussion depends on words, and words are necessary," said Vinoba.

"Not too many words, otherwise discussion loses significance," K replied. "Discussion implies. . . ."

Before Krishnaji could proceed, Vinobaji said, "Sharing experiences."

"Yes, and also to penetrate deeply. Experience is limited—I distrust basing action on experience."

"Is that because experience conditions man?" asked Vinobaji.

"Yes," replied K, "that is why it is important to have a free mind a mind that is not full of experience, but free to see beyond experience. One has to die to experience every day. One is always translating experience in terms of the old. As a Hindu I translate it in terms of Shiva, Krishna—but they are just words."

"The division taking place as Hindu, Muslim, Christian has to be wiped out," said Krishnaji.

Vinobaji responded, "Yes."

"You say 'yes,' but it is a verbal statement. Do you cease to be a Hindu? In science, one drops past experience, to discover a new insight. From the very beginning one should be taught to be free of conditioning—as a Hindu, Muslim, Christian. None of us let go. We only pretend to do so.

"One has to cease to be Hindu or Muslim; one has to be a human being. But that is very difficult. Thinking about being free leads you nowhere.

"First, one must be free. Freedom first, not through thinking about freedom."

Vinobaji asked his comrades to ask questions, but they were hesitant. Vinobaji said to Krishnaji that most people don't want to question, but come for *darshan*. The discussion moved away from the serious, and Vinobaji asked Krishnaji, "How much time do you spend in India?"

"Six months."

"Do you take exercise?"

"A little, I walk."

One of Vinobaji's followers asked, "What is the meaning of self-realization?"

"What does it mean to you?" was the reply.

"Union with Brahman—with God," said one of Vinobaji's disciples.

"God is a phrase. To realize God, you must have a free mind, a good mind that does not follow anybody. A mind that has no guru, no system. Try it."

"How does one get such a mind?" came the reply.

"There has to be self-knowledge. Not knowledge of the Atman, but how one thinks, why one thinks—how one acts. What is the 'oneself?' I am not speaking only of the conscious self, but of the deep levels of the unconscious. What is needed is a revolutionary mind. You cannot have that by *sadhana*. If you see only through one window, your view is limited."

"Is it not possible for philosophy to be taught?" asked one of Vinobaji's followers.

"There is a right way of thinking. Does it matter who listens?" said Krishnaji.

"Perhaps he feels that you should come out as a preacher," Vinobaji intervened.

"Me, Sir! I am talking—that is my life. Do you want me to do it traditionally?"

"Perhaps you are doing in your way what he wants you to do."

"Sir, there is no my way, your way, his way. There is only one way." Krishnaji was uncompromising.

"I think in one way, you think in another. We mislead a whole generation. One has to be free, man has to be free to speak of God. The Communists say there is no God, you say God is. You are both conditioned. You are both saying the same thing. That is the calamity. There is no your or my way of meditation. There is only meditation."

"When you speak this way in the U.S.A., people must appreciate what you say," said Vinobaji.

"In the West the welfare state looks after minimum needs. People are turning to belief, to Christianity, as people here turn to Hinduism. What is the difference? In India economic reform has become all-important—reform and the welfare state is the function of government. But a reformer has nothing to do with religion. A religion is connected with reform and religion with something very different.

"Religion is the source of life, not reform. I am not against reforms. They are necessary. But religion is different.

"I know some Communists in Europe. They are very interested in me up to a point. So also Catholics, up to a point—so are Hindus, up to a point. That is why I am an outsider, whether I am in Europe,

U.S.A., or India. Do you have anything in this country except politics? Why is there nothing deeply creative?

"Why have the majority of thinkers in India given themselves to reform? Reform is a small thing. In the small, the great can never be included. In the great, the small can be included. Wherever I come to India, people ask me why I am not concerned with poverty, corruption? I ask, Why don't we tackle these problems from a different angle? Surely it is the political approach that distorts.

"And why do so-called spiritual minds concern themselves with reform? Reform is not going to lead to deep revolution."

"What do you conclude from this?" asked Vinobaji.

"Not conclude, but observe," answered Krishnaji. "There is a deep contradiction in the Indian mind. We talk about ideals and do the opposite. We are inhibited from becoming something because we feel we should not be ambitious. So frustration leads to superficial reformation and we pursue that with passion. I say, act and observe the result. But tradition and the gurus say the opposite. In this country one sees frustration, contradiction, and the sense of being a very old race. We search for God, but we have not lived life. That may be the reason we turn to the superficial, which we call 'reform.' "

"Are you more appreciated in Europe?"

"I abhor appreciation."

"Do they grasp your thought more?"

"It is the same as in India," replied Krishnaji. "Some minds are serious. People take politics very seriously in India. Politics is most destructive. When people say they are working for peace, for reform, it is always the 'I' that is important. People who touch politics cannot have a fresh mind. The world needs fresh minds, clear minds, not minds that are conditioned by being Hindus or Muslims.

"If you are a Hindu, you can't love. Love requires freedom. The other day a *sannyasi* came to see me. He had been to Amarnath. He spoke of the various sects of *sadhus*. I asked him, 'What do they do?' He said, 'Nothing—but they know Brahman. They live alone. They meditate.' I said, 'With all their beliefs, the load they carry, they can never be alone.'

"But you have to be alone to find the real—totally alone. It is difficult in an old country with its stress on gurus, tradition."

Krishnaji pointed to the people who surrounded Vinobaji. "Are all these your followers? Too bad."

"I don't know why they are my followers," commented Vinobaji.

"In India there is a desire for the authority of a guru. They feel that with guidance, they will not fail to find truth. They are not prepared to make mistakes. It is all childish," said Krishnaji.

"But children, as they are, to be as children becomes them," was Vinobaji's comment.

"Then let Vinobaji deny the follower," swiftly came the reply.

"Every man thinks his search is unique." Vinoba was following his own stream of thinking.

"The search for God isn't linked to success. God may be a being without end. The mind abhors the sense of no ending," said Krishnaji.

"You mean there is no object of search? You cannot search to find God?!" Vinobaji was aroused.

"Yes, otherwise it would be a trivial God. People go to Amarnath to find God. What does it mean? We have banished love, beauty; banished individual thinking, every form of intellectual, emotional curiosity and replaced it with acceptance of authority, systems; denying the mind the space to enquire. What have we done with real creation? We say that to realize God we must don the saffron robe, deny sex, deny the senses, refrain from looking at the clouds, at nature. We say we must meditate. Such meditation is mesmerism."

"What is the place of religion in the progress of a nation?" asked one of Vinobaji's followers.

"What is a nation? What is society?—a relationship social, cultural? If that relationship changes, society changes." Krishnaji paused for a while, then said, "The discovery of reality and its relationship to our daily life is religion. There is no one today who says, 'I am not a Hindu, not a Muslim, but a human being, concerned with the whole problem of man, with the ravaging of the earth, with the atom bomb, with brotherhood.' These are very serious problems and there are not six people who are concerned about them."

"But I have found that the Indian mind has been ready as never before, to grasp new ideas, to shed nationalism and come out of a narrow life." Vinobaji was on the defensive.

"I understand. But, it requires more than that. The mind has become so mechanical. It needs and seeks a goal in life. We follow paths to a goal. We never question. We are too respectable. But one must have a free mind, not a mind burdened with tradition, with the past. Extreme freedom is needed. But the moment you think you are free, you are not free. One has to unearth oneself, unravel oneself, delve into the corners of one's mind—ignite the mind." Krishnaji was pushing further and Vinobaji, perhaps to counter the force of the energy generated, broke into the trivial.

"I am told that you have not given public talks for one year," said Vinobaji.

"Yes, I have not given public talks for one year. I have kept quiet. But that is not because I have taken any vows."

"I am glad I have seen you today. I have been longing for this. Do you know any Indian language?" The discussion was becoming casual.

"I tried to learn Hindi. My native tongue is Telugu, but I left speaking it when I was a boy."

"You are not too old to learn an Indian language," said Vinobaji.

"I am trying to learn Sanskrit—for the fun of it," Krishnaji responded.

"If you speak English, few people in India will understand," said Vinobaji.

"I know. But, if you use traditional words, they have traditional connotations and you cannot proceed."

"Connotations are attached even to English words," Vinobaji said.

"Break them," came the response.

"I find that when you translate Sanskrit words into English, you have to really understand. But if you translate Sanskrit into Hindi or Marathi, you can keep the same word without understanding its depth."

Krishnaji and Vinobaji parted with smiles and *pranams*, and the next day Krishnaji returned Vinobaji's call. Vinobaji spoke of his *Bhoodan Yatra* pilgrimage.* He said, "God, whom I seek, is everywhere—I am not going to Amarnath. People say I am not doing the right thing, I should go. Swami Vivekanand went there." The previous day's discussion had touched some instinctive responses. He said, "Yesterday, we had a very good talk. It was so illuminating. These thoughts have guided me for many years. It was long before I went to Gandhiji. I went to see him when I was twenty. I went to see and hear. He never told me or anybody to accept his thoughts."

"Quite," said Krishnaji.

"You also had an occasion to meet him?"

"Thrice—once in London with Dr. Besant."

"I get very little time to read. Still I read," said Vinobaji.

"I hardly read, except one or two casual books. You leave early in the morning?" The talk was again at the superficial level.

"Half past four. I walk ten miles a day," said Vinobaji. "You write books?" he enquired.

---

*Bhoodan: "gift of the land"; Yatra: "pilgrimage."

"Yes," replied Krishnaji.

"Who publishes these books?" asked Vinobaji.

"The talks and discussions are published in India."

"There are many people in the Bhoodan movement who have read your books," said Vinobaji.

"That is what Rao and Achyut tell me."

Vinobaji pointed to Mahadevi Tai. "She doesn't know English."

"Too bad. I don't know Hindi—so we can't converse," said Krishnaji.

"But you are learning Sanskrit—for the fun of it."

"It is very beautiful, a marvelous language," was Krishnaji's response.

"Every word in Sanskrit is based on some root word. Latin and Sanskrit belong to one family. Your word 'ignite' in Sanskrit is *agni*, as flame. The root meaning of both are the same."

They parted in friendship.

Later, on the evening of August 14, Vinobaji spoke to crowds that had gathered to hear him at Pahalgam. A different direction was present in his talk, and he acknowledged that this was the influence of Krishnaji's meetings with him. He said that men like Krishnaji were the sentinels—their voices and statements were warnings, and must be listened to with gravity. Some months later, a friend was to tell Vinoba Bhave that Krishnaji had remarked, "Vinoba says he agrees with me, but goes on doing his work as before. So his saying that he agrees has no meaning."

Vinoba responded, "Krishnaji is right."

Many years later Nirmala Deshpande told me that Vinobaji had said, "Krishnamurti may deny the role of the World Teacher, negate the church built for him, deny his role as the supreme guru, deny being the divine Krishna; but Dr. Besant could not be denied her role as Yashoda, the foster mother of Krishna, the divine cowherd."

# Part 4

## THE RIVERS OF INSIGHT
### 1960–1962

# CHAPTER 20

# "Through Negation
# There Is Creation."

By the middle of August Krishnaji began to feel unwell. His urinary tract was inflamed, he had a high fever, and was extremely weak. As medical facilities were rudimentary in Pahalgam, Madhavachari brought him down to New Delhi, where he was examined thoroughly by Shiva Rao's doctors. They found a kidney infection and prescribed antibiotics. Krishnaji's highly sensitive body, unused to strong drugs, reacted violently. Those were anxious days. I was away in the United States during his illness, and only heard about it on my return in the third week of September. Kitty and Shiva Rao nursed him with great devotion. After some days, he was better. He returned to Srinagar, to a lovely cottage on Dal Lake that belonged to Dr. Karan Singh (who would have been Maharaja of Kashmir if princely titles had not been abolished).

By the middle of September the fever was back. The damp climate had brought on an attack of rheumatism, and for ten days Krishnaji was racked by joint pain. Madhavachari nursed him, assisted by Parameswaran.

Krishnaji wrote to Kitty Shiva Rao on September 27, 1959:

My dear Kittyji,

I have never written to thank you and Shiva Rao for the care and trouble you took while I was ill in Delhi. It was not negligence but I haven't been able to write. You know all that has happened so I won't go into all that. It has been dreadful ten days and Mamaji has been very disturbed by it all. But everything is better. I can hold a pen and move about. All this has completely exhausted one and now, one must step out of all this. Sorry to have caused you concern and bother. Everything is under control and so things will be all right.

Madhavachari wrote to me with a report on Krishnaji's health. He said Krishnaji had been so weak in Pahalgam that he had to be carried to the bathroom.

On September 27 I received a letter from Krishnaji in which he wrote of the pain he had suffered. It had been agonizing, he said, and this was the first day he could hold a pen. He went on to ask Nandini and me to come to Srinagar and be with him in this quiet and beautiful place. He went on to say, "This has been a great trial for Mamaji." Krishnaji had been taking homeopathic medicines for his trouble, and in his letter of October 4 he asked me to consult L. K. Jha, who had been treating him. He wondered whether he should continue taking alfalfa tonic and beri beri vulgaris, and for how long. The homeopathic medicines seem to have suited him.

I wrote to Krishnaji, suggesting that he come down to Delhi and from there go to Bombay for a complete medical checkup.

On October 5 Krishnaji wrote that he was much better and that he did not think it would be necessary for him to go to Bombay for a thorough examination by doctors there. He also wrote that he was suffering from rheumatism, but felt that it was due to the almond milk he had been drinking. He expected to be in Srinagar till October 21.

Krishnaji recovered, and in early October he even began holding discussions with small groups of people who gathered to see him. Amongst them was a tall, erect *sannyasi* dressed in Kashmiri robes. He had a silent presence, a dignity and otherness that arose from deep inward enquiry. His name was Laxman Joo, and he was the last of the great living exponents of Kashmir Saivism, a school introduced by Abhinav Gupta in Kashmir in the eleventh century. Laxman Joo told me many years later that he had gone to hear Krishnaji in Karan Singh's cottage, and his words had filled him with a vast ecstasy.

Krishnaji came down to Delhi with Madhavachari in the third week of October. He often went for walks on the central vista in New Delhi. On one walk he spoke to Madhavachari and me of awareness as a state of being awake in the present; a state where seeing and listening operated fully and intensely, as in one stream. Where the mind had no shape, no contour of word and meaning; no limits to contain what was revealed. He spoke of a mind that was not concerned with judging, holding, or leaving, where there was "seeing, listening; listening, seeing." "There is," he said, "an explosive quality in listening." Speaking of the act of seeing, listening, he said that "it activates the senses. Seeing without word creates energy. It is a state of understanding of scientific spirit being religious spirit. Listening which receives small and great, ugly and beautiful. Which does not reduce everything to name, form and word. Such a mind is overflowing." He said that the night before he awoke from some great depth, with the word "Lord of the World" resounding in him. There was tremendous light, stronger than the sun.

Soon the fever recurred, but Krishnaji was well enough to travel with me by air to Bombay on November 4. Though he had been ill and was physically weak, the six months of relative solitude had recharged the mind. A vital stream of energy was flowing through him, the mind was wide awake. On the plane he told me of his meeting with Vinoba Bhave and what they had discussed. He said, "What is necessary is to further the mind, and the mind cannot be furthered if there is an end in view."

"What relevance has that to action?" I asked.

Krishnaji responded, "Don't you think that in furthering the mind you do act, but in a different way altogether? To be a revolutionary, you have to see further than the immediate. If you want to further the mind and have object in view, you are limiting the mind. Vinoba has drawn a circle round himself and he remains at the center of it."

In Bombay he was examined by Dr. Nathubhai Patel, who had treated him when he was ill in 1955. Dr. Patel found that there were still pus cells in the urine, and the urinary tract was again inflamed. He was a little worried about Krishnaji's loss of weight—he had lost twenty-five pounds since the beginning of the year. He had been on a very strict diet, and Dr. Patel asked him to give it up and start eating nourishing food—curds, butter, cereals, and ripe bananas. The doctor felt that the rheumatism was probably due to some viral infection, and prescribed some pills and injections. Krishnaji liked the doctor; in a letter to Kitty Shiva Rao he wrote, "Dr. Patel is very good, no fuss and unnecessary remarks. He says, I must put on weight."

From Bombay Krishnaji went with Madhavachari to Rishi Valley, where he recovered rapidly. By November 22 he wrote from Madras:

My dear Kittyji,

Thank you very much for your letter which was waiting at Bombay. I hope, you and Shiva Rao are well and that the new house is pleasant and quiet.

Mama and I have been talking about plans; the doctors seem to think that it would be wiser not to undertake big public talks. I think it is wiser too, so we can only have small, limited group discussions. Mama will let you know when we are both coming North, Mama and I.

You know these black shoes I sent from England, some months ago, are for Shiva Rao and they are not meant to be kept in the safe. Pupul is bringing another pair, brown, for Shiva Rao. She is coming back to Delhi next week I think.

Plenty of rains here; it must be cool and pleasant in Delhi.

With much love to you both.

Krishna

Over the years Sunanda had suffered three miscarriages. At Rishi Valley, she discussed once again her sorrow at her incapacity to have a child. Krishnaji said, "Motherhood is a primordial movement. It is not like the movement of ambition, of becoming. Motherhood is a natural instinct. Everything blooms in a woman—her body, her emotions. Has your body accepted the fact, or your mind?" he asked. "Has it left a mark on the body? If the body accepts it, then there is no conflict between body and mind." They had talked at some length. Sunanda had wept, and he had wiped her tears.

"How will you find out if any scar remains? Whether there is a yearning still lying dormant in consciousness? You have to bring it to the surface, allow it to speak to you, to communicate its intimations."

On walks, he would point to a baby, or a woman heavy with child, and say to Sunanda, "Observe the woman and the child. Don't feel ashamed of the feelings that arise. Don't be intellectual. Listen to your responses. Be awake to every response. See it through completely. Do it now."

She had listened, and commented that she had accepted the fact of remaining childless. He had refused to let her proceed. "Acceptance, adjustment, rationalization are escapes. They have no place. You are being self-defensive. Look at the fact without emotion or sentiment—otherwise you close the door of perception." After some time, he told her, "Listen to your loneliness, frustrations, comparisons. If you so listen, something happens, the ache of the denial of personal motherhood dies."

On November 22 Krishnaji went to Madras, where he was to hold seven discussions. Professors, students, and professionals, as well as members of the Theosophical Society, attended the discussions, which were held under ancient rain trees. The scent of pine, the thunder of falling mountain springs, the astonishing green of young paddy, and an ancient sense of pilgrimage permeated his words. They had a translucence, a lucidity and purity; insights sparkled, the sensory perceptions were tender with creation.

"What I would like to communicate to you is a total self-abandonment on the instant. For abandonment you need passion. Do not be afraid of the word. For, in seeing this, we may solve the one central problem 'of me and my urges.' "

He spoke of a tree with its trunk, its roots, its branches, its leaves, as a totality, and asked, "By some miracle, by some way of looking at the clouds, some instant of cleaving perception, could one see? Could the mind be extraordinarily sensitive to every movement of thought and feeling?

"The timeless is whispering around every corner, it lies under every leaf. It is open not to the dehydrated human being who has suppressed himself and no longer has any passion. But to the mind, which is in a state of meditation, moment to moment."[1]

In another discussion he said, "I think it would be marvelous if without words one could convey what one really feels about the problem of existence. I wonder whether it is not possible to go beyond the frontiers which the mind has imposed, beyond the narrow limits of one's heart and to live there; to act, feel, think; while carrying on one's own activities?"

When questioned on the need for regular practice, he said, "Practice for ten thousand years, you will still be within the field of time, of knowledge.

"The self, the 'me' is restless. Roaring down like a river, living, moving, being. Self-knowing is extraordinarily swift in its perceptions. Accumulation of knowledge gives birth to the 'me.' "

Questioned on death, he spoke of "death and life walking together." The fear of complete loneliness, isolation, of not being anything, is the root of self-contradiction. Creation is in ending, not in continuity.

"If there is a living coming to an end from moment to moment, there is an extraordinary state of being nothing. Of coming to the abyss of an eternal movement and dropping over the edge, which is death. I want to know all about death, because death may be reality, God, that extraordinary something that lives and moves."

In December 1959 Krishnaji went to Bombay. By then he had completely recovered and it was decided that he give eight talks. Like a fast-moving current, new insights of the teaching were flowing through consciousness, washing away the impurities, the problems and conflicts of everyday living. Krishnaji's language was tender, vast perceptions and depths were evident. Like the waters of the snow-fed springs and rivers of Achebal and Pahalgam, insights were generated that had to travel far, exploring, finding new channels, generating life. At the talks and in the small discussions he was to speak of the urgency that rested behind asking the right question. It was this, he was to say, that brings about right perception. "A perceiving mind is living, moving, full of energy.

"There are no answers to life's questions. The state of mind that questions is more important than the question itself." Speaking of conditioning and freedom from bondage, he said, "If it is a right question, it will have no answer, because the question itself will open the door. But, if it is a wrong question, you will find ways and means to solve the problem and so remain in bondage. For he who asks the question is himself the bondage."

He spoke of "efficiency, essential in technology; but in the within of man, in the world of the psyche, is tyranny." For when "means are used for ends, means strangle you."

At another talk he spoke of an exploration into the within. "To uncover is to discover, but to accumulate what you discover is to cease to discover." He was speaking in the tree-filled compound of the J. J. School of Art. Crows nested in the trees on evenings, and his words were interspersed with their harsh cries.

"Have you ever listened to the noise of a crow? Actually, listened to it without shutting it out as ugly. If you are capable of so listening, there is no division between the noise and what is being said. Attention implies a clarity of altogetherness, in which there is no exclusion." He dwelt on the altogetherness of a mind, a mind that had no past, no future; it was a feeling, a fullness with no center.

"I have nothing to offer," he continued. "If you are listening, you are already in that state." "No guru is going to tell you that you are doing well. That you may go to the next examination. You are listening to yourself and that is an art."

He saw that any change with motive was a seeking of power, and asked, "Can the mind, without motive, let go? That is real renunciation. Keep the mind clean, alert, watchful, observe every thought, see its significance without motive, urge, or compulsion, then there comes an energy that is not your own, which descends upon you. There is a limitless being, and in that energy is reality."[2]

A sense of flux permeated his words. He explored the nature of the verb as an unbroken movement, a total state containing past, future, and an active present. "We are not concerned with being, but with having been and becoming. There is an active present, a state of being, a living, active state."

He spoke of listening as a state of comprehension, of being, in which all time was included.

Then he asked, "With the understanding of the verb, let us examine the nature of the self. The self is me."

On January 10 he spoke of sorrow. To end it, sorrow has to be embraced, lived with, understood; one has to become intimate with sorrow. Running away from sorrow is what one knows; it is an escape from it. Understanding of sorrow is an explosion, a revolt, a tremendous discontent in everything. To understand death and sorrow one must have a burning urge, an intensity, and face the fact. Death is unknown, as sorrow is; but to know the nature, the depth, the beauty, and loneliness of sorrow, is its ending. "Benediction comes when there is a state of nonreaction. It is a benediction to know death because death is the unknown."[3]

Seeing the intense, sorrow-laden, tormented faces in his audience, he spoke on January 17 of learning to play with a problem. Unless you can play, you will never find out. If you don't know how to smile, not only with your lips but with your whole being, with your eyes, your mind, and heart, then you don't know what it is to be simple and take delight in the common things of life." And later, he laughed with joy and said, "Unless you are capable of laughter, real laughter, you don't know what sorrow is. You don't know what it is to be serious."[4]

Speaking of meditation, he said, "For most of us, what is explored is not important; therefore, it does not open up the capacity to enter into 'what is.' Life is an extraordinary thing—we call the past the time before, and the future as the time after; can one go into it through the present? Truth has no future, no past, no continuity. Meditation is the state of living in which the frontiers of the mind break down. There is no self, no center, and, therefore, no circumference."

He explored the nature of negative thinking. Positive thinking, as an assertion, is destructive to enquiry. "Through negation there is creation," he said. "Whatever is born of a mind, that is completely empty, is creation. Out of that arises negative thinking. Such an approach, based as it is on attention, can have no measure. The mind that goes into itself deeply enters on a pilgrimage of enquiry from which there is no return." For this one needs to be completely alone—no companionship, no dependence, no attachment, thought, or memories; a total denial of everything. "To open the door to the eternal, the journey into the self is the only way."

Krishnaji returned to Europe in March 1960. On reaching Rome, he felt very unwell and entered the Bercher Brenner Clinic in Zurich. There, after a detailed medical examination, they put him on a special diet.

Later, he went to Ojai, where he was scheduled to give eight talks. Suddenly, after the third talk, he announced that he would give only four.

# CHAPTER 21

# "The Mind That Goes into Itself Deeply Enters on a Pilgrimage from Which There Is No Return."

Krishnaji returned from the West in the autumn of 1960, having sensed the volcanic energies being released in the new scientific and technological mind. With the eye of prophesy, Krishnaji looked into the years that lay ahead. He perceived the accelerated pace of change that was to come about with the unlocking of the mysteries of nature, and the invention of tools and systems that would transform society and environment and generate enormous pressures on humankind. He also appeared aware of a rapid trend toward chaos and violence.

Madhavachari had come to meet him in New Delhi and was staying with me. In the evenings we took Krishnaji to the Buddha Jayanti Park, which he loved, and we walked amongst the rocks, trees, and bushes. One evening he began to speak of the nature of creation, of negation being the source of creation.

"Creation can only be when the mind is completely empty; whatever is born of that emptiness is negative thinking. It has no root, no source." He was to enquire into a state in which the frontiers of the mind broke down. So that in such a state there was no self, no center, and no circumference. "Most of us have never wandered into ourselves." He said, "Never look without calculations," and spoke of intelligence as the tool of enquiry: "The probing is with nothing into endless being."

In January 1961 Krishnaji was in Bombay, where he gave ten talks and held small group dialogues. Like the churning of the oceans of mind in the archaic myth of creation, jewels of insight were arising. With immense passion, Krishnaji said, "The world is becoming something totally new. Space is being conquered, machines are taking over, tyranny is spreading." Sensing the limitations of the minds that listened to his words, and their incapacity to comprehend the enormity of the winds of change, the growing inhumanity and callousness, Krishnaji sought to convey the urgency he felt.

"Something new is going on of which we are not aware. . . . You are not aware of the movement, the significance, the flow, the dynamic quality of this change. We think we have time. . . . There is no time, . . . the house is burning."[1]

"Wandering about the land [in India]," he observed an appalling death of human integrity. He spoke with passion of the demand for a new mind, "a good mind which held pity, affection, compassion. The old mind could no longer deal with the challenges that were so intricate, so subtle, so diffused." A new enquiry was needed. "Can one wipe out everything? And start anew?"

"How do you enquire?" asked Krishnaji. For him, there were three ways: "It is possible, it is not possible, it may be possible." The first two responses were an ending of enquiry, for they were limited by their certainties and so were held in time. It was only in a tentative delving into "the may be possible" that true enquiry was revealed. At his talks, in discussions, at the breakfast and lunch table, he spoke again and again of the need for a new mind; a mind that could only arise "out of the void, out of complete negation, in a state of revolution, when the mind is completely alone."

He spoke of exploration as a negative awareness in which there was perception without recording; a state of pure seeing without opinion, judgment, or conclusion. Moving away from the step-by-step observation and enquiry of the 1950s, he explored the new mind with its capacity to comprehend the whole; this was only possible "when the mind is not concerned with the particular; then comprehending the whole, it can play with the particular.

"One has to see inwardly and outwardly. That seeing brings an extraordinary energy. In that seeing, there is an awareness that there is no outer and inner, they are really one continuous movement. It is the tide going out and the tide coming in." Seeing that his listeners were perplexed, he said, "Time prevents perception. A mind that thinks of distance as space from here to there, as becoming, as achievement, such a mind cannot see a thing totally."

He was probing into "mind," discovering insights of the "new" as he observed. "The quality of going beyond itself belongs to the new mind, which is free of time; time as an inner psychological process. The time of the psyche brings about fear and so limits the flow. To understand the enormous pervasive nature of fear, to see the complexities in which mind is entangled, you must understand time. Fear and time go together." Perceiving the shadows on the faces of his listeners, Krishnaji said, "Fear is the destructive energy in man, it withers the mind."

Speaking to small groups, he had gone deep into the nature of the challenges facing humankind. He said that the crisis was of a different dimension to that faced earlier. In these talks in Bombay, Krishnaji was penetrating deeply into the nature of the scientific mind and the religious mind; the only two minds that could survive in the future. He asked himself, "Can the scientific mind with its logic, its investigation into matter, energy, enter into the religious mind?" and answered, "When the scientific mind breaks through the limitations of the known—then perhaps it approaches the religious mind."

He probed further. "The scientific mind with its logic, its precision, its enquiry, investigates the outer world of nature, but this does not lead to an inward comprehension of things; but an inward comprehension brings about an understanding of the outer. We are the result of the influences of the outer. The scientific mind is precise and clear in its investigation. It is not a compassionate mind, for it has not understood itself.

"What is the true religious spirit?" he asked. "Obviously, not the man who believes—who goes to temples and churches. Nor is the reaction to that the religious spirit. It is only when one denies all belief or nonbelief, when there is a seeing of the fact and the falseness of belonging and reaction, that the mind is in a state of negation, which means the mind is alone, it has no authority, no goal; therefore, it is not in a state of fear, which is reaction.

"The religious mind is not ritualistic. It is capable of thinking precisely, not in terms of the negative and positive; therefore, that mind has within it the scientific mind. But the scientific mind does not contain the religious mind, because it is based on time, knowledge; it is rooted in success and achievement.

"How does the religious mind enter the unknown?" He was questioning himself aloud. "It cannot come to the unknown except by 'jumping.' It cannot calculate and enter the unknown.

"The religious mind is the real revolutionary mind. It is not a re-

action to what has been. The religious mind is explosive—creative . . .
It is in a state of creation.[2]

"The religious mind is the only mind that can respond totally to
the present challenge and to all challenges, at all times." He paused
for a long time to permit the words to sink deep. "Can this mind be
so solitary, solid in its aloneness, like fire?"

Again he questioned himself. "How can radical transformation from
the roots of one's being come about? How can one recognize a religious
mind? How does one recognize a saint? What does the word 'recognize'
mean? To see again? Can one explode the pattern we have of a saint?
You must explode the pattern to find the religious mind. Then there
is no saint. He may be around the corner, unrecognized."

His questioning continued. "Can one observe without reaction? To
observe without the center is the negative process. The mind is a slave
to words. Can it be free of them?" Seeing the strained look on the faces
of listeners, striving to reach the essence of his questions, he smiled,
drawing the audience close to him. "Can you play with this a little?

"To find out whether there is God or no God, or if there is something more than thought, you must shatter the whole background,
must you not? Seeing the truth that any conditioning is destructive to
perception, can the mind break through without reaction? That breaking through opens the whole field of self-knowing."

In a public meeting he was asked, "How did the first mind come
about?" His answer denied all theoretical speculation. "The fact is we
are here. To investigate origins, you have to investigate what you are
now. Is there a beginning and an ending? Do not ask what is the beginning. We started the discussion with time and the timeless; that
brings us to existence, to living, to what we are. Can we be ruthless
in our investigation of what we are? Can we understand what is the
present? Then we will touch the beginning and ending of all things.
To question rightly is to see that there is no beginning, no ending. To
understand this extraordinary sense of timelessness, you have to understand the mind in the present. The human mind, as it is now, is
the result of environment. The mind has to extricate itself from all
influences to find the 'timeless.'

"To understand time, not put it aside, not create a theory about it,
you have to investigate your own mind, grow aware of the extraordinary impact of influence. Time is the influence of a thousand yesterdays. There is not only chronological time, time by the watch, but
there is time as memory, stretching backwards and forwards. This
memory is unconscious, buried, hidden deep in the vast recesses of

one's mind. There is time, from place to place, from here to there, and there is time as becoming. I am this and I shall be that. This reaching into the future to become introduces the permanent and the transient.

"There is time when you sow—time when you reap." He probed into inward time as memory, with its extraordinary complexity and subtlety. "Can we investigate into the self like the scientist?" he asked.

On another evening he explored the nature of the observer and the observed. The distance between the observer and the observed creates duality. "It is only when the mind observes itself as being conditioned that there is no observer. Can the mind observe itself as the observer? It is not a rare thing. When you are angry, passionate—in that state there is no observer, nor the observed as thought."

Speaking of the unknown, the void, from which alone the new mind could emerge, he said, "The mind cannot come to it; the mind that measures itself in time must wipe itself away and enter into that, without knowing that. You cannot know it. It has no color, no space, no shape. You cannot make a statement about it. All you can do is to jump out of the old, then you won't even know, for you are part of that extraordinary state."

He was holding the problem of the scientific mind and the religious mind in consciousness; his mind awake, listening to the intimations of the "new mind."

He was to discuss the question again and again. "What is needed is a new mind that functions wholly. The scientific mind is directive; the religious mind explodes without direction. Self-knowing is essential; because it is only a mind in self-knowing, because it is understanding itself, that it withers away, for the new mind to be.

"What is demanded is a fertile mind. Fertile in the sense of rich, in which a seed can grow, be nurtured, carefully watched over; a mind that is deeply enquiring, searching, looking, watching. Only that mind, exquisitely pliant, not tethered to anything, is sensitive. The fertile mind is empty, like the womb before it conceives. Can you take one thing? Take envy—understand it and go through it ruthlessly. Put your teeth into it and strip the mind of envy. Take stock of yourself, day after day, minute after minute, to ruthlessly penetrate this appalling thing—envy."

Like a shaft of fire, penetrating, his words dispelled shadows in the within. "The mind is a vast thing. It is not a spot in the universe. It is the universe. To investigate the universe demands an astonishing energy. It is energy greater than all rockets, because it is self-perpetuating, because it has no center. This is only possible when there is an enquiry into the inner and outer movement of the mind. The inner, the racial unconscious, in which are the urges, compulsions, the hidden dark fears, is the story of man. How do you observe? How do you listen? If the observation, the listening, is direct, then you are observing negatively. Then the mind has no conclusions, no opposites, no directives. In that looking it can see what is near and what is far away. In that there is an ending. Such a mind is the new mind. It has exploded without direction. Such a mind is the religious mind."

Then he opened up the nature of such a mind, a mind for which there has to be hard, arduous work. "But," he said, "you cannot watch from morning till night. You cannot be vigilant, never blinking for the whole day. So play with it. Play with it lightly. To question 'how am I to be aware' is to create conflict. But as you are playing, you learn.

"The mind that explodes without direction is compassionate, and what the world needs is compassion, not schemes.

"The new mind is not within the field of knowledge. It is that state of creation which is exploding. For that, all knowledge has to come to an end.

"The new mind cannot come into being with authority, with masters, with gurus. With a burnt-out mind, you cannot come to the new mind. You need a fresh, eager, live mind." He then held out the key. "What releases energy is direct perception. The greater part of the brain is the residuary animal and the remaining part undefined. We live our life in the very small part. We never investigate. Sensitivity arises when you watch a tree, bird, animal, ant. Watch how you walk, bathe, dress; watch yourself being important. If you so watch, if you so observe thought and every emotion, flowering, then the brain is very sensitive; out of that, the flowering of the mind begins. That is mutation.

"To watch, to observe everything, is to be aware of totality, never to limit any thought, to let everything flower. A mind that is completely quiet, without any reaction, is only an instrument of observation. It is alive, sensitive.

"Mutation is only possible when you have brought this about through awareness, without effort. The challenge of the present time and of every instant, if you are awake, is to respond totally to something that is new.

"Creation is not invention. The universe is not made of invention."

# CHAPTER 22

# "Be Awake."

Krishnaji left India for Rome in the middle of March 1961. A few days before his departure Nandini had been talking to him in his room at Himmat Nivas in Bombay. Krishnaji was sitting cross-legged on his bed, Nandini on the mat-covered floor close by. Suddenly, in the middle of the conversation, he stopped speaking; his straight back became still, his eyes closed, and like a swift moving tide, she felt it, pouring in through the doors and windows—rivers of silence that bathed her body, entering the pores of her skin, saturating her. She too became totally still and died to the world. She does not know how long it lasted. Suddenly, she heard the voice of Krishnaji and grew aware of her surroundings. She had felt the strength needed to hold this silent roaring wind, and commented on it.

For some time after that Krishnaji was far away. Krishnaji's long periods of rest and the silences of Ranikhet and Kashmir had triggered the awakening of these immense rivers of energy. Insights awakened and converged that were to flower in the "notebooks" Krishnaji was to start writing in the spring of 1961.

From the plane on his way to Rome on March 25, Krishnaji wrote to Nandini:

Half an hour out of Bombay, at 35,000 ft., the sky was blue, so blue, so intense, so pale, so soft that it brought tears to one's eyes, at one time the blue was almost black; we were so high, the plane so steady and the sea so far below, there was a strange sense of peace and incomprehensible vastness from horizon to horizon, there was this cloudless dome of intense blue; at the horizon, the blue was almost tender green. It was a marvelous sight, something incredibly beautiful. In the cabin it was freshly cool, almost cold, which revived one after the heat. It took some time to come back to oneself and I am sorry if I made a nuisance of myself before leaving. It was bright and warm when we arrived but it has become cold and rainy.

Writing to Nandini from Rome, he said:

Resting and doing nothing must have pushed the body to the limit and now it is flat. Hope you are well. Don't please do these exercises with any strain; if there's a strain, the exercises are not being done properly. Give complete attention and things will come right. Don't settle down; keep the flame alive. It has been altogether strange and don't get lost in trivialities; don't let yourself be drowned; keep awake; be in a state of complete attention.

Signora Vanda Scaravelli, an old friend of Krishnaji's, was a remarkable woman, with the fire, eccentricity, quickness of mind and body of the fine-bred Italian. She met Krishnaji in Rome, and after a few days was to travel with him to Il Leccio, near Florence. Later, in Geneva, he underwent a complete medical checkup at the Bercher Brenner Clinic.

In May, Krishnaji was in London. Miss Doris Pratt, the representative of K. W. I. in England had arranged for his stay in a house near Wimbledon Common. She was there to look after him. He held meetings with and gave talks to a small group of specially invited people. In the evenings he went for long walks alone on Wimbledon Common. On May 12 he wrote to Nandini:

The wheels* of Ooty are working, unknown to any, and other things are taking place. It is so extraordinary, and words seem so futile. Days are too short and one lives in a day, a thousand years. Keep alive, aware and don't let anything whatsoever smother the flame. Don't let a single thought escape without observing from where it came, its motives, and significance. Keep awake.

Another letter arrived from Wimbledon on May 18:

As one grows older, as the mind gets more set and more mechanical, it is very important to break down every pattern of thought and feeling—to be aware of every movement of thought, to watch ceaselessly, never to allow moods to gather strength or allow the physical to cloud the clarity of the mind. Don't let the flame die down or let the smoke of everyday events smother it. Strangely the things that happened at Ooty are taking place, though no one knows about it—it is very strong. The wheels of Ooty are working powerfully. I am surprised.

These references to Ooty were to occur again on June 1, when he wrote from London:

Don't be smothered by mediocrity and by everyday events of nothing. Be

---

*His use of the word "wheels" refers to the *chakras*.

intense and don't let the flame die. Everything is well here. The wheels of Ooty are working furiously and painfully.

Miss Pratt had noticed that Krishnaji was undergoing some mysterious experiences. In a letter to Rajagopal she described what was happening. She questioned Krishnaji, and he told her that there was nothing anyone could do except keep quiet, relaxed, and not worry; but he said not to let anyone touch him. She went on to say that she felt she was an onlooker at a most profound and tremendous mystery.[1]

Krishnaji flew to Ojai via New York on June 14. My daughter Radhika, who was working for her Ph.D. at Bryn Mawr, came to see him on June 16. In a letter to Nandini, Krishnaji said:

Saw Radhika—looks well and we had a long talk. Life is short and there is so much to discover not outwardly but within. There are vast unexplored regions within and don't let a day go by without discovering something. Be explosive inwardly and then the outer things will take care of themselves.

On June 17, the day before he left for Ojai, he began to write a record of his pilgrimage into the vast oceans of "otherness." The immense insights and the perceptions without horizons that he was to write about in the *Notebook* were unfolding.

The letters to Nandini started again in July from Ojai. On July 4, he wrote to her:

You may remember that two days before I left, you were aware of that strange energy in the room. To stand it one has to be tremendously "strong." You used that word. Be of it. For that's here now and the wheels of Ooty are working. Don't get entangled, be aware of deep thoughts and feelings. Be direct simple and clear.

The letters continued. On July 19 he wrote from Gstaad:

Fear really destroys and perverts all seeing. It breeds illusion; it dulls the mind, it destroys dignity. Search it out—be open to it. Don't find excuses for it. Go into it ruthlessly. Be aware of every form of fear and wash it away. Don't let it remain with you for a single minute. There is no innocency [sic] where there is fear, jealousy, attachment. Be burningly aware of it. The wheels of Ooty have been working.

Signora Scaravelli, his hostess in Gstaad, has described Krishnaji's states of consciousness while he was at Chalet Tannegg.* They were

---

*Chalet Tannegg is in Gstaad, Switzerland. Krishnaji lived there every year in the months of July and part of August till 1983 as a guest of Signora Vanda Scaravelli. During this period he held talks and discussions in Saanen.

similar to and yet different from what took place at Ootacamund. The intense pain was absent. The states of otherness and benediction arose in his walks, in the house, while he was awake, or as he awoke from sleep. Vanda Scaravelli sensed the sacred presence that was around and within him. She spoke of the face-changing and of an awareness, a simultaneous feeling of emptiness and fullness. All the time he was giving talks in Saanen. They were not independent of his states. All separation between these mystic happenings and his daily life appears to have ended.

On July 18, while in Gstaad, he wrote in the *Notebooks:* "Our eyes and brain register the outward things, trees, mountains, swift running streams; accumulate knowledge, technique and so on. With that same eyes and brain, trained to observe, to choose, to condemn and justify, we turn inward, look inward, recognize objects, build up ideas, which are organized into reason. This inward look does not go very far, for it's still within the limitation of its own observation and reason. This inward gaze is still the outward look and so there's not much difference between the two. What may appear to be different may be similar.

"But there's an inward observation which is not the outward observation turned inward. The brain and the eye which observe only partially do not comprehend the total seeing. They must be alive completely but still; they must cease to choose and judge but be passively aware. Then the inward seeing is without the border of time-space. In this flash a new perception is born."[2]

As far as we know, this was the last occasion when he was to experience such events. In later years other states of vastness and emptiness were to arise, he was to faint and be out of his body; but these processes appear to be of another nature.

K came back to Rishi Valley in the late autumn of 1961. Dr. Balasundaram was principal. The relationship between the students, the teachers, and the principal was warm and friendly; there was a living quality in the atmosphere. K sensed this and responded with passion and abundance. He had an immense empathy with the land and the surrounding hills. He could see Rishi Konda from his window, and the dialogue with the "sculptured" hill had commenced. To K the state of well being of the valley and its inhabitants was communicated in the intensity of the benediction that flowed from the hill. Local legends spoke of seers and sages who lived on Rishi Konda. At night inexplicable lights appeared and traveled across the slopes.

K continued to write his *Notebook*. A great benediction comes

Krishnaji at Rishi Valley School: addressing
a gathering of students in the early 1970s; in
discussion with a student in December 1982;
listening to a music concert in December
1980 (Photo: M. A. Hamid).

Krishnaji in November 1982, holding the hand of Maya, a Rishi Valley student. Pointing to the pole that separates them, he comments "the eternal problem."

Krishnaji in December 1982 with G. Narayan, the principal of Rishi Valley School and Radhika Herzberger, the director of studies.

Krishnaji in discussion with Pupul Jayakar and Achyut Patwardhan, Rishi Valley, December 1984.

Krishnaji in December 1981 writing at his desk in his bedroom at Rishi Valley.

Krishnaji in November 1982 with Palghat Mani Aiyar, a Master of percussion in residence at Rishi Valley School.

Krishnaji and Asit Chandmal at lunch in a hotel at Gstaad, Switzerland in July 1982.

Krishnaji at Rishi Valley School, December 1980, bidding farewell to Rajiv Gandhi and his mother Indira whom he was later to succeed as prime minister of India. (Photo: M. A. Hamid)

Krishnaji with Achyut Patwardhan in New Delhi, November 1981.

Mahesh Saxena in Vasant
Vihar, Madras, January 1986.

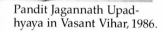

Pandit Jagannath Upad-
hyaya in Vasant Vihar, 1986.

Nandini Mehta in Bombay,
January 1981.

Krishnaji with Indira Gandhi and Pupul Jayakar at Rishi Valley School. (Photo: M. A. Hamid)

Vasant Vihar, the headquarters in Madras
of the Krishnamurti Foundation India.

Krishnaji listening to music
after a Sunday talk in Bombay,
February 1980. (Photo: Asit Chandmal)

Krishnaji with the members of the Krishnamurti Foundation India, December 8, 1985: (from left to right, front row) R. R. Upasini, Dr. Parchure, Pt. Jagannath Upadhyaya, Krishnaji, Dr. Krishna, G. Narayan; (second row) Padma Santhanam, Prema Srinivasan, Sunanda Patwardhan, Achyut Patwardhan, Radhika Herzberger, Pupul Jayakar, Nandini Mehta, Anantaswamy; (standing) Amarendra Roy, Mahesh Saxena, Pama Patwardhan, Dr. Hiralal, Kabir, Asit Chandmal, Rajesh Dalal, Ahalya Chari, Sathe, Murali Rao, Meheralli, and to the extreme right is Parmeshwaran, Krishnaji's cook who served K and the Riski Valley School since the early 1950s. (Photo: Mark Edwards. Copyright © The Krishnamarti Foundation)

A child approaches Krishnaji with a flower at the end of his last talk, which ends with silence. (Photo: Asit Chandmal)

The last talk in Vasant Vihar, Adyar, Madras, January 3, 1986. (Photo: Asit Chandmal)

Krishnaji, January 10, 1986, on his last walk on the Adyar Beach—a strong wind sweeps his hair back like a comet's tail. (Photo: Asit Chandmal)

through his words. Whatever was in him and around him penetrated the soil of the valley and is still felt by many sensitive visitors. "For the otherness was there, and coming up the valley; it was like a curtain of rain but only there was no rain; it was coming as a breeze comes, softly and gently and it was there outside and inside."[3]

Radhika and I were with Krishnaji in Rishi Valley for the period he was there. K went for long walks alone or with Dr. Balasundaram and Radhika. The trees that had been planted in the late 1940s were now full grown; the wells had made possible the planting of paddy; the valley was alive with green, sap-filled shrubs; the paths were fragrant with white flowers shed by avenues of cork trees.

The children who had gathered on the hilltop at Astachal to witness the sun sink below the horizons felt the colors explode within them. They were silently aware of the stranger in their midst and the skies that were ablaze to welcome him. K later wrote in the *Notebook*:

The earth was the colour of the sky; the hills, the green, ripening rice fields, the trees and the dry, sandy river-bed were the colour of the sky; every rock on the hills, the big boulders, were the clouds and they were the rocks. Heaven was the earth and the earth heaven; the setting sun had transformed everything. The sky was blazing fire, bursting in every streak of cloud, in every stone, in every blade of grass, in every grain of sand. The sky was ablaze with green, purple, violet, indigo, with the fury of flame. Over that hill it was a vast sweep of purple and gold; over the southern hills a burning delicate green and fading blues; to the east there was a counter sunset as splendid in cardinal red and burnt ochre, magenta and fading violet. The counter sunset was exploding in splendour as in the west; a few clouds had gathered themselves around the setting sun and they were pure, smokeless fire which would never die. The vastness of this fire and its intensity penetrated everything and entered the earth. The earth was the heavens and the heavens the earth. And everything was alive and bursting with colour and colour was god, not the god of man. The hills became transparent, every rock and boulder was without weight, floating in colour and the distant hills were blue, the blue of all the seas and the sky of every clime. The ripening rice fields were intense pink and green, a stretch of immediate attention. And the road that crossed the valley was purple and white, so alive that it was one of the rays that raced across the sky. You were of that light, burning, furious, exploding, without shadow, without root and word. And as the sun went further down, every colour became more violent, more intense and you were completely lost, past all recalling. It was an evening that had no memory.[4]

In his talks to the children and teachers K questioned the place of knowledge in the transformation of man. The minds of the children were alive, quickened by direct contact with K's presence, the bene-diction, an ocean in which he walked and talked. The clarity and depth of the insights revealed in the talks were startling. These talks were later to appear in *Krishnamurti on Education*. In the talks K emphasized the two instruments available to the human mind: knowledge, which enables one to gain mastery over the material environment; and intel-ligence, which is born of observation. To the child he said, "A new mind is only possible when the religious spirit and the scientific atti-tude form part of the same movement of consciousness." To K they were not separate movements that had to be fused, but a new move-ment inherent in intelligence and in the creative mind.

K denied all hierarchical relationships. To him right communion was only possible when the teacher and student functioned at the same level, communicating through question and counterquestion, until in the act of learning the problem was explored fully and understanding illumined the mind of the student and teacher simultaneously.

Speaking to the child of fear, K said, "When you see fear, enquire into it, face it, then it goes away." He explored with the child the complex problem of fear. He unraveled the enormous darknesses of fear and the nature of becoming with delicacy and lucidity. He spoke of time by the watch and inner time, which is created by the psyche, as becoming the "I shall be." Projection into the future is the root of fear.

A child asked him about death. "There are two kinds of death," he said. "Bodily death and death of thought." The body, the physical organism, has to end. "We are not afraid of that. We are afraid that thought as the 'me,' which has lived, acquired money, family, the 'me' that wants to become important, will end." He asked the child, "Do you see the difference between the physical dying and the 'me' dying?" Children listened, the seed of intelligence was planted, on rich earth or barren rocky soil—only the future would reveal.

He introduced the child to self-knowing and meditation. At the end of one talk, he said, "First of all, sit completely quiet, comfortably, sit very quietly, relax. Now, look at the trees, at the shape of the hills, and look at the quality, the color, of the trees. Do not listen to me. Watch and see those trees, the yellowing trees, the tamarind, and then look at the bougainvilleas. Look not with your mind, but with your eyes. After having looked at the colors, the shapes, and the shadows of the trees, of the hills, the rocks, then from the outside move to the inside. Close your eyes, close your eyes completely. You have finished looking at things outside, and now with your eyes closed, look at what is happening inside. Watch what is happening inside you. Do not think, but just watch. Do not move your eyeballs, just keep them very very quiet. There is nothing to see now, you have seen all the things around you, now you are seeing what is happening inside your mind. And to see what is happening inside your mind, you have to be very quiet inside. And when you are quiet, do you know what happens to you? You become very sensitive, you become very alert to things outside and inside. Then you find that the outside is the inside. Then you find out that the observer is the observed."[5]

He spoke with the same directness to the teacher as he did to the child. He spoke of the urgency and necessity to have a long vision, in which the little things are contained. He explored with tactile subtlety the many darknesses of the mind.

K's final talk, "On Flowering," is perhaps one of the most daring and explosive of any talk on education.

"Can frustration flower?" he asked. "How do you question so that frustration unfolds, so that frustration flowers? It is only when thought flowers that it can naturally die. Like the flower in a garden, thought must blossom, it must come to fruition and then it dies. In the same way, thought must be given freedom to die. And the right question is whether there can be freedom for frustration to flower and to die?"

A teacher asked what he meant by "flowering." Krishnamurti answered, "Look at the garden, the flowers in front over there! They come to bloom and after a few days they wither away, because it is their nature. Now, frustration must be given freedom so that it blossoms.

"Your question was: 'Is there a momentum which keeps moving, keeping itself clean, healthy?' That momentum, that flame which burns, can only be when there is freedom for everything to flower— the ugly, the beautiful, the evil, the good, the stupid—so that there is not a thing suppressed, so that there is not a thing which has not been brought out and examined and burnt out. And I cannot do that if through the little things I do not discover frustration, misery, sorrow, conflict, stupidity, dullness. If I only discover frustration through reasoning I do not know what frustration means."

The teachers were unable to understand, and questioned further. "You see," responded K, "to you flowering is an idea. The little mind always deals with symptoms and never with the fact. It does not have the freedom to find out. It is doing the very thing which indicates the little mind, for it says, 'It is a good idea, I will think about it,' and so it is lost for it is then dealing with idea, not with fact. It does not say, 'Let it flower, and see what happens.' Then it would discover. But it says, 'It is a good idea, I must investigate the idea.' "

He told the teachers that most people were prisoners of little things. Then he asked, "Can I see the symptom, go into the cause, and let the cause of flower? But, I want it to flower in a certain direction, which means I have an opinion on how it should flower. Now, can I go after that? Can I see that I prevent the cause flowering because I am afraid I do not know what will happen if I allow frustration to flower? So, can I go into why I am afraid? I see, that so long as fear exists there can be no flowering. So I have to tackle fear, not through the idea of fear, but tackle it as a fact, which means, can I allow fear to blossom?

"All this requires a great deal of inward perception. To allow fear to blossom—do you know what that means? Can I allow everything to blossom? This does not mean I am going to murder, rob somebody, but can I just allow 'what is' to blossom?"

Seeing that they still did not understand, he asked, "Have you grown a plant? How do you do it?"

A teacher replied, "Prepare the ground, put in manure. . . ."

K continued, "Put in the right manure, use the right seed, put it in at the right time, look after it, prevent things from happening to it. You give it freedom. Why do you not do the same with jealousy?"

"The flowering here is not expressed outside like the plant."

Krishnamurti said, "It is much more real than the plant you are planting outside in the field. Do you know what jealousy is? At the moment of jealousy, do you say it is imagination? You are burning with it, are you not? You are angry, furious, why do you not pursue it? Pursue it not as an idea, but actually. Can you take it out, look at it, and see that it flowers? So that each flowering is a destruction of itself and, therefore, there is no 'you' at the end to ask who is observing the destruction? In that is real creation."

The teachers again asked, "When the flower blossoms, it reveals itself. What exactly do you mean, Sir, when you say that when jealousy blossoms it will destroy itself?"

Krishnamurti said, "Take a bud, an actual bud from a bush. If you nip it, it will never flower, it will die quickly. If you let it blossom, then it shows you the color, the delicacy, the pollen. It shows what it actually is, without your being told it is red, it is blue, it is pollen. It is there for you to look at. In the same way, if you allow jealousy to flower, then it shows you everything it actually is—which is envy, attachment. So, in allowing jealousy to blossom, it has shown you all its colors, it has revealed to you what is behind jealousy.

To say that jealousy is the cause of attachment is mere verbalization. But, in actually allowing jealousy to flower, the fact that you are attached to something becomes a fact, an emotional fact, not an intellectual verbal idea. And so each flowering reveals what you have not been able to discover; and as each fact unveils itself, it flowers and you deal with it. You let the fact flower and it opens other doors, till there is no flowering at all of any kind and, therefore, no cause or motive of any kind."[6]

Seeing the look on the faces of the teachers, Krishnaji said, "In the very act of your listening, the flowering is taking place."

Krishnaji's relationship to the schools was undergoing deep change. He saw the school as an oasis where the teaching could be cherished and kept alive, whatever the disorder and violence in the world. A new generation, the new mind, had to come into being; and for that not only had the teacher and the taught to have listening minds and eyes that could see with a long vision, without identification and fragmentation, but the ground had to be ploughed and the seed sown, the land made holy with benediction.

Radhika and I traveled with Krishnaji in the car from Rishi Valley to Madras. Aldous Huxley and his wife were in India, and were to visit Madras as Krishnaji's guests later in the month. I had promised to help make their stay in Vasant Vihar, a spartan household, comfortable. The furniture in the rooms at Vasant Vihar had to be rearranged, and some sophistication brought into the serving of meals. On reaching Madras, however, there was a telegram awaiting me; my husband had fallen ill, and so Radhika and I left immediately for Delhi.

Krishnaji arrived in Delhi later from Madras with Madhavachari. Devastated by personal sorrow, I went to see Krishnaji. He overwhelmed me with his affection, held my face so that my eyes could not escape the intense depth of his eyes, and repeated the facts of my bondage and the illusions and hopes that refused to be allayed. Suddenly, it was over. Some blockage within me was swept away in the rivers of energy that flowed from him. In the following years I was to meet him several times alone, they were meetings regarding the schools or concerning the teaching; it was very seldom that I was to raise a personal problem.

Later in 1962, the decision taken by Radhika, my only child, to marry a young philosopher from the United States had shattered me. I was deeply attached to her, and my response to the proposed separation was inevitable. My body and mind were ravaged. I could not bear to accompany her to America, where she was to marry. I saw her to the airplane and then fled from the rest of the family, seeking to be alone, away from everything familiar.

From Calcutta I went to Birbhum, and on my return read the newspaper headlines. Emergency had been declared in India. China had broken through India's defenses and was at the gateways. The eyeball-to-eyeball confrontation of Kennedy and Kruschev over the Cuban missile crisis had shaken the world. The point of no return had been reached. I looked at the headlines, and the ground collapsed under me. I had to face the fact that I might never see my daughter again.

I sat through the whole night holding the anguish, letting the agony flood consciousness, refusing to turn away with hope. Anxiety, despair, memories arose; the sense of forever; the terror of the word paralyzed me, but I saw it arise and let be. By the morning the love for my daughter was still as deep, but the pain and anguish that arose at the thought of the possible ending of the relationship was quenched. Attachment had lost one peg to which it was rooted. Now there remained only my dependence on the guru, and that also was soon to be challenged.

Radhika met Krishnaji in Gstaad on her way to the United States in November 1962. Krishnaji wrote to me from Chalet Tannegg that he had met Radhika and gone for a long walk with her. "It was good that we met," he said. Knowing what her going would mean to me, he wrote, "It must be a great trial to see Radhika go away."

# CHAPTER 23

# "Happy Is the Man Who Is Nothing": Letters to a Young Friend

Between 1948 and the early 1960s, Krishnaji was easily accessible and many people came to him. On walks, in personal meetings, through letters, the relationships blossomed. He wrote the following letters[1] to a young friend who came to him wounded in body and mind. The letters, written between June 1948 and March 1960, reveal a rare compassion and clarity: the teaching and healing unfold; separation and distance disappear; the words flow; not a word is superfluous; the healing and the teaching are simultaneous.

Be supple mentally. Strength does not lie in being firm and strong but in being pliable. The pliable tree stands in a gale. Gather the strength of a swift mind.

Life is strange, so many things happen unexpectedly, mere resistance will not solve any problem. One needs infinite pliability and a single heart.

Life is a razor's edge and one has to walk on that path with exquisite care and with pliable wisdom.

Life is so rich, has so many treasures, we go to it with empty hearts; we do not know how to fill our hearts with the abundance of life. We are poor inwardly and when the riches are offered to us, we refuse. Love is a dangerous thing, it brings the only revolution that gives complete happiness. So few of us are capable of love, so few want love. We love on our own terms, making of love a marketable thing. We have the market mentality and love is not marketable, a give-and-take affair. It is a state of being in which all man's problems are resolved.

We go to the well with a thimble and so life becomes a tawdry affair, puny and small.

What a lovely place the earth could be, for there is so much beauty, so much glory, such imperishable loveliness. We are caught in pain and don't care to get out of it, even when someone points a way out.

I don't know, but one's aflame with love. There is an unquenchable flame. One has so much of it that one wants to give it to everyone and one does. It is like a strong flowing river, it nourishes and waters every town and village; it is polluted, the filth of man goes into it but the waters soon purify themselves and swiftly move on. Nothing can spoil love, for all things are dissolved in it—the good and the bad, the ugly and the beautiful. It is the only thing that is its own eternity.

The trees were so stately and strangely impervious to man's tarred roads and traffic. Their roots were deep down, deep in the earth, and their tops stretched to the skies. We have our roots in the earth, which we have and must have, but we cling or crawl on the earth; only a few soar into the skies. They are the only creative and happy people. The rest spoil and destroy each other on this lovely earth, by hurt and likewise gossip.

Be open. Live in the past if you must, but don't struggle against the past; when the past comes, look into it, not pushing it away nor holding to it too much. The experience of all these years, the ache and the joy, the sickening blows and your glimpses of the separation, the far-away sense, all these will add enrichment and beauty. What is important is what you have in your heart; and since that is overflowing, you have everything, you are everything.

Be alert to all your thoughts and feelings, don't let one feeling or thought slip by without being aware of it and absorbing all its content. Absorbing is not the word, but seeing the whole content of the thought-feeling. It is like entering a room and seeing the whole content of the room at once, its atmosphere and its spaces. To see and be aware of one's thoughts makes one intensively sensitive, pliable, and alert. Don't condemn or judge, but be very alert. Out of separation, out of the dross comes pure gold.

To see "what is," is really quite arduous. How does one clearly observe? A river when it meets an obstruction is never still; the river breaks down an obstruction by its weight or goes over it or works its way under it or around it; the river is never still; it cannot but act. It revolts, if we can so put it, intelligently. One must revolt intelligently and accept "what is" intelligently. To perceive "what is" there must be the spirit of intelligent revolt. Not to mistake a stump needs a certain intelligence; but generally one is so eager to get what one wants, that one dashes against the obstacle; either one breaks oneself against it or one exhausts oneself in the struggle against it. To see the rope as the rope needs no courage, but to mistake the rope for a snake and then to observe needs courage. One must doubt, ever search, see the false as the false. One gets power to see clearly through the intensity of attention; you will see it will come. One has to act; the river is never not-acting, it is ever active. One must be in a state of negation, to act; this very negation brings its own positive action. I think the problem is to see clearly, then that very perception brings its own action. When there is elasticity there is no question of right and wrong.

One must be very clear within oneself. Then I assure you everything will come right; be clear and you will see that things will shape themselves right without your doing anything about it. The right is not what one desires.

There must be complete revolution, not only in great things, but in little everyday things. You have had that revolution, don't settle back, keep at it. Keep the pot boiling, inwardly.

I hope you have had a good night, pleasant sunrise out of your window and you were able to see the evening stars peacefully before you went to sleep. How little we know of love, of its extraordinary tenderness and "power," how easily we use the word love; the general uses it; the butcher uses it; the rich man uses it and the young boy and girl use it. But how little they know of it, its vastness, its deathlessness, its unfathomability. To love is to be aware of eternity.

What a thing is relationship, and how easily we fall into that habit of a particular relationship, things are taken for granted, the situation accepted and no variation tolerated; no movement towards uncertainty, even for a second, entertained. Everything is so well regulated, so made secure, so tied down, that there is no chance for any freshness, for a clear reviving breath of the spring. This and more is called relationship. If we closely observe, relationship is much more subtle, more swift than lightning, more vast than the earth, for relationship is life. Life is conflict. We want to make relationship crude, hard, and manageable. So it loses its fragrance, its beauty. All this arises because one does not love, and that of course is the greatest thing of all, for in it there has to be the complete abandonment of oneself.

It is the quality of freshness, of newness, that is essential, or otherwise life becomes a routine, a habit; and love is not a habit, a boring thing. Most people have lost all sense of wonderment. They take everything for granted, this sense of security destroys freedom and the wonderment of uncertainty.

We project a far distant future, away from the present. The attention to understand is always in the present. In attention there is always a sense of imminence. To be clear in one's intentions is quite an arduous task; intention is as a flame, ceaselessly urging one to understand. Be clear in your intentions and you will see, things will work out. To be clear in the present is all that one needs, but it is not quite so easy as it sounds. One has to clear the field for the new seed and once the seed is planted, its own vitality and strength creates the fruit and the seed. Outward beauty can never last, it is marred always if there is no inward delight and joy. We cultivate the outer, paying so little attention to the thing inside the skin; but it is the inner that always overcomes the outer. It is the worm inside the apple that destroys the freshness of the apple.

It needs great intelligence for a man and woman to be forgotten, to live together, not surrender to each other or be dominated by one or the other. Relationship is the most difficult thing in life.

How strangely one is susceptible to an atmosphere, one needs a friendly tension, a sense of warm attention in which one can freely and naturally blossom. So few have this atmosphere; and so most are stunted, physically as well as psychologically. I am very surprised that you have survived without being perverted in that peculiar atmosphere. One can see why you were not utterly destroyed, spotted and twisted; outwardly you adjusted as rapidly as possible, inwardly you put yourself to sleep. It is this inward insensitivity that saved you. If you had allowed yourself to be sensitive, inwardly awake, you couldn't have stood it and so there would have been conflict and you would have broken down, been marked. Now that you are inwardly awake and are clear, you have no conflict with the atmosphere. It is this conflict that makes for perversion. You will always remain unscarred if you are inwardly very alert and awake and warmly adjust to things externally.

Substitutes soon wither away. One may be worldly even though one has a few things. The desire for power in any form; the power of the ascetic, the power of a big financier or the politician or the pope is worldly. The craving for power breeds ruthlessness and reemphasizes the importance of oneself, the self-expansive aggressiveness is in essence worldliness. Humility is simplicity, but the cultivated humility is another form of worldliness.

Very few are aware of their inward changes, setbacks, conflicts and distortions. Even if they are aware they try to push them aside or run away from them. Don't you do it. I don't think you will, but there is a danger of living with your thoughts and feelings too closely. One has to be aware of one's thoughts and feelings, without anxiety, without pressure. The real revolution has taken place in your life, you should be very much aware of your thoughts and feelings—let them come out, don't check them, don't hold them back. Let them pour out, the gentle as well as the violent ones, but be aware of them.

Occupied with what are your desires, if you have any? The world is a good place, we do everything to get away from it through worship, prayer, our loves and fears. We don't know whether we are rich or poor, we have never gone deep down into ourselves and discovered "what is." We exist on the surface, satisfied with so little and made happy and unhappy by such small things. Our petty minds have petty problems and petty answers, and so we spend our days. We don't love, and when we do it is always with fear and frustration, with sorrow and longing.

I was thinking how important it is to be innocent, to have an innocent mind. Experiences are inevitable, perhaps necessary; life is a series of experiences, but the mind need not be burdened with its own accumulative demands. It can wipe off each experience and keep itself innocent—unburdened. This is important, otherwise the mind can never be fresh, alert and pliable. The "how" to keep the mind pliable is not the problem; the "how" is the search for a method, and method can never make the mind innocent; it can make it methodical, but never innocent, creative.

It began to rain yesterday afternoon and how it poured last night. I have never heard anything like it. It was as if the heavens opened. There was extraordinary silence with it, the silence of weight, a great weight pouring itself on the earth.

It is always difficult to keep simple and clear. The world worships success, the bigger the better; the greater the audience the greater the speaker; the colossal super buildings, cars, aeroplanes and people. Simplicity is lost. The successful people are not the ones who are building a new world. To be a real revolutionary requires a complete change of heart and mind, and how few want to free themselves. One cuts the surface roots; but to cut the deep feeding roots of mediocrity, success, needs something more than words, methods, compulsions. There seem to be few, but they are the real builders—the rest labor in vain.

One is everlastingly comparing oneself with another, with what one is, with what one should be, with someone who is more fortunate. This comparison really kills. Comparison is degrading, it perverts one's outlook. And on comparison one is brought up. All our education is based on it and so is our culture. So there is everlasting struggle to be something other than what one is. The understanding of what one is uncovers creativeness, but comparison breeds competitiveness, ruthlessness, ambition, which we think brings about progress. Progress has only led so far to more ruthless wars and misery than the world has ever known. To bring up children without comparison is true education.

It seems strange to be writing, what seems so unnecessary. The thing that matters is here and you are there. The real things are always alike, so unnecessary to write about or talk about; and in the very act of writing or talking something happens to pervert it, spoil it. There are so many things that are said apart from the real thing. This urge to fulfill, which burns so many people, in small ways and big ways. This urge can be satisfied in some way or the other, and with satisfaction the deeper things fade away. That is what happens in most cases, does it not? Fulfillment of desire is such a small affair, however pleasant; but with its fulfillment, as it keeps on satisfying itself, routine, boredom sets in and the real thing fades away. It is the real thing that has to remain and the wonder of it is, it does—if there is no thought of fulfillment but just seeing things as they are.

We are so very seldom alone; always with people, with thoughts that crowd in, hopes that have not been fulfilled, or are going to be—recollections. To be alone is essential for man to be uninfluenced, for something uncontaminated to take place. For this aloneness there seems to be no time, there are too many things to do, too many responsibilities and so on. To learn to be quiet, shutting oneself in one's room, to give the mind a rest, becomes a necessity. Love is part of this aloneness. To be simple, clear, and inwardly quiet, is to have that flame.

Things may not be easy but the more one asks of life, the more fearful and painful it becomes. To live simply, uninfluenced, though everything and everyone is trying to influence, to be without varying moods and demands is not easy, but without a deep quiet life, all things are futile.

How clear the blue sky is, vast, timeless and without space. Distance and space is a thing of the mind; there and here are facts, but they become psychological factors with the urge of desire. The mind is a strange phenomenon. So complex and yet so essentially simple. It is made complex by the many psychological compulsions. It is this that causes conflict and pain, the resistance and the acquisitions. To be aware of them, and let them pass by and not be entangled in them, is arduous. Life is as a vast flowing river. The mind holds in its net the things of this river, discarding and holding. There should be no net. The net is of time and space, it is the net that creates here and there; happiness and unhappiness.

Pride is a strange thing, pride in small things and big things; in our possessions, in our achievements, in our virtues, pride of race, name and family; in capacity, in looks, in knowledge. We make all this feed this pride, or we run to humility. The opposite of pride is not humility—it is still pride, only it is called humility; the consciousness of being humble is a form of pride. The mind has to be something. It struggles to be this or that, it can never be in a state of nothingness. If nothingness is a new experience, it must have that experience, the very attempt to be still is another acquisition. The mind must go beyond all effort only then . . .

Our days are so empty, filled with activities of every kind, business, speculation, meditation, sorrow, and joy. But in spite of all these, our lives are empty. Strip a man of position, power, or of money, what is he? He had all that show, outwardly, but he is empty, shallow, inwardly. One can't have both, the inner and other riches. The inner fullness far outweighs the outer. One can be robbed of the outer, outer events can shatter what has been carefully built up; but the inner riches are incorruptible, nothing can touch them, for they have not been put together by the mind.

The desire to fulfill is very strong in people and they pursue it at any cost. This fulfillment, in every way and in any direction, sustains people; if fulfillment fails in one direction, then they try in another. But is there such a thing as fulfillment? Fulfillment may bring a certain satisfaction, but it soon fades away and again we are on the hunt. In the understanding of desire the whole problem of fulfillment ceases. Desire is effort to be, to become, and with an ending to becoming the struggle to fulfill vanishes.

The mountains must be alone. It must be a lovely thing to have rain among the mountains and the rain drops on the placid lake. How the smell of the earth comes out when it rains and then there are the croakings of many frogs. There's a strange enchantment in the tropics, when it rains. Everything is washed clean; the dust on the leaf is washed away; the rivers come to life and there is the noise of running waters. The trees put out green shoots, there is the new wild grass where there was barren earth; insects by the thousands come out from nowhere and the parched earth is fed and the earth seems satisfied and at peace. The sun seems to have lost its penetrating quality and the earth has become green; a place of beauty and richness. Man goes on making his own misery, but the earth is rich once again and there is enchantment in the air.

It is strange how most people want recognition and praise—to be recognized as a great poet, as a philosopher, something that boosts one's ego. It gives great satisfaction but it has very little meaning. Recognition feeds one's vanity and perhaps one's pocket, and then what? It sets one apart and separation breeds its own problems, ever increasing. Though it may give satisfaction, recognition is not an end in itself. But most people are caught in the craving to be recognized, to fulfill, to achieve. And failure is then inevitable, with its accompanying misery. To be free of both success and failure is the real thing. From the beginning not to look for a result, to do the thing that one loves, and love has no reward or punishment. This is really a simple thing if there is love.

How little attention we pay to things about us, to observe and to consider. We are so self-centered, so occupied with our worries, with our own benefits, we have no time to observe and understand. This occupation makes our mind dull and weary, frustrated and sorrowful, and from sorrow we want to escape. As long as the self is active there must be weary dullness and frustration. People are caught in a mad race, in the grief of self-centered sorrow. This sorrow is deep thoughtlessness. The thoughtful, the watchful are free from sorrow.

How lovely a river is. A country without a rich, wide, flowing river is no country at all. To sit on the bank of a river and let the waters flow by, to watch the gentle ripples and hear the lapping of the ripples on the bank; to see the wind on the water making patterns; to see the swallows touching the water, the water catching insects; and in the distance, across the water, on the other bank, human voices or a boy playing the flute, of a still evening, quietens all the noise about one. Somehow, the waters seem to purify one, cleanse the dust of yesterday's memories and give that quality to the mind of its own pureness, as the water in itself is pure. A river receives everything—the sewer, the corpses, the filth of the cities it passes, and yet it cleanses itself within a few miles. It receives everything and remains itself, neither caring nor knowing the pure from impure. It's only the ponds, the little puddles that are soon contaminated, for they are not living, flowing, as the wide, sweet-smelling flowing rivers. Our minds are small puddles, soon made impure. It's the little pond, called mind, that judges, weighs, analyzes, and yet remains the little pool of responsibility.

Thought has a root or roots, thought itself is the root. There must be reaction or otherwise there's death; but to see that this reaction does not extend its root into the present or into the future is the problem. Thought is bound to arise, but to be aware of it and to end it *immediately* is essential. To think about thought, to examine it, to play around it, is to extend it, to give it root. This is really important to understand. To see how the mind thinks about thought is to react to the fact. The reaction is sadness and so on. To begin feeling sad, to think of the future return, to count the day, etc., is to give root to the thought concerning the fact. So the mind establishes roots, and then how to root them out becomes another problem, another idea. To think of the future is to have roots in the soil of uncertainty.

To be really alone, not with yesterday's memories and problems but to be alone and happy, to be alone without any outward or inward compulsion, is to let the mind be uninterfered. To be alone. To have a quality of love about a tree, protective and yet alone. We are losing the feeling for trees, and so we are losing love for man. When we can't love nature, we can't love man. Our Gods have become so small and petty and so is our love. In mediocrity we have our being, but there are the trees, the open heavens, and the inexhaustible riches of the earth.

You must have a clear mind, a free untethered mind; this is essential, you cannot have a clear, penetrating mind if there is fear of any sort. Fear clogs the mind. If the mind does not face its own self-created problems, it is not a clear, deep mind. To face its own peculiarities, to be aware of its urges, deeply and inwardly, to acknowledge all this without any resistance, is to have a profound and clear mind. Then only can there be a subtle mind, not merely a sharp mind. A subtle mind is a slow, hesitant mind; not a mind that concludes, judges, or formulates. This subtlety is essential. It must know to listen and to wait. To play with the deep. This is not to be got at the end, but this quality of the mind must be there from the very beginning. You may have it, give it a full and deep chance to flower.

To go into the unknown; to take nothing for granted, not to assume anything, to be free to find out, and then only can there be depth and understanding. Otherwise one remains on the surface. What is important is not to prove or disprove a point, but to find out the truth.

All idea of change or the truth of change is seen when there's only "what is." The "what is" is not different from the thinker. The thinker is that "what is," the thinker is not separate from that "which is."

It's not possible to be at peace if there's any kind of want, any hope for some future state. Suffering follows if there's any want, life is generally full of want; even to have one want leads to endless misery. For the mind to free itself from that one want, even to know that one desire needs attention, and that is quite an affair. When found, don't let it become a problem. To prolong the problem is to allow it to take root. Don't let it take root. The one want is the one and only pain. It darkens life; there's frustration and pain. Just be aware of it and be simple with it.

Through this estate runs a stream. It is not quiet water running peacefully to the big river, but a noisy cheerful stream. All this country around here is hilly, the stream has many a fall and at one place there are three falls of different depths. The higher one makes the noise, the loudest, the other two are not valuable but are on a minor key. All these three falls are spaced differently, and so there is a continuous movement of sound. You have to listen to hear the music. It's an orchestra playing among the orchards, in the open skies, but the music is there. You have to search it out, you have to listen, you have to be with the flowing waters to hear its music. You must be the whole to hear it—the skies, the earth, the soaring trees, the green fields and the running waters, then only you hear it. But all this is too much trouble, you buy a ticket and sit in a hall, surrounded by people, and the orchestra plays or someone sings. They do all the work for you; someone composes the song, the music, another plays or sings, and you pay to listen. Everything in life, except for a few things, is second-, third-, or fourth-hand—the Gods, poems, politics, music. So our life is empty. Being empty we try to fill it—with music, with Gods, with love, with forms of escape, and the very filling is the emptying. But beauty is not to be bought. So few want beauty and goodness, and man is satisfied with second-hand things. To throw it all off is the real and only revolution, and then only is there the creativeness of reality.

It's strange how man insists on continuity in all things; in relationships, in tradition, in religion, in art. There's no breaking off and a beginning new again. If man had no book, no leader, no one to copy, no one to follow, to example, if he was completely alone, stripped of all his knowledge, he would have to start from the very beginning. Of course this complete stripping of himself must be wholly and fully spontaneous and voluntary, otherwise he would go mad, force himself into some kind of neurosis. As only a few seem to be capable of this complete aloneness, the world carries on with tradition—in its art, its music, its politics, its Gods—which everlastingly breed misery. This is what is happening in the world at the present time. There is nothing new, there is only opposition and counteropposition—in religion the old formula of fear and dogma continues; in the arts there is the endeavor to find something new. But the mind is not new, it is the same old mind, ridden with tradition, fear, knowledge, and experience, endeavoring to search the new. It is the mind itself that must denude itself, wholly, for the new to be. This is the real revolution.

The wind is blowing from the south, dark clouds and rain, everything in putting forth, reaching out and renewing itself.

The farmer about here had a beautiful rabbit, alive and kicking. His woman carried it to him and one of the women said, "I cannot look," and the man killed it, and a few minutes later that which was alive, with a light in its eyes, was being skinned by the women. Here they are used to killing animals, as elsewhere in the world, religion does not forbid them to kill. In India where for centuries, children are told, at least in the South among the Brahmins, not to kill, how cruel it is to kill, there are many children who when they grow up are forced by circumstances to change their culture overnight. They eat meat, they become army officers to kill and be killed. Overnight their values change. The centuries of a particular pattern of culture is overthrown and a new one taken on. The desire to be secure, in one form or another, is so dominant that the mind will adjust itself to any pattern that can give it security and safety. But there is no security; and when one really understands this, there's something totally different, which creates its own way of life. That life cannot be understood or copied; all that one can do is to understand and be aware of the ways of security, which brings its own freedom.

The earth is beautiful and the more you are aware of it, the more beautiful it is. The color, the varieties of greens, the yellows. It is amazing what one discovers when one is alone with the earth. Not only the insects, the birds, the grass, the varieties of flowers, the rocks, the colors and the trees, but thoughts, if one loves them. We are never alone with anything. With ourselves, or with the earth. It is easy to be alone with a desire, not to resist it by an action of will, not to let it run away into some action, not to allow its fulfillment, not create its opposite by justification or condemnation; but to be alone with it. This brings about a very strange state without any action of will. It is that which creates resistance and conflict. Being alone with a desire brings about a transformation in the desire itself. Play with this and discover what happens; don't force anything, but consider it easily.

Education? What do we mean by it? We learn to read and write, acquire a technique necessary for a livelihood, and then we are let loose on the world. From childhood we are told what to do, what to think, and inwardly we are deeply conditioned by social and environmental influence.

I was thinking, can we educate man on the outside but leave the center free? Can we help man to be free inwardly and be always free? For it is only in freedom that he can be creative and so be happy. Otherwise, life is such a tortuous affair, a battle within and so without. But to be free inside needs astonishing care and wisdom; but few see the importance of this. We are concerned with the outer and not with creativity. But to change all this, there must be at least a few who understand the necessity of this, who themselves are inwardly bringing about this freedom. It is a strange world.

What is important is a radical change in the unconscious. Any conscious action of the will cannot touch the unconscious. As the conscious will cannot touch the unconscious pursuits, wants, urges, the conscious mind must subside, be still, and not try to force the unconscious, according to any particular pattern of action. The unconscious has its own pattern of action, its own frame within which it functions. This frame cannot be broken by any outward action, and will is an outward act. If this is really seen and understood, the outward mind is still; and because there is no resistance, set up by will, one will find that the so-called unconscious begins to free itself from its own limitations. Then only is there a radical transformation in the total being of man.

Dignity is a very rare thing. An office or a position of respect gives dignity. It is like putting on a coat. The coat, the costume, the post gives dignity. A title or a position gives dignity. But strip man of these things, and very few have that quality of dignity that comes with inward freedom of being as nothing. Being something is what man craves for, and that something gives him a position in society which it respects. Put a man into a category of some kind—clever, rich, a saint, a physicist; but if he cannot be put into a category that society recognizes, he is an odd person. Dignity cannot be assumed, be cultivated, and to be conscious of being dignified is to be conscious of oneself, which is to be petty, small. To be nothing is to be free of that very idea. Being, not of or in a particular state, is true dignity. It cannot be taken away, it always is.

To allow the free flow of life, without any residue being left, is real awareness. The human mind is like a sieve which holds some things and lets others go. What it holds is the size of its own desires; and desires, however profound, vast, noble, are small, are petty, for desire is a thing of the mind. Not to retain, but to have the freedom of life to flow without restraint, without choice, is complete awareness. We are always choosing or holding, choosing the things that have significance and everlastingly holding on to them. This we call experience, and the multiplication of experiences we call the richness of life. The richness of life is the freedom from the accumulation of experience. The experience that remains, that is held, prevents that state in which the known is not. The known is not the treasure, but the mind clings to it and thereby destroys or defiles the unknown.

Life is a strange business. Happy is the man who is nothing.

We are, most of us at least, creatures of moods and a variety of moods. Few of us escape from it. With some, it is caused by the bodily condition, with others it is a mental state. We like this up and down state, we think this movement of moods is part of existence. Or one just drifts from one mood to another. But there are few who are not caught in this movement, who are free from the battle of becoming, so that inwardly there is a steadiness, not of the will, a steadiness that is not cultivated, nor the steadiness of concentrated interest, nor the product of any one of these activities. It comes upon one only when the action of will ceases.

Money does spoil people. There is a peculiar arrogance of the rich. With very few exceptions, in every country, the rich have that peculiar atmosphere of being able to twist anything, even the Gods, and they can buy their Gods. Riches is not only of wealth, but the capacity of being able to do things. Capacity gives man an odd sense of freedom. He also feels he is above others, he is different. All this gives him a sense of superiority; he sits back and watches other people squirming; he is oblivious to his own ignorance, the darkness of his own mind. Money and capacity offer a very good escape from this darkness. After all, escape is a form of resistance, which breeds its own problems. Life is a strange business. Happy is the man who is nothing.

Take things easily, but inwardly with fullness and alertness. Don't let a moment slip by without being fully aware what is happening inwardly and about you. Often this is what it is to be sensitive, not to one or two things, but to be sensitive to everything. To be sensitive to beauty and to resist ugliness is to bring about conflict. You know, as you watch you will perceive that the mind is always judging—this is good and that is bad, this is black and that is white—judging people, comparing, weighing, calculating. The mind is everlastingly restless. Can the mind watch, observe, without judging, calculating? Perceive without naming and just see if the mind can do that.

Play with this. Don't force it, let it watch itself. Most people who attempt to be simple begin with the outer, discarding, renouncing, and so on; but inwardly the complexity of their being remains. With inward simplicity, the outer corresponds to the inner. To be simple inwardly is to be free from the urge for the more, which does not mean to be satisfied with "what is." To be free from the urge for the more is not to think in terms of time, progress, getting there. To be simple is for the mind to free itself from all results, is for the mind to empty itself of all conflict. This is real simplicity.

How can the mind battle between the ugly and the beautiful, clinging to the one and pushing away the other. This conflict makes the mind insensitive and exclusive. Any attempt on the part of the mind to find an undefined line between the two is still part of the one or the other. Thought cannot, do what it will, free itself from the opposites; thought itself has created the ugly and the beautiful, and good and the bad. So it cannot free itself from its own activities. All that it can do is to be still, not choose. Choice is conflict and the mind is back again to its own entanglements. The stillness of the mind is the freedom from duality.

There is so much discontent and one thinks an ideology, communism or other, is going to solve everything, even banish away discontent, which of course it can never do. Communism or any other organized religious conditioning can never do away with discontent; but one tries every way to smother it, to shape it, to give it content, but it is always there. To be discontented, one thinks, is wrong—normally not right, and yet one cannot do away with it; it has to be understood. To understand is not to condemn. So really go into it, watch it without any desire to change it, to channelize it. Be aware of it as it operates during the day, perceive its ways and be alone with it.

Freedom comes when the mind is alone. Just for the fun of the thing, keep the mind still, free of all thought. Play with it, don't make it a very serious affair, without any struggle, be aware and let the mind be still.

There is frustration as long as one is seeking fulfillment. The pleasure of fulfillment is a constant desire and we want the continuity of that pleasure. The ending of that pleasure is frustration in which there is pain. Again the mind seeks in different directions fulfillment and again it meets frustration. This frustration is the movement of self-consciousness which is isolation, separation, loneliness. From this the mind wants to escape again into some form of fulfillment. The struggle to fulfill brings the conflict of duality. When the mind sees the futility or truth of fulfillment, in which there is always frustration, then only can the mind be in that state of loneliness from which there is no escape. When the mind is in this state of loneliness, without any escape, then only is there freedom from it. Separation exists because of the desire to fulfill; frustration is separation.

No shocks must ever take place now, even the fleeting ones. These psychological reactions affect the body, with its adverse effects. Be very strong inwardly. Be firm and clear. Be complete; don't try to be complete, be complete. Don't depend on anyone or on anything or on any experience, or memory; the dependence on the past, however pleasant, only prevents the completeness of the present. Be aware and let that awareness be intact and unbroken even if it be for a minute.

Sleep is essential; during sleep one seems to touch unknown depths, depths that the conscious mind can never touch or experience. Though one may not remember the extraordinary experience of a world that is beyond the conscious or the unconscious, it has its effect on the total consciousness of the mind. Probably this is not very clear, but just read it and play around it. I feel there are certain things that can never be made clear. There are no adequate words for them, but nevertheless they are there.

Especially with you this is important, to have a body that will not be subject to any illness. You must easily, voluntarily put aside all the pleasurable memories and images, so that your mind is free, uncontaminated for the real thing. Do, please, pay attention to what is written. Every experience, every thought must end each day, each minute, as it arises; so that the mind does not put out roots into the future. This is really important, for this is true freedom. Thus there is no dependence, for dependence brings pain, affecting the physical and breeding psychological resistance. And as you said, resistance creates problems—to achieve, to become perfect, and so on. In seeking is involved struggle, effort, endeavor; this endeavor, this struggle, invariably ends in frustration—I want something or I want to be something—in the very process of getting there is the craving for the more, and the more is never in sight and so there is always a sense of being thwarted. So there is pain. So once again one turns to another form of fulfillment, with its inevitable consequence. The implication of struggle, of effort, is vast, and why does one seek? Why does the mind everlastingly seek and what makes it seek? Do you know or are you aware that you are seeking? If you are, the object of your search varies from period to period. Do you see the significance of search, with its frustrations and pain? That in the finding of something that is very gratifying there is stagnation, with its joys and fears, with its progress and becoming? If you are aware that you are seeking, is it possible for the mind not to seek? And if the mind does not seek, what's the immediate, actual reaction of a mind that does not seek?

Play with this, find out; don't force anything, don't let the mind coerce itself into any particular experience, for then it will breed for itself illusion.

I saw someone who is dying. How frightened we are of death; what we are frightened of is living; we do not know how to live; we know sorrow and death is only the final sorrow. We divide life, as living and dying. Then there must be the ache of death, with its separation, loneliness, isolation. Life and death are one movement, not isolated states. Living is dying, dying to every thing, to be reborn every day. This is not a theoretical statement but to be lived and to be experienced. It is will, this constant desire to be, that completely destroys the simple "being." This "being" is totally different from the sleep of satisfaction, fulfillment, or the conclusions of reason. This being is unaware of the self. A drug, an interest, an absorption, a complete "identification" can bring about a desired state, which is still self-consciousness. True being is the cessation of the will. Play around with these thoughts and experiment happily.

It is a cloudless morning, very early, the sky is so pure, gentle and blue. All the clouds seem to have gone, but they may come up again during the day. After this cold, this wind and this rain, spring will burst forth again; spring has been gently going on, in spite of the cold winds, but now every leaf and bud will rejoice. What a lovely thing the earth is! How beautiful are the things that come out of it—the rocks, the streams, the trees, the grass, the flowers, the endless things that she produces—only man grieves, he alone destroys his own species, his own kind; he alone exploits his neighbor, he tyrannizes and destroys. He is the most unhappy and most suffering, the most inventive and the conqueror of time and space. But with all their capacities, in spite of his lovely temples and churches, mosques and cathedrals, he lives in his own darkness. His gods are his own fears and his loves are his own hates. What a marvelous world we could make of it, without these wars, without these fears. But what is the use of speculation; it's no use at all.

The real thing is man's discontent, the inevitable discontent. It is a precious thing, a jewel of great worth. But one's afraid of it, one dissipates it, uses it or allows it to be used to bring about certain results. Man is frightened of it, but it is a precious jewel, without value. Live with it, watch it day after day, without interfering with its movements, then it is as a flame burning away all the dross, leaving that which is homeless and measureless. Read all this wisely.

The rich man has more than enough and the poor man goes hungry, looking for food and struggling and working all his life. One who has nothing makes of his life or allows life to make itself rich, creative, and another who has all the things of this world, dissipates and withers away. Give one man a piece of earth, he makes it beautiful, productive, and another neglects it and allows it to die, as he himself dies. We have such infinite capacities, in every direction, to find the nameless or to bring about hell on earth. But somehow, man prefers to breed hatred and enmity. It is so much easier to hate, to be envious, and as society is based on the demand for the more, human beings slip into every form of acquisitiveness. And so there is everlasting struggle, which is justified and made noble.

There is the unlimited richness of a life without struggle, without will, without choice. But that life is impossibly difficult when our whole culture is the outcome of struggle and the action of will. Without the action of will, for almost everyone living, there is death. Without some kind of ambition, for almost everyone, life has no meaning.

There is a life without will, without choice. This life comes into being when the life of will comes to an end. I hope you don't mind reading all this; if you don't mind then read it and listen to it with pleasure.

The sun is attempting to break through the clouds, probably it will manage to break during the day. One day it is spring and the next day it is almost winter. The weather represents man's moods, up and down, darkness and temporary light. You know, it is strange how we want freedom and we do everything to enslave ourselves. We lose all our initiative. We look to others to guide us, to help us, to be generous, to be peaceful; we look to the gurus, masters, saviors, meditators. Someone writes great music, someone plays it, interpreting it in his own way and we listen to it, enjoying it or criticizing it. We are the audience watching the actors, football players, or watching the cine-screen. Others write poems and we read; others paint and we gape at them. We have nothing, so we turn to others to entertain us, to inspire us, to guide or save us. More and more, modern civilization is destroying us, emptying us of all creativeness. We ourselves are empty inwardly and we look to others to be enriched and so our neighbor takes advantage of this to exploit, or we take advantage of him.

When one is aware of the many implications involved in looking to others, that very freedom is the beginning of creativeness. That freedom is true revolution and not the false revolution of social or economic adjustments. Such revolution is another form of enslavement.

Our minds make little castles of security. We want to be sure of everything, sure of our relationships, of our fulfillments, hopes, and of our futures. We build these inward prisons and woe to anyone that disturbs us. It is strange how the mind is ever seeking a zone where there will be no conflict, no disturbance. Our living is the constant breaking up and the rebuilding, in different forms, of these zones of safety. Our mind then becomes a dull and weary thing. Freedom consists in having no security of any kind.

It is really astonishing to have a still and a very calm mind, without a single wave of thought. Of course, the stillness of a dead mind is not the calm mind. The mind is made to be still by the action of will. But can it ever be profoundly, right through its whole being, silent? It is really most amazing what happens when the mind is, thus, silent. In that state all consciousness, as knowing, recognizing ceases. The instinctual pursuit of the mind, memory, has come to an end. And it's very interesting how the mind begins to do its best to capture that worldless state, through thinking, verbalising, perfecting symbols. But for this process to come to an end, naturally and spontaneously, is like dying to everything. One does not want to die, and so there is always an unconscious struggle going on, and this struggle is called life. It is odd how most people want to impress others, by their achievements, by their cleverness, by their books—by any means to assert themselves.

How is everything? Are your days swifter than a weaver's shuttle? Do you live in one day, a thousand years? It is strange, for most people boredom is a very real thing; they must be doing something, be occupied with something, an activity, a book, the kitchen, children, or God. Otherwise they are with themselves, which is very boring. When they are with themselves they get self-centered, crochety, or become ill and ill-humored. An unoccupied mind—not a negative blank mind, but an alert passive mind, a totally empty mind—is a sweet thing, capable of infinite possibilities. Thoughts are wearisome, uncreative, and rather dull. A thought may be clever, but cleverness is as a sharp instrument—it soon wears itself out, and that is why clever people are dull.

Let there be an unoccupied mind without deliberately working for it. Let it happen rather than cultivate it. Read this with awareness and let it take place. Hearing it or reading about the unoccupied mind is important, and how you read and how you listen.

What is important is to have the right kind of exercise, good sleep, and a day that has significance. But one slips so easily into a routine, and then one functions in the easy pattern of self-satisfaction, or in the pattern of self-imposed righteousness. All their patterns invariably lead to death—a slow withering away. But to have a rich day, in which there is no compulsion, no fear, no comparison, no conflict, but to be simply aware, is to be creative.

You see, there are rare moments when we feel this, but most of our life is made up of eroding memories, frustration, and vain efforts, and the real thing goes by. The cloud of dullness covers everything and the real thing fades away. It is really quite arduous to penetrate through this cloud and to be in the simple clarity of light. Just see all this and that is all. Don't try to be simple. This trying only breeds complexity and misery. The trying is becoming and the becoming is always desire, with its frustrations.

How important it is to free oneself from all emotional, psychological shock, which does not mean that one must harden oneself against the movement of life. It is these shocks that gradually build up various psychological resistances that also affect the body, bringing various forms of illness. Life is a series of events (wanted and unwanted); and as long as we pick, choose which we shall keep and which we shall discard, there must inevitably be a conflict (of duality) which is the shock. These series of checks harden the mind, heart; it is a self-enclosing process and so there is suffering. To allow the movement of life, without choice, without any particular movement, desirable or undesirable, to take root needs enormous awareness. It is not a matter of trying to be aware all the time, which is wearisome, but seeing the necessity of the truth of awareness, then you will see that the very necessity operates without your forcing yourself to be aware.

One may travel, be educated in the best of schools, in different parts of the world; have the best of foods, instruction, climate; but does all this make for intelligence? One knows of such people, and are they intelligent? The Communists are trying, as others, like the Catholics, to control and shape the mind. The very shaping of the mind does have certain obvious effects—more efficiency, a certain quickness and alertness of mind—but all these different capacities do not make intelligence. The very learned people, those who have plenty of information, knowledge, and those who are educated scientifically, are they intelligent? Don't you think intelligence is something entirely different? It is really the total freedom from fear. Those whose morality is based on security, security in every form, are not moral, for the desire for security is the outcome of fear. Fear and the constraint of fear, which we call morality, is really not moral at all. Intelligence is the total freedom from fear, and intelligence is not respectability, nor is it the various virtues cultivated through fear. In understanding fear there is something which is wholly different from the formulations of the mind.

It is good to experiment with identification. How do we experiment with anything? From the most simple to the most complex. We say this is mine—my sandals, my house, my family, my work, and my god; with identification comes the struggle to hold. Containing it becomes a habit. Any disturbance which might break that habit is pain, and then we struggle to overcome that pain. But identification, the feeling of the mine, belongs to something that continues. If one really experiments with this, just being aware, without any desire to alter or choose, one discovers so many astonishing things in oneself. The mind is the past, the tradition, the memories which are the foundation of identification. Can the mind, as we know it now, function without this process of identification? Find out, play with it; be aware of the movements of identification with the common daily things, with the most abstract. One finds out odd things, how thought fades, how it plays tricks upon itself.

Let awareness pursue thought through the corridors of the mind, uncovering, never choosing, ever pursuing.

It is especially difficult, as one is placed, not to desire, crave for certain things, happenings; not to compare. But whatever the condition, desires, cravings, comparisons continue. We always crave for more or for less, for continuity of some pleasure and the avoidance of pain. What is really quite interesting is this: Why does the mind create a center, within itself, round which it moves and has its being? Life is a thousand and one influences, innumerable pressures, conscious and unconscious. Among these pressures and influences, we choose some and discard others, and so we gradually build up a center. We don't let all these pressures and influences pass by, unaffected by them. Every influence, every pressure affects us, the effect is called good or bad, we don't seem to be able to watch, to be aware of pressure, and not take part in it one way or the other, resisting it or welcoming it. This resistance or welcome makes for the center from which we act. Can the mind not create this center? The answer can only be found through experimentation, not through any form of assertion or denial. So experiment and find out. With the ending of this center there is true freedom.

One does get agitated, anxious and sometimes frightened. These things do happen. They are the accidents of life. Life is a cloudy day. It was clear and sunny the other day, but now it is raining, cloudy and cold; this change is the inevitable process of living. Anxiety, fear suddenly comes upon one; there are causes for it, hidden or fairly obvious, and one can with a little awareness find those causes. But what is important, is to be aware of these incidents or accidents and not give them time to take root, permanent or temporary. One does give root to these reactions when the mind compares; it justifies, condemns or accepts. You know, one has to be on one's toes all the time, inwardly, without any tension. Tension arises when you want a result, and what arises again creates tension which has to be broken. Let life flow.

It is so fatally easy to get used to anything, to any discomfort, to any frustration, to any continued satisfaction. One can adjust oneself to any circumstances, to lunacy or to asceticism. The mind likes to function in grooves, in habits, and this activity is called living. When one sees this one breaks away from all this and tries to lead a life which has no meaning, no moorings, no interests. Interests, if one's not very alert, bring us back to a pattern of life. In all this you will see the will, the directive, is functioning, the will to be, to achieve, to become and so on. Will is the very center of the chooser and so long as will exists, the mind can only function in habits, either self-created or imposed. Freedom from will is the real problem. One can play various tricks upon oneself, to be free from will, the center of the me, the chooser, but it will go on under a different name, under a different cloak. When one sees the real significance of habit, of getting used to things; choosing, naming, pursuing an interest and so on; when there is an awareness of all this, then the real miracle takes place, the cessation of will. Experiment with this, be aware of all this, from moment to moment, without any wish to arrive anywhere.

Southern skies and northern skies are so extraordinarily different. Here, in London, for a change, there is not a cloud in the tender blue sky and the towering trees are just beginning to show their green. It is spring here, just about beginning. Here it is grimy, the cheer in the people is not there, as in the South.

A quiet mind, but very alert, watchful, is a blessing; it is like the earth, rich with immense possibilities. When there is such a mind, not comparing, not condemning, then only is it possible for the immeasureable richness to be.

Don't let the smoke of pettiness smother you and let the fire go out. You have to keep going, tearing away, destroying, never taking root. Don't let any problem take root, finish with it immediately and wake up every morning fresh, young, and innocent . . .

Be wise and definite about your health; don't let emotion and sentiment interfere with your health nor belittle your action. There are too many influences and pressures that constantly shape the mind and heart, be aware of them, cut through them and don't be a slave to them. To be a slave is to be mediocre. Be awake, aflame.

Face the fear, invite it, don't let it come upon you suddenly, unexpectedly, but face it constantly; pursue it diligently and purposefully. Hope you are well and don't be scared by all that; probably it can be cured and we will go after it. Don't let it frighten you.

Deeply, inwardly, there may be a slow withering away; of this you may be unconscious or, being conscious, negligent. The wave of deterioration is always on the top of us, it does not matter who it is. To be ahead of it and meet it without reaction and be out of it requires great energy. This energy only comes when there is no conflict whatsoever, conscious or unconscious. Be very awake.

Don't let problems take root. Go through them rapidly, cut through them as through butter. Don't let them leave a mark, finish with them as they arise. You can't help having problems, but finish with them immediately.

There has been a distinct change in you—deeper inward vitality, strength and clarity—keep it—let it function—give it an opportunity to flow extensively and deeply. Don't, whatever happens, be smothered by circumstances, by the family—by your own physical condition. Eat properly, exercise, and don't become slack. Having come to a certain state, keep going, don't stay there—either go forward or you retrogress. You can't be static. You have ridden on the inward wave for so many years, withdrawn, inward, but now from that inward movement you must go out—meet more people—expand.

Have done a great deal of meditation and has been good. I hope you are doing it too—begin by being aware of every thought—feeling—all day, the nerves and the brain—then become quiet, still—this is what cannot be done through control—then really begins meditation. Do it with thoroughness.

Whatever happens don't let the body shape the nature of the mind—be aware of the body, eat right, be by yourself during the day for some hours—don't slip back and don't be a slave to circumstances. Be tremendous—be awake.

# Part 5

## CHANGING HORIZONS
### 1962–1977

CHAPTER 24

# "People Who Are without Creativity Build Dead Institutions."

Krishnaji left India in March 1962. One period of his dialogue with the land of his birth and his friends was over. He would never be the same again. The Krishnaji who had laughed with us, walked with us, been overwhelmed by the beauty of the land; who had looked at the poor and the rich with compassion; listened to the voice of thousands; healed inwardly; taken the hand of a friend and led him through the labyrinth of the mind, pointing out, discussing, taking over the burdens of pain and sorrow—this Krishnaji would vanish. A new Krishnaji would emerge—stern, impatient, questioning. All personal relationships would undergo transformation. He would be compassionate, but he would also be the teacher, demanding answers to fundamental questions. All great laughter and play had ended.

From Bombay he flew to Rome. He was met by Signora Vanda Scaravelli. On his arrival Krishnaji fell seriously ill, first with fever and then with an attack of mumps and kidney trouble.

The discontent and the distance between Krishnaji and Rajagopal and his friends in Ojai was increasing. A new group of people vitally interested in Krishnaji and the teaching had come together in Europe. The first Saanen gathering in Switzerland, which Rajagopal reluctantly permitted to be organized in 1961, had drawn people from all parts of the world. Krishnaji sensed a new movement in the West, and his response to the situation was total.

He was not to return to India in the autumn of 1962. In his talks with Vimla Thakkar at Gstaad and later in Rome, he had spoken of his deep apprehensions about India. That the Chinese attack had distressed Krishnaji deeply was apparent from his letters. He was worried about India. After the talks in Saanen, Krishnaji was ill again. He wrote to me of being worn out, traveling, speaking, meeting people. His system, the muscles and the membranes, needed toning up. So he decided not to return to India in the winter of 1962, but to stay on through the year in Italy, resting, regaining his vitality, and conserving his energy. In the traditional language of India, he went into retreat, generating *tapas*.*

Krishnaji returned to Delhi on October 21, 1963, after eighteen months in Europe. In the car on the way from the airport, he spoke of not being in contact with people. While abroad, India had rarely been in his consciousness. On his arrival in India, one sensed that the spontaneous flow of feeling that India evoked through the years was missing. He seemed distant.

Madhavachari was in Delhi, and every evening we walked with Krishnaji in the Buddha Jayanti Park. I asked Krishnaji why various people could follow his teaching up to a point and not further. He said, "That is so," and appeared very grave as he walked ahead of us; on his return we carried on from where we had left the conversation. He felt that man lacked an energy that knew no conflict; energy that knew the discipline of attention and of total denial. He said it was necessary to deny at the very depths of the self.

During later walks he began questioning the fact of Krishnamurti. How did it happen? Why was the vacant, stupid boy not conditioned by the Theosophical Society and its rituals; or by life in the West? I asked him whether he knew when illumination took place. He said, "No. But how did it happen? Is it what the Theosophists say, that the body of Krishnamurti is the vehicle of Lord Maitreya? Is it reincarnation? Why did Krishnamurti's mind work innocently, directly? Why did he question everything?"

In the early 1960s Buckminster Fuller met Krishnaji in India. "Bucky," as his friends called him, was a designer who had revolutionized structures and designed for a future culture and way of life; he was at once a philosopher, a scientist with vision, creative vitality, and a holistic view of people and their needs. I knew Bucky well, and he telephoned me when he heard Krishnaji was in Delhi to suggest a

---

*Tapas*: severe austerities; also, the generation of an energy that does not dissipate.

meeting with "that marvelous, beautiful, wise person." I arranged a dinner at which both men were present. Bucky entered the room bouncing a yo-yo. Krishnaji was shy and a little withdrawn, his response in those days when he met a formidable intellect. Bucky started to talk. He talked before dinner, he talked at dinner, he talked after dinner. Krishnaji listened, hardly saying a word. Still Bucky talked. After Krishnaji left to return to Kitty Shiva Rao's house, where he was staying, Bucky turned to me and thanked me for the meeting and commented, "What a marvelous, wonderful, wise person Krishnaji is."

From Delhi Krishnaji went to Rajghat, Varanasi. Achyut, who had worked at Rajghat for several years, spoke to Krishnaji while he was there of Vinoba Bhave and his work of Bhoodan, the distribution to the landless of gifts of land, in the villages of India. Achyut felt immense sympathy for the direction and ethos of Vinoba's work; to him work for the poor and oppressed was integral to a religious life and could not be separated. Krishnaji's response, however, shook Achyut deeply.

Krishnaji said, "After all these years, how can you be such an ass? Why are you fooling around? Look, my boy, if you were not to have met me, you would be in 'sarvodaya,'* cleaning the bottoms of village children. It may be right to do that. But you are not in Rajghat to do that. You are self-righteously trying to change society. But deep change must start with man."

Achyut said he could not understand what Krishnaji was saying. Annie Besant had told Achyut, "If you don't understand Krishnaji put what he says on a shelf, but never reject him." Achyut had learned from the seer never to say yes to anything unless he actually perceived the truth of it. So he took six months off from his work in Rajghat and went to the Himalayas, to Lohaghat, Pithoragarh, and asked himself, "Am I too attached to Krishnamurti and Rajghat?" He also explored his motives for work amongst the poor. He began writing down his thoughts every morning, and soon found a direct perception of mind and the movement of thought. Perception brought freedom.

Achyut returned to Rajghat in 1964. That winter he met Krishnaji again and discussed his insoluble conflicts. Krishnaji said, "Nothing is happening to you in Rajghat, so you should go. Rajghat is not helping you to flower." Achyut left Rajghat in 1965 without bitterness. He went into retreat, observing total anonymity. He lived in an isolated house

---

*Sarvodaya: Sarva means "all"; udaya arising. Therefore sarvodaya is the awakening or arising of humankind. It was a movement initiated by Gandhiji to eradicate poverty in village India and so lead to a regeneration of the people of India.

on the outskirts of Bangalore, wandered from place to place, trying to cut away at roots.

His brother, Rao Sahib, was very upset. He felt Achyut had been let down. Thirteen years of Achyut's life had been dedicated to Rajghat and to Krishnaji's work, and Rao Sahib felt Achyut had come away empty-handed. Rao Sahib was slowly moving away from Krishnaji. Deeply devoted to him personally, with a passionate, emotional response and a need to be near Krishnaji, he stubbornly denied himself. He was aware that something had awakened within him, but refused to acknowledge any insight into the teaching. Caught in conflict, he withdrew, tended his roses, and refused to acknowledge his confusion. But one could sense the deep hurt and pain. The tensions were to affect his health, and he developed high blood pressure, and heart disease.

By 1963 Krishnaji was expressing a general dissatisfaction with India. He had started asking questions which were to persist for many years. Krishnaji felt the need for action and was ruthlessly questioning himself and those around him. He said that he had been speaking in India for thirty years and nothing had happened. "There is not one person who is living the teaching." He appeared impatient with the old and felt the need for young people around him. Krishnaji was critical of Madhavachari, who was stubborn and refused to change his ways of functioning. The circle of people around Krishnaji was limited. Madhavachari ran the foundation like a sergeant major. Madhavachari, Achyut, and Rao Sahib were increasingly in conflict.

In December 1964 I was in Madras, staying at Vasant Vihar. Krishnaji very often had supper with us. Achyut Patwardhan, Madhavachari, Nandini, and Balasundaram were present. Rao had not come from Poona. A discussion began after supper. I asked, "What is the one action necessary for there to be a breakthrough in the mind? The exploration that had to be done, has been done. There is self-knowing awareness, the eyes are open, the ears listen, the mind is awake. Yet there is no totality of perception and compassion. One total action appears needed to break through." Krishnaji said it must be so. He felt it was a good question and we should go into it, discuss it.

Again, the next night, we tried to discover what is that one action. Krishnaji said, "Perception—can perception and the movement of the heart be one?"

"Perception that is rich with essence—how does it arise?" I asked.

Krishnaji said, "It must be an act of tremendous simplicity." He was quiet. The very discussion created an atmosphere of energy in the room. Like a flame, it seared through the corridors of consciousness. There was deep, limitless silence. It was too much for the body. We had been sitting straight-backed, cross-legged around Krishnaji. My body could not bear the intensity in the room and sought the support of the wall. Krishnaji sat erect, his back straight, his head unmoving. We sat, and time ceased.

In 1963, amongst the many people who had gathered at the Rajghat camp, was a tall, rather solidly built but good-looking young man named Alain Naude, a South African musician. He had attended Krishnaji's talks in Saanen in the summer of 1963 and had met Krishnaji several times. Soon afterward he severed his connection with South Africa.

Naude had followed Krishnaji to India in the winter of 1964 and 1965, and soon Krishnaji spoke to some of us of the possibility of Naude taking over as his secretary, traveling with him round the world, dealing with his correspondence, encouraging young people to listen to Krishnaji, and so forth.

By the autumn of 1965 Naude joined Krishnaji as his secretary while Krishnaji was in Europe; and when Krishnaji came to India in October 1965 he was accompanied by Mary Zimbalist, Naude, and George Vithoulkas, a homoeopath from Greece, who in later years was to become very well known. Krishnaji was to give talks in Delhi and from there travel to Varanasi.

The Rajghat visit proved disastrous. Krishnaji had written to Madhavachari, and in his innocence had suggested that Madhavachari arrange for the stay of Mary Zimbalist, Naude, and George Vithoulkas on the campus of Rajghat, as they were his personal guests. Madhavachari's concept of comfort was antedeluvian, and so were his aesthetics.

In India the toilet has always been regarded as a focus of pollution. Orthodox Hindus were expected to bathe each time they used the bathroom. Achyut Patwardhan told us that he could remember a time in Varanasi when Brahmins used to carry an extra *dhoti* with them when they left the house, and a bath would follow in case they needed to visit a friend's facilities. Through the years I had remonstrated with Madhavachari about the need for minimum amenities in the toilet, but to no avail. To him a flush or a washbasin were unnecessary luxuries;

a bucket and a metal water pot had sustained Indian needs for centuries, and he saw no reason to change.

In the 1960s at Rajghat minimum facilities were available only in the house where Krishnaji lived. Mary Zimbalist, a product of New York society, reared in the most rarified of atmospheres and used to luxurious living in the homes of her father and her husband, was put into a room where the toilet had no flush, the bathroom had no basin, and the freshly whitewashed room had paint splashed on the window panes. Krishnaji had come personally to see the rooms arranged for his guests, and there was an explosion. He was horrified. Mary Zimbalist moved to a room in Krishnaji's house, but Madhavachari was unruffled.

The relationship between Krishnaji and Madhavachari grew increasingly difficult.

Since the 1960s Krishnaji's attitude to the schools, people, and work had undergone a major change. He was demanding a continuous revolution. He saw a rapid decline in India; the schools had to awaken from their lethargy. The stagnation he sensed had to end. No strong current of creative change was visible. "Move," he kept saying to the members of the Foundation and to the teachers of the schools. "If you stay where you are, you will decline, grow crystalized." There had to be continuous movement within oneself and so in one's work. In one of his letters to us he wrote, "Having come to a certain state, keep going, don't stay there. Either go forward or retrogress. You can't be static." An explosion was necessary in Krishnaji's institutions, changes had to take place. In India the mountains move when the energy of a single person is awake.

I visited Krishnaji in Gstaad in the summer of 1965. Krishnaji had been given a Mercedes for his use. He took me for a drive; in spite of lack of practice, he drove round the hairpin turns with a masterly control and stability. It was marvelous to observe him handling the machine.

I was again in Gstaad in the summer of 1966 on my way back to India from the United States. Krishnaji spoke to me of the young people who were being drawn to the talks in the United States. Naude had arranged for Krishnaji to speak at some of the great universities. The young were in revolt against the existing American culture and wanted "instant Nirvana." Electrified by Krishnaji's presence, they flocked to hear him. Then, unwilling to accept the austerity and rigor of self-knowing, and denied psychedelic experiences of consciousness, they drifted away to more amenable gurus who promised them bliss. In Saanen, a large number of young people initially came to the talks; but it was a casual crowd, few of them seriously delved into themselves or joined Krishnaji's work. But the Saanen gatherings were soon to become a meeting place for serious people from Eastern and Western Europe; people concerned with the enormous challenges to humankind and who sought a new way of life.

Naude continued to accompany Krishnaji on his visits to India, and was with him in the winter of 1966. Each visit saw a deterioration in the relationship between Krishnaji and Madhavachari, and a widening of the gulf between Krishnaji and the Indian foundation. Krishnaji had been told in Europe that the Indian foundation was supporting Raja-gopal in his stand against Krishnaji. That the Indian Foundation was parochial, narrow, arrogant, self-satisfied in its outlook.

In India, he continued to question sternly. He had been speaking for thirty years and what had happened? He refused to compare it to other countries or situations. A new question had emerged. "What will happen when I die? Who is there to hold these places?" There were no answers. An enormous pressure was building up amongst all of us.

The situation was very strange. This great teacher, who on the platform spoke with passion about a mind that knew no conflict, who himself was free of pressure, was posing questions that generated enormous pressures amongst his close associates. It was to be some years before we were to understand the nature of Krishnaji's question, and the energy generated by deep listening and holding the question in consciousness.

In January 1967 a major clash took place at Rishi Valley between Alain Naude and Madhavachari. Krishnaji was very disturbed. He spoke to me at length of his deep concern. Vasant Vihar in Madras seemed a dead place. There was little activity, and few people came to read or discuss. "People who are without creativity build dead institutions," he said.

That winter, Naude did not accompany Krishnaji to India. Since 1963 Krishnaji had been having discussions with Madhavachari, pointing out to him the major changes that were necessary in the functioning of the Foundation. On reaching Madras in the winter of 1967, he asked Madhavachari to share the work of the Foundation with Galloway, a Scotsman, who had recently retired from the chairmanship of Binnys, one of the more important British companies operating in India. He also suggested that Madhavachari take the assistance of Smt. Jayalaxmi in maintaining the garden and the house at Vasant Vihar. Madhava-chari's response was noncommittal.

Smt.* Jayalaxmi, a South Indian Iyengar Brahmin with a remarkable business acumen, especially in real estate, and an equally remarkable knowledge of South Indian classical music, had begun visiting Vasant Vihar in the early 1960s. She was steeped in the Iyengar Brahmin tra-dition, a red *tilak* on her forehead, she wore her deep emerald or *arakh* red *saree* in the Iyengar style, draped across the body. She was soft-spoken, but tough in her responses and actions. She would drive Krish-naji to the beach every evening when he was in Vasant Vihar, and wait in the car while Krishnaji went for his walk on the Adyar beach.

For us in India, 1967 was a year of gloom. Krishnaji appeared ag-itated and critical. There was a sense of flux in his words; a feeling was evident that major changes were in the offing. Addressing the Foundation for New Education in Bombay on February 9, 1967, Krish-naji had spoken with passion of his apprehensions regarding the Foun-dation in India. We who listened felt choked and could hardly speak.

Krishnaji said, "I want to say certain things, and what I am going to say is in no spirit of criticism or condemnation. I really do not have, in my heart or mind, any sense of judgment. So, that must be clearly understood from the beginning.

"I have been talking now for over forty-five years. Rishi Valley and Rajghat came into being with one intention. These two places were to have been the center of the teachings and, if I may use the word with-out being misunderstood, holy places. I think it about time we took stock of what is actually happening; whether these two places are the centers of these teachings. And whether there is that sense of 'other-ness' in these two places.

"I have used an expression which may have given rise to misun-derstanding. I have said that the schools 'must be saved' as an oasis in this country; saved from the chaos that is going on all around. Be-cause I really feel most profoundly and I get rather stirred up about it, so forgive me if I speak hesitatingly, I feel that the flowering, after all these years, is still not taking place.

"And, I may never come back, I may die. If I do come back, as I was telling Mama [Madhavachari], it will be for a short time, not for these five months at a time. Physically I cannot do it any more, because I am not sleeping very well and I am getting too tired.

---

*Smt. is the shortened form of *srimati* or "auspicious one." It is used as a prefix to a married woman's name.

"So, you will have to consider that I am gone. Anything can happen. I can die. The decision may be taken, not by anybody else but by me, alone, never to return, or to return for very short periods. I do not know what is going to happen in the future, and I really mean this.

"So, can these two places be saved? You understand? Not saved from Balasundaram, or someone else, or from corruption or things like that, but saved as an oasis?

"As I was telling Kittyji this morning, and also Pupul at lunchtime, we have to do something very very drastic. I do not know what you are going to do. My days are limited, probably ten years more or less, and I want to concentrate everything I have and not waste my energy. I am speaking sanely, unemotionally, not sentimentally.

"So, what are we going to do to 'save' these places? Please understand what we mean by that word 'save.' To save in the sense of making them [an] oasis in this mad world. And, if I do not come back, if I die, what is going to happen?

"After forty years, what have we produced? You all have given a great part of your life to this—and what has happened? If you say, 'we are doing our best' or 'we are doing everything we can,' then somehow that is not good enough any more. I am not saying what you are doing is right or wrong. I do not feel that way, but what are we going to do?" There was a long pause.

"The same thing has happened at Ojai. You may know that there is a disturbance between the K. W. I. as it is now, and myself—and there is trouble. We all started out together to build something deep, something lasting, something worthwhile *there* as well as *here*. But there it is not flowering either.

"So, what can we do here? What can we do to save these places so that they become an oasis for these teachings? How can we make it into something really worthwhile? I have talked to Mama many times about this, for several years, and I say to myself now, 'What are we going to do?' "

Madhavachari was interrupting Krishnaji with explanations and excuses, but Krishnaji was not prepared to listen to him.

"I understand all that you are saying," he continued. "We have discussed this together several times at Rajghat, at Rishi Valley. For seven years now, we have discussed this. I am asking what are we going to do now? Forget the past, forget that I said this and you said that, forget that 'we are doing our best.' The *only* question is, 'What are we going to do?'

"Take it, Mama, I may die tomorrow, I don't intend to, but if I die, what will happen? Will you carry on just as before? Put it to yourself, Mama."

Madhavachari said, "I think when a great crisis like that comes . . ."

"It is *here*, Mama." Krishnaji said.

On Krishnaji's return to Europe in early 1968, we heard that a new group had formed around him. Krishnaji sent a telegram to Madhavachari, asking him to hand over Vasant Vihar to Galloway. Madhavachari replied that although he held a power of attorney from Rajagopal, he had no legal rights to hand over Vasant Vihar to Galloway. He said Krishnaji might have the moral authority, but the legal rights rested with Rajagopal. Krishnaji was very distressed with Madhavachari's response.

Balasundaram was in Paris, and soon was to go to Saanen to meet Krishnaji. Kitty Shiva Rao had written to Krishnaji that if Krishnaji so wished, she would get all the members of the Indian Foundation to resign. Krishnaji had not responded.

By the time Krishnaji met Balasundaram, a formal announcement had been made at the Saanen gathering in which Krishnaji stated that he was severing all connections with K. W. I. in Ojai, and that a new Foundation was to be formed in Europe, to carry on his work.

By now Brockwood Park in England had been purchased and the Krishnamurti Foundation was soon to be registered in England. Balasundaram found Krishnaji critical of the Indian Foundation; Naude was present at Krishnaji's meeting with Balasundaram, taking notes. After some discussion, it was finally decided that Balasundaram would be secretary, and that I should be asked to take over as president of the Indian Foundation.

Balasundaram returned to India soon afterwards. By late August 1968 he and I went to Vasant Vihar and asked Madhavachari to hand over Vasant Vihar either to the Foundation for New Education or to Smt. Jayalaxmi. Madhavachari refused. He left Vasant Vihar, sent back his power of attorney to Rajagopal, and handed over Vasant Vihar to Rajagopal's attorneys.

In October 1968 we received a bewildering letter from Krishnaji which shook the Foundation to its roots.

Members of the Foundation,

When Dr. Balasundaram came to Gstaad this summer, we spoke at great length about the necessary changes that have to take place in the Foundation for New Education, before it can be associated with the Krishnamurti Foundation in England, and thereby linked to the work which we are doing throughout the world.

Mr. and Mrs. Moorhead also came to Gstaad and we went over the same points with them, and we were all very clear as to what was needed. It would seem that there is now some misunderstanding in the Foundation about these points, and so we thought it would be useful to put them down again.

The Krishnamurti Foundation was formed in London on the 28th of August, this year, to direct and coordinate the diffusion of the teachings throughout the world. We worked for many months on the statutes of the Krishnamurti Foundation to make quite sure that it would respond exactly to our needs, that no one person or group could seize control of it now or later, and that it was entirely responsible to me and subject to my wishes.

I would like to make it clear that the Krishnamurti Foundation is simply an office, simply an efficient instrument to do material things. It is not in any way an "organisation" in the sense in which I use that word so often when I speak against organisations. It is not a psychological organisation. Belief and following are not involved, nor hierarchy. It is simply a committee responsible to me which will see that the teachings, publishing, etc. are diffused according to my wishes. It is an international committee, and the members on it all feel that they represent every country and not simply their own country.

If the work in India and in particular, the work of the Foundation for New Education is to be associated with the work throughout the world, certain conditions must absolutely be fulfilled. This is perhaps not the right occasion to go into a lengthy list of mistakes made in the past, but as I have said often, the Foundation for New Education has not functioned as I wished, nor has it really done what I wanted it to do. Therefore, we drew up a list of requirements with Dr. Balasundaram and I have seen this list and prepared it with him and others, and it is accurate and authentic. He will show it to you if he has not already done so.

The main thing on it is the absolute necessity that the Foundation for New Education be comprised exclusively of these people who do, actively and intensively, give their work, their energy, and their time to the schools, people who actually work at the schools and do the job. No personalities are involved in this, nor is any criticism intended against anybody in particular.

We feel sure that all those to whom the teachings mean something will implement this. If this means that they resign, this too will be an act of intelligent cooperation.

With much affection,
J. Krishnamurti."

An urgent meeting of the Foundation was called by us in Rishi Valley. Rao Sahib Patwardhan, Achyut Patwardhan, and Sunanda Patwardhan had already resigned; their letters were placed before the meeting. Madhavachari tendered his resignation, and Balasundaram was appointed secretary along with his role as principal of the Rishi Valley School. Kitty Shiva Rao, unable to bear the pressure being generated, also resigned, and I was elected president. Although Kitty Shiva Rao and all the remaining members signed the reply to Krishnaji, it was left for me to draft it. It was a difficult letter to write. He was the teacher, loved and evoking great devotion amongst all of us. But the challenge his letter posed left us with no alternative. It was necessary in the light of our intelligence to communicate our love and yet refuse to be placed in the impossible situation the letter demanded. We wrote:

My dear Krishnaji,

The F. N. E. in its meeting considered with deep gravity the points sent by you through Dr. Balasundaram and Mr. Moorhead and also your letter to the Foundation. In keeping with the spirit of these points and as an expression of our own deep concern that the F. N. E. should reflect your teachings and provide a fitting situation where your teachings can take root and flower in the minds of the young; a reorganisation of the structure and operation of the F. N. E. has been evolved and accepted. It will be implemented.

For many years, the F. N. E. has been associated with you and your work. Its members have sat with you, and with joy and devotion and attention have listened to what you have had to say. That they have failed to put through the teaching in the field of education is a measure of their inadequacy but not of their lack of interest and devotion to you and the teaching. The two places, Rishi Valley and Rajghat, were set up for the purpose of implementing your teaching in the field of education—the F. N. E. has not at any time deviated and will not deviate, from this intention.

There are however some points arising out of your recent communications which have caused deep hurt to the members of the Foundation. The implication seems to be that the present F. N. E. is inadequate to be associated with the Foundation set up for your work, and that the reorganised F. N. E. will have to achieve some grade before it can be associated with the Krishnamurti Foundation and your work. Who will apply this test?

We extend to the Krishnamurti Foundation our cooperation in the work of the dissemination of your teachings; a cooperation based on complete equality, with F. N. E. functioned as a free and independent body. In saying this, we would like to express to you once again our deep and unwavering intention to do whatever possible to see that these two institutions fulfill the purpose for which they were intended.

With affectionate regards,
Yours

We had assured Krishnaji of our deep ties with him, but refused to accept the judgment of any organization on our right to be associated with Krishnamurti's work.

The links with the guru were under strain, and a new relationship had to emerge. There was no reply to our letter, but we were to soon learn that a Krishnamurti Foundation had been registered in England with Krishnamurti as the president, and a Krishnamurti Center set up in Madras with Smt. Jayalaxmi as the Indian representative of Krishnaji in India, responsible for Krishnaji's work throughout the country.

For me, it was a period of deep inward search. In June of that year I went to the United States and had written and later telegraphed to Krishnaji at Brockwood that I would like to see him. I received no reply. I passed through London enroute to the United States, and while in New York heard from friends that Krishnaji had been in London for a day while I was there. Deeply hurt, I faced the fact that the guru had disappeared. My dependence on him was revealed in the intensity of the pain the incident evoked. I faced the fact that the guru had indeed disappeared. Abandoned, in darkness the seed of the teaching sustained me. I received no answers, but as I observed relentlessly, I felt the muscle and tone of my brain gain resilience and strength; still capable of holding impossible questions.

As president of the Krishnamurti Foundation India I wrote to Krishnaji in late December 1968, inviting him to speak in India. He wrote back on January 16, 1969, from California thanking me for officially inviting him to India. He asked Kitty Shiva Rao and me to be responsible for the talks and for the bulletin which he wanted to be brought out in India. He said he would be in India from December 1969 through February 1970.

Not a trace of the letter of 1968 and its content was to appear in Krishnaji's subsequent letters. The letter from Ojai was the first I had received since September 7, 1966. On June 2, 1969, Krishnaji wrote again of the need for India to raise funds for two return tickets— Naude's and his from Europe to India; Ojai could not provide the tickets because funds were low.

The news that Krishnaji had severed all connections with Naude reached us in India in late August 1969. It was a major surprise. It was unbelievable that a few months earlier, Naude could have had such influence, and yet had disappeard from the scene with such immediacy.

I had last seen Rao Sahib in late spring 1969 in Poona, where he was living. He was mortally ill, but waited for me at the door of his house—wearing, in his inimitable way, his white starched cap at a slant. Seeing me he smiled, picked a parijataka flower, and gave it to me.

Suddenly, towards the end of August, Rao Sahib Patwardhan suffered a severe cerebral hemorrhage. Achyut had warned me of the seriousness of his illness, and I was prepared for the news of his imminent death. But I found myself unable to see him in a coma, with tubes stuck into him. I knew his immense pride; he would have been devastated to have been so exposed. He lingered for two days, dying on August 29. I went to Poona, reaching the day after his death and cremation. His death left me desolate. He had been a beloved friend, warm, affectionate; it was the end of a precious relationship, and I mourned for him. One chapter of my life was over.

# CHAPTER 25

# "It Is Necessary to Ask Questions to Which There Are No Answers."

While I was in Poona I had asked Achyut and Sunanda again to rejoin the Foundation. Sunanda agreed. Achyut, though he did not formally join, agreed to help in every way.

Achyut, Sunanda, Nandini, and I met Krishnaji at the airport in the winter of 1969 when he arrived in Delhi. Rao's absence made the occasion particularly poignant. Krishnaji looked at us and said gravely, "So you have not all deserted me."

We held discussions with K on the future of the Foundation for New Education and its relationship with the Krishnamurti Center in Madras. Jayalaxmi was with us in New Delhi, and here too Krishnaji hesitated. It was finally decided that the Foundation for New Education would be renamed the Krishnamurti Foundation of India. This was necessary to reflect the nature of change in the work. The Foundation was no longer to be a body concerned only with schools and other educational institutions, and with holding and protecting the land, but would take over the work of the spread of the teaching. The change of direction would determine change of membership and function. In England Krishnaji had agreed to be president of the Krishnamurti Foundation; we strongly opposed this in India. To be head of a foundation was to accept total responsibility for its functioning, legally and morally. We felt Krishnaji was the great teacher and should not be so burdened. Our discussions were incomplete and were to continue later.

Krishnaji went to Bombay enroute to Madras. While in Bombay he stayed at Himmat Nivas. One night at supper, at which Nandini, Asit

Chandmal, and I were present, Krishnaji started talking about the Theosophical Society and Annie Besant. This was the first time in twenty-one years that he had spoken to us at length of the Theosophical Society.

Krishnaji was exploring the mystery that surrounded the discovery of the boy, Krishnamurti. He was probing delicately, tuning the ear to intimations and insights that might arise in discussion. His statements on the Theosophical Society were clear and precise. He made no comment as to whether they were true or illusion. Sensing the "otherness" in Krishnaji, we listened, asking few questions and letting him speak.

Krishnaji said that the Masters had told C. W. Leadbeater to find a boy who was a Brahmin, who came from a good family, and who had a "face as described." It was the duty of the Theosophical Society to protect the body of the child, and to provide an atmosphere of complete security for two years. If the body was prepared and ready, Lord Maitreya would give the boy the mind. When Leadbeater saw Krishnamurti on Adyar beach, he perceived that there was no selfishness in the boy's aura.

Krishnaji asked himself how it was that the boy remained unaffected in spite of being given everything he wanted—from orange juice to a Rolls Royce—and in spite of being treated by the people around him in a special way. Nobody was allowed to sit on his seat, or touch his tennis racket; tremendous care was taken to see that the body remained sensitive. He was not allowed to drink alcohol or eat meat or meet people who were coarse or unrefined. Krishnaji then advanced several theories to explain how the boy remained untouched. Was it that, through birth and rebirth, the child had evolved to perfection? Or had the Lord Maitreya protected the body till it was mature? Had the boy been born without a formal character or personality, allowing him to remain vague, untouched by his earlier years with his father, the school, the doctrines of the Theosophical Society, the luxury of the life he lived in England?

He then spoke of the Theosophical Society hierarchy—the highest was the "Lord of the World," then the Mahachohan, then the Buddha. The Bodhisattva Maitreya was considered equal to the Buddha. Below them were the Masters; each with a different name—one a Tibetan Lama, another an Indian aristocrat, another a Polish count.

The boy, who was totally innocent and unaffected, still had to be protected so that evil could not touch him, could not enter him.

Suddenly, in the middle of the conversation, Krishnaji stopped speaking. He said, "We are speaking of dangerous things. It can bring it into the house." The voice of Krishnaji was strange, his body gathered itself together. "Can you feel it in the room?" The room was pulsating. Strong forces were alive and in movement. Krishnaji was silent for a long time. When he started speaking again, the atmosphere in the room was transformed; there was silence, an active quality of goodness.

Krishnaji continued. Mrs. Besant had insisted that two initiates accompany Krishnaji all the time. She said, "Since you are always alone within, you must never be physically alone." There was a reservoir of the good in the boy that should not be contaminated. He said he needed protection even in 1969, for his character was still unformed. "The other night, while meditating, I could see that the boy still existed exactly as he was, nothing had happened to him in life. The boy is still as he was. The body still needs to be protected from evil." He paused again, and said, "I still feel protected."

He then spoke of the early years, when the boy Krishnamurti's body had to be completely protected and given security for two years; but the mind was not to be touched, for "the Lord would give him the rest." There were long silences between his sentences. K said the body had to go through a lot of pain (as in Ojai and Ootacamund) because there were still imperfections in the brain.

We then asked Krishnaji about the many undesirable people who through the years had come around him. Asit Chandmal asked, "How does the good allow evil in the form of a human being to come near?"

"I can't push away anybody or anything," K said. "I can't say 'go away'; it has to leave me. Isn't it strange that it does?" He then asked, "What is the force which completely protects something so that it is innocent and unaffected. You must be extremely careful if you open the door; evil or good can enter. Evil finds it easy to enter, the good much more difficult. Evil is not the opposite of the good," he repeated. "There is no relationship between the two."

Krishnaji then went on to speak of the initiations he had gone through in the Theosophical Society. According to the secret doctrines of the Society, there were three initiations. After two, things could still go wrong. But, after the third, the being could not be affected by anger, sex, money. They were all too trivial.

It was nearly midnight before Krishnaji went to bed.

From Bombay Krishnaji went to Madras. In his public talks and discussions there he raised a fundamental question: Is there such a thing as an individual, or is man merely a movement of the collective?

Insights into the nature of the collective revealed that it was made up of tradition, beliefs, knowledge, and the experience of the book. Krishnaji said that to be an individual, there had to be a revolution in the collective as revealed in knowledge and tradition. And so man had to discover his own incorruptibility.

"It is necessary to ask questions," Krishnaji said. "Questions to which there are no answers. So that the question throws man back on himself and the way the structure of thought operates. The hand that seeks to throw away or reject is the same hand that itself holds."

Later, during a walk in Bombay, he said that "the act of seeing and listening activates the sense. Seeing, without the word as thought intervening, creates energy."

He also spoke about the urgency "to know the self as it is, not as one wishes it to be, which is illusion, an ideal and fictitious. It is only that 'which is' that can be transformed, not that which you wish to be. The understanding of what you are—ugly, beautiful, wicked, evil—understanding without distortion is the beginning of virtue. Virtue alone gives freedom."

Krishnaji's interest in exploring the traditional Indian approach to liberation was evident from the autumn of 1970. He was in Delhi, and on our walks and in discussions he spoke of the tenacity of the Hindu mind, which despite conquest and repression had kept alive the ancient teachings.

We talked over the ancient role of the Brahmin; there was arrogance, evident in his refusal to accept money for giving knowledge. His gift of teaching had to be a free gift. As a Brahmin, he would not accept *dakshina*, charity. He felt he had a right to be supported by the state. Poverty was his birthright; so was learning. In time this pride had led to great Brahminic arrogance and corruption and with it degeneration.

Indian myth delighted Krishnaji. He often made me repeat the legend of Narada, the semicelestial musical mendicant and busybody who traveled ceaselessly, carrying the gossip of the world of the gods from one god to another.

Narada, anxious to learn the secret of Vishnu's *maya*, came on Vishnu as he rested in a grove of trees. After the salutations were over, Narada asked the god of the blue waters the secret of his *maya*—the web of illusion that covered the world of man and his actions. Vishnu agreed to teach it, but told Narada that as he was thirsty, would he first fetch him some water. Narada wandered into the forest seeking a homestead. After some time he came to a house and knocked at the door. It was opened by a ravishingly beautiful young woman who smiled at him with her large lotus eyes as she turned to fetch the water. Narada was infatuated, and lingered for days in her company.

Time passed. Narada married his love and, as year followed year, children were born. Narada lived in bliss with his wife and children. A year came when it rained incessantly, the waters of the rivers over-flowed their banks and a gigantic flood swept away Narada's house and the surrounding trees. Holding his wife by one hand, clutching a child with the other and with yet another child perched on his shoulder, Narada waded through the waters to reach higher ground. But soon the waters reached his chest, and then his chin. One by one the children who clung to him were swept away, until only his wife remained. It was night and the darkness added to the terror that engulfed him; the waters continued to rise and his wife, unable to hold on to his arm, was separated from him and the waters claimed her. Then Narada, alone, lifted his arms and cried out to the gods. Suddenly, a voice was heard. "Ten minutes have passed. Where is my glass of water?"

We were meeting in the home of B. Shiva Rao in Lodi Estate. Every morning we discussed Indian traditional thought; Tantra, the awak-ening of *kundalini*, yoga and energy, beauty, perception, and the "back-ward-flowing movement." One of the discussions was on death. Shiva Rao was critically ill on the day of the discussion, and the doctors were with him. Krishnaji had sat with him for some time, holding his hand. Shiva Rao's heart was failing, and he was not expected to survive.

That morning in the discussion Krishnaji was very serious. When we started speaking of death, he said that Shiva Rao would not die, but would recover. Without attaching much significance to his remark, he went on to say that no one had ever died under the same roof while he was living in the house. As he was then seventy-five years old, the statement was staggering.

The discussion on death started with a query. "There must be a way of learning how to die?"

Krishnaji said, "We put death beyond the walls, beyond the move-ment of life. It is something to avoid, to evade. The question is, What is living and what is dying? The two must be together, not separate. Why have we separated the two? Can one learn about living and so learn about death? Learning is always in the active present. Unless the brain perceives directly, it can never understand. But there is nothing to learn. There is no death when the mind is free of the known.

"Death says, you cannot touch me, you cannot play tricks with me—the mind is used to tricks—carving something out of experience. Death says, you cannot experience me—death is an original experience—a state I do not know—I am starkly frightened."

The discussions continued, and when K went to Madras another group gathered to meet with him. One of the participants was George Sudarshan, a young physicist teaching at Austin University in Texas. They discussed, in Sudarshan's words, "the Second Law of Thermodynamics." Krishnaji spoke of time, and of how the observer and the observed were one.

"The observer separates himself through images, conclusion, and so creates space and time. That is one of the major fragmentations. Can the observer look at 'what is,' without the observer, who is the maker of time, space, distance? The observer is time." George Sudarshan found that he could not immediately connect with Krishnaji and the special meaning he gave to words. George Sudarshan still had to grow familiar with Krishnaji's language, but he had been deeply moved by Krishnaji and had felt an overflowing sacredness in his presence.

I had a car accident near Madras and suffered a cracked vertebra, so I could not go to Rishi Valley, where Krishnaji was to continue his discussions. I was carried by air on a stretcher to Bombay, where I was in bed for three weeks. But I insisted on participating in the Bombay dialogues. When Krishnaji met me in Bombay his response to my accident was totally unexpected. He caught me by the shoulders and shook me, saying I had no business to be irresponsible with my body. I took a deep gulp and girded myself for our discussion, which would cover topics of immense diversity and depth. The way of dialogue and the energy generated by serious enquiry was being revealed. After two hours of discussion, I would go to my bedroom and collapse with pain. Krishnaji must have noticed it, but made no comment.

Krishnaji was happy with the quality of our dialogues; he had sensed in them a new approach to the teaching. He took a copy of them back with him when he left India, as he felt that they should form the basis of his new book. The dialogues were corrected in India and published under the title *Tradition and Revolution*. It was the first major book of Krishnaji's dialogues. There was a recognition in the book of the importance of dialogue in awakening the questioning mind, and an awareness that there were no answers to life's fundamental problems. There was only awakening of intelligence and the constant asking of fundamental questions.

By the spring of 1971 tensions between India and Pakistan had built up. Like a tidal wave, lean, dark-skinned, liquid-eyed, men, women, and children refugees poured over the border from East Pakistan into West Bengal. The sheer weight of their numbers had led to a collapse of all civic amenities, and by October, ten million refugees were flooding the Eastern countryside. It was a disaster for India.

In June 1971 I had gone abroad. Before leaving, I had met my old friend Indira Gandhi. She said, "If people in the U.S.A. ask you of the situation, tell them that Indira Gandhi says, with all solemnity, that in one year there will not be a single refugee remaining on Indian soil." The threat of war was a reality, the situation grim.

Krishnaji was to have come to India from Rome towards the end of October. But on October 19 he wrote from Paris that the local newspapers were full of the possibility of war between India and Pakistan, and he had been told that with the hysteria of war flooding the country he would not have the freedom to speak in India. He asked us to consider seriously whether he should come. Letters from Rome soon followed. In a letter dated October 28 Krishnaji wrote that the newspapers reported that in India the smell of war was in the air. He reminded me that, "You have, as you said, taken the responsibility of protecting this body and I also have a responsibility towards its protection. All this may jeopardize the work in India. So Pupul, consider all this and a wise decision must be reached by us all."

I wrote him a letter, assuring him that even if there were a war he would have no problem leaving India. On November 3, he wrote from Rome:

. . . war or no war, the situation is this and I haven't written to you before about it as I was hoping there would be a change for the better. Eve[r] since this summer after Gstaad, my body is getting more and more tired. It has reached a point of exhaustion. Since I have been here I have been vomiting every day, little sleep and spend most of the day in bed and had to cancel two talks here that they were planning. Add to this, the body has become hypersensitive. It needs total and complete rest. If I come to India in this state, I am sure it will fall ill which would be no good to anyone. My teeth have been troubling too. I was hoping very much that things would improve during these three weeks in Rome but unfortunately it has not, if anything more worn out. So it is wiser that I don't come to India this winter. I am very sorry not to, but there it is, this body must be kept going as long as possible. It is, I feel, our responsibility.

From here I shall go back to Brockwood and then on to California. Mrs. Zimbalist is with her family in America. I have to write to find out if she can have me at Malibu. I want to go somewhere where the body can be at rest and quietly "disappear." I hope you understand. I will keep in touch with you, dear Pupul.

Nandini and I were deeply concerned about his health, and on November 8 we spoke to him on the telephone. Soon rumors started in India that K was very ill and in hospital. We telephoned to Malibu, where K was resting in Mary Zimbalist's house, and got a reassuring reply.

In the autumn of 1971 I had an attack of cardiac insufficiency while I was in Bombay. It was accompanied by high blood pressure, and I was in bed for several weeks. Meanwhile my husband, who was in Delhi, again fell seriously ill. His lungs were very weak and he suffered from severe emphysema. We took him to Bombay for treatment, but his condition continued to deteriorate. I was traveling constantly between New Delhi and Bombay.

On July 23, 1972, his condition suddenly grew critical. That night I rested in the corridor outside his room. At a little after midnight I was called in. Jayakar was semiconscious; he was speaking, but one had to bend near to catch his words: "Help me, hold my hand, help me." I do not know whether he recognized me. I had taken his hand. Nandini had come into the room and she took the other hand.

The body had grown still and the voice silent, but the pressure of his hand was still there. The room was totally still, so was the mind. In the enormous silence one felt a presence take over, carrying him gently across the threshold. Suddenly, the hand grew slack. The worn face lost its look of intense suffering; he looked young, beautiful, untouched by his disease. Who was I to mourn? My daughter Radhika had come into the room. She saw him "sleeping," and it was a moment before she realized that death was our companion. The silence that had awakened that night stayed with me in the days that followed. Later I came away to Delhi, and the quietness rested in me.

One night in October I awoke, fear exploding within me. My window was open and in the darkness I felt a presence waiting outside. I was choked with fear. I put on the light and stayed up all night, afraid to close my eyes—for with darkness, the presence was there. For ten days this continued. I would fall off to sleep and awake to a torrent of fear, the presence waiting outside in the darkness. No observing within was possible. The intensity of fear was annihilating me; I was a wreck and I could not sleep for over a fortnight.

Krishnaji came to Delhi in the autumn of 1972, and I went to see him. He asked me in great detail of the manner of Jayakar's death, the moment of death and the state of my mind. We talked of it, we sat quiet with it, but after that day he never mentioned the fact of Jayakar's death again. One aspect of my life was over, I had to be free of the past and move on. Later I spoke to him of the fear that had awakened in me and was destroying me. He listened with gravity, held my hand, and made me sit silently with him. We sat for a long while.

The discussions had started, and one of the discussions was on fear. Krishnaji said fear existed when there was a feeling of complete isolation, of utter helplessness. I responded that one could deal with conscious fears, even allow them to flower and end. But one appeared helpless with unconscious fears, with the primeval darkness that lay at the root of existence.

"Does the unconscious hold these fears?" asked Krishnaji. "Does the unconscious invite these fears or does it gather them from the environment? Are they in the inherited genes?" he asked. "Why do we consider the unconscious as the storehouse of fear?"

"Fear is always there, it is in a crisis that you become aware of it," I said.

As discussion flowed, it reflected the dark, nameless fears that lurked as shadows in the brain. Sensing this, Krishnaji asked, "Is it that the whole structure of the cell is frightened of not being? Is fear part of human existence? Is it part of the tiniest living thing, the minutest cell? If so, why should I have to create a crisis to deal with fear?" There was silence.

"A gesture, a thought, a word, a look, a whisper brings about fear. Fear is here, in the without and the within." As he spoke, it was there around us and within us. "Why don't we contact fear before the challenge?" he asked. "Is the conscious mind frightened to face fear?" Then, sensing the atmosphere and seeing the enormity of the problem, he said, "Let us go slowly, we are tracing a rocket.

"What is required," he said, "is real simplicity, not analysis. Fear of not being is a part of our blood cells. It is our inheritance. I say it is there under the carpet, lift it and look. It is there. When the conscious mind is awake in itself, it is not frightened. Why should I be frightened if fear is part of my being?"

There was little we could say to contribute to the discussion. Suddenly, he spoke. "Can the mind be completely motionless? Then let fear come, let it arise. When the mind is awake, what then is the central root of fear?" As he spoke, there had been deep ending of the rising spiral of fear. The brain was still, so was the body.

"Has this state ever arisen to you, Sir?" I asked. Again he was silent.

"Several times, many times, when the mind is completely stable, without any recoil, neither accepting nor denying, nor rationalizing nor escaping, when there is no movement of any kind. We have got to the root of it, have we not?"

I had listened. I came away seeing that freedom from fear was not in any action from within or without, but could only be when the brain was totally still. The quietness generated by dialogue remained with me, and I slept that night without fear. Cataclysmic, primeval fears have not arisen within me since that dialogue. The few fears that have arisen have been at the surface level of consciousness and so possible to deal with.

In the days that followed K was to speak to me of the nature of loneliness. It was an extraordinary state of being, completely isolated. It was the essence of the self—the "me" with its web of words in which the mind is caught. He asked me to face complete inward loneliness; only in that was there freedom from fear.

"To be free of fear is to be free of time" he said. I received those words and held them close.

CHAPTER 26

# "Love Does Not Suffer."

The war with Pakistan in 1971 and the formation of Bangladesh had been a traumatic experience for the subcontinent. Krishnaji, on seeing us in 1972, had spoken with passionate concern about the war. He asked us why we did not protest strongly against war, which was the ultimate act of violence; whatever the circumstances, war could not be countenanced. We tried to explain the presence of 10 million refugees on Indian soil, the pressure generated, and the problems inherent in the situation. But Krishnaji would not waver from his position.

At his talks and small discussions we noticed that his language and use of words had changed. He was going into the root meaning of words, drawing clear distinctions between brain, mind, and consciousness. In one of his talks in Delhi he said that the brain cells had been conditioned for thousands of years, and that unless there was a breakthrough in that conditioning disaster was inevitable. "The world is afire. Can the brain, the whole human structure, undergo a tremendous revolution, a great mutation? Can there be a holistic living rather than the fragmentary?"

There was a great sadness in Krishnaji. On November 19 in New Delhi, he said, "It is one of the greatest sorrows in the world that one wants to convey something tremendous with one's heart and mind and you don't receive it. That is sorrow not only to the speaker, but to you who listen." Sensing the increasing violence that lay in the future, Krishnaji spoke of man as being caught in the corridor of opposites— hate and love, violence and nonviolence. But the truth was in "what is," which is violence. He investigated thought and its structure; thought was the past as memory, thought was time.

"Now can the mind, the brain cells themselves which are the product of time as evolution—can the brain cells themselves and the total mind, that is the body the movement of desire, the movement you know as thought, the whole thing—be completely still? And it can only be still when you have understood the value of thought where it is important and where it is unimportant. Without understanding the structure and nature of thought you will not come upon this silence naturally.

"And silence is necessary. When you look at a cloud and the beauty of the light in that cloud, if your mind is chattering, wandering, speculating, verbalizing, it cannot see the beauty of the cloud. The mind must be quiet and it will be quiet when you have denied or put aside control, authority; all the things which man has put together in order to find truth or enlightenment, things which are the fabrications of man, therefore caught in time. And to find that which is not of time, which has no measure, which is not nameable, the mind must be completely still. That means can that brain—please follow this—the brain which has demanded absolute security, otherwise it cannot function freely, effectively—can that brain be completely secure, so that it can operate without friction?

"When you see that, then there is clarity in observation and learning, which is the act of intelligence. In observing that which is false the brain cells become quiet, and with that the mind naturally, easily, sweetly—without any effort—is extraordinarily quiet. And in that stillness of mind there is no time. It is not a question of, 'Can the mind sustain or maintain or continue in that silence?' That question is a desire of thought, which wants to pursue that silence as pleasure.

"In that silence there is no observer, no experience, but only that quality of complete and total silence. In that silence the door is open. What lies beyond the door is indescribable, it cannot be put into words."

In the summer of 1971 I was in the United States. After my official work was over, I spent a holiday with my daughter in California. She was to tell me of a very unusual lecture she had heard in Toronto. The speaker was Ivan Illich. He had been ordained into the Jesuit order and had spent several years in South America. Differences had arisen between him and the church in Rome and he had, after great travail, left the Jesuit priesthood and started living in Mexico at Cuernavaca. There, as he was to explain later in India, he established a center, an empty space where people could meet.

His Toronto lecture had been on "Deschooling Society," and Radhika gave me a copy of the book. Its originality and intensity intrigued me, and on my return to India I gave the book to Indira Gandhi. She read the book, thought it relevant to the Indian situation, and arranged for Illich to be invited to India. He was to tell me later that he hesitated before responding to a government invitation, but ultimately agreed. We had a common friend, Dorothy Norman, and he brought me a letter of introduction from her.

Illich came to dinner at my house in Delhi in the late autumn of 1972. He had a remarkable presence and I responded eagerly to the challenge of his words. Soon we established a rapport and became friends. Indira Gandhi had asked me to help plan his programs and I had suggested that he visit Rajghat and meet Krishnaji.

On November 27, Ivan Illich was in Rajghat. He was staying in the room over the guest house; the river Ganga in all its majesty lay before it. He was having his meals with Krishnaji and the first meeting between the two took place in the afternoon. It was a seminal meeting of two minds; Krishnaji with an observing mind, alive, perceptive, and Ivan Illich, erudite, rational, rooted in the finest traditions of Western thought, yet prepared to listen. The river Ganga listened to the dialogue as it had listened through the centuries to the sound of voices questioning, listening, and counterquestioning.

Although the minds of Krishnaji and Illich flowed as two distinct streams, they came together in their shared passion for transformations and the need to free man from illusion.

I introduced Illich to Krishnaji, and spoke of his criticism of modern society and his concern with restructuring society and its tools. Krishnaji and Illich discussed the chaos and corruption of contemporary education in the world. Illich spoke of his concern with liberating the individual from the illusions about what he owed society. Krishnaji had been listening, trying to contact the man behind the words. Sensing that the minds were not meeting, Krishnaji pointed to the river. "There lies the Ganga. It is flowing and all human beings are being driven by the flow of the stream—surely the individual is one who steps out of the stream. The word 'individual' means one who is not divisible, who is whole—not fragmented."

The river was soon to become the shifting metaphor, around which the dialogue moved; voices coming together and moving apart.

Illich too was trying to establish contact and to feel his way into the new relationship. He said he had spent some hours on the riverbank, watching people bathing, praying, living in the same river, below the burning *ghats*. He had witnessed people come out of the river to sit quietly on its banks and had felt the resignation that arose within them, an acceptance that the river would carry them away again, one day. He mused on modern technological society to which India was becoming slowly a slave and so losing its touch with life, and the pervading feeling in the world that technology could rechannel the river.

"But the river could not be rechanneled," said Krishnaji. "Will it not be the same water? There is only one action for the human being to step out of the stream, to never go back or form another stream." Illich's response was to quote a poem from Mexico written in the Navajo style, the first line being repeated and meditated upon:

> Only for a short time have you loaned us to each other.
> Because it is in your drawing us that we take shape.
> It is in your painting us that we get form.
> It is in your singing to us that we get voice.
> But only for a short while, have you loaned us to each other.
> Because even as lines drawn in crystaline obsidian disappear
> and as the green color of the Quetzalcoatal feathers fade
> and as the waterfall subsides during the summer—so we
> too disappear.
> Only for a short while have you loaned us to each other.

On the banks of the Ganga, Illich had witnessed an affirmation of life which he felt could not be recreated in modern terms. He had sensed the weight and depth and rootedness of a civilization of which the river was a symbol.

There was a great anguish in Illich for the loss of ancient traditions. Modern man, industrial man, whose values had been institutionalized, felt that he could take people from the old stream and insert them into a new stream. But the stream into which he hoped to place people was a lifeless one. It was illusory and abstract. That was the great corruption. He spoke about modern education which tried to create a new consciousness, the illusion that you can step out of the river of tradition, to create a new kind of current; a current that would create a new humanity.

For Krishnaji, the river symbolized all traditions, modern as well as ancient. To him traditions, however noble, however ancient, conditioned man. "If I had a son, for I feel they are my sons whether in England, France, or here, I would feel responsible to help them to get out of these two streams or those seemingly running parallel to each other." Was it not necessary, he asked, for young people to be free of all streams?

Krishnaji and Illich shared a sense that compassion was essential and that it did not demand of people that they change into "this or that." Illich had sensed the rootedness of Indian women and remarked on it, and the danger of their losing this contact with tradition and life. He felt grateful for his own roots in certain traditions. He did not want to let go of the great help and discipline that traditions sometimes give.

To Krishnaji, however, all discipline, control was violence. It is only when man felt responsible that he was free, compassionate. Freedom and compassion were one thing. "We have tried for the last fifty years to see if a few could get out of the stream, get out without motive." He spoke of learning as the essential factor for freeing of mind, a learning that creates its own momentum.

Along the riverbank, a dog had started to bark and the sounds of the outer world of Varanasi entered the room.

Krishnaji developed the theme of compassion. He asked Illich whether he saw that freedom and compassion and the sense of not belonging went together. Illich said yes, for to belong gave people the feeling of power; not to belong meant powerlessness. Krishnaji felt that to belong gave people the sense of changing, producing, acting. "Can one say, Let me not belong, and see what happens? Most people are Catholics, Buddhists, Hindus, and the tradition of that is destroying them." Illich discussed the possibility of setting up enclaves, communities outside the stream; but they agreed that historically such communities have not worked. Krishnaji spoke of the terrible things happening in the world. He asked, "What can we do?" Illich felt that possibly it was because the world's elite lived on belief in the "better"— better education, better health. To him the concept of the "better" was a falsification of consciousness.

"You see, Sir, we are second-hand human beings—all knowledge is second-hand. To be free of the second-hand is not to belong to a thing—not to accumulate knowledge," said Krishnaji.

Illich asked whether not accumulating knowledge meant immediate experience. Krishnaji set experience aside. To him experience was dangerous. "When the mind is totally awake, why do you need experience? The whole world is concerned to experience, to acquire knowledge, to be attached within the stream and so to belong."

But Illich felt committed to the little streams, those rich traditions that have given form to human life, forms that if permitted to "become gods or hierarchies" could be as destructive as other destructive streams. In that sense of belonging he was prepared to be second-hand. He felt a responsibility to help people become critical and felt ashamed of affirming a rootedness in those little traditions, even if it meant being partially second-hand.

"Wait, wait," said Krishnaji. "Let us go slowly. One belongs to something because, in oneself, one is lonely, afraid. The whole psychological phenomenon is going on inside the skin, it makes one belong to something, the big stream or the little stream or the latest *ashram*—the latest guru. Do you follow? One goes back to the church or to Buddhism or whatever. It is only when you see this inwardly, with clarity, that you don't belong to anything and therefore you have rejected all the things that man has put together—ideation—formulas—concepts—beliefs—because they are all part of the stream."

Krishnaji turned to what for him was the central issue. "There has to be right perception. I would like to say to people, 'Look, just look, don't argue, don't translate, don't say this is right, that is wrong. Don't ask how shall I live, if I don't belong. Just look—have an eye that has no corruption in it.' "

Illich's concern was to show people what they could not do. To Krishnaji to know what not to do, was to do the right thing.

Illich perceived this instantly. A new movement had started. He felt responsible for translating in extremely lucid terms what they were talking about into concrete knowledge. To Krishnaji, that came later. It was first necessary not to belong to any society, any nation. The mind had to extricate itself. It had to be free to look and that freedom was action. The very seeing was action.

Krishnaji said that nationalism divides man. But Illich's response to this was equally intense. He again emphasized the need for roots, which meant much more than being held in nationalism. Krishnaji said he too had roots because he was born in India into the Brahminical fold. That root—it might be thousands of years old—was his conditioning, but so long as the mind was so conditioned it was not free. It was the past as thought that essentially divided man. Thought was knowledge. "If I want to live with you in peace, thought must come to an end. That in which I have my roots prevents my relationship with you."

To Krishnaji, observation without the introduction of thought was necessary; that alone was total action. Illich said he had begun to understand. The problem was one of language. But to him the danger was that the younger generation had lost the capacity to distinguish and to deny the false.

Drawing the strands of the discussion together and responding to Illich's concern with roots, Krishnaji said, "When I step out of that stream, I am not fragmented—not contradictory—I am whole—the whole has no root."

Illich felt the intense need for roots, he was not prepared to let go.

Krishnaji felt that without a solution of this central problem, there could be no flowering of man. The flowering had to take place. Illich felt there was little hope of solving the central problem. He was prepared to accept and live and die with something short of perfection. Krishnaji and Illich had come to a parting of ways.

For Krishnaji, Illich's response was not good enough. Suddenly he started to speak of the central issue as an ending to suffering. He could not visualize life as meant for perpetual suffering.

To Illich, suffering had to be accepted. "Why?" asked Krishnaji, "Should human beings suffer psychologically?"

"Because God accepted it," said Illich.

Krishnaji was merciless in his enquiry. "Why should man suffer?" For man to accept suffering psychologically was the essence of his ignorance. Why should human beings suffer? Because they were ignorant? Because they were in conflict? Because they were contradictory in themselves?

Illich was equally passionate. He said that he believed suffering was the human condition.

"Ah, that's it," said Krishnaji.

Illich felt the need to recognize his conditioning fully, lucidly, and sensitively, and be shaped by this conditioning. But Krishnaji refused to accept that sorrow was essential to the human condition.

The two minds were face to face. Illich asked, "What does compassion then mean?"

Like a rush of water came the reply. "Compassion means passion for all; love, Sir, does not suffer."

They parted. As we walked silently to his room, Illich plucked a jasmine flower and gave it to me. It was an eloquent gesture. The next day he was to meet Krishnaji again, but I was not present.

# CHAPTER 27

# "The Observer
# Is the Observed."

In June 1973 the first international meeting of the Krishnamurti Foundation was held at Brockwood Park. Achyut, Sunanda, Balasundaram, and I represented India. While introducing us to the members from the American and the English Foundations, Krishnaji said of Achyut, "How shall I introduce Achyut? He was one of the people responsible for driving the British out of India."

We discussed the question of copyright and publications. There was a major difference of opinion where the copyright should vest. Ultimately, it was decided that while the copyright continued with the English Foundation, the Indian Foundation would have the right to publish from Krishnaji's talks and discussions in India, as well as bring out an international publication once in three years.

Krishnaji had no possessions save his clothes and his watch. However, he had indicated in his will that his body after his death should be cremated wherever he died, and no monument built over his ashes. At this point, seeing the sadness on our faces, Krishnaji joked, "If I die in England, you can cremate me in 'Golders Green and scatter my ashes there.' "

I felt I was choking. I told him not to be flippant, that his body was sacred and no feet should tread where the ashes of his body had fallen. "We shall take the ashes and scatter them in the rivers of India." He immediately became very grave, turned to the others and affirmed, "This body is sacred." It was so decided, that his ashes be sent to India and would ultimately flow in the rivers to the ocean.

On November 17, 1974, Krishnaji arrived in New Delhi on his way to Varanasi. I had arranged for a pass to meet him in the lounge within the customs enclosure. I saw the Maharshi Mahesh Yogi standing nearby; he was garlanded and surrounded by his disciples. Sitting in the lounge awaiting Krishnaji's luggage I asked, "Was the Maharshi with you on the plane?" Krishnaji smiled. He had boarded the plane at Rome, and as he walked to his seat he had passed a bearded figure sitting cross-legged on a tiger skin. K vaguely recognized the man, but he could not quite place him. Some time later the hostess had come to him holding a rose and asked whether he was J. Krishnamurti. When Krishnaji said he was, she had handed him the rose saying that the Maharshi, who was in the plane, had sent his greetings and the rose. Krishnaji conveyed his thanks. A few hours later he had gone to the toilet and, returning, had passed the Maharshi's seat. The Maharshi sprang to his feet. After they had folded their palms in *namaskaras* to each other (the traditional form of greeting in India between friends, strangers, young, or old people), the Maharshi pointed to a seat next to him and suggested that they talk for a while. So Krishnaji sat down. After a few pleasantries, the Maharshi said that he was going to Nepal to announce a world revolution in consciousness and suggested Krishnaji accompany him and join him in his work, as together he felt they could change humanity. Krishnaji had politely declined, saying that he had a number of engagements and so begged to be forgiven. Maharshi had continued to urge him, as he felt that what he was doing was more important. The conversation had continued for an hour, after which they parted and Krishnaji returned to his seat.

In November 1974 Krishnaji was again in Varanasi. At a small discussion held on November 19 in his sitting room overlooking the Ganga, I asked, "Could we identify the main elements in the teachings?" We had heard him for twenty-five years. Many of us could give substance to the whole field of self-knowledge, but the question remained: "What is the teaching?"

Krishnaji was taken by surprise; he was quiet, letting the question unfold. Finally, he said, "I don't know. I can't put it in a few words, can I? I think the idea of the teaching and the taught is basically wrong, at least for me. I think it is a matter of sharing rather than being taught, partaking rather than giving or receiving. And so, can we share something which is not in the field of time, thought, and direction? Can we share, or are we all so conditioned that we don't know what it means to share?"

We then discussed at length the question of participating, sharing, and receiving. Krishnaji said, "There is no teacher and the taught. Is it a matter of compassion?"

Then, as the energy generated by dialogue intensified, Krishnaji suddenly commented, "You were asking, 'what is the teaching?' Right? I say, the teaching says, 'Where *you* are the *other* is not.' "

We listened, the mind silent with the purity of K's insight. Then the ripples of thought started again. We discussed the quality of listening and the maturing of the mind.

"Would you say," K asked, "that the mind must be free from any movement as accumulation, as knowledge, as direction, as will? Movement implies time. Time is movement. I am asking—is time necessary to see? Or, is it not necessary? Then how does a mind, the whole structure of the mind, which is evolved through time, see that which is not of time? You see the paradox?" he queried. "So can you die to all the things you have acquired—pleasure, pain, hurt?"

"Do you go through that exercise?" I asked.

"Of course not. Those exercises, practices are trivial. The mind, the brain, is evolved through time. It is recorded in time. Can that mind see that which is not time? Obviously not. Then, what is it that perceives something which is not of time? Find out."

Some days later we held the first of the discussions with the Buddhists. Amongst the group that had gathered was Rimpoche Sandup. A *bhikshuk* (monk) from Tibet, clad in red ochre, with a grave demeanor and an ageless face, he was the director of the Institute of Tibetology at Sarnath. Pandit Jagannath Upadhyaya of the Sanskrit University, a Socialist and a scholar of Nagarjuna, other pandits from the Sanskrit University, and Krishnaji's companions participated.

Describing it later, Rimpoche Sandup said that when he had asked Krishnaji a question, Krishnaji had negated the question and in turn challenged the Rimpoche. He was bewildered, he could not comprehend Krishnaji's approach. At the end of the discussion, and later, as he heard Krishnaji over the years, the lama came to realize that fundamental questions had no answers, but still had to be asked. "Krishnaji," he said, "never provides an answer, never puts anything into a person. But his challenge touches a germinating point within, which enables the listener to awaken and for 'what is' to unfold."

Rimpoche Sandup said, "If you feel the compassion that flows from Krishnaji, you will see there is no limit to him. Most teachers have a limited approach, but Krishnaji's approach is without limit." He was deeply touched by Krishnaji, his presence and his words. "The more one has insight and tries to touch Krishnaji, the further he recedes; the greater Krishnaji's insights. You can never hold him, never get near him. For there is no end, no limit to him."

Rajesh Dalal, a young technocrat who had just graduated from the Indian Institute of Technology, Kanpur, came to Rajghat to hear Krishnaji speak. Attracted by the depth and relevance of Krishnaji's teaching, he was the first of the young academics and professionals to turn away from a career and join as a teacher in Krishnaji's schools.

Krishnaji's visit to Rajghat in November 1976 led to Rajesh's first meeting with him. He went to Krishnaji's room, rather excited, a little nervous at the idea of meeting the "great one." Krishnaji met him at the door, took him by the hand, and led him to the veranda overlooking the Ganga and the garden. They sat on a divan, and Krishnaji said, "Sir, please don't feel shy." He started to ask about Rajesh's life, where he was born, the house he lived in, his parents, his school. His presence was so reassuring that Rajesh rambled on, talking about himself; in his words, "forgetting who I was talking to. It was like talking to someone who was an intimate close friend. When I told him that in school and college I had always played with objects, people, ideas, numbers, words, and so on, he seemed to be happy and said, 'That is good.' "

Krishnaji suddenly became very quiet and serious. Rajesh grew acutely conscious of the silence and was deeply affected by it. He became aware of the sun setting and "the radiance of the pink gold of the ripples in the water." He perceived the movement of the peepul leaves as the breezes played through them and listened to the sound of the peacock's call. They sat about four minutes without a word. Rajesh looked at Krishnaji once or twice, expecting him to break the silence, which he was finding too much to bear. He was beginning to realize the immensity of the person sitting beside him, and the intimacy which they had shared gave way to a feeling within him of immense awe. He saw Krishnaji as part of the river, of the peepul tree and the birds flying over it. "It was the awe which you feel when you are face to face with something unknown—something very profound."

Suddenly, he heard Krishnaji's voice. "Look Rajesh, the world is in darkness. It is mad. The violence you see all around you is crazy. And these places—Rajghat, Rishi Valley, Brockwood Park, and Ojai—have to become centers of light. The older people have messed everything up. They have not done it. And the new people, young people have to do it. You understand? I hope you have not come here to experiment for a year or two but are committed to this." When Rajesh assured

Krishnaji that this was the only thing that truly and deeply mattered in his life, there was a gentle yet enigmatic smile on Krishnaji's face.

By then it was time for Krishnaji to go for his walk. Krishnaji stood up swiftly and went into his room to get his shoes. Rajesh watched the way he stood, sat, wore his shoes, climbed down the stairs, and walked. He saw a very alert man, eighty-one years of age; by contrast, Rajesh could not help observing how sloppy and careless he was—and he was only twenty-three. Rajesh suddenly grew aware of all that he had to learn from this man. And as if he had sensed Rajesh's thoughts, Krishnaji said, "We will meet more often. I will see that you are with us in Madras and Rishi Valley."

To Rajesh it was a downpour of affection and blessing. He experienced a quiet alertness and went back to his room very aware of everything around him—the roses, boats on the river, and squirrels playing with each other. The mind was more alive than it had ever been.

In 1979 Krishnaji was to hold discussion with the teachers of Rishi Valley. Rajesh Dalal participated. Krishnaji spoke of the need to create trust in the student. Rajesh, sitting to K's right, was particularly attentive that day. The whole question of the student having deep trust and confidence in the educator was, Krishnaji said, "central to the process of education." He kept challenging his audience, throwing problems back to them, forcing them to enquire and respond from depth.

Rajesh told me, "I was alert, watching and listening. When suddenly Krishnaji turned to me and asked, 'Rajesh, what do you say?' I kept quiet, not feeling the need to respond. Again, after five or ten minutes, he said to the teachers, 'Sirs, will you come down from your platforms and tell your students that you are just like them—that you have fears, jealousies, hurts, and so on and that you don't know what to do. They will then see that you are honest and trust you. Will you do this?' Perhaps I had been waiting to hear something more profound than this. Also I felt I already had such a relationship with my students. So, I spoke out and my voice was charged with emotion. 'Sir, I have done that. But, that is not good enough. You can't keep saying I am confused and have fear. You have to be free of fear, if the student is to trust you.' "

Rajesh continued. "He turned to me, held my hand, and said, 'Rajesh, do it now.' His gaze and his words were like a noose choking me. It was a strange experience. The intensity of it stunned me and I could not speak. He immediately realized it and, turning his gaze away from me, began to discuss with other teachers. But he kept on gently and affectionately stroking my hand, as if to say, 'My boy, I understand what you have been through.' "

Seeing that Rajesh was living a life of total abstinence and chastity, and sensing the tensions that were arising, K spoke to him of sex. Krishnaji said, "Sex is like a tender flower, an intense flame, delicate and rare. It has to be nurtured and cherished. You have to be specially watchful when it is not operating as nature intended. To let sex function freely is to dissipate energy; to suppress it brutally is to destroy something delicate and intensely beautiful. So watch it with warmth, nurture it, let it discover itself and unfold—neither denying it nor succumbing to it."

Krishnaji kept telling us, "Challenge me. Take. Your challenge is not great enough."

We were in Madras and he had started discussing the rapidity of change that was taking place in the world. In the West, from the middle of the 1960s, a reaction against growing materialism and consumerism had led to an immense ferment amongst the young. An appalling emptiness was permeating all aspects of life. The pressure being generated by the ravaging of the environment and the unlocking of the mysteries of nature and their reckless use as toys of technology could not be sustained by the existing resources of young minds and bodies. The abnormal was becoming the norm.

Like a wave, confusion and chaos were overtaking adolescent boys and girls, who were in revolt. Vast numbers of these "flower children" had taken to the road; like the fakir or the mendicant, they were the new barefoot wanderers of the earth. They homed for India, meeting from all over the world in Nepal, Varanasi, Goa. They were sowing the seeds of a new culture, however abnormal, seeking to reestablish their communion with nature and man. They sought it in drugs, in music, in yoga, in sex. Antiwar, anticompetition, antihypocrisy, anti the "more" of acquisitive society, they were concerned with loving and being. Striding continents, even in their failures they had brought to the human situation a gentle, anguished interval. But they were a lost generation.

We discussed the cultural revolution in China. The experiment of millions of young people invading the environment had been awesome. It was an action bereft of all compassion, and the element of ruthlessness inherent in it was terrifying. It too had failed and left behind disaster and destruction.

Krishnaji asked us what was happening to the young in India. We told him of the Naxalite movement. It had started in rural West Bengal, but had rapidly penetrated universities, drawing into its ambience the young student, the unemployed intellectual, as well as boys and girls from affluent families in revolt against the status quo. Young, ruthless, violent, their concerns were with the destruction of existing values and economic structures. Ironically, young academics and professionals from the same milieu, dazzled by the explosions in science and technology and the unlimited opportunities that appeared on the Western horizon, were turning West, seeking to share in a seemingly limitless pot of gold.

In rural India one felt the immense winds of change. Power was passing into the hands of new caste groups, the so-called backward were coming to realize the power of the vote. In cities a growing corruption was taking over.

A general destructive violence, a fragmentation at all levels, and a growing lack of sensitivity was permeating the landscape of India. Krishnaji said he had seen this coming. As he traveled round the country he noticed the general decline in values and the tendency to shirk responsibility. "One observes this not only in the newspapers, but from what is happening around us socially; what is happening at the periphery of life, but also from what is happening inwardly. One sees disintegration, overpopulation, callousness, a growing indifference to man and environment." His passionate demand for a revolution in the ground of the mind was unallayed.

While in Madras Krishnaji, in his public talks and discussions, raised a fundamental question: Is there such a thing as an individual, or is man merely a movement of the collective? Insights into the nature of the collective reveal that it is made up of tradition, belief, knowledge, and the experience of the book. Krishnaji said that to be an individual, there has to be a revolution in the collective as revealed in knowledge and tradition; and so man has to discover his own incorruptibility.

It is necessary to ask questions: "Questions to which there are no answers. So that the question throws man on himself and the way the structure of thought operates."

From Madras Krishnaji went to Bombay. Perceiving that for millennia man has searched for freedom in the outer and inner, Krishnaji probed into the whole problem of living, learning, and observing. He said, "To learn is to observe and to act." Like the scientist observing through the microscope, he asked the audience "to observe, to watch

things as they are, not twist them to suit inclinations or prejudices."
He spoke of man's quest to be free of sorrow and violence.

Man had pondered over this question of violence for millions of
years—violence as opposed to peace, aggression as opposed to compassion, goodness as opposed to evil. Human beings had lived with
this question. "Why?" he asked. "We must answer this question, not
verbally, but in our own hearts, not explain it away or justify it, but
see that we are not violent, in our speech, in our gestures, in our
activity.

"If you observe," Krishnaji said, "man lacks a sense of beauty—
beauty as sensitivity not only physically, but also of the heart and
mind. To be sensitive is to be intelligent. Can one be aware of the
extraordinary beauty of the earth, the richness of a rice field, the beauty
of a face, of a smile, and the sadness of tears? Without such understanding not only the beauty that the eye sees, but the beauty of clear
unspotted perception, man can never be free of violence. To understand violence, one has to be free of the word. And one cannot be free
if there is no sensitivity to the beauty of everything about you. There
must be freedom to find out what love is. You know, the word freedom
is a dangerous word. Freedom for most people means to do what they
would like to do, a freedom from social restrictions, social morality.

"Freedom from something is one thing, and freedom for itself another. Only in negation is there freedom. By learning about disorder,
there is order. To learn about fear and violence needs a very subtle
mind. With the dying is the living. You must die to yesterday, to live
today, and then there is love. You have been given a piece of earth
and what are you to do with that earth? To grow plants on it, you
must have energy, passion, drive, intensity. If you live this way, then
the treasure you have discovered becomes clear, vibrant, alive.

"To live in the present is to see in the microscope, not according
to your wish or my wish, to see in the microscope how the past flows
through the present and explodes into the future. But as long as the
mind is caught in the image of the past, how can the heart live in the
present? And love is the present, not the tomorrow."

As he spoke, the mind, listening with great intensity, was one with
his words.

"What have you done with your life?" he asked. "Don't say, 'I am
going to fulfill next life.' There is only the present, the beauty of the
present, the richness of the present. You have had this life, this extraordinary thing called life in which there is sorrow, pleasure, fear,

guilt and all the tortures and the loneliness and despair of life and the beauty of life. And what have you done with it? A life was given to you, the most precious thing in the world, and what have you done? You have distorted it, tortured it, torn it to pieces, divided it, brought about violence, destruction, hatred, lived a life without love, without compassion, without passion.

"The question is asked and the answer lies only in the present, not in tomorrow or in the past, which raises the question, what are you doing 'now' with your life? And if you can answer this, you will find out what love is." The passion, the intensity of his concern was as a breeze that enveloped us as we listened, quickening the brain cells, making innocent the mind.

Krishnaji was also holding his small group discussions. He asked us, "Has religion failed in India? In India *sannyas*, *ashrams*, have become a form of religious revolt. Go to the moon, live under the sea, transplant the human heart; without compassion the problems of human existence continue. Could we observe with eyes that have never been spotted, made narrow with callous indifference? For this, to see the whole, a different quality of mind was needed."

In the discussions we were exploring the nature of the observer and his relationship to the observed, a central point of K's teaching. Krishnaji said, "In the very act of observing object there is the process of naming which clogs perception. In this very act, nature of what is observed, is undergoing change."

He spoke of insight as born of the observing mind. It is when the mind, heart, body are made one in attention that the division between religious perception and scientific truth disappears. "Freedom from the known exists within the brain cells. When grooves cease to exist, the brain is alive. In this state there is a physical transformation."

In his discussions Krishnaji denied his role as teacher and his listeners as disciples. He spoke of "learning," a state where the relationship of the teacher and the disciple undergoes a total change. Learning needs energy and intense curiosity and a freedom to explore. This comes with observation, a state in which all authority and all hierarchy in terms of the psyche ends. He spoke of himself as a mirror in which the listener sees himself, with a vision that is not distorted or conditioned.

"The act of learning is the act of living. Learning is a quality of mind, an attitude that is more important than what is learnt."

In his talks he elaborated on the discussions. Speaking of the brain and its need for security, he said, "The brain demands security and order, it also demands harmony. Without harmony, there is no security. Harmony means order, and the brain lives and it has lived for thousands of years in disorder, which means contradiction. Therefore [it is] in conflict not only within, but outwardly; and in this conflict, both inward and outward, it has found some kind of security. It accepts conflict as a way of life, and in that it has found security. Though it brings great disorder, though it brings destructiveness to itself, it has accepted this chaos, this confusion, because it doesn't know what to do. That brain which has been conditioned for millions of years to accept values that really bring disaster to itself, is conditioned that way, and it accepts that conditioning and lives in that conditioning as security.

"Look," Krishnaji continued, "you have accepted nationality, haven't you? But if you observe, that security brings war. When you accept nationalism, and you accept it because you have found security in it, that security is completely destroyed because nationalism invariably divides; and where there is a division there must be conflict. So your nationalism, in which the brain has found security, is bringing about its own destruction.

"Our brain, the brain cells, have themselves been conditioned for thousands and millions of years. And if there is no breakthrough in this conditioning, there will always be disaster, there will always be sorrow, there will always be confusion, there will be no harmony.

"And the world is afire. The house is burning and you have to respond to it with a fresh mind. Not according to your own conditioning. Therefore the question is, can the brain, can this whole human structure, undergo a tremendous revolution, great mutation, so that it is a fresh mind?" He paused.

"Watch this very carefully. You have taken the ideal of nonviolence. It is one of those extraordinary tricks you have played on yourself and all the teachers and the mahatmas have taught endlessly about it. Now watch it, go into it, learn about it, put your heart and mind into it. You want security; that is the very basis of the brain. So you seek security in an idea or in an ideal of nonviolence. So there is a division between violence and the ideal, and therefore contradiction, therefore hypocrisy, therefore disorder and pretension. When the real thing is violence, you are pretending there is nonviolence. So the brain cells seek out of this incapacity to deal with violence, an ideal, and therefore division follows and there is contradiction and conflict.

"So, you see there is security only in the truth that life has no security, but is a constant movement. That is the truth, and in that truth there is security.

"Have you learnt?" he asked. "In that learning about truth, the whole structure, the whole response of the brain cells undergoes a tremendous change. It lives in a total dimension of movement, a whole movement, not a fragmentary movement. Order, which is harmony, has no blueprint. Order, which is harmony, comes only when there is freedom from disorder. Order comes only when there is understanding, learning about the disorder. And out of the learning about disorder—not the learning how to bring order into disorder, which you can never do—out of that learning comes order, naturally."

Krishnaji explored the words "watch," "observe," "learn." "Is the observer, the one that learns, is he different from the thing he is observing or learning from? The fact that there is always the observer and the observed, in essence is division, disorder. As long as there is the observer, the experiencer, the thinker, the one who says 'I am learning' and divides himself from the observed, the experiencer and the thing from which he is learning, as long as there is this division, it will invariably bring about conflict, as all divisions do, and therefore confusion and therefore disorder."

Then he asked his listeners whether they observe disorder as an outsider looking in, or do they see that there is no observer at all? "Do you see that you are disorder?" He was speaking with pauses in between. "If you are the observer, watching the disorder in yourself and round about you, you are separate from the disorder; and therefore you who are watching, to bring about order, and therefore you are bringing about disorder because there is separation.

"So how you look at disorder matters enormously. If you look at it from the outside as though you are independent of it, as though you have nothing to do with it or as though you are going to bring about order, the 'you' is a fragment of other fragments. Is the 'you' who are looking at disorder different from disorder? You are part of that disorder; otherwise you wouldn't know it; otherwise you wouldn't recognize disorder. You are part of that disorder, you the observer are the creator of that disorder.

"If you see the truth of it, you are free. Because it is only the truth, which has nothing to do with pleasure or pain, the learning and seeing the truth, [which] frees the brain cells from their conditioning, therefore the brain is then a new brain.

"Do you see the beauty of this? You know, just as to see the beauty of a palm leaf in the clear sky, to see it, not as an observer with all his peculiar knowledge and impotence, but to look at it without the observer, to see the extraordinary movement of that palm leaf—so in the same way, to look is to learn. And in the learning is the total movement of life in which there is no fragmentation, and therefore it is a life of great harmony, and harmony means love."

# CHAPTER 28

# "The Pebble in the Pond"

In 1977, with the defeat of Indira Gandhi, I had resigned from the chairmanships of several government boards and societies and returned from Delhi to Bombay, where I was to live in an old, rented flat on Malabar Hill. I had been actively working in many organizations since long before independence, and this was the first time in thirty-five years that I found myself with nothing to do. I was still president of the Krishnamurti Foundation, but I sensed a breath of discontent amongst several of my colleagues.

From early 1978 I grew aware of an ebb of energy within me. The acuteness and altogetherness of my senses were blurred and losing vitality. I had started writing, but words came with difficulty.

I wrote to Krishnaji in California at Malibu, where he was staying. His reply was immediate.

My dearest Pupul,

Since you have written about yourself, may I point out certain things and I hope you won't mind.

I don't think it's old age that deteriorates the mind but you have had many psychological shocks. You have been deeply hurt and if I may point out, you haven't healed them, seen beyond that. Consider what I am writing seriously.

Now, you have to become deeply aware, not intellectually. Aware of your body; you have let it go; aware of what you eat and how much you eat; exercise, etc. Train that body, you have neglected it; then its own intelligence will take over.

You have, if I may point out, cultivated the intellect, with its arrogance and neglected the other side of it which is love, compassion. Naturally, one cannot and may not cultivate love but one must be wholly aware of this. If one may point out, give your complete and therefore choiceless attention to all this.

Of course, there's old age, with all its troubles but they are normal and natural. But these should in no way interfere with the mind and its beauty; though they are interrelated, the mind is infinite.

Sorry to write like this! I wanted to put it in as few words as possible. You will understand all this and with what love one's writing this. Be well, Pupul and see you fairly soon.

With love,
J. K.

Krishnaji arrived from England in the late autumn of 1978. He traveled directly from Delhi to Varanasi, accompanied by Mary Zimbalist. I followed him to Rajghat, Varanasi, where I was to stay in a small cottage on the edge of a cliff, overlooking the Ganga. The river was low, revealing banks planted with brilliant yellow mustard. Sunsets and sunrises intoxicated the waters; birds nested in the overhanging trees and sounds of Tulsidas's "Ramayan" floated down the river. But the passion that the river had awakened in me in earlier years was absent. When I talked with my colleagues I again felt a discordant chord.

Krishnaji had been warm and affectionate when he met me, but with him too I felt a distance. After a few days I went to see him. I was hesitant at first, but after some time I told him that I felt I was ageing, the brain was losing its edge and its capacity to penetrate and delve. There were few fresh insights. He was sitting at some distance from me. For some time after I spoke, we sat silently. Then he said, "I have noticed over the last two years that you have not been to see me."

I was close to tears. I looked up and found his eyes mirroring me. "When the brain cells deteriorate, they can never be renewed," he said. "When a relationship is broken, it can never be restored." He stopped speaking, perhaps listening to my unspoken response. Then he continued. "But a new cell in the brain has to be born, a new relationship come into being. In that is the renewal." I listened. There was no reaction, no protest. Not a thought arose nor the need to question him further. I sat quietly, then went to my room.

I spoke little during those days at Varanasi. Soon, in early December, I left Varanasi to go to Rishi Valley.

My brain had rested. There had been no immediate clarity or energy, but the chaos within the brain, the feeling of an ebbing tide, had ended. I could look again at trees; observe the shape of boulder against boulder changing color in the sun, listen to the distant sounds of children, look at the butterflies that swarmed over wild flowers in the valley; but the distance between my colleagues and me continued.

One morning I awoke from a deep sleep. Krishnaji had been ill and was resting in his room. I went to him and found him lying in bed. I said, "Krishnaji, I have been pondering over what you said to me in Varanasi. I have also been going into my being president of the Krishnamurti Foundation, and I feel deeply from the bottom of my heart that you should be the president. I opposed your being president since the early 1970s, as I felt that you would have to bear the responsibilities, legal and otherwise, if you were president. This burden I felt should not be placed on you. But I feel now that it would be right for you to be the head of K. F. I."

He closed his eyes, placed the palms of his hands on his breast, and lay silent for sometime. "You feel it from the depths of yourself?"

"Yes."

"Then leave it alone, the answer will come," he said, his eyes still closed.

Later, he gathered the members of the Foundation present in Rishi Valley and said, "Yesterday Pupul came to me and said from the bottom of her heart that she felt K should be the president of the K. F. I. I have not answered but left it, for in my own peculiar way, an answer will come." But, he said, he would like to make his position clear.

"In 1928 K dissolved the Order of the Star and said all organizations condition man; spiritual, political, or connected with social reform; organizations do not bring freedom. Man has become more and more an organized man.

"What shall I do?" he asked. "I am not an organization man. I do not conform to a pattern. So what is our relationship? Must the K Foundation exist at all? The schools have taken over the Foundation. The Foundation has not taken over the schools. What is the function of the Foundation—are we clear—why should the Foundation exist? Its purpose was to hold the lands and to see the schools keep in the right direction.

"Pupulji pointed out that for years she had opposed my being the president—I understood. She says that I should now accept and I ask what is my function and my relationship to the whole setup in India—and what do you all think is my responsibility? Bear in mind, K dissolved all organizations with which he was connected. He says no organizations will help the world. Rajesh said the Krishnamurti Foundation in India was not an organization, but it was also not a directing force in the right sense.

"So if K becomes president, what will happen? Bearing in mind that I will be in this country only for three months. I can't say carry on and come back and say, 'It's not moving in the right direction.'

"What is your relationship with me? Do we trust each other, that we will do the right thing in all circumstances?"

I said that each one of us had a relationship with Krishnaji, and because of that we had a certain relationship to each other. We were responsible to Krishnaji. But when Krishnaji was away, we did not feel responsible to each other.

Achyutji said, "We are responsible to the teaching, which is the source."

"I feel his being president might resolve the impasse that exists in the Foundation," I said. "There are barriers. The impasse has to be broken."

Krishnaji said, "Break it. Where does K come in?"

We then discussed the nature of cooperation—to work together in cooperation, not for an ideal, not about something, but simply to work together, to cooperate. The discussions were to continue for the next two days.

After the meetings I went to his room; my eyes were alight, free of burdens. I said to him, "Do you realize, with my ceasing to be president of the Krishnamurti Foundation India, I am completely stripped of everything?"

He said, "Yes, I know," and was silent.

Without a word said, a new relationship of trust and a limitless friendship with Krishnaji was born. Speaking to me of the nature of trust, he said, "It is only possible when the brain sheds its burdens, is free." Soon I was to start writing a book on Krishnaji. I spoke to him of my intention, and he had responded with warmth.

In connection with the book I was writing, one morning at Rishi Valley in December 1978 I asked Krishnaji whether I could explore his mind and unravel the way it operated. He readily agreed. I asked him questions, he listened with intensity to the question, and out of that intensity the response arose. One could feel the strength and density of the mind and the depth from which he spoke.

I said, "I have heard you for over thirty years. You say there is no way to truth, no method involved. But as I observe you, a certain process has revealed itself. I would like to explore your mind because I feel that the probing of your mind, and the way it operates, may reveal the nature of right observation and enquiry. And that is where we are getting bogged down. Now, how do you receive a question which is put to you? Could we go into the state of the mind that receives a question?"

"Right. How does K receive a question? How does K, when a question is put to him, proceed with the answer? I think he would say, first there has to be innocence. That is to say a listening without any conclusion, without any barrier and because there is no hindrance, the mind is . . . could I use the word empty? The mind is empty, in the sense that in it there are no preconceived answers, no remembrance of previous answers, and therefore no further recording of those answers."

I pressed on. "Now in that state, what is the function of attention? There is a function of attention, which is that of searching. If attention does not search, what happens to the question? The mind may receive the question in emptiness, but what actually happens to the question? Because you do respond." I was challenging him.

K answered, "When a question is put, there is a hearing of it, not only with the ear, but also the hearing of it without the usual process of hearing. It is like a seed put into the earth and the earth then acts upon the seed and the seed acts upon the earth and gradually out of that comes forth a plant, a flower, and so on. So, when a question is put, it is heard with the ear and there is also a state in which the hearing is not with the ear and out of that there is the answer."

"When one observes you, one feels that your eyes are participating in the listening process," I said. "You have a listening eye, if I can so put it. Now, you have said there is a listening with the ear and there is a listening without the ear. Is it that a new instrument has come into being? An instrument, not in the sense of a physical growth in the brain cells, but a new capacity?" I had started probing.

"I think so, Pupulji. I would like to answer this by bringing in another word, 'insight.' Insight is a state of mind in which there is no remembrance, there is no conclusion, there is no sense of anticipation, there is no quality of reaction, and a great deal more is involved in that word. Now when you ask a question, there is a hearing with the ear and there is also a hearing with the non-ear, which means the mind is in a state when there is no remembrance, no conclusion, no previous record of that question and therefore there is no reply to that question according to previous memory. That not being there, there is insight into the question." Krishnaji was exploring his mind.

"Does the hearing with the non-ear come into being with the very ending of the process of the mind? Or is it something else?"

"When there is insight of that kind, the brain cells themselves undergo a change. When there is insight, that insight transforms the brain cells." He was perceiving his mind as he spoke.

"You have said there is hearing with the ear and there is a hearing with the non-ear, and that insight brings about a change in the brain cells. Does insight arise because of the hearing with the non-ear? Can you open up this non-ear hearing?"

"Let us see. First there is the hearing with the ear, which we all know; and the hearing with the non-ear, which is a state like that of a tranquil pond, a lake that is completely quiet and when you drop a stone into it, it makes little waves that disappear. I think that is the hearing with the non-ear, a state where there is absolute quietness of the mind; and when the question is put into the mind, the response is the wave, the little wave. I don't know if I am making it clear."

"Is the pond the matrix of the mind?" I asked.

"What do you mean by matrix?"

"Is it 'mind' only?"

"I don't quite see that," said Krishnaji. "I will have to go into it. When you say is it 'mind' only, what do you mean?"

"Is it the totality of what has been? You have said earlier that consciousness is its content."

"Yes." Krishnaji was listening intensely.

"The receiving into . . . "

"Now wait a minute. Look at it. Consciousness is fragmented; and when you put a question to that fragmentary consciousness, the answer will be fragmentary."

"When the question is put, and is received as in a pool, is it the totality which receives?" By now my mind had caught the stillness, and the questions I asked were arising out of Krishnaji's responses.

"I think that is really quite interesting, and we should go into it. Can the mind be so extraordinarily receptive that it has no barriers and the past does not enter into it?"

"The past being the fragment?" I sought clarification.

"Yes, the past is the fragment. And can the past not come into it at all?"

"You say there is a listening with an ear and there is a listening with the non-ear. Has that listening the same quality as the listening we know? Or is it of a different nature?"

"Of a different nature, obviously."

"What is the difference?" I was pushing.

"Listening with the ear or hearing with the ear, and the response from that listening to a question will necessarily be fragmented. Right? That is obvious. But when there is a listening with the non-ear, that state of listening is not fragmented. Listening with the ear implies a recording and a remembrance from past knowledge. It is experience answering the question. In the other, there is no past involved at all. Therefore it is not a fragmentary answer. I think that is right."

"Is that non-ear listening different from that which receives?"

"I don't quite follow," said K.

"A question is put, it is received with the ear, but there is also a non-ear listening. Now is that non-ear listening, the same as the state which receives?" All anchors within me had ceased.

"Yes, must be, of course. A pond is absolutely quiet, a question is dropped into the pond, the pond is pure water without all the pollution that man has put into it, which is the past. The pond is clear, clean water, and into that water a question is put as a pebble and the reply is the wave. I think that is how it functions."

"As there is a non-ear listening, is there also a non-eye seeing?"

"Yes," said Krishnaji. "You are using the word 'eye' in the sense of the visual, the optical? Yes."

"Can we go into the nature of that?"

"Let us see. The hearing with the non-ear and the seeing—the visual seeing without the past interfering with the seeing—are the same. The hearing without the ear and the seeing, the visual seeing, the optical seeing, are both the same." Krishnaji was clarifying as he responded. "What is important is the non-remembrance without the past interfering."

"Sir, tradition maintains that the outward movement of the eye is the movement of naming. The optical movement which turns back, breaks through the naming process, breaks the naming process, dissolves the naming process. Is that so?" I was back to memory, to a process familiar in yoga.

"Let us see if I have understood the question rightly. Are you saying there is the optical vision going out and then the coming back from the outward movement to the inner movement?"

"No," I said. "There is the movement, outer, which we all know, which is the movement of seeing, registering, focusing, etc. Then there is for the *sadhaka*, that is for the man who is seeing, a movement in which the very optical seeing is thrown within, breaking the naming process, the divisive process. It is a backward-flowing movement."

"The forward movement and the backward movement?"

"It is not the forward movement turning backwards, but the optical sense which moves out, and another movement in which it does not move out."

"I understand. It is not like a tide which is going out and coming in. There is only a going out."

"And another movement altogether, which is optically drawing in."

"So that is what tradition says. What do you say?" asked Krishnaji.

"The looking-out focuses."

"By looking out, you mean the looking at the tree?"

"The looking within ends focusing, ends the very instrument which focuses." I was trying to reveal a state of perception.

"I must understand this very clearly," said K. "You say this looking within is not with the movement of the eye which looks, observes the external world, but a looking within, which is not the ebb of the tide. There is the seeing, going out and the coming in. But is this an entirely different way of looking inwards?"

"The looking inward is not the tide," I responded.

"Is not the tide?"

"But the looking inward can be a tide."

"Of course. That is the danger of it. The tide goes out and the tide comes in."

"You can look with the same . . . "

K broke in, "I know it can be the same water. Whereas this going out optically and the looking within are two different, entirely different processes. Is that so? You see, I question this whole thing. I wonder if there is a looking within. Can we explore that?" He paused. "Does looking within imply a movement of thought?"

"No, Sir."

"Then if there is no movement of thought, then what do you mean by looking within?" The instruments of enquiry were very subtle.

"Looking within is the seeing of 'that which exists' at a particular instant. There is no within and without in that state."

"That is the whole point. Now let us be very clear. What you are saying is that the outward-looking and the inward-looking are not the tide going out and the tide coming in. The inner-looking is not the reaction to outer-looking. The inward-looking is entirely different from the outer-looking. You are saying that inward-looking dispels the whole structure of thought. That is what you are saying." He paused. "I question that." He paused again. "I question whether there is an inward-looking at all. Let us go easy. Wait, I am just exploring, Pupul. I am not saying it is so or not so. What is it to look inward? One can look inwardly from what you have said, into the whole movement of thought. Right? Is that inward-looking?"

"I would say it is inward-looking, because in it there is a physical looking."

"Yes, in the outward seeing."

"And a nonphysical looking. That is, the looking is physical, but what is seen is nonphysical. Thought is not a thing which can be seen."

"All thought is a material process," Krishnaji said with precision.

"But it cannot be seen."

"Yes. But it is a material process—the remembrance, the recording of knowledge; all that is a material process."

"Yes, that may be so, but there is a difference between the state of seeing the microphone and seeing the flashing movement of the mind."

"But the flashing movement of thought is still a material process." Krishnaji was adamant.

"Yes, all right. It is a material process. Is its existence in a dimension which we call the within?"

"Within? I question the whole thing." A new element had entered, revealing the illusion of outer and inner.

"It is somewhere, Sir."

"Yes, but why should it be within or without?"

"Because it is not without, it is not something visible 'without.' "

"It is not visible as one's face is visible in the mirror. Thought cannot be perceived with the eye as you perceive your face in the mirror. So, is that which is not perceivable in the mirror what you call the inner?"

"Yet it exists," I said.

"Yes, but I would question whether it is the inner at all."

"You can take away the word inner and substitute another word." I was forcing the challenge.

"No, no."

"Where is it?"

"I am going to tell you something. I believe the Eskimoes, when they use the word thought, they mean something outside."

"Yes."

" . . . Look at it carefully, look at it. Think about it."

"I understand, Sir. I see what is something outside. It is a physical seeing. The nature of thought itself I can never see with the same optical . . . "

"That is very simple. I can see my face in the mirror. I cannot see thought in a mirror. That is simple."

"Where do I see thought? What is this 'seeing,' then?" I asked.

"That is it. I don't think there is 'seeing' at all."

"But you have kept on saying there has to be 'seeing.' "

"Seeing? Seeing the flower," said Krishnaji.

"Seeing also anger."

"No, I only said 'seeing.' "

"You said something just now. You said, 'I don't think there is a seeing at all.' Can that be investigated?"

"I must be very clear on this point," said Krishnaji. "First there is a hearing by the ear and there is a hearing without the ear, which is a state like a mill pond that is absolutely still without a single movement. There is no air that ruffles it. And when the question is put in it, it is like a piece of stone thrown in a still pond. The waves are the answers."

"Which the question itself throws up?"

"Yes, that is what we said from the beginning. When you approach the question afresh, the very throwing of the question into the mill pond produces the answer. There is no entity that answers. That is very important. Now bearing in mind that the seeing of the face in the mirror is clear, but the seeing of thought is not possible, what is 'the seeing of thought?' "

"What is it that actually takes place?" I asked.

"That is what we are going to find out," answered K. "First let us be clear. There is no 'seeing' of thought. For that implies that there is a seer and thought as separate. The seeing of the face in the mirror is clear. The mirror cannot reflect thought. 'The seeing' of thought implies that there is a seer and thought. But the seer is thought. So there is only thought, which cannot be seen in the mirror. So for me there is no inward looking."

"Then what do you mean when you talk of 'seeing of' what is?"

" 'Seeing of what is' is not only to observe with the visual, optical eye, optical nerve, but also to hear 'what is' without the ear; 'what is' implies all that, 'seeing,' 'hearing.' "

"But you say thought cannot be seen." I pressed him.

"No. Thought cannot be seen with the inward look."

"By what then is thought seen?"

"Thought cannot see. . . ."

"It is not seen by the inward look, it is not seen as you see in the mirror and yet you say there is a 'seeing.' "

"No, I wouldn't use the word 'seeing,' " said K.

"Then what word would you use?"

"I would say, 'thought being aware of itself.' "

"Thought being aware of itself?" I asked.

"Of its own activities."

"But you have been talking, all these years, of 'seeing what is.' "

"I spoke of seeing what is happening, actually, inwardly, not the observation of 'what is' happening with an optical eye or with another thought. When you say 'seeing,' it implies that."

"What is that state?" I queried.

"That is what we are enquiring into. If you say 'seeing' inwardly, I say that you are bringing a dual state into that which is seen. Right?" Krishnaji's mind was piercingly subtle.

"Can there be 'seeing' without a dual state?" I asked.

"Yes, this 'seeing' implies a state where there is no opposite."

"Because such seeing has the same quality as the lake."

"Yes, that is why when you speak of inward looking, there is something artificial in that approach. Thought itself has to be quiet. I think it works like the lake. And when you put a question from that, the question is answered from the lake."

"But, Sir, anger arises, or jealousy arises. It is a material thing?"

"Absolutely."

"I grow aware and it is already over. Because I cannot 'see' that which is over."

"Look, you say jealousy arises and there is the watching of it."

"Can there be a watching of the actual state of jealousy arising? If so, it would not arise."

"No," answered K. "The fact is, jealousy arises. Jealousy is a reaction which we name. Before you name it as jealousy, can that reaction be watched? Not as a watcher watching. You understand what I am saying? But the watching in which there is no opposite? Can I just see the reaction? By the 'seeing' of the reaction I mean the 'seeing,' 'observing' without the eye or the ear. The observation of the arising of that reaction is the non-hearing, is the hearing without the ear, the seeing without the eye. Does it sound crazy?

"Now, let us be clear," he continued. "We are saying, a question is asked and that question is like a stone dropped into a mill pond and the mill pond is absolutely quiet. The very answer is the dropping of the stone into it, otherwise the pond is quiet.

"Now what we are talking about is not the tide going out, the tide coming in. But of an observation of 'what is' without a previous remembrance associated with 'what is.' That's all."

"Then it is neither optical nor auditory."

"Absolutely."

"But yet you have used the word observing . . . "

"Observing in the sense that in such observation there is no remembrance of the thing which is being observed. I am right in this, let me go slowly. In the process of observation, there is no center from which it is being observed, the center being memory, various conclusions, hurts. There is no point from which 'it' is being observed. Right? And in this observation there is no conclusion, there is no association with past events, which means the 'seeing' is as quiet as the mill pond. The 'what is' is the challenge, and can the mill pond which is quiet respond as the challenge drops into it?" The ripple of the mill pond was responding.

"The ripple is the response?" I asked.

"The ripple is the response. That is a marvelous thing."

I asked, "Now, I have observed you listening to your own response, with the same awareness as you listen to a question. Do you listen to your responses?"

"I listen to it to see if what is said is accurate."

"You listen to your own responses; and to you, your responses and the responses of another person are at the same level."

K said, "But if you are talking seriously and you are listening to the questioner and responding, there is an act of listening—in both directions—not the listening to your or my response, there is only listening."

"You listen," I responded, "and if what is said is not so, you move away. There is a total flexibility, if I may so put it. There is no taking of answer and holding to it."

"You see if the pebble is very light, the ripple is a tiny wave," explained K. "But if it is a small rock which is thrown, there are a great many waves. So, the act of listening is not only to the person challenging but also a listening to the answering. It is a total state of listening to the questioner and the person who replies. When the person's reply is not quite as it should be, because there is listening, there is a withdrawal from that. And then you change and you move. So I have discovered something. There is no inward looking or listening. There is only looking and listening."

"I have to go into this at depth. I am just taking it in." I paused. "What is the mill pond?"

"First of all," K asked, "whose mill pond? The mill pond of your mind, K's mind, or the mill pond of a person who is agitated?"

"We are talking of Krishnaji's mill pond," I said, "because what is being attempted is to see how far one can go into investigating your mind."

"I understand. You are asking what is the state of the mill pond that apparently K has. I don't think K is aware of this mill pond."

"What are you aware of?"

"It is important to understand that if K is aware of it, it is not a mill pond. Wait, wait. Yes, that is right."

"Now, if I may ask, what is the inner nature of yourself?" I was challenging K's mind to see how far he would reveal its nature. There was a pause. Then, from a great depth, Krishnaji spoke. "I have never asked myself what is the mind, the inner nature of K. If I reply 'nothing,' which means 'not a thing,' would that be acceptable? There is nothing. Would you comprehend the state of K's inner being, which is nothing, which is absolutely nothing? It is like measuring the immeasurable. I am not saying my mind is immeasurable—but it is like measuring the immeasurable."

My eldest sister had died of a heart attack in 1976. My mother could not contain the shock. Her body and mind broke down, and she suffered a minor stroke. She was devoted to Krishnaji and had acted as his hostess on many occasions. He wrote her a note enclosed in a letter to Nandini in which he asked after her well being, sent his love, and expressed his gratitude for the hospitality and affection she had given him over the many years. We read the letter to her, and she managed to smile. She recovered but remained very weak.

In January of the following year, when Krishnaji was in Bombay, he came to see her. She was in bed, life was gradually ebbing away; but she had bathed before Krishnaji came and her white muslin *sari* covered her head. Seeing him, her face and eyes filled with life. He held her hand for over an hour and spoke to her with unbounded attention. She said to him, "My daughter is dead."

"I know, Amma," he replied. "We all have to die." Her mind had become quiet, and although she never recovered, her inward suffering ended. She died gently, without disturbing any of her children who were sitting in the next room. She was alone when she slipped away.

The Krishnamurti Foundation in the United States had arranged a seminar for scientists and philosophers in the spring of 1976 at Arya Vihara in Ojai. Sunanda, her husband, Pama, and Krishnaji's nephew Narayan were there. Balasundaram, who was also to go, developed jaundice and had to cancel his travel arrangements.

Krishnaji spent time in Ojai with Sunanda; they went for walks together, he talked to her at length, discussing the work at Vasant Vihar; giving of himself in full measure. She came back to India aglow with his benediction.

On June 3, 1976, I had written to Krishnaji about my mother's health and my meeting with Sunanda:

I have been in Bombay for the last two weeks because of my mother's illness. It has been a very difficult period. She had a urinary infection with complications in the lungs and for the last week has been unable to speak or take any nourishment or water by mouth. The doctor feels it may be a partial paralysis of the throat. She is receiving nasal feeding and for the last 24 hours appears to be better. She has started forming words which though indistinct yet are recognizable. She has forgotten the immediate past and keeps asking for Moon. There is a certain desperation in her questions.

I met Sunanda and Pama when they were passing through Bombay and we had a long talk. I am deeply happy that they are going to Vasant Vihar and I hope that everything will be well there with them and that the work in Vasant Vihar will flower. I am going to Madras on the 6th for a meeting of the Krishnamurti Trust. On an earlier visit Radha and I had gone over the repairs to be done as suggested by you, and I think work on that must already have started.

I feel one with you that the Secretary of the Krishnamurti Foundation India should not be the same as the Principal of Rishi Valley School. This had been decided when you were here over a year ago. After Balasundaram met you abroad last year you had written to me that Balasundaram had explained to you that the Secretaryship was just a technical thing and that in your view all activities of the Foundation should be shifted to Rishi Valley, which should become the centre of the work. I do not have the letter with me here, but when I return to Delhi I will send you a copy of your letter. I had sought clarification from you whether in the light of what you felt the Secretary and Principal should be one and you had clarified the position and said that they should not be one. At the meeting of the Foundation last year when the matter of appointing the Secretary came up, it was found that Balasundaram would have to continue for a year as Secretary till the case was over as he was the principal plaintiff in the case and the Powers of Attorney were in his name. To make a change in midstream would cause many complications. All the Foundation members had agreed to this. Legally the Secretary of the Foundation is appointed every year at the annual meeting which is held in Oct/Nov. I had discussed the matter with Balasundaram and he had himself suggested that he should not continue as Secretary. I have always felt that Pama is the right person to take over the Secretaryship, and it is with this in mind that I had persuaded him to join the Foundation.

By December Pama Patwardhan had taken over as Secretary from

Balasundaram, and Sunanda and Pama went to live at Vasant Vihar. The house was in shambles, there was no money, and they faced a herculean task to build the place anew. Sunanda was to take the responsibility for the work of publications and soon a bulletin was to appear. In the years that followed, Vasant Vihar, the headquarters of the Krishnamurti Foundation in India, became a center for K. F. I. publications, the archives, and the teachings. *Tradition and Revolution, Krishnamurti on Education*, various talks, and Indian editions of Krishnaji's works were published.

# CHAPTER 29

# "Riding the Back of a Tiger."

I first met Indira Gandhi in 1931 at Anand Bhawan, her family home at Allahabad. I was sixteen, she fourteen. I was in love, igniting fires in that ancient town; but I remember Indira as fragile, withdrawn, an austere young girl living in enclosed spaces of fantasy. I continued to meet her over the years at the home of her aunt Krishna Hutheesing. It was there in Bombay that her son Rajiv was born on August 20, 1944. In 1955, after I came to live in Delhi, Indira and I became friends. She was the official hostess of her father, Prime Minister Jawaharlal Nehru, and they lived at Teen Murti House, the residence of the Commander-in-Chief prior to independence.

Indira continued to hide behind an aloof exterior; a sensitive, eager human being, she tuned to the unusual, to people and to events in the outer world. Krishnaji and his teachings were part of my waking existence, and I often spoke to her of self-knowing and perception. She would listen intently, but was guarded in her responses. It was only when barriers were lifted that she began to ask me of the nature of self-knowing and of an observation that was free of the observer. She shyly spoke of her own finely honed perceptions. While young, she found herself watching herself speak; saw things behind her; was aware of events she could not possibly have seen; had often experienced exalted sensory perception. "You know Huxley's doorways of perception?" she said. "I saw the world with the same fierce intensity, but hid my perceptions, as people laughed at me and did not understand."

From childhood she felt she could "drown in color." For years a certain color would overwhelm her. Strong reds, oranges of all tones, and dusty pinks evoked deep responses. Yellow and green awakened energy, blue was alien.

When she became prime minister in 1966 her vulnerability lessened.

Indira's first meeting with Krishnaji was at dinner at my house in the late 1950s. Indira appeared shy and hesitant to speak. Krishnaji was also shy, but soon started relating anecdotes. One Zen tale in particular delighted her. Two Buddhist monks came to the bank of a river and found it flooded and difficult to cross. A woman was waiting on the banks and she begged them to help her across, as her children were alone and hungry. One monk refused, the other picked her up and crossed the stream, holding her on his back. When they had crossed and were on their way again, the first monk protested vehemently. He was horrified that a monk should touch a woman, let alone carry her on his back. The second monk turned to him and said, "You mean you still carry the woman in your mind? I left her behind on the riverbank long ago."

In the winter of 1970 Krishnaji came to dinner at my flat. Indira Gandhi, Karan Singh of Kashmir, my sister Nandini, G. Parthasarthi,* and Jim George, the high commissioner for Canada, were present. The talk at the table turned to the youth of the world. The young in the West were in revolt, had refused to accept the mores of their fathers, had denied all security, and become wanderers—traveling to distant countries, sharing, smoking hashish, breaking all taboos, seeing and tasting the world. Someone at the table asked, "Why are the youth in India so concerned with security?" K spoke of a growing materialism in India; we discussed the fact that the young in India seemed to be losing their roots, turning to the affluent West for their outer and inner needs. Krishnaji asked, "Why is there deterioration in India at all levels of society?"

Indira listened, but seldom spoke. Karan Singh was in a mischievous mood, and asked Krishnaji, "Is it true that no politician can perceive truth?" Indira was listening, and later wrote to me:

Thank you for the interesting evening.

As usual the food was delicious. I broke my rule of having only salad at night and ate far too much!

I was very glad of the opportunity of meeting Krishnaji again. His views are always stimulating. After a while it seemed as if we were all questioning at him. But can the situation of the young rebels in the United States or France be equated with the situation here? In these countries, many of these young people belong to the richer families and can well afford the time to sit on the beach and meditate. In India, the compulsions are many—earning one's living, supporting one's family. Because of my family and the special circumstances

---

*G. Parthasarthi was then a friend of Indira Gandhi. A senior diplomat, he has held very important assignments in Russia and the United States. In 1986 he was advisor to Prime Minister Rajiv Gandhi.

in which I grew up, my personal experience is also entirely different to that of others. But if I say so, it might seem as if I am setting myself apart. This is just loud thinking.

Indira had apparently made no special impact on Krishnaji. He did not comment on their meeting.

I left India for Europe and the United States in early June 1975. While I was in Paris I learned of the decision of the Allahabad High Court that Indira Gandhi's election had been declared null and void on what appeared to be a technical point, and that she had been debarred from seeking election for six years. The *Times* in London, commenting on it, had compared it to a "parking offence." The unbelievable had happened and no one could foretell what lay ahead.

While in England I went to stay at Brockwood Park with Krishnaji. He was very concerned for the future of India. We had long talks. Indira Gandhi had appealed the judgment and had been granted stay of the order; she could continue to hold the office of prime minister but could not vote in the Lok Sabha,* as she was no longer a member. The British press was seething with speculation as to whether she would resign before the appeal was heard.

The day after I reached New York, a state of emergency was declared in India and the news of the arrests reached us. Far away, with little access to accurate information, we heard rumors that civil war had begun. I went to the Indian Permanent Mission and tried to phone through and speak to Indira Gandhi. To my amazement it was possible to reach her, and she came on the line. I told her of the rumors and the total absence of accurate information. She tried to reassure me; a state of emergency had been declared, she said, and many people, including Jai Prakash Narain and Morarji Desai had been detained. She told me that there was a threat of widespread violence, and stressed that the emergency was for a short period of time.

I did not go to Gstaad to see Krishnaji on my return journey, nor did I phone him from London. I was very confused and knew that Krishnaji would be greatly distressed by events in India.

In New Delhi many people spoke to me about the emergency—a few in support, a large number in anger and with passion. Fear and tension were growing. I met Indira at Parliament House, where I spoke of the prevailing atmosphere and my sorrow that this should happen in a government of which she was the head. She listened intently and

---

*Lok sabha is the Hindi word for parliament.

replied that I could not know the extent of the violence inherent in the situation nor of the dangers, internal and external, that faced the country. She spoke of the railway strike the previous year, which had triggered violence and instability.

She also referred to Jai Prakash Narain's Total Revolution movement, around which a large number of young people rallied. At first nonviolent in its approach, by 1975 it had been infiltrated by many undesirable elements. Jai Prakash, she said, was an idealist and appeared totally unaware of the danger. But if these forces were allowed to strengthen their position, the country would face disaster.

I expected emergency to be lifted on August 15—Independence Day—and went to the Red Fort* to hear her speak. But just before she appeared on the ramparts she received news of the assassination in Dacca of the then president of Bangla Desh Mujib-ur-Rehman and his family, including his very young son. All her dormant fears and anxieties were awakened. She was certain that the murders were part of a major plot to destabilize the subcontinent and that she, her sons and her grandchildren were the next target. The emergency continued with traumatic results for both ruler and ruled.

Soon after, I received a letter from Krishnaji:

I am writing to you about a very serious matter, not only to you personally but also as the President of K. F. India. From the various reports in the American, English and French papers it appears that India has become a "totalitarian state," thousands are being put in prison, freedom of speech and freedom of the press is almost gagged. I do not know what your position is? The Foundation is not political and is in no way connected with any kind of political group, left or right. I want to ask you what is K's position if and when he comes to India, knowing that he will talk about freedom at all levels, which K has been doing in all the talks here, freedom of speech, freedom of thought, freedom of expression. And if he addresses public meetings they are bound to ask him certain questions and he will have to answer them. He feels he cannot modify what he says for any reason whatsoever, to suit any government or any group of people. He has not done so in the past, he cannot limit himself to the dictates of any group, political or otherwise. He cannot allow himself to be put in prison or be prevented from leaving the country once he comes. I would also like to point out that K will not accept special favours or have an exemption made in his case . . . [He ended his letter with the words:] Please Pupulji, this is a sacred matter and your responsibility must be equally sacred.

---

*The Red Fort is a monument built in the seventeenth century by Shah Jahan. From its ramparts the prime ministers of India address the nation on Independence day, August 15.

In my reply, I gave him an accurate account of the situation in India, but assured him that he could never be jailed in India. The culture of this country made the voice of the truly religious teacher a light that could not be extinguished. By August 20, I received a second letter. His extreme concern was evident, and introduced a new question: "What is the purpose, the value, and the benefit of my coming to India?"

Apart from personal feelings and affection which has [sic] its own significance, as the physical organism is now over 80 I have been considering how best the next 10 or 15 years should be spent. As I have repeated and can repeat it again without boredom, I have spent more time and given more talks in India than anywhere else. I am not concerned with the results, what effect the Teachings have in India, how deep the roots have penetrated, but I think one has the right to ask and should ask, as I am asking, why there is not in India after all these years one person totally and completely involved in these Teachings, living them and dedicated entirely to them. I am not in any way blaming any of you, but if I may, I would urge you to give your most serious attention to this.

He went on to ask me if I would indeed retire from my other work by March 1976, as I had told him. He ended the letter with these words:

As it may become more and more difficult to speak freely in India, you have to consider how best K can spend the rest of his life most usefully for the Teachings. I am also pointing this out to the group in America and in England. All this should in no way be construed as a personal matter but as what is right and good for the Teachings as a whole. The whole thing, I am afraid, in India is being worked out at personal convenience and it is too bad this is happening after 40 years.

I was overwhelmed by the letter. To me, at the time, it seemed evident that Krishnaji had rejected India and the people who had been his companions for many years. In Bombay I spoke to Nandini, and she felt as I did that Krishnaji's dialogue with India was over.

I wrote back to Krishnaji expressing my deep distress. I said I was stunned by his letter. Balasundaram, who was with Krishnaji in Brockwood when my letter reached him, wrote to me that Krishnaji was puzzled and kept on asking, "What has stunned Pupul?" Krishnaji had been holding detailed discussions with Balasundaram on what was needed to be done in the Indian Foundation. Soon it became clear that Krishnaji had finally decided not to return to India in the winter of 1975. He had also canceled his annual visit to Rome, but was to return to Malibu in California.

I received a long letter from Krishnaji dated November 10 from Malibu, where he was staying at the home of Mary Zimbalist. Like a child he asked, "You wrote from Delhi that you were stunned by a long letter which I had written you in which, among other things, I said that it was all run in India on personal convenience. In all your letters you do not say what stunned you. I would like to find out why you felt that way." I replied that the first impact of his letter was that he had abandoned India and did not intend coming back. There were many questions which needed to be answered, but there appeared to be no point in going into details and seeking clarification. It was the first impact of the letter that was crucial.

The emergency had been on for over a year and though I was aware of the strain and anguish it had caused Indira, I also knew she had been tough, turning a blind eye to many happenings reported to her. As the emergency gathered momentum, for the first time in her life she lost her intuitive contact with the people of India. She was isolated and suspicious and would not countenance any criticism, even when her close friends brought her concrete evidence that officials had overstepped their authority. It was only by the autumn of 1976 that the anger and fear felt by people started to reach her.

It was about this time that I spoke to Indira about the possibility of Krishnaji speaking in India in the winter of 1976. She said, "He is most welcome to come to India and he can speak freely." She knew of Krishnaji's passionate concern for freedom; he was a religious revolutionary, and for him life without freedom was death. Krishnaji arrived in India in October 1976 and stayed with me at 1 King George's Avenue.

On October 27 Indira arrived at my home for dinner at 7:30, wearing a sari printed in soft pinks. The other guests included Achyut; Nandini, her daughter Devi, and her granddaughter Aditi, a young and exquisite dancer; Sunanda and Pama Patwardhan; and L. K. Jha. Indira told us it was her birthday according to the Indian calendar. She expressed a desire to speak with Krishnaji, and was with him in his sitting room until nine.

At dinner she was very silent, hardly aware of what was happening around her. Achyut, who had been passionately critical of the emergency, was silent, even grim. L. K. Jha and Krishnaji did most of the talking. Krishnaji did not look at Indira or talk to her throughout dinner. He sensed that she was vulnerable, and did not wish to intrude.

During dinner Krishnaji, to lessen the tension, started relating his many anecdotes of Saint Peter and heaven. I remember one in particular. A very rich man who had given to many charities died. When he approached the gates of heaven, he met Peter guarding the doorways. The man gave his credentials, and Peter said he could enter the gates; but before he did so, would not he like to see what it was like down below? The rich man said, "Sure, is it easy to get there?" Peter replied, "Just press the button and the elevator will take you down." On going down, the gates to the underworld opened and the rich man saw a flower-filled garden with running water and beautiful women waiting to receive him with choice wines and rare foods. After spending some time in the most wonderful surroundings, he returned to Peter to tell him that the underworld was a better place, more fun, and he had decided to go there. Peter said, "Sure, I thought you would feel that way." So the rich man pressed the button and went back to the underworld. When the door opened, the garden had vanished and two hefty bullies were waiting for him and started beating him up. The man tried to stop them; in between the blows, he gasped, "What has happened? I came here only a few minutes ago and I was met with open arms!" "Ah," said the ruffian, administering another blow. "Then you were a tourist."

Everyone laughed, and even Indira could not help smiling—though she seemed preoccupied and far away. Then Indira joined the conversation and told a story of the astronauts who, on their return from outer space, went to visit Kruschev, and were asked by him in secret, "When you were up in the heavens, did you see mysterious lights, strange beings? Did you see a great, mysterious white-bearded figure surrounded by light?" The astronauts said, "Yes, comrade, we did," and Kruschev said, "I was afraid so." Then he warned them, "This is between ourselves, don't tell a soul." Later, the astronauts went round the world and visited the pope. After their devout formalities were over, the pope took them aside and said, "My sons, when you were up there, did you see lights or come upon a vast figure with a white beard?" They replied, "No father, we saw no lights nor did we see a bearded figure." And the pope said, "Ah, my sons, I thought so. But on your soul don't tell this to anyone." Everyone at the table laughed, but L. K. Jha looked embarrassed—for Krishnaji had told him the story, he in turn had repeated it to the prime minister, and now it had come back to Krishnaji.

After dinner, when everyone had left, Krishnaji took me to his room and told me that Indira was going through a very difficult period. For a long time after they met, they had sat silently. He could feel that she was very disturbed. She told him that the situation in India was explosive. Krishnaji had sensed something very fine within her, which politics was destroying. He also hinted at a current of violence that surrounded her.

The next morning the prime minister wrote to me to say that Krishnaji had promised to meet her again, and she wanted me to arrange a suitable time. I had telephoned Seshan, her special assistant, when suddenly at eleven o'clock a car arrived at the door with Indira in it. There was no security, and it was only some time later that her escort car with its anxious security personnel arrived.

Indira spent over an hour with Krishnaji. She came out of the room visibly moved, and tears were streaming down her face. When Indira saw that my grandniece Aditi was in the sitting room, she quickly took control of herself, asked Aditi what she was reading, and spoke to her for a few moments. I saw Indira quietly to her car.

During the months Krishnaji was in India, he held Indira in his consciousness. He asked me many questions about her and her early life. He had been deeply touched by her ability to listen and her refusal to react or defend herself. He told me that she was possibly the only person in her position who was prepared to listen. Most people were either arrogant in their positions and so could not listen, or broke under adversity and cracked up. She appeared different. He was to write to her before he left Delhi.

Years later, after her son Sanjay's death, I asked Indira whether she cried easily. She thought for a while then said, "No, sorrow does not bring tears. But when I am deeply moved, especially by great beauty, I weep." She said she had cried when she met Kamakoti Sankaracharya of Kancheepuram* and that she had wept copiously when she came to see Krishnaji at 1 King George's Avenue in November 1976. "I sobbed and could not stop my tears. I have not cried like that for years." She also told me something of what happened during the conversation. Krishnaji and she had spoken of the events in India over the last few months, and Indira had said, "I am riding the back of a tiger, but I do not know how to get off its back." Krishnaji replied, "If you are more intelligent than the tiger, you will know how to deal with the tiger." She had asked him what she should do. He refused to tell her, but said that she should look at the conflicts, the actions, the wrongs as one problem, and then act without motive. He said he did

---

*The Kamakoti Sankaracharya of Kancheepuram is in the direct line of successive teachers or preceptors going back to Adi Sankara, the first Sankaracharya, who taught in about the eighth century A.D. Kamakoti is the name of the village in Kancheepuram district of Tamil Nadu, South India, where his religious center is located.

not know the facts, but that she should act rightly, without fear of consequence.

In later years she told me that it was on October 28, 1976, the day she met Krishnaji for the second time, a frail movement had awakened in her, suggesting an end to emergency, whatever the consequences. She had mulled over this feeling, talked to a few people close to her, and finally took the decision to call for elections.

Krishnaji was in Bombay, about to leave for Europe, when the announcement was made that Indira had ordered the release of people held under the Maintenance of Internal Security Act, and had also announced elections. Krishnaji was very happy and spoke to me at length. He told me that he would have liked to have seen her before he left India. He was even prepared to go to Delhi, but I dissuaded him, knowing that she would be greatly preoccupied with the coming struggle. The day before he was to leave, he asked me to keep him informed about Indira. Then suddenly he asked, "What happens if she loses?"

# CHAPTER 30

# "She Is Very Vulnerable."

Krishnaji heard of Indira's defeat while in Ojai, California. In his letter to me dated March 22, he wrote, "She is out of the political world now and I wonder what she is going to do. When you see her, please give my love to her, will you?" On March 31 he wrote again. "I have received your letter after the election. I am glad you were with her when the news came. I feel somewhat responsible in this event. As I told you in Bombay, she may be defeated. Anyhow, please give her my love." In the letters that followed, he continued to enquire about her.

I stayed on in Delhi until late May, though I resigned from all the positions I held with government. Indira had shifted from the prime minister's residence to 12 Willingdon Crescent. The pressures and tensions were mounting. I would find her sitting alone in the darkness on the veranda on a hot summer evening, looking out into the summer night of an Indian garden. I would sit with her, but few words were said. Sometimes I would share her frugal meal and go home.

One evening I found her looking unduly exhausted. I knew she had been to call on one of the leaders of the new government. I asked her whether she had felt great hostility when they met. "Yes," she said. "I got a terrible allergy, while he was talking—the insides of me got swollen. I hadn't enough handkerchiefs, my nose was running."

On some days she would suddenly arrive at my house "to sit quietly." She appeared totally unafraid for herself, but was extremely anxious for her son, Sanjay. She had been told by the few people who remained with her that he would be arrested and tortured in jail. I did not know how to comfort her.

I left for Bombay in early June, as I had nowhere to live in New Delhi. Soon after I left, Indira was arrested. She spent a night in the police lock-up, but was released by the magistrate the next morning.

Krishnaji heard the news of Indira's arrest in London on BBC, and he immediately wrote to me to enquire of her well-being. With the pressures mounting against her and Sanjay, Indira wrote to Krishnaji; but with no staff to assist her, the letter was understamped and went by surface mail. When I met her in August, she said she had not received a reply to her letter. Knowing that Krishnaji would have replied, I wrote to him enquiring whether the letter had reached him. His response was immediate; her letter had not reached him. It only reached him much later, when he returned to India; the letter had been redirected to him from Brockwood. Her letter to him of June 21, 1977, read as follows:

Respected Krishnaji,

Pupul has sent me your address.

I want to write but I don't know what.

I thought I had acquired a measure of quiet within myself but it is obviously not sufficient for the sort of pressures that I am now experiencing. I have smiled through the longstanding campaign of calumny against me and my family. This continues. In addition we are constantly watched, followed and harassed.

She went on to speak of Sanjay and the threats of criminal charges being made against him. The letter ends, "Sanjay himself, though subject to such hardships and humiliations—raids on his premises, CBI questioning and the actual case, is behaving with dignity and equanimity."

People who had been close to her when she was prime minister began to abandon her, and she was deeply hurt. She did not know what the future held for her. She was aware the Janata government sought revenge and would go all out to humiliate and persecute her. She was apprehensive for Sanjay.

Krishnaji arrived in India in early November. From Bombay he was to go to Varanasi, but an acute water shortage there made him cancel his visit.

My ground-floor flat in Dongersey Road, Malabar Hill, where Krishnaji was to stay in Bombay, was in a horrendous state of disrepair. The day before his arrival part of the plaster from the roof had fallen near my bed, barely missing my sleeping body. It was impossible to get it repaired before he came. To add to my despair, on the morning of his arrival workmen started digging up the road in front of my gate, and no telephone calls to the Municipal Corporation could stop them. No one could even advise me as to who was responsible, and I was help-less. So Krishnaji came to a house in which the plaster was falling, and a ditch was being dug in front of the gate. A plank had been placed over the ditch, and wooden poles supported the portico and the back veranda to save them from collapsing.

Soon after he arrived, K started asking questions about Indira. He told me that before he left India in February 1977, he had a sudden perception in which he foresaw Indira's defeat. He went on to say that she would face travail, tribulation, and violence in the years ahead.

A few days after his arrival I had a telephone call from Delhi that Indira was to come from Bangalore to Bombay with the sole purpose of meeting Krishnaji. It was to be a private visit. She came to the house and walked out of the car, amused at having to "walk the plank" to enter the house where I lived. She spent over two hours with Krishnaji, while the director general of police, who was there for reasons of se-curity, waited in the corridor. When she came out she took me aside and told me that Krishnaji had asked her to stay another day, and she had agreed. Could she stay? She hoped it was not too much trouble.

I immediately agreed, though with inward trepidation, and began to plan the details. When the director general of police heard this, he was horrified. He told me it was impossible to provide adequate se-curity to protect this flat. It was on the ground floor, with a number of windows opening on to the road. He begged me to persuade her to go back to Delhi. He was very nervous and genuinely afraid. By then several Congress leaders started coming to see her. They were all crowded into the third bedroom, while Indira met them individually in the sitting room.

It was finally arranged that she go back to Delhi. By then people had come to know that Indira was in the flat, and crowds had gathered outside. Before she left late in the evening, Indira enthusiastically ate cucumber sandwiches and *patodi*, a succulent Gujarat savory made with graham flour. I drove with her to the airport—the plane was several hours late.

In the spring of 1978 I traveled around Karnataka with Indira, seeing temples and visiting *maths* or monasteries. We had stopped for lunch at Mulabidri, an ancient Jain religious center. A vast collection of Jain *tirthankara* images carved out of emerald, ruby, sapphire, crystal, obsidian, jade, agate, and other semiprecious stones had been brought out from the strong rooms to be shown to the ex-prime minister. From the tenth century, merchants trading in the Far East brought back with them treasures carved in the form of the standing Jain images to offer at this ancient shrine.

We ended our journey at Mercara in a rest-house nestled amongst gardens and huge trees. Here Indira was to write her book *Eternal India*. She would discuss the book with us and spend the morning writing; at times she would relax and talk. Writing the book had awakened many memories, and had also helped her to investigate herself. She told me, "When I go for a trip, I observe everything that takes place, everything that passes my car. The car often has no springs and is uncomfortable on *kuccha* or mud track roads. I watch the villages, the way people dress, their faces, their expressions. I have always watched. As a child, I was full of curiosity, I was interested in everything: birds, insects, animals." She loved to walk barefoot, especially when she was in the mountains. She said, "Gandhiji used to say, 'Walk barefoot because the poor have no shoes,' but to me walking barefoot is to feel the earth, the touch of it."

Krishnaji returned to India in early November 1978. He did not stop in Delhi on his way to Varanasi. From there he went south to Rishi Valley via Calcutta. While in Rishi Valley I got a phone call from 12 Willingdon Crescent in New Delhi that Indira was proposing to visit Rishi Valley and hoped to meet Krishnaji. She had never been to the valley, and thought a few days there would be restful. She had just won the fiercely fought election at Chikmagelur, and tensions were mounting as the date for the opening of Parliament drew near.

The day before she was to arrive, I received another phone call to say that the privilege motion to expel her from Parliament and jail her was gathering momentum, and the next few days would be critical; naturally, she had to abandon the trip. I came down from Rishi Valley and flew to New Delhi and was present in the Lok Sabha when the battle was fought. She was arraigned by Parliament, expelled, and sent to prison until Parliament adjourned. She was in Tihar Jail for a week. From there she wrote me this note, scribbled on a crumpled and stained piece of paper:

Pupul dear

You looked positively ill the other day and I have been worried about you. You are anxious about me—but why? Physically and mentally I am well. My cough and cold are much better. I am e[n]sconced (it sounds a good word but the spelling escapes me for the moment) in a large barracks all by myself with two matrons taking turns to look after me. It is fairly clean but indescribably ugly, the fittings unfunctional and badly made. They have made a bathroom for me and I had hot water in the morning. It is quiet and peaceful. I am reading and if the mood comes, may be able to write. I have brought an odd selection of books—all birthday gifts.

Love

Indu.

Have finished hastily as my food has come.

Soon after she was released, she decided to visit Krishnaji in Vasant Vihar, Madras. Elaborate arrangements had been made for her security. She was to have lunch with Krishnaji, stay the night at the State Rest House, and return to Delhi next morning.

The airport was a seething mass of people who had come to receive her. She came out of the plane looking a little tired. She was coming from Karnataka where the opposition parties had organized some violent stone-throwing.

Krishnaji was at the porch and took her to his room on the first floor of Vasant Vihar. I waited in a nearby sitting room. Some time before she left, he called me in. Indira had distressed eyes, but smiled when she saw me. After a while she said, "Krishnaji has been asking me to leave politics. I have told him I do not know how. There are twenty-eight criminal cases against me." She turned to Krishnaji and said they had brought a criminal charge against her for having stolen two chickens, and a summons was being issued against her, demanding that she appear to answer the charge. She paused, searching for the right words. "I have told Krishnaji that I have only two alternatives, to fight or to let them destroy me like a sitting duck."

I took her to my cottage, where she had a wash and relaxed before lunch and told me of her life in jail. She would wake up at five in the morning, exercise, drink cold milk that had been brought to her by her daughter-in-law Sonia the evening before, and go back to bed until seven. She then bathed, and after that read. Ironically, she had been given the same ward that had been used by George Fernandes.* There were two matrons with her all the time. The ward was ugly. Sonia brought her meals cooked at home. The jail authorities only allowed her a limited number of books, a situation she found irritating. She had no self-pity of any sort.

Towards the end of the conversation she said, "When I saw Krish-

---

*George Fernandes, a socialist, was one of the most aggressive opponents of Indira Gandhi. He was a member of Parliament for several years and was a minister in the government of Morarji Desai, after Indira Gandhi and the Congress were defeated in 1977.

naji in Delhi in 1976, he asked me if I realized that, if I acted rightly, I would have to face the consequences? They would try to destroy me."

By one o'clock we had gone back to the house for lunch. Besides Indira and Krishnaji, there was Mary Zimbalist. Krishnaji played the host. It was heart-warming to see the exquisite courtesies with which he filled this role; he was attentive to what she said, watched the way the food was served, discussed international affairs, spoke of the problems facing humanity.

During lunch Mary Zimbalist asked Indira, "What was it like in prison?"

"Not comfortable," came the prompt reply. Indira went on to say that they had provided a wooden bed, but no mattress. She had used the blankets to keep out the light from the barred windows. She had received two telegrams while in jail, from unknown people. The first said, "Live frugally"; the other advised her to count the bars in the window. She had actually counted them.

M. S. Subbulakshmi, one of the best-known singers of the carnatic music of South India, a woman whose melodious voice is in harmony with her dignity, was to give a concert for Krishnaji at Vasant Vihar that evening, and he invited Indira. She replied that she had several meetings in the evening, but would try and come if she could get away.

A large number of people had come to hear the music. Krishnaji was sitting on the floor slightly behind the first few rows, and there were chairs against the wall. Subbulakshmi was singing when Indira came, and sat down on an empty chair near the door. Seeing her, I got up and sat in the chair beside her. I could see that everyone in the room was aware that she was there and were watching her closely. Krishnaji had noticed her presence, but sat without movement. After about an hour, she got up and quietly slipped out by the side door. I followed her and found him waiting. He had seen her leave and had swiftly moved to the porch, to bid her goodbye. He was very affectionate, took her hand, and said, "Au revoir, Madame. Be well. We shall meet again."

The repression and harassment against Indira and her family in 1979 were to become counterproductive. After emergency, the people of India had rebelled against her, but they were not prepared to see Indira humiliated. To them she was Jawaharlal's daughter, courageous beyond measure. One evening after her defeat, she had told me that she was a survivor. Life had been so tough in her childhood that traits necessary for survival had developed within her. She could bear hardships, deprivation, and live a life of austerity. This instinct for survival made her shed what was unnecessary and develop the faculties needed to meet danger; it enabled her to sense the change of mood amongst people in India. With the Janata Government* breaking up, shrewd and insightful politician that she was, she was quick to act. She toured the country vigorously, speaking at small and large gatherings. The three years of severe persecution, of isolation, of seeing people betray her out of fear or for gain, of being hunted and having to use all her senses to protect herself and her son, had left her wary and watchful. By the time Krishnaji returned to India at the end of 1979 elections had been announced. She wrote a letter to him, expressing her inability to meet him, as she was traveling continually.

I was on the plane to Delhi when the election news came in: She had won with an overwhelming majority. I went to her next morning. Barricades had been put up around 12 Willingdon Crescent and huge crowds were milling around. She embraced me and tears brimmed over. Although she had known the tide was in her favor, the shock of victory took some time to register.

I went to Bombay, and Krishnaji arrived there the next day. We spoke of Indira and her future. One morning he called me to his room; he was grave and silent. We sat quietly. He then told me that Indira would face great sorrow in the year to come and I should be in Delhi as much as possible. He said, "It is a strange coincidence that you should be so close to an outsider like me and also be a friend of the prime minister. By very watchful of yourself. Such situations just don't happen. Be deeply aware of every thought and action." His words penetrated deeply, though I could give him no reply. I was aware that he sensed some darkness overshadowing Indira, but he did not speak of it.

I started going to Delhi regularly beginning in February, though I did not take up any work in the government until late September. I was in Kashmir in June, staying with Governor L. K. Jha, when the news came by phone that Sanjay had been critically injured in an airplane accident. I took a plane to Delhi immediately. On the plane I

---

*After the emergency ended, the opposition leaders came together to form a single party under the name of the Janata Party. *Janata* means "people." The Janata Party was inspired by the most respected Gandhian leader, Jai Prakash Narain; the new party fought the elections in 1977 against Indira Gandhi and the Congress Party. The Janata Party was victorious and a new government was formed under Morarji Desai, the veteran leader of Gujarat. Most of the members of the Janata Party had earlier been members of the Congress; many of them had fought in the freedom struggle against the British, but broke away from the party.

met Dr. Karan Singh, who told me that he had confirmation from Delhi that Sanjay was dead. Krishnaji sent a telegram, which I later gave to Indira.

I had written to Krishnaji giving him news of Indira and the catastrophe. He wrote back immediately from Gstaad: "It must have been a terrible shock for her and I hope she is recovering." I had suggested that he write to her on how to face death. He replied, "I have just answered that question in the public meeting. I feel it would not be right to send her a message on meeting death. I could talk to her, which would be totally different from a written message. I hope you understand this."

As days passed Indira's body, which had stood the shock of Sanjay's death with a straight back and dry eyes, started to express its anguish. Her lips, which in the early years had contradicted the warmth of her eyes, lost all toughness. Her hair became unruly, brushed back from her forehead; her step was heavy.

She began to receive all manner of telegrams and letters containing astrological forecasts of disaster and danger to Rajiv. Some astrologers claimed to have actually forecast the day of Sanjay's death, several months earlier. It was obvious that the fresh astrological forecasts were sent to break her spirit. I suggested that she throw the letters out of the window. She hesitated. Then with anguish she said, "If I had died, it would have been right. I am over sixty and have lived a full life. But Sanjay was so young." We were at dinner; Rajiv was grim, Sonia in tears, Sanjay's young widow Maneka absent. Indira got up, saying she had four more hours of work that night. As she walked to the door, her shoulders were bent, her body drooped, she looked aged and bone weary.

Krishnaji arrived from Brockwood in early November 1980. From Madras he went to Colombo, Sri Lanka, where he was to give four talks. By the fourth week of November, Krishnaji was in Rishi Valley. The members of the American and British Foundations had come to the valley for the joint meeting that was to take place later in Madras. In December I got a message that Indira Gandhi was coming to visit Krishnaji at Rishi Valley with Rajiv and Sonia and their children Rahul and Priyanka. Krishnaji was puzzled that a prime minister would come such a long distance to visit him and see the valley. He spoke to me of the special quality of the feelings he had for her. It had been nearly two years since he had first met her. During that time she had known great triumph and the devastating sorrow of the sudden loss of her son.

The prime minister had issued instructions that it was a private visit and that she did not want the ministers and other representatives of the state legislature to crowd the campus. She had also told the security staff to keep off the campus, as she realized that Krishnaji would be sensitive to guns and uniforms. The collector of the district and the police officials were in a state of despair. Police had to be there, but they had to be located so that they became invisible. It became a game of finding a suitable bush behind which to hide—one stout inspector of police even tried to hide behind a slender eucalyptus tree. Nearly five hundred security personnel were hidden on the campus.

Indira's plane landed at an airstrip some miles from the campus. I climbed into her car and we drove to the gates of Rishi Valley, where the villagers, children of the school, and teachers had gathered, with garlands. She stopped the car, got out, and mingled with them.

I took her to see Krishnaji, who was waiting on the doorstep of the old Guest House. They spent a few minutes together; then, while Krishnaji returned to his room, we drove her round the campus. We showed her the school buildings, the farm, the rice fields, the village school. She was very watchful, observing the trees, the lush crops, and workers' homes. We stopped at a small children's hostel and she went in and spoke to the children. She did not comment, but I could see that she was impressed. At the end of the drive we reached the assembly building, where she and Rajiv planted ficus bengamina trees.

After the tree planting, we entered the assembly hall. Krishnaji came in silently and sat next to Indira. There was absolute silence. Then, with perfect intonation, the children chanted Sanskrit *slokas*. As they ended, Krishnaji turned to Indira and asked her to speak. She said she could not do so before Krishnaji. So he went and sat cross-legged on the low platform and spoke a few words to the children. When he finished, she took off her shoes and went on to the platform, sat down, and gave a short, simple talk.

She then walked with Krishnaji to the old Guest House. I followed with her family. Tea, *dosas*, and *jalebis* were served in the large open space near Krishnaji's room. Rishi Konda was hidden by the tall trees, the branches of which framed and even entered into the open room. Parameswaran, the master chef of Rishi Valley, was famous for his *dosas*, and Indira and the family ate them with enthusiasm. Krishnaji noticed that she needed to wash her fingers and asked Parameswaran for a finger bowl. No such vessel was available, so a soup plate with water was brought in which Indira washed her hands. Krishnaji looked at me; Indira noticed the look and smiled.

She then asked whether she could speak to Krishnaji, and he took her to his room. Rajiv and Sonia went to see the school, while Rajesh Dalal took the children hiking. Indira was with Krishnaji for some time. Later, they went for a cross-country walk. The security police were hidden behind bushes on the route they were to follow. They walked through mango groves, towards Rishi Konda; the sun was setting behind the hill, and the sky was molten. Indira kept pace with ease and Krishnaji was walking fast.

In the evening there was a concert under the banyan tree and later a moonlight dinner. Indira was relaxed, told anecdotes, and joined freely in the conversation. I had arranged her room with some care— a window opened onto Rishi Konda, which was visible through plants and wild flowering grass. She noticed the plants and the hill and the atmosphere created in the room, and commented on the peace and infinite quiet in the valley. Next morning, she had breakfast with Krishnaji.

In the eighteen hours she had been in Rishi Valley, an unwavering compassion had flowed from Krishnaji, enveloping her. I do not know if she was aware of the timeless energies that emanated from him, healing body and mind. A *Rig Veda* text speaks of the place "Where Oshadies or herbs and plants are found, there the wise man is the healer, of evil and disease."

I accompanied her back to Delhi. She slept deeply on the plane without waking. It seemed to be the sleep of healing.

Indira had brought away within her the silences and the compassion of the valley. It soon became evident that her senses were quickening. A young, vulnerable look was replacing the ravaged face. Her step had grown light and her shoulders straight.

# CHAPTER 31

# "Don't Hold Memories of Her in Your Mind, that Holds Her to the Earth. Let Her Go."

Krishnaji returned to Delhi by Lufthansa on October 26, 1981; he had been ill and was very weak. Asit accompanied him. The president of India, Shri Sanjeeva Reddy, a former student of the Rishi Valley School, had sent a message through one of his aides that he would like Krishnaji to stay with him when he was in Delhi. The problem of his doing so had been explained to the president and it had been decided that he would host a lunch for Krishnaji when he was in Delhi.

The day after his arrival, Krishnaji began to talk to me about Indira. He wanted to know what kind of mind she had. Was there in her the sense of the global? Was she aware of the crisis facing humanity? I had answered that I felt she had a sense of the global and could see problems in a totality. Krishnaji then asked if she could cease to be national. I said, no, she could not do that and remain prime minister. He then started talking of the arms race. He was greatly disturbed at the dangers facing humanity. He also had forebodings about Indira. There was increasing corruption and violence in India, and the violence would accelerate. "Could she act and control it?" he asked. "She is very vulnerable."

I then asked him, why, for the past several years, he had been so concerned about Indira. What did he find in her? He pondered, questioned himself, and said it was a new question; he appeared intrigued by it. He had held her in his consciousness for some time. He felt he could silently commune with her. We were interrupted, and the discussion remained unfinished.

Indira had invited Krishnaji to tea, and was waiting for him on the porch. They were together for two hours, at the end of which she came into the dining room, where I was waiting with Sonia and Maneka, and asked for the time. When she heard it was seven thirty, she laughed and said she had lost all track of time and had missed a meeting. She took the children into the room and they were introduced to Krishnaji. A little later, Indira came to the door to see us off. Krishnaji was very silent on his return. Later, he was to tell me that he had felt great tension in the house; strong, suppressed emotions and some latent hatred. He had asked Indira whether there were problems in the family, and she had replied, "The usual quarrels, as in all families." But Krishnaji was not satisfied. He felt that there was violence and something very wrong in the atmosphere.

On November 2 we went to lunch at Rashtrapati Bhavan, the president's residence. Achyut, Narayan, Nandini, and I accompanied Krishnaji, who wore a red-bordered *dhoti* and a *kurta* made of a rough, bark-toned handspun *tussar*.* An *angavastram* rested on his shoulder. Tall, straight-backed, silent, with grave demeanor and liquid, compassionate eyes, it was a luminous sage who entered this symbol of imperial splendor. The president, Sanjeeva Reddy, received Krishnaji with great respect, as is the tradition of this country. S. Venkataraman, who had known Krishnaji for several years, started a conversation. Indira came in a few moments later. Like a nimble girl, her eyes sparkling, she ran to greet Krishnaji.

At lunch, she insisted on speaking to Krishnaji in French. Krishnaji's French was perfect, and there was a sophistication in him that delighted Indira. She was aware that the president was intrigued and very curious. He kept bending over to listen and appeared frustrated, as he could not understand what was being said. After lunch Krishnaji was seen off at the door of Rashtrapati Bhavan by the president. It had been a memorable, though amusing, interlude.

Krishnaji returned to Delhi from Varanasi in early December 1981. Indira came to dine at the house. It was the day of the Qutub Minar tragedy; a stampede in the dark spiral staircase of the Qutub (a tower of victory built by the twelfth-century ruler Qutbudin Aibak) had

---

*A non-mulberry silk; the cocoons of *tussar* are reared on trees and gathered by tribal men and women to be sold in tribal markets.

trapped a school party, and forty-five children had been killed. She had come straight from the scene of the accident, from the horror of mutilated bodies and hysterical, grieving parents. Her face was taut and grim, her eyes shadowed. Krishnaji had heard of the disaster and met her at the door. She was with him for over an hour. When they came out for dinner, her face had softened, though the eyes still held the agony of what she had seen.

The conversation at dinner turned to the extrasensory, magical happenings in India. Krishnaji told a story of the early 1920s, when he and his brother Nitya were in Varanasi. A very poor man had walked into the compound where they were staying. After talking to them for a while, he had asked for a newspaper and placed it at some distance. He had then asked Krishnaji to keep watching the paper. K watched as it grew smaller and finally disappeared. The magician refused any money for this feat, and walked away.

L. K. Jha said that in Darbhanga, where he was brought up, there was a tantric who was the family guru. After a theft the guru had called L. K., who was a young boy, and put the eyewash *kajal* (collyrium) on his thumb. He asked him to look intently at the *kajal*. As L. K. looked, the black vanished and he saw a man walking toward a haystack to hide something. The man turned, and the boy saw the face clearly. Later, he had described the face to the guru, the thief was apprehended, and the object discovered in the haystack.

Indira told the story of what happened at 12 Willingdon Crescent. Narain Dutt Tiwari (who is at present chief minister of Uttar Pradesh) had brought a man dressed in a simple *dhoti* and *kurta* to see Indira. He was known as "Balti Baba" or the "Bucket Sage." He asked for a bucket of water and suggested that Indira write a question on paper. As she was hesitant, Narain Dutt Tiwari wrote out the question in Hindi, folded it, and placed it below the bucket. Balti Baba then asked for another clean sheet of paper and some milk. The paper was placed in the water within the bucket and milk was poured over the water and paper. They waited for about two minutes. The paper was then taken out of the water. Writing in Hindi had appeared on both sides of the paper. Though smudged, it was easy to read and had given a relevant answer to the question. Balti Baba said this capacity or *siddhi* had come to him without his having performed any meditative practices. It was the will of the goddess and could disappear as easily as it was given to him. He was humble about his powers and reiterated that he was in no way responsible for what had happened.

Soon it was my turn. I recounted the strange happenings in Himmat

Nivas, Dongersey Road, when Krishnaji was staying there as my guest. One morning two men dressed in saffron robes knocked at the door. One was old and walked with the aid of a stick; the other was young. The young man said that they had come from Rishikesh and were going on a pilgrimage to Rameswaram. As they were walking along Ridge Road in Bombay, the older *sannyasi*, who was renowned for his insights, had felt the presence of a profoundly great Being in the neighborhood. He had come to this house, the presence of the Being illuminating his way. He told me he wanted to meet the Mahatma who dwelt within. Knowing Krishnaji's attraction for the saffron robe, I asked them to come in and spoke to Krishnaji, who immediately came out of his room and sat with them on a mat.

Krishnaji held the hand of the old *sannyasi*. For a while they sat silently, then the old man turned to me and said, "Daughter, get me some water." I brought a bottle of water and some glasses. He then asked me to get a *thali*, a metal container, and to pour the water over his hands so that it collected in the vessel. He then asked us to sip the water. To my amazement, Krishnaji sipped it; the *thali* was passed round and everyone had a sip. It was plain water. Then the *sadhu* asked me to throw away the water and repeated again the pouring of the water over his hands into the vessel. He again asked us to sip; and when I tasted the water, I found it had the fragrance and taste of rosewater. No one commented.

The old *sannyasi* then turned to me and said, "*Dakshina do*, Give me alms." I felt annoyed; but as Krishnaji, who was observing closely, was present, I felt I could not refuse. So I gave him 50 rupees. He said, "No, give me a hundred." By now, I was quite angry and felt I was being duped; I saw that Krishnaji was watching me. So I gave the old man 100 rupees. As I handed it over, the *sannyasi* handed back the money, saying, "Take it back, daughter. I was testing you." Immediately, my Indian background responded. I told him that once *dakshina* had been given, it could never be taken back.

The old *sadhu* said, "I am pleased with you, ask for whatever you wish." The offer was terrifying. I said, "There is nothing I want." The old man blessed me, then turned to Sunanda. "You have no children— ask for a child." It was true she had longed for a child, but she too replied, "Swamiji, I do not wish for anything." He then turned to Balasundaram and said, "You too don't have a child. Ask." Balasundaram was dazed and shook his head. Krishnaji had been watching with great intensity.

And now the old *sannysasi* turned to Krishnaji, bent low, asked for his blessing, made his *pranams*, and said he would resume his journey. After the two saffron-robed swamis left, Krishnaji turned to me and said, "Did you taste the rosewater?" All of us said we had felt its fragrance and its taste. Krishnaji said, "How did the old boy do it? I was watching him closely. He could not have introduced anything into the water."

Indira lingered after dinner, loath to leave. But it was late, and soon she said goodbye to Krishnaji and went home. He was smiling and happy for her.

Indira wrote to Krishnaji in June 1982. The letter went astray, and she wrote again in July.

Dear Respected Krishnaji,

Pupul has sent me your letter of the 21st June. I am sorry that my previous one did not reach you. Apparently, the British do not live up to the image of their efficiency which they have propagated in India.

There was nothing much in the letter. Just my deep appreciation of your concern and I am deeply in need of it just now. This is a depressing time. Has the world come to a dead end? More and more people are realising what is wrong and what can be done. Yet, we drift in the opposite direction. A handful of people have the power to affect the lives of all other millions who inhabit this earth. The few are too wrapped up in themselves and what they consider their immediate interests in terms of place and time, and the many are willing to be pushed along in the illusion that they are free and guiding their own lives. The world needs your spirit of compassion and direction to look within themselves and the courage to act accordingly.

With warm regards,

Yours sincerely,
Indira

Indira was to visit the United States. Before she left she had gone on a short holiday with the family to Kashmir. The wave of despair had been dissipated. She wrote to me, "I took the family up to Kashmir for a couple of days. Actually, there was only one full day of what can be called rest and relaxation but it was wonderful change. We stayed out at Dachigam—a sanctuary, did a lot of walking and stalked wild bear in the forest. Besides, the beauty of the valley is in itself a tonic. I had two brief meetings with Pandit Lakshmanjoo. The first time, he offered me his usual Paratha and several Bulbuls came to sit on my shoulder and knee to share it."

By early November 1982 Krishnaji was back in New Delhi. He was to meet Indira again at dinner at 11 Safdarjung Road. Rajiv had accompanied his mother. Earlier she had told me that, for the last few weeks, she had not been able to sleep and was waking between two and three every morning, with a feeling of great uneasiness. There were rumors in Delhi that her opponents had been indulging in all manner of plots and black magical rites to destroy her. For three nights she had dreamed of an old, hideous hag who wished to harm her but could not succeed, for a luminous being with a beard was protecting her.

Indira wanted to see Krishnaji once again before he left Delhi three days later. The meeting was difficult to arrange, as Krishnaji was giving his public talks on the next two days. It was finally decided that he would go to her residence to meet her after his last talk on Sunday. We were very surprised, as he never went anywhere after a talk.

Indira was waiting for him that Sunday evening. During their conversation, she said that the uneasiness that woke her at night had disappeared and so had the dreams. She was sleeping soundly. The atmosphere in the house had grown quiet. Krishnaji was to comment on it to me later. During the meeting, Krishnaji asked her whether she was securely guarded. She replied there were vast numbers of guards, but she was certain that very few of them would risk their lives to protect her.

Krishnaji soon left Delhi for Madras. Indira wrote to him, questioning him on the nature of truth and reality. He had responded immediately. I do not know whether the correspondence went any further, but it was clear the inner enquiry that had been dormant in Indira for years was reawakening.

For Indira, 1983 was a year of destiny. She was to play a vital role on the world stage; but within India, storms were gathering. The countries bordering on India were in ferment. As Indira's horizons extended, the burdens and responsibilities increased; and with it came extraordinary demands on her time and energy. To meet this challenge, from June 1983 she had imposed a rigorous discipline on her body, eating frugally to strip herself of every extra ounce. Her energy was legendary—her work day stretched to over eighteen hours. Exquisitely groomed, two silver streaks of hair swept back from her forehead, giving the slim, taut body dignity and elegance.

Her speech reflected her ever-extending concerns. Aware of the unprecedented crisis that threatened to annihilate the world, there was a passionate urgency in her call for total disarmament. From insights gleaned in solitude, she voiced her concern for those essential links needed to bind the world and its resources into one unfragmented whole.

Humanity, heritage, ecology were words that had acquired for her a new and poignant meaning. The protective walls that she had built around her in her childhood had been broken; she was vulnerable and awake.

By the winter of 1983 it was apparent that the country was to face grave dangers. The problem of Punjab was becoming increasingly serious. Krishnaji had met Indira in early November, and they had talked at length. At Rishi Valley he gave me a letter to give to her, along with a parcel of custard apples. She replied on December 26, 1983:

Respected Krishnaji,

Pupul brought your greetings and the custard apples. Sustenance for the soul and the body! Thank you for the thought.

I don't know what to write because I am so full of anguish. I have the feeling that I have strayed onto an unknown planet. Advice and the desire to dominate have been with us since the world began, or rather since the human race began, but never on this scale and at such peril. Yet, how many care for anything but the immediate and they do not even try to understand that. So many people come to your lectures but what do they do afterwards? At home or at work? It is indeed difficult to keep hope or faith.

I had meant only to let you know that I had received your message and how much your thoughts mean to me. I'm sorry, I've rambled on, at the same time there are few people to whom one can talk and with you one does not need to talk.

I treasure our brief meetings.

With warm regards and good wishes,

Indira

With the inevitability of epic tragedy, her life was moving towards its destiny. Deeply aware of the direction and flow of events, Krishnaji reached out to her to convey the depth of his feeling and concern. He offered to come to see her at any time, if it would help.

My dear Indiraji,

I was so glad to get your letter which Pupulji brought a few days ago.

I am very sorry indeed that you are disturbed and distressed. The world is upside down, terrible things are happening; threat of nuclear war, murder, torture, and all the unspeakable things that are taking place. It is all becoming more and more insane, and I am most concerned that you are involved in all this.

As you will not be able to read my handwriting, I hope you will not mind my resorting to a typewriter.

If it is in any way, "in any way," helpful to you, I'll come to Delhi. Pupulji and I have talked the matter over. I am leaving India on the 15th of February. Pupulji can always give you my programme.

I hope you are well.

Please accept my love.

J. K.

I took the letter to her. She put it aside to read later and we talked for a while. Her energy was at an ebb and she spoke of the dangers that lay ahead. She had premonitions of disaster and spoke of forces seeking to destabilize the country.

Outwardly, she was calm, and I commented on it. She replied, "At times the sea has no ripple, but deep within it are stormy movements."

She had not seen her grandson Varun for nearly a year, and I was aware of the sorrow the separation had evoked in her. After Sanjay's death, for the twenty months Varun had spent in the house, he had slept in his grandmother's room; I had sat with her when she played catch with the child, acted the grandmother, cuddled him, and spoke baby talk with him. She refused to admit it, but the decision of Maneka to deny the child all visits to her after March 1983 had wounded her deeply.

She wrote to Krishnaji on January 29, and I took the letter with me to Bombay.

Respected Krishnaji,

Thank you so much for your letter.

It is most considerate of you to offer to come to Delhi. I am truly over-whelmed. Meeting you is a special experience, but I would feel guilty asking you to interrupt your programme in Madras to come here when we are in the midst of a cold wave. I should certainly have found time for you but these two months are particularly rushed ones for me with many formal functions and visitors.

No day goes by without some news which adds to one's concern for the future. The American scientist, Prof. Morrison has been explaining to me in greater detail the implications of the "nuclear winter."

I shall be in Bombay for a Naval function on Sunday, the 12th and Monday, the 13th February. If it is convenient to you, I could drop in on the 12th after 8.00 p.m. or on the 13th after 6.00 p.m.

I hope you are keeping well.

With warm regards,

Indira

Krishnaji was staying at Sterling Apartments, Peddar Road, Bombay, where Indira came to see him on the evening of February 13. She spent a little over an hour with him. He came down in the lift to see her to her car, and held her two hands as they parted. This was the last time they were to meet.


The situation in Punjab, already murky, soon exploded. Threats to the life of Indira Gandhi and her son Rajiv had started pouring in. By February, with the murder of Atwal, a senior police officer, as he was leaving the Golden Temple after offering prayers, the situation became critical. By early April I was in Washington, D.C.; Krishnaji had arrived in New York, where he was to give talks. I told him over the phone of developments in India.

He asked me whether he should speak to Indira Gandhi on the telephone. My nephew Asit Chandmal was in New York with him, and finally, after much difficulty, he got through to her. Krishnaji had never learned to speak on the telephone, and the conversation did not proceed very far; but he sent Indira his love and she responded with deep emotion. I spoke to her shortly afterward; she thanked me over and over and over again.


I was to head a delegation to Delphi, Greece, to attend a seminar on culture to be held there in early June. The night before my departure, I heard Indira speak on television. From the supreme gravity of her speech and the tone of her voice, I sensed that the country was to go through fire in the near future. I asked my secretary to cancel my departure to Athens, as I felt I should not leave Delhi. The next day I had a phone call from Dhawan, Indira's personal assistant. He said the prime minister wanted to know why I had not gone to Athens. I said I would explain when I saw her that evening.

When I met her, she was insistent that I go. "Everything is all right, Pupul," she said. "Go." She had a letter which she had written to the president of Greece, and asked me to deliver it to him with her personal greetings. I met her again the evening before my departure. She was detached and quiet. I had a feeling that the critical decision had been taken; having taken it, she had stepped back, for the future was no longer within her control. I sat in her room and we spoke of Greece—its art, its transforming light, and the beauty of its landscapes. Later, I had dinner with the family. When I reached Rome the next day, it was to hear that troops had entered the Golden Temple.

October is a tender month in Delhi. The damp heat wanes and morning dew ushers in the winter. Warm shawls emerge from clove-scented wrappers, and festivals celebrate the harvests of the fields of the vast countryside.

I saw Indira several times during October 1984, the last month of her life. We sat together in her study, she was at peace with herself, had laid aside her burdens and barriers. During the last few weeks she had once again been meeting physicists, philosophers, and poets and, on November 3 she was to lunch at my house with Krishnaji and the Dalai Lama. For her, this month was an interval, an in-between month, a period for renewal; for, by November, preparations for the election would commence. That evening we discussed symbols, and I told her of the Bhadrakali Shrine in North Canara (the local name for the west coast of Karnataka and North Kerala), where there was no image or icon. The great Mother as energy was symbolized within the shrine as a highly polished bronze mirror in which the worshiper saw his or her own face reflected, igniting a journey into the pathways of self-know-ing. A journey of austerity and aloneness; for there was no other, nei-ther god nor guru.

The symbolism aroused her. She was quick to respond, refreshed from exposure to a new movement; a fresh spring. Awake to intima-tions, a memory arose and she started speaking of a day in her life when she felt an overwhelming surge of joy. It had no cause, but the explosion was of such intensity that she felt the earth would open and swallow her up. The ecstasy had transformed her face, and people commented that she looked radiant. When she felt that she would dis-appear into the earth, it was not a death wish. She said she had never been afraid of dying at any age. "I have felt it as a natural process, a part of life. One lives a certain number of years, and then you die"— she was not afraid. She spoke of a need to return to roots; of Indian thought that maintained "light is within you," and the need to find a way to discover it.

I saw her for the last time on the evening of October 26. She was to visit Srinagar the next morning. She had never been there in au-tumn, and she was eagerly looking forward to seeing the chinar leaves change color. She wanted to lie in the sun and see the green of the leaf turn rust, vermilion, and gold; the brown of a falling leaf. Perhaps it was the end of life in the leaf that made her pursue the question of death. For as she mused she said, "My father loved rivers, but I am a daughter of the Himalayas and I have told my sons"—for a moment she appeared to have forgotten that Sanjay was dead—"that my remains should be scattered on the snow-tipped Himalayas." As I was leaving, she called out to me, "Remember what I said, Pupul, remember."

Krishnaji, with Mary Zimbalist, arrived late that night. He was scheduled to give one public talk on November 4, on the same platform as the Dalai Lama. News of this talk had traveled to many Buddhist centers in India and abroad, and a large number of Buddhist monks were expected to attend. On the evening of October 30, Krishnaji, after an early supper, insisted that the book I was writing about him be read aloud. Mary Zimbalist read part of the book, which dealt with the early years of his birth and childhood. Later, I took over.

Krishnaji had been totally still during the reading. He only interrupted once when he heard me read the passage on Alcyone, in which I had said that the word Alcyone meant "kingfisher," the calmer of storms. He interrupted to correct me. "No," he said, "it means 'the brightest star in the Pleiades.' " As the reading continued, the room awoke as if there was a presence there, listening. As I continued, the feeling of presence was overpowering, and soon my voice stopped. Krishnaji turned to me, "Do you feel It? I could prostrate to It?" His body was trembling as he spoke of the presence that listened. "Yes, I can prostrate to this, that is here." Suddenly he turned and left us walking alone to his room.

Indira Gandhi was shot by two of her security guards October 31 at 9:20 A.M., as she was walking from her residence to her office. Riddled by bullets, she fell mortally wounded to the earth, surrounded by growing things. She fell close to the grove of kadamba saplings she had planted that rainy season, after the June tragedy in Punjab.

On hearing the news I rushed to her house only to find barriers going up. Indira's grandchildren Rahul and Priyanka were alone with a friend. They did not quite know what had happened, but I was told that Sonia had rushed Indira to the hospital. The atmosphere in the house was turgid with an undercurrent of violence and fear. Sharada Prasad, her Principal Information Adviser, was in the office, and he told me what had happened. Before going to the hospital, I sent a message back to Krishnaji that Indira had been shot. I returned home late at night and found Krishnaji waiting up for me. Seeing me, he took me to his room and asked for the details of what had happened. My family said that on hearing the news, Krishnaji sat through the day in my sitting room overlooking the garden; he had watched the trees and birds, hardly speaking and eating little. At four in the afternoon he had felt Indira's presence and had commented on the need for silence within the mind to enable her to be at peace. I could see that he was deeply moved. Late the next night he was to say, "Don't hold memories of Indira in your mind, that holds her to the earth. Let her go." His hand made a gesture towards space and eternity.

# Part 6

## THE SUMMATION OF THE
## TEACHING 1978–1985

# CHAPTER 32

# "Can You from Today Look at the Thirty Years as the Past? Not from the Thirty Years Look at Today?"

In the early summer of 1978, I was in England at Brockwood Park. While there, I held two dialogues with Krishnaji. From around 1970 I had felt a change in Krishnaji's teaching. His contact with the scientific community, in discussions and seminars, had introduced into his vocabulary a greater precision. He was examining the root meaning of words; carefully defining his use of the words brain, mind, consciousness. He was no longer exploring step by step into thought or into problems like fear, jealousy, anger. The expressions he had used in the late 1940s and 1950s—"the thinker and thought are one"; or "the need to observe thought, see it arise, see it disappear, to pursue it till it ends"; or "to listen and perceive the crucial instant of the arising of thought"—were not evident in the talks after the mid 1970s. By 1978 he was speaking of a totality of seeing, a holistic seeing.

I told him that I had listened to him for thirty years, and I felt that there had been a change in the teachings. "Could the holistic arise without step-by-step observation of consciousness?" I asked. "Have you moved away? Has there been an unfolding or a change?"

Krishnaji pondered my question, then said, "Unfolding would be correct; the teaching is in the same direction, it is holistic rather than an examination of detail. It is direct, simple, and comprehensive."

I asked whether the total immobility of the mind he now spoke about was possible without the earlier observation, questioning, examining? Krishnaji was listening carefully, as he always did in dialogue. He said, "Total ending of thought is immobility, is silence; thought as time has to stop."

I asked him, "If time is the movement of becoming, without the observation of that movement of becoming in consciousness, could becoming end? Without the thirty years of listening, observing the outer and the inner, could there be an end to becoming? Is there not a fundamental change in the teaching?"

Krishnaji's response was startling. He said, "Can you from today look at the thirty years as the past? Not from the thirty years look at today?"

For a moment, I was puzzled by the distinction—"Without the yesterday, can one look back at yesterday?"

"When you look from today to yesterday, you look with a different mind, with eyes in which you don't hold yesterday," he said.

"I had a yesterday," I said. "Therefore, from today, I can look back at the yesterday."

"How do you look at the past from today?" Krishnaji asked. "Inbuilt is holistic seeing. That seeing and listening from today to yesterday is immobility. The present holds the totality of the past. Is that so?" Krishnaji questioned. "And what do we mean by the present? Is it possible to apprehend, have an insight into the whole immediately?" Krishnaji was questioning himself as his responses arose.

"Without the step-by-step, self-knowing, exploration, examination into consciousness, how is it possible?" I refused to move away from my position. Then, suddenly, I saw it. To see from today to the thirty years was to end the linear, the sequential. It was to see with depth into depth. To see back, or to see from the thirty years to today, was to see step-by-step, to see with time as the measure.

"Now, how shall we explore?" asked Krishnaji.

"Thirty years ago you took us by the hand and explored into consciousness; today, you have taken away your hand," I said.

"We are more mature," Krishnaji said.

"What has brought about that maturity? The thirty years?" I asked.

"No—no—no."

I said I saw three distinct periods in the teaching. The early days, when Krishnaji spoke of self-knowing, of the thinker and thought as one, of freedom from judgment and condemnation. In the 1960s he had moved to a denial of the individual as separate from the stream of humanity; from the step-by-step approach Krishnaji had moved to the urgency for a revolution in the human stream. He had stopped speaking of any specific problem like greed or hatred. In the past he had used words such as brain, mind, thought, consciousness interchangeably, as the past, as memory. In the 1970s his terminology had become more precise. He was probing into the nature of observation and the illusion that underlay the division between the observer and the observed. By 1978 he appeared to be concerned with universals, and with a holistic perception.

"When Krishnaji says that holistic perception is possible 'now,' what triggers it? What gives maturity to the eye and the ear to listen, without the past of thirty years?" I asked.

"How can a blind man see light?" asked Krishnaji. "Without preparation, can there be a holistic view? Without detailed exploration, can one see the totality of all existence? Can one see the wholeness of consciousness? I say, yes, it is possible."

"Was the position of thirty years ago, then, not true?" I asked.

"No, I won't say that," said Krishnaji. "The position then was true."

"Was the perception of the thinker and thought as one a total perception, as true as this today?" I questioned.

"But I question whether K went through all that. What he said then was out of totality as what he says now. That detailed examination was born from a totality of perception," Krishnaji said.

I was not satisfied, and pursued the enquiry. "Can the person who comes to the teaching for the first time understand becoming, without seeing becoming as a movement in consciousness?"

"You are asking whether you have to go through school, college, before your final examination?" Krishnaji responded.

"I know you will say process is time. But I say it was total then as it is now. If you say that one can journey straight into holistic seeing as you showed us then, can you show us now?" I challenged Krishnaji.

Krishnaji asked, "Can one observe without the past? Can one have insight without the weight of yesterday? Insight is instantaneous. Perception of totality is an instant perception. If that is so, what is the need for preparation?" One could feel the tautness of the still mind. "Insight is possible only in the instant. The instant is not contained in time. X cannot see that. He says, 'Tell me what to do?' K says, 'Observe the thinker and the thought as one.' Is X listening, or is a process of abstraction taking place, which puts X away from instant perception?"

"You may deny the thirty years, but it is there. The mind that has listened for thirty years is capable of receiving what you say today."

Krishnaji asked, "What is listening? Why haven't people seen when this person says, 'Insant perception is totality?' "

"It is like asking you to 'give me insight,' " I responded.

"Nobody can give another insight. You ask, can you give it to me? What is your reaction to the statement, 'No time, no evolution can give it to you?' "

"Yes, that is so," I said.

"To that K says, 'Listen, nobody can give it to you.' If you listen, it must have a tremendous effect. Your whole attention is gathered in listening. In listening, there is no time."

"Do you think it is possible without delving, without enquiry, to so listen?" I asked.

Krishnaji was speaking with great urgency and passion. "Delving won't bring listening. What has happened to your mind when you listen? It means I have to abandon everything. The whole dependency I have cultivated for millennia."

"Do you say there has been no change in the teaching?" I asked.

"None at all," said Krishnaji.

There was silence in the room. "Has there been an inner change in you during these years?" I spoke with great hesitation. There was a long pause. Krishnaji appeared to be looking within, going deep into himself.

"Let me observe. I have never been asked this question. From the beginning or from thirty years has there been an inner change? No," Krishnaji said, "I think there has been no fundamental change. That is immobility."

For some time again there was silence. Then Krishnaji turned to his personal physician, Dr. Parchure, and G. Narayan and asked them, "What do you say to this statement that perception of the total is immediate? That time is not necessary. Preparation is not necessary. Do you ask, 'What am I to do? What is the next instruction?' To which the reply would be 'listen.' Have you listened accurately to that statement? Time, preparation, the whole process of evolution is unnecessary. If you so listen, you have the whole perception."

He turned to me. "So, Pupulji, the fact is, our whole attitude is based on evolution—becoming, growing, achieving, ultimately reaching. I think that basic assumption is radically false."

"I see the truth of that. I can listen to that without a ripple in consciousness," I said.

"If you so listen, what takes place?" Quietness flowed. Out of great depth, Krishnaji spoke. "What takes place if the Buddha says to me, 'Ending of sorrow is the bliss of compassion'? I am one of his audience. I don't examine this statement. I don't translate the statement into my way of thinking. I am only in a state of acute total attention of listening. There is nothing else. Because that statement has enormous truth, tremendous truth. That is enough. Then, I would ask the Buddha, 'I am not capable of that intense capacity of listening, so please help me,' and the response is, 'First listen to what I am saying. There is no outside agency that the mind or thought have invented.' But I am frightened, for I see it means giving up everything that I cling to. So, I ask, 'How am I to be detached?' The moment I say 'how,' I am lost. He says, 'Be detached,' but I am not listening. I have great reverence for him, but I am not listening. Because attachment has a tremendous place in my life. So, he says, 'Throw it out, throw it out, in one instant.' " He paused for a long time. "The moment you have perception into the fact you are free of the fact."

"Is it a question of seeing the totality of that statement of the Buddha, 'Be detached,' without the words?" I asked.

"Of course, the word is not the thing. The statement, the flowering is not the thing. There must be freedom from the word. Intensity of listening is the crux of it," Krishnaji said.

"What is it that gives one that intensity?" I probed.

"Nothing." The statement was absolute. "Our whole way of thinking is based on becoming, evolving. It has nothing whatsoever to do with enlightenment.

"The mind is heavily conditioned. It does not listen. K says something totally true. Something immovable, irrevocable, and it has tremendous weight, like a river with volumes of water behind it. But X does not listen to that extraordinary statement. You asked a question: 'Has there been a fundamental change in K from the 1930s, 1940s?'

"I say, no. There has been considerable change in expression. Now, if you are listening with intensity, then what takes place when a statement is made—that time, process, evolution, including knowledge— has to be abandoned. Will you listen to that? If you do, you are actually abandoning them. After all, listening, seeing totally, is like thunder or lightening that destroys everything. To go through the whole process is not to deny this instant thing."

"That's it—you have now said it."

"What?" asked Krishnaji.

"It means going through the whole thing, without denying the instancy," I said. "That doesn't mean time is involved."

"But man translates it as time," said Krishnaji.

The next day at Brockwood we discussed the possibility of defining his terms so that confusion did not arise amongst his listeners. Through the years many of his words had changed meaning. We began with the words consciousness, thought, brain, and mind. We discussed consciousness, and he asked, "How do you define it?" I said that consciousness was the sense of existing, of being. The sense that one "is." We then explored the relationship of thought to consciousness. "Thought is not concerned with the totality of consciousness, but with parts of it," Krishnaji said.

"But is it through thought that consciousness reveals itself? The part is revealed in the 'now' as the fragment," I responded.

"Does thought reveal the part? Thought is a fragment. Can thought, which is a fragment, see the whole of consciousness? 'I am hurt'—that feeling is a part of consciousness. Thought is a broken piece in movement. That fragment, that thought, cannot see the whole. Thought does not see it is hurt; it says, 'I am hurt.'" Krishnaji was elaborating.

"But that is a thought formation," I said.

"The name—the form—the environment are the structure of the 'I.' Thought does not say it is hurt."

"Who says it?" I queried.

"Look at it factually," said Krishnaji. "I am hurt—in explaining that hurt, thought thinks it is different from the structure it has built, which is hurt. Thought can never be aware of the total content of consciousness. It can only be aware of the fragment. What is the total content of consciousness? You say consciousness implies existence—what will give holistic meaning to consciousness?" Krishnaji asked.

"Has it a holistic meaning?"

"Consciousness is the totality of life. Not only my life, your life, but the life of the animal, the tree; the totality of all life," said Krishnaji.

"You are using the word consciousness very differently to what you said in the early 1950s."

"Yes, I am moving away from what I had said earlier," Krishnaji said.

"Is consciousness the totality of life?" I enquired again.

"I am feeling around. I am asking, is consciousness the totality of life? I think consciousness can be global, but it is still limited." Krishnaji was probing.

"What you say is very new. Can we pursue it? Consciousness is the totality of life. Is it different from my experience of life?"

"Your experience of life is the experience of every human being. It may have different colors, but it has the same direction. Your life is the life of man, of humanity, basically you are not different from mankind. Your consciousness is the consciousness of mankind. Mankind goes through travail—Doesn't everything go through travail—the animal, all nature?"

"Do you mean consciousness is the whole phenomenon of life—of existence?"

"What do you mean by phenomenon?" Krishnaji was still looking into the question.

"That which can be perceived by the senses."

"That is only part of it," said Krishnaji.

"What is the other part?" I asked.

"All accumulated knowledge, experience, the psychological agonies of man which you cannot touch or taste. Psychological turmoil, anxiety can affect the organism of man and plant. That is the process of mankind. It is global. It is the common fate of man."

"How can thought be aware of the totality of consciousness?"

Krishnaji paused to let the question sink in. "If thought cannot be aware, then what perceives the totality? There must come into operation a factor that sees the totality. If it is not thought—Is it the mind? Is it the brain cells?"

"As they exist today, the brain cells carry memory. The brain as it is, cannot perceive the totality of consciousness," I answered.

"As thought cannot see it. The movement of the brain cannot comprehend totality. Can the mind perceive totality? Then what is the mind? Pupulji, let us be more tactile. Find out whether there is a movement beyond consciousness. Do we understand the movement of thought as an activity of the brain? Is it that a part of the thinking within the brain fabricates a perception that is beyond this consciousness? I don't think it can see that as it is 'now.' " He paused. "What is the mind? Is the mind intellect? Part of it is, of course, the intellect. Can the intellect perceive?"

"Is intellect separate from thought?" I asked.

"It is not. Intellect is the most extraordinary thing we have. We worship the intellect, but can it perceive the totality of consciousness? The intellect is the product of thought. Can the mind perceive the totality?" Krishnaji was still probing.

"You are using mind as if it were an instrument. You say it can perceive. Is the mind an instrument or a field?"

"Is the mind the field? Is it the whole field—or part of the field?"

"Does the mind include intellect, and what part do the senses play?" I asked.

"I don't think emotions—sensation—can possibly bring about a perception of the whole."

"Would you rule out the place of the senses as such?"

"No, I don't rule them out."

"Are they being wrongly used?" I asked.

"When thought identifies itself with sensation, then it becomes the 'me,' " said Krishnaji. "You say the mind is the field, the matrix. A field circumscribes. The mind includes the brain, thought, emotion, intellect. Is time part of the field—part of the mind?" Krishnaji was extending the area of investigation. "If time is not part of my mind, is sensation part of mind?"

"Are we discussing senses identified with desire building up the structure of the self, or have the senses any other role?" I asked.

"Yes. I see the germ of what it is. To observe with all your senses— in that there is no identification. The question is, can you look with all your senses awakened?"

"Can you look and listen in one instant of time?" I asked. "Is it possible to observe with all your senses, and in that state is there any movement of thought at all?"

Krishnaji continued to probe as he questioned. "When there is movement of thought, then it is one particular sense operating. Can I find out if there is a totally different dimension? A state where consciousness as we know it ceases?"

"You have examined and negated all the known instruments we have. The only instrument you do not negate is the movement of the sensory."

"How can I negate the senses?" Krishnaji spoke.

"It is the senses that may have the capacity to be free from illusion."

"This is only possible when the sensory as identification with thought is understood. Then the senses do not produce the psychological structure, as the 'me.' The movement of thought, emotions, as fear, hate, attachment, are going on in the brain endlessly. We want to bring about order in it. What instrument or quality is necessary to move out of this enchaining circle of consciousness?" Krishnaji asked.

"The last question is very valid."

"I am trying to convey that there must be total order for the cosmic to be. I see that there is total disorder in everyday life. Order is necessary. What will bring order?"

"There is only one instrument which has a possibility of being free of taint."

"The senses?" asked Krishnaji.

"Otherwise you have blocked every instrument the brain has."

"Have we not also blocked the senses?" asked Krishnaji.

My daughter Radhika had been abroad since 1957—first as a student and, after her marriage, as a resident in the United States and later in Toronto, Canada. Her roots were deep in India and in Krishnaji's teaching, whom she had listened to from the age of ten. The essence of what he had said had been held within her through the years with a simplicity and a childlike quality. She had occasional meetings with Krishnaji in India and the United States, but in a gesture of self-protection she had kept away from him, to conserve the way of life to which she was committed. Married to a professor, she had lived in a world of scholarship and books. But, deep within her, she was aware of the mediocrity of her life and values; an immense nostalgia for the luminosity which she was letting go by was deep within her.

In December 1978 she came with her two daughters to Rishi Valley to be with Krishnaji, and returned in the winter of 1979. She met Krishnaji several times; he overwhelmed her by his attention and she was profoundly moved by his presence.

In 1980 and 1981 her husband, Hans Herzberger, accompanied her to India, and she lived and taught in Rishi Valley. It was during this period that she discussed with Krishnaji the possibility of her return to India and to Rishi Valley. I kept out of the talks, as I did not wish my attachment to her to cloud her decision. Her husband, comprehending the goodness in Radhika and sensitive to the atmosphere that emanated from Rishi Valley, agreed to work on the modalities of her coming to India. Krishnaji did not influence her, but spoke to her at length of her life and the teaching. Radhika and her family went from Rishi Valley to Oxford, where her husband was a visiting Fellow at All Souls College. She visited Brockwood Park several times, meeting Krishnaji. Her decision to return to India was firm. By the spring of 1982 she had completed her Ph.D. in Sanskrit and Buddhist Studies, and by the autumn of 1982 she was in Rishi Valley. Her husband had come to an arrangement with his university to teach for one term and to spend the second term doing research in his own field, which was philosophy.

In the last four years a number of young, highly qualified people have joined the schools—Rishi Valley; the Valley School in Bangalore; Rajghat Varanasi; The School in Madras; and Bal Anand, the school for underprivileged children in Bombay, which Nandini has run for the last thirty years. A new awakening is evident.

# CHAPTER 33

# "Energy Is Cosmos, It Is Also Chaos. That Is the Source of Creation."

Krishnaji returned alone to India in early November 1979. We were at the threshold of a pivotal decade. In the 1980s the world was to change traumatically. A revolution was taking place in the environment and in the minds of humankind. The search for artificial intelligence was soon to become a central concern of technological research; microchips would become cheap to produce, leading to a revolution in communications; genetic engineering and cloning were to make rapid advances, clouding the future of man, yet promising great benefits to mankind. The tools for untold good or evil were available.

I joined Krishnaji in Madras. Asit Chandmal was there, so were the Patwardhans, Radha Burnier, and Ahalya Chari, a well-known educator who left her government post in the 1970s to join the Krishnamurti Foundation. The instant we saw Krishnaji we felt the power of his presence and the endless energy flowing from him. His mind appeared to have weight and density and an immense immobility. I had seen the emphasis of his teaching change over the years. The urgency had shifted from individual transformation, to the questioning of the fact of individuality, and a positing of a stream of human consciousness in which deep revolution had to take place. To him the individual was one who stepped out of the stream.

Now perception had swept aside all limitations, to include the universe and its boundless energy.

Even though he had flown nonstop from London via Delhi to Madras, he did not appear fatigued, but was eager to begin discussions with us. That afternoon at lunch, we started to talk.

The question posed was, "What is the one thing I would demand, seeing the degeneration in India? Is it possible to help? What is the central thing?" The conversation then moved around the table to an identification of the problem. Krishnaji said, "India has lived all these centuries on ideas. She has to move from a life based on ideas, which are non-facts, to seeing of fact only." He then asked, "How did this boy get it?" We saw that there was no point in giving explanations. The weight and density of the question was meant to be held in the mind without the mind searching for solution.

Krishnaji was questioning the problem of India; but the atmosphere became so charged that one saw that India was oneself, and that he was addressing the question to each one who listened. For "you" were India.

By November 28, 1979, we were in Rishi Valley. Radha Burnier had come from Madras to spend a few days with us. Krishnaji at breakfast one morning asked Radha Burnier whether she was standing for president of the Theosophical Society. She said she did not know. He said, "What do you mean by you do not know?"

Suddenly, the atmosphere grew charged with a new energy. Krishnaji said, "Mrs. Besant intended the land at Adyar to be meant for the teaching. The Theosophical Society has failed, the original purpose is destroyed." He spoke of the true religious spirit that probed, questioned, and negated. He said America had not got it. Europe had not got it. In India it has been wiped out and destroyed. Yet it was there in India, waiting in the soil. "Can we do something about it?" he asked.

For the first time the emphasis was not on the individual, but on land, the earth—the physical land of India and the sacredness of it and the capacity for it to hold the source of creation. It was as if Krishnaji had found something precious; there was great joyousness in him, as if the long-awaited time had come. We hardly spoke. He turned to us, searching for confirmation. "Pupulji," he questioned "what do you feel?" When I said that this was a new mystique, he did not deny it. Later he again spoke of the Theosophical Society and of Radha Burnier becoming president. I asked him, "At one point you say that Radha is deeply in the Krishnamurti Foundation, at another point you say that she should stand for presidentship of the Theosophical Society. How do you reconcile these two statements?"

He said, "I can say it, others can't." He repeated, "I can say anything." It reminded me of the verse from *Brihadaranyaka Upanishad* which, speaking of the illumined one, says, "Therefore let a Brahmana after he has done with learning, desire to live as a child. When he has done with the state of childhood and with learning then he becomes the silent meditator. Having done with the meditative and nonmeditative states then he becomes a Brahmana. However he behaves he is such indeed."

Krishnaji went on to speak of India as the ground on which the sacred could flower, though it has been destroyed by the ugliness of politics, corruption, and destruction of values. India was the ground where the seed had been sown. In spite of all that had happened, the ground was still there. He said he felt something was waiting. I asked if the ground he spoke of was physical ground, or did he mean something else? He said he meant the earth and the sacredness of it. He felt that this ground had been prepared.

The atmosphere was pulsating, strong, alive. At one point he said, "They found me two angels—I have gathered many more through the years." He was laughing; there was great laughter, and in between he kept on saying, "I am very serious." He had not laughed like this in years. "Now I find that I can do without some of them." He turned to Radha and said, "Can I give you two?" He was laughing, joyous, but deeply serious, suggesting something.

He said many people had told him not to come to India. He had always felt the sacredness of the land and had loved to come. Something had been destroyed in India, but a presence waited in the land. "The benediction of the timeless is waiting, the ground is ready. Can we create something that is of this benediction?"

What came through was a depth and immensity. It was a prophecy that a sacred energy was alive again in the Indian soil.

Every morning at the breakfast table, questions were asked and insight flowed. We probed, paused, questioned. Krishnaji's mind was immense and charged with mystery. One morning, speaking with great intensity, Krishnaji conveyed a way of perception, of challenge and response from a state that lay beyond the mind, beyond brain, memory, all responses of consciousness. "A state that comes into being in listening at great depth; where consciousness and its movement do not obstruct. A state where seeing is whole, inclusive, nonfragmented, a state of no movement from or towards; beyond matrix and all racial memories of man." Krishnaji also spoke of mind which comes into being when there is complete trust. This was only possible when the mind had shed all burdens, was free. "This state is not a state of the ending of thought," said Krishnaji. "It is not the gap between thoughts, but a listening that has the whole weight and depth of the million years of man, and goes beyond. A state that can be touched at any instant. It is like tapping the energy of the universe."

We spoke of the place of the guru and whether the role of the guru had validity. I said to Krishnaji that, looking back from today to the many yesterdays, I saw clearly that for me Krishnaji was the guru. Krishnaji intervened and asked, "What do you mean by guru?" Radha Burnier said, "He who points the way." There were other comments. I said, "He who awakens. Krishnaji awakened me. There was an eye into eye looking. Such looking is rare." I asked, "What was your role in 1948—did you not awaken?" Krishnaji said, "The approach of the awakener and the awakened is wrong. When there is light and I am in darkness and move into the light there is no separation. There is just light. Where is the awakener? Some stay in the light, some wander away, that is all." A little later he said, "I am not saying I am the light."

Another morning at breakfast we discussed the brain and the possibility of transformation of the human brain. Krishnaji said he had been discussing the brain with scientists. He had understood them to say that "every cell in the human brain holds memory of the million years of man." Then Krishnaji asked, "Can there be a total transformation in that?"

As discussions continued, Krishnaji's concern with the brain and its operation was evident. His perception had shifted to an enquiry into whether the movement of memory within the brain cells could end. It was only then that a whole new way of perception could emerge.

Someone asked whether Krishnaji's touch and contact could release energy held in an object, and in turn could that object communicate wholeness, sacredness? Could it heal, protect? Krishnaji said from boyhood he could read other people's thoughts, heal people. He had been given objects to magnetize, to make potent with energy. But the boy Krishnamurti was not interested in these powers.

He spoke of an immense reservoir of energy which must exist. "Can man reach it and let it operate?" he asked. Asit said, "Surely a boy who had no evil in him, no self, was a very rare being; he could touch it, but could that energy be contacted by ordinary beings?"

"I think it is possible, Sir," Krishnaji said with heistancy.

Krishnaji was in a very strange state. He spoke of an approach to the sacred with a mind that could receive, but did not want power, position. What was necessary was an absolute purity of mind.

I asked whether anything else was necessary, and asked him the nature of this purity of mind. Krishnaji said, "The purity of my mind is not the purity of 'the mind.' The purity of *the mind* is the mind of the universe. That is sacred." I then asked whether the human being who had purity of mind, was a vessel that could receive. "As it is possible to give energy to an object, can a human being communicate wholeness, can you give the other?"

Krishnaji said, "No. However pure, the brain is still matter, it is still mind. The other is the universe. It is immense."

Krishnaji refused to be caught in discussion. He asked himself, "Is there an ultimate beyond which there is nothing? A ground from which everything is, behind and beyond which there is nothing, no cause?"

We then discussed the sacredness of Rishi Valley. I said in India there was such a thing as a *Punya Sthal*—a sacred site. Gods could come and go, but the sacredness of a site continued.

Krishnaji said, "I feel the soil of Rishi Valley has this special quality. It is," he said gravely, " 'the *Sthal* of all *Sthals*.' "

I said the whole valley was a sacred site. It had been impregnated with Krishnaji's presence and his words. Rajghat also had that sense of the sacredness. "One has to see," said Krishnaji, "that this feeling is not destroyed."

Krishnaji said he was greatly tempted to stay on in Rishi Valley. He felt strongly about it. Asit asked Krishnaji why he could not live in Rishi Valley and let people come to see him there from all over the world.

Krishnaji was quiet, then said, "My life has been one of physical movement. It is important for me to stay here, but I cannot. For God's sake, tread lightly on this soil."

Later, Krishnaji was to say, "Energy is cosmos, it is also chaos. That is the source of creation. Anger is energy, sorrow is energy—but there is supreme order. Can it be established in Rishi Valley?"

# CHAPTER 34

# Negation and
# the Ancient Mind

In January 1980 Krishnaji held a discussion at Vasant Vihar with friends who had been closely associated with him for several years. We spoke of the Rishi Valley School and its students and what needed to be done there. Suddenly, the quality of the discussion was transformed, an urgency and passion arose in Krishnaji's questions. Speaking with the purity of fire, Krishnaji's words burned away the accretions that clouded the mind. He spoke of a total negation of all that man had thought, said, or done.

It started with a simple query: "How is Narayan actually going to help the students—not just talk to them, but to awaken intelligence, to communicate what it is to penetrate at great depth?"

Narayan replied, "I am going to meet them every day in smaller groups, both teachers and students." He knew this would not satisfy Krishnaji, but there was nothing else he could say.

"How will you do it? Merely talking to them or having discussions is not going to bring this about. How will you make them sensitive, alert?"

"There has to be a basic order and sensitivity." Narayan continued to hedge.

Krishnaji kept on probing. "There has to be a different element in it all. There has to be a brain that is extraordinarily good. But that is not enough. What is necessary is to bring about a genius. The demand is that there has to be good brain, capable of sustained argument; a human being who has great affection, love. Apart from all this, there must be in him something totally unworldly. How did K happen to get it? Do you understand my question?"

"You have asked this question several times. But I have never understood the relevance of it. It is not known how Krishnaji came upon it, but how can it happen to some of us?" I intervened.

"Is K a biological freak?" Krishnaji continued his questioning.

"I can't answer that," I said. "It may be so. I find that you are questioning and pushing much deeper. Is it that you have reached a new milestone in your teachings? You used to say, 'If you are traveling south, can you change direction and travel north?' Now you ask, 'Can the mind of Narayan, the mind of Sunanda, be basically in the same state as Krishnaji's mind?' " I countered.

Krishnaji continued his enquiry. "Can we give a boy or a girl a sense of freedom, the feeling that they are 'protected'? That they have a special role in life, that they are special human beings? I am trying to find out, Pupul, what is the catalyst, what is the thing that changes the whole mind, the whole brain?

"I am asking, can there be a quality of otherness? Can there be the other dimension so that the mind is quick, the brain is quick, the senses are alert? So that there is never a point at which the brain rests, but is moving, moving, moving? I would like the student to have such a movement. I would discuss with him. I would walk with him, sit silently with him. I would do physically anything to kindle this thing in him. But will he move? Or is the material, the brain material itself, so slow that it cannot follow quickly, run quickly? Is it possible for Narayan, who is a student at Rishi Valley, to be an extraordinary being so that he is aware of the trees, the feeling of the earth, and also have a brain that is extraordinarily quick? Can he listen to something that is true? Can there be a breakthrough so that there is a sense of vitality, energy, drive? I would like him to have it, and I say to myself, what shall I do and can I do something for him to have this?"

Again he was quiet, and then asked, "Is it in my hands at all? Or is it that a door needs to be opened by both of us? A door which is not his door or my door, but the door has to be opened. I have a feeling that there is something waiting to enter, a Holy Ghost is waiting; the thing is waiting for you to open the door, and it will come. I don't know if I am conveying anything?

"So I say, Narayan, do all those things. Sit quietly, see how you behave, how you look at a tree, at a woman, go through all that. But that is not enough. There is a sense of benediction waiting, and we are not moving towards it. We are all fussing around, sitting around. What you are doing is necessary, but it is not enough."

Rajesh interrupted. "What is the state of the mind which realizes that what it does is not enough?"

"It is obvious, Sir. Millions have meditated. The Catholic monks, the *sannyasis* have meditated, but they have not brought benediction.

"Now, what can I do in my relationship to Narayan? He is my student. He is willing to do all the things I speak about—to observe, be silent, talk, read, look around, feel the beauty of the earth. But there is another quality which is demanding something, and that demand is not to be found in his talking, discussing, seeing. And the benediction does not enter."

The intensity in each one of us had deepened. Narayan asked, "When you say the door has to be opened, can you say what it is?"

"I am deeply concerned that this should happen to Narayan," said Krishnaji, "and I ask what am I to do to precipitate this thing?"

"Perhaps there is something from our side which is blocking us. There is an inexpressible quality, a boundless quality in you, and I feel that we are not putting out our hands," Achyut said.

"You do put out your hands, but it is not taking place. It may be we are condemned, and so it is only for the very, very few. With the Buddha there were only two after fifty years—Sariputta and Mogallanna—that may be the lot of man," Krishnaji mused.

"Is there any quality of renunciation necessary?" asked Achyut.

"I don't think it has anything to do with renunciation. Man has starved; sat alone in the mountains; he has done everything to have that something; but apparently it does not happen that way. So I say perhaps he should go quickly through with this watching, observing silence, and end it. And I ask, what is the most important thing? Is it energy? The missionary has immense energy when he goes around preaching, and yet this thing is not there." Krishnaji was questioning himself deeply.

"Is it my passion that can transform Narayan? If Narayan stayed with me, listened to all the discussions, pushing, challenging all the time within himself, would that do something? You understand?" Again he paused and was silent. Then, from a vast depth, he said, "Or has there to be the negating of everything, the role of the *sannyasi*, the monk who keeps silence right through his life, who sits by himself; has all that to be dropped? Can you deny all that?

"For centuries man has struggled, and yet the other thing has not happened. And can Narayan say, 'I see all that and I won't touch it. It is finished'?" Suddenly, there was an immense quickening. "I am the saint; I am the monk; I am the man who says, I will fast, I will torture myself physically, I will deny all sex; I am that man. I say I have finished with all that, but I am all that because my mind is the human mind which has experimented with all that and yet has not come upon this benediction. Therefore I won't touch all that. It is out.

"Are you following? Can you do this? Do you understand what I am saying, Rajesh?"

"I am just listening."

"That is not good enough. I don't have to sit quietly the rest of my life. The Trappist monks have done that, why should I do it? I see the saints, the people who starve, who torture themselves, who study great books, who meditate; I see that I am all that. Because they have done it, my brain is part of that doing. Therefore I have done it, I don't have to go through it all." The awakened insight was probing.

"Is it possible to negate it with the same urgency as the man who studies, takes vows? Is it with the same urgency you see this and negate it? But after negating it, does urgency rest?"

"It may be, Sir, when we negate, we are also negating the urgency.

"What remains at the end of negation?" I asked.

"I see your point. I see everything. Man has seen and done everything from the beginning of time. He has done everything to get this blessedness, the unnameable. I see it in front of me and I cannot go near it. I can't do anything about it." Krishnaji was immovable.

"You have also through these years spoken of self-knowledge, of the flowering of 'what is.' You have said watch, examine, investigate. You now seem to be getting to a point of negating all that."

With intense passion and urgency Krishnaji said, "I have negated. I see that all that does not lead anywhere. You understand what I have done? I have negated everything man has done, toward reaching that. Do you follow what I am saying? And I say to myself, can Narayan do this? He is my student in Rishi Valley and I ask, can he do it?

"Does that negation indicate a maturity, a tremendous maturity? Is it real maturity to say that all the things man has done have not brought about benediction and so I am not going to go through it all?

"Is that what is missing? Is it the sense of great maturity without going through all that?

"I see the gurus and the immaturity which goes with them. I see that I should not follow. But seeing that, do I settle down and begin to go downhill? Do I become sluggish or lazy?

"The man who says, 'I have tried all this and negated,' he is moving. If you do not move or move in a narrow circle and spend your time comparing what K says with what the Buddha says, at the end of that, what is left?

"We have to deny knowledge, deny everything.

"Narayan, my student at Rishi Valley, can I show you this act of total denial?"

"Does that mean I deny you? Look at what you are saying." I could not help interrupting.

"Yes, you have to deny me," was Krishnaji's response. "What I say is, you cannot deny truth, but you have to deny everything else. I deny everything that man has sought, to get this. I deny the saint who has tortured himself, the Trappist monks who have kept absolute silence. They have done everything in the exercise of that and I deny what they have done. Can you so deny? Is it the lack of a total denial the reason why the door is not open?"

"In my younger days, when you broke away from the order and you said truth is pathless, I really felt very confused. I am getting the same feeling now because I feel that no path will lead to it," lamented Achyut.

"We started by asking whether the teachers of Rishi Valley, Rajghat, could communicate with students and help them to be awake. Narayan said he would discuss with them, talk with them in small numbers. If necessary, he would sit silent with them, watch birds, be sensitive. But I see it does not bring that perfume. See what the monks and other human beings have done to get this extraordinary intelligence, and they have not got it. So why should we go through it? So I deny all the things that man has tried to do, to get it. So my mind, my brain, is free from experiment." Krishnaji was opening the windows of his mind. "I think that is the clue. These people have experimented for years in forests, but they have not got it. Why should I go through all that?"

"What you are saying is, the mind has to be in a state of no direction in which to turn, no enquiry which thought has pursued," I said.

"In that state, see what the brain is. It is no longer in a state of experimentation or investigation." He was speaking, but there was no movement away from the depth and passion of the perception. "People have investigated and they have all failed. They have tried getting drunk, tried sex, tried drugs. I see all that. Why should I go through all that? So I see and I deny. It is not blind denial. The denial has tremendous reason, logic behind it. Right? And so my mind, the brain, is totally mature. Do you follow what I am saying? Are you in that state? Please answer me. This is a challenge. You have to answer. Are you still experimenting?" He paused.

"In this denial I include the Theosophists with their hierarchy, with their Masters. I am through with all that.

"Is it that total denial that is necessary to help the boy, the student to see and jump out of it? Then the brain is absolutely steadfast, because it is not looking in any direction. It has turned its back completely on all direction. What do you say, Narayan? You are my student in Rishi Valley."

"The lack of strength of the body and the mind creeps in," said Narayan.

Krishnaji said, "I am eighty-five and I say, you have to deny. For centuries man has said he must control his body, see that it does not interfere. Can you deny all that? If you cannot so deny, I say to you, why can't you deny?"

"Do you come back to knowledge, discussion, etc.?" Narayan was dodging, unable to face the absolute negation. Krishnaji said, "That is a triviality. My concern is to see that the student does not go through with all this struggle. That the mind is mature, alive. Can I do this with ten boys or girls? You are then bringing about a group of boys and girls who are totally different."

"How does one meet all the problems of adolescence?" Again Narayan was trying to move away.

Krishnaji said, "A boy who is with us from the age of five suddenly changes when he is thirteen or so. I want to prevent that. I am going to find out what happens. I want to prevent the coarsening."

"No educator has done this," was Narayan's comment.

Krishnaji said, "I am going to deny all educators. I want to find out. Is it puberty, sex? Is it a sense of manhood that makes him coarse? You can see the transformation at that period of his life. I want to prevent it. I think you can prevent it. You can see to it that physically he matures very very slowly."

"What does that mean?" asked Rajesh.

"Don't you know what it means? Why is it that a boy or a girl, up to a certain age, has a sense of lightness and then becomes coarse? Is it the physical organism which is concerned with procreation? Is it that which causes the change? If it is so, can that take place much later in life? Narayan, I am sorry to bully you. But can you deny all that you know?"

"I would still study."

Krishnaji said, "Study. But you know at the end of forty years, you are where you are, right? Study, practice abstinence, celibacy, take vows; do all that, but it does not lead you anywhere. Why should I go through all that? I am part of the human being who has done all that."

"I feel, Sir, that all these things have limited effects. They will not lead me to that. I take exercise, etcetera, but they don't lead to that," Achyut commented. He continued, "You look after your body with vigilance. There is a balance. By denial I understand that there is negation, but all that has a place. There is great diligence."

Achyut was attempting to diffuse the gathered energy. But Krishnaji was immovable. "That diligence does not come through any of this. My brain is the brain of humanity. I am absolutely certain of that. So, being the brain of humanity, my brain has done all this. I don't have to go through it all. Do you know what that means?"

The *Vedas* speak of the great teacher taking his disciple within himself, as an embryo. For three nights holding him in the darkness of the within, the gods gather to witness the birth. Krishnaji was in a sense doing that with us, drawing close the people sitting around him, enabling their minds to directly touch his mind, all division was ending. Krishnaji said, "I think we are opening the door slightly. Do you see what we are doing? Move. This chapter has not been studied so far. K has not gone through all these disciplines. Why should he?"

"Where do you get your perceptions?" asked Narayan.

Krishnaji said, "By not doing any of this."

"By not doing will I get it?" asked Narayan.

Krishnaji's voice came from depth, it was held in eons. "No. The brain itself says that it is so old, and that brain says it won't remain with knowledge. Do you see what has happened to this brain? It is like an immovable rock. It is steadfast, which does not mean that it is stagnant. It is not going to sleep. Do you see what happens to a brain that says, 'I am humanity, and what humanity has done, I have done'? And I see that it does not produce benediction and therefore all that has been done, has no meaning." There was a long pause. Krishnaji said, "Is there a clue in all this? See what has happened to the brain. It has moved out of its circle. Do it now. Move out of that circle which man has woven around himself.

"Now, can you do this to the student? Will you create something, a school that has never existed before?"

A few days later Krishnaji took me to his room and said to me, "I have been wanting to tell you something. At Rishi Valley a strange thing happened. One night I awoke feeling the whole universe converge into me. An entering of everything and the traveling deeper and deeper into a depth without end." His face was immensely serious as he spoke, luminous with light.

# CHAPTER 35

# "One Touched the Source of the Energy of All Things."

From the moment Krishnaji came to Bombay, he was afire and communicated his intensity. Relentless in his questioning, at breakfast one morning he asked, "Is it possible for the brain, which is memory, completely to be free of memory? Is there in the brain a faculty capable of totally transforming itself? What happens when you hear a question of this nature?" He kept silent for some time, and our minds too grew silent.

"Is the mind of man deteriorating because it is a millennia of tradition and memory?" There was an intense silence and a receding of Krishnaji's consciousness to vast depths, and it is from this depth that he spoke. "Is there a faculty in the brain which can change the nature and structure of the brain so that it frees itself of the past, so that it is alive and new?

"Since Rishi Valley—and I am not saying this is any personal sense and not exaggerating—every night the brain has been 'breaking' and entering into something immense. I have been watching this, as if I were watching an operation on someone else."

Aware of the immensity that rested in Krishnaji, I asked him if he would meditate aloud. He agreed. This took place at Sterling Apartments, Bombay, toward the end of January 1980.

"The last four months or so, there has been a peculiar activity going on, as though the brain was being washed out—a purgation taking place—and I wondered what it was about. Recently, when I was in Rishi Valley, a peculiar thing happened. For several nights, one actually touched the source of the energy of all things. It was an extraordinary feeling; not from the mind or brain, but from the source itself. And that has been going on, in Madras and here. It is as though one was totally isolated—if one can so use that word without a sense of withdrawal. There was a sense of nothing existing except 'that.' That source or feeling was a state in which the mind, the brain, was no longer in operation—only that source was in operation. This may sound odd and crazy, but it is not. I said to myself that I must watch carefully whether I am deceiving myself or am caught in illusion, a desire for that which began and the desire wanting to multiply it, change it. I have been watching very carefully to see that desire does not enter into it at all. Because the moment desire enters, it becomes a remembrance and the energy is gone, the original thing is gone. So I am extremely careful to see that that thing remains pure. The word pure means clear, unspotted, not corrupted. It is like pure water, distilled water, a mountain stream which has never been touched by human mind or hand.

"I have been very careful about this. I have found recently that the brain is losing—I must be very careful how I put this—losing its own volition, its own activity. Just listen for a minute. I do not know whether it is common to the lot of man, that for as many years as I recollect, I go for a walk for three or four hours and there is not a single thought in that time. This is not an invention, this is not a wish product. And 'that' has been going on, when I go for a walk it is always there.

"The mind, the brain, is so accustomed to remembrance, to experience, knowledge, memory. It has to find its own tranquility . . . so that the origin, the beginning is not interfered with. The words in the Bible and other religious books of the East are that the beginning was chaos and out of that chaos came order. I think it is the other way. I may be wrong, but the beginning was order. Man made chaos. Because creation cannot be chaos. *Chaos* means disorder, and Genesis says there was chaos, darkness; out of that chaos God created order. I am sure that is not so. There must have been total order; the earthquakes, the upheavals, the volcanoes, were all order. I think we have lost that sense of total, complete, original, blessed order. We have lost it, and the darkness of chaos has been created by man.

"It is not that the beginning was chaos. That is impossible. Even if there is God—I am using God in the ordinary sense of the word—and he created original chaos and out of that created order, the origin must have been order. It could not be disorder and out of that to create order. The beginning must be order. And man called it chaos and out of that man brought about tremendous disorder.

"Now he seeks to go back to that origin, that order. That state must be something of immense benediction, an immense, timeless, incorruptible state, otherwise it is not order.

"So can man get back to that?

"It can never be experienced. Because experience implies recognition, remembrance. It is not a thing that you go through as 'I remember.' 'This' is outside the realm of all experience, outside all knowledge, totally beyond all man's endeavor.

"But man is left with his senses, and his desires and the vast accumulation of knowledge gathered in the brain.

"So, the question is, can one wipe out the tremendous accumulation of a million years?

"I think it is possible when all the senses are totally awake and excellent. Then there is no center from which an experience can take place. As long as there is a center there must be experience and knowledge. When there is no center, there is a state of nonexperience, a state of observation, when all the senses are highly awakened and functioning, superbly sensitive, then in that state, there is no center as the 'me' involved. It is this center as the 'me' that creates desire. This state, this center, cannot reach that state—the beginning.

"Man cannot aspire or sacrifice or discipline to reach anywhere near it. So what is he to do? It is very important to understand desire. If that is not completely understood, the subtlety of desire is immense and therefore it has extraordinary, immense possibilities of illusion.

"Desire, will, time, must come to a complete end. That is, the mind, the brain, must be absolutely pure—not pure as no sex, no ugly thoughts—but the brain must be completely empty of knowledge. A state where thought can never arise—unless necessary. So that thought has its own responsibility, so that it can only act in certain directions.

"A brain that is free from all experience, and therefore knowledge, is not in the field of time, therefore has come to the beginning of all things. You cannot explain all this to people. But they should listen to it—you follow?"

"You have said the senses are not evil—but the senses create knowledge?" asked Achyut.

Sunanda wondered, "What is the relationship between the state of the mind and that?"

"This cannot go to that, that which is non-time. The mind which is free from all experience, a mind that has never experienced—is like a vessel, it can receive that. But this cannot go to that."

"What is the relationship between the vessel and 'that'?" asked Sunanda.

"None. What are you talking about?" Krishnaji was in a state of exaltation. "Desire of the senses—desire that comes from the center has to be completely emptied. There is no movement towards 'that' which means an end to time. Any movement in any direction is time. Man has made great struggle to reach that. It is not possible. Desire which is so subtle and therefore the creator of illusion, must end. The brain has to be free of desire. There can be no pattern, no direction, no volition, no desire."

We had touched something, and I spoke. "That is creation. There is no 'has been' in that. There is only beginning. There is only the state of beginning."

"Ah, wait—watch it carefully. There is always a state of beginning, watch it, watch it Pupulji, remain there. When you say this, what does it mean to the people who listen to you?" Krishnaji's mind was feeling around.

"What are the implications of this? The ending is always the beginning? Right? What does it mean?" asked Asit.

"It means the ending of attachment. That is the beginning. Look, Sir, with the ending of a problem, the mind is empty. To have no problem, at all, is to have no experience. But I am an ordinary man. I have all kinds of fears, desires, I carry them all my life and I never say—can I end one thing? Attachment, jealousy."

"The mind is still full of thought," said Asit.

"The mind is full of thought because the senses are not fully flowering. The senses create thought. Senses create experience, which is knowledge, memory—thought. When the senses are fully flowering, what happens? There is no center as desire," said Krishnaji.

"What are the implications of that in my daily life?" Asit queried.

Krishnaji replied, "In your daily life, your main concern is whether your senses can flower. All your senses, not just sex, not just eyesight, not just hearing with the ear. Can you look at a woman, with all your senses? Then you lose the center; experience does not exist. Right?"

"What interferes in the flowering of the senses?" again Asit asked.

"There is nothing that interferes. We have never allowed the senses to flower. We have operated with thought as the medium of action. But we have not enquired into the origin of thought deeply. If I had no senses I would be a piece of rock, with vibrations, or a mass of flesh. But the moment the senses begin comes appetite, sex—I start moving in a narrow groove. You have to go into that deeply so that all the senses are operating. Tradition denies the senses—therefore there is always . . . "

Asit interrupted. "If I may ask what is the relationship between a piece of rock that has no senses, to all my senses operating? Rocks have no senses."

"I am not so sure that rocks have no senses—matter is merely the wheel of energy," said Krishnaji.

"Is it a question of the entering of this limitless energy? A question of the amount that can enter into rock, or the senses that are half awakened or fully awakened? Is the limitless energy always there to enter? Is it the amount that can be received that makes the difference?" asked Asit.

"My concern is to find if my senses can flower because from that everything arises," said Krishnaji.

Asit pushed further. "Do the senses become dull because of lack of attention?"

"You are not aware of the senses. You are the senses. All the associations that have become strengthened become tremendous. Is love a movement of the senses?" asked Krishnaji.

"Does attention awaken the senses?" asked Asit.

"Attention means care, responsibility, affection, no motive," Krishnaji pointed.

"So daily life," said Asit.

"When problems arise—totality of senses not operating. When the senses are awakened and there is no center, there is a beginning and an ending.

"Psychological problems do not exist in the state of no center. Don't say 'I must be aware'; then you are lost. Yesterday, when we were walking, you were telling me of the computer. The brain was listening, it didn't record. There was a sense of a pouring out, something pouring down to the brain. When something is actually taking place there is no feeling; when there is actually fear, there is no feeling. Fear arises a second after. The moment you are not apprehending there is fear," said Krishnaji.

"There must be something in that state," Asit persisted.

"This cannot be answered," said Krishnaji.

"Is there a complete renewal?" asked Asit.

"A renewal of the brain? Yes, the brain cells are cleansed. They don't carry ancient memory," said Krishnaji.

"Your brain does not carry any ancient memory? The million years are wiped away?" I asked.

"Otherwise there is only darkness," said Krishnaji.

Days later, when we were at the breakfast table, I asked whether Krishnaji was pointing to a new use of the senses. When the senses are fully flowering, in a state of simultaneity, the center ceases. I asked him whether in this state the thrust of the "I" consciousness, which gives direction to the mind, dissolves? This wholeness of sensory intelligence negated the dividing line of outer and inner, the yesterday and tomorrow.

"See it, Pupulji, see it," Krishnaji said. "There is only being and beginning."

In the days that followed Krishnaji spoke again and again of that which lies beyond creation itself. He said, "Order is the beginning, the source of an energy that can never diminish. To investigate it there must be an investigation of the senses and desire. That blessedness of order is when the mind does not have a single desire and the senses are operating fully, totally." I asked Krishnaji whether he was saying essentially the same as he had said in previous years, but using new words; or were these insights entirely different? He said, "This is entirely different."

I observed from Rishi Valley and Madras that, when he spoke of the seed, the millennia-old brain of man, the beginning, creation, his face changed.

# CHAPTER 36

# "Doubt as the Essence of Religious Enquiry"

On the way from London to Colombo on November 1, 1980, Krishnaji came to Madras accompanied by Mary Zimbalist. Their luggage had been misrouted, and Mary Zimbalist was left with only the overnight bag she carried with her. Krishnaji was distressed for Mary, concerned about her, and his frail body appeared agitated. That evening he did not go to the beach, but walked on the circular path that goes around Vasant Vihar.

The next morning a significant discussion took place over the breakfast table, which revealed insights into his relentless questioning. Krishnaji's question that day was whether the Indian mind was degenerating. Achyut spoke of a meeting Krishnaji had with Jawaharlal Nehru and Acharya Kripalani in 1931, at which he had been present. Achyut said, "Nehru and Kripalani* felt that it was essential for India to be politically free before a regeneration in the Indian mind could take place." Krishnaji had said that if they ignored inner regeneration in the struggle for Independence, India would lose its way. Nehru was young; his alert and attentive mind understood the importance of regeneration, but felt that political freedom had to be, for the Indian mind to flower; to have the space in which it could enquire. At the time Achyut had agreed with Nehru.

But Krishnaji's response to Nehru was that India had stood for the religious spirit throughout history. "Buddhism spread from India to China, Japan, the whole of the East and Far East. What is the rela-

---

*A prominent member of the Congress Party and President of the Indian National Congress for several years, Kripalani was a senior leader in the freedom struggle against British rule.

tionship of that religious core of India to the world today?" he had asked Jawaharlal Nehru.

Achyut had been speaking with deep emotion. Krishnaji had listened quietly to what Achyut said, then turned to us and asked, "Is the core alive? The Western world, the Christian world, had a religious core that rested on faith. In India at the heart of religion was the denial of everything but 'that.' Now is that religious core, the seed, disappearing? If it still exists, what is its response to the West and its values?"

Krishnaji said to Achyut, "You spoke of this country having a different soil. The ancients used the word *Tat* or *Brahman* to express it. In ancient times religion was not based on caste or ritual. This concern with the core had lead to a different way of life. Now, is it possible for the seed that has laid dormant in the soil for centuries to awaken?"

"It is the seed awakening that is life, and that responds—the flowering of the seed is the response," I said, then went on to speak of my recent visit to Varanasi some weeks earlier. I had discussed Krishnaji and the teaching with Pandit Jagannath Upadhyaya. A Mahayana scholar in the Nagarjuna tradition, he had participated in discussions with Krishnaji. He had said, "We have to understand the dialectics of Krishnamurti, but the core of Krishnaji is beauty, a total overflowing of Being." Then he said many of his comrades, anguished with the present trends in Hinduism, had turned to Buddhism for sustenance; they had held dialogues to ask themselves what the Buddha would say if he were amongst them today. They came to see that what Krishnaji was saying was what the Buddha would have said.

Krishnaji heard me patiently, but was not prepared to accept what I was saying. "You are not answering my question," he said. "You are all Indians, conscious of Indian culture. You have to answer this question. You are aware of what is going on in India, the various gurus, the cults, and also you must have a feeling of the core from which great things took place. What relationship has that core, if it still exists, to the West and to Western religion and culture which is based on faith, belief?" Then Krishnaji asked, "If there is no relationship, then is that the point from which a new regeneration can emerge?"

"If that core, that center, has disappeared in India, is it in that, that the East and the West are coming together?"

"Apparently," he said. "From the beginning of time, the people of India had something which was genuine, true. They were deeply religious in the true sense of the word. There were the Buddhas and the pre-Buddhas who had left their imprint on the soil of India. The present world of astrologers, gurus—does that indicate that the depth of the real thing is going?

"In the Christian world doubt had never been part of religion. Here doubt, as part of religious enquiry, has always existed. Is that capacity to doubt being dissipated? Is that disappearing and gradually become faith?

"Do you see that doubt in religious enquiry is one of the most extraordinary things that existed in India? Christianity was based on faith; doubt, skepticism, questioning were denied. They were regarded as heresy. In India and in the Asiatic world doubt was one of the principles of religious investigation. Is that doubt disappearing, and therefore is India joining the Western stream? Or if doubt still exists, is it being smothered and are we losing the vitality of it? Doubt as an extraordinary purgation."

"Doubt is becoming a formal questioning," said Radha Burnier.

"I am speaking of real doubt, with the immense energy that lies behind it. What do you say, Pupulji? You are a mixture of both the East and West."*

"When you use that word 'doubt,' it is an immense thing. But I cannot answer your query whether it still exists or not," I said.

"The Theosophical Society and Amma had that quality at the beginning. Dr. Besant left Christianity, she left her husband; there was doubt, and then she got trapped in organizations and lost vitality. But the Indian mind, the original mind, emphasized doubt. Doubt with its clarity, doubt with its immense vitality purges the mind of illusions. Is India losing that? You follow? Because it is only through doubt that you come to the Brahman, not through acceptance of authority," said Krishnaji.

"That is what the Buddha also said," said Radha.

"Are we losing that? Not the few of us. But the Indian mind. Is it losing that quality, that quest for clarity?" Krishnaji was pushing the question.

Radha responded, "I still think that in India doubt exists, but this doubt has become a tradition. We question in a formal sense. In the West this takes the form of scientific search. Doubt is that which has not been corroborated by experiment. The Indian mind has turned in the direction of scientific search."

---

*Born in a Brahmin family, free of all ritual and belief yet rooted in Indian heritage, educated in England, I symbolize to K a mind that could span the bridge between East and West.

"The Western tradition of conformity has also entered the Indian stream," added Achyut.

"Krishnaji has brought into his teaching a new factor: doubt that does not move toward an answer. When you use the word 'doubt' within the Indian context, immediately out of doubt springs search," I said.

" 'What am I, who am I?' This is the Indian question. This is not a question with a direction," commented Achyut.

"Of course. If you have doubt with direction, then it has an entirely different meaning," said Krishnaji.

"Doubt without being followed by search has not existed in the Indian stream. In Krishnaji's doubt is an immediate immobility of the mind," I said.

"I am asking a really very serious question. I want to find out if in India the mind is being caught and carried away by the materialistic wave. That wave is threatening the Western world, expressing itself through technology, materialism, nationalism. The Western mind is moving in the direction of the outer, and it dominates the world. So is India losing something which was there? From what one can see, it appears to be losing it."

Mary Zimbalist queried, "Are you asking whether the other spirit which underlays India is failing? How does one tell that?"

"Can you answer that question? Can you feel, probe into it? Can Pupul or Achyut have a feeling of what is happening in this country? Can you take the outer as a measure and move to the inner?" Krishnaji asked. "The other was always there. I am saying something very simple. India moved from a center and that center spread all over the Asiatic world through inner search, dance, music, and cultural expression. The Western world was centered in belief, which is so superficial. That superficiality, that materialism, is that conquering this? It is very significant to see this. Can one see the outer manifestation of this in India, through its bureaucracy, technology, science, nuclear energy; following the ways of the West; and so is the pristine, original core of this country gradually withering away? India was centered on one thing. And therefore she had a fire which spread throughout the world. Now what is happening to the Indian core?" Krishnaji's passionate question and the fire of his attention was igniting our minds.

"Would you not say that in India the spirit has turned to the other? It has become adulterated. It is no longer a force. So what is the difference between India and the West?" Mary spoke.

"I would not say that this field has been corroded in the last fifteen years. I would not say that," I said.

"I hope not. But I won't accept your statement. I am questioning it. I want India to be that. So I say I hope she is not going to lose it. If it is lost, it is lost. I don't want her to lose it, because then it is the end of everything."

"Either you bring what you are saying into the comparative field of time and question whether earlier there were more people concerned with the core, or you can only put the question. Are there people today who take their stand in this?" I asked.

"Outside of those people who have been exposed to Krishnaji in India, are there people who take their source, their energy from doubt?" asked Achyut.

"There have been times in the history of this country when energy has exploded in great manifestations. When you say India is deteriorating, a hundred years or more ago was there religious doubt then and what was its nature? So don't put the question in terms of linear time. Can one ask the question are there people today who have the capacity to ask this question?" I said.

"There have been various factors also that have contributed to the wearing away of this spirit. The Bhakti movement with its emphasis on belief and faith, which existed for a number of centuries, could be compared to Christianity. Then the modern, scientific approach has reduced all nature to experiment. All this has cut the source at the roots," said Radha.

"In the past there were only a few who were the aristocrats of the spirit who took their stand on the formless," I said.

"But the elitist dominated the culture that exploded," said Achyut.

"Buddha arose and talked. It was three hundred years before the teaching was established," I said.

"Don't say you cannot answer my question." Krishnaji wouldn't let go. "I have been questioning this for years. This time as I flew into Bombay I was again asking that question, is the West conquering the East? The West has the capacity to organize, bring people together, it has technology, communication, etcetera. It has been capable of building systems to a marvelous extent. Here it was not based on organization or system. There were people who stood alone."

"There is a field of good and the field of evil. The challenge really is what is possible to make that field of good potent," I said.

"No, the good cannot be potent. Good is good," responded Krishnaji.

"Take it that the center is corroded. What is the response?"

"Then we can say it is finished, let us do something about it. But if you say it exists then we just carry on," said Krishnaji.

"If I admit it is finished?" I asked.

"Then that which has an ending has a new beginning. If it has ended, then something tremendous is taking place," Krishnaji said.

"That is the major difference between you and others. I was brought up in a tradition which believed in this source and everyone thought about revivalism, saying that it existed. You are the only person who is asking whether the seed is alive or not," said Achyut.

I added, "As long as Krishnaji is there, how do I say the seed is corroded?"

"I also fail to see how doubt has completely ended and a new thing has started," said Radha.

"When something has ended a new thing is taking place," said Krishnaji.

"You can ask, is there doubt in me? I can answer that directly; but when you ask me has that seed been corrupted, I can never answer that."

"I am afraid if doubt has ended in India, then it is a terrible thing," said Krishnaji.

"If I deny the seed I have denied everything," I said.

"I am not talking of denying. I am asking you a question. The West is enormously powerful with science, technology, organization, communication, war, all that. That enormity has smothered that which is not enormous. Right? Is the core of India so enormous within, that it can counter that and see that it is not touched by all that? Do you see what I am saying? It is not a geographical question. I am talking about the Indian mind that has produced the *Upanishads*, the Buddha. India has been the storehouse of something very very great. The West, with its emphasis on faith and its materialism, is destroying that greatness."

"I cannot answer your question," I said.

"You have got to answer. It is a challenge you have got to meet. It is a challenge that every Indian must meet," said Krishnaji. "Pupul, it is very interesting, the human mind is asking itself this question: 'Is there a mind that is incorruptible?' Is that mind being destroyed by the West?

"Religion in the West is based on faith and belief with all its implications. To be caught in faith or belief is the ending of doubt. Religious enquiry in India was not based on faith, so it could move in any direction. Free of direction, there was a different movement taking place; this is the essence of the Buddhas, the pre-Buddhas. Is that essence gradually being corroded by the West? Or is that essence expressing itself now? Not as the Buddha or Maitreya—these are but names: but is that essence expressing itself?"

I responded, "That essence is incorruptible. Therefore it cannot be corroded. The Indian mind today is conditioned. The only thing which one can say is that that mind, because it has been tuned to the 'other' for centuries, may have a proclivity to the 'other.' "

"And so the possibility of mutation. I think this mind has a greater possibility of mutation. This is not denying the West. We are not talking of the East and the West as opposites; we are talking of a quality of mind that has no direction."

"Would you say the conditioned mind can have nothing to do with 'that'?" asked Radha.

"The conditioned mind can have nothing to do with 'that,' but 'that' can have something to do with 'this.' So I am asking, is the mind of India—not my mind or your mind, but the mind that has evolved through five thousand years, the mind of the Buddha—can that mind ever be conditioned? The Indian mind groping for that, doubts, questions. You say, Pupul, that is the mainstream of the Indian mind. Are we in those waters of enquiry? Or are we floating in words, symbols, myths, ideas, theories?"

On the evening of November 4 at supper in Vasant Vihar, Krishnaji began discussing perception and wholeness. I said I had been attempting to understand the holographic model, in which a fragment contains the whole.

Krishnaji said in total perception there was the wholeness of mankind. He spoke of a perception of sorrow, in which there was total freedom from sorrow; in such a perception human consciousness was renewed. Then he asked himself, "Is that so? In one perception of sorrow, is there the whole content of human sorrow?"

We started questioning him and he said, "If you see the whole movement of pleasure—sexual, sensual—you have understood the whole content of consciousness."

"Could we be so aware of the body, the mind?" Achyut asked.

"Could there be an exploration of attention?" Krishnaji questioned. "We have said, 'attend.' But we have never probed into attention! What is it to attend?" Some of us responded, but Krishnaji continued to question.

"What takes place as attention probes into iself? If you are so attending, all your senses are completely awake. It is not one sense attending, but the totality of all the senses. Otherwise you cannot attend. When there is one sense that is highly cultivated and the others are not, one cannot attend. Complete sensory activity is a state of attention. Partial sensory activity leads to concentration. Attention has no center. Attention is a flowing from itself, it is moving, never still; it flows, moves, goes on. Attention gets more and more—not more in a comparative sense, but as a river that has behind it a vast volume of water; a tremendous volume of energy, of attention, wave upon wave upon wave, each wave a different movement. We have never enquired what takes place beyond attention. Is there a total summation of energy?" Scientists had told him that energy and matter were one. The wave still was energy, it could never be still.

"In penetrating into a wave of perception as energy, extraordinary things go on. There is a sense of soaring ecstasy; a feeling of limitless space; a vast movement of color." He paused. "Color is God;" he said, "not the gods we worship, but the color of the earth, the sky, the extraordinary color of a flower."

Asit asked hesitatingly, "Would you include aroma?"

"Of course, color is aroma," Krishnaji said.

He was probing as he spoke. "Can one see completely with all the senses? See not with the eyes alone, but with the ears; to listen, to taste, to touch? There has to be harmony. This is only possible when there is no center, no movement."

"Watch yourself one day," he said to us. "Look at the sunlight and see whether you can see with all your senses, completely awake and completely free. Which leads to an interesting fact: Where there is disharmony, there is the self."

"Attention is complete harmony. There must be a great volume of energy gathered through harmony. It is like the river Ganga. Attention is a movement to eternity."

That evening was historic: Krishnaji walked again on the grounds of the Theosophical Society at Adyar. We accompanied him. Radha Burnier was with him in the car. They were met at the gate by the vice president of the Theosophical Society. Krishnaji was garlanded with pink roses. Radha and Krishnaji walked by the road to the seashore, past the headquarters building. Krishnaji walked past his old room; on his return he took the path along the river. It was lovely land. The trees were beautiful; the people who lived there were seeking refuge from the travails of the world. Krishnaji's return held a great poignancy.

Every day while he was in Madras, Krishnaji drove through the Theosophical Society compound to Radha's house, and from there he walked on the beach. One evening on returning from his walk Krishnaji spoke of two young fishermen—slender, tall, and dark-skinned boys.

With ease and immense skill they prepared their catamarans for launching; turning the rudder towards the sea, jumping in and pushing the boat swiftly into the dark, unknown sea. Krishnaji was deeply moved.

Later in the year Krishnaji was to go to the Theosophical Society to have lunch with Radha Burnier. Before lunch she took Krishnaji to the main Theosophical Society building where Dr. Besant had had her room and where she had lived. He first visited his own room, which overlooked the river and the sea. He stood before the window, gazing across to where the river meets the sea. Later he was to say that he did not remember it. Then he went to the room of Dr. Besant. Carefully he stood before her *chowki* with its little desk, and walked around the room, quiet, listening. Suddenly, he stopped before a large photograph of Leadbeater which hung on a wall. "This was not there in my time," he said. Radha Burnier said it had been placed there many years later. For minutes Krishnaji stood before the portrait, gazing at it; then suddenly he raised his hand and said, "Pax, pax." Then he turned to Radha Burnier and walked out of the room.

# CHAPTER 37

# "I Suddenly Saw the Face."

The government of Sri Lanka had invited Krishnaji to be a state guest when he gave his talks in Colombo. A number of his friends accompanied him to this emerald island. Mary Zimbalist, Nandini, and I stayed with Krishnaji there at Auckland House, the official guest house of the Sinhalese government. Every effort had been made by the Sinhalese government to welcome Krishnaji. He was invited by the president to tea, met the prime minister, and was interviewed several times by the press. The talks were attended by a vast number of people—monks and laymen, Sinhalese and Tamilians, ministers and clerks gathered to hear the man of wisdom.

Asit Chandmal was also in Colombo. He had been in California and had met scientists and technologists working on the frontiers of the new sciences. He spoke to Krishnaji of the electronic age into which man was being catapulted; of the amazing capacities and skills of the new computers and the search for the ultimate intelligence machine.

Computer scientists were pursuing the possibility of creating artificial intelligence. They were studying the human brain, to see how it worked and whether it could be reproduced. Japanese scientists were deeply involved. IBM had already started the search. Krishnaji listened eagerly; his mind instantly perceived the dimensions and directions of this new intelligence, the magnificence of man's inventive drive, and with it the enormous dangers to the survival of humankind. Realizing that man was soon to be challenged at unprecedented levels, he questioned Asit relentlessly.

Later, we held discussions on the computer and the human brain. K said, "The brain has an infinite capacity. That immense capacity is being used for material purposes." He saw with great clarity that with the inventive capacity, certain faculties of the brain would in a short time be taken over by the machine.

"Ceasing to function, would these faculties wither or shrink?" he asked. "Would the brain slowly atrophy? Man has to either explore within, so that he can use these new tools rightly, or perception, compassion and the essence of humanity as we know it, will cease to be. There are only two options open: Either we commit ourselves to the whole range of entertainment outwardly, or we turn within."

Krishnaji was afire with the question. He discussed it in Colombo with us and later in Rishi Valley and Madras. For over two years, this problem of the human brain and the challenge of the machine taking over the processes and faculties of the brain was Krishnaji's main concern.

One morning I asked Krishnaji for a meeting, as I needed some answers to questions that puzzled me. He was in a strange state; he seemed outside himself. I questioned him about his position that there were no footholds to truth. I said, "Most other systems of meditation state require the need for support at the early stages. You have repeatedly said that there are no steps, no levels. The first step is the last step. But going into your historical past, as well as in casual conversations, I have observed that you have gone through all the *kriyas*, the actions known to religious tradition. You have tested yourself, you have denied your senses; tied a bandage for days on your eyes to see what it is to be blind. You have fasted for days, you observed silence, *'maun'*, for over a year in 1951. What was your reason for this silence?"

"Probably it was to find out if I could keep quiet," said Krishnaji.

"Did it help at all?"

"Not a bit," was the reply.

"Why did you do it?"

"I have done crazy things—eaten so that I did not mix protein with starch; eaten only vegetables; then only protein."

"Do you put silence in the same category?" Nandini asked.

"You mean I did not talk to anybody—are you sure? It was never anything serious. There was no spiritual intention behind the silence."

"In the experience that took place in Ooty, you still saw visions. Do you ever see visions now?" I asked.

"No." He appeared unsure. "Wait a minute. Sometimes I do. What do you mean by visions—pictures, images? You see, it must have been a very strange thing when they picked me up. As far as I remember,

Master K. H. and the Buddha were always there somewhere in my mind. Their images used to follow me for a considerable time."

"You have talked about a face being with you, which merged into your face."

"That is right."

"I am asking you today, is that face still with you?"

"Yes, occasionally. I must go into this. Why are you asking all these questions?"

"I want to write an accurate account, not only of events; events are very inconsequential from my point of view."

"Right from the beginning, C. W. L. and Amma had said the face has been created for many, many lives. I was too young to know what they were saying, but apparently the face impressed them tremendously. They said it was the face of the Maitreya Bodhisattva. They used to keep repeating this, but it meant nothing to me, absolutely nothing. Many, many years later, after the death of my brother, and many, many years after that—I can't tell you when, but one morning I suddenly saw the face, a most extraordinarily beautiful face, that used to be with me for many years. Then gradually that face disappeared. It all began after the death of the brother."

"Let us pursue the question of the visions," I said.

"For many, many years I was not really all there. Sometimes, even now, I am not all there. Ojai was totally independent from C. W. L. At Ootacamund it was totally independent of Rajagopal and Rosalind. After I moved away from Ojai—after 1947 to 1948, things started happening, like seeing this extraordinary face. I used to see it every day—in sleep, while walking. It was not a vision. It was like that picture, an actual fact."

"You saw it even when you were awake?" asked Nandini.

"Of course, on my walks it was there."

"We saw it in Ooty. A tremendous change taking place in your face," I said.

"That is true."

"And you said the Buddha was there. You say that occasionally you still see visions."

"The other night in Madras I woke up with this face."

"So it is still there."

"Of course."

"I would like to get a feel of it," I said.

"Yes. Which is, it is not a vision. It is not something imagined. I have tested it out. It is not something that I wanted. I do not say, 'What a beautiful face'—there is no wish to have it."

"What happens to you when you get these visions?"

"I look at the face."

"Does anything happen to you?"

"I don't know. It is like cleaning the body and the face and the air. I have seen the face in the dark, in the light, while walking. You may say that this is all cuckoo. But it is so. I have never done anything for any spiritual reason."

"Before the mystical process that happened in Ojai, in your letters to Lady Emily, you said you were meditating every day?" asked Mary Zimbalist.

"All the meditation was on Theosophical Society lines. I did it because I was told to do it. It was part of the Theosophical Society belief, but it meant nothing to me. I did all that automatically."

"When you 'grew up, came to,' was it in a flash or was it something which matured without your knowing?" I asked.

"In a flash, naturally. I used to have a horror of vows, fasts, vows of celibacy, vows not to get angry. I never took any vows. If I did not like a thing, that was the end of it. If I liked it, I went on with it."

"When one reads the *Notebook* and then reads the talks of 1948, one finds there has been a major leap in the teachings. Is there a leap taking place all the time?"

"Yes, it is happening all the time, in my brain, inside me. After traveling this time from London to Bombay and then to Madras, that first night in Madras, I felt the brain exploding; there was an extraordinary quality, light, beauty. This is happening all the time, but not every day. That would be a lie. What is necessary is quietness . . . "

"I realize that things happen when you are alone. It happened when you were supposed to be very 'ill' in 1959, in Srinagar and later in Bombay. I have never been certain whether you have an illness or something else. At the end of any serious illness, you give extraordinary talks."

"Illness may be a purgation," said Krishnaji.

"I know you have been ill on two occasions in Bombay. I have been present. There is a strange atmosphere when you are ill."

"I remember your being ill in Bombay," Nandini spoke. "You had bronchitis. We had to cancel the talks. You had 103-degree to 104-degree temperature. Suddenly you wanted to throw up. So I ran to get a basin. I held your hand. I saw you were about to faint. I called out and you said, 'No, no.' Your voice had changed. Your face had changed. The person who sat up was different from the person who had fainted. You were cured.

"You told me not to leave the body alone; just to be there. You said, 'Never be anxious near me; never get worried, don't allow too many people to come near me. In India they never leave an ill person alone.' You asked me to sit down quietly and then you said, 'I must tell you something. Do you know how to help a person die? If you know that someone is about to die, help him to be quiet, help him to forget his accumulations, to be free of his worries, of his problems, to give up his attachments, all his possessions.' You were silent and then you said, 'It is just stepping over.' And your face lit up. 'If you can't do that, you are where you are, you remain where you are.'

# CHAPTER 38

# "Is It Possible to Keep the Brain Very Young?"

On January 14, 1981, Krishnaji gave a public talk in Vasant Vihar, Madras. Speaking of the brain, he asked, "Is it possible to keep the brain very young? Is it possible for the brain to rejuvenate itself? This brain which is so old, with its infinite capacities; a brain that has evolved in time through social, economic pressures; the brain which is an extraordinary instrument, which controls all thinking, all activities, all our sensory operation; can that brain become totally innocent? I use the word 'innocent' in the sense that it cannot be hurt." He asked each person in the audience not to agree, but to observe their own mind, the brain, which is very very subtle. "Can we," he asked, "challenge the brain itself to find out whether it has the capacity, the energy, the drive, the intensity to break down this continuity of the past so that in the very ending, the brain cells themselves undergo a change, a transformation?" He was probing deeply.

"Thought is a material process; thought is the outcome of memory, experience, knowledge, stored up in the brain cells, in the thinking process itself. And it has functioned in a particular direction, continuously evolving. Thought, memory is a part of the brain. The brain is material; this brain contains memory, experiences knowledge, from which comes thought. So thought has its continuity, based on knowledge, which is the past; and that past is operating all the time, modifying itself in the present and continuing. In this continuity it has found immense security through beliefs, illusion, knowledge. In this faith there is a sense of being protected, of being 'in the womb of God.' This is an illusion. Any disturbance in that continuity is the challenge;

and when it cannot respond properly, it finds its security is disturbed." He paused and was silent, listening to himself.

"Watch this in yourself, watch carefully. We are asking whether the brain—which is the brain of all human beings, evolved immemorial times, conditioned by cultures, religions, by economic, social pressures—whether that brain, which has had a timeless continuity till now, can discover an ending of continuity as time?" He asked the listeners not to be stimulated by the speaker, for then the listener was dependent on him. "Then the speaker becomes your authority, your guru. The demand is that you be a light to yourself, not accept the light of another."

He discussed death as a total ending and destruction of the brain, an ending to a continuity of life. "To understand this," he said, "can we examine 'what is'? The 'what is' of your life, your everyday life? Throughout the ages we have clung to a continuity of life. We have never asked what is the meaning of death. We have put death in opposition to life. But continuity implies time. The movement of thought. Time means movement. From here to there—to psychologically reach from that which is not beautiful to that which is beautiful.

"To find out what death is, can that continuity end? Can the sense of duration end?" He paused.

"Death says to you, 'end it,' end your attachments completely, because that is what is going to happen when you stop breathing. You are going to leave everything behind.

"So death implies the ending of attachment. It is only in the ending that there is a beginning.

"It is only then that the brain can discover for itself a quality of movement that is totally free of the past."

Krishnaji asked his listeners a question. "If there is no ending, what happens to the mind, to the whole movement of consciousness, yours or mine, to the consciousness of man? What happens to our daily life? Life is like a vast river in which there is pain, sorrow, anxiety. When the part dies, the stream goes on. Manifestation of the stream is you, with your name, and so on. But you are still part of this stream. And we are saying, can you end that stream? Do you follow? Because the 'me' is the continuity. The 'I' is the beginning not only genetically, but of that which is handed down generation after generation from millennia. It is a continuity, and that which is continuous is mechanical. You observe a person who has insulted you or praised you. The brain registers. So you never actually see. This registration is what gives continuity.

"We are laying the foundations to discover what is meditation. The understanding of ourselves is part of this meditation. In the understanding of sorrow, pain, fear, anxiety, you see that consciousness is its content, as tradition, anxiety, name, position. Can this consciousness in which is the brain, which is part of the mind, part of consciousness—can this consciousness realize its content, realize its sense of duration, and taking one part of that consciousness as attachment, end it voluntarily? That means, can you break continuity? Which means, is it possible to register only what is necessary and nothing else?

"Knowledge is always limited. So the brain, having found security in the movement of knowledge, clings to it and translates every incident, according to the past. In the movement of ending of continuity is complete order. This insight is the revolution in the structure of the brain."

Krishnaji's words flowed. "It is the brain that puts everything in its right place. Then, in total insight into the whole movement of consciousness, the activity and structures of the brain undergo a change. When you see something for the first time, a new function begins to operate. Your arm, this arm was developed because of function. So when the brain discovers something new, a new function is born, a new organism comes into being.

"It is necessary for a mind, for a brain to become very young, fresh, innocent, alive, youthful. This is only possible when there is no psychological registration," said Krishnaji.

Then he spoke of love and meditation. "Has love a continuity? Is love desire? Can love come into being like fresh morning dew? It cannot. If love has a continuity, please go into it. Love does not exist in your heart, that is why the world is in such a mess.

"To come upon love, the whole stream of consciousness must come to an end. Consciousness being your jealousy, your antagonism, your ambition, your desire for becoming bigger, your desire for seeking power. Where there is any sense of egotism, the other is not. And the essence of egotism is the process of registration. The ending of sorrow is the beginning of compassion.

"Now, can we talk of meditation? There are several things implied in meditation. There must be space; not physical space only, but space within the mind. All our minds are occupied. This occupation is like a housewife with her cooking, with her children, like a devotee with his god, a man with his occupation, with his sex, with his job. In that the mind is wholly occupied, therefore there is no space in it. If there is no order in your relationship with your wife, with your children, forget about meditation. But absolute order can look to cosmic order. That order has relationship with cosmic order. Cosmic order means the setting of the sun and the moon, the marvelous sky of the evening with all its beauty. But merely examining the cosmos, the universe, through a telescope is not order. Order is here, in our life. Then that order has an extraordinary relationship with the universe."

One evening a barefoot, bearded *sadhu* wearing an earth-colored robe and a cloth tied round his head, spoke to Achyut, and later in the week he met Krishnaji. He belonged to the ancient Siddha sect and lived with a guru in Anantpur District. His guru was old and had told his disciple that he had felt the mystic presence of a great being who was teaching in the world. "I am dying," the guru said, "so he will be your guru, find him." The disciple had wandered, searching for the true teacher. He had visited all the *ashrams*, but was not satisfied. Then in Madras he had heard of Krishnaji and had come to the talks. Feeling that he had found what he sought, he returned to his guru and described what he had seen. The guru had confirmed his insight and had asked him to return to Madras and Krishnaji. Later, in Madras, the *sadhu* heard that his guru had died.

This *sannyasi* had secret knowledge of plant alchemy and the use of herbs in medicinal recipes. He knew the time of the day or night when the plants were to be collected, how stored, and the *mantras* that were to accompany the making of the potion. A great element of magic was present in what he said: that plants had intelligence and awareness. They revealed themselves only to those who approached them rightly. He told Achyut, "A plant wrongly approached, with greed or desire, vanishes and cannot be found. Plants and herbs have to be talked to. Their permission must be taken before touching them, they have to be addressed with humility—'Do you permit me to touch you, would you like me to wait?' They give light and fragrance to those who commune with them." His words were reminiscent of the mysterious sacredness and wonder for plants as life-givers, protectors, holders of energy that is found in the hymns of the *Atharva Veda*. Krishnaji was very interested in the man and his sensitivity and relationship to plants.

Achyut sent him out to carry Krishnaji's teachings amongst Siddhas and wandering sects of *sadhus*.

# CHAPTER 39

# "The Nature of God"

In early 1981 I was asked by Indira Gandhi to be chairman of the advisory committee set up to organize the Festival of India celebrations in England.* In this connection, I visited England in May. After my official work was over, I went to Brockwood Park to meet Krishnaji. I asked him whether we could continue our dialogues, and he agreed. The first afternoon we discussed "the nature of God." A few members of the Brockwood Park School were present.

I asked Krishnaji whether it was possible to inquire into "the nature of, call it God—call it creation—the ground of Being?"

"I think it is possible" Krishnaji responded, "if one can free the mind of all belief—of all traditional acceptance of the word 'God' and the implications and the consequences of that word. Can the brain and mind be totally free to investigate that which the Israelis call the 'nameless,' the Hindus 'the Brahman,' the 'Highest Principle?' The whole world believes in the word 'God.' Could we put away all beliefs? Only then is it possible to investigate."

"But 'God' is a word; in it there is a storehouse of content. Therefore when the mind says it is free of belief, what does it exactly mean?"

"Human beings say they believe in God," answered Krishnaji. "God is omnipotent and omnipresent, he exists in all things. There is a traditional acceptance of that word with all its content. Can one be free of the million years of this tradition—consciously as well as unconsciously to be free of that word?"

"At one level," I said, "it is possible to say that one is free. If you

---

*The Festival of India celebrations, organized by the government of India, were a major cultural manifestation which included dance, music, theater, exhibitions of the classical and rural arts and life, science and technology, street performers, seminars, films, and so forth.

were to ask me do I believe in God, do I believe in Krishna, Rama, or Shiva, I would say no. But that is not the final thing."

"No," said Krishnaji.

I continued. "There is a feeling that God goes far beyond all words, that it is integral to the fact of life itself. Before I go into the origins of that word I have to enquire into the state of my mind which says the outer beliefs are out for there is a sense that without 'it' nothing could exist. That it is the ground."

"Shall we discuss the ground from which everything originates?" asked K. "How does one find out? One can only find out when one is absolutely free, otherwise one cannot. Our consciousness is so loaded, crowded."

I asked, "Is there a possibility of being in which any movement of the mind as belief is out; belief in any particular God is negated?"

"Does one negate it verbally or deeply at the very root of one's being? Can one say I know nothing and stop there?" Krishnaji responded.

"I can't say I know nothing," I answered. "But I can say that the movement of belief in a particular God, does not arise in the mind. Therefore there is nothing outer to negate as belief. But I still do not know the state of 'I know nothing,' which is a very different state from the outer movement as belief."

"How does one proceed?" K asked. "Could we negate completely the whole movement of knowledge? Negate everything except the knowledge of driving a car and all technological knowledge? Could one negate the feeling that one knows? The whole accumulated experience of man, which says there is God or there have been prophets and seers who have said there is no such thing as God. Can one negate the knowledge of all that one knows?"

"One has comprehended the way of negating the rising movement."

"Do you mean the rising movement of thought as belief?" asked Krishnaji.

"Yes, but the depths, the dormant, the million years that form the matrix of one's being, how does one touch that?"

"Could we begin not by enquiring into whether there is God, but ask why the human mind has worked, struggled with becoming? Becoming not only outwardly, but inwardly. *A* becoming that is based on knowledge, on constant movement, an uprising movement—the being somebody." Krishnaji was entering into the question.

"Now, are the two related? We started with an investigation into the nature of God and we spoke of the matrix and becoming. Are they related?"

"Aren't they related?" Krishnaji asked. "I think they are. Let us look at it. I may be wrong. My being is essentially based on what I have understood, not verbally, but the feeling in me that there is something enormous, something incredibly immense. I am looking about that part of my being, that knowledge, tradition that is the matrix, the ground on which one stands. So long as that is there, one is not actually free. Can one investigate into that?"

"Sir," said Mary Zimbalist, "there is a heritage of that in every human life. Is that different from human instinct to which heritage attaches? Is it only heritage handed down, or is it a deep movement that is innately in the human mind apart from all influence?"

"Are you saying, is this inherent in man?" Krishnaji asked her.

"Is there an inherent movement in every human being towards some unknown being which is sought? Something that is beyond what one is taught, beyond what one picks up through one's heritage?" she enquired.

"Is it genetic?" asked someone else.

"Genetic involves time and the movement of growth, evolution. Now, can one totally empty all that, the accumulation of a million years? I am speaking of the most deep-rooted, something that is unconscious; deep things are always so. I think if we want to investigate, that must go too," said Krishnaji.

"Can one go to the end of the unconscious mind?" I asked. "Is it possible, without the unconscious being exposed, for it to end? How does one experience that which one cannot formulate? That which lies beyond the total particulars of any one person's knowledge?"

"Don't you have the feeling, the insight into this question, that there must be the total negating of all things, or the beginning of all things?" asked Krishnaji.

"I comprehend the negation of all that rises in the brain. But the layers of the unconscious, the ground on which one stands, can one negate that? Perhaps one is asking the wrong question. Perhaps there can never be a negation of that. How can one negate that?" I was trying to understand.

"Just a minute. Man has tried in several ways to find this. He has fasted, he has tortured himself, but he is always anchored to something."

"Yes."

"One can be free of anchors from most things. Can one be free from the question?" Mary asked.

"Oh, yes, oh, yes," said Krishnaji.

"Then how can Pupul ask that question?" Mary wondered.

"No," said Krishnaji. "That is the whole point. Can one do such a thing first of all? Is it possible to be so totally 'non-movement'? Otherwise movement is time, thought, and all that. Complicated things are involved in this. First of all, why do we want to find the meaning of God? The meaning behind all this?"

I answered, "There is a part of us which is still seeking."

"Yes, that is it. We never say 'I don't know.' That's a state of mind that is absolutely motionless. To say 'I don't know.' " He paused. "I think that is one of our difficulties. We all want to know—which means, to put God into the bay of knowledge."

"Look Sir, isn't there in the ear listening, in the eye seeing—in the word said—the whole content of what God is? Is it not necessary to wipe out this matrix?" I enquired.

"Can you wipe out the matrix?" Krishnaji asked.

"I don't know."

"When you use the word 'matrix,' what do you mean by that?" asked Krishnaji.

"I only know that beyond the horizons of my mind, of the obvious beliefs, there are depths and depths in me. You use a very significant phrase somewhere, 'to play around with the deep.' So you also point to depths which lie beyond the surface arising. Is this depth within the matrix?" I enquired.

"No, no—can't be," said Krishnaji. "That is why I am asking, why do I want to find out whether there is something beyond all this?"

"Because, Krishnaji, I can do nothing about this matrix," I said.

"I wonder what you call matrix?" asked Krishnaji.

"This depth which I cannot bring to the surface, into the daylight of consciousness, of perception, of attention. This depth which does not come within the purview of my eyes and ears, but still is there. I know it is there. It is 'me.' Not being able to see it, touch it, I have a feeling that perhaps if there is a right listening to the truth . . ." I was trying to communicate.

"Let us go into it. Is that depth—if I may use that word for the moment—is that depth measurable?" asked Krishnaji.

"No," I replied.

"Then why do you use the word 'depth'? Depth means measurable."

"I am using the word depth to connote something that is beyond my knowledge—you see, if it is within the contours of my horizon, available to my senses, then it is measurable. But if it is not available I can do nothing about it. I do not have the instruments to reach it."

"How do you know that there is this depth? Is it not imagination? Do you know it as experience?" Krishnaji asked.

"Yes."

"Ah! be careful, be careful."

"The problem is—if I say yes, it is a trap. If I say no, it is a trap."

"I want to be quite clear, Pupulji, forgive me, that we both understand the meaning of our words."

"Surely, Sir. A word can be said from the surface mind and it can be said with a great weight behind it. I am saying that this ground contains the whole history of man. It has great weight and depth. Can I not go into it without your asking me whether it is imagination? Can't you feel that depth?"

"I understand, Pupulji, but you see . . ." He paused. "And that depth—is it the depth of silence? Which means the mind, the brain is utterly still—not something that comes and goes."

"How can I answer that?" I asked.

"I think one can—if there is no sense of attachment to it. No sense of memory involved in it. Pupulji, let us begin again. The whole world believes in God. In Ceylon they were very upset when I said the word God is put together by thought. Do you remember? The whole world believes in God. Unfortunately, I don't know what God is. Probably I can never find out." He paused. "And I am not interested in finding out. But what I am concerned with is whether the mind, the brain, can be totally, completely free from all accumulated knowledge, experience? Because if it is not, it will function always within its field, expanding—contracting—vertically, horizontally—but always within that area. It does not matter how much one accumulates, it will still be within that area. And if the mind moves from that area and says, 'I must find out,' then it is still carrying the movement, the mind, with it. I don't know whether I am making myself clear?" There were great pauses between Krishnaji's words.

He continued. "So my concern is whether the brain, the mind, can be completely free from all taint of knowledge. To me that is tremendously significant, because if it is not, it will never be out of that area, never."

"You speak of any movement of the mind—any movement."

"Yes. Any movement out of that area is to find that the brain is still anchored in knowledge and seeks further knowledge about God. So I say my concern is whether the mind, the brain is capable of being completey immovable? When you put a question of that kind either you say, 'It is not possible' or 'It is possible.' But if you deny the possibility and the impossibility of it, then what is left? Do you follow? Can I have insight, the depth of insight into the movement of knowledge so that the insight stops the movement? Not I who stop the movement nor the brain that stops the movement. In that is the ending of knowledge and the beginning of something else. So I am concerned only with the ending of knowledge, consciously, deeply. There is this enormous feeling that comes of oneness, a harmonious unity, and if it is simulated there is no point, then you perpetuate yourself—Right?" Again he paused and listened.

"The 'me' is the essence of knowledge," he continued. "I doubt everything man has put together, including myself. That is a very cleansing attitude. So we start with the extraordinary feeling of not knowing anything. If we could say, 'I know nothing,' in the deepest sense of the word—it is there—you don't have to do anything."

Krishnaji challenged me. "Look Pupulji, suppose this person were not here. How would you deal with this problem? How would you deal with this problem of God, belief? How would you actually deal with it without any reference to anybody?"

"Yes, even to do that is possible," I responded.

"Let us move from there. Each one of us is totally responsible. We are not referring to past authorities or saints. Each one is totally responsible to answer this question. You have to answer it."

"Why should I have to answer it?" I asked.

"I will tell you why. You are part of humanity and humanity is asking this question. Every saint, every philosopher, every human being, somewhere in his depths, is asking this question."

"Sir, is this question not somewhere, in a sense, wrong?" asked Mary.

"I said so. But you have to answer it without any reference to what has been said or not said. I come to you with these questions. I ask you as a human being. To me, these questions are tremendously important."

"May I ask you something? How does one take a question like this and leave it in consciousness?" I asked.

"Pupulji, either you have never thought about it, or you have thought about it and gathered tremendous information from books—maybe this is the first time you are facing this question. Go slow, go slow."

"You have a way of taking a question, asking it, and then, without any movement of the mind, remaining with it." I refused to be turned away.

"Yes, that would be right."

"That is what I want to know. One asks the question and there is movement of the mind towards it. With you, when such a question is put, there is no movement of the mind towards the question."

"You are right. Now are you asking how to get it?" asked Krishnaji.

"I know I can't get it," I said.

"No. You are right to ask that question." He addressed everyone. "Do you understand what Pupulji said? Do it, do it. I am asking you as a human being, and human beings have asked these questions for a million years. I come to you and put this question—are you ready to answer or do you hold the question quietly? Hold it, do you understand? And out of that very holding without any reaction, any response, comes the answer. Right?"

"Could you say something about the nature of that holding?" asked Scott Forbes, a member of the faculty at Brockwood Park School.

"A cup holds water. A pond is a receptacle that holds water, a holding without any wave, without any motive or movement, without any sense of trying to find an answer."

"Sir," said Mary, "with most of us we may not try to find an answer, we may first remain quietly with an unanswered question, but sooner or later comes an answer that may not be something from the deep wells of the unconscious and wells up to fill that space."

"I know. Now just a minute. I ask you a question. 'Do you believe in God?' I am asking that question. Can you say you don't know or you don't believe or do you say, may be? Without saying anything about it, can you look at the question? Can you? If you ask a devout Christian, immediately he would say, 'Of course I believe in God.' If you went to India and asked, immediately there would be a reaction. It is like pressing a button. For me, I really don't know whether there is God or not."

"In holding, isn't there an enquiry?" Scott spoke again.

"You see—unless you understand this, it can lead to a great deal of misunderstanding. Sir, computers can be programmed by ten different professors, with a great deal of knowledge. They can hold tremendous information. Our brains are trained that way, they have been programmed for thousands of years, and that brain replies immediately to a question. If the brain is not programmed, it is watching, looking. Now can our brains be not programmed?"

"But this activity of looking around is not the holding? Can you say something about the holding?" Scott continued.

"You say it." Krishnaji was pushing.

"I have nothing to say."

"Push, push." Krishnaji said.

"As the cup holds water or the earth holds the pond, is there something that holds like the cup and the earth?"

"No. Pupulji asked me a question which was depth. You received that question. What was your response?"

"Which question, Sir?" asked Scott.

"From the depth—layer after layer, from the depth, the ground. Now, what was your reaction to that?"

"You see, Sir," I intervened, "when a question is normally put, it is like grains of sugar being dropped on the ground—the ants from all over come towards it. It is the same with the mind; when a question is put, movements, responses are awakened that gravitate toward the question. Now the question is can the question be put without these movements?"

"Without the ants, yes. I am told that when the brain is not operating—is quiet—it has a movement of its own. We are talking of the brain that is in constant movement, the energy of which is thought. Is thought the problem? How will you deal with this question? Can you question thought completely? Don't complicate it. I ask you a question. Don't answer immediately. Look at it, hold it. This is not an examination. Can one have a mind that is capable of not reacting immediately to a question? Can there be a delaying reaction, perhaps holding the question indefinitely?

"Let us go back, Pupulji. Is there a state of mind that is out of time? Is that a state of profound meditation? A meditation in which there is no state of achievement, there is nothing. That may be the ground, the origin of all things, a state in which the meditator is not."

"May I ask, is the meditator not the ground?"

"Obviously not."

"Without the meditator, can the ground be?"

"If the meditator is there the ground is not."

"But without the meditator, can there be meditation?" I asked.

"I speak of a meditation without the meditator."

"Meditation is a human process," I said.

"No," said Krishnaji.

"Let us investigate this if we may. Meditation cannot be free of individual being. There can be no meditation without the meditator. You may say the meditator is not the ground."

"No, just a minute. So long as I am trying to meditate, meditation is not," Krishnaji said.

"Yes," I agreed.

"Therefore there is only a brain, mind, that is in a state of meditation."

"Yes."

"Now that is the ground. The universe is in a state of meditation and that is the ground, that is the origin of everything. That is only possible when the meditator is not."

"And that is only possible when there are no anchors."

"Absolutely. In that there is absolutely freedom from sorrow. That state of meditation has come with the complete ending of the self. Beginning may be the eternal process, the beginning, an eternal beginning. How is this possible? Is it at all possible for a brain, for a human being to be so completely, utterly free of the meditator? Then there is no question whether there is God or no God. Then that meditation is the meditation of the universe." He paused.

"Is it possible to be so utterly free? I am asking that question. Don't reply, hold it. Do you see what I mean? Let it operate. In the holding of it, energy is being accumulated and that energy will act, not you acting. Do you understand?" After a long pause, Krishnaji asked, "So, have we understood the nature of God?"

# CHAPTER 40

# "The Meaning of Death"

The next morning we discussed death. I began the dialogue by asking the question that lies at the very depth of the human mind, the "coming to be and the ceasing to be," life and death.

"It is around these two, the wonder of birth and the fear of death, that man's life rests. At one level we understand birth and death. But it is only the superficial mind that understands. It is imperative to understand at depth the meaning of existence, that which is held between birth and death and the fears, the darkness that lie in the ending of anything."

Krishnaji listened as he always does, with his whole body and mind. He asked, "Why do you use the word 'problem'?"

"In themselves, birth and death are not a problem; but the mind can never leave them alone. The mind clings to one and rejects the other. The problem is because of the shadows that surround the word 'death.' There is joy and splendor in the word 'birth,' the coming to be and there is the urge to hold to it at any cost and the urge to evade 'death.' " I was trying to open up the problem.

"I understand that."

"Out of this arises sorrow, out of it arises fear, out of it all demands," I continued.

"So what is the question?" asked Krishnaji.

"How do we explore the word 'death'? How can we be free of the darknesses that surround the word? How can the mind look at death with simplicity and observe it for what it is?"

"Are you including in your question the whole process of living, with its confusion, complexities, and the ending of that? Are you concerned to find out what it means—death and this long period of struggle, misery, etc., to which we cling? Are you asking a question regarding the whole movement of life and death?" Krishnaji was widening the question to include a nonfragmented wholeness.

"There is a whole movement of existence which includes life and death," I said. "But if you make the field too wide, we cannot get to the depth of sorrow, of ending. There is such anguish in something that 'is' and something that 'ceases to be.' Something that is marvelous, fills one's life, and the sorrow that lurks behind—for that which is, must end."

"Now, what is ending?" Krishnaji asked.

"Something that exists and ceases to be—ceases to be eternally," I answered.

"Why do you use the word 'eternally'?" questioned Krishnaji.

"Sir, something 'is,' and in the very nature of its 'isness' lurks the ending of that, the ceasing of that for eternity. There is no tomorrow in ending." I was listening very intently.

"Now, just a minute. Ending what?" The probing had started.

"Ending that which sustains. The sorrow is the ending of that which sustains."

"The ending of sorrow, but the ending is not eternity?" asked Krishnaji.

"No, the sorrow which arises when something that was so marvelous ends."

"Wait a minute. Is it so marvelous?" asked Krishnaji.

"Let me be more direct. You are, and that you should not be—that is great anguish," I said.

"You are and—" Krishnaji was still hesitant, trying to get me to see the problem with an absolute clarity.

"Not you are—You, Krishnamurti, are, and in that statement there is the tremendous anguish of Krishnaji ceasing to be," I said.

"Are you speaking of the anguish of Krishnaji ending, or Krishnaji himself ending? You follow?"

I did not follow, and asked, "Why do you make the distinction?"

"Death is inevitable to this person," said Krishnaji. "To him it does not matter. There is no fear, no anguish. But you look at that person and say, 'My God, one day he is going to die.' So the fear, the anguish, is your anguish," said Krishnaji.

"Yes, it is my anguish."

"Now, why?" questioned Krishnaji.

"It is. Why do you ask why?"

"I want to know why, when a human being dies, beautiful, ugly—the whole of human existence is contained in that—he dies and it is inevitable. I look at that person, I love that person, he dies, and I am in anguish. Why? Why am I desperate, lonely, in sorrow? We are not talking intellectually, but actually. I have lost that person, he has been dear to me, my companion, and he comes to an end. I think it is really important to understand ending, because there is something totally new when there is an ending to everything," said Krishnaji.

"Isn't it inevitable—he was the perfume of my existence," I said.

"Yes, I loved him. With him I felt full, rich. That person comes to an end."

"Isn't that sorrow?" I asked.

"It is. My son, my brother dies, it is tremendous sorrow. It is as though the whole of existence had been uprooted, a marvelous tree torn down in an instant. I shed tears, there are anxieties, and my mind then seeks comfort and says I will meet him in my next life. Now I am asking myself, why does man carry this sorrow with him? You see, I am in sorrow because I have never understood deeply what is ending. I have lived forty, fifty, eighty years; during that period I have never realized the meaning of ending. The putting an end to something I hold dear. The total ending of it—not the ending of it, to continue it in another direction—"

"What makes the mind capable of ending? What comes in the way?" I asked.

"It is fear, of course. Can one end something without any motive or direction, without attachment, with all its complexities, with all its links to memory, to experience, knowledge? Death comes . . . after all, it is an ending of knowledge, that is what one is clinging to—the knowledge that a person dies, and I have looked after him, cherished him—in that all conflict is involved. Can one end totally, absolutely to the memory of that?" He paused. "That is death." Krishnaji was speaking very slowly, feeling his way into the immense question.

"Is there, as you have said, 'living to enter the house of death'?"

"Yes," he answered.

"What does it exactly mean?"

"To invite death while living. This does not mean to commit suicide or take a pill and exit. I am talking of ending—not only the depth of it, but the actual ending of something I have cherished. I cling to that memory and I live in that memory. I cherish it, and therefore I never find out what it means to end. There is a great deal in that. To end every day, everything that you have psychologically gathered," said Krishnaji.

"Attachment has to end?" I asked.

"That is death," said Krishnaji.

"That is not death," I countered.

"What would you call death? The organism coming to an end? Or the ending of the image I have built about the person who dies?"

"If you reduce it to an image, then I will say the image I have built about you. But it is much more than that," I said.

"There is much more than that. But I am enquiring. I have cherished you, and the image of you is deeply rooted in me. You die and that image gathers strength, naturally. I put flowers before it, write poetic words to it, and I am in sorrow. I am talking about the ending of that image. This mind cannot enter into a totally new dimension if there is a shadow of memory lurking. If the mind has to enter the timeless, the eternal, it must not have an element of time in it. I think this is logical. What is it you object to?" asked Krishnaji.

"Life is not logical, rational," I explained.

"Of course it is not. But it is in the ending of everything that you have gathered, which is time, that you understand that which is everlasting, without time. The mind must be free of time, and therefore there must be ending." The words were perfectly tuned.

"Therefore there is no exploration into ending?" I asked.

"Oh, yes, there is," said Krishnaji.

"What is exploration into ending?" I asked again.

"What is ending? Ending to continuity? The continuity of a particular thought, a particular desire? Or is it that which gives life a continuity? In birth and in dying, in that great interval there is deep continuity. It is like a river, the volume of water makes the river like the Ganga, the Rhine, the Amazon. But we live on the surface of this vast river of life and we cannot see the beauty of the depths, if we are always on the surface. The ending of the continuity is the ending of the surface."

There was a long pause. For me, there had been a sinking to vast depths. From there I asked, "What dies?"

"All that I have accumulated, both outwardly and inwardly. I have built a good business, I have a nice house, nice wife and children and my life gives continuity to that. Can one end that?" said Krishnaji.

"But you mean to tell me that with the death of the body of Krishnamurti, the consciousness of Krishnamurti will end? Please, Sir, there is great weight in this question," I said.

"You have said two things, the consciousness of Krishnamurti and the body. The body will end, that is inevitable—disease, accident, and so on. So what is the consciousness of that person?" asked Krishnaji.

"Unending, abounding compassion. Suppose I say that," I said.

"I wouldn't call that consciousness."

"I am using the word 'consciousness' because that field is associated with the body of Krishnamurti. I can't think of another word—can I say, the mind of Krishnamurti?"

"Keep to the word 'consciousness' and let us look at it. Consciousness of a human being is its content. The content is the whole movement of thought, the learning of language, beliefs, rituals, dogmas, loneliness, a desperate movement of fear, all that is consciousness. If the movement of thought ends, consciousness as one knows it is not."

"But thought as a movement in consciousness as we know it does not exist in the mind of Krishnaji," I said. "Yet there is a state of being that manifests itself when I am in contact with him. Therefore—"

"Consciousness as we know is a movement of thought. It is a movement of time," Krishnaji intervened. "See that very clearly. When thought comes to an end, not in the material world, but in the psychological, consciousness as we know it is not."

"You can use any other word, but there is a state of being that manifests itself as Krishnamurti. What word shall I use?"

"I am not asking you to change the word. But say, for example, in real meditation you come to a point that is absolute. I see it, I feel it, to me that is a most extraordinary state. I contact it. Through you I feel this immensity. And my whole urge, striving is to capture that. You have it, not 'you' have it—It is there—It is not Pupulji having it. It is not yours or mine. It is there," said Krishnaji.

"It is there because of you?" I asked.

"No, it is not there because of me. It is there." Again there was a long pause. The mind was touching something.

"Where?" I asked. Krishnaji listened, and let all time held in the question end.

"It has no place," he said. "First of all, it is not yours or mine."

"I only know that it is manifested in the person of Krishnamurti. Therefore when you say it has no place I cannot accept it," I said.

"Because you have identified Krishnamurti with that?" asked Krishnaji.

"But Krishnamurti *is* that?" I responded.

"Maybe. But K says that it has nothing to do with Krishnamurti or anybody. It is there. Beauty is not yours or mine. It is there, in the tree, in the flower."

"But, Sir, the healing and the compassion which is in Krishnamurti is not out there. I am talking of that," I said.

"But this is not Krishnamurti." He pointed to his body.

"It is manifested in Krishnamurti and it will cease to be manifested. That is what I am talking about," I said.

Krishnaji's response was swift. "I question that. It may manifest through X. That which is manifested or is manifesting does not belong to X."

"It may not belong to X," I began.

"It has nothing to do with X."

"It may not belong to Krishnamurti. But Krishnamurti and that are inseparable," I said.

"Yes. But you see, when you identify that with the person, we are entering into something very delicate." The tentacle was probing.

"I want to go into it slowly. You see—take the Buddha—whatever the Buddha consciousness was, it was manifested through him and it has ceased to be," I said.

"I question that the consciousness of Buddha ceased when he passed away. It was manifested through him, and you say when he died that disappeared."

"I have no knowledge to say it disappeared, but it could no longer be contacted."

"Naturally not," Krishnaji said.

"What do you mean by 'naturally not'?" I asked.

"Because he was illumined. Therefore it comes to him. It was. There was no division. And when he died his disciples said, 'He is dead and with his death that whole thing is over.' I say it is not. That which is good can never be over. As evil—if I can use that word without too much darkness in the word—evil continues in the world. Right? That evil is totally different from the good. The good manifests, the good will always exist, as the evil—which is not the opposite of the good—continues."

"You say that great illumined compassion does not disappear, but now I can contact it?" I persisted.

"Yes. But you can contact it when that person is not. That is the whole point. Krishnamurti has nothing to do with it," said Krishnaji.

"When you say, 'be a light to yourself,' is it involved with contacting 'that' without a person?"

"Not contacting, but receiving, living it. It is there for you to reach out and receive. But thought, as consciousness as we know it, has to come to an end. Thought is really the enemy of that. Thought is the enemy of compassion. And to have this flame, it demands not sacrifice, not this, not that, but an awakened intelligence which sees the movement of thought and the very awareness ends it. That is what real meditation is."

"What significance then has death?" I asked.

"None. It has no significance, because you are living with death all the time. Because you are ending everything all the time. I don't think we see the beauty and importance of ending. We see continuity with its waves of beauty, its superficiality."

"I drive away tomorrow, do I cut myself completely from you?" I asked.

"No, you cut yourself away from that eternity, with all its compassion, if you make me a memory." He paused. "I meet the Buddha. I have listened to him very deeply. In me the whole truth of what he says is abiding, and he goes away. He has told me very carefully, 'Be a light to yourself.' The seed is flowering. I may miss him. He was a friend, somebody whom I really loved. But what is really important is that seed of truth which he has planted—by my alertness, awareness, intense listening, that seed will flower. Otherwise, what is the point of somebody having it? If X has this extraordinary illumination, a sense of immensity, compassion, and all that, if only he has it and he dies, what is the point of it all? What?"

"May I ask one question? What is the reason, then, for his being?" I asked.

"What is the reason for his being, for his existence? To manifest that?" There was a pause, then Krishnaji said, "To be the embodiment of that, why should there be any reason? A flower has no reason, love has no reason, it exists. I try to find a reason and the flower is not. I am not trying to mystify all this. It is there for any one to reach out and to hold. So, Pupulji, death and birth—which must be an extraordinary event to a mother, and perhaps to a father—birth and death are far apart and all the travail of continuity is the misery of man. It is when continuity ends each day that we are living with death. That is a total renewal. That is something which has no continuity. That is why it is important to understand the meaning of ending totally. Can there be an ending to experience, or that which has been experienced and remains in the mind as memory?" He paused. "Could we go into the question whether a human being can live without time and knowledge apart from physical knowledge?"

I challenged him. "Isn't the living with ending the core of this question? That is, when the mind is capable of living with ending, it is capable of living with the ending of time and knowledge. Is it that you can do nothing about it? Is it that you have to listen and observe and do nothing else? Now I am getting to something rather difficult. There is the stream of knowledge. When I ask, 'Can I be free of the stream?' is it not one element of the stream of knowledge asking that question?"

"Of course, of course," Krishnaji responded.

"Then in that there is no meaning. The stream of knowledge, because it is challenged, responds. The only possible answer is the listening to the response."

"A throwing up, a listening, a flowering, and a subsiding," said Krishnaji from great depth.

"Is there anything else for man to do but to be awake to this arising?"

"And falling? Are you asking to really understand—we will call it goodness for the moment. Can you do anything? Is that what you are saying? I am not entirely sure of that."

"That is what I wanted to know—tell me."

"Isn't that rather an ultimate statement? I can do nothing about it," said Krishnaji.

"No, Sir, either I can do or . . . "

"Let us find out," said Krishnaji. You could feel the tentative probing mind.

"Either I can do, then the next question is, 'What can I do?' "

"What makes you say you cannot do?" asked Krishnaji. "Let us investigate together. What makes you say you can do nothing about it? About what?"

"About this arising from the stream. That is what we are talking about. There is a stream of knowledge. Either I am separate from that stream—"

"Which you are not," said Krishnaji.

"In investigating, I see, I am not."

"I understand that. If you make the statement 'I am the stream of knowledge and I can do nothing about it,' then you are playing with words."

"Then what is possible? What is the state of mind?"

"That is better," Krishnaji interrupted.

"That is sensitive to the arising and the falling," I said.

"If it is sensitive, there is neither arising nor ending," said Krishnaji.

"We don't know that state—the fact is, there is arising," I said.

"Can't you do something about the arising? Can't you do something without trying to change it, modify it, or escape from it? Can one see the arising of anger and be aware of that? Can one let it flower and end? Can one see anger arise and not get violent about it? Can one watch the movement of it, let it flower, and as it flowers it dies?"

"The mind that is capable of observing, how does anger arise at all?"

"It may be that the mind has not understood the whole movement of violence," said Krishnaji.

"Now, how does one observe something without the observer? Or does one observe with the observer?"

"The human mind has separated itself as the observer and the observed," said Krishnaji.

"I can observe anger arising, watch its manifestations—not interfere with its manifestations—and watch it subside," I said.

"That you can do something about it."

"The mind we call awake, that is what it does."

"Only the mind that sees that it can do nothing is motionless.

"So, have we, in this dialogue, seen the meaning of death?"

# CHAPTER 41

# "Learn to Die to Yourself Completely."

On October 22, 1981, Krishnaji arrived in Delhi with Asit Chandmal. Krishnaji had been ill in Brockwood a few days earlier and had also pulled a muscle in his back. He was looking very frail and had lost a great deal of weight. He had aged and his shoulders were bowed. He wanted to talk seriously to us in the afternoon. At about 4:30 P.M. he started talking to Nandini and me. He said that a fortnight back he was in Brockwood; he had been quite ill and in bed for a month. One night he awoke with a feeling of being completely well. Every organ in his body was healthy and awake. In that state he had a sense that the door of death was open. He was stepping through, completely awake and completely still. At one instant of death, however, the door closed. He did not close the door, the door closed.

He then turned to me very seriously and said, "Death can come at any moment." He asked me how I was physically. I said I had not been too well. He said, "You have to be well. You have to outlive me." And then he said strange words, which he repeated, "Learn to die to yourself completely." The frail body was shaking, yet there was a roar of thunder in his words.

From Delhi Krishnaji came to Varanasi. His first talk was exalted. He spoke about "the teaching as the mirror in which you see 'what is' reflected. The teaching is perception within you, of the actual."

Krishnaji said, "See, ask, what is religion, what is thought? See thought arising, watch it—without that all else is illusion and becoming. The truly religious mind is concerned with discovery and the understanding of what Truth is.

"Look," he said, "find out the origin, the beginning of thought, operating in time. For millennia, man is caught in pattern, in knowledge. There is no freedom in pattern, in knowledge." He spoke of the future of man—of computers taking over the inventive capacity of the brain. Scientists were pondering the ultimate intelligence machine— mother computers that could possibly create future computers. Computers in the future would invent gods, create philosophy. "Then, what is man?" Krishnaji asked. "The only thing man can do which the computer cannot is look at the evening star.

"There are only two alternatives for man: Either he commits himself to entertainment outwardly, as sport, religion, ritual, or he turns inward. The brain has an infinite capacity, now used technologically. The brain is occupied by the material—when this function is taken over by the machine, the brain will wither. Only religion can bring about a new culture. A religion that is totally independent of superstition and ritual. For that one has to uncover that which is beyond time, beyond thought."

At lunch Jagannath Upadhyaya was present. He had just been given a Nehru Fellowship and was going on his first trip abroad, visiting Buddhist centers in several countries. Krishnaji asked how he would communicate with academics, for Panditji knew no English, though he could understand the spoken word. Panditji replied that he would converse with his counterparts in Sanskrit. Soon Krishnaji began advising the Pandit on what clothes he should wear in Europe. Jagannath Upadhyaya was bewildered and overwhelmed when Krishnaji asked Achyut to make a list of clothes for him to take, including woolen longjohns. Krishnaji was very concerned that Upadhyaya would suffer because he would not be able to stand the winter abroad.

We then discussed the morning talk. Upadhyayaji said he had discussed the talk with his friends and they felt that, for the first time, they had actually contacted what Krishnaji said. In the beginning of the 1950s, when pandits of Varanasi had first heard Krishnaji, the Buddhists held that Krishnaji was speaking Buddhism, the Vedantins that he was in the stream of Vedanta. Later, Upadhyayaji felt that Krishnaji was more in the stream of Nagarjuna. Again, at a later period, he felt that Krishnaji's word was what Nagarjuna would have said had he been alive today. It was relevant to the contemporary moment. Since Madras last year, Panditji had been thinking anew. He could no longer make any statement on Krishnaji, he was still probing. Krishnaji said he had talked a great deal; there were a number of books. People referred to them as "Krishnamurti's teachings." "The teachings were not the book," he said. "The only teachings were, 'Look at yourself. Enquire into yourself—go beyond.' There is no understanding of the teaching, only understanding of yourself. The words of K were a pointing of the way. The understanding of yourself the only teaching."

Questioned, Jagannath Upadhyaya explained to Krishnaji the nature of Nagarjuna's negation. It was the negating of all doctrine, belief, including the doctrine of the Buddha. Krishnaji was very interested. Later, he asked Upadhyayaji, "How do you approach a problem?" Upadhyayaji could not understand. Krishnaji kept on probing. He said, "In the approach is the answer, not away from it." Jagannath Upadhyaya said he understood verbally.

On November 24, 1981, Achyut, Rimpoche Sandup, and I had lunch with Krishnaji. The Rimpoche's face was very grave. We spoke of Tibet and the possible return of the Dalai Lama. Krishnaji asked questions on the various schools of Buddhism in Tibet. Suddenly, the Rimpoche said, "For the last few days I have known great sorrow. I have meditated—looked, listened, but it is there." He had tears in his eyes and deep sorrow on his face. We talked of the ending of sorrow and the holding of sorrow in the mind and what it involved. Krishnaji suddenly put his two hands over his heart and said, "It is here." I asked him to elucidate that gesture. He said, "First of all, one must observe, see with great care the mind and its functioning, listen to what is within and without; out of this arises sensitivity and in sensitivity there arises insight. That insight alone will wipe away sorrow."

A day earlier we had, at a small discussion, spoken of time and knowledge. "Can the brain be free of time as becoming—can it change its dependence on psychological time?" I said that when one looked at the teaching, it had first concerned itself with individual transformation. He spoke of the mind of man, the million years of man's history, contained in the brain cells and the transformation in the brain cells. The birth of the global mind demanded an urgency, a revolution in the human condition. In the last few years Krishnaji had denied any place to the individual. He had gone beyond "man" and the human condition. He had been speaking of the universe, and a sense of the cosmic had entered his teachings. Krishnaji was asking, "What is man's relationship to the universe?" I again asked Krishnaji, "Has there been a change in your teachings?" He pondered for a few moments, then said pointing to the river Ganga, "at the source, that river is one drop—it is the Ganga."

He spoke of the meditation of the universe as the ground of creation. Meditation being a state without horizons, space without limit, and an ending of time. The words "timeless eternity" were part of his vocabulary. He brought into his teachings the logic of Buddhism, and with the ending of logic and thought he probed into space, using intelligence as the instrument. "The probing is with nothing, into wordless endless being."

"Can one hold that in consciousness?" he asked. "Then, what is consciousness?"

On a walk, he said, "The enquiry within is infinite. You must be alone, stripped, then you can take a journey into the unknown." He was still probing, feeling out, he continued to question.

Another afternoon at lunch he was pondering the immensity of time and its implications. He asked, "Is inner time a fact? Is there the arrow of time within?" He spoke of creation as total destruction. "In life there is both creation and destruction—the very act of listening is the miracle, it is light in darkness. In it is mutation and deep uprooting. Could one in the act of listening, explore into oneself?" he asked.

While in Rajghat, Krishnaji probed into the nature of attention. He asked us, "What is it to attend?" He said that the "total attention of one thought unfolds the whole nature of thought."

I said that for such a total attention, the mind had to have weight. Every attention gave depth to the ground of the mind. Krishnaji refused to accept that the many acts of attention gave depth to the mind. "No preparation is necessary," he said.

I asked him, "What gave the mind the swiftness, the insight to perceive that in one thought, all thought is revealed?" Krishnaji spoke of the necessity for the brain cells to be totally still. I said there was an inherent tendency in the brain to move. In asking the brain to be totally still, Krishnaji was going against the nature of the brain.

"Mutation is immediate," Krishnaji said. "The question is, what makes it take place?"

"Biologically, mutation is possible when there is a tremendous necessity for such mutation; or, with the ending of a particular function of the brain, the cells wither away and a new cell is born," I commented.

"The absolute necessity to change creates the biological need to find the new. As knowledge cannot transform man, I ask, is there an action that is not based on knowledge?"

Krishnaji's attention was cleaving into mind, establishing a direct contact, touching the minds around him.

I said, "I have to observe the mind, to see its traps. That is insight."

Krishnaji interrupted me. "No, you are a traditionalist. You are speaking of years of preparation to see this. I say, insight is the perception of this pattern. Insight breaks the pattern."

I said, "The word 'insight' is an interesting word. It implies sight into the within. Insight is to turn your face away from the known."

Krishnaji said, "Yes. The brain is conditioned to a pattern. The very biological necessity makes it to break the pattern. The insight needed to see this does not need training, nor time."

I said, "I am not speaking of continuity as time, but insight as a deepening of the mind."

Krishnaji said, "Deepening is time. See what is implied in what you are saying."

I said, "You are speaking of the mind being totally still. Twenty years ago when you asked such a question, my thoughts moved towards the question. This no longer happens. The brain is still and listens. There is a difference in quality between the two states. How can you deny the twenty years?"

Krishnaji said, "Time makes the brain duller and duller. I question the whole concept of time to get anywhere. I don't accept inner time."

"I am not talking of it as practice," I said.

"But you are giving strength to time," said Krishnaji. "How does the river in flood flow?" he asked. "Yet the first few drops are the river."

Achyut spoke, "You are so relentless in your logic. There is such immensity in what you say. Yet, I see that there is a blockage in me that comes in the way of my understanding you."

Krishnaji replied, "Could you consider denying time? Not time as the linear stream, but psychological time as becoming. Can you so deny time that it ceases in your brain? We are speaking of the psychological process of time as a movement from here to there." He paused. "Can you listen quietly?" he asked. "Can you accept time as sunrise and sunset and say, there is no other time?" he paused. "Don't say 'yes.' Do you see that this implies that there is no psychological future? It means the past has its own action, but not as the movement of time, as becoming something. I am asking you 'now.' I say, there is no preparation for insight. Do you see that? Can you see immediately, without time?"

I said, "One can see that the brain cells and thought are one. The brain cells for millennia have been conditioned to move in a pattern. Krishnaji said to me some years ago that the brain cells could not renew themselves, but a new cell had to be born."

Krishnaji said, "Transformation cannot take place in the old cell, nor in thought. The new can have no relationship to the old. All change, the movement from one corner of the brain to another, is not renewal. Find out, whether it is possible to break conditioning and discover something totally new."

I said that in total attention was the ending of the old. I could not know or contact the brain cells, I could only know thought. Any operation of attention has to be on thought. Then I asked, "We have said that movement is inbuilt into the brain. Can that brain, which for millennia has known movement, not move?"

"Yes, now we are getting it," said Krishnaji. "Can one see the brain cell as thought? Can one see that attention can only act on thought? And that transformation cannot act and has no relationship with thought? The old has to end."


I returned to New Delhi and was at the airport to receive Krishnaji when he arrived with Achyut from Varanasi on the last day of December 1981. They both stayed at my house at 11 Safdarjung Road. It was the first time that Krishnaji, Achyut, and I had been alone together, staying in the same house, and Krishnaji commented on it.

The next morning after breakfast we went into the sitting room and Krishnaji began talking of Mrs. Besant and Leadbeater. His great love for Mrs. Besant was evident. He told us that, as a child, he had many extrasensory powers—the capacity to read thought, or what was written in an unopened letter. He could make objects materialize, see visions, and foretell the future. He had the power of healing. But he had put all these powers aside naturally. He had never felt any interest in them. We tried to pursue the topic, when all of a sudden he asked, "Do you believe in mystery?"

"Yes," I said. "When we see you and talk to you seriously, a mysterious atmosphere comes into being."

Krishnaji said, "Yes, that is so."

I said, "There is a feeling of touch without anyone being there—a feeling of presence."

"It is in the room," said Krishnaji. "I don't know whether you feel it—what is that?" and then a strange look entered his eyes. "I must be awfully careful about this." He stopped speaking suddenly, then said, "You ask—I won't ask."

I said, "What is it?"

"Be careful. When we talk of this, either we are imagining it or . . . "

"What takes place—is it linked with you?"

"Yes, obviously." Krishnaji's mood was changing, he was speaking from great depth, as if traveling swiftly vast spaces within. "I think there is a force which the Theosophists had touched but tried to make into something concrete. But, there was something they had touched and then tried to translate into their symbols and vocabulary, and so lost it. This feeling has been going on all through my life—it is not. . . ."

"Linked with consciousness?" asked Achyut.

"No, no. When I talk about it, something tremendous is going on. I can't ask it anything," said Krishnaji.

Through windows, doors, silence poured.

"All your illnesses have been very strange. Every serious illness has been followed by a fount of new energy," I said. There was a long pause.

Krishnaji suddenly asked, "What are we talking about?"

"Is it something outside of you? Does it protect you?" I spoke hesitatingly.

"Yes, yes—of that there is no question—absolutely."

"Every time it takes place—does the nature of it change?"

Krishnaji said, "No, no . . . "

"Does it intensify?" I asked.

"Yes, it intensifies." Again there was a long pause.

Then, as if hesitating to use words, Krishnaji said, "Is it an external thing happening inwardly? The universe pouring in—and the body cannot stand too much to it. As I am talking, it is very strong. Five minutes ago, it wasn't there. When young they told me, 'Be completely like an open channel—don't resist.' " Only later did I wonder who 'they' were."

"Has it any relationship to the word Maitreya Bodhisattva?" Achyut asked.

"Is Maitreya Bodhisattva fictitious? Did C. W. L. invent it? Did the boy live with that name unconsciously? Or is it something totally different from their indoctrination?" Krishnaji appeared totally absorbed in the query.

"Does the word Maitreya mean anything to you?" I asked.

"No," Krishnaji answered.

I persisted. "Why do you say, 'No.'? You, who say there is no psychological memory, why do the words 'Maitreya Buddha' have an effect on you?"

"You remember Abanendranath Tagore's 'Buddha'—That picture had an extraordinary effect on the boy. He did not know what Buddhism was." Krishnaji paused. "But, the feeling of the Buddha has always been there. A feeling of enormity."

"A feeling of enormity? Can we go with that? Is that feeling outside you? Or is it within? Is the body not able to take it?"

"Don't think I am crazy. I have never felt as I feel now. That the universe is so close, as though my head was stuck in the universe. Does it sound crazy?" Krishnaji asked shyly.

"Are you saying that all barriers have ceased?"

"You see, the words 'Buddha,' 'Maitreya,' have lost meaning. I have a feeling that all verbal sensation has ended."

"You said something about being very close to the universe?"

Krishnaji laughed. "Yes, my head is in it."

"That comes through in the talks. The center of your teaching has moved to a cosmic position," I said.

Then he used strange words. "Or it may be nothing at all. It may be a tentacle that is feeling around. I am not getting to the clarity of it. Now, this room is filled with it. Whatever it is, it is throbbing with it. The more I watch, it is there—the intensity of it. I could sit here with you two and go off. Be with that enormous thing and let it operate. It is a mystery; the moment mystery is understood, it is no longer mystery. One cannot understand the mysterious—it is too infinite. It is like looking around the corner. Do you see?"

"I have a curious feeling that I want to penetrate that mystery. Do you follow? And yet there is a certain hesitancy to go near it. You cannot touch it. It is there. It is mysterious. On the platform it is something different. Or probably, it is the same thing."

# CHAPTER 42

# The Limits of Thought

In the third week of January 1982 Krishnaji was in Bombay, staying at Sterling Apartments. After the Sunday talk on January 24, Krishnaji, Nandini, and I were at dinner. We were discussing cancer, and I remarked that if it was not in its early stage, I would not permit my body to be destroyed by the new therapies, which were more destructive than the disease. I would prepare myself for death. K said a society had been started in the West where people claimed the right to die. A manual had been brought out which gave details of the easiest way to die. It prescribed the taking of sleeping pills, a large dose, then the slipping of a plastic bag over the head, with a rubber band round the neck; the person could lift the band and let in air, if he felt suffocated. As he fell asleep the hand would fall and next morning the person would be dead. Nandini heard this and a look of great fear came over her face. "No, no," she said unconsciously. We looked at her and I asked her a little sharply why she was reacting? Had she ever thought of committing suicide? She hesitated, pulled herself together, paused, and said, "Once. As K spoke I felt the suffocation."

We discussed fear and its nature. I asked Krishnaji whether he had ever known fear. He paused, pondered. "Many things can happen at night; darkness invites many things." In his life he had not known fear, but evil existed. Evil had a presence and was always waiting to find a chink through which to enter.

K said, "Fear attracts evil. To talk about evil is to invite it." Suddenly, Krishnaji became strange and far removed. He drew his arms close to himself, drawing his body into the smallest possible space. Then he said, "Do you feel it in the room?" His face had changed. The room was charged with power. Then K said, "Before we sleep, I will have to dispel it. Protect this place." He would not say what he would do, but something had to be done. A little later he got up and walked round, circumambulating each of the rooms. Devi and Ghanshyam, Nandini's children, had come into the house. They sensed something, and did not enter the room where we sat. A little later, Krishnaji came back to the dining room. He was serene, his face beautiful, his eyes limpid. The atmosphere had totally changed. Whatever was there had been totally wiped away.

Over the years Nandini and I had often talked of Krishnaji's attitude to good and evil. He had told us, "Evil is a fact. Leave it alone. Your mind should not play with evil. Thinking about it is to invite it. Hatred, jealousy, attract evil. That is why it is important for the mind and body to be still and silent and not let any strong emotions arise, without watching relentlessly. Deterioration walks one step behind you. No matter who you are." Through the years I had noticed that when strong emotions were at play amongst people around him, or when any question arose concerning evil, his voice changed, his eyes withdrew, he would draw his body close together, the atmosphere grew turgid, to totally dissipate a few moments later.

For him, as there was a reservoir of the good, there was also lurking darkness. The two were not related. Evil looked for a foothold to enter; therefore the need for watchfulness. "Have you ever observed a cat watching a hole into which a mouse has hidden? Watch any strong feeling like that, without the eyes moving away," he was to say.

In the summer of 1982 I was in London in connection with the Festival of India, with which I had been closely associated. From London I had gone to Brockwood Park and had spent a week with Krishnaji. During one of his conversations with me, we discussed insight and the mind. We talked of the Indian mind, the place of myth. I said, "The modern mind has no density or weight." He replied, "What is necessary is to have an ancient mind, not a mind that is superficially East or West. Insights give strength to the mind. Most people feel they have strong minds. But with a strong mind, you cannot probe. Strange things are happening. I wake up at night with immense action within the head. I feel every cell in my body, living, dancing, throbbing."

I asked Krishnaji whether he would accept the fact that there was an Indian mind. The Indian mind might have within it the same tendencies as the Western mind—the same greed, jealousy, anger—but the ground from which these two sprang was different. I went on to say that, being differently conditioned, these two minds complemented each other.

Later, Krishnaji said that when he was in India he had witnessed a growing materialism. He then asked me, "What is the concern of the

Indian mind today?" I replied that it was difficult to say. There had been vast changes in recent years. There was growing violence, an increase of materialism, and a movement towards consumerism. The technological culture had penetrated to some depth into the Indian mind and environment.

Krishnaji then asked what was the basic difference between the two minds. For centuries, the Indian mind had a certain edge that enabled it to delve; but it lacked precision, the capacity to take an abstraction and transform it into concrete solution. The Western mind had precision; rooted in logic and reason, it had turned to the outer, to the transformation of the environment. Krishnaji said technology had possibly brought the Indian mind to the earth. He questioned, however, whether thought was ever of the East or West. "There is only thought, expressions may differ. Has the Indian mind a tendency for inward search?"

"Yes," I said, "just as the Western mind has a proclivity to move and function in the outer environment. The inner environment has been the concern of India."

"Concern of a very few people," commented Krishnaji.

"But it is only the few that create culture. How does culture come into being?" I asked.

We then discussed what had divided the two minds, what led the Indian and the Western mind to move in different directions. Krishnaji spoke of climate, political directions, concern with worldly affairs, which led in the West to the inventive mind. In India, with its ancient civilization, the highest concern had been with a religious life and inner enquiry.

"Somewhere along the line, people of one racial stock seemingly divided," I said. "The West turned to outer discovery, in their dialogue with nature. Out of this emerged very significant truths concerning science and technology. India also had a dialogue with nature, but it was of a different order."

"Are you saying," asked K, "that the Indian mind is more concerned with religious matters than the West? In India the concern with religion has been deep. Indian tradition has maintained that the understanding of the Self, of the Universe, of the Highest Principle, is the most significant pursuit."

"There is a swiftness with which the Indian mind starts an inner enquiry. The great insights are different in the West and India," I said.

"In the East, in religious matters, doubt, skepticism, questioning form the base of religious enquiry. In the West, faith is all important," K commented.

"Both cultures today are in crisis," I said.

"Yes. Human consciousness, human culture is in crisis."

"Would you distinguish consciousness from culture?" I asked.

"No, they are the same," said Krishnaji.

"The crisis is at the very root of the human mind. Human beings feeling an inadequacy, turn to other cultures."

"I am questioning whether in their search away from the materialistic outlook, they are not being caught in superstition, by romantic ideas, gurus? If human consciousness is in crisis, as it is, the question is can the crisis be resolved, or is it inevitable that human beings can never go beyond their limitations?"

"The outer and the inner, the material and the search within, are two mirror images," I said. "If man has to survive, can these two be brought together? Or can a human culture come into existence which could sustain and contain the two?"

"What do you mean by the word culture?" K asked.

"Everything the brain contains," I responded.

"The training of the brain and the refinement of the brain; the training of the brain in action, in behavior, in relationships, and also a process of enquiry that leads to something untouched by thought. I would say that is culture," commented K.

"Would you include enquiry in the field of culture? Isn't culture a closed circuit?"

"You can make it that, or you can go beyond," said K.

"As it exists, culture is a closed circuit," I said.

"What is culture?" K asked again.

"Perceptions, the way we look at things, thoughts, feelings, attitudes; the operation of the senses. You can keep on adding to this," I said.

"Include in it religion, faith, belief."

"The content can keep on growing, but within a contour. When you talk of search, would you include it in culture?" I asked.

"Of course," said Krishnaji. "I am enquiring with hesitation and skepticism whether the brain evolved through thousands of years, having experienced untold sorrow, despair; attempting to escape from its own fears through every form of religious endeavor; whether that brain in itself can ever change? Can it bring about a mutation in itself? Otherwise anything new, a different culture, can never be."

"If it does not bring about a mutation in itself, is there anything else?" I asked.

"The Hindus have asked this question centuries ago, whether there is an outside agency, the Highest Principle which can operate on the conditioned brain?" Krishnaji said.

"Or is it that it can awaken something within the brain?" I queried.

"There are two possibilities: Either there is an outside agency, as energy, operating; or, from within the brain cells, there is an awakening that transforms." Krishnaji continued his enquiry into whether there is an outside agency that would bring about a mutation in the brain cells that were conditioned.

I was listening deeply, watching within and responding from the listening. "The fact is that the energy in nature, the flow rarely touches the brain cells. There are so many obstacles one has built; that the flow of energy from nature, never seems to touch and create."

Krishnaji suddenly asked, "What are we discussing?"

"The possibility of a human culture that is neither of India nor of the West; which contains all mankind and its insights. The division between the within and without ends. Insight is insight, not insight into outer or inner. If the instrument is the brain, something has to happen in the brain," I said.

Krishnaji's response was to ask whether it could happen without the idea that there was an outside agency that would bring about mutation in a conditioned brain. Or could the conditioned brain awaken to its own conditioning, perceive its own limitations and stay there? "All the time we are trying to do something. And I ask, is the doer different from that which is done? I see that my brain is conditioned and that all my activities, my relationships, are limited. I see that limitation must be broken down. But the 'I' is operating on the limitation. And the 'I' is limited. It is not separate from the limitation which it is trying to break down. The limitation of the self and the limitation of the conditioning are not separate. The 'I' is not separate from its qualities."

"From what it observes?"

"One part observes the other part," was Krishnaji's response.

"You say that, but we are all the time trying to operate on the other," I said.

"All life is that. Apart from the world of technology, the brain is conditioned in this tradition that the actor is different from the action. So conditioning goes on. But when one realizes that the actor is the action, then the whole outlook changes. We are asking Pupulji what brings about a change in the human brain."

"That is crucial: What is it that makes the division end?"

"Man has been the same for a million years—and, psychologically, we are as primitive as we were. We have not basically changed very much. We still kill each other; we seek power, position. We are corrupt. Human beings are the same today psychologically as they were. What will make humanity change all that?"

"Insight?" I asked.

"Is so-called culture preventing insight?" asked Krishnaji. He said that a few people had gone into this question of insight in India, while the rest just repeated. "Tradition is a dead thing, and India lives with this dead thing. Here too, tradition has tremendous power."

"In the West there are the few who have great insights into science," I said.

"Yes. But what will make human beings bring about a mutation in themselves? Culture is trying to bring about certain changes in human behavior. Religions have said don't kill, and man kills. There are the edicts, the sanctions, and we are doing quite the opposite," said Krishnaji.

"Cultures have collapsed."

"That is what I want to find out. Whether cultures have collapsed and so man can't turn to them any more. So man is now at a loss. What will bring about a mutation in the brain cells?" Krishnaji's passionate concern was evident.

"We were saying that the Indian matrix may be different to the Western matrix. But the problem is identical. How do we bring about a mutation in the human matrix, the human brain?" I asked.

"After all, Indians suffer there as the European suffers; the despair, misery is the same. So let us forget the East or West and see what prevents this mutation taking place."

"Is there any other way but perceiving the actual?"

"That is what we have been saying for years. The actual is more important than the idea. The ideal concepts have no value at all because they move away from 'what is.' Apparently, it is tremendously difficult not to have ideals," said Krishnaji.

"In perceiving the actual, is there no movement of the brain?" I asked.

"That's all I'm saying. If one observes very carefully, facts in themselves bring about a change. Human sorrow is not Western or Eastern. We are always trying to move away from sorrow. Can we understand the depth and meaning of sorrow? Not intellectually understand, but actually delve into the nature of sorrow? Sorrow is not yours or mine, so what is blocking the human brain from enquiring deeply within?"

"You use the word delving, enquiring into oneself. Both are words connected with movement—yet you speak of the ending of movement. Of course . . . of course . . . movement is time . . . movement is thought. There has to be the ending of movement. Can that really end or we think it can end? We divide the entity that enquires and the entity that is to be enquired into. That is my objection—that is the major block."

"When you use the word 'enquiry,' do you use it as perception?" I asked.

"Perception—watching," was Krishnaji's response. "What will make human beings change in the way they behave? Very simply put, what will change all this appalling brutality? Who will change it? Not the politician, not the priest—not the people who talk of environment, ecologists and so on. They cannot change the human being. Who will change him if man himself will not do so? The church has not succeeded in changing man. Religions have tried to transform the world, humanize man, make him more intelligent, more affectionate. They have not succeeded."

"We see all this, Krishnaji, but that itself does not bring man to perception of fact," I said.

"What will make him have this perception? You may have it—but if I don't have it, what effect has your perception on me? I am asking a deeper question. Why are human beings, after millennia, like this? Why is there one group against another group, one tribe against another tribe, one nation against another nation? A new culture, will that bring about a change? Does man want to change? Or does he think it's all right, man will evolve at a certain stage. Meanwhile, we are destroying each other."

"What is the actual moment of facing a fact? What is the actuality of it?" I asked.

"What is a fact? Fact is that which has been done and which is being done now. The acting now and that which has happened, is the fact.

"Let us be clear. When we see the fact, the fact of yesterday or last week, the incident is over, but I remember it; the memory is stored in the brain. What is being done now is also a fact, colored by the past, controlled by the past. Can I see this whole movement as a fact?"

"Would you say that seeing it as a fact is seeing without accretion?" I asked.

"Seeing without prejudice."

"Without anything surrounding the fact."

"That's right, which means what?"

"Negating all responses that arise."

"Negating the remembrances."

"Which arise out of it," I interrupted.

"Now is that possible?"

"That is possible. Attention itself dissipates the movement."

"That means, can the brain be so attentive that the incident that happened last week is revealed? You do not carry on the remembrance. But what happens is, my son is dead and I suffer. And the memory of that son is so strongly imprinted in my brain that there is a constant arising of suffering which is remembrance."

"Out of that is the movement of pain. Attention ends not only the pain, but the arising." I was probing.

"Go into it a little bit more," Krishnaji said. "What does that mean? My son is dead. I remember him and there is the thought of him standing near the piano or the mantlepiece. There is this constant remembrance flowing in and flowing out."

"The negating of the pain and the dissolving of this, doesn't it have direct action on the brain?" I asked.

"Which means what? My son is dead. That's a fact. I can't change the fact. He's gone. It sounds cruel to say it, but he's gone. But I'm carrying him all the time. Right? The brain is holding it as memory and carrying it all the time. I live on memories, which are dead things. Memory is not the actual. There has to be an ending. My son is gone. It doesn't mean I have lost my love for him."

"But what remains?"

"May I say something without being shocking?" asked Krishnaji. "Nothing. My son is gone—which is not an assertion of cruelty or denying my love. What has ended is not the love of my son, but the identification of love with my son."

"You are drawing a distinction between love of my son and love."

"If I loved my son in the deepest sense of the word, I love humanity. If I loved my son, I love the whole world. I love the earth, the trees, the whole universe. What takes place when there is a pure perception of fact, without any bias, without any escape? Can one see the fact completely? Is that possible? When I am in sorrow, I am lost. It's a great shock, and at the moment of death you can't say anything to the person who is in sorrow. But as he comes out of his confusion, loneliness, despair, sorrow, then perhaps he will be sensitive enough to see this fact."

I asked whether the perception of the fact needed a great watching. "You can't tell a person who has never watched to end sorrow."

"That would be cruel. But a man who has observed, has enquired into death, and sees that it is common to all humanity, to the man who is sensitive—he wants to find an answer."

I began, "Sir, at that level how simple it is—"

"We must keep it simple, not bring into it intellectual theories and ideas."

"Is the mind afraid of the simple?" I asked.

"We are so highly intellectual. To make things complex is part of our education, part of our culture. Ideas are tremendously important. To us they are essential—"

"To you the highest point of culture is the dissolution of the self. When you speak of the dissolution of the fact, it is essentially the dissolution of the self."

"Yes. But the dissolution of the self has become a concept, and we worship the concept. They do this all over the world. Concepts are put together by thought. What will make human beings throughout the world behave, not my way, not your way, but so that they do not kill, they have affection. Nothing has succeeded. Knowledge has not helped man."

"Living the way man does, fear is his shadow."

"And man wants to know what the future is," said Krishnaji.

"As part of fear?" I asked.

"Because he seeks security in so many things and they all fail, and he feels there must be security somewhere?" He paused. "I question whether there is security—anywhere?"

"What is the action of the dissolution of the fact, on the brain cells?" I asked.

"I would use the word insight. Insight is not a matter of memory, knowledge, or time, which are all parts of thought. I would say insight is the total absence of the whole movement of thought, time, and remembrance. So that there is direct perception. Can I see that I have been going north for the last ten thousand years? That my brain is accustomed to going north? Then someone comes along and says, 'That will lead you nowhere. Turn east.' When I turn east, the brain cells change. If I see the whole movement of thought as limited and I see thought will not solve any of my problems, then I stop going north. In the ending of the self is the ending of a movement that has been going on for thousands of years. That is insight. That brings about a change or a mutation in the brain. I think one sees this very clearly. But will that perception make humanity change? What will make my son, my daughter change? They read this, and they continue their old way. Is the past tradition so strong? I have thought of myself for the last thousand years, and I am still thinking of myself. I feel I must fulfill myself. This is my condition. This is my tradition. Is the past so tremendously strong? And the past is incarnating all the time. Is that part of culture—to continue in our condition?"

"I would say that is part of culture," I said.

"Look at it. I have been watching this very seriously. How strong tradition is. I am speaking of tradition as a continuity of the past, carrying on in its own momentum. And we are that. Our culture, our religious concepts are our tradition. So what is the brain to do?"

"I have a feeling, Sir, that we talk of observing thought, but that is an entirely different thing to the actual state of attention."

"That is thought being aware of itself. The central issue is that the world has become more and more superficial, more and more money-minded, identified with the me-me-me."

"It is so easy to turn what you say into a concept. But can there be a culture which is living, because it is living with insight?"

"I wouldn't use the word 'culture.' "

"You started with the word 'culture' as something that contains more than just a human culture—which perhaps is the culture of the mind. In such a state what happens to all the civilizations the world has seen and known and contains?"

"Which means, Pupulji, 'What is freedom?' Are we aware that we are prisoners of our own fantasies?"

"I think we are."

"If we are aware—they are burnt out."

"You don't admit an in-between state. That is the whole problem."

"The man who is violent and tries to be less violent in an in-between state, is violent."

"Not necessarily. Is there not also in what you say the whole movement of time and thought?"

"Which is what? Thought is limited. I know thought enquiring into itself is limited."

"The difference is, Sir, I might see this—but the attention necessary for it to remain alive in my waking day may not be there. The capacity, the strength of that attention may not be there."

"That passion, that sustained movement of energy is not dissipated by thought, by any kind of activity, and that comes into being when you understand sorrow. In the ending of sorrow there is compassion. That intelligence, that energy, has no depression."

"You mean it neither rises nor falls."

"No, to rise or fall you must be aware that it is rising, falling, and who is it who is aware—"

"But is it possible throughout the day to hold that?" I asked.

"Just be aware, not hold it. It is like a perfume—it is there. You don't hold it. That is why I think one has to understand the whole conditioning of our consciousness. I think that is the real enquiry. The real exploration is into consciousness, which is the common ground of all humanity. And we never enquire into it. We never say, 'I am going to study this consciousness that is "me." '

"And to be free of the self is one of the most difficult things, because the 'me' hides under different rocks, in different crevices."

# CHAPTER 43

# "How Far Can One Travel?"

The next morning Krishnaji walked in while I was drinking my early cup of morning tea. We started talking. We were to have a dialogue later in the day and Krishnaji said, "Pupul, could we discuss to the limits of thought and travel beyond?"

He was in an exalted mood. I had a bad cough and did not feel particularly bright that morning. I did not think of the topic we were to discuss, nor did I try to awaken the brain in any way.

Later, as Krishnaji and I sat down facing each other, I still did not know what I was going to say. Then I started speaking, and the words flowed as if they had been programmed. I was fluent, lucid; there was depth of probing and an extensive seeing. I said that recently I had read of a rocket that would travel to the outer reaches of the universe and there would be no end to its journey. There would be no friction, no time, and so no ending. I asked, "Is there in the ways of the self, in the human mind, in the human brain, a within of things? Are there vast, immeasurable spaces that lie in the within of nature?"

"Are you asking whether within the human brain—I would like to use 'mind' as separate from 'brain'—whether there is or there can be a space without end, an eternity out of time? We could speculate about it, but speculation is not actuality."

"But it was an insight into the possibility of exploring outer space that enabled man to explore outer space. If we do not posit a thing, we cannot explore and prove that it is so," I said.

"Are we speculating, or are we really enquiring whether there is such immensity, whether there is a movement that is not of time, a movement that is eternal?"

"For this enquiry we must pose the question. What comes out of it will determine whether the question is speculation or enquiry."

"We have posed the question whether the brain can realize the truth, that there is eternity or no eternity. How do we begin to enquire? How do you feel into this question diligently, a question that has been asked by man for thousands of years? Is man bound to time forever? Or is there—or can there be—actually within the brain a realization, for itself, that there is a state of eternity?"

"How do you proceed into this? You started by drawing a distinction between the brain and mind. Would you elaborate?"

"The brain is conditioned. That conditioning is brought about by knowledge, memory, experience. The brain is limited. So to discover something new there has to be a period, even temporarily, when thought is not in movement, when it is in abeyance."

"The brain is a material thing, it has its own activity."

"Yes, an activity that is not imposed by thought," said Krishnaji.

"For us, the operation of the brain has been the operation of thought," I said.

"Yes, the movement of the brain, the part of the brain being used, is conditioned by thought. Thought is always limited, conditioned to conflict. That which is limited must create conflict. Mind is a totally different dimension that has no contact with thought. Let me explain. The brain which has been functioning as an instrument of thought, that brain has been conditioned; and so long as that part of the brain remains in that state, there is no entire communication with the mind. So when there is no functioning of thought, there is communication, which is a totally different dimension; that can communicate with the brain using thought."

"You are postulating a state outside the realm of thought?" I asked.

"That's it. That is outside the realm of time," said Krishnaji.

"As time and thought seem to be the essential core of this problem, perhaps if we could go into the flow of time, we could discover at what instant interception is possible."

"What do you mean by 'interception'?" asked Krishnaji.

"I am not talking of the interceptor, but of a direct contact which is the ending of time. Isn't time from a past immemorial, projecting into a future which is without end?"

"No, the future is conditioned by the past."

"So, unless the human being ends, ceases to be—"

"Ceases to be conditioned," said Krishnaji.

"But you will still use thought. Its content will undergo change, but the mechanism of thought will continue," I said.

"Now, thought is the chief instrument we have. After thousands of years of friction, wars, that instrument has been made dull. It cannot go beyond its own tether. Thought is limited, it is conditioned and in a perpetual state of conflict."

"I had used the word 'interception' to signify contact with the movement from the past, as the yesterday."

"As the today," said Krishnaji.

"What is the today? How do we contact the today?"

"Today is the movement of the past modified. We are a bundle of memories, which is what? The past, present, future is a movement of time—thought. How do you realize it?"

"Is there not such a thing as a tactile touch with it?"

"How do you touch this thing? How does one have contact with the fact that I am a whole series of memories, which is time—thought?"

"Let us be concrete. The thought that I go away this afternoon and I will be leaving you is a fact."

"It is an actuality."

"Out of that is born a certain nostalgia of leaving you, which is emotional, psychological, which covers up the fact. What has to be contacted, surely, is not the fact that I am going away, but the pain of my going."

"The pain of going, of a thousand centuries of pain, anxiety, aches. Is that separate from you who feel it?" Krishnaji spoke.

"It may not be separate. How do I touch it?" I asked.

"What do you mean?" asked Krishnaji.

"It is only in the present that I can contact the whole of this edifice," I said. "The now contains the past, future, and present."

"The present is the past and the future. The present is moving. The present is a thousand years of the past being modified, and the future is 'now,' the present."

"The present is also not static. The moment you try to see it, it is gone. So what is it that you actually observe?" I asked.

"The fact that the present is the whole movement of time and thought. Can one see the truth of that? Can one have insight, perception into the fact, that the now is all time and thought?" asked Krishnaji.

"Does that perception emanate from the brain?"

"Either it emanates from perceiving, or the perception is an insight that has nothing to do with time and thought," said Krishnaji.

"Does it arise within the brain?" I asked.

"Yes, or does it arise outside the brain?" said Krishnaji. "Is it within the sphere of the brain, or is there insight that comes when there is freedom from conditioning? This insight, this mind, is supreme intelligence," said Krishnaji.

"I don't follow."

"The brain is conditioned by time and thought. So long as conditioning exists, insight is not possible. You may have an occasional insight, but this insight we speak about is the comprehension of totality, a perception of completeness. Right? This insight is not bound by time—thought. That insight is part of that brain which is a different dimension."

There was a pause. The listening had been at great depth.

"Without sight there cannot be insight," I said. "So seeing, perceiving, listening seem to be essential to insight. The word 'insight' is the seeing into. Is it seeing into seeing?"

"No. Seeing, comprehending the totality, the vastness of something. Insight is possible only with the cessation of thought and time. Thought and time are limited. Therefore in such limitation there cannot be insight," said Krishnaji.

"To understand what you say, I have to have an open ear and eyes that see. Out of sound, form, arises a seeing that goes beyond. You talk of insight, but insight cannot arise without sight."

"Insight cannot arise so long as there is time, thought."

"Which comes first? I cannot start with insight. I can only start with observation," I said.

"You can only start by seeing that psychological time is always limited, and so whatever it does will be limited. Time and thought have brought havoc in the world. You can see that. The question is, Can that limitation ever end? Or is man to live forever in that condition?"

"What is the relationship of the brain cells to the senses? What takes place when you hear a statement like this: that time, thought are limited? It is like telling me, 'You are an illusion.' Pupul is a psychological bundle consisting of the past, of time and thought."

"The self is part of the psyche, and whatever it does is limited," said Krishnaji.

"Then what is wrong with that?" I asked.

"Nothing. If you want to live in perpetual conflict," said Krishnaji.

"What is the nature of this ending you speak about?" I asked.

"What is ending?" Krishnaji turned back the question to me.

"To see that the flow ceases to flow," I said.

"Yes, to see that time and thought cease psychologically," said Krishnaji.

"There is a point of perception, which is a point of insight. In what time-space do I see it?" I asked.

"Look, Pupul, let us be simple. Time and thought have divided the world. Can't you see the fact of that?"

"No, Sir. I don't see the fact. The moment I see the fact, I would stop time and thought. If it is such a simple thing—but it is not. It has such devious ways," I said.

"Can you have an insight that the movement of thought and time, at whatever level, at whatever realm, in whatever area, is a realm of endless conflict?" Krishnaji asked.

"You can see it outside in the world," I said.

"If you see it outwardly, then inwardly can you see that the psyche is time and thought. The divisive psychological movement has created the outer divisive fact. The feeling that I am a Hindu; I feel secure in the word, in belonging to something, this is the factor of division and conflict."

"All this can end. One can see it as a movement of time, thought, but within it all, there is a sense of 'I exist.' That is essentially the problem. Why don't I see it?" I asked.

"Because I have thought of the psyche as other than the conditioned state," said Krishnaji. "I have thought that there is something in me, in the brain, which is timeless, and if I could reach that everything would be solved. That is part of my conditioning. I feel God, the Highest Principle, will protect me."

"What is the nature of the ground from which insight springs?" I asked.

"Insight can only take place when there is freedom from time and thought," said Krishnaji.

"This is an unending process."

"No, it is not. To live in peace is to flower, to understand the extraordinary world of peace. Peace cannot be brought about by thought," said Krishnaji.

"Is it the brain that listens to what you say?"

"Yes. Then watch what happens."

"It is quiet. It is not rattling, it is quiet."

"When it is quiet and listens, then there is insight. I don't have to explain in ten different ways the limitations of thought."

"Is there anything further?" I asked hesitatingly.

"Oh, yes, there is. A great deal more. Is listening a sound, a sound within an area, or am I listening to what you are saying without this verbal sound? If you want to convey something more than words, then if there is sound in my hearing, I can't understand the depth of what you are saying. The present is the 'now.' In that is the whole movement of time thought, the whole structure of time—thought ends. The 'now' then has a totally different meaning. 'Now,' then, is 'nothing.' Nothing in the sense that zero contains all the numbers. So 'nothing' contains all. But we are afraid to be nothing."

"When you say nothing contains all, does it mean the whole racial environmental—nature—cosmos?" I asked.

"Yes, yes. Do you see the fact that there is nothing? The self is a bundle of memories; memories that are dead. They function, but they arise from a past that is over. If I have insight into that, it ends. I see that in the 'now' there is 'nothing.'

"You said something about sound and listening. Yes, it is possible to so listen, when the mind itself is totally still."

"We won't speak of the mind, but when the brain is absolutely quiet, therefore there is no sound made by the word. This is real listening. The word only tells you what I want to convey. I listen to what you say."

"Brain has no other action than listening?" I asked.

"When the brain is active, it is noise. It is very interesting to enquire into sound. Pure sound can only exist when there is space and silence. Otherwise it is just noise. Can we come back to our question? All education, knowledge, is a movement in becoming, psychologically as well as outwardly. Becoming is the accumulation of memory. This we call knowledge. So long as that movement exists, there is fear of being nothing. But when one sees the illusion of becoming, and that becoming is endless time, thought, and conflict, there is an ending of that. An ending of the movement of the psyche which is time-thought. The ending of that is to be 'nothing.'

" 'Nothing' then contains the whole universe. Not my petty little fears, anxieties, sorrows. After all, Pupulji, 'nothing' means the entire world of compassion. Compassion is 'nothing,' and therefore that 'nothingness' is supreme intelligence.

"But we are frightened of being nothing. Do I see that I am nothing but a walking illusion, that I am nothing but dead memories? So can I be free of memory as time-thought and see the fact that as long as there is this movement of becoming, there must be endless conflict, pain?" He paused, he was speaking from depth.

"Astrophysicists are trying to understand the universe. They can only understand in terms of the material world, in terms of their limitations. But they cannot understand the immensity of it; immensity as a part of the human being; not only there, but here"—he placed his hands on his chest—"which means there must be no shadow of time and thought. That is real meditation. That is what *Sunya* means in Sanskrit.

"We offer a hundred commentaries, but the actual fact is, we are 'nothing' except a lot of words. Can one grasp that the zero contains all the numbers? So in 'nothing,' all the world exists." Like a thundering river, the insights were flowing.

"But in life, when I suffer or there is fear, it is the only thing I know. But I don't see that they are all petty little things. How do you listen to all this? What is it you realize? If you could put it into words, it would be good. What is it you feel? The people who are going to read this, what are they going to feel? It may be rubbish, it may be true; what do you capture or realize? Do you see the immensity of all this?" Krishnaji paused for a long time.

With great hesitation, I said, "This implies an ending of the psychological nature of the self."

"Yes. I have asked a question. It would be very helpful to all of us if, as you listen to this, you could say what is your response. What is the perfume of all this?"

I could not find words to speak. "Don't ask me that question. Because anything I say would sound *totally* inadequate. Because as you were speaking, there was immensity," I said.

"Yes. I could feel the tension of that. Is it temporary? Is it for a moment, then gone? Then again the whole tension of remembering it—capturing it," said Krishnaji.

"No. One has moved away from that," I said. "Another thing one realizes. The most difficult thing in the world is to be totally simple."

"Yes. If one were really simple, from that one could understand the whole complexity of life. But we start with complexity and never see the simplicity. We have trained our brain to see the complexity, and try to find an answer to the complexity. But we don't see the extraordinary simplicity of facts." Again there was a pause.

"In the Indian tradition, out of sound were born all the elements, the *Panch Maha Bhutas*," I said. "Sound that reverberates and is yet not heard."

"That is it. But after all, in the Indian tradition the Buddha, Nagarjuna, said man must deny the whole thing. Nagarjuna denied everything, every movement of the psyche. Why have they not pursued that?" Krishnaji asked. "Not by denying the world, you can't deny the world. But they have denied the world. But by the total negation of the 'me.' "

"Renunciation is the negation of the 'me,' " I said. "Basically, renunciation is never in the outer."

"Renunciation is in the within. Don't be attached even to your loincloth. I think we are caught in a net of words, we do not live in actualities. I suffer, and the way to end that is not to escape into illusion. Why have human beings not faced the fact and changed the fact? Is it because we are living with ideas, ideals—unrealities? We are living with the history of mankind. Mankind is me, and the 'me' is endless sorrow. And so if you want to end sorrow there has to be an ending of the 'me.' " Krishnaji was exploring as he spoke.

"It is really the ending of time, isn't it?"

"Yes. Ending of time-thought, that is, to listen without sound. To listen to the universe without sound." He paused. Krishnaji was far away. "A doctor in New York said the fundamental issue is whether the brain cells, which have been conditioned for centuries, could bring about a mutation? I said it is possible only through listening. But no one is willing to listen in its entirety. If man really said, 'I must live peacefully,' then there is peace in the world. But he doesn't want to live in peace. He is ambitious, arrogant, petty. So we have reduced the vastness of all this to some petty reactions. Do you realize that, Pupul? We have such petty lives—from the highest to lowest." He paused.

"What is sound to you, Sir"? I asked. Again there was a long silence, out of which Krishnaji spoke. "Sound is the tree. Take Indian chanting, Gregorian chanting, they are extraordinarily close together. You listen to the sound of waves, of strong wind, the sound of a person you have lived with for many years, you get used to it all.

"But if you don't, then sound has an extraordinary meaning. Then you hear everything afresh. You tell me time and thought are the whole movement of man's life. You have communicated a simple fact. Can I listen to it without the sound of the words?

"Then I have captured the depths of that statement, and I can't lose it. I have listened to it in its entirety. It has conveyed the fact that it is so and what is so, is absolute always. In the Hebraic tradition it is only Jehovah the Nameless One who can say 'I Am,' that is the *Tat Tvam Asi* in Sanskrit."

# CHAPTER 44

# "The Good Mind"

While in Bombay in January 1983, Krishnaji started speaking of "the good mind." Nandini and I were having supper with him. The evening before in his talk, K had asked, "How do you look at the vast movement of life? Do you see that you are a human being related to all human being? The body does not divide. It never says, 'I am.' It is thought that separates." He had been speaking of the chaos in the world, and asked whether man ever questions the root of all the chaos. "How do you approach the problem? How do you come in contact with such a problem?" He was drawing us into contact with his mind. "Can you come close and be open to the question? But if you keep away from the question, you are not open, you are not alive to the question. Can you approach the question with no direction, no motive? Motive distorts perception. To find out what is the root of chaos, the mind must be free."

K said to us, "Most people would consider a good mind to be a mind that has read a great deal, that is full of knowledge about many things. A mind like Aldous Huxley's, Gerald Heard's, and others—they had encyclopedic minds. In India, would the good mind be the Brahminic mind? I am using the word 'Brahminic' to include the stream that has cultivated the brain through centuries; to describe a brain that has become very sharp, but has not lost the quality of depth within it. You can make an instrument very sharp; it can cut, but it has also to be used for delicate things. Do you understand? Is such a mind a good mind?" He paused. "A good mind must be related to action, to relationship. It must be related to depth. Great scientists sometimes lead the most shoddy lives. They are ambitious, greedy, they fight each other for position and acclaim. Would you say they have good minds?"

I replied, "A good mind does not mean a good life. The scientist may be a great scientist, but as a human being he may be a disaster. You see, Sir, a really good mind must be able to brood within itself. Perhaps out of this brooding, there is insight."

"Yes." K continued, "Would you say a good mind has no center from which it is acting?" He was speaking with many pauses, as always when discussing something serious. "The center being the self." He posed the question and answered it himself. "A good mind has no self. When a mind is in a state of complete attention, attending, listening, then there is no place in it for the self. The self manifests itself afterwards. The clue is listening. It is one of the great sustainers of the brain." Krishnaji had been listening and pondering, then spoke. "You see, a good mind must have compassion. It must have a great sense of beauty and be capable of action; there must be a relationship which is right. Is it impossible to find such minds? Aristotle, Socrates—they had good minds."

"They had minds that could question, cleave into matter, energy. The mind has to have a wholeness to it." I was challenging Krishnaji.

"Would you say a good mind is a holistic mind?" K asked.

"When you said in your talk yesterday that the body does not divide, it was a statement that had never been made before. You went on to say that with the mind, the instrument that has been trained in the technological, in the understanding of great knowledge, with the understanding of the technique of doing things—with that technical mind, man turns to sorrow. And so sorrow does not end. For there is no relationship between the two. How did these insights arise? Your mind throws up insights all the time. How do they arise? Do the insights arise when you are sitting on the platform, or do you think it out earlier?"

"Insights arise all the time," K paused. "They arise all the time when there is serious talk." Then again he grew quiet. "You see, if you define it too much—the good mind—then you wipe away everything. So we should not define it too clearly. Then it limits it."

"And yet logic is essential—the mind must move step by step. I wonder what they will make of your mind in centuries to come," I queried.

"Can we say, a healthy, good mind has an originality that goes contrary to the current?" Krishnaji ignored my query and continued to question. "Socrates? He stood for something," said Krishnaji.

"One is talking of a mind from which compassion flows—otherwise what does it matter?" I asked.

"How does such a mind come into being?" Again K questioned. "Is

it the result of tremendous evolution of a group of minds—the enquiring mind, which has cultivated the brain, morality, austerity, for
centuries? They may not all have been austere, but inside them there
was that inner movement going on. We have to enquire whether such
a long background of enquiry produces the Buddha."

"Is there a density and insight to the background mind—the racial
mind?" I asked.

"Of course," said K. "Or there is a reservoir of the good which has
no relationship to evil. That reservoir exists and, given the opportunity,
brings the Avatar, whatever that may mean. Right? Or is it the other?
Is it a group consciousness, that for centuries has thought and thought
and thought about 'that,' and that might have produced the Buddha?"
He paused. "I was thinking the other day—the Egyptians in 4500 B.C.
had the calendar. It didn't happen at once. They must have had tremendous backgrounds to have produced it. Maybe the Indians contributed to it. It may be the same thing—these vast insights."

"The converging of them?" I asked.

"I think the good mind must be *absolutely* free. It may meet fear,
but there has to be an energy that wipes it out. Could the scientists
store such energy?"

I questioned him. "Science has nothing to do with otherness? Can
the scientist end his self-centered concern? Can he wipe it out? It is
self-centered activity that is the problem. Is it dependent on what you
do?" My role was to ask the right question.

"No. You see, they say the Buddha left his house, became a *sannyasi*, fasted, ultimately got to Buddhahood. I don't accept that. The
fasting, the austerities, have nothing to do with the other." Krishnaji
pondered.

"The Buddhists would maintain that the Buddha might have gone
through all that—but Buddhahood has nothing to do with that. But
could he have danced his life through and come to that?" I asked.

"You see, we have made austerity a becoming to 'that.' "

"But is there no gathering of energy necessary for 'that'? 'That' only
becomes possible when you start seeing that energy is not dissipated.
That is essential," I said.

"Be careful. 'That' means a sense of self-awareness. Don't say for
that you *need* energy." The subtlety of K's mind was being revealed.

"But there has to be preparation of the ground."

"Of course."

"Your eyes and ears have to be open. It may have nothing to do with morality. But the energies that are constantly being dissipated by gossip, trivialities, self-concerned activity, have to cease," I said.

"That—yes," K responded. "But if you say all self-centered activities must end, then there is a relationship between 'that' and the other. There is no relationship."

"It cannot mean that you can dissipate energy."

" 'That must end'—You can't say that." K would not move.

"Then what can you say, Sir?" I asked.

"I am self-centered, and you tell me, 'That must end'—That is also a becoming," K was pushing.

"Right. So is your teaching to be viewed in a different way? Is it a teaching of awakening to life, in which self-centered activity arises—the outside world enters, sorrow arises?"

"And you wipe all that out?" asked K.

"Whatever comes is wiped out," I said.

"Not wiped out," K persisted.

"Whatever 'is,' is observed; there is listening, seeing."

" 'What is' has no intention or becoming." K was unmoving.

"But it is a flow in which everything is?"

"Yes."

"I see that your teaching is not the ending of becoming, but the observation of becoming. There is a difference between ending of becoming and seeing 'whatever is.' "

"Yes, seeing and moving out of it." Krishnaji's mind was like an open flower.

Later, I was to comprehend the nature of this seeming contradiction. The observing of the river filled with impurities—without in any way demanding, hoping to change its nature—dissolves the impurities, leaving the river clear and unpolluted. The subtlety of the teaching was absolute.

A discussion in Bombay later in the week went into the challenge of biogenetics and its ability to transform man. Krishnamurti said, "If it is possible to manipulate the genes, then what is man? Human beings have been programmed in many directions, now the genetic engineers want to program man in other directions. But still man is programmed." K was pondering, brooding.

"Is there such a thing as psychological evolution?" he asked. "Genetic engineers can concern themselves with changes in values, but it is a journey from the known to the known. Can genetic engineering lead to an extension of the brain? Can it enable simultaneity to operate, or is it concerned with introducing a set of values which man has determined? Genetic engineering can only operate with what is within the known."

Achyut Patwardhan intervened. "All scientists accept what they see as the limits of their telescope."

But Krishnamurti's questions were to himself. He asked, "Is the self part of the genetic process or part of the psychological process?" He paused and let the question sink deep. "The same technological mind which evolved and discovered the nuclear bomb is now asking the genetic question and undertaking research into the genes. But it is the same instrument. The technological revolution led to the atom bomb, evolution has not changed man. Only one part of man's brain is operating. This imbalance is causing great havoc. The question now arises, 'Can man be helped through genetic engineering to change?' "

He was speaking slowly, probing into the question at depth. Some questions were raised in the middle of the discussion. K let them be and suddenly interrupted, saying, "Can we discard evolution?" The participants were silent, then started questioning.

"That would amount to a quantum leap. In what direction? Wisdom is needed." And, "If it continues to be a leap in evolution, man who determines the genetic direction, must have already taken the leap to know." Again Krishnaji broke in. "Is it possible to change man immediately, and not through the genetic process? Is it possible to stop evolution in any direction?"

"It may be possible with the individual, but not with the mass," was the reply.

"What is the mass?" K asked.

"The many."

"Why are you concerned with the many? Are you separate from the mass?" K countered. Again there was silence.

"Is it possible to stop time, which is evolution?" K had gathered the threads and was moving into the question. "Which means what? Genetic engineering needs time. It is part of evolution. The crisis is here now. Is it physical or psychological? Is it in the consciousness of man? Where is the crisis? Is it in the technological world? A crisis is a fire, and the mind has to have an immensity which the crisis demands."

He said, "The intense drive of thought in the direction of technology has led to tremendous discoveries. There seems to be no end to this problem-solving drive. We use the same drive to tackle psychological problems of greed, hate, fear. There is no evolution in the psyche. Greed and fear cannot dissolve into their opposites. This is the fallacy and the great illusion. Becoming is illusion. Greed can only grow and strengthen in its own nature; it can never become non-greed.

"So is it possible to discard the idea of evolution in the psyche? Can one end thinking in terms of time as becoming? Mutation is that. In that is fundamental change."

During his stay in Bombay he was to speak of "living lightly as a guest in one's house, or in one's body. To be a guest is to have no sense of attachment; to step lightly on the earth."

He also spoke of a new use of the senses, "so that in functioning the sense organs do not destroy energy, but let it flow. Eternity," he said gravely, "is that timeless flow."

# CHAPTER 45

# "What Is Time?"

From the early 1960s Krishnaji had been greatly concerned with the problem of time. He had spoken of the many dimensions of time at the breakfast table, on walks, and in his talks and discussions. In early November 1983, when we were together in my house at 11 Safdarjung Road, New Delhi, he continued to question.

"What is time?" Krishnaji asked. "Can we be simple and go as deeply into the nature of time as possible? We know a whole series of continuous time movements. We know physical time and psychological time as becoming, and the movement of not becoming. Between the 'what is' and 'what should be' is time. Physical time is distance, from here to there. Now, is physical time related internally to psychological time?"

I replied, "Knowing physical time by the clock, one applies time as a reaching out, in the inner. The illusion is the introduction of the concept of physical time to the within and the shaping of the structure of the within, on the basis of the linear movement of physical time. The measure of becoming is the measure of inward time."

"When the outer movement is extended to psychological states, the illusion of time enters. The idea of growth in the outer extends to the inner." As Krishnaji spoke, he was listening deeply, listening to us and to himself. The listening was itself a probing.

"The movement of becoming is the 'I should be.' It is a process of fantasy; it builds from illusion to illusion. The mind ruminates. 'What will be—then what will happen?' Anxieties—fears are part of its structure.

"The brain extends the physical time into the inner psychological sphere, because the brain is conditioned to linear time in the outer. As it is conditioned to that, it accepts psychological time in the within. I am questioning that illusion that conditions the brain. The brain is accustomed to the movement of becoming. It looks at itself as a movement in time. It operates in this illusion. The brain is evolved in time, and so looks at everything in terms of time. 'I am, I was,' modified into, 'I will be.' Now I ask, is that so? Is there a tomorrow in the psyche?" Krishnaji asked.

"There is a physical tomorrow, therefore psychological tomorrow is inevitable," I said.

"That is continuity," Krishnaji intervened.

"I exist; therefore there will be tomorrow. Why do strong feelings of fear get entangled in the projection of the tomorrow?" I asked. There was silence for some time.

"There is no time," Krishnaji said suddenly. "Physical time we know as movement. There is no way of measuring physical time without movement. If there were no movement in the psyche, as thought, the wheel of time ends.

"Look at it," he said. "Movement is time. Movement is thought. Thought is a material process. That is simple. Why do we complicate it? Can you accept this even logically?"

"What does it mean to accept a statement logically?" I asked.

"To see that any psychological movement is the process of becoming. Now, is there a movement where no time exists?" he asked. "If you sit in a dark room, without movement, without thought, is there time? This is also so in the within. When there is no thought, no movement in time, the outer and inner is the same movement."

"There may be an ending of physical movement in the brain, for a moment, but the action of time as duration, as continuity, is an activity that operates in every cell of my body. It also acts in the brain. The action of time is inevitable." I said

"The brain is a physical thing. The brain grows old. It deteriorates. The question is whether the brain needs to deteriorate?" Krishnaji enquired.

"If it is a material process, as material as the fact that my hair grows gray—it must deteriorate. How is it possible that one part of the organism can remain unaffected?" I asked.

"You say the brain grows senile. Senility is the physical aging by time. To me the brain need never grow old," Krishnaji said.

"How do you distinguish between the brain and other organs? How can the brain alone have the capacity for renewal?" I asked.

"Are we clear what is meant by time? It is the same movement in the outer as in the inner. They are not separate. Millennia through millennia, that movement has continued. The question is, Can that movement stop? That constant movement is decay, is the factor of deterioration, both organically and in the psyche."

"The brain receives physical stimuli so it will always respond as movement to the challenge," I said.

"Go slow, go slow," said Krishnaji. "There is reaction and action—otherwise the brain is dead. But that action in itself has little significance."

"The brain cannot be wholly still," I said. "Does aging arise because of movement or friction?" I asked.

"Movement, as we know it, is friction. Movement is the deteriorating factor. It is like a piston in an engine. Any movement in the brain physically wears out the brain. It is the psychological process that affects the body and the brain. It is not the other way around," said Krishnaji.

"Can there be movement without friction?" Asit spoke.

"If there is no psychological movement, then movement is as in absolute space, there is no friction," said Krishnaji.

"And yet there is tremendous movement in outer space."

"When psychological movement is not, time as becoming is not. But one can sit very quietly in a dark room for twenty years and the brain will go on aging—for thought, as becoming, continues to operate. But when thought is quiet, without movement, then the psyche has no time. If there is no movement as thought, there is no becoming. Becoming creates duality. Therefore there is conflict, deterioration, time. Time is the barrier, is limitation. Only a spaceship that is moving without friction can go to the limitless. If friction as movement, as psychological time, stops, is there a factor of deterioration?" Krishnaji asked.

"When the brain is quiet, does the body function naturally?" Asit asked.

"Yes, the body has its own intelligence," said Krishnaji. "Is this an actuality? Can the brain ever be without movement except for its own natural movement? Psychological movement is interfering with the body. Can that movement stop? That in turn implies, can there be no accumulation of any kind?"

"What distinguishes the negation or denial of all time as movement?" I questioned. "How is one aware of time?"

"I am aware of it when there is a challenge," said Krishnaji.

"The brain reaches out, looks backwards or forwards, and asks questions." I continued the enquiry.

"That is movement," said Krishnaji.

"But actually the brain is chewing the cud all the time," I said. "When the brain is not seriously challenged, it plays games with itself. It throws up memories."

"The brain is memory," said Krishnaji. "Remorse, guilt, are a constant movement in the brain, as memory. The brain is memory, a movement from the past through the present to the future."

"Continuity is that. The brain creates memory. Does it play with it?" asked Asit.

"The brain survives through memory," said Krishnaji.

"We know the function of the heart. It is to pump blood through the arteries and veins. What is the function of the brain? Is it to create knowledge as stored memory?" asked Asit.

"What is the movement that must stop? Or do you say that all movement must stop?" I asked.

"The brain feels that in memory is security," said Asit.

"In the ending of this movement, does a new movement come into being, which makes it totally secure? Is there a movement outside time?" I asked.

"Don't put that question," said Krishnaji. "As the heart functions naturally, so the brain has its own movement—when memory does not interfere. The brain has its own movement on which it has superimposed memory. Listen," he said, "the heart doesn't remember. The heart beats without remembrance. The brain can function without movement, if allowed to do so by thought. The heart doesn't pump because of knowledge."

"To draw similarities between the heart and brain is not correct," I said. "The physical brain has evolved out of memory, out of man's capacity and experiences. It can only survive through hoping, seeking survival."

"Does the brain teach the body to survive?" asked Asit.

"Is the brain we know built out of memory? There is a part of the brain one is not aware of. When the wholeness of the brain operates, it has no limits," I said.

"The brain teaches the hand skills. Thought itself creates memory to survive," said Asit.

"The whole brain is not linked to memory," I said.

"The brain has sought security through knowledge," said Krishnaji.

"Has the human brain become bigger because of this capacity? Is mutation within the brain? Surely mutation cannot be outside the brain?" I asked. "What mutates?"

"Knowledge has made the ground of the brain very limited. Knowledge is discovering that the ground of the brain which it has created is not stable and feels that friction as movement is necessary for the brain to survive. So what does it do?" Krishnaji said. "It sees there is no security in knowledge. The brain realizes its foundation in knowledge is very weak."

"Can it see that there may be a different ground altogether?" Asit spoke.

"The brain, as it functions, can never let go of the past. All movement is time. So I ask, does one remain in the old house?" Krishnaji asked.

"When I don't move there is no ground on which the old house can arise. To move away from the unstable ground creates the new ground," said Asit.

"Any movement means duality," said Krishnaji.

Asit continued, "When there is no time, there is no space. If there is no movement, there is no time. When there is nothing in space—no object, no thought—where is time? But what I say is at the intellectual level."

"If there is no measure, is it the same brain that functions without movement? When the brain is silent, the mind operates. That is the intelligence of the universe." Krishnaji had taken a vast leap, and we were left far behind. We had no words. Later, I broke the silence. "Is intelligence a faculty of the brain?"

"Intelligence is that which sees the movement of continuity, sees it as the process of aging. The intelligence that sees this, is outside the brain," said Krishnaji.

"If the brain cannot reach it, who or what is it that sees the limitation of the brain? To see that, the brain must have contact with that," said Asit.

"The brain in its functioning has its own intelligence. That limited brain has no relationship to the other," said Krishnaji.

"Then what is it that can stop the movement of the brain?" asked Asit.

"Its perceiving, its own inadequacy," said Krishnaji.

"If the brain is only a movement of time, then what sees its own limitation?"

Krishnaji spoke out of a long silence. "Would you accept insight as the operation of the whole brain?"

"Is the operation of insight then not connected with the narrow operation of the brain?" I asked.

"An insight into the operation of limitation frees the brain from limitation. Insight can only arise when there is no memory, and so no time," said Krishnaji. "When the whole brain is operating, it has no direction. It is free of the past. Insight is mind operating on brain." Again there was silence.

"The brain is limited. How can the mind operate on the brain?" I asked.

"K has watched carefully, without motive. In that watching there is tremendous attention. It is like light focusing. That attention, the depth of it, is mind. That attention focuses light on the limitations of the brain. Love is outside the brain. Love is not a sensation. Insight is not a sensation. It is not a reaction. We have come to an ending," said the sage.


I was traveling by air to Madras from New Delhi on December 28, 1983. I had been correcting my manuscript, when suddenly the vital difference between sermon and dialogue became clear. In the West, dialogue had seldom played a major part in awakening religious enquiry. It had been used in philosophic dissertation, the Socratic dialogues had concerned themselves with discovery of truth through logic and rigorous enquiry. But the intensity of enquiry that had been generated by Socrates remained a sounding board for the framework of logic and reason. At the end of the dialogue, reason was established. What of the other participants—did the two streams become one in their flow? Did all division end?

In most religions the truth was a revealed truth, established through doctrine, of Bible or Koran, its acceptance based on faith. Any hint of doubt or questioning was regarded as heresy; this was so amongst the Cathars of France, the early Coptic sects, the Gnostics. The truth of the church was not the truth that arose out of pristine perception and self-enquiry and the energy generated by dialogue.

Indian religious enquiry had from the earliest times perfected dialogue as an instrument of probing the within of things; using logic to its ultimate limits as a tool, it could free itself of logic and delve beyond.

Krishnaji had given to dialogue a depth and dimension. Through listening at great depth, duality ended and the doors to the within of the mind and nature opened. The quality, the perception, and the spaces of the mind changed. If one observed, in listening to a sermon or a lecture there was an acceptance or a rejection, even a questioning; thought was in abeyance, interspersed by thought wandering, caught in becoming, as the past or the future.

In serious religious dialogue the ear is open, energy is gathered, the senses awake, operating simultaneously; attention fills the mind. Held in attention, the mind rests undifferentiated. From this ground all responses are possible. To participate at depth, there has to be listening at depth. In this state the questioner and listener lose their separate identities.

I was hesitant, uncertain of the implications of what had arisen. On reaching Vasant Vihar, I spoke of it to Krishnaji. Like quicksilver his mind awoke to the full implications of what I had been feeling out. He was totally awake, eager to pursue the subject, to open it up and probe into the question.

That afternoon we began a discussion on the nature of intense dialogue and its role in freeing the brain from time.

Krishnaji said, "We will talk about time and dialogue as between two religious people. Religious in the sense of people who are free from all tradition, free from authority, from all systems. In such dialogue there is a questioning and an answering; the answering provokes a further question; and so the question is kept rolling. In such dialogue there is a state of listening where the two people disappear and only the question remains."

"Dialogues need not mean two people," I said. "Essentially, its meaning seems to be a probing into something through a listening and challenging situation. I see that all problems that arise in the brain are born of time. They arise because of the need to change 'what is.' The movement of the brain which wished to change 'what is' into something else creates time."

"Physical time is sunrise and sunset," said K. "The covering of one point to another point. Psychologically, time is to become something. Time is the whole process of evolution, both the psychological and physical.

"My question is, is there a totally different time? Time as nonmovement? Time as we know it is movement, the division between one action and another action; time is hope; time is the movement of the past, through the present, to the future. Time is the movement of fulfilling, achieving, becoming. Time is thinking about something and acting. The interval is time. I am asking, Is there a time that does not belong to any of these categories at all?" Krishnaji had plunged into the question.

"You say the time you speak of does not belong to the category of movement. Does it belong to the category of matter?" I asked.

"Not as I understand it. I have been told matter is solidified, manifested energy. Time as the tree growing," said Krishnaji.

"The brain is matter. In that matter, evolution must exist," I said.

"Of course. We were monkeys; after millions of years we are *Homo sapiens.*" said Krishnaji.

"We link that evolution with the content within the brain. The brain is matter. Evolution is inherent in the brain. The content of the brain is memory. We link evolution in the brain with evolution in memory." Listening, the response arose.

"I see what you are talking about. Has memory evolved through a process of evolution?" Krishnaji asked.

"The problem arises because we apply to memory the same rules as we apply to matter," I said. "Evolution is inherent in matter. The problem is we take the content of the brain which is memory and feel that there is an entity that can change that content. The whole process of becoming is that. That is the time of the within, time of the interior."

"But all evolution implies time," said Krishnaji.

"We apply evolution, which is inherent in the brain substance, to its content. Is there evolution in the time within?" I asked.

"Evolution is time." Krishnaji would not move.

"If evolution is time, why should it not be applicable to becoming?" I asked.

"Becoming implies time. I am this, I will be that. Pupulji asks whether the content of the brain is part of the process of evolution?" He had turned to the others.

"No. The brain itself is a product of time as evolution. But is the content of the brain, which has been a gathering of experience through millennia, identical with the nature of the brain stuff itself?"

"It is simple to understand that becoming is illusion. But there is something much more than that. You imply that there is an outer time of the watch and an inner time of becoming. Then you ask, Is there another time that does not belong to these two categories? Time and space are one. Time and matter are one." I pushed.

"Time is matter. Time is manifested energy. The very manifestation is a process of time," said Krishnaji.

"So time cannot exist without manifestation?" I queried.

"We know time as past, present, and future," said Krishnaji.

"We project time into the future. What is the nature—the perception of that instant in which is reality?" I asked.

"I see that the future is the past modifying itself in the present.

That is time. I will do—I will become. Now, is there a timeless action that is perception—action without interval?" Krishnaji had begun the question which was the opening of the doorways.

"What is it that is modified in the present?" I asked.

"Thought," said Krishnaji

"Can we examine that instant when modification takes place?" I asked.

"I am afraid of what might happen tomorrow. Tomorrow is both the present and yesterday. The present, the 'now,' is both the past and the future," said Krishnaji.

"Does perception in the present negate both the past and the future?"

"That perception requires an ending of the past. Perception is timeless. Right. You perceive that you are full of prejudices, knowledge, conclusion, beliefs and with that you look at the present and that present is modified by the challenge. You might alter it, but you remain in the same field," K responded.

"Yes, this is a state where there is no point of perception. But to understand the time which does not belong to this stream is obviously to understand the perception of the 'now,' " I said.

"Perception is not of time. It does not contain the past," said Krishnaji.

"What is the 'now'? "

"I will tell you. The 'now' is the past and the present. The 'now' is all time as past time, future time, and present time," said Krishnaji.

"Can one experience past time? Can one experience future time? What is the experiencing of all time?" I was challenging Krishnaji.

"You cannot experience that. To experience that implies the experiencer, who is experiencing in time." The response came swiftly.

"Therefore, when you say the 'now' is all time—what do you actually mean?" There was a long pause. "Is there an actual contact with the 'now'?" I asked.

"The past has created the present," Achyut spoke.

"That is easy to see. I am trying to delve deeper. Krishnaji says the past and the present are both contained in the 'now.' I say what is this 'now'?" I was pushing as far as I could.

Sunanda intervened. "Pupul, look at it. The 'now' is 'what is'—the whole of the past is in 'what is.' "

"But what is 'what is'?" I asked.

"How do you assert that the past is contained in the present? Do you actually experience it, or is it a theory? This is my question. Pupulji is asking, What makes you say the past is contained in the present? Is it an idea, theory, or do you have insight into that?" Krishnaji was questioning himself.

"Let us see what Krishnaji is saying," I said. "He asks, 'Is there a time which is not linear time, nor the time of becoming? Is there a time which is independent of both these times?' "

"That is all," said Krishnaji.

"Only perception or revelation can bring it about in the present. How do I come to the 'now' of experience?"

"You cannot come to it. You cannot experience it. You cannot conceive it.

"See what has happened. You cannot experience it, but your brain is conditioned to experience, to knowledge. It is conditioned to measurement through words. This cannot be approached that way. Right? That is the religious mind. It has wiped out theories, ideas. We are dealing with actualities. Right? That's where religious enquiry begins." Krishnaji was at the center of the enquiry.

"Is it possible to probe into this time you speak about?" I was hesitant.

"It is possible in the sense that you may use words, but words are not the thing."

"You cannot divide past, present and future with words?" Sunanda spoke.

"Yes. But the question remains," said Krishnaji.

"Yes, the question remains. That is what is extraordinary. The question remains, but the questioners do not remain," I said.

"Yes, the questioners cease to exist," Krishnaji spoke.

"But is it a verbal question at all?" asked Radhika.

"What does the question operate upon?" asked Asit.

"Let us enquire. We are saying time is evolution. Time is becoming. Time is from here to there—physically and psychologically. We know that process of becoming and nonbecoming—the positive and the negative—and we proceed along these lines all our life. Then someone comes along and asks, 'what for?' He has left me with that question. We ponder over it and say, 'Let us look at it; let us find out.' We see there is time between seeing, thinking, and being. That interval is time. It is in the field of time. You also see that all time is contained in the present. Pupul then asks, 'Can we explore into the present?' I say, 'No.' If you experience it, the experiencer is the past and the experience itself is of time. What is the state of the brain that has put away all theories and conjectures? What is the state of the brain that sees perception and action as one? It sees that there is no interval, and so no time. Perception is free of time. What is that state which is the 'now'? Perception is the 'now.' Perception is not of time. There is no 'I will learn to perceive.'

"What is perception? It is not of time. Can one experience that? It is not possible. Perception has no perceiver. Perception is 'now'—therefore it is timeless. Therefore action born of perception is timeless." The question had flowered.

"Therefore, in that perception, the past and future are totally annihilated?" I asked hesitatingly.

"Perception of what?" asked Asit.

"What is the necessity for perception to perceive, Sir?" asked Sunanda.

"In the state of dialogue," we asked the question.

" 'What is the now,' K says, 'It contains the past, present and future.' Then the brain asks, 'How do I contact it?' And he says, 'It cannot be contacted. There can only be perception.' Now the listening, taking in of that perception wipes out past and present." I was tentatively feeling my way into the question.

"You see, it is happening now. Listening is not of time. If I listen, it is 'now.' Listening has no time. Therefore there is no horizontal time." Krishnaji spoke.

"What is the enquiry, then?" asked Asit.

"Out of questioning, listening arises; out of listening, question arises," I said.

"Don't theorize." Krishnaji was quick to see that my response lacked depth.

"I am not theorizing."

"Perception is timeless."

"Then I ask you a question. Is it possible to probe?" I said.

"I say, yes. In probing the mind rids itself of all concepts, all theories, all hopes, desires. It is now in a state of purity. In that state you can enquire. I tell you, 'Love is not of time.' How do you listen? What is your response? You hear words, words have meaning. You interpret them according to your capacity. Can you listen to the truth of that without the word?" Krishnaji asked.

"You can't listen like that. You listen to the words," said Asit.

"The word is not the thing," Krishnaji said.

"I listen to the word, but do not understand," Asit reiterated.

"Come, have a dialogue with me." Krishnaji was drawing his listeners towards him.

"If I may say something, how do you listen? Isn't that the crucial question?" I asked.

"You cannot listen to words without translating them," Asit spoke.

"In a dialogue with Krishnaji you listen without thought operating, and yet comprehend fully what he is saying. There is a listening at such depth, that it opens up the question," I said.

"What do you mean by comprehending?" asked Sunanda.

"Can you have a dialogue with the question, 'Love is not of time'?"

"Don't verbalize. We have all been trained to be highly intellectual. A poor man who does not seem bright, he will understand a simple statement," said Krishnaji.

"How can there be enquiry in a state of attention?" asked Asit.

"Just listen. You tell me, 'Love is not of time.' To me, that is a tremendous fact. I say I really don't understand it, and you tell me you won't understand it, the way you want to understand it. Do you get what I am saying? You want to understand it through the intellectual process, through argument, through a verbal process of reaction. But you won't understand it that way. You say, 'That is the only instrument I have.' I say there is a totally different instrument. You say, 'Tell me about that instrument.' I say, 'Put aside your capacity, your knowledge that is time,' " said Krishnaji.

"Are you saying, 'Put aside your intellectual instrument,'?" asked Asit.

"Of course not," said Krishnaji. "I said, 'Put aside knowledge.' Knowledge is evolution. Is there a comprehension, an insight, an immediate perception, without the word, without bringing all knowledge into it? I say, yes. Can there be a state where there is pure perception of something and can you probe into that perception?"

The discussions on time were to continue in Madras. At a seminar on January 4, 1984, at Vasant Vihar, the subject was discussed again. Professor George Sudarshan and Pandit Jagannath Upadhyaya were present.

"The question has been raised by our friend on the functioning of different kinds of time. That is, is there a time which comes into operation, which functions even when becoming ceases to be? That when cause and effect have ceased, when normal process of causation, of memory and expectation, anticipation—all the background accumulated over one's lifetime or even before that—have been given up, drop off: Is there still a kind of time in which events unfold?" George Sudarshan commenced, unfolding the question.

I added, "Krishnaji also spoke of the arising of a perception which simultaneously negates that arising, a simultaneity of arising and negating; and what is the nature of time, in relationship to the 'now'?"

"We have said, 'The present, which is the past, is also the future.' We also said that time is not only becoming, anticipation, hope, but also time is the holding—the sense of possessing, the sense of accumulating knowledge and living with that knowledge; that also is time. And we asked, Is there any other time movement? Is the movement of thought a material process; thought which is also movement? So, time and thought are similar. There is physical time, from here to there.

"You are now asking a question: 'Is there a nonmovement when one has stepped out of psychological time? Is there a movement which is totally different from the movement of time and thought?' " The Master had commenced the enquiry.

"Do you speak of the brain ceasing to function, or the mind ceasing to function?" enquired Sudarshan.

"I would like to separate the brain and the mind. The brain is conditioned. The mind is outside the brain. Mind, for me, is something totally unrelated to the conditioned brain and therefore something which is not measurable by words or by thought. Whereas the brain activity and the wastage of the brain activity is measurable and measure is time. Now any function arising from accumulated knowledge is the known—as myself, my ego, my self-centered activity. Now, is it possible not to be self-centered? Can one ask this question: Can one be free of the self, entirely?

"The self, the 'me,' is the product of time—evolution. It is the activity of the self-centered brain as my position, my power. It is the 'me.' And as long as there is that 'me' which is accumulated knowledge, memory, experience, there is the limitation of time," Krishnaji said.

Jagannath Upadhyaya asked, "One may speak of time in whatever way one likes—time as thought, time as movement, etcetera. There is time as the coming into existence and time as ceasing to be, which is the process of becoming in which we live. But behind it, is there mind, in which there is no arising and ending? If it is so, then it is outside us, one cannot do anything about it. We can't act upon it or investigate it?"

"No, we can't. As long as the self, the 'me,' is arising, dying, arising, ending, and again arising, this constant process of becoming is time."

"Not only becoming but being," explained the Buddhist.

"When Upadhyaya speaks of being, he means 'I am.' There is a becoming, but there is also the sense of 'I am.' " Radha Burnier had joined the dialogue.

"We see this process of arising, becoming—thought arising, thought ending—when this stops, what happens?"

"How do you know it stops?" asked Krishnaji.

"To put it simply, when becoming comes to an end, is there Being?" Radhaji continued.

"What do you mean by Being?"

"The sense of 'I am,' " offered Achyut.

"Existing," I intervened.

"What is existing? The moment you acknowledge you are living, you set the whole process of the self in operation."

"No, I won't accept that," I said. "With ending, becoming ends. To most of us it is possible for a thought projection to end, which is for becoming to end. But that state is not a dead thing. It is a state of existing."

Sudarshan enquired, "When you talk about Being, is it a statement about a condition or function or are you talking about an object? If it is Being, by definition it is an object."

"I am not talking about Being as object."

"So, when you talk about living or Being, to the extent that there is no separation of a knowing person from the rest, to the extent that there is *vyaapti*, complete identification, without claiming anything for yourself, there is no separation between you and anything else," said Sudarshan.

"Why do you deny Being? Being in the sense that something 'is.' Do you say there is nothing?" I asked.

"There is no difference between Being and becoming. When becoming ends, being ends," responded the Pandit.

"Yes," said Krishnaji.

"Becoming and being are the same. Where there is becoming and being, there is the self with all its activities, etcetera, and when it ends, that also ends. But when there is the end of all this, of thought, etcetera, then is there something which sustains, in which everything is sustained?" asked Jagannath Upadhyaya.

"If I may ask, what is the distinction you draw between becoming and being?" I asked the Pandit.

"In Sanskrit they are not two words. *Bhava* means both being and becoming," Radhaji explained.

"Panditji says that what you call intelligence is unrelated to intellect.

Only when this intellect recognizes that it is fragmented and is limited that it ceases and intelligence is born," said Achyut.

"I would like to go into becoming and being a little more. Being is a state of nondifferentiation."

"Why do you differentiate between being and becoming?" Krishnaji enquired.

"There is a state from which things arise and into which things disappear," I said.

"Which is the self?" Krishnaji spoke.

"In a state of attention, a state of awareness, what is there?" I enquired.

"In attention there is no self," said the Master.

"Then what is the nature of attention?" I asked.

"Are you asking what is the nature of attention or whether there is a ground or stratum from which attention springs?" Radhaji turned to me.

"Attention has no background." Krishnaji brought us back to the central question.

The scientist Sudarshan began to explore. "There are two kinds of functioning in the physical universe. One is a functioning which is labeled by discrete events in which you have a chronology, you have a sequence of things, and then you construct laws connecting the events. And so you say the wind is caused by differences in temperature, and you find one event causing another event which is causing another event, and you are able to understand a number of things. Then there is another kind of functioning in which you don't differentiate, for example, an object which is moving freely; and it was a great discovery of physics when people decided that free motion does not require an explanation. You don't ask why it is continually moving; you attribute it to the nature of things, you say that it is the nature of objects to move. And one can enlarge, generalize the scope of the thing so that no system functions in a sense without this thing. An isolated system—isolated in the sense that there is no other; a complete system has no history, has no events in it. Events come when you are putting the system which is functioning by itself, within the matrix of something else, and then you say something which is moving in a closed fashion, is really not natural because we like to think straight. So we ask the question: Why is it not moving straight? So chronological time of unfolding takes place when you have an incomplete system, incomplete in the sense that there are ideals for the behavior of the system, which are not external to the system, and when you measure the actual performance of the system against these ideals, then you talk about events taking place and chronology. But when the system is complete within itself, it is not featureless, but its functioning has no chronology, there are no events within the system. Unfortunately, we are so used to the idea of chronology that natural evolution is always very puzzling: an evolution in which there are no happenings. So, whenever there is a motion which contains things taking place but to which we cannot put definite cause and effect, we feel very anxious, we feel that we do not fully understand. We want to break it up, discretize it.

"Perhaps these two possible kinds of unfolding may be useful as models for this discussion. There is one kind of time—physical time in which events take place, in which the second law of cause and effect takes place. Another time in which you cannot say what is the cause and what is the effect, because there is no breaking up of events with regard to that." Sudarshan stopped.

"When does that take place?" asked Krishnaji.

"When the system has no ideal to compare itself with," said Sudarshan.

"Which means what?" Krishnaji was pushing.

"We refer to it as a closed system, but we mean it may be a complete system," said Sudarshan.

"In all systems—bureaucratic, scientific, religious—is there inherent decay, entropy?" enquired Krishnaji.

"Yes."

"So, as long as the brain is collective, it forms a system."

"Quite right."

"So, inherently in the collective is a process of decay, degeneration takes place?" enquired Krishnaji.

"Krishnaji, I am concerned about your attention to the brain. The brain is also part of the physical system and I do not have to pay that much more attention to my brain than I do to trees or to birds," said Dr. Sudarshan.

"No," Krishnaji said.

"Sometimes I use them, but then sometimes I use the tree also. So, why should I feel so attached to what happens in my brain—thought waves and the functioning of the various interconnections and so on? Should I be too concerned about what the brain is doing?" asked Sudarshan.

"As long as my brain is conditioned, the brain becomes very limited. The brain has an infinite capacity, and that capacity is being denied by its own limitation. You are a scientist and I am not. You have acquired tremendous knowledge and have occasional insights into something. You keep moving, adding. This addition is the factor of conditioning. Obviously. And therefore the brain becomes limited and that addition is the self. We won't go into different terminologies. As long as the self is there, the self is a system, and the self is a factor of deterioration," Krishnaji said.

"That is what we call the self with a little 's' rather than the big 'S,' " said Sudarshan.

"The self is self, not the big 'S' or small 's.' I am using it only in one context, the small 's.' For me, there is no big 'S,' " Krishnaji said.

"Going back to what Pupulji said, Sir, you said that attention has no background," prompted Radhaji.

"Here is a scientist. What is attention to you, Sir? Be simple." Krishnaji turned to Sudarshan.

"Well, I would say attention is when there is no separation, when there is no identification of anything else; including perception of any entity. Attention is one, in which there are no anticipations and there are no memories."

"Which means what? There is no background?" asked Krishnaji.

"No background. I feel that that is the simplest statement. In attention there is no background because background assumes a matrix, an ideal. In attention there is no comparison. Attention is one without the second," said Sudarshan.

"When there is attention, there is no background. We were discussing time. I say love has no time. Love has no reminiscences. Love is not the activity of desire or pleasure. The activity of desire and pleasure involves time. Love has no time," Krishnaji spoke.

"This is a mighty leap," I commented.

"It is a *Brahmastra*. It is a weapon which annihilates everything," Upadhyaya commented.

But Krishnaji would not accept this statement. "It is approachable," he said. "I don't put something on a pinnacle and then say it is unapproachable."

"Has love an arising and an ending?" asked the Pandit.

"No. If there is an arising and ending, it is not love."

"Then it is beyond discussion," said Upadhyayaji.

"What is a dialogue? A dialogue is—you question and I answer; so, you and I are forgotten. We don't exist. Only the question remains. And if you leave the question, it flowers, it has vitality, it provides an answer," Krishnaji spoke. "Has Panditji understood my answer?"

"He accepts what you say—that there is a question and an answer flows, but he says, "What has this to do with love?" Radha Burnier spoke.

"I make a statement—'Where love is, time is not.' You listen, you question it, and I reply. There is a connection, both verbal and non-verbal, and the question remains, the fact remains. If you let it remain, it begins to move."

"You say love has no time," I asked.

"See the beauty of it."

"It is a fine question and no response arises to it, but there is still the question," I said.

"Then remain with that. Pupul, take a lotus, look at it."

"I look."

There was a long pause. Then Radha Burnier turned to Jagannath Upadhyaya and said, "In looking there is no question."

"I don't know how to respond to Krishnaji's question." Sensing a certain barrenness in the dialectics, Krishnaji suddenly dropped the discussion and took one of his great leaps. "Death has no time."

"Out of kindness for us, could you make these leaps a little shorter? Because already Panditji is saying that he is finding it difficult to respond to your statement, which he may completely agree with, identify with. How do we relate this particular statement to the question of 'being, becoming'?" Sudarshan intervened.

"It seems to me that before we move to death, let us talk about love, and its relation to the question," Sudarshan continued. "You have previously said that when there is a dialogue between two or many people, and the purpose is actually in the dialogue, the persons cease and the question remains and it moves around, it speaks through various people and its own vitality functions. I think Panditji is saying that he does not know how to respond, not because he disagrees with you—not that what you say is a *Brahmastra*, the ultimate weapon which destroys everything including the launching pad—but how is he to respond to your earlier question that the dialogue has a vitality of its own?"

"Have you understood it?" Krishnaji asked Sudarshan.

"Yes."

"Then explain it to Panditji," Krishnaji said.

"I think Krishnaji is saying that the purpose of the dialogue is not for a person to ask questions and for the other person to answer, but for the question and answer to come around, and in a sense move by itself between people. So it is not one person giving information to another person, but it is a case of the question itself answering itself, using people's voices as the instrument. But we have always the feeling that it must be in terms of a catechism—a question and answer. Krishnaji is saying that if there is a time when the question ceases, that too is a very valuable time, that too is in fact very natural. In a sense, what it shows is an image, an echo of what he was talking about earlier— namely, is there a being at this point or is there a becoming or is there something which is other than the two? Looked at from one point, there is being; looked at from another point, when all questions cease, then who is there to ask any question, who is there to understand? That holding the question, or holding the answer if there is no question, is itself in a sense a dialogue. It is a meditation in which no words are spoken because it is *yato vaacho nivartante*, a state where words do not reach."

"Yes. So, let us talk about death. What, according to the Buddhists, to Nagarjuna, is death?" Krishnaji spoke.

"By whatever cause life came into being, by the same cause life comes to an end; that is death," said the Buddhist.

"I exist because my father and my mother met, and I was born. I live eighty-nine years or one hundred years. At the end of one hundred years, I die. There is a causation and the end of causation. Right? Is that what you call death?" Krishnaji asked.

"This causation is not at the level of things, that is, at the biological level; but it is at the memory level, at the thought level. Nagarjuna says in that movement is past, present and future."

"If you say that past and present contain the 'now,' that now is death. Becoming and dying. Is that death?" asked Krishnaji.

"Yes," said Jagannath Upadhyaya.

"That is logical," Krishnaji said.

"Yes, logical."

Krishnaji continued, "It is an intellectual concept."

"Yes."

"That doesn't interest me," said K, "I am dying."

"At every moment there is an ending; each moment is separate. There is a death all the time," said Upadhyayaji.

"But I have a son who is dying and I am in sorrow, I shed tears. I am lonely, depressed. You come along and speak of causation. But I am in pain. What are you going to do about it?"

"Whatever comes into being ends from moment to moment," Upadhyayaji said.

"I have heard all that before," said Krishnaji. "But I am in sorrow."

"But what connects the moments together is memory," said Upadhyayaji.

"All right. I come to you and you explain that. I say, 'Go to hell.' "

I intervened. "Jagannath Upadhyaya says that none of the Buddhist teachings have dealt with death, except as a rising and ending."

Krishnaji said, "I was with a man, Sir, some years ago. He was dying. His wife came and said, 'He is asking for you.' I went to him, sat next to him, and held his hand. And he said, 'I am dying, don't preach philosophy to me. I am dying, and I don't want to die. I have lived a fairly good life, a fairly moral life, I have got my family, my memories, all the things that I have accumulated, and I don't want to die. But I am dying.' What is your answer to that? Don't come to me with your 'beginning and ending.' "

"The answer is, he has to die," said Upadhyayaji.

"Oh, God!" cried Krishnaji. "Is that what you say to your son, to your wife, to your husband? 'He has to die'? Of course he has to die. He has got cancer, he has got tuberculosis, a disease. He is quite young, and he says, 'My god, help me to understand.' "

"But death is part of life," said Panditji.

"Panditji, are you saying there is no ending to sorrow?" I tried to clarify the position.

"Unless the cause of sorrow is eliminated, it cannot end," said the Buddhist Pandit.

"But the man who is dying hasn't eliminated it. You have to deal with this man who is dying. Nobody has held his hand. So I hold his hand and he has the feeling that there is love. I do not talk to him about a beginning or ending," said Krishnaji.

"What is the difficulty here? He may die or not die. He will die sometime. But we are dying at this moment, we are dying to this feeling. We are in sorrow, there is no question of that. The question is not whether our brother is dying. It is we who are in sorrow, and we are asking for help, for support. He wants consolation. But I am not giving him a thing. We cannot give him life. He who is dying is not dying outside of himself, he is dying within himself and it is his problem.

"Is the question how you deal with that person?" Sudarshan enquired.

"No," said Krishnaji, "it is how you deal with death."

"In the process there are two things. One is my feeling that my friend is dying and that he is afraid, he is unhappy and unwilling to die. The other is what can I do to give him help at this point. Which of the two aspects are we discussing?"

Krishnaji replied, "Both. I want to know about death. I am going to die. I'll be eighty-nine in May—probably I will live another ten years. I am not frightened. I don't want anybody's help. I have lived with death and life together, all the time, all my life. Because I don't own anything, I don't possess anything inwardly. I am dying and living at the same time. There is no separation for me. I may be living in illusion, but take it as it is.

"But my friend is dying. Nobody has loved him and he has loved nobody. What the Buddha said, does that help? He wants somebody to love him, be with him. Somebody who says 'Look, we are together in this. You are lonely and what does it mean when death comes?' I see him utterly lonely, separated from anybody else. And there is dreadful fear. And you come and speak of beginning, ending. I say, for God's sake!"

"If I love, can I give it to him? Is it something which can be given?" asked Jagannath Upadhyaya.

"No," said Krishnaji, "he is with me, not that I give him love. It is not something I give.

"Because he is ill and is going to die, and he does not want to die, how do we give him love? Love cannot transcend causation; it cannot be outside cause and effect. However great or deep compassion may be, it cannot be independent of causation," said Upadhyaya.

"Sir," said K, "he is not interested in your philosophy. He is not interested in what the Buddha said. He is dying. Don't tell him of beginning, arising, and ending. He is not interested in that. We go to the dying with a lot of words and these words are like ashes to him, including Buddha's words. He is dying and says, 'My God! What of my life? Don't talk to me about all this.' Can one come with nothing and hold his hand? Can one say, 'My friend, when you die, a part of me is also dying. I have never met you before. But your wife came to see me and she asked me to visit you. So, we both are going to die today. I know what it means to die. I have lived my life dying and living, never separating the two. Each day I die.' So I say to my friend, 'Let us die. I understand your fear.' Then death is not fear."

# CHAPTER 46

# "The Lineage of Compassion"

In April 1984 I was in Arya Vihara in Ojai. The book of memoirs was nearing completion, but what of the ending? The river was in full flood. Was it possible to distill the essence of the teaching? At times it appeared so lucid, clear, simple, and then so distant, immense, universal that it defied a unified perception of it. I sought clarity, the key to the ending. At Pine Cottage on April 28 I met Krishnaji. His hair was white, time had left its mark on the face, but the eyes that mirrored mine were of the boy Krishnamurti in the photograph taken after his first initiation; eyes that were limpid, untouched, eyes that had never looked back in time.

I asked him what was the summation of his teaching? To me it was vast. It integrated and included the teachings of the Buddha and Vedanta. He could negate the super-Atman, the Brahman, but in the very negation, he emanated an energy which those words conveyed. That led me to the often-asked question, "Who is Krishnamurti? What is his lineage?" Was he a breakthrough in evolution? It would take centuries to comprehend the challenge Krishnamurti had posed to the human brain—to the root of the human mind.

Suddenly Krishnaji caught my hand. "Keep it—keep the challenge—work with it—forget the person." His touch was charged with the strength of nature, as found in storms in oceans. "Look what religions have done: concentrated on the teacher and forgotten the teaching. Why do we give such importance to the person of the teacher? The teacher may be necessary to manifest the teaching, but beyond that, what? The vase contains water; you have to drink the water, not worship the vase. Humanity worships the vase, forgets the water."

My body, mind responded. "Even to start real enquiry into the teaching is a breakthrough in consciousness."

"Yes, that is so," Krishnaji said. "The human tendency is to center everything around the person of the teacher—not on the essence of what he says, but the person. That is the great corruption. Look at the great teachers of the world—Mohammed, Christ, and the Buddha too. Look what their followers have made of it? Buddhist monks are violent, they kill. Contrary to all that the Buddha had said.

"The manifestation has to take place, through a human body, naturally—the manifestation is not the teaching. We must be extraordinarily impersonal about all this. To see that we do not project the teacher because of one's love and affection for the person, and forget the teaching. See the truth in the teaching, the depth in it, go into it, live it, that is, what is important. Does it matter?" Krishnaji asked, "If the world says of K, what a wonderful person he is—who cares? If K is a breakthrough, the word is not his measure. The word is not important. If I were living in the time of the Buddha, I may be attracted to him as a human being, I may have great affection for him, but I would be far more concerned with what he says. Look Pupulji, our brains have become so small by the words we have used. When one speaks to a group of scientists, specialists in various disciplines—one sees that their lives have become so small. They are measuring everything in terms of words, experiences. And it is not a matter of word or experience. Words are limited; all experiences are limited. They cover a very small area."

He was hesitant. "Let us start anew. The self is a bundle of memories. The self is the essence of knowledge. Knowledge is always in the field of time. K is saying that the self is inherited and accumulated memory. When the self is not, time is not. Energy has no past. But man has emphasized the past. When there is that energy, not bound by the self, energy has no time. It is energy."

"But in all manifestation, is a time not born, limited to that manifestation?" I asked.

"Yes. Manifestation needs time. Therefore, having manifested as a flower or a tree, as a human being, that energy is limited. When the self is not, it is a state totally out of time. I am questioning whether the evolution of the brain is to continue as it is now, modifying, growing, gathering, more and more knowledge? I see something very interesting. Meditation as it is known is practice, discipline, recitation of mantras. It is based on knowledge. So it is a very small affair. Is there a meditation that is not based on knowledge, not deliberate? So long as consciousness exists, consciousness must mean manifestation. There must be time. Therefore this meditation can only be when consciousness, as we know it, ends.

"For the last year, there is a state, not measurable by words, not in the field of knowledge, immense, totally out of time. It is there, when I close my eyes to do my exercises, when I go for a walk. I watch, I am skeptical to see whether it is fanciful or reality."

Krishnaji had moved out and was free of the discussion; a new state was evident.

"That must be totally altering the nature of the brain," I commented.

"Probably it does."

"Can it touch the brain of humanity?"

"Yes, yes." Krishnaji's voice was flowing, deep and compassionate. Then suddenly he asked me, "Pupulji, you have read the ancient texts, you have discussed with pandits, what do you contact?"

I let the question float; then, hesitantly, I spoke. "You see, Krishnaji, I have read the ancient texts, but I bring to the texts the listening which has come through listening to you. I so listen to the texts, and because there is that state, I can touch something, get close to it."

"Why." Krishnaji spoke—it was not a question, but a way of moving me into the journey.

"Because touching 'that' does not lie in the word. You speak and the mind, because it is quiet, feels close to 'that.' Now when I read the ancient texts and the mind is quiet, or when I sit alone in the garden and hear birds sing, or the touch of the wind, I may feel a closeness to 'that.' "

"Does the person of K become important?"

"No. The energy emanating, certainly is important. You draw us in, the moment the mind is quiet. I am beginning to see something, the energy in this mind, as it is, is not capable of touching 'that.' It can go so far and no further. This also I understand, to allow the self as little space as possible."

"Yes," Krishnaji laughed. "Allow it as little play as possible."

"I see that there is very little of the personal Krishnamurti left."

"Yes."

"You feel it, the moment you touch the gateways of your mind; the ground is saturated with 'that.' "

"Yes."

"In the last year or so, you have tried—no, 'tried' is not the right word—to bring people closer and closer to 'that.' " I paused. "But then there is the blockage of evolution that is karma."

"As you sow, so shall you reap," Krishnaji laughed again.

"Karma, which is the essence of what you were, so you are and so you will be. I see also that one has to let thought flow, let it be very fluid, not let it crystalize. One has to uproot thought, unearth it."

"Uproot it, that is right."

"So that it sits lightly in the mind."

"Just a minute." K interrupted my flow. "How would you communicate what you are saying to fifty people, or five thousand?"

"The key to communication is observation. Nothing else is needed."

"How do you answer, who is the observer?"

"The only answer is to observe. To be open, to discover. How extraordinary is this journey of discovery, the insights into the endless."

As I left the room, the question again arose in my mind: Who is Krishnamurti? What is his *gotra*, his lineage? Out of the question, the answer arose: All humankind. Because in every human being is the capacity to break through bondage; to be in the lineage of impersonal compassion.

Later I asked him of the nature of the word *samadhi*. He said, "The brain is silent throughout the day; a word is said and the brain sees instantly the whole content of it. The brain does not accumulate. What arises is full. There is no movement within the brain as time, but there is an infinite movement, the rhythm of the brain. There is a sense of timeless, eternal protection."

On May 11, 1985, Krishnaji turned ninety years old. That day I was with him at Arya Vihara in Ojai, and in the morning I knocked at the door of his room overlooking the pepper tree, where sixty-three years earlier he had undergone his mysterious transformations. At my knock Krishnaji opened the door. I bent to touch his feet; but he laughed and embraced me instead. Nothing special happened that day. He was ninety and another day passed.

# CHAPTER 47

# "No Beginning, No End": Krishnamurti at Ninety

In the *Bhagavad Gita* Arjuna asks Krishna of the nature of the Steadfast, illumined Being. "How does he walk, how does he talk, how does he conduct himself?"

The same question is asked by many people who have seen and heard Krishnaji speak. This chapter perhaps provides some answers to the question, and yet it remains an incomplete answer, for the mystery of Krishnamurti remains unfathomed.

At ninety, Krishnamurti's day is little different than it has been for forty years. In India he awakes at sunrise, lies in bed, every sense of the body awake, but without a single thought arising until there is a coming to, from vast distances. He starts the morning with yogic *asanas* and *pranayam*. For thirty-five minutes he does his *pranayams*, his breathing exercises, and forty-five minutes are spent on yoga *asanas*, the physical stances—toning the body, the nerves, the muscles and the cells that form the skin tissue, the opening of every cell of the body so that it breathes naturally and in harmony.

At eight o'clock Krishnamurti has a breakfast of fruit, toast, butter, and whole wheat. His breakfast sometimes includes South Indian *idlis* or *dosas*, steamed rice cakes with coconut chutney. At the breakfast table in India his close associates gather to discuss education and the schools, consciousness, the seed of disintegration in man, computers, and the role of artificial intelligence. He asks for news of the international world and of India. The state of the country is freely discussed; the violence, the corruption, the decay of values; the future of man or the mutation of the human mind. Every problem is raised and probed;

everyone participates; a sense of order and quiet pervades even the discussions.

He is quite childlike in his attitude to situations, especially political; but a supreme gravity is evident in his concern with the psyche or the spaces within the mind. He frequently pauses, letting the mind rest with questions, responding with passion and dignity.

When he is to hold his morning dialogues, the breakfast session is short. We disperse to meet again at 9:30, when the small group gathers to participate in the dialogues. The discussions continue until eleven, after which individuals with special problems or sorrows can speak to him. At times he takes them into his room for a few minutes. When there are no group discussions, his talks with his associates continue for two or three hours. We discuss death, the nature of God, the problem of the observer and the observed. Some of the most intense insights have been revealed at these sessions.

Around eleven-thirty he goes to his room and lies down for half an hour with the *Economist, Time,* or *Newsweek,* picture books of trees, mountains, birds, or animals, or a mystery novel. He rarely reads serious books, but is very well informed on the state of the world, on advances in science and technology, and the degenerating processes corroding man. At noon he has an oil massage and a very hot bath. Lunch is at one o'clock. He eats Indian food, but nothing fried, and very few sweets. He likes hot pickles and permits himself tiny portions. Again at lunchtime there are discussions, and guests are often invited.

The conversation varies from international affairs to scientific discoveries, war, nuclear disarmament and its insoluble problems. Krishnaji has an intense curiosity and questions deeply. New discoveries in science fascinate him. At times he is prophetic and feels into the future. His statements are far ahead of his time. He has insights into the significance of world events and can relate them to a global totality. He often asks visitors, "What is happening in the country? Why has it lost all creativity?" No answer satisfies him. The serious individual is made to hold this impossible question within and so be awake to its intimations. The question of degeneration in the inner processes has to be asked and the mind must remain with the problem, ponder on it.

His span of attention is formidable. He once said to me that some questions have to be held in the mind for eternity.

At lunch Krishnamurti continues the question he has discussed over the breakfast table, and sometimes he tells stories—anecdotes of his encounters with wild animals, or stories of St. Peter and heaven and hell, Russia and the commissars, which he repeats with eloquence, zest, and good humor. He is completely without malice. With strangers he is shy, and someone else has to fill in awkward silences.

For years he saw vast numbers of people. *Sannyasis*, Buddhist monks, *siddhas*, wandering yogis converge on him, seeking answers or solace. He never refuses to see them. The saffron or ochre robe of the ascetic evokes deep compassion within him. In the early 1970s two Jain monks had started visiting him every year. Their appointment had to be fixed a year ahead, with the exact date, time, and place. For during the *Chaturmas*, the four months of the monsoons, the monks rested and all wandering ceased. After the four months were over, the two monks would start their pilgrimage to meet Krishnaji, sometimes walking seven hundred miles to be in Bombay on the appointed day. One of the monks had leukemia, the other was very young and had beautiful eyes. They tied white cotton masks around their mouths, to ensure that even while breathing they did not harm an insect. They could not speak English, and I had to translate what was said. I sat on the door sill, while they shared a mat with Krishnaji; for by monastic ordinance they were not permitted to sit on the same mat as a woman. They were passionate in their queries. Young, they had harshly denied their bodies, and the promised liberation was not forthcoming. Krishnaji was very gentle with them and long discussions took place. One year, these white-clad monks did not appear for their appointment. It is difficult to say what happened. Perhaps the head of their order, sensing a rebellion against authority, had refused them permission to hold their meetings with Krishnaji.

After lunch Krishnaji rests. At about four he starts seeing people again. A woman going blind comes, and he places his hands on her eyes. A visitor who has lost a child sits with him, and he holds her hand and symbolically wipes her tears, healing her inwardly; a young man, bewildered, lost in this violent world, seeks answers.

Beginning in the late 1970s he saw fewer people, but at ninety he is again available to those who seek him out; he never closes his doors on anyone—the young man with hallucinations, in communication with satellites; the woman in sorrow; the adolescent; the old; the blind. He is never too busy or too tired.

His name and teachings are known throughout the country, amongst *ashrams* in the Himalayas as much as amongst academics. The Buddhists in India still speak of him as a great teacher in the Nagarjuna tradition; the Hindu gurus and *sadhus* speak of him as a great liberated being in the Advaita or nondual tradition. They accept him as a most profound teacher of the age.

When the sun is about to set, he goes for a walk. At ninety his strides are long, his body still erect and straight. His close friends, their children and grandchildren walk with him. Sometimes he holds the hand of a little child and walks and laughs with her. He walks three miles, breathing in the earth, the trees, listening to distant sounds. There is very little conversation. At times he prefers to be alone, his mind far away. He has said that not a single thought touches his mind during these walks.

At home again he washes, and does some more *pranayam*. He eats a light supper—salad, fruit, nuts, soup, vegetables. On rare occasions he sits over the dinner table with a few friends and hints of an eternity that lies beyond the mind. The hands assume the role of the teacher. His voice changes, fills with power and with volumes of energy; silences sweep into the room.

A river of quietude flows within him. His mind never crystalizes. He is prepared to listen to any criticism. I remember one day in 1978 in Colombo when he and I were staying in the same house. He had been restless. I said to him, "Sir, you are agitated." He did not answer me. We started discussing something else. In the evening at supper, he turned to me and said, "You said I was agitated. This afternoon I took the question to bed with me. I asked myself, 'Am I agitated? Is it because of dependence?' And suddenly I saw it. To seek an answer is to give agitation root in the soil of the mind; and it was over. I will not be agitated again. I have been watching and listening to everything, to my body, my mind, to root out any trace of agitation."

He is open to all challenges. He never stops observing, listening, questioning. Krishnaji's mind holds few symbols, yet he has a close personal identity with rivers. In 1961, speaking in Bombay, he described the Ganga: "It may have a beginning and an end. But the beginning is not the river, the end is not the river. The river is the flow between. It passes through villages and towns, everything is drawn into it. It is polluted, filth and sewage are thrown into it, a few miles later it has purified itself. It is the river in which everything lives, the fish below and the man who drinks the water on top. That is river. Behind it is that tremendous pressure of water, and it is this self-purificatory process that is the river. The innocent mind is like that river. It has no beginning, no end—no time."

He wastes no energy when he walks, talks, or works at some inconsequential occupation—polishing shoes, picking up a stone and removing it from the pathway. As he grows old, the tremors in his hands have increased, the highly sensitive body's response to the world of noise and pollution. He has often suffered from mysterious illnesses. He becomes delirious, his voice changes, he sometimes becomes as a young child, he asks strange questions, faints easily, particularly when he is near to people he can trust; he often cures himself.

His relationship with nature, trees, rocks, and the earth has special significance; he has the ability to enter into spaces within nature, to feel life move. Lately he has started to speak of the sound that reverberates within a tree, when all outer sound ends.

Animals and birds trust him. I have seen him sit alone in a garden throwing parched rice on the grass; birds pick the rice within a few inches of his body, and some alight on his shoulder. Describing himself, he misquotes Browning: "shy like a squirrel, wayward like a swallow."

By ten-thirty he is asleep. Just before he falls asleep the whole day and his actions pass swiftly through his mind; in a flash the day and its events and all the yesterdays are quenched. In sleep Krishnaji's body, like a bird, folds in on itself. He does not like to be woken up suddenly. He says he very rarely dreams. When he arises there is barely a wrinkle on the sheet.

He is prepared to try all kinds of herbal and Ayurvedic remedies; he shies away from any modern drugs. He has fads about food; at times he mixes milk and orange juice, at other times he gives up milk; at other times he lives on raw foods. These food fads are smiled at by his friends. He never lets anyone touch his feet. If anyone does so, he himself bends and touches the feet of the other.

At his public talks, some of which are attended by about seven thousand people, he still wears a broad, red-bordered *dhoti* and long, honey-toned robe. Krishnaji walks to the dais surrounded by people but untouched by them. As he sits on the platform, Krishnaji's presence reaches out and draws his listeners close to him.

He begins to speak. The back is erect, the voice is clear, permitting every nuance to flower. The face is untouched by time. His hands rest in his lap; occasionally they move, assuming symbolic postures, like flower buds opening to light. For almost two hours the vast audience is silent, with hardly any movement. When the talk is over Krishnaji sits still for a minute, then folds his hands in *pranams* and the crowds surge towards him. His body trembles with the energy that has flowed through it. He reaches out with both his hands and allows them to be held by those that can reach him. Slowly he extricates himself.

Krishnaji gets down from the platform. People press on the tiny passage through which he passes; they bend to touch his feet, he touches their faces to his hands. He does not draw away his hands, but keeps them extended on either side. Like a lion he walks, slowly, with immense dignity. The eyes turn to meet hundreds of eyes surrounding him. A stampede seems inevitable, but the silence of his presence creates order. People move back. He walks alone. In the car, when his companions try to pull up the window, he stops them. His arms reach out through the windows. All the way to the gate, men and women press on the car, touching his hands, putting them to their eyes. A policeman, seeing the pressing crowd, orders them to move. Krishnaji stops him, takes his hand and holds it. The policeman flings aside his baton and prostrates himself at Krishnaji's feet. Krishnaji lifts him up and, still holding his hand, enters the car. As the car moves, the policeman runs with it, refusing to let go the hand.

Children wait at the flat on Peddar Road with a garland of sweet smelling interwoven jasmine and roses, floral pearls, rubies and emeralds. He takes it with grace, wears it round his neck for some moments before giving it to the children near him.

Staying with him in close proximity has always been arduous. He is ablaze, and the bodies of his associates take a little time to get used to his presence. He sometimes questions his friends, demanding that they be attentive and observe. He watches carefully whether they react strongly to people and statements. It is not possible for deteriorating minds to linger round him—one either moves or is left behind. Vast volumes of energy flow; one must be of it or have no place.

His body is frail, but his mind never slackens. He has said that as he grows very old a limitless energy operates through him. The urgency has increased, so has the drive. Nothing seems to tire him. He pushes the body, walking faster, testing himself, so that most people half his age cannot keep up with him. It is only when he is doing nothing, lying in bed, that he looks frail and aged. His hands tremble, his body shrinks. But in discussion, at breakfast or lunch, on his talks, every wrinkle is wiped away. The skin is translucent, it appears ethereal, lit from within.

At ninety Krishnaji continues to travel, to speak, to search for minds that are awake and capable of perceiving with clarity. Such perceptions, flowering without shadow, transform the brain.

In 1980 Krishnaji told me that when he stopped speaking, the body would die. The body has only one purpose: to reveal the teaching.

# Epilogue

"But how shall we bury you?"
"Any way you like," said Socrates, "that is if you can catch me and I don't slip through your fingers."

—PHAEDO, *The Last Days of Socrates*

The story of Krishnamurti has ended. On February 17, 1986, at 12:10 A.M. Pacific Standard Time, he died at Pine Cottage, Ojai, where he had been mortally ill for five weeks with cancer of the pancreas. He died in the room facing the pepper tree, under which, sixty-four years ago, he underwent vast transformations of consciousness.

He was cremated in Ventura, California. His ashes were divided into three parts: for Ojai, India, and England. In India they were consigned to the river Ganga: midstream at Rajghat, Varanasi; at Gangotri, the source of the river in the deep Himalayas; and at Adyar beach in Madras, where they were taken in a slim catamaran over the turbulent waves to be immersed in the ocean.

Krishnaji had said before his death that the body after death was of no importance. Like a log of wood, it had to be consumed by fire. "I am a simple man," he said, and like a simple man should be his ultimate journey. There were to be no rituals after his death, no prayer, no fuss, no great ceremonial processions. No memorials were to be built over his ashes. Under no circumstances was the teacher to be deified. The teacher was unimportant; only the teaching was important. It was the teaching that had to be protected from distortion and corruption. "There is no place for hierarchy or authority in the teaching; there is no successor and no representative who will carry on these teachings in my name now or at any time in the future." However, he enjoined on his associates that the foundations that bore his name in India, the United States, and England should continue, as should the schools founded under his guidance.

His ashes were brought by plane to Delhi. I received them at the foot of the plane and drove straight back to my home. As we entered the gate, a sudden heavy shower of rain with hail fell. It continued to fall for a few minutes, until the urn had been placed under a banyan tree in the garden. Then, as suddenly as it had begun, the rain stopped.

It was in Rougemont, Switzerland, in July 1985 that the first intimations of his approaching death arose within Krishnaji. I had met him at Brockwood Park late in September. He had waited for me in the little kitchen off the West Wing of the old house. He said he had to tell me something very serious. "Since Switzerland, I know when I am going to die. I know the day and the place, but I will not disclose it to anyone." He went on to say, "The manifestation has started to fade."

I was stunned and sat silent.

He arrived in New Delhi on October 25, where he was to rest for a few days before leaving for Varanasi. On October 29 he met R. Venkataraman, the vice president of India and a close friend, and Rajiv Gandhi, first at lunch at the home of the vice president and later at dinner at my home. This was the first time Krishnaji had met with Rajiv since Indira Gandhi's death the previous year, and there was a poignancy in the meeting.

From Delhi Krishnaji traveled to Varanasi, where a camp attended by three hundred people had been organized. The monsoons had been bountiful and there were signs of new life sprouting on tree and bush; brilliant yellow-and-green mustard plants had started to appear on the river bank. The festival of Diwali was celebrated while Krishnaji was in residence; thousands of oil lamps were lit at the house where Krishnaji dwelt and the river was bright with floating oil lamps flickering in the evening breeze.*

Krishnaji spoke to the gathering, held discussions with the pandits of Varanasi and the scholars in the Vedantic and Buddhist tradition, and discussed the future of Rajghat with the members of the Foundation. Professor Krishna, a teacher of physics at the Benares Hindu University, whom Krishnaji had known for several years, agreed to give up his job and take charge as the Rector of the Rajghat Education Center. Two pilgrims, R. Upasani and Mahesh Saxena, walked with Krishnaji as he circumambulated the land, looked and smiled at pilgrim and peasant, listened to the pulse of this ancient city.

Upasani had lived for three decades in Rajghat, tending the soil;

---

*Diwali, the festival of lights, is celebrated on the darkest night of the month, four months after the monsoons are over and the earth awakens to new life. It heralds the sowing of seed and is a celebration to invoke the presence of Laksmi, the goddess of prosperity. Even the poorest villager lights a clay oil lamp so that the goddess does not pass by his home without entering it.

his care and concern had brought him close to Krishnaji and Mahesh Saxena, the newcomer, former head of the central police in Delhi. Vulnerable and passionate, Saxena had resigned his job, donned a robe, and become a seeker. For several years he lived in the Himalayas, then started to wander until he came to Rajghat. His presence and intensity swept him into Krishnaji's proximity, and soon he too was to join the Foundation, to become its secretary.

From Rajghat Krishnaji traveled to Rishi Valley, where he held discussions with educators and students. The rains had been plentiful; the arid soil had awakened, the fields were green, and a vast number of saplings planted by children covered the rocky hillside.

His walks were becoming shorter and he was losing weight at an alarming rate. Going to his room one day, Radhika heard Krishnaji chatting to a Hoopoe bird: "You and your children are certainly welcome to come in here. But I can assure you that you won't like it. In a few days I'll be gone, the room will be locked, the windows shut, and you will not be able to get out." When she entered the room she saw the bird, framed by the picture window, sitting on the branch of the spathodia tree, its crest fanned out, listening to Krishnaji, who lay on his bed talking in measured tones. Krishnaji said that the bird liked the sound of his voice, and had been sitting listening to him for some time. Very often when small groups of us sat on the carpet with Krishnaji in his room, the bird would swoop down against the window, peck at the glass pane, and generally make a racket. Krishnaji would say, "Here comes my friend."

He cut short his stay in Rishi Valley and came to Vasant Vihar in Madras, where he held three public talks. Here too, the rains had preceded him. The garden was lush and heavy yellow blossoms had appeared on the tabubea argentina, blossoming out of season. Krishnaji had a high temperature, but he refused any medical intervention and continued his talks. Vast crowds attended the talks, for it was clear that Krishnaji was ill and this might be his last visit. He spoke on death and creation, on that which lies beyond beginning and ending. The immense energy that used to flood the body and the voice that would reverberate in the atmosphere was now in low key; the frail body, though radiant and erect, trembled as if unable to hold the power and thrust of the energy pouring through it. After the talk Krishnaji asked his audience to sit quietly and meditate with him.

A child walked up with a white champak flower. He turned and smiled as he took it. The child smiled. The sermon ended with the silence and the smile. He had said it was the last talk.

During the days that followed he met his friends and associates from the Krishnamurti Foundation in India, sometimes alone, sometimes in a group. He spoke to them of many things, of schools and study centers and silence. Toward the end of the last gathering he said: "Be absolutely alert, and make no effort."[1] Asit asked if those were his last words to us, and he smiled.

He decided to return to Ojai on January 10. That evening he went for his usual walk on the Adyar beach. A large number of his friends walked with him. A strong breeze swept his hair like a comet's trail, back from his face, exposing his high domed forehead. He had the look of an ancient sage of the forests. He walked on the beach where he had been "discovered," adopted, and initiated. Here by the sea, at Adyar, seventy-five years ago, when Halley's comet last entered the orbit that would carry it towards the sun. On his return he asked his friends to wait for him at Radha Burnier's house within the Theosophical Society compound. Krishnaji lingered on the beach, facing the roaring sea. Then he turned to each of the cardinal directions and paused for a minute; quietly he entered the gate and returned.

That night, an hour before his departure, he came down from his room. He was dressed immaculately in Western clothes, his tweed coat thrown over his arm and a red printed silk scarf—a present from me—around his neck. He greeted his friends, who stood in a semicircle; then he came to me and shook my hand. "How do I look?" he asked. "Forty," I responded. I remarked on his scarf. "My favorite one," he replied. He knew that it was the last time he was to meet many of his friends who stood before him. But he had cut away all emotion, all sorrow and sense of separation. This was his final benediction. That night he left via the Pacific, flying direct to Los Angeles.

In Ojai his condition grew critical and his illness was diagnosed as cancer of the pancreas. I arrived there on January 31 to find him desperately ill. His highly vulnerable body, so carefully protected through the years, was ravaged by the violence of the disease. On the first day he saw us as if through a haze. He had lost all sense of time and place. But the next day he rallied, and I found his mind lucid, the eyes clear and fully awake. I read to him the letters I had brought with me from Nandini, Sunanda, and Prime Minister Rajiv Gandhi, who had sent a personal message. Krishnaji held my hand; the grip was firm and a great flow of love reached out to me. He said he was too weak to write, but sent his love to all his friends in India.

During the next three or four days his strength returned. He asked to be taken in a wheelchair to the pepper tree. There he sat alone and bade farewell to the mountains of Ojai, the orange groves and the many trees.

He also walked with some support to the living room and lay on the sofa gazing into the fire. He saw a film on television that evening and the doctors felt that there might even be a remission in the disease. To me he said, "Come and see me tomorrow and all the days that you are here." So I saw Krishnaji every morning. I would sit by his bedside, hold his hand with both of mine, and be silent with him.

I noticed the books by his bedside, books in English, Italian, and French—Palgrave's *Golden Treasury*, *The Oxford Book of English Verse*, Italo Calvino's stories, the *Berlitz Dictionary of Italian*, Alphonse Daudet's stories, Gustave Doré, and Lawrence Durrell's *Alexandria Quartet*.

On Sunday, February 9, the tumor restarted its relentless attack and Krishnaji was back in bed, desperately ill. I could not see him that day. The next morning he sent for me. He said, "I had gone for a long walk in the mountains. I got lost and they could not find me. So I could not see you yesterday." For an instant the face was young, supremely beautiful.

I saw Krishnaji around one o'clock on the day of my departure on February 16. I sat with him for some time. He was in great pain, but his mind was clear and lucid. I said I would not say goodbye, for there would be no separation. With great effort, he lifted my hand to his lips. The grip was still firm. He lay cradled in a silence which enveloped me. As I was leaving, he said, "Pupul, tonight I shall go for a long walk in the mountains. The mists are rising." I left his room without turning back.

That night, at nine o'clock Pacific Standard Time, Krishnaji slept, to start his long walk into the high mountains. The mists were rising, but he walked through the mists and he walked away.

# Notes

## 1. "In Space One Is Born and Unto Space One Is Born."

1. Mary Lutyens, *Years of Awakening* (London: John Murray, 1975), 2; also, B. Shiva Rao, *Birth and Early Years*, no date, manuscript on Krishna's early life. Archives of the Theosophical Society, Adyar, Madras.
2. Sarvapalli Radhakrishnan, "The Principal Upanishads," *The Chandogya Upanishad* 7.12.1, 480.
3. Naraniah's account of Krishna's childhood was taken down in 1911 by Mrs. Katherine Taylor, an English Theosophist living in Adyar. The statement is signed by Naraniah and witnessed by Von Mannen and Mrs. George Gagorin. Archives of the Theosophical Society, Adyar, Madras.
4. Ibid.
5. She spoke of her feelings to her neighbor, who would later become the grandmother of Radha Burnier. Burnier, who belongs to a prominent family of Theosophists, was one of the group who came close to Krishnaji in India. As of 1986 she was president of the Theosophical Society.
6. J. Krishnamurti, *Autobiography*. Krishna started to write his autobiography in 1915 at Varengeville in Normandy. He wrote his reminiscences up to 1911. (Adyar, Madras: Archives of the Theosophical Society.)

## 2. The Theosophical Society and the Occult Hierarchy

1. Annie Besant, *Autobiography* (Adyar, Madras: Theosophical Publishing House, 1939), 326.
2. Annie Besant, conclusion of two lectures given in the Hall of Science, London, on August 4 and 11, 1889, under the title, "Why I Became a Theosophist." Archives of the Theosophical Society, Adyar, Madras.
3. Jawaharlal Nehru, *An Autobiography* (India: Allied Publishers Private Ltd., 1962), 15–16.
4. Gregory Tillet, *The Elder Brother* (London: Routledge and Kegan Paul, 1982), 102.
5. J. Krishnamurti, *Autobiography* (Adyar, Madras: Archives of the Theosophical Society, n.d).
6. Mary Lutyens, *Years of Awakening* (London: John Murray, 1975), 41–42.
7. Tillet, *Elder Brother*, 135.
8. Ibid., 125.
9. Annie Besant, "On Krishnamurti," *The Theosophist* (March 1986), 207. Originally published in 1923.

## 3. The Dream: "Is That You My Lord?"

1. This conversation between Krishnaji, Pandit Jagannath Upadhyaya, and a small group of members of the Krishnamurti Foundation India took place in Vasant Vihar,

Madras, in January 1985. It was transcribed by Sunanda Patwardhan. Archives of the Krishnamurti Foundation India, 64/65 Greenways Road, Madras.

2. Archives of the Theosophical Society, Adyar, Madras. Original letter K&R Archives, Ojai, California.

3. Ibid.

4. Ibid.

5. Ibid.

6. *Atharva Veda Samhita*, vol. 1, translated by William Dwight Whitney (Varanasi: Motilal Banarasidas, 1962), 150.

7. From my diaries. Krishnaji to George Sudarshan at Brockwood Park at the time of the gathering of scientists in October 1974.

8. Arthur H. Nethercot, *The Last Four Lives of Annie Besant* (London: Rupert Hart Davis, 1963), 159.

9. Esther Bright, *Old Memories and Letters of Annie Besant* (London: Theosophical Publishing House, 1936), 134.

10. Archives of the Theosophical Society, Adyar, Madras. Originals K&R Foundation, Ojai, California.

11. Ibid.

12. Ibid.

13. Ibid.

14. Ibid.

15. Archives of the Theosophical Society, Adyar, Madras. Original with K&R Foundation, Ojai, California.

16. Ibid.

17. Ibid.

18. Ibid.

19. Ibid.

20. Arthur H. Nethercot, *The Last Four Lives of Annie Besant* (London: Rupert Hart Davis, 1963), 229.

21. Mary Lutyens, *Years of Fulfilment* (London: John Murray, 1983), 6.

22. "Theosophy in India," *Literary Digest* (1974). Archives of the Theosophical Society, Adyar, Madras.

23. Mary Lutyens, *Years of Awakening* (London: John Murray, 1975), 136.

24. From my diaries.

## 4. "Mother, Please Touch My Face. Is It Still There?"

1. Report of the Star Congress, Ommen, 7. Archives of the Theosophical Society, Adyar, Madras.

2. For a detailed account see Mary Lutyens, *Years of Awakening* (London: John Murray, 1975), 153–157.

3. Archives of the Theosophical Society, Adyar, Madras.

4. Ibid.

## 6. "I and My Brother Are One"

1. Gregory Tillet, *The Elder Brother* (London: Routledge and Kegan Paul, 1982), 218.

2. Mary Lutyens, *Years of Awakening* (London: John Murray, 1975), 215.

3. Arthur H. Nethercot, *The Last Four Lives of Annie Besant* (London: Rupert Hart Davis, 1963), 367.

4. "Nitya died less than four months after these words were said." Editor's comments. George Arundale, writing in the *Herald of the Star* (January–December 1925): 359.

5. Nethercot, *Last Four Lives*, 369.

6. Tillet, *Elder Brother*, 220.

7. Archives of the Theosophical Society, Adyar, Madras.

8. B. Shiva Rao manuscript, "The Krishnamurti Story," no date. Archives of the Theosophical Society, Adyar, Madras.
9. Archives of the Theosophical Society, Adyar, Madras.
10. Ibid.

### 7. "The Personality of J. Krishnamurti Has Been Swallowed Up in the Flames."

1. Archives of the Theosophical Society, Adyar, Madras.
2. J. Krishnamurti, *The Kingdom of Happiness* (Adyar, Madras: Theosophical Publishing House, n.d.), 86.
3. Mary Lutyens, *Years of Awakening* (London: John Murray, 1975).
4. Ibid.
5. Esther Bright, *Old Memories and Letters of Annie Besant* (London: Theosophical Publishing House, 1936), 168.
6. Annie Besant in a letter to George Arundale dated 12-10-1926, *Theosophy in India* (January–December 1933).
7. From my diaries.
8. Lutyens, *Years of Awakening*, 241.
9. Ibid.
10. "Who Brings the Truth?" no date. Archives of the Theosophical Society, Adyar, Madras.
11. Arthur H. Nethercot, *The Last Four Lives of Annie Besant* (London: Rupert Hart Davis, 1963), 396.
12. Ibid, 394–395.
13. Arthur H. Nethercot, *The Last Four Lives of Annie Besant* (London: Rupert Hart Davis, 1963), 409.
14. Archives of the Theosophical Society, Adyar, Madras.

### 8. Krishnamurti in Ojai: The Forgotten Years, 1938–1947

1. Arthur H. Nethercot, *The Last Four Lives of Annie Besant* (London: Rupert Hart Davis, 1963), 449.
2. *The Theosophist* (April–September 1934): 454–455.
3. Letters to Padmabai Sanjiva Rao with Smt. Sudha Raman, Mysore. Archives of the Krishnamurti Foundation, Adyar, Madras.
4. From my diaries. Krishnaji in conversation with Nandini and me.
5. A. K. Ramanujam, *Speaking of Siva* (London: Penguin Books, 1973), 44.
6. Sybille Bedford, *Aldous Huxley—A Biography* (New York: Alfred A. Knopf/Harper & Row, 1974), 154.
7. Anita Loos, *Kiss Hollywood Goodbye* (London: Penguin Books, 1974), 154.
8. Christopher Isherwood, *My Guru and His Disciple* (London: Magnum Books Methuen Paperbacks Ltd., 1981), 50.
9. From my diaries.
10. Bedford, *Huxley*, 126.
11. Isherwood, *My Guru*, 304.
12. Henry Miller, *The Books in My Life* (London: Village Press, 1974), 153.

### 9. The Gathering of Friends

1. J. Krishnamurti, *Commentaries on Living* (London: Victor Gollancz Ltd., 1977).

### 10. "You Are the World."

1. From my diaries, Bombay, 1948.
2. Ibid.
3. J. Krishnamurti, *J. Krishnamurti's Talks in Bombay, 1948* (Madras, India: Krishnamurti Writings, Inc., 1950), 105.
4. J. Krishnamurti, *Commentaries on Living* (London: Victor Gollancz Ltd., 1977), 72.
5. From my diaries, 1948.

6. Krishnamurti, *Talks in Bombay, 1948,* 4, 5.
7. From my diaries, 1948.
8. Krishnamurti, *Talks in Bombay, 1948,* 8.
9. From my diaries, 1948.
10. Ibid.
11. From my diaries.
12. Ibid.
13. J. Krishnamurti, *Tradition and Revolution* (New Delhi: Orient Longman Ltd., 1972), 24.

## 11. "Go and Make Friends with the Trees."

1. J. Krishnamurti, *Commentaries on Living* (London: Victor Gollancz Ltd., 1977), 29.

## 12. "There Was the Face Beside Me."

1. Asit Chandmal, *A Thousand Moons* (New York: Harry N. Abrams, 1985), 16.

## 14. "Under the Last Rays of the Sun, the Waters Were the Color of Newborn Flowers."

1. J. Krishnamurti, *Commentaries on Living* (London: Victor Gollancz Ltd., 1977), 88.

## 16. "Religion Comes When the Mind Has Understood the Workings of Itself."

1. From my diaries. A conversation with S. M. Joshi at Rajghat, Varanasi, in 1983.

## 17. "The Mind Seemed to Expand without an End."

1. J. Krishnamurti, *Commentaries on Living,* 2d series (London: Victor Gollancz, 1978), 241–242.

## 18. "Can There Be Action without Consequence?"

1. From my diaries. I was present at the discussion.
2. Apa Sahib Pant of the Indian Foreign Service, retired and living in Poona, sent a letter to me describing the meeting between Krishnaji and Dalai Lama. Apa Sahib was present.
3. The account regarding Vimla Thakkar and Krishnaji was told to me by Dada Dharmadhikari, a close associate of Vimla Thakkar, at his son's residence in Bombay. Dada Dharmadhikari, one of the leaders of the Sarva Seva Sangh movement, died in 1986. Vimla Thakkar left Vinobaji and began lecturing on her own search and liberation. While in India she lives in Mount Abu and Dalhousie. She wrote a book on her meeting with Krishnaji, entitled *On an Eternal Voyage.*

## 19. "To Speak with the Whole Head"

1. Nirmala Deshpande is the daughter of P. Y. Deshpande. She lived in Vinobaji's ashram in Paunar in Maharashtra and functioned as his secretary. She accompanied the sage of Paunar wherever he traveled, taking down notes of his important conversations, and meeting visitors on his behalf. She was present at the meeting between Krishnaji and Vinobaji and took down the discussion.

## 20. "Through Negation, There Is Creation."

1. J. Krishnamurti, *Krishnamurti's Talks, Madras, 1959* (Madras: Krishnamurti Writings Inc., 1961), 98.
2. J. Krishnamurti, *Krishnamurti's Talks, Bombay, 1960* (Madras: Krishnamurti Writings Inc., 1961), 27.
3. Ibid., 37.
4. Ibid., 46.

## 21. "The Mind That Goes into Itself Deeply Enters on a Pilgrimage from Which There Is No Return."

1. J. Krishnamurti, *Krishnamurti's Talks, Bombay, 1961* (Madras: Krishnamurti Writings Inc., 1961), 52.
2. Ibid.

## 22. "Be Awake."

1. Mary Lutyens, *Years of Fulfilment* (London: John Murray, 1983), 108.
2. J. Krishnamurti, *Notebooks* (London: Victor Gollancz Ltd., 1976), 26.
3. Ibid., 158.
4. Ibid., 188–189.
5. J. Krishnamurti, *Krishnamurti on Education* (New Delhi: Orient Longamns Ltd., 1974), 23–24.
6. Ibid., 104.

## 23. "Happy Is the Man Who Is Nothing": Letters to a Young Friend

1. Nandini Mehta, Bombay.

## Epilogue

1. Asit Chandmal, "The Last Walk," *Bombay Magazine* (March 7, 1986).

# Index